T0262095

IET COMPUTING SERIES 42

Computer Vision and Recognition Systems Using Machine and Deep Learning Approaches

Other volumes in this series:

Computer Vision and Recognition Systems Using Machine and Deep Learning Approaches

Fundamentals, technologies and applications

Edited by
Chiranji Lal Chowdhary, Mamoun Alazab,
Ankit Chaudhary, Saqib Hakak
and Thippa Reddy Gadekallu

The Institution of Engineering and Technology

Published by The Institution of Engineering and Technology, London, United Kingdom

The Institution of Engineering and Technology is registered as a Charity in England & Wales (no. 211014) and Scotland (no. SC038698).

© The Institution of Engineering and Technology 2021

First published 2021

This publication is copyright under the Berne Convention and the Universal Copyright Convention. All rights reserved. Apart from any fair dealing for the purposes of research or private study, or criticism or review, as permitted under the Copyright, Designs and Patents Act 1988, this publication may be reproduced, stored or transmitted, in any form or by any means, only with the prior permission in writing of the publishers, or in the case of reprographic reproduction in accordance with the terms of licences issued by the Copyright Licensing Agency. Enquiries concerning reproduction outside those terms should be sent to the publisher at the undermentioned address:

The Institution of Engineering and Technology
Michael Faraday House
Six Hills Way, Stevenage
Herts, SG1 2AY, United Kingdom

www.theiet.org

While the authors and publisher believe that the information and guidance given in this work are correct, all parties must rely upon their own skill and judgement when making use of them. Neither the authors nor publisher assumes any liability to anyone for any loss or damage caused by any error or omission in the work, whether such an error or omission is the result of negligence or any other cause. Any and all such liability is disclaimed.

The moral rights of the authors to be identified as authors of this work have been asserted by them in accordance with the Copyright, Designs and Patents Act 1988.

British Library Cataloguing in Publication Data
A catalogue record for this product is available from the British Library

ISBN 978-1-83953-323-5 (hardback)
ISBN 978-1-83953-324-2 (PDF)

Typeset in India by MPS Limited
Printed in the UK by CPI Group (UK) Ltd, Croydon

Contents

17 Automated detection of defects and grading of cashew kernels using machine learning **439**
S.V. Veenadevi and C. Srinivasan Padmavathi

About the editors

Chiranji Lal Chowdhary is an associate professor in the School of Information Technology and Engineering at VIT University, where he has been since 2010. He received a B.E. (CSE) from MBM Engineering College at Jodhpur in 2001 and M. Tech. (CSE) from the M.S. Ramaiah Institute of Technology at Bangalore in 2008. He received his Ph.D. in Information Technology and Engineering from the VIT University Vellore in 2017. From 2006 to 2010, he worked at M.S. Ramaiah Institute of Technology in Bangalore, eventually as a Lecturer. His research interests span both computer vision and image processing. Much of his work has been on images, mainly through the application of image processing, computer vision, pattern recognition, machine learning, biometric systems, deep learning, soft computing, and computational intelligence. He has given few invited talks on medical image processing. He is the editor/co-editor of five books and is the author of over 40 articles on computer science. He filed two patents deriving from his research.

Mamoun Alazab is an associate professor at the College of Engineering, IT, and Environment, Charles Darwin University, Australia. His multidisciplinary research in cyber security and digital forensics focuses on cybercrime detection and prevention including cyber terrorism and cyber warfare. He works closely with government and industry on projects including IBM, the Australian Federal Police (AFP), the Australian Communications and Media Authority (ACMA), the United Nations Office on Drugs and Crime (UNODC), and the Attorney General's Department. He is a Senior Member of the IEEE and founding chair of the IEEE Northern Territory (NT) Subsection. He holds a Ph.D. degree in Computer Science from the School of Science, Information Technology, and Engineering, Federation University of Australia.

Ankit Chaudhary is an assistant professor at the Department of Computer Science, University of Missouri at Saint Louis, USA. His research focuses on data science, computer vision and cyber security. He has authored three books. He is an associate editor and on the editorial board of several International Journals. He is a member of the IEEE. He received his Ph.D. degree in Computer Engineering from CSIR-CEERI, India.

Saqib Hakak is an assistant professor at the Canadian Institute for Cybersecurity, the University of New Brunswick, Fredericton, Canada. His current research interests include fake news detection, security and privacy, anomaly detection, natural language processing, and applications of AI. He has worked on numerous industrial projects involving IBM Canada, and TD Bank, Bell Canada. He received a complimentary ACM professional membership based on his services to the research community. He holds a Ph.D. degree from the Faculty of Computer Science and Information Technology, University of Malaya, Malaysia.

Thippa Reddy Gadekallu is an associate professor at the School of Information Technology and Engineering, VIT, Vellore, India. His areas of research include machine learning, deep neural networks, internet of things, and blockchain. He holds a Ph.D. degree in Data Mining from VIT, India.

Preface

Computer vision is an interdisciplinary scientific field that deals with how computers can gain high-level understanding from digital images or videos. It seeks to understand and automate tasks that the human visual system can do. To imitate human sight, computer vision must obtain, store, interpret, and understand images. It is an artificial intelligence system used in various applications such as convenience stores, driverless car testing, day-to-day medical diagnostics, and crop and livestock safety monitoring. The incredible growth in approaching this milestone was made possible in the iterative learning process through neural networks, machine learning, and deep learning methodologies.

Machine learning research and its application, especially with deep learning methods, have seen inspiring improvements in recent years. With this edited volume entitled "Computer Vision and Recognition Systems Using Machine and Deep Learning Approaches," we attempted to collect some quality chapter based on computer vision and recognition systems. Computer vision is the field of computer science that focuses on replicating parts of the complexity of the human vision system and enabling computers to identify and process objects in images and videos in the same way that humans do. Also, computer recognition systems are one of the most promising directions in artificial intelligence.

In this edited book, we address one of the critical components for understanding the potential of artificial intelligence, which is to give machines the power of vision and recognition. We plan to present topics devoted to advanced computer vision and recognition methods, technologies and applications which will facilitate ongoing attempts to understand and solve problems in this field.

The chapter "Computer vision and recognition-based safe automated systems" (Chapter 1) presents the automation appears to be one of the most exciting regions for recently developed artificial intelligence solutions, primarily computer and machine vision frameworks. Among the most important problems in automation is the protection of human–computer and human–machine interactions, which necessitates the "explainability" of techniques, which also precludes the use of any deep learning-based solutions, regardless of their success in computer vision applications. This chapter addresses the issues involved with computer vision and recognition-based safe automated systems.

The chapter "DLA: deep learning accelerator" (Chapter 2) introduces deep learning accelerator's (DLA) communication infrastructure which connects the processing elements (PE). Trained models' traffic distributes on PEs using communication infrastructure, which can inspire various structures and designs such as application-specific integrated circuit (ASIC) and field-programmable gate array (FPGA). This chapter describes various approaches and investigate their impact on DLA-based system's efficiency, which included data-flow mapping, data-flow stationaries, traffic patterns, and partitioning methods.

The chapter "Intelligent image retrieval system using deep neural networks" (Chapter 3) discusses the image retrieval system using convolutional auto-encoders and improving an image retrieval system's usability using generative adversarial networks (GANs). In convolutional autoencoders, the autoencoder's encoder portion is used to compute the latent space representation, which quantifies the content of the image in a feature vector.

The chapter "Handwritten digits recognition using dictionary learning" (Chapter 4) deals with a convolutional neural network model to compare the performance of deep learning with that of dictionary learning for handwritten digits recognition. The obtained results and their comparisons with benchmark methods confirm the effectiveness and robustness of the proposed approaches for recognition of the handwritten numbers. This chapter also complements the chapter "Handwriting recognition using CNN and its optimization approach" (Chapter 5) discusses several state-of-the-art handwriting models, namely Flôr, Bluche, and PuigCerver models with the modified data set.

The chapter "Real-time face mask detection on edge IoT devices" (Chapter 6) introduces the advent of deep learning and GPU compute availability, deep learning methods became very popular for real-time detection tasks. Real-time object detection needs to process a stream of images or videos. One more chapter addressing the issues with "computer vision and recognition-based safe automated systems" is involved in this edited volume.

The chapter "Current challenges and applications of DeepFake systems" (Chapter 7) provides an overview on various challenges the human race faces because of the DeepFake technology and the limitation of different forensic tools available to analyze and forecast the challenging future and understand the solutions incorporated to secure the current data situation.

The chapter "Vehicle control system based on eye, iris and gesture recognition with eye tracking" (Chapter 8) provides a study of the eye tracking and head motion identification approaches. Examples of various implementation areas are also discussed in both innovations, such as cooperation with the person and computer systems, driver assistance systems, and assistive technology.

The chapter "Sentiment analysis using deep learning" (Chapter 9) analyzing sentiments using computational techniques is one of the prominent area of research these days. This chapter will propose the novel method of classifying the opinions by automatically training the classifier. The details of the layers and other parameters will be discussed in the chapter highlighting on the learning is achieved through word representations. The accuracy achieved using several information retrieval metrics will be illustrated using visualization tools.

The chapter "Classification of prefeature extracted images with deep convolutional neural network in facial emotion recognition of vehicle driver" (Chapter 10) discusses a study on pre-feature extraction with different models of convolution neural networks (CNN) and demonstrates its benefits through the use of face emotion classification problems. Gaussian filter with canny edge detection, most significant bit (MSB) plane slicing, and Gabor filter with element-wise maximum feature extraction are the pre-feature extraction techniques.

The chapter "MobileNet architecture and its application to computer vision" (Chapter 11) deals with the Mobile Net architecture that is built especially for its use on mobile devices. Along with the overview of mobile vision architecture, this chapter focuses on Mobile net applications. This chapter provides an overview of mobile vision architecture and its application.

The chapter "Study on traffic enforcement cameras monitoring to detect the wrong-way movement of vehicles using deep convolutional neural network" (Chapter 12) describes various vehicle detection and monitoring techniques to perform various operations such as counting vehicles, detecting vehicles, and wrong direction detection.

The chapter "Glasses for smart tourism applications" (Chapter 13) includes highlights such as navigation, interpreting text from images, plant and animal identification, face recognition and other essential highlights like note-taking, time, weather forecast and playing music. All these functions are included on a glass frame which can project the necessary information images onto the glasses. All controls depend on speech recognition and the output is on either visual or sound.

The chapter "Renal calculi detection using modified grey wolf optimization" (Chapter 14) presents the grey wolf optimizer-based support vector machine method is proposed for the detection of renal calculi. The proposed method utilizes the preprocessing step, which consists of two main sub-processes as filtering and histogram equalization. These methods are used to enhance the image quality by removing speckle noise and normalizing the images. This method is expected to aid medical image diagnosis systems with better speed and reliability.

The chapter "On multiclass aerial image classification using learning machines" (Chapter 15) introduces to benefit readers, who are interested to abreast themselves of recent research in area of object detection and classification from aerial images using deep learning methods and their efficiency. The challenges faced respective training issues and testing metrics, available databases and development platforms with useful applications are also discussed in this research.

The chapter "Machine learning methodology towards identification of mature citrus fruits" (Chapter 16) discusses research to provide a software solution for identification of mature citrus fruits with the approach of machine learning algorithm. Image processing techniques are used with multiclass support vector machine (SVM) for segmentation of the fruits. The feed-forward neural network is used to locate the fruit in three dimensions. The result of this would be the detection of fruits and cluster of fruits on the images.

The chapter "Automated detection of defects and grading of cashew kernels using machine learning" (Chapter 17) provides an overview on a cashew defect detector and segregation of high-quality cashew images which primarily is based on leveraging image processing and machine learning techniques for cataloging cashew kernel quality which plummets production expenditure.

I am very thankful to all the contributors of this edited volume for their willingness to participate in this project, their patience and valuable time. I am also grateful to Val Moliere, the IET Senior Commissioning Book Editor, for her encouragement to organize and edit this volume, as well as Olivia Wilkins, the IET Assistant Editor, for her support of this project. I would also like to express my gratitude to Srinivasan N of MPS Limited for his efforts with the final typesetting.

Chiranji Lal Chowdhary
31 March 2021

Chapter 1

Computer vision and recognition-based safe automated systems

Chiranji Lal Chowdhary[1], Harpreet Kaur[2], Dharm Singh Jat[3] and Abhishek Ranjan[4]

Abstract

Computer vision, pattern recognition, deep learning (DL), expert systems, cognitive computing, and the Internet of things are some of the innovations and terminologies that have sprung up as artificial intelligence (AI) has grown in popularity. Among these, computer vision is one of the innovations that allow computers to perceive and comprehend the visual world. Computers recognize and classify artifacts using digital images and DL representations. Computer vision technologies have exploded in popularity in the fields of automation and logistics. Despite these challenges, automation appears to be one of the most exciting regions for recently developed artificial intelligence solutions, primarily computer and machine vision frameworks. Amongst the most important problems in automation is the protection of human–computer and human–machine interactions, which necessitates the "explainability" of techniques, which also precludes the use of any DL-based solutions, regardless of their success in computer vision applications. To automate some aspects of the manual labor involved, robotic platforms have been created. Traditional analytic methods are used by many of the current systems. Usually, automation is not end-to-end, necessitating user involvement to transfer vials, create analytical methods for each compound, and interpret raw data. This chapter is addressing the issues involved with computer vision and recognition-based safe automated systems.

Key Words: Safe automation; computer vision; recognition; artificial intelligence; deep learning; machine learning; robotics

[1]School of Information Technology and Engineering, Vellore Institute of Technology, Vellore, India
[2]Electrical Engineering Department, Chandigarh University, Mohali, India
[3]Faculty of Computing and Informatics, Namibia University of Science and Technology, Windhoek, Namibia
[4]Dean and Head of Maseru Campus, Botho University, Maseru, Lesotho

1.1   Introduction

In recent years, computer vision technologies are applied and used to address industry safety issues. There is a lack of theoretical connections between computer vision technologies and secure automated systems notwithstanding technical advances. Big data and its closely related technologies such as cloud computing, Internet of things (IoT), and artificial intelligence (AI) have achieved enormous attention in the past decade. Artificial intelligence branches that mimic human intelligence include machine learning, computer vision, and robotics, as shown in Figure 1.1. The advancements in both hardware and software for data will together benefit a wide range of fields, including design, construction, and maintenance of underground infrastructure [1].

A primary example is the use of computer vision technology in production facilities, which now has the ability to achieve automatic safety enforcement that is

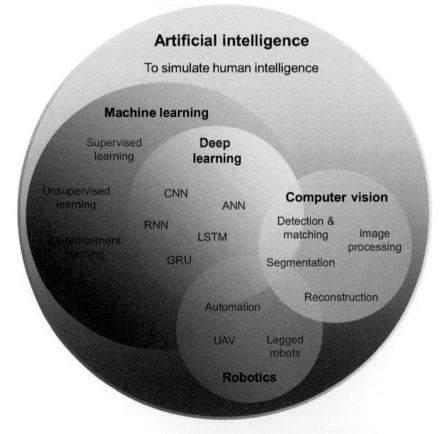

Figure 1.1   Artificial intelligence types include machine learning, deep learning, computer vision, and robotics. Adapted from [2]

superior to that of a human counterpart. Computer vision technologies had exploded in popularity in the fields of automation and robotics, as well as other related fields such as mechatronics, intelligent transportation and logistics, biomedical engineering, and industry 4.0 [3].

Meaningful physical observation and mining the electronic health record (EHR) for evidence of mobility incidents are two existing strategies for tracking patient mobility. These approaches are time and labor intensive, susceptible to erroneous documentation, and have a substantial time lag between patient treatment and reporting. By passively collecting data from the clinical environment and applying machine learning algorithms to identify and measure patient and staff movements automatically, computer vision technology (CVT) provides an alternative solution [4–6].

1.1.1   Role of computer vision in automation

A broad range of manufacturing and customer-related applications use AI-based computer vision systems. It normally results in improved productivity and creativity, expanding the limits of what is possible in the automation industry. Computer vision systems powered by AI boost the production process in the automotive industry, where any mistakes can be costly in a highly competitive industry. In the automotive industry, there are several benefits of using AI-powered computer vision algorithms and applications [7]. Following are the points of benefit for using computer vision in safe automated systems:

- Excellent level.
- Enhanced performance.
- Flexibility of production.
- More complete and trustworthy information.
- Constricted industrial examination.
- Lesser capital equipment and production costs.
- Compact floorage.
- Reduced percent of defective goods.

Computer vision systems are gaining popularity in a variety of fields, especially in the field of industrial automation. They employ image capture and processing technology for visual analysis and control, and they draw on a variety of engineering disciplines such as optics, computer science, industrial automation, and mechanical engineering [8–11].

1.1.2   Organization of the chapter

The organization of this chapter is as follows. Section 1.2 presents a literature survey of safe automation systems. The applications of computer vision technology in automation are discussed in Section 1.3. Section 1.4 shows the points to ensure safety during coronavirus disease 2019 (COVID-19) using computer vision approaches. Finally, the conclusion and overall discussion are presented in Section 1.5.

1.2   Literature survey of safe automation systems

Chen *et al.* [12] proposed a computer vision algorithm for individual vehicles to automatically identify traffic signal light status to facilitate their decision makings for traffic safety. To improve countdown time recognition, the authors created an adaptive threading method using the nearest neighbor interpolation algorithm. The developed method can be used to improve vehicle-crossing protection and operational efficiency at intersections by combining it with other detection and control algorithms.

Park *et al.* [13] worked on a computer vision-oriented method for flood depth estimation with flooded-vehicle images on a ground-level view. Three main processes were used over vehicle objects, and they are (1) segmentation, (2) image retrieval, and (3) flood depth estimation. A region-based convolution neural network (R-CNN), feature maps from VGGNets, and the flood depth were deliberated by comparing the flood objects with three-dimensional (3D) rendered images.

Reggiannini *et al.* [14] studied the saliency concepts and various related applications for production with underwater vision. These tasks were challenging and demanding of specific algorithms and approaches. Heimberger *et al.* [15] proposed a new automated parking system. It was designed and implemented based on computer vision approaches. A latest research direction is in automated driving in industry and academia. An automated parking system is an important product for completely autonomous driving systems. Vital camera systems were used for attending a range of automated parking to complement robustness to systems based on active distance measuring sensors such as ultrasonic and radar. The computer vision modules realized the parking use cases for 3D reconstruction, parking slot marking recognition, free space, and vehicle/pedestrian detection.

Trivedi *et al.* [16] proposed investigations into the role of computer vision technology in developing safer automobiles. A vision system was considered to detect and track roads for vehicles by avoiding hitting with obstacles or pedestrians and also observing inside the vehicle to monitor the concentration of the driver and even predict her intentions. Systems-oriented methods were used for designing computer vision technologies that will make cars safer. The system was broken down into three parts: climate, car, and driver. A novel sensory systems and algorithms capture not only the vehicle's dynamic surround information but also the drivers' state, purpose, and activity patterns.

Loce *et al.* [17] provided a review of computer vision techniques for three main transportation problems: safety, quality, and protection and law enforcement. Security, reliability, law enforcement, energy conservation, and pollution reduction are only a few of the noble goals of smart transportation networks. In this transportation evolution, computer vision plays a critical role. Intelligent sensing and processing technologies were developed by video imaging scientists for a broad range of applications and services.

To automate some aspects of the manual labor involved, robotic platforms have been created. Many current systems, on the other hand, rely on conventional analytic techniques such as high-performance liquid chromatography, which necessitate precalibration for each compound and can be resource intensive. Shiri *et al.* [18] proposed a closed-loop, modular robotic device with integrated solid and liquid dosing capabilities that uses computer vision and iterative feedback to effectively test caffeine solubility in a variety of solvents.

Computer vision is a valuable method in both industrial production and mobile robots, according to Grilo and Figueiredo [19]. Since human vision is the most important sense for providing environmental information to the brain for decision-making, machine vision is quickly becoming the most important artificial sensor in the fields of industrial quality assurance and mobile robot trajectory management. Cheng *et al.* [20] used computer vision in industrial GUI automation. We build smart machines and robots to replace manual labor in the pursuit of Industry 4.0. Various fundamental technologies can be used to simplify the user interface.

Modern machine vision methods are now opening new doors in automated optical image object recognition. Deep learning (DL) and sparse representation are two computer vision methods that are commonly used in the computer vision community for object and texture detection, with promising results in optical images. In the case of X-ray testing, a thorough evaluation is needed [21–31].

1.3 Application of computer vision technology in automation

Nowadays, the application field of AI-based computer vision technology is in the automotive sector. The main points [32] are as follows:

1. Vision-guided machine automation: This is a robot's computer vision that makes the machines more flexible to perform the repeating tasks with increased efficiency.
2. Inspection automation: Component inspections are conducted by computer vision systems 24 h a day, 7 days a week, in a quick and reliable manner that increases performance and product quality.
3. 3D vision automation: Moving, tracking, and precisely localizing moving objects in 3D space are made possible by AI-based computer vision cameras.
4. Automation in a car: Vehicles, pedestrians, and other objects can all be identified with the right algorithms, a strong processor, and a handful of image sensors mounted on a vehicle. However, you can read traffic lights, lane markers, road signs, and road surface conditions.
5. Automation for safer human–robots interaction: Computer vision application powered by AI determines the exact location and direction of the human. Interactions are more fluid, versatile, and safe because of this capacity to respond to human trajectories.

Technology has come a long way in terms of advanced robotics and automation. Machines can now 'see' pictures, process information, and behave in the same way that humans can. Computer vision is a complex technique that allows machines to see and process information. It is a field that combines solid mechanics, neurobiology, and other factors to teach a computer to recognize pictures, videos, or patterns and respond appropriately [32]. New technological developments in computer vision and recognition lead to a safe automated system. Following are the latest such advances.

1.3.1   Using face ID in mobile devices

Face ID is Apple's facial recognition technology, which debuted with the iPhone X in 2017. The technology replaces the Touch ID fingerprint scanning system. This is a face unlock feature [33] which is being used in every Android and iPhone device after once launched. This approach is providing more security to these devices. This is based on computer vision and recognition system which permits the phone device to recognize the facial features (Figure 1.2), matching it with database and finally allow unlock the phone if the new captured face is matching with stored images.

1.3.2   Automated automobiles

In India, automobile accidents are one of the leading causes of death [34]. Every year, an estimated 1.3 million people die in traffic accidents around the world [35]. These staggering statistics illustrate the need for increased caution among drivers and pedestrians. To address such issues, companies such as Tesla have decided to develop self-driving vehicles [36]. Individuals will feel more secure and healthy when driving due to this automation technology.

Figure 1.2   Face ID unlock feature on cell phones

Sensing pedestrian gestures, understanding traffic signals, controlling speed in congested areas, and maneuvering in an emergency are all possible with computer vision (Figure 1.3). Waymo [37] is an example of a business that uses robotics and automation to reduce the number of people involved in car accidents.

1.3.3 Computer vision in agriculture

Agriculture is the reason we can eat nutritious food, but it has always gone unnoticed in the region. Farmers work tirelessly to successfully water crops, spray insecticides, and maintain a high level of turnover. Growing crops on a wide scale is a very hectic operation that cannot be done by a small team.

As a result, computer vision was used to relieve farmers of some of their responsibilities. Drones (Figure 1.4) have been invented by companies like Slantrange using industrial automation to inspect acres of agricultural land, detect crop water levels, and control damage [38]. The sensors can distinguish between crop qualities and distinguish between good and bad yields.

Farmers no longer have to worry about their crops being destroyed due to human error due to intelligent automation. In addition, this computer vision system monitors weather conditions in order to alert farmers to hailstorms or other severe weather. Drones that are regulated by computers are often used in the United States, but they need to be popularized in India as well. Farming provides a living for 70% of the Indian population, and it is past time for the government to take steps to improve their working conditions.

Figure 1.3   Automated car

Figure 1.4   Computer vision in agriculture

1.3.4   Computer vision in the health sector

A patient's life can be lost in a matter of minutes if a diagnosis is made incorrectly. In medicine, computer vision has the highest degree of accuracy and efficacy. It makes early diagnoses, decreases the chances of false-positive tests, and keeps track of the health of the patient. For example, if a patient's blood pressure drops suddenly, the automation technology will automatically sound an alarm and prescribe the necessary medications (Figure 1.5).

Computer vision is also used in specialized fields such as nuclear medicine, which treats medical problems with protons. It also aids in the provision of high-quality body scans and photographs for a clearer understanding of a patient's issues.

1.3.5   Computer vision in the e-commerce industry

Online shopping has been on the rise since the release of COVID-19. Customers prefer to shop online rather than go to stores. This resulted in a significant increase in traffic, which was efficiently managed by most web pages using computer vision software.

Every item is organized by category using intelligent automation, making it easier for customers to search the items. Furthermore, it displays objects based on your preferences, preventing you from browsing through random goods. Computer vision allows for smooth payment transfers in addition to keeping consumers hooked (Figure 1.6).

Customers became irritated as a result of the COVID-19 restrictions, which included long payment lines in shopping malls and shopkeepers who were constantly bickering. On the other hand, they do not have to deal with any of these

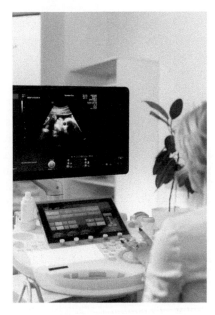

Figure 1.5   Computer vision in the health sector

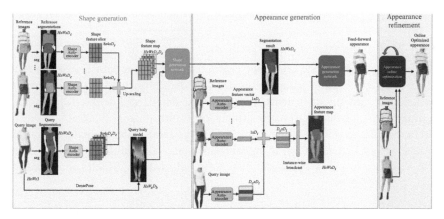

Figure 1.6   "Virtual try-on network" used by Amazon researchers

problems while shopping online. Robotics and automation played the main role in building the best customer experience.

Computer vision is a rapidly developing field that has yet to fully replace conventional technology. However, as time passes, respectable businesses are gradually moving to automation technology. This is due to the fact that in the tech world, change is the only constant, and brands must keep up with the new tools and apps. India, too, will begin researching and investing in computer vision, whether today or tomorrow, in order to build a safer and more prosperous future.

1.3.6   Generating 3D maps

It would make it possible for self-driving cars to gather visual data in real-time. The cameras mounted on such vehicles can capture live video and use computer vision to generate 3D maps. With these maps, autonomous vehicles can better understand their surroundings, spot obstacles in their way, and choose alternate routes.

Self-driving cars can use 3D maps to anticipate collisions and can deploy airbags to shield passengers instantly. This approach increases the safety and reliability of self-driving vehicles. As a result, technology will assist in the development of safe autonomous vehicles that prevent collisions and protect passengers. As a result, computer vision will assist in the development of self-driving vehicles that can prevent collisions and protect passengers in the event of one.

1.3.7   Classifying and detecting objects

Self-driving cars may use technology to identify and track various objects. The vehicle will use light detection and ranging (LiDAR) sensors and cameras to measure distance, with the former using pulsed laser beams. The information collected can be used in combination with 3D maps to detect objects such as traffic lights, cars, and pedestrians. These high-tech vehicles process data in real-time and make decisions based on it. As a result of computer vision, self-driving cars would be able to detect obstacles and prevent collisions and accidents.

1.3.8   Congregation data for training algorithms

Using cameras and sensors, computer vision technology can collect vast quantities of data, such as location information, traffic conditions, road maintenance, and crowded areas, among other items. These specific details will help self-driving cars use situational knowledge to make critical decisions as quickly as possible. This information can be used to train DL models in the future. For example, a thousand computer vision images of traffic signals can be used to train DL models to detect traffic signals while driving. It can also assist self-driving vehicles in classifying various types of items.

1.3.9   Low-light mode with computer vision

Self-driving cars use different algorithms to process low-light images and videos than they do for daylight images and videos. Low-light images can be fuzzy, and such data may not be precise enough for these vehicles.

When the computer vision senses a low-light situation, it will automatically turn to low-light mode. LiDAR sensors, thermal cameras, and high-dynamic-range imaging (HDR) sensors can all be used to gather this information. These devices can be used to produce high-resolution images and videos. Using computer vision technology, self-driving vehicles can be rendered intelligent, self-reliant, and dependable. However, the vehicles could face additional difficulties during construction.

1.4   Ensuring safety during COVID-19 using computer vision

1.4.1   AI started from bringing humans closer to forcing them in keeping apart

As technology crept into our lives, it was almost unanimously done under the slogan "technology will bring us all closer together." Now, in the COVID-19 era, technology has been charged with a much more important task: holding us all apart. This has resulted in a search for innovations that can help us stop the spread of the virus while still helping us to return to growth and prosperity. AI is leading the way, allowing us to work smarter and safer in these uncertain times.

Many of the technologies at the forefront of the war to stop the spread of COVID-19 make use of key elements of computer vision technology, which enables computers to create an artificial interpretation of sequences of images using AI [39].

1.4.2   Access control through computer vision

In the midst of a pandemic, touch-screen and other types of biometric access are still seen as unnecessarily dangerous, as maintaining adequate cleaning and hygiene of these high-touch surfaces is virtually impossible. However, many companies and industries continue to place a high value on safe and stable access control.

Fortunately, central processing units (CPUs) and graphics processing units (GPUs) have progressed to the point that they can now perform rapid, touchless image recognition. The device uses artificial intelligence to quickly scan facial expressions from a safe distance in order to establish identity and access authorization. This removes the need for high-touch surfaces such as keypads and thumbprint scanners, as well as face-to-face human security checkpoints, making security personnel safer and more effective [39].

1.4.3   Thermal fever detection cameras

When offices and workplaces reopen, everyone is struggling to come up with instructions for identifying people who might be infected and stopping them from spreading the virus further. Temperature increase is a universal indicator; however, manually monitoring the temperatures of hundreds or even thousands of people in places such as airports, office buildings, and other high-volume areas is virtually impossible and extremely hazardous.

There is a modern solution to this issue. With AI software and thermal imaging sensors, thousands of people's temperatures can be processed in seconds with no physical touch. This eliminates the need for long queues to enter the office, which wastes both time and money. It also provides more reliable and quicker performance [39].

1.4.4   Social distancing detection

When it comes to stopping the virus's tide, proper social distancing has been a major failure point. Although we hope that people will respect the 6 foot rule, it can be difficult to do so, particularly when people return to their old "natural" environments like the office.

To overcome this, several businesses are currently using AI to detect when people are getting too close together using cell phone cameras and other mobile technologies. The algorithms will send a warning to remind people to step back based on the distance between people in the camera frame or the proximity of mobile devices to each other, giving companies an additional degree of peace of mind [39].

1.4.5   Sanitization prioritization

Sanitizing high-traffic, high-use areas is critical to halting the virus's spread. The algorithms can monitor which areas have had the most interaction and therefore require the most urgent or regular cleaning by incorporating AI technology into existing systems such as surveillance cameras and other devices. This eliminates the guesswork involved in keeping a clean and secure atmosphere for both consumers and employees [39].

1.4.6   Face mask compliance

Aside from AI's ability to monitor temperatures, maintain social distance, and even ensure proper sanitation, there is one crucial factor that scientists have repeatedly stressed is critical to preventing the virus's spread. Face mask enforcement of 100 percent is the solution.

Businesses, on the other hand, are having a hard time ensuring that staff and consumers are adequately dealing with this rule, either by not wearing masks at all or by wearing them incorrectly. AI will serve as your quicker, sharper eyes once more, scanning and monitoring every face to ensure proper enforcement and alerting businesses and security to security breaches.

The critical tasks needed to build healthy companies and workplaces can now be done without the high risks associated with placing workers on the front lines of compliance. Instead, AI technology will help us begin to reconnect while keeping us safe apart [39–40].

1.5   Discussion and conclusion

Computer vision in autonomous vehicles has the potential to contribute to the design and creation of advanced and next-generation vehicles that can navigate around obstacles while keeping passengers safe. Passengers may be transferred to their destination without the need for human interaction. Autonomous vehicles, on the other hand, are still in their infancy and will take some time to be deployed on congested city streets. Even a small fault in the vehicle's design or development may result in fatal accidents and life-threatening circumstances.

The industrial applications of a general-purpose machine vision system were listed. The current state of machine vision inspection technology and study is discussed. The image creation and visual process, computational methods and algorithms, depth details, image representation, modeling, and matching must be considered in the design and operation of a vision system.

Further advances in AI would result in more self-sufficient, highly accurate computer vision technology, completely disrupting the low-qualification job market and introducing previously unknown automation. Furthermore, it will provide unparalleled productivity in life-changing domains such as healthcare diagnostics, food industry precision agriculture, climate change monitoring, public safety, and national security.

In the post-COVID industrial world, vision intelligence will be critical. With the increased adoption of digital transformation in the last 9 months, the urgent need for advanced automation in the manufacturing sector, a rise in demand for vision-guided quality inspection systems, and growing favorable government measures for worker protection, we expect the market to expand exponentially.

References

[1] Huang, M. Q., Ninić, J., and Zhang, Q. B. "BIM, machine learning and computer vision techniques in underground construction: Current status and future perspectives." Tunnelling and Underground Space Technology. 2021; 108: 103677.

[2] Chowdhary, C. L., Mittal, M., Pattanaik, P. A., and Marszalek, Z. "An efficient segmentation and classification system in medical images using intuitionist possibilistic fuzzy C-mean clustering and fuzzy SVM algorithm." Sensors. 2020; 20(14): 3903.

[3] Somayaji, S. R. K., Alazab, M., MK, M., Bucchiarone, A., Chowdhary, C. L., and Gadekallu, T. R. "A framework for prediction and storage of battery life in iot devices using DNN and blockchain." 2020. arXiv preprint arXiv:2011.01473.

[4] Yeung, S., Rinaldo, F., Jopling, J., *et al.* "A computer vision system for deep learning-based detection of patient mobilization activities in the ICU." NPJ Digital Medicine. 2019; 2(1): 1–5.

[5] Das, T. K., Chowdhary, C. L., and Gao, X. Z. Chest X-ray investigation: A convolutional neural network approach. In Journal of Biomimetics, Biomaterials and Biomedical Engineering 2020; 45: 57–70.

[6] Chowdhary, C. L., Das, T. K., Gurani, V. K., Ranjan, A., and Swarnalatha, P. "An efficient approach for lung nodule detection on CT images." Research Journal of Pharmacy and Technology. 2018; 11(8): 3263–3267.

[7] See https://medium.com/computer-vision-technology-drives-the-future/how-computer-vision-reinvents-the-automation-5f02b75e9b16 [Accessed on March 31, 2021].

[8] See https://www.einfochips.com/blog/catching-up-with-latest-trends-in-industrial-automation-machine-vision/ [Accessed on March 20, 2021].

[9] Vasnani, B. K. "Image caption generation with beam search." Intelligent Systems: Advances in Biometric Systems, Soft Computing, Image Processing, and Data Analytics. 2019; 257.

[10]   Senthilkumar, M., and Chowdhary, C. "An AI-based chatbot using deep learning." Intelligent Systems: Advances in Biometric Systems, Soft Computing, Image Processing, and Data Analytics. 2019; 231.

[11]   Chowdhary, C. L., and Mouli, P. C. "Image registration with new system for ensemble of images of multi-sensor registration." World Applied Sciences Journal. 2013; 26(1): 45–50.

[12]   Chen, X., Chen, Y., and Zhang, G. "A computer vision algorithm for locating and recognizing traffic signal control light status and countdown time." Journal of Intelligent Transportation Systems. 2021; 1–19.

[13]   Park, S., Baek, F., Sohn, J., and Kim, H. "Computer vision–based estimation of flood depth in flooded-vehicle images." Journal of Computing in Civil Engineering. 2021; 35(2): 04020072.

[14]   Reggiannini, M., and Moroni, D. "The use of saliency in underwater computer vision: A review. Remote Sensing. 2021; 13(1): 22.

[15]   Heimberger, M., Horgan, J., Hughes, C., McDonald, J., and Yogamani, S. "Computer vision in automated parking systems: Design, implementation and challenges." Image and Vision Computing. 2017; 68, 88–101.

[16]   Trivedi, M. M., Gandhi, T., and McCall, J. "Looking-in and looking-out of a vehicle: Computer-vision-based enhanced vehicle safety." IEEE Transactions on Intelligent Transportation Systems. 2007; 8(1): 108–120.

[17]   Loce, R. P., Bernal, E. A., Wu, W., and Bala, R. "Computer vision in roadway transportation systems: A survey." Journal of Electronic Imaging. 2013; 22(4): 041121.

[18]   Shiri, P., Lai, V., Zepel, T., *et al.* "Automated solubility screening platform using computer vision." iScience. 2021. 102176.

[19]   Grilo, F., and Figueiredo, J. "Computer vision in industrial automation and mobile robots." In Introduction to Mechanical Engineering (pp. 241–266). Cham: Springer; 2018.

[20]   Cheng, Y. P., Li, C. W., and Chen, Y. C. "Apply computer vision in GUI automation for industrial applications [J]." Mathematical Biosciences and Engineering. 2019; 16(6): 7526–7545.

[21]   Samantaray, S., Deotale, R., and Chowdhary, C. L. "Lane detection using sliding window for intelligent ground vehicle challenge." In Innovative Data Communication Technologies and Application (pp. 871–881). Singapore: Springer ; 2021.

[22]   Chandrasekhar, U., and Chowdhary, L. "Classification of ECG beats using features from two-stage two-band wavelet decomposition." Journal of Theoretical and Applied Information Technology. 2013; 49(3).

[23]   Acharjya, D. P., and Chowdhary, C. L. "Breast cancer detection using hybrid computational intelligence techniques." In Handbook of Research on Emerging Perspectives on Healthcare Information Systems and Informatics (pp. 251–280). IGI Global; 2018.

[24]   Chowdhary, C. L., Goyal, A., and Vasnani, B. K. "Experimental assessment of beam search algorithm for improvement in image caption generation." Journal of Applied Science and Engineering. 2019; 22(4): 691–698.

[25] Mery, D., and Arteta, C. "Automatic defect recognition in x-ray testing using computer vision." In 2017 IEEE winter conference on applications of computer vision (WACV) (pp. 1026–1035). IEEE; 2017.

[26] Chowdhary, C. L. "3D object recognition system based on local shape descriptors and depth data analysis." Recent Patents on Computer Science. 2019; 12(1): 18–24.

[27] Chowdhary, C. L., Sai, G. V. K., and Acharjya, D. P. "Decreasing false assumption for improved breast cancer detection." Journal of Science and Arts. 2016; 35(2): 157–176.

[28] Chowdhary, C. L., and Acharjya, D. P. "Singular value decomposition: Principal component analysis-based object recognition approach." Bio-Inspired Computing for Image and Video Processing. 2018; 323 .

[29] Chowdhary, C. L. "Application of object recognition with shape-index identification and 2D scale invariant feature transform for key-point detection." In Feature Dimension Reduction for Content-Based Image Identification (pp. 218–231). IGI Global; 2018.

[30] Jain, T. "Meenu. Automation and integration of industries through computer vision systems." International Journal of Information and Computation Technology. 2013; 3(9): 963–970.

[31] Chowdhary, C. L., Muatjitjeja, K., and Jat, D. S. "Three-dimensional object recognition based intelligence system for identification." In 2015 International Conference on Emerging Trends in Networks and Computer Communications (ETNCC) (pp. 162–166). IEEE; 2015.

[32] See https://xane.ai/5-intelligent-automation-and-computer-vision-applications/ [Accessed on March 31, 2021].

[33] See https://en.wikipedia.org/wiki/Face_ID [Accessed on March 31, 2021].

[34] Dandona, R., Kumar, G. A., Gururaj, G., *et al.* "Mortality due to road injuries in the states of India: The Global Burden of Disease Study 1990–2017." The Lancet Public Health. 2020; 5(2): e86–e98.

[35] See https://www.cdc.gov/injury/features/global-road-safety/index.html [Accessed on March 31, 2021].

[36] See https://www.washingtonpost.com/technology/2020/10/21/tesla-self-driving/ [Accessed on March 21, 2021].

[37] See https://www.theverge.com/2021/3/8/22315361/waymo-autonomous-vehicle-simulation-car-crash-deaths [Accessed on March 31, 2021].

[38] See https://medium.com/aerial-acuity/drones-in-agriculture-then-and-now-ebde3df01667 [Accessed on February 11, 2021].

[39] See https://www.customhouseinc.com/post/creating-a-safer-workplace-during-covid-19-using-computer-vision [Accessed on March 31, 2021].

[40] Panigrahi, R., Borah, S., Bhoi, A. K., *et al.* "Performance assessment of supervised classifiers for designing intrusion detection systems: A comprehensive review and recommendations for future research." Mathematics. 2021; 9(6): 690.

Chapter 2

DLA: deep learning accelerator

*Seyedeh Yasaman Hosseini Mirmahaleh[1]
and Midia Reshadi[1]*

Abstract

Machine learning algorithms-applications (ML) have been deployed to support growth by employing the Internet of things (IoT) in various technologies and aimed at full smart cities. Graphic processing unit (GPU)-based systems or GPU–central processing unit (CPU)-based systems were aimed to implement various MLs' computations including deep neural networks (DNN), convolutional neural network (CNN), and recurrent neural network (RNN), which have utilized parallel computations in multiply-accumulate (MAC) operations. GPU-based systems satisfied flexibility for implementing different MLs and supporting their training and inference phases, whereas increasing neural network's layers remains its energy efficiency problems caused by enhancing memory accesses. According to deploying high accurate image processing, and pattern and speech recognition-based applications and grow up their complexity, some methods had to be considered to tackle the problem. Hence software (SW), hardware (HW), and SW-HW approaches have been proposed to face the challenges, which consist of memory capacity, delay, energy consumption, and bandwidth requirement. One of the approaches is the deep learning accelerator's (DLA) communication infrastructure which connects the processing elements (PE). Trained models' traffic distributes PEs using communication infrastructure, which can inspire various structures and designs such as application-specific integrated circuit (ASIC) and field-programmable gate array (FPGA). As an example of DLA's efficiency, ASIC-based designs have less flexibility and reconfigurability compared to network on chip (NoC) and FPGA-based communication structures and can only support a specific purpose such as image processing. In this chapter, we will focus on hardware approaches to improve the GPU-based system's energy efficiency and performance in the inference phase, which is described as a deep learning accelerator including memory, communication infrastructure, and PEs. We first explain different communication network's role in improving or deteriorating data transfer of

[1]Department of Computer Engineering, Science and Research Branch, Islamic Azad University, Tehran, Iran

trained DNN models between memory and network, and processing elements. Next, we will describe various approaches and investigate their impact on DLA-based system's efficiency, which have included data-flow mapping, data-flow stationaries, traffic patterns, and partitioning methods.

Key Words: Deep learning accelerator; data-flow mapping; communication infrastructure; traffic pattern

2.1 Introduction

The highlight role of deploying Internet of things (IoT)-based smart cities and the Internet of medical things (IoMT)-based applications increased by employing machine learning algorithms to analyze and infer the edge nodes' monitored information. Growing up, the image processing's accuracy and applications affected increasing neural networks (NNs)' layers besides deploying IoT and IoMT. To support the different machine learning algorithms (RNN, DNN, and CNN) and the NN with many complex layers, GPU and GPU–CPU-based systems utilize parallel computations, including MAC operations. Parallel computations enhanced memory accesses, which remains energy efficiency problems for GPU and GPU-CPU-based systems in the inference phase, whereas these systems have high flexibility to support MLs [1–3]. Hence deep learning accelerators have been proposed to face the problems caused by increasing NNs' layers, which consist of the energy consumption, delay, memory capacity, and bandwidth requirements. DLA approaches consist of DNN pruning, employing binary weights, software, SW-HW, and hardware methods, which we focus on HW-based deep learning accelerators and analyze their role in tackling the challenges [4–5].

Different methods have been presented to accelerate deep learning, including three-dimensional memory (3D memory), communication infrastructures, embedded memory (such as eDRAM), and various mapping algorithms [6–10]. Different structures have proposed connecting DLA's components, including ASIC, FPGA, and NoC-based designs, and we will investigate their weaknesses and advantages in improving or deteriorating energy efficiency problems [1]. Deep learning accelerator-based systems have aimed to confront the challenges caused by increasing DNN layers and their complexity. In contrast, their flexibility is challenging due to the support of the different NN-trained models. Some approaches proposed to improve DLAs' flexibility besides reducing memory accesses, energy consumption, delay, and memory and bandwidth requirements included mapping and stationary methods [11–15]. Various technologies were employed to communicate structures such as optical, optical-electrical, through silicon via (TSV) interconnections, and photonic and interposer-based networks that were affected to speed up them and to face energy efficiency problems [10,16]. According to DLAs' flexibility problem, traffic distribution and data transfer methods can improve their flexibility, including flow and data-flow mapping, stationaries, and partitioning approaches.

In this chapter, we follow hardware-based DLAs' purpose and describe different architectures to accelerate the inference phase and their impact on solving energy efficiency challenges in addition to the approaches for improving deep learning accelerator-based systems' flexibility.

2.2   ASIC-based design accelerator

We consider a scenario for analyzing ASIC-based deep learning accelerators and their characteristics to satisfy flexibility besides facing energy efficiency problems. This section first demonstrates an ASIC design to accelerate the inference phase of deep and convolutional neural networks and evaluates its efficiency and possible weaknesses points to follow the issue.

Figure 2.1 shows a fully connected neural network including one input layer, seven hidden layers, and one output layer that is trained gradient-distance-based method according to Matyas standard function [17]. We start the ASIC-based design scenario with a simple architecture for NN in order to evaluate the design's performance in improving the inference phase's energy efficiency, as shown in Figure 2.1. The presented NN's neurons are mapped on a set of PEs using transferring data from the global buffer to multilevel switches (MLSs) in order to data transaction to processing elements by MLSs. To propose an ASIC design for improving latency and total energy, we have two choices that consist of weight, neuron, and layer pruning before mapping and providing an energy-aware algorithm to analyze MLSs' performance and removing the components according to the algorithm feedbacks.

First, a set of weight data are transferred from global buffer to PEs using multilevel switches, in which MAC or multiply operations are performed into processing elements, as shown in Figure 2.2. The proposed neural network consists

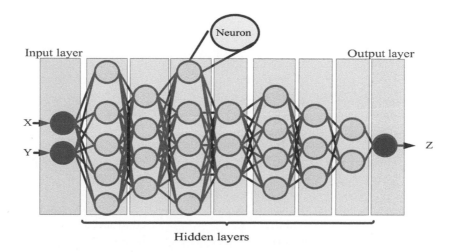

Figure 2.1   A fully connected NN's architecture

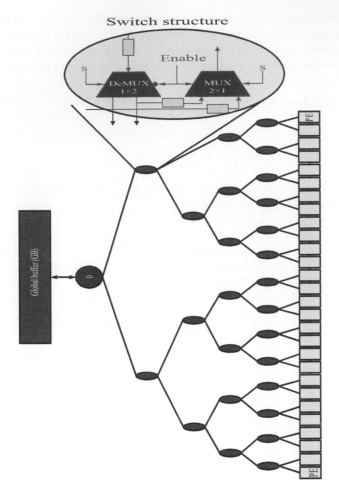

Figure 2.2   ASIC-based design for DLA

of 28 neurons, in which two, 25, and one neuron are located on input, hidden, and output layers, respectively. Therefore, we consider 28 processing elements for performing neurons' operations that are connected and related to each other by the links with high bandwidth. The accumulated partial sums (Psums) are transferred from PEs to the global buffer using middle multilevel switches including multi-plexer and demultiplexer for data transactions on the duplex links.

The MLSs' structure is inspired by a binary tree to distribute NN's traffic onto PEs that its root (switch 0) is a hotspot point due to direct connection with GB and two switches in the next level, and transacting maximum flow. The proposed structure just supports and accelerates the neural network, whereas its efficiency is reduced for other neural networks with different architectures and standard func-tions because of changing the number of NN's neurons and more or fewer computations than the trained neural network based on Matyas function. With increasing multiply operations for other NNs, 28 PEs cannot support their MAC operations that have led to a decrease in DLA's efficiency. Reducing MAC operations leads to an increase in the number of idle PEs, and hardware and static power consumption overheads.

In the pruning method after mapping, we remove the weak weights, neurons, and layers, where their value is closed to zero. The pruning method maintains the margin error rate for the NN without losing accuracy and also improves NN's performance due to removing the elapsed time and total energy for transferring weak weights and neurons with Psums close to zero, as shown in Figure 2.3. This method reduces GB accesses, total delay, and MAC operations' energy consumption by removing 34 weak weights and five neurons from the NN architecture. We map the pruned NN on the DLA for analyzing and estimating its efficiency in improving latency and total energy.

In employing an energy-aware algorithm-based method, the DLA's components with minimal energy consumption are identified using the algorithm after simulating its behavior induced by distributing the NN's traffic, which is removed from the structure before fabricating.

Figure 2.4 illustrates the impact of performing the energy-aware algorithm on recognizing the components with minimal cost, which are determined by green color and are removed from the structure before fabricating. This method can reduce cost overhead compared to the pruning method before mapping according to

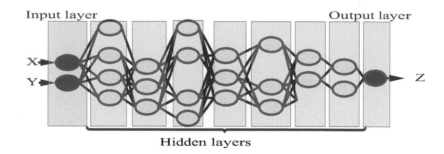

Figure 2.3   The pruned neural network's architecture

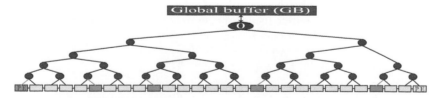

*Figure 2.4   Determining low-energy components with green color after
performing the algorithm*

removing the static power consumption of switches and processing elements, whereas this overhead is not significant.

As shown in Figure 2.5, DLA has an impressive effect on improving the inference phase's efficiency for the neural network after removing hardware overhead, whereas the structure supports the proposed NN and its flexibility is challenging for other NNs with different architectures.

The DLA's structure can be optimized by presenting a flow mapping method and a traffic pattern to distribute the neural network's weights and inputs onto PEs, which can remove more low-energy components from the accelerator design according to identify them by the energy-aware algorithm. Also, we can increase the DLA's flexibility using programmable fully connected multilevel switches to support NNs with different architectures while their wiring overhead increases cost including total delay, energy, and area consumption. Figure 2.6 shows the proposed DLA based on a reconfigurable design including the programmable fully

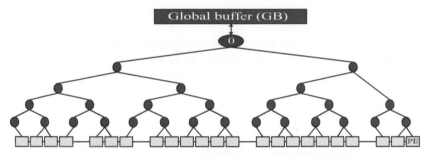

Figure 2.5   Customized structure of the ASIC-based DLA

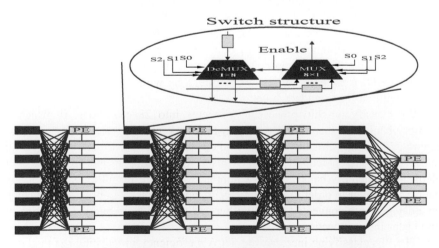

Figure 2.6   ASIC-based DLA with programmable switches

connected MLSs. We classify the 28 processing elements into four categories that consist of eight PEs because of performing 8-bit multiply or MAC operations. The reconfigurable structure is customized by employing energy and delay-aware intelligent algorithms for learning and recognizing hotspot paths and low-energy components, which are almost observed in transferring data of the different NNs. The identified low-energy components are removed from the design before fabricating and its flexibility is increased compared to the initial provided DLA architecture (Figure 2.5). Nevertheless, this structure likewise faces the initial proposed ASIC design in case of following the specific application's purposes and improving its efficiency.

To map deep and convolutional neural networks' data flow on ASIC-based DLA such as the proposed structure, we utilize the internal buffers into PEs for reusable data storage including Psums and synaptic weights, which decreases memory accesses and its negative factors including total delay and energy. Memory structure affects improving ASIC-based DLA's efficiency and facing its problems, which consists of utilizing 3D memory, embedded dynamic random access memory (eDRAM), static (SRAM), data buffering into PEs, and volatile memory [18]. Processing-in-memory (PIM) method has a significant effect on reducing communication delay and power consumption as an ASIC approach for increasing the energy efficiency of CNNs and DNNs' inference phase by classifying data into two categories of low and high reusable data [19–20]. Nevertheless, ASIC-based designs just follow specific purposes such as speech recognition and have less flexibility than FPGA and NoC-based DLAs, in which the issue is investigated in Sections 2.3 and 2.4.

2.3 FPGA-based design accelerator

This section focuses on FPGA-based DLA's performance in speed up the inference phase of deep and convolutional neural networks and reducing latency caused by data transfer, processing, and traffic distribution. To follow the issue and analyze FPGA-designs' role, we consider the proposed NN architecture in Section 2.2 (Figure 2.1) for mapping its dataflow on a deep learning accelerator that its structure is based on a field-programmable gate array. Its programmability feature leads to enhance DLA's flexibility to support the NNs with different architecture and trained with various standard functions.

We classify on-chip processing elements into 28 categories, in which the memory banks are shared between them to reduce memory accesses, as shown in Figure 2.7. Partial sum and accumulation operations are performed by PEs that the reusable data are shared between them using transferring Psums from processing elements to memory banks. In this example, we inspire from the number of NN's neurons per layer in order to classify PEs, in which the located processing elements on a category are connected to each other and utilized from internal buffering and on-cluster interconnections.

The PEs classifying increases the DLA's efficiency in reducing the total delay and energy consumption induced by on-chip and off-chip memory accesses.

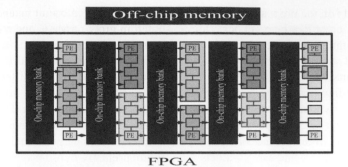

Figure 2.7   *FPGA-based design for DLA*

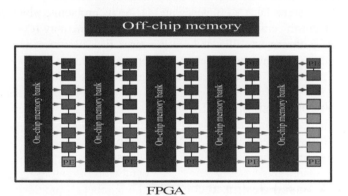

Figure 2.8   *Green, orange, and red color demonstrate the standard, medium, and critical situations of the component after analyzing performance by an intelligent algorithm*

Nevertheless, the proposed structure for an FPGA-based DLA and classifying can only support the neural network, whereas a reconfigurable architecture has to present for increasing its flexibility to satisfy other NNs' energy efficiency.

Its reconfigurability feature has a highlighted role in switching on the new relationship between lookup tables (LUTs) and programmable gates for providing the different structures to support the various architecture of NNs. This characteristic gives an opportunity to present a flexible method for classifying PEs based on CNN and DNN architectures and their traffic. Also, an intelligent algorithm can help to detect onboard hotspot paths and reconnect between components and reprogram them for normalizing flow on an FPGA board. Figure 2.8 demonstrates the role of an intelligent algorithm for identifying hotspot paths and idle components on the proposed FPGA-based DLA that standard, medium, and critical situations for different components are illustrated in green, orange, and red colors. The algorithm utilizes analyzing energy consumption, total flow, and delay parameters for identifying critical paths and idle components, which can employ the Fuzzy approaches to determine the three situations. To recognize the situation of different components, we reprogram the gate array or redesign the structure to distribute flow and achieve a standard or medium situation.

The fixed FPGA's characteristics lead to reduce flexibility compared to NoC-based DLAs, which we can propose a state-of-the-art design for FPGA's structure to accelerate CNN and DNN models with minimal energy consumption. To optimize an FPGA-based DLA's efficiency, providing an approach (such as data-flow mapping, partitioning, and clustering methods) has less cost than presenting a novel design for FPGA's structure. The case studies proposed different approaches to accelerate deep and convolutional neural networks' inference phase on FPGA families-based designs such as employing Zynberry and highlight roles of its modules in increasing energy efficiency compared to GPU and GPU-CPU-based systems [21]. Its programmability feature increases flexibility compared with the ASIC-based design for deep learning accelerators.

2.4 NoC-based design accelerator

Network-on-chip was proposed as a scalable on-chip communication infrastructure to reduce interconnection delay and energy consumption of transferring data between PEs. Shared bus-based systems face bandwidth requirement and arbitration mechanism problems and also increasing the number of processing elements reduces the bandwidth's efficiency and system performance. Therefore, communication infrastructures affect improving or deteriorating deep and convolutional neural networks' efficiency with reducing or increasing total energy and communication delay. In this section, we investigate NoC-based DLA's role in tackling energy efficiency problems for implementing DNN and CNN models by GPU and GPU-CPU-based systems. To analyze the issue, we first map the proposed NN's data flow (Figure 2.1) on a mesh network and investigate its impact on improving total delay and energy. This section evaluates the impact of different on-chip networks with different topologies (Regular and irregular) on speedup DNNs' inference phase.

We consider a mesh network to follow the purpose of investigating NoC-based DLA's efficiency in improving CNN and DNN models' performance according to its features including the high bisection bandwidth, existing different deadlock-free routing algorithms, and its planar structure [22]. The proposed neural network's weights and inputs are transferred from the global buffer into the mesh topology' PEs that left-side partition's processing elements are connected to the shared bus and are the source or destination nodes for right-side partition's PEs, as shown in Figure 2.9(a) and (b). The designation nodes are located on the right-side partition

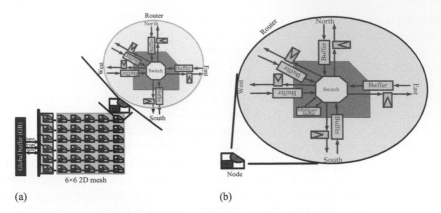

Figure 2.9   NoC-based DLA: (a) 6 ×6 2D mesh without multicast buffer and
(b) the mesh's router structure with employing multicast buffer.
Adapted from [14,15]

and perform multiply or MAC operations. As shown in Figure 2.9(a), we unicast the
NN's traffic onto processing elements of the mesh that its dimension is determined
according to the number of NN's PEs and its layers. Its high bisection bandwidth
leads to speed up data transfer between PEs, whereas distributing traffic in unicast
increases GB accesses and total hop counts between source and destination nodes.

Therefore, the proposed NoC-based design only satisfies flexibility, reconfigurability, and scalability features to accelerate a neural network, whereas lack of multicasting traffic is challenging for the proposed DLA because of increasing memory
accesses in unicast traffic distribution. We have to propose a structure or method for
NoC-based DLA, which consists of the multicasting traffic feature besides its flexibility, reconfigurability, and scalability. Providing a novel design for the router can
support the NN's traffic distribution in multicasting which this structure is simpler
than the baseline router according to employ XY-based routing algorithm. The multicast buffer first receives flit from input links and copies it on the other links, in which
Figure 2.9(b) demonstrates the switch structure with a multicast buffer. Transferring
the received flits to other links of the router creates an opportunity for multicasting
traffic on the adjacent nodes by utilizing the multicast buffer, which this feature can
help to distribute the similar weights on a set of the network's PEs in parallel con-
currently. NoC-based DLA's structure with multicast buffer has a highlighter role in
improving the NN's performance than the proposed structure without employing the
multicast buffer because of reducing global buffer accesses and facing its problems.
We propose a 6×6 2D mesh for transferring the NN's weights and inputs onto the
network's PEs, which consists of 36 processing elements and routers with multicast
buffer, as shown in Figure 2.10. The number of processing elements and the network
dimensions is determined by the NN's characteristics including the total number of
neurons and layers, which are based on ifmap, filter, channel, and kernel sizes for
deep and convolutional neural network models.

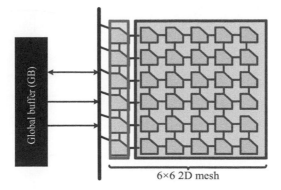

Figure 2.10   The NN traffic distribution on the mesh network

First, the neural network's similar weights are multicasted on a set of PEs, and next inputs are distributed onto the mesh's processing elements in order to perform multiply and accumulate operations. The computed Psums of the neuron in a layer are transferred to the next layer's neurons and follow the process to reach the output. We distribute the NN's partial sums on the mesh topology instead of computing Psums into PEs for estimating communication delay and energy that are demonstrated by the NoC-based DLA's efficiency using a mesh network. The yellow-color nodes illustrate the network's PEs that the neural network's traffic is distributed onto them. The data-flow mapping method can have an impressive effect on improving the deep learning accelerator's performance by reducing total hop counts and flows.

The mesh-based deep learning accelerator utilizes scalability, reconfigurability, and multicasting features to support the different trained models and improve their performance, which a partitioning method can create a flexible structure for the DLA. Nevertheless, its arbiter circuit and crossbar switch structures lead to hardware overhead for a mesh with large scale dimension to support CNN and DNN models. We demonstrate that providing a very simpler design for switches than baseline crossbar switches eliminates hardware overhead. The switch structure consists of a 4×1 multiplexer and a 1×4 demultiplexer that transfers data on a link based on four address lines' value, as shown in Figure 2.11(a). A switch selector is utilized to transfer data on corresponding rows and columns of destination nodes instead of employing the baseline router's arbiter circuit with less hardware overhead compared to its complex structure [14,15]. A row and column decoders, and multiplexers are included a simple structure for the switch selector because of utilizing an XY-based algorithm and a simple arbitration mechanism. Figure 2.11(b) shows a sample of switch selector structure that determines corresponding rows and columns of destination nodes due to the address line and set enable signal [14].

By presenting a simple structure for the switch and employing a switch selector instead of an arbiter circuit, a mesh-based DLA improves CNN and DNN models'

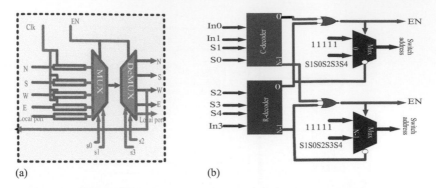

(a)   (b)

Figure 2.11   The switch and switch selector structure for the mesh-based DLA:
(a) switch structure and (b) switch selector. Adapted from [14]

efficiency with the minimal cost including hardware overhead. The planar mesh's structure creates an opportunity to distribute trained models' traffic on the network's processing elements in four directions that its feature reduces total hop counts and flow on the mesh's nodes. Its flexibility, reconfigurability, scalability, and multicasting traffic lead to increase energy efficiency and reduced communication delay for different deep and convolutional neural network's models compared to ASIC and FPGA-based DLAs.

The various topologies have been proposed as an on-chip communication infrastructure, which is classified into two categories including regular and irregular networks such as C-Mesh, torus, fat tree, binary tree, butterfly, Bene's, clos, octagon, hypercube, and SPIN [22]. Also, the researchers proposed novel structures as an NoC that included the hybrid architecture and technology such as wireless/wireline-based mesh, three-dimensional mesh, 2.5D mesh, and Eyeriss network [11,23,24].

A binary tree can be an appropriate structure for an on-chip communication network for mapping the trained models' data flow onto its MAC units compared to other proposed topologies (except for the mesh network) according to its minimum wiring overhead. The binary tree's nodes can distribute CNNs and DNNs' traffic onto MAC units to perform the operations and speed up the inference phase by employing extra links' high bandwidth, which have switch's role to data transaction. Also, the network's node structure can consist of the internal buffer, switch, and PE, in which neural networks' data flow is mapped onto processing elements and transferred to next level nodes of the tree by their switches.

We evaluate the binary tree's efficiency in improving deep and convolutional neural networks' performance, whereas its node structure includes processing element, switch, and buffer. To follow the purpose, we map the neural network's weights and inputs (Figure 2.1) onto a binary tree's PE, as shown in Figure 2.12. The number of levels and nodes of the binary inspires the number of layers and neurons of the neural network that yellow-color nodes demonstrate the network's utilized nodes for processing or transferring data.

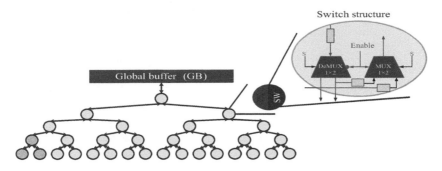

Figure 2.12   NoC-based DLA with a binary tree

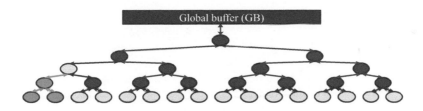

Figure 2.13   The situation of the binary tree's nodes and components after analyzing simulation results

According to propose an NoC-based DLA, employing the pruning method before mapping leads to ASIC-based design to accelerate the NN and customize the DLA structure, in which the issue was investigated in Sections 2.2 and 2.3. Therefore, we can simulate the DLA architecture, distribute the NN's traffic onto PEs, and estimate the total energy and delay caused by transferring data on the network's processing elements. The DLA's efficiency can be improved after analyzing the simulation result and providing a data-flow mapping approach to reduce energy consumption and latency. Also, a delay-energy-aware algorithm affects increasing the NoC-based deep learning accelerator's efficiency using identifying hotspot-paths, high-energy components, and the network's idle nodes.

By recognizing idle nodes and high-energy components, presenting a flow mapping or employing the extra links with high bandwidth or both methods have a significant effect on improving the DLA's performance by utilizing idle nodes and flow uniform distribution on the binary tree's nodes. Figure 2.13 shows idle and high-energy components of the NoC-based DLA's binary tree with green and red colors, respectively, which are identified after simulating the design and distributing the NN's traffic. The DLA's cost can be reduced by employing extra links between the left and right references per level with high bandwidth, which utilizes it to achieve the root of the binary tree, as shown in Figure 2.14.

Nevertheless, a baseline binary tree's structure cannot support a DNN or CNN's traffic as an on-chip communication network and leads to the deteriorating

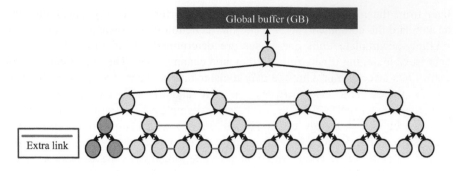

Figure 2.14   Optimized the NoC-based DLA with binary tree

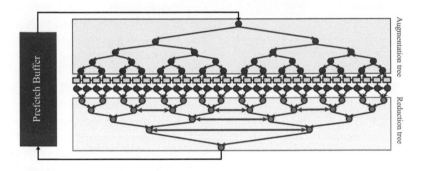

Figure 2.15   MAERI deep learning accelerator. Adapted from [25]

deep neural networks' efficiency according to increased communication delay including queue, processing, and internal buffering delay. This structure utilizes a memory element with high capacity into each node to temporary data storage of MAC operations and waits to release other nodes for transferring data between GB and binary tree's PEs that lead to enhance its cost. According to the existing characteristics, employing high bandwidth-extra links and idle nodes has no significant effect on improving the DLA's efficiency because of increasing the binary tree's nodes with raising the number of layers and neurons of the neural networks.

A state-of-the-art structure for a binary tree as a communication network affects increasing CNN and DNN energy efficiency, reducing communication delay, and supporting the various trained models' traffic with high flexibility and low cost. The structure has to eliminate high flow and data transfer rate on the connector links between a binary tree's levels to distribute traffic from root to PEs and transfer accumulated Psums from processing elements to global buffer.

Figure 2.15 demonstrates the MAERI network as an NoC-based communication infrastructure to accelerate deep and convolutional neural networks, which include reduction and augmentation trees to reduce the flow on connector links between different levels of the tree and global buffer. The network's nodes transfer data from the global buffer to MAC units to perform multiply operations and accumulate the computed Psums using the reduction tree, in which the number of multiply-accumulate units and nodes are determined considering DNN's characteristics including ifmap, filter, kernel, and channel sizes. The high bandwidth of extra links affects improving the data transfer rate between the root and the next layer's nodes, and also between the left and right references per layer. Nevertheless, its root nodes flow overhead and employing extra bandwidth have a negative impact on energy efficiency and also its data computation dependency increases communication delay. According to the proposed DLA's structure, the trained models' traffic is only distributed in one direction of the network's nodes. To improve MAER's performance, an energy and delay-aware algorithm affects reducing total energy and delay identifying idle virtual neurons and assigning them to map the trained models' data flow based on their characteristics that consist of the input feature map, filter, channel, and kernel sizes. Recognizing the number of idle virtual neurons and MAC units, and the suitable number of neurons for different deep and convolutional neural network' models help to traffic uniform distribution on the network, which improves MAERI's efficiency.

Figure 2.16 shows classification of MAERI's multiplayer switches to introduce virtual neurons on the reduction tree that accumulates the computed partial sums and transfer to the prefetch buffer by the reduction tree's root node.

According to baseline binary tree and MAERI network structure, data-flow mapping, stationary, and partitioning methods have not significantly affect their performance to implement the inference phase of machine learning algorithms.

A suitable structure for designing a deep learning accelerator has to include the flexible, reconfigurable, scalable, and traffic distribution in multicasting features to support various ML algorithms (DNN, CNN, and RNN) without losing or falling energy efficiency. Also, a DLA's structure has more efficiency on speedup DNN and CNN's inference phase and reduce latency with high flexibility in case of supporting flow mapping, stationary, and partitioning methods, which is faced with

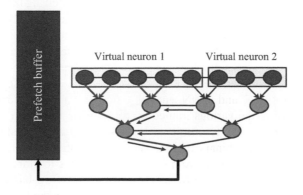

Figure 2.16   Virtual neuron assignment on MAERI's reduction tree. Adapted from [25]

different neural network architectures such as a sparse deep and convolutional neural network. On-chip communication infrastructure has a highlighted role to satisfy the characteristics to propose a design for a deep learning accelerator with high energy efficiency and flexibility. NoC-based DLAs have a highlighter role than ASIC and FPGA designs to speed up the inference phase due to reduced interconnection delay and communication energy. The mesh network can be a suitable communication infrastructure for an NoC-based DLA in case of providing a simpler structure of the routers and switches than its baseline architecture, which leads to improve the deep learning accelerator's performance with high flexibility and minimum cost.

2.5   Flow mapping and its impact on DLAs' performance

This section is aimed to analyze the role of flow and data-flow mapping methods in improving deep learning accelerators' performance with different structures including ASIC, FPGA, and NoC designs. Flow and data-flow mapping are the techniques for transferring data from off-chip or on-chip memory to the processing elements that are improved communication delay and energy using reducing memory accesses and interconnections between PEs. The approaches affect on reducing or increasing a DLA's efficiency in case of its compatibility with the deep learning accelerator's structure [26]. A flexible and reconfigurable structure can support flow and data-flow mapping methods with more efficiency compared to inflexible and un-reconfigurable designs according to presenting a set of PEs with high communication between them in order to map flow or data flow on them.

Flow and data-flow mapping's impact on ASIC-based DLA: An ASIC design follows a specific purpose and its connections are based on the application's characteristics such as a pruned neural network.

We consider a scenario for mapping the NN's data (Figure 2.1) onto ASIC-based DLA (Figure 2.2) to analyze its role in improving or deteriorating performance. As shown in Figure 2.17, we first broadcast the similar weights onto DLA's processing elements and classify the related inputs to them into two categories for

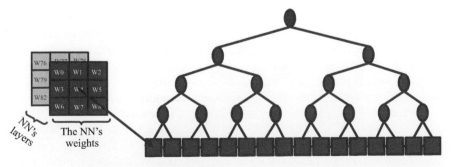

Figure 2.17   Broadcasting the neural network's similar weights onto the DLA's PEs based on WMIS method

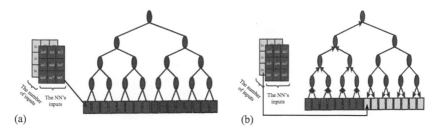

Figure 2.18   *Multicasting the neural network's inputs onto the DLA's PEs based on WMIS method: (a) multicasting inputs onto PEs using left-references of the tree and (b) multicasting inputs onto PEs using right-references of the tree and transferring Psums to GB using the tree's left references*

multicasting them onto PEs using the tree's left and right references, respectively. Figure 2.18(a) and (b) demonstrates multicasting of the neural network's inputs onto the DLA's processing elements. We name the data-flow mapping approach to weight and multicasting inputs stationary (WMIS), which can also be employed after customizing DLA's structure (Figure 2.5).

WMIS method affects improving the DLA's performance with uniform distributing flow onto its processing elements and reducing global buffer access by broadcasting similar weights and multicasting related inputs to them onto two different classified PEs. After releasing the tree's root node and performing multiply and accumulate operations into the first category of processing elements, the computed Psums are transferred to GB using left-references of the tree, which are reduced total delay and energy. The data-flow mapping approach has an impressive effect on improving the performance of deep learning accelerators that their design is inspired by tree structure as a communication infrastructure. We analyze data-flow mapping's role in increasing or deteriorating ASIC-based DLAs' performance by employing tree structure as a communication platform, whereas ASIC designs for deep learning accelerators can be very vast and diversified to satisfy the specific application's purposes.

According to ASIC-based designs' characteristics, WMIS is not a generalized method to support all ASIC-deep learning accelerators and has a negative impact on their efficiency, as an example, the approach has not affected the performance of the DLA with fully connected switches (Figure 2.6). We analyze flow or data-flow mapping's impact on the fully connected switches array's efficiency (Figure 2.16) that its hieratical structure creates a restriction to broadcast a neural network's data. We multicast the NN's similar weights (Figure 2.1) per layer onto the DLA's processing elements (Figure 2.6) and its inputs are transferred to PEs, which multicasting similar weights is based on the different levels of MLSs, as shown in Figure 2.19(a) and (b). The data-flow mapping method reduces global buffer accesses to read similar weights using multicasting them onto the deep learning accelerator's PEs, which we name the approach to multicast weight stationary (MWS).

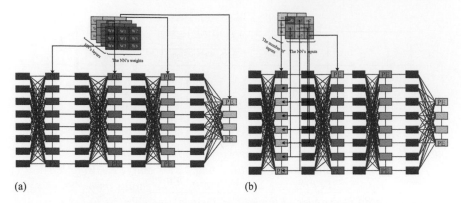

Figure 2.19   Multicasting the neural network's similar weights and distributing
its inputs in unicast onto the DLA's PEs based on MWS method:
(a) multicasting the NN's similar weights onto PEs and
(b) unicasting inputs onto the DLA's PEs

MWS method has less impact on improving an ASIC-based DLA than WMIS because of increasing GB accesses for MWS compared to WMIS. Also, WMIS's efficiency in reducing communication delay is more than MWS according to MLSs' structure between the processing elements, whereas transferring data between PEs for fully connected multilevel switches is faster than WMIS. The observations prove that we cannot propose a generalized method for flow or data-flow mapping on ASIC-based DLA and are dedicated to a specific design for a deep learning accelerator.

The programmable gates' features and on-board data storage sources of FPGA-based design create an opportunity for providing a different effective data-flow mapping to improve the performance of deep learning accelerators due to the highlighted role of the communication infrastructure to support the issue. We illustrate the impact of dedicated memory elements and data-flow mapping methods on increasing FPGA-based DLA's efficiency by presenting a scenario to analyze the issue, which consists of mapping the neural network's data (Figure 2.1) onto the deep learning accelerator's PEs (Figure 2.7). We dedicate the four global buffers to similar weights storage and broadcast them onto processing elements, in which Figure 2.20 demonstrates the provided process. After distributing the NN's weight onto PEs, the four GBs are reset and are dedicated to the NN's input storage for multicasting them onto the DLA's processing elements, as shown in Figure 2.21 (a)-(b). We again reset GBs after multicasting inputs onto the processing element and the computed Psums are transferred to the global buffers, which the process is performed in hieratical due to data dependency between the different levels of the neural network. We just multicast the related inputs to the broadcasted similar weight, whereas other NN's inputs are distributed in unicast onto the processing elements.

The data-flow mapping increases the energy efficiency by reducing on-chip and off-chip memory accesses by broadcasting similar weights onto the DLA's

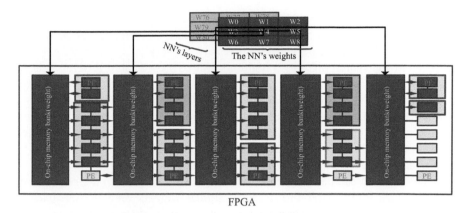

Figure 2.20   Broadcasting the NN's similar weights onto PEs

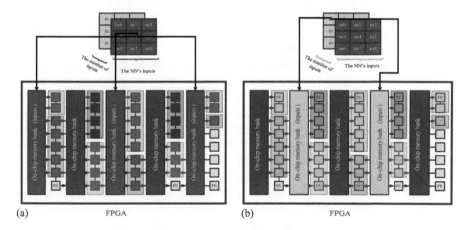

Figure 2.21   Multicasting the neural network's inputs onto the DLA's PEs:
(a) multicasting inputs onto a set of PEs after resetting tree GBs and
(b) multicasting inputs onto a set of PEs after resetting two GBs

processing elements instead of distributing them in unicast and also multicasting inputs. Also, dedicating global buffers to specific data storage (such as weights storage) leads to a decrease in off-chip memory accesses and bandwidth requirements. Similar weights are assigned to the similar value or nearest values to each other that considering similar them has no negative impact on the neural networks' accuracy and performance.

In a deep and convolutional neural network, their data reusability features (such as reusable synaptic weights and Psums) affect reducing memory access and facing its problems using internal or shared flash memory into or between processing elements to reusable data storage. We utilize the feature to propose a flow or data-flow mapping method to improve a deep learning accelerator's performance by multicasting them onto a related set of PEs to the computed partial sums and synaptic weights. The experimental and analytical results demonstrate employing distributed and shared memory's highlight role to provide an effective method for mapping data flow and also lead to reduce flow overhead to access on-chip memory. As shown in Figures 2.20 and 2.21, distributing on-chip memory banks and sharing them between processing elements help to broadcast the neural network's weight and multicast its inputs onto the FPGA-based DLA's processing elements, which is generalized to map different CNN and DNN models and improve their performance.

This method can be assigned as the weight stationary (WS) method according to distributed inputs after broadcasting similar weights onto the deep learning accelerator's PEs and generalizing it for mapping different trained models. Nevertheless, the fixed components and the number of programmable gate array characteristics of an FPGA-based design create a restriction to provide the different flow or data-flow mapping, which has less efficiency in improving a deep learning accelerator's performance than NoC-based DLAs. Indeed, its less flexibility leads to a challenge to propose different partitioning and mapping methods with a high impact on the DLA's performance.

To analyze flow or data-flow mapping's role in increasing NoC-based DLA's efficiency for facing GPU and GPU-CPU-based system' problems, we map the neural network's data flow (Figure 2.1) onto the deep learning accelerators' PEs (Figures 2.9, 2.14, and 2.15). The NN's similar weights broadcast onto the processing elements that distribute on them using the left and right references of the tree, as shown in Figure 2.22. We demonstrate the data-flow paths on the DLA with red-color arrows, which illustrates different data-flow mapping methods for DLAs with tree-based communication infrastructures in ASIC and NoC-based designs. The inputs of the neural network are distributed in multicast onto the tree's processing elements using the left and right references, respectively. Figure 2.23(a)-(b) shows multicasting the related inputs to broadcasted similar weights after distributing them on the tree's nodes. According to the tree structure, the distributing process is performed in a hieratical that utilizes the extra links to reduce

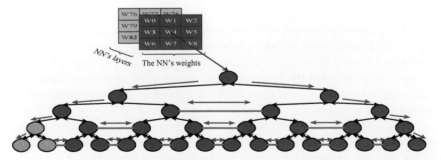

Figure 2.22   Broadcasting the NN's similar weights onto the DLA's nodes

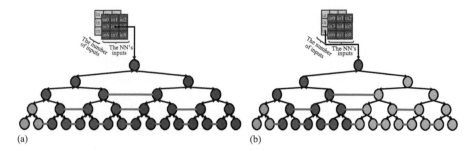

(a)   (b)

Figure 2.23   Multicasting the neural network's inputs onto the tree's nodes after broadcasting weights: (a) multicasting inputs onto the nodes using left-references of the tree and (b) multicasting inputs onto the nodes using right-references of the tree

communication delay and energy caused by transferring data between the root and other nodes.

With broadcasting the NN's similar weights onto the tree's nodes, the root node' flow, global buffer, and off-chip memory access are reduced, which leads to increase energy efficiency and decreased latency. The data-flow mapping method leads to flow and traffic uniform distributions onto the tree's nodes including switch, buffer, and PE. Also, multicasting the related inputs to similar weights reduces the total delay and queue's wait time to release the sources in order to employ them for transferring data from the tree's nodes to global buffers.

First, we employ the left-references of the tree to multicast the inputs onto its nodes and next multicast them onto the nodes using its right-references, in which the computed Psums are transferred to GB after releasing the root node.

To map deep and convolutional neural networks' data flow, the node's internal buffer is employed to their reusable data storage in temporary besides buffering data until releasing the sources of the next level of the tree for transferring them to the next level's nodes. Nevertheless, the nodes' structure reduces the levels of the tree due to place a processing unit besides a switch per node, whereas its feature imposes flow overhead on the connected links between different levels and provides a flow or data-flow mapping method with high efficiency. Therefore, separating the PEs units and employing a reduction tree to accumulate partial sums, and transferring them to on-chip memory reduces the flow overhead and creates an opportunity to present an efficient data-flow mapping to improve the NoC-based DLA's performance.

By combining a reduction and augmentation trees in the MAERI structure, the NoC-based deep learning accelerator's flow overhead is reduced that utilizes the tree structure as an on-chip communication network [25]. To provide a data-flow mapping method for improving MAERI's performance, we first analyze the impact of the different proposed strategies on improving or deteriorating the DLA's efficiency, which is presented according to the number of idle virtual neurons, MAC units, and the total number of multiply-accumulate units. A delay and energy-aware algorithm affects detecting the suitable number of virtual neurons that reduces latency and total energy of distributing the trained model's traffic onto MAERI's MAC units. By analyzing the simulation results of mapping the deep and convolutional neural networks' data flow including total delay and energy after performing the algorithm, we determine a margin for the suitable number of virtual neurons and propose a data-flow mapping method, which satisfies a DLA's purposes with high flexibility and efficiency. DNNs and CNNs' data flow are mapped on the deep learning accelerator based on the determined suitable number of virtual neurons and their characteristics including input feature map, kernel, filter, and channel sizes (Figure 2.24).

An on-chip communication with a planar and scalable structure has significant potential to support different data-flow mapping and partitioning approaches to improve an NoC-based DLA's efficiency in reducing communication delay and energy of implementing DNNs and CNNs' inference phase with high flexibility. To investigate a planar and scalable network's role for following the issue, we map the neural network's data flow (Figure 2.1) onto the mesh-based DLA's PEs (Figure 2.9).

First, the NN's similar weights are distributed in multicast onto processing elements because of the impossibility of broadcasting traffic in a mesh network due to its structure. We multicast the related inputs to the distributed weights onto the mesh's PEs after transferring them from the global buffer to processing elements that the shared bus connected nodes have a distributor's role, as shown in Figure 2.24(a) and (b). This method affects reducing memory access, total delay, and energy caused by transferring data from GB to processing elements, in which the partitions' dimensions are determined due to the neural network's characteristics including the number of layers and neurons. To improve a mesh-based deep learning accelerator's performance, the traffic pattern, partitioning, and data-flow mapping methods have a highlighted role in facing energy efficiency problems with high flexibility, which we provide the traffic patterns based on global buffer accesses. The planar and scalable features consist of distributing traffic from

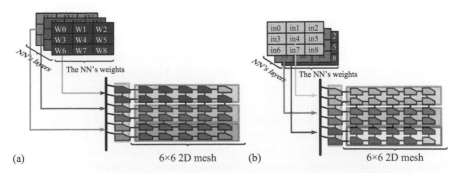

Figure 2.24   Multicasting the neural network's weights and inputs onto the mesh network's PEs: (a) multicasting similar weights onto PEs and (b) multicasting inputs onto PEs

different directions of the mesh network and increasing processing elements to support deep and convolutional neural networks' models without losing performance. Distributing DNNs and CNNs' traffic in different directions of the network is a feature that leads to reducing total hop counts between source and destination nodes, and also improving interconnections' delay and energy consumption. A suitable partitioning method reduces total hop counts to data transfer between GB and distributor the network's nodes, and its processing elements and also affects providing a data-flow mapping approach with high performance in improving the DLA's efficiency. According to the mesh's structure, employing the distributed on-chip memory in different directions of the network has a highlighted role in reducing total hop counts to local buffer accesses.

Figure 2.25(a) and (b) demonstrates the impact of the partitioning method and employing distributed local buffers to improve a mesh-based DLA's performance. The network is partitioned according to the destination nodes' location on the mesh that is distributed the neural network's traffic onto them, as shown in Figure 2.25(b). We determine the partitions' dimensions based on the minimum total hop counts between source and destination nodes, which depends on distributed local buffer access mechanism and traffic pattern. The NN's weights are transferred to left and right local buffers from main memory and distributed onto the processing elements that are located on the network middle partitions. After transferring the neural network's weights to PEs, these buffers are reset and loaded with input data. The partial sums are accumulated and transferred to the Psum buffer from the lower partition's nodes. The data transferring process between main memory, distributed local buffers, and PEs is performed by providing a bus scheduling method.

With comparing total hop counts between two structures of the employing local buffers and partitioning, and baseline design, observations illustrate reducing

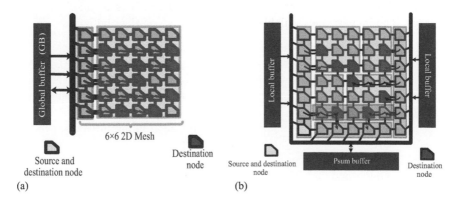

(a)   (b)

Figure 2.25   *Multicasting the neural network's weights and inputs onto the mesh network's PEs: (a) multicasting the NN's traffic onto the mesh's PEs with baseline structure and (b) multicasting the NN's traffic onto the mesh network's PEs with partitioning based design*

total hop counts for partitioning-based design compared to its baseline structure. Therefore, partitioning methods and employing local buffers affect increasing an NoC-based DLA's efficiency besides an effective data-flow mapping approach with improving total delay and energy by reducing total hop counts. These approaches are utilized to improve the NoC-based DLA's performance for mapping the neural network's data flow.

To map the trained models' data flow onto a mesh's processing elements, MAESTRO [27] creates an opportunity to determine a suitable number of PEs to support different DNN and CNN models by importing the characteristics, which are included if map, filter, kernel, and channel sizes using describing their loops. According to the explained approaches, we can improve a deep learning accelerator's performance after determining its design type (ASIC, FPGA, and NoC), communication infrastructure, and the required number of processing elements utilizing existing methods.

Comparing ASIC, FPGA, and NoC-based designs' weaknesses and advantages, analyzing their features demonstrates than an NoC-based DLA has a highlighter role in facing GPU-based system's problems to implement DNNs' inference phase than the other designs according to support the flow or data-flow mapping and partitioning methods. However, an on-chip communication network's type of NoC-based DLA has an impressive effect to satisfy an accelerators' purposes and increases its efficiency with high flexibility.

2.6   A heuristic or dynamic algorithm's role on a DLA's efficiency

This section follows investigating an algorithm's impact on optimizing a deep learning accelerator's design to improve its performance to implement deep and convolutional neural networks' inference phase. We analyzed a heuristic or dynamic algorithm's role for improving ASIC, FPGA, and NoC-based designs without providing an example case for investigating its performance on identifying critical paths in a design and deciding about increasing the DLA's efficiency.

In this section, we present a dynamic energy-aware algorithm (DEAA) to analyze its impact on optimizing an ASIC-based DLA, in which a DNN model's data flow is mapped on the deep learning accelerator's PEs. The algorithm consists of two-phase that collect initial information of DLA's performance (total delay and energy) using analyzing its simulation result after distributing the trained model's traffic, in phase 1.

The DLA structure utilizes a binary tree as a communication infrastructure for transferring DNNs and CNNs' data to its nodes to perform MAC operation, which consist of a processing element, internal buffer, and a switch (such as node's structure in Figure 2.12). The binary tree includes eight levels and 256 nodes, which we determine its characteristics and the suitable number of nodes using the MAESTRO tool, as shown in Figure 2.26 [27]. The ASIC-based DLA follows a specific application's purposes and satisfies them (such as image processing) that is

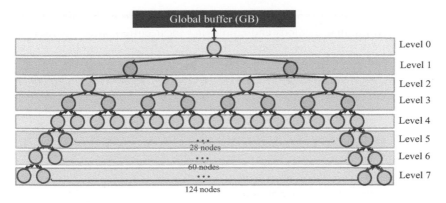

Level 0
Level 1
Level 2
Level 3
Level 4
Level 5
Level 6
Level 7

28 nodes
60 nodes
124 nodes

Figure 2.26 *ASIC-based DLA with a binary tree as a communication infrastructure which node structure consists of the internal buffer, PE, and switch*

presented to speed up the DNN model's inference phase and increase its energy efficiency [1,8]. Therefore, the ASIC-design can be optimized to support the specific application using flow uniform distribution and pruning the tree's idle components by two-phase DEAA with minimal hardware overhead and high performance. DEAA's phase 2 utilizes the collected initial information to decide about the tree's components, which have to be pruned for reducing the DLA's cost.

In phase 1, we simulate the DLA and distribute the trained model' traffic onto nodes for collecting initial information including identifying maximum-energy nodes and links, and idle components. A threshold's value is determined using computing an average value between the minimum and maximum-energy nodes and links (EN_{min}, EN_{max}, EL_{min}, and EL_{max}) and identifying high-energy components where $EN>EN_{Thr}$ and $EL>EL_{Thr}$ conditions are met. Figures 2.27 and 2.28 demonstrate the defined dynamic two-phase energy-aware algorithm's parameters and phase 1 of DEAA's steps to collect initial information about the deep learning accelerator's efficiency with analyzing the simulation result, respectively. The threshold's value can be changed where $EN \geq EN_{max}$, $EL \geq EL_{max}$, $EN \leq EN_{min}$, and $EL \geq EL_{min}$ conditions are met and evaluated the nodes and links' energy consumptions after changing EL_{Thr} and EN_{Thr} values. Also, analyzing simulation results affects recognizing the idle components that impose hardware overhead and static power consumption, which improves the DLA's performance by removing them from the ASIC-design.

To evaluate the tree components' energy consumption after simulating and mapping the deep neural network's data flow on its nodes, we consider a margin to determine maximum and minimum values for the node and link's energy consumption and utilize them to analyze the DLA's performance. DEAA employs the values to detect low and high-energy nodes and links and also identifies the tree's idle component for pruning them in phase 1.

Algorithm 1 dynamic energy-aware algorithm (DEAA)
// Definitions:
//EN_i: node j's energy consumption and $i{\geq}0$
//EL_j: link j's energy consumption and $j{\geq}0$
//EN_{max}: maximum-energy node and $EN_{max}{\geq}$ initial maximum value for node's energy consumption
//EN_{min}: minimum-energy node and $EN_{min}{\leq}$ initial minimum value for node's energy consumption
//EL_{max}: maximum-energy link and $EL_{max}{\geq}$ initial maximum value for link's energy consumption
//EL_{min}: minimum-energy link and $EL_{min}{\geq}$ initial minimum value for link's energy consumption
//EN_{Thr}: a threshold value for nodes' energy consumption
//EL_{Thr}: a threshold value for link's energy consumption
//X: x dimension of input matrix and $X \geq 0$
//Y: y dimension of input matrix and $Y \geq 0$
//ICS: the size of input channel and $ICS \geq 0$
//W_X: x dimension of filter (weight) matrix and $W\_X \geq 0$
//W_Y: y dimension of filter (weight) matrix and $W\_Y{\geq} 0$
//WKS: the size of weight kernel and $WKS \geq 0$
//NN: total number of the tree's nodes and $NN{\geq}0$
//NLK: total number of the tree's links and $NLK{\geq}0$
//NL: total number of the tree's levels and $NL{\geq}0$
//NNL_i: the number of the tree's nodes in level l and $i{\geq}0$
//EIN_i: node i's energy index and $EIN_i{=}0$
//EIL_j: link i's energy index and $EIL_j{=}0$
//IN_i: the idle node i's index and $IN_i{=}0$
//IL_j: the idle node j's index and $IL_j{=}0$
//α: the node's static energy consumption
//β: the link's static energy consumption
//k, z: are counter index $k{=}0$ and $z{=}0$

Figure 2.27   Definition of DEAA's parameters

By determining the low and high-energy components, we can define another data-flow mapping method to transfer the deep and convolutional neural network's data from global buffer to the tree's nodes, which lead to flow uniform distribution and improve the DLA's performance.

As shown in Figure 2.28, we recognize the idle components where $EN_i \leq \alpha$ and $EL_j \leq \beta$ conditions are met and α and β values are defined as the static energy consumption of the node and link, respectively.

In phase 2, the algorithm decides about the pruning binary tree and mapping the DNN model's data flow onto the pruned tree's nodes after identifying low and

```
1: procedure DEAA (X, Y, ICS, WKS, EN_max, EN_min, EL_max, EL_min)

2:   //Start phase 1 // Analyzing energy consumption and identifying idle components, low and high-energy nodes and links

3:        EN_Thr = (EN_max + EN_min)/2  // Computing and determining a threshold value for node's energy consumption

4:        EL_Thr = (EL_max + EL_min)/2  // Computing and determining a threshold value for link's energy consumption

5:        for (i=0; i++; i≤ NN)

6:            for (j=0; j++; j≤ NLK)

7:                Investigating the node and link's energy consumption after mapping

8:                if (EN_i≥ EN_Thr) // investigating the node's energy consumption after mapping based on the condition

9:                    EIN_i=1; // labaling the node as an high-energy component

10:               End if;

11:               if (EN_i≥ EN_max) // exchanging EN_max with EN_i based on the condition

12:                   EN_max←EN_i;

13:               End if;

14:               if (EL_j≥ EL_Thr) // investigating the link's energy consumption after mapping based on the condition

15:                   EIL_j=1; // labaling the link as an high-energy component

16:               End if;

17:               if (EL_i≥ EL_max) // exchanging EL_min with EL_j based on the condition

18:                   EL_max←EL_j;

19:               End if;

20:               if (EN_i≤EN_min) // exchanging EN_min with EN_i based on the condition

21:                   EN_min←EN_i;

22:               End if;

23:               if (EL_i≤ EL_min) // exchanging EL_min with EL_j based on the condition

24:                   EL_min←EL_j;

25:               End if;

26:               if (EN_i≤α) // identifying the idle node

27:                   IN_i←1;

28:               End if;

29:               if (EL_j≤β) // identifying the idle link

30:                   IL_j←1;

31:               End if;

32:           End for;

33:       End for;

34:       Return

35: // end phase 1;
```

Figure 2.28   Phase 1 of DEAA

high-energy components in phase 1, as shown in Figure 2.29. The deep neural network's data flow is again mapped onto the pruned tree's nodes and simulated for investigating the impact of removing idle components and distributing flow on them in uniform on improving the DLA's performance.

After pruning the tree based on identifying idle components by performing DEAA, 88 nodes and 176 links are removed from the DLA structure, which reduces their hardware overhead and static energy consumption, and increases the deep learning accelerator's efficiency. Therefore, the binary tree structure is replaced with the ASIC-based communication infrastructure after pruning which design is inspired by the tree structure, as shown in Figure 2.30.

DEAA demonstrates a highlighted role of a dynamic or heuristic algorithm to improve the performance of a deep learning accelerator which positive impact is

```
36: // Start phase 2 // Pruning the tree by removing idle components, and Mapping the DNN's dataflow onto the pruned tree's nodes
37:         for (i=0; i++; i≤NN) // Pruning the tree's idle nodes
38:             for (j=0; j++; j≤NLK) // Pruning the tree's idle links
39:                 if (IN_i=1)
40:                     Removing IN_i as an idle component
41:                 end if;
42:                 if (IL_j=1)
43:                     Removing IL_j as an idle component
44:                 end if;
45:                 if (EIN_i=1)
46:                     HENI←1; // setting the index of the high-energy node (HENI)
47:                 end if;
48:                 if (EIL_j=1)
49:                     HELI←1; // setting the index of the high-energy link (HELI)
50:                 end if;
51:             end for;
52:         end for;
53:     Reset the link's number and node's number after pruning the tree
54:     if ((HENI=1) OR (HELI=1))
55:         Change dataflow mapping method to flow uniform distribution
56:     for (k=1; i++; i≤W_C) // mapping the rows of filter matrix on the ASIC-based DLA's processing elements
57:         for (z=1; j++; j≤WKS) // considering kernel size for mapping
58:             for (i=0; i++; i≤NN)
59:                 N_i← W_X_{k,z} // mapping the rows of filter matrix on the tree's nodes
60:             end for;
61:         end for;
62:     end for;
63:     for (i=1; i++; i≤ICS) // mapping the rows of input matrix on the ASIC-based DLA's processing elements
64:         for (j=1; j++; j≤IKS) // considering kernel size for mapping (input kernel size)
65:             for (i=0; i++; i≤NN)
66:                 N_i← X_{k,z} // mapping the rows of input matrix on the tree's nodes
67:             end for;
68:         end for;
69:     end for;
70: // end phase 2
71: end procedure
```

Figure 2.29   Phase 2 of DEAA

not restricted to ASIC-based design. As shown in DEAA, providing and employing an adapted dynamic or heuristic algorithm to a DLA's structure has an impressive effect on optimizing the deep learning accelerator's design, presenting a suitable flow or data-flow mapping method, and improving the performance with high flexibility.

2.7   Brief state-of-the-art survey

This section presents a brief overview of the case studies in the field of different acceleration methods to speed up the deep and convolutional neural networks' inference phase and facing GPU-based systems' problems.

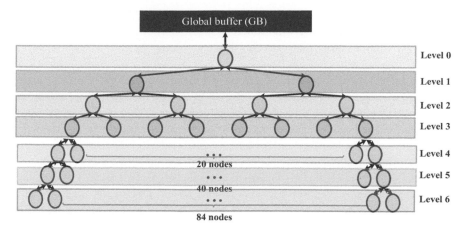

Figure 2.30   ASIC-based DLA after pruning the tree

The tensor processing unit (TPU) was employed as a systolic array-based structure to accelerate DNN models' inference phase by replacing 8-bit multiply operations to 16 and 32-bit multiplies without losing accuracy that was provided by Google and affected on improving implementing GoogleNet's performance [28]. The accelerator improves the performance of different deep neural network's models, whereas it has a highlighter role in increasing energy efficiency and speeding up the inference phase for GoogleNet than other DNN models according to its ASIC-based design and its structure compatibility (its dimension) with the trained models. Nevertheless, the DLA follows output stationary (OS) data-flow mapping methods to transfer data between processing elements that lead to computation dependency and negative impact on its performance. Various proposed deep learning accelerators' structures were inspired by the systolic array structure as a communication infrastructure, and their flexibility, scalability, and reconfigurability are challenging for them to support different CNNs and DNNs with high efficiency [28,29].

DianNao families [6–9] utilized ASIC-based structure, embedded memories, and optical-electrical connection to provide DLAs and accelerate implementing CNN and DNN models with reducing main memory accesses. The families' deep learning accelerators also exploited synaptic weights' reusability in convolutional neural networks to internal buffering them in temporal and confronting main memory access problems. TETRIS [10] employed 3D technology-based structure and improved communication delay and energy caused by transferring the trained models' data between PEs according to TSV link features including low energy consumption and high bandwidth, which some DLAs likewise utilized the technology to increase their performance [16].

Eyeriss [11] and Eyeriss v.2 [12] focused on a hybrid network as a communication infrastructure and data-flow stationary's influence to accelerate the inference phase of deep and convolutional neural networks, whereas their horizontal shared buses and increasing MAC operation's complexity are challenging for their scalability and energy efficiency. MAERI [25] combined a reduction and augmentation trees to distribute the trained models' traffic on MAC units and accumulate the partial sums and transfer them to global buffer, which the DLA's structure support dense and sparse deep and convolutional neural networks' models with high performance according to employ the extra links. Nevertheless, the deep learning accelerator only distributed NNs' traffic on the multiply-accumulated units in one direction of the DLA's network according to the tree structure. Simba [30] proposed a chiplet-based structure to speed up the inference phase of deep neural networks and learning and support the different machine learning algorithms with high flexibility, which have to increase the number of chiplets to satisfy ML algorithms' purposes and it also leads to reduce energy efficiency.

Also, some case studies focused on NN-based approaches to tackle some problems caused by deploying IoT and other ML-based applications, which can affect improving the performance of IoT's sensor level besides DLA-methods [31]. A predictor model approximated the lifetime of a battery in the Internet of things and proposed a principle component analysis (PCA)-based solution to reduce time complexity and increase life time battery's efficiency for performing real-time monitoring applications at sensor level without losing accuracy. The researchers utilized a model to predict a dataset in order to improve encoding for increasing information security in network instruction systems, which can increase the efficiency of a DLA-based system by reducing the dimension of deep neural networks and their imposed dataset [32]. According to utilize PCA method's benefits, the preprocessing dataset and classifying them likewise reduced the dimension of a DNN to recognize three-dimensional objects with high accuracy, which can employ in a deep learning accelerator before mapping a NN's data flow onto PEs and discard its computational complexity related to data classification [33]. Therefore, the mentioned case studies demonstrated the positive impact of employing NN-based approaches in DLA-based systems before mapping the neural network's data flow onto a communication network's processing elements that are led to improve the performance of a deep learning accelerator.

According to GPU-based systems' energy efficiency problems, the different DLA-based systems have been proposed to reduce energy consumption and communication delay, which we introduced some highlighted deep learning accelerators due to their impact on tackling the problems.

References

[1]   Chen, K.C., Ebrahimi, M., Wang, T.Y., and Yang, Y.C. "NoC-based DNN accelerator: A future design paradigm." In Proceedings of the 13th IEEE/ACM International Symposium on Networks-on-Chip. October 17, 2019 (pp. 1–8).

[2]   Nabavinejad, S.M., Baharloo, M., Chen, K.C., Palesi, M., Kogel, T., and Ebrahimi, M. "An overview of efficient interconnection networks for deep neural network accelerators." IEEE Journal on Emerging and Selected Topics in Circuits and Systems. 2020;10(3):268–82.

[3]   Daneshtalab, M., and Modarressi, M, editors. *Hardware Architectures for Deep Learning*. Stevenage: The Institution of Engineering and Technology; 2020.

[4]   Samajdar, A., Mannan, P., Garg, K., and Krishna, T. "Genesys: Enabling continuous learning through neural network evolution in hardware." In 2018 51st Annual IEEE/ACM International Symposium on Microarchitecture (MICRO). October 20 (pp. 855–866). IEEE; 2018.

[5]   Cavigelli, L., Magno, M., and Benini, L. "Accelerating real-time embedded scene labeling with convolutional networks." In Proceedings of the 52nd Annual Design Automation Conference. June 07 (pp. 1–6). 2015.

[6]   Chen, Y., Chen, T., Xu, Z., Sun, N., and Temam, O. "DianNao family: Energy-efficient hardware accelerators for machine learning." Communications of the ACM. 2016;59(11):105–12.

[7]   Liu D, Chen T, Liu S, *et al.* "Pudiannao: A polyvalent machine learning accelerator." ACM SIGARCH Computer Architecture News. 2015; 43(1): 369–81.

[8]   Du, Z., Fasthuber, R., Chen, T., *et al.* "ShiDianNao: Shifting vision processing closer to the sensor." In Proceedings of the 42nd Annual International Symposium on Computer Architecture. June 13 (pp. 92–104). 2015.

[9]   Luo, T., Liu, S., Li, L., *et al.* "Dadiannao: A neural network supercomputer." IEEE Transactions on Computers. 2016;66(1):73–88.

[10] Gao, M., Pu, J., Yang, X., Horowitz, M., and Kozyrakis, C. "Tetris: Scalable and efficient neural network acceleration with 3d memory." In Proceedings of the Twenty-Second International Conference on Architectural Support for Programming Languages and Operating Systems. April 04 (pp. 751–764). 2017.

[11] Chen, Y.H., Krishna, T., Emer, J.S., and Sze, V. "Eyeriss: An energy-efficient reconfigurable accelerator for deep convolutional neural networks." IEEE Journal of Solid-State Circuits. 2016;52(1):127–38.

[12] Chen, Y.H., Yang, T.J., Emer, J., and Sze, V. "Eyeriss v2: A flexible accelerator for emerging deep neural networks on mobile devices." IEEE Journal on Emerging and Selected Topics in Circuits and Systems. 2019; 9(2):292–308.

[13] Kwon, H., Samajdar, A., and Krishna, T. "Rethinking nocs for spatial neural network accelerators." In 2017 Eleventh IEEE/ACM International Symposium on Networks-on-Chip (NOCS). October 19 (pp. 1–8). IEEE; 2017.

[14] Mirmahaleh, S.Y., Reshadi, M., Shabani, H., Guo, X., and Bagherzadeh, N. "Flow mapping and data distribution on mesh-based deep learning accelerator." In Proceedings of the 13th IEEE/ACM International Symposium on Networks-on-Chip. October 17 (pp. 1–8). 2019.

[15] Mirmahaleh, S.Y., Reshadi, M., and Bagherzadeh, N. "Flow mapping on mesh-based deep learning accelerator." Journal of Parallel and Distributed Computing. 2020;144:80–97.

[16]   Firuzan, A., Modarressi, M., Daneshtalab, M., and Reshadi, M. "Reconfigurable network-on-chip for 3D neural network accelerators." In 2018 Twelfth IEEE/ACM International Symposium on Networks-on-Chip (NOCS). October 4 (pp. 1–8). IEEE; 2018.

[17]   Mirmahaleh, S.Y., and Rahmani, A.M. "DNN pruning and mapping on NoC-Based communication infrastructure." Microelectronics Journal. 2019; 94: 104655.

[18]   Hayashikoshi, M., Suzuki, J., Watanabe, Y., *et al.* "Processing in-memory architecture with on-chip transfer learning function for compensating characteristic variation." In 2020 IEEE International Memory Workshop (IMW). May 17 (pp. 1–4). IEEE; 2020.

[19]   Wang, Y., Chen, W., Yang, J., and Li, T. "Exploiting parallelism for CNN applications on 3D stacked processing-in-memory architecture." IEEE Transactions on Parallel and Distributed Systems. 2018;30(3):589–600.

[20]   Peng, X., Liu, R., and Yu, S. "Optimizing weight mapping and data flow for convolutional neural networks on processing-in-memory architectures." IEEE Transactions on Circuits and Systems I: Regular Papers. 2019;67 (4):1333–43.

[21]   Guo K, Sui L, Qiu J, *et al.* "Angel-eye: A complete design flow for mapping cnn onto customized hardware." In 2016 IEEE Computer Society Annual Symposium on VLSI (ISVLSI). July 11 (pp. 24–29). IEEE; 2016.

[22]   Jerger, N.E., Krishna, T., and Peh, L.S. "On-chip networks." Synthesis Lectures on Computer Architecture. 2017;12(3):1–210.

[23]   Choi, W., Duraisamy, K., Kim, R.G., *et al.* "On-chip communication network for efficient training of deep convolutional networks on heterogeneous manycore systems." IEEE Transactions on Computers. 2017;67(5):672–86.

[24]   Guirado, R., Kwon, H., Abadal, S., Alarcón, E., and Krishna, T. "Dataflow-architecture co-design for 2.5 D DNN accelerators using wireless network-on-package." . 2020. arXiv preprint arXiv:2011.14755.

[25]   Kwon, H., Samajdar, A., and Krishna, T. "Maeri: Enabling flexible dataflow mapping over dnn accelerators via reconfigurable interconnects." ACM SIGPLAN Notices. 2018;53(2):461–75.

[26]   Krishna, T., Kwon, H., Parashar, A., Pellauer, M., and Samajdar, A. "Data orchestration in deep learning accelerators." Synthesis Lectures on Computer Architecture. 2020;15(3):1–64.

[27]   Kwon, H., Pellauer, M., and Krishna, T. "MAESTRO: An open-source infrastructure for modeling dataflows within deep learning accelerators." 2018. arXiv preprint arXiv:1805.02566.

[28]   Jouppi, N.P., Young, C., Patil, N., *et al.* "In-datacenter performance analysis of a tensor processing unit." In Proceedings of the 44th Annual International Symposium on Computer Architecture (pp. 1–12). 2017.

[29]   Samajdar, A., Zhu, Y., Whatmough, P., Mattina, M., and Krishna, T. "Scale-sim: Systolic cnn accelerator simulator." 2019. arXiv preprint arXiv:1811. 02883x.

[30]   Shao, Y.S., Clemons, J., Venkatesan, R., *et al.* "Simba: Scaling deep-learning inference with multi-chip-module-based architecture." In Proceedings of the 52nd Annual IEEE/ACM International Symposium on Microarchitecture. October 12 (pp. 14–27). 2019.

[31]   Reddy, T., RM S.P., Parimala, M., Chowdhary, C.L., Hakak, S., and Khan, W.Z. "A deep neural networks based model for uninterrupted marine environment monitoring." Computer Communications. 2020;157:64–75.

[32]   Khare, N., Devan, P., Chowdhary, C.L., *et al.* "Smo-dnn: Spider monkey optimization and deep neural network hybrid classifier model for intrusion detection." Electronics. 2020;9(4):692.

[33]   Chowdhary, C.L. "3D object recognition system based on local shape descriptors and depth data analysis." Recent Patents on Computer Science. 2019;12(1):18–24.

Chapter 3

Intelligent image retrieval system using deep neural networks

*Shubham Gujar[1], Rutuparn Pawar[1]
and Yogesh Dandawate[1]*

Abstract

In the past decades of the digital era, the amount of electronic data such as text, audio, images, and many more have increased to tremendous amounts. A study reveals that the number of cameras in the world exceeds the number of eyes. Reports suggest there will be approximately 7.4 trillion images generated by the end of 2020. An image retrieval system is used to search for images similar to the query image in a large image database. An image retrieval system will assist in the processing, organizing, and handling of image data efficiently. Companies such as Google and Pinterest use image retrieval systems to provide users with related images.

In the year 1970, a text-based image retrieval technique was implemented where images were first annotated manually and then searched using a text query. This method was extremely time-consuming, labor-intensive, and prone to errors in annotation due to human perception's subjectivity. In the early 1980s, a content-based image retrieval (CBIR) system was introduced which used visual features extracted from an image. This method used traditional image processing tools for understanding the color, texture, and shape-based features of the image. This approach had problems such as inappropriate and limited feature representations which resulted in less efficient and non-generalized algorithms.

Advancement in deep learning (DL) related to image processing has given rise to better processing of image data. Deep learning was inspired by the working of the biological neural network. It is widely used for classification tasks and achieves state-of-the-art performance.

Today, we use convolutional neural networks (CNN) to perform image retrieval tasks. CNN is a variant of DL and is widely used for computer vision applications because of its inherent ability to extract features from an image.

[1]Department of Electronics and Telecommunication Engineering, Vishwakarma Institute of Information Technology, Pune, India

CNN has also shown prominent results as compared to traditional image processing techniques. In a CNN, convolutional layers are used for feature representation and extraction. After the features are extracted, distance metrics are used for measuring the similarity between the query image and the images from the database. Generally, similarity metrics such as Euclid distance, Cosine distance, and Manhattan distance facilitate finding similar images from the database.

Further, the authors will discuss the image retrieval system using convolutional auto-encoders and improving an image retrieval system's usability using generative adversarial networks (GANs). In convolutional auto-encoders, the autoencoder's encoder portion is used to compute the latent space representation, which quantifies the content of the image in a feature vector. The query image's feature vector is compared with the feature vectors of all the images in the database to find similar images. GANs can produce an image from text or a simple sketch. Alternatively, GANs can be used to create an image with new features. The image generated by a GAN can be used for image retrieval thereby adding a method to query an image retrieval system.

Convolutional neural networks, convolutional auto-encoders, and GANs are the three prominent methodologies for image retrieval that are to be discussed by the authors.

Key Words: Content-based image retrieval (CBIR); generative adversarial network (GAN); convolutional neural network (CNN); deep learning; image retrieval; deep neural network (DNN); crime scene investigation (CSI); autoencoder

3.1   Introduction

The amount of electronic data has increased exponentially in recent years. Cheap and readily available data storage and management facilities have greatly influenced data collection with various formats such as text, image, audio, etc. Reports from Internet World Stats claim to have almost 4.8 billion active Internet users as of July 2020 [1]. A similar report released in May 2020 by Statista forecasts that the total amount of data created, captured, copied, and consumed in the world to reach 59 zettabytes in 2020 [2]. According to Internet Live Stats, Google itself handles 1.2 trillion searches every year and about 4.2 million search queries every minute [3]. Reports suggest approximately 7.4 trillion images generated by the year 2020 and 60,000 images to be uploaded by Instagram every minute [4].

The image retrieval system works by providing the user with a similar output image from the large databases using a single query input image. Image retrieval system will facilitate the users for better accessibility and usability of the images data from the database. Images retrieved using this system can be further used for medical imaging, education, satellite imagery, etc. [5]. An image retrieval system is commonly defined as a computer system used with a large digital image database for browsing, searching and retrieving images as per user requirements. Image retrieval is a challenging task and much research is being carried by many renowned researchers in the computer vision domain.

Few key factors must be considered for working with designing for image retrieval system and they are as follows:

- Efficiency: The image retrieval system will be practical enough when the image database has a variety of images in large amounts. With that, the user query image should also be retrieved in a computationally efficient manner to make its application fast, robust and reliable.
- Distinct: The image retrieval system must consider distinct images.
- Positional accurate: The system must consider spacial features or a region-based approach also into consideration for object detection.
- Insensitive to change in illumination: The system must be robust enough for efficiently and automatically evaluating query image features irrespective of any illumination disturbance. Also, the system must work under all lighting conditions.
- Invariant to change in scale/resolution of an image: The query image can be of any scale or resolution or even cropped or zoomed, the output of similar images must not be influenced by the scale or resolution of the query image.
- Rotation invariant: The query image can be rotated at any angle or flipped or even shifted, the output must not be influenced by rotation.
- Invariant to viewpoint changes: The system must be insensitive to query images taken from different positions of a camera [6].

With the development of image processing technology in the digital era, the image retrieval system has become a very active and popular research area. The main motive of research on this system is to manage, create, and handle the image database query accurately and efficiently. During the initial phase of research, three distinct methodologies were envisioned for image retrieval systems: text-based image retrieval (TBIR), CBIR, and semantic-based image retrieval system [7].

In the late 1970s, the text-based image retrieval (TBIR) method was being experimented with. It is based on an annotations-based approach where a database has to be created of images and its annotations depending upon the keywords, features or description of that image. This is a text-based approach and annotations are done manually. Furthermore, each image must be annotated using different keywords, this makes the system labor intensive, time-consuming, costly and practically impossible to keep up with the annotation demand. It was highly impractical to use TBIR systems for large databases. The keywords were language or culture-dependent reducing the scalability of the system. A drawback of the system was that it finds similar images from the database based on the keywords and not from the image's visual features. This system was not capable of providing rich images with more details related to a specific domain.

Content-based image retrieval (CBIR) system is used for image retrieval based on the content existing in the images. Image processing techniques are used for this purpose; however, they could not provide effective results and its implementation was difficult. The images were considered to have a few fundamental components as contents such as shapes, color, and textures. Image processing methodologies using such fundamental components as descriptors for image retrieval from the large dataset provided inaccurate results. More complex or human-like descriptions were not considered as fundamentals which were later commonly known as high-level descriptors. These high-level descriptors were crucial, and traditional image processing tools failed to consider such high-level descriptors with the fundamentally considered descriptors for image retrieval.

The authors propose to discuss a novel methodology for image retrieval systems using CNNs which have brought a revolution in the computer vision domain with robust and state-of-the-art techniques. Furthermore, the authors have discussed methodologies for image retrieval system using an unsupervised learning approach namely autoencoder and generative adversarial network.

3.2 Conventional content-based image retrieval (CBIR) system

In the early 1990s with the advancement in the digital era and Internet culture, requirement for robust image retrieval system was growing. The CBIR system was implemented, depending on visual features of an image and overcame the drawbacks faced by the TBIR systems. CBIR is a very fast-growing research area and is commonly known as query-based image content (QBIC) and content-based visual information retrieval (CBVIR).

IBM was the first company to come up with a commercialized approach to CBIR. Kato *et al.* [8] were one of the researchers who initiated the CBIR system using graphical features such as color and visual impressions for sketch-based image retrieval tasks. CBIR system mainly dealt with low-level features such as color, shape, texture, and retrieved similar images based on only these attributes. Shape-based features are extracted using position detection via moment evaluation and contours, colour-based features are extracted using color transformation and using colour histogram, while texture-based features are extracted using image processing techniques such as frequency transformation, Gabor transformation, wavelet transformation, and energy-mean histogram (Figure 3.1) [9].

These image processing tools and methods were implemented for feature extraction with development in the CBIR domain. The user has to give an input query image to the CBIR system where then the query image is converted into a feature vector which will eventually be compared with all the feature vector of the images in the database and index out the most similar images from the database (Figure 3.2). CBIR system also had some evident drawbacks. The images were retrieved only on the basis of low-level features such as color, shape, and texture and had less similarity between the retrieved images. The major drawback of the CBIR system was the evident processing gap between the low-level and high-level features for spatial representation. Due to these drawbacks, many researchers also approached combining TBIR and CBIR systems for robustness and improved efficiency.

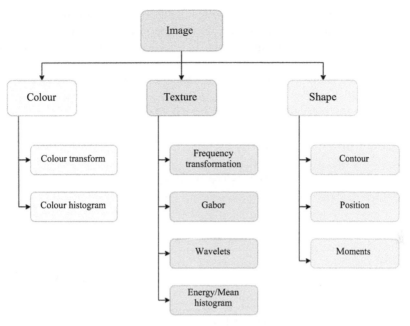

Figure 3.1   Various methodologies and techniques for finding descriptors used in traditional CBIR systems. Adapted from [9]

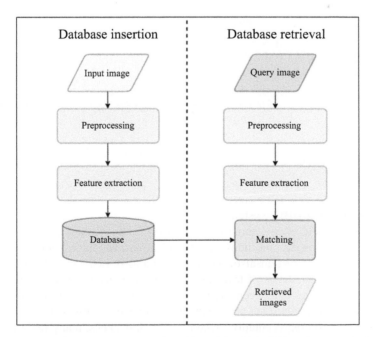

Figure 3.2   Illustrating the usage of extracted features using CNN. Adapted from [9]

Human understanding of the image differed from that with computer-processed low-level feature understanding. This drawback generated an unconventional gap that leads to the CBIR model's bad performance. Humans understand the high-level features such as nose, lips, eyes, etc. from an image containing a face but the CBIR system has understanding limited to color, shape, and texture in the image.

3.2.1   Semantic-based image retrieval (SBIR) system

Semantic-based image retrieval system (SBIR) was developed to deal with this semantic gap between low-level and high-level features. The main motive was to process image based on human perception high level features more than CBIR low level features and minimize the semantic gap. For example, if the user wanted to find an image of the beach, the query would be sea, sand, clouds and not blue, or sandy. Low-level features were then further mAP with high-level concepts by combining semantic image extraction descriptor with the annotation process. Firstly, the features would be extracted based on low-level features such as color, shape, and texture, then a corresponding patch or region would be formed by clustering them together. This patch or region has to go for the image keyword annotation process, where a keyword would be given to each patch or region in the image. The annotation process would be manual, semi-automatic or completely automatic.

A human can interpret images based on high-level structures and low-level structures, whereas a computer can only interpret low-level features because of the way images are stored in computer memory. Using SBIR region, object-based annotations were made along with low-level features for better understanding, interpretability, and user-friendly experience. SBIR system had drawbacks too. This system was more reliable and efficient when queried with a keyword and had poor results when queried by image. The keyword annotations may be required to be done manually which was time-consuming, labor-intensive, costly, and difficult to implement on a large database. Automatic keyword annotations tools were not developed enough to provide a reliable experience. SBIR system showed good results as compared to TBIR and CBIR but was time-consuming and too many complex image processing involved which made the implementation difficult [10].

3.3   Deep learning

Learning is fundamental for living creatures. Specifically, for human beings; the newborn baby learns to sit, stand, walk, and eventually run. Learning is considered crucial for growth and development. Learning to survive in critical conditions will lead to the evolution of a particular species. In 1940, McCulloch *et al.* [11] initiated findings by analyzing neuroscience and biological study, after that the research work for DL started. In 1982, Hopfield *et al.* [12] proposed Hopfield architecture which turned to be noteworthy research in DL soon, it was the start of 2006 and DL took place in the research domain and Deep Belief Network was proposed by Hinton *et al.* [13] Google,

Facebook, and Microsoft achieved many noteworthy achievements in the field of artificial intelligence (AI) using DL. Google's AlphaGo defeated Lee Sedol in a Go competition. DeepDream Google's initiative can classify images and also generate artificial paintings. Deep Text by Facebook can interpret the texts in post format and multiple languages. However, DL seemed difficult at the time due to a smaller number of reliable and structured data and less computing power. Efficient data storage pipelines were missing in multiple areas. CPU was used for the processing which was slow and training of the Neural Networks Architecture was costly. Later, parallel processing using GPU was started, which made the neural network architectures' training with large parameters a lot easier.

Deep learning, for computer vision, in particular, has revolutionized the area of machine learning in recent years [14]. It was the biological neural network that inspired the building of artificial neural networks. It will not be false if we say that computer vision using DL is a simulation of the virtual computer world's biological vision.

Today's initiatives such as DeepMind and GPT3 technology are unique and have brought a revolution. A pocket-size mobile phone has the implementations of AI used for assisting photography, auto-suggesting search query, filter spam emails, and many more. The CNN (Convolution Neural Network) has improved image processing technology's performance and made tasks such as object detection and object classification. The RNN (Recurrent Neural Network) has helped improve time-series analysis for weather prediction, stock market analysis, and even the outbreak of the COVID19 virus. The LSTM and BERT model architectures have brought revolution where a machine can write an article and have its views on an issue. Automatic image caption generation is also possible due to DL [15]. Automatic poetry generation is also one of its applications. Intrusion detection systems are also getting popular along with its applications with DL [16,17]. The most common applications of DL are using supervised learning where large labeled data are available which are then put forward for training through a deep neural network architecture and results are acquired. In unsupervised learning, data are not available in a labeled format, but the model is trained over a deep neural network and results are achieved.

We need vast amounts of labeled training samples to create an image retrieval system with DL, but the resulting classification accuracy is truly amazing, even beating humans at it. The amount of digital content, including images on the Internet, has increased tremendously. The simplest way to locate highly correlated images within a short time is through image retrieval systems. In the field of information processing, numerous studies have shown the usefulness of DL. The common opinion about the impact of adding DL into image retrieval systems is that it provides tremendous improvement over the traditional approaches. Our day-to-day needs have flooded many databases in volume and variety, ranging from music, videos, blogs, documents, and other digital data. Intelligent image retrieval systems add efficiency to search engines by giving a very helpful hand to users searching for images. Such systems' success and effectiveness are due to their ability to return convenient information from infinitely large storage. Given the advances in the field of DL in various application domains such as machine vision, natural language processing, and speech recognition, DL was extended to the field of information retrieval. Deep learning has significant relevance to image retrieval systems because feature extraction by employing CNN is quite efficient and shows impressive results.

3.4   Image retrieval using convolutional neural networks (CNN)

Neurons that have trainable weights and biases connect to make an artificial neural network (ANN). Each neuron is given some inputs, performs a dot product on input and weights, adds the bias, and then uses an activation function to generate an output. ANN can be considered a fairly complex mathematical function that provides a solution with the help of artifacts learned from the dataset while training.

An ANN observes entries in a dataset at one entry at a time. The neurons in the hidden layers adaptively modify the previous layer's information using a mathematical equation determined by weights, biases, and the activation function. The ANN then determines the error it made while giving a result using a cost/error function and utilizes backpropagation or similar optimization techniques to improve its learning by taking errors into account. The errors are mitigated by calibration weights and bias thereby modeling nonlinear and complex relationships. ANN finds extensive applications in several aspects of banking, business analytics, defence, education, finance, medicine, and many more [18].

Implementing machine learning, especially DL models, has become easier because of PyTorch and TensorFlow platforms. Multiple organizations have successfully used these platforms for deploying multiple real-world applications. TensorFlow has shown optimized performance for computation hence is more suited for real-world applications with constraints on computational resources.

A CNN, also referred to as ConvNets, is a class of neural networks that use convolution and pooling layers and a fully connected neural network to perform signal processing, especially image processing. A CNN employs convolution to convert low-level features in the image to high-level features such as horizontal edges, vertical edges, and many more. Today, deep CNNs have outperformed traditional algorithms for image processing since they deal with an image similar to the human perception of vision, thereby dealing with the semantic gap [19] that the earlier algorithms could not overcome.

CNNs gained popularity when Alex Krizhevsky *et al.* [20] developed a CNN that won the ILSVRC held in 2012 by dropping the top-5 classification error record from 26% to 15%.

LeNet, ZFNet, GoogleNet, VGGNet, and ResNet are examples of CNN architectures. Most of them were winners or runners-up of the ImageNet Large Scale Recognition Challenge (ILSVRC). ILSVRC is an annually held competition for computer vision algorithms. It can be considered the Olympics of computer vision where algorithms on computer vision tasks compete for proving themselves to be the best.

A CNN requires a fixed input image size. This constraint is required to make sure that the network converges while training. A nonlinear activation function is used to add nonlinearity to the model since linear models usually do not generalize while training. ReLu is the most general activation function used in CNN since it is better than other nonlinear activation functions such as sigmoid, tanh, and others [21].

The convolutional layer, pooling layer, and fully connected layer are three types of layers that combine to build ConvNet architectures. The convolutional layer, as its name suggests, operates convolution. The convolutional layer's parameters consist of a collection of learnable kernels. A convolutional layer detects local structures and maps them to a feature mAP. The number of kernels applied determines the depth of the output feature maps. This is the core CNN layer that gives a CNN the inherent ability to extract features from an image. At the end of the convolution operation, the feature mAP is passed to the ReLU activation function. ReLU (rectified linear unit) provides nonlinearity and rectification to the CNN model. Most recent CNN architectures utilize rectified linear unit layers or equivalent since they deal with vanishing gradients and are computationally inexpensive. The pooling layer performs downsampling leading to a reduction in the spatial size of the activation maps. Pooling layers are generally used after multiple convolutional layers to reduce computational space and time complexity that gets added to architectures due to the convolutional layers. They also minimize the possibility of overfitting the CNN while training. The pooling operation has translational invariance, that us, it preserves the detected feature even though it disrupts the feature's spatial information. The most popular reduction methods are max pooling and average pooling. In max pooling, the largest value with the window is taken while in average pooling, a mean of all the values in the window is taken. Recent CNN architectures tend to use max-pooling or its variants over average pooling since it has better performance and leads to faster convergence [22]. The fully connected layer is similar to an artificial neural network and maps the earlier layers' features to a class probability distribution.

Connecting multiple convolutional layers followed by pooling layers results in the conversion of low-level features into mid-level features and then eventually into high-level features thereby replicating the process vision perception by a human inside a machine. The following image illustrates low-level features' conversion into high-level features in the convolution and pooling layers of a VGGNet (Figure 3.3).

Semantic-based image retrieval systems could not achieve results for query by image because of the semantic gap. Deep learning can extract better features from an image than traditional hand-crafted features. Today, features extracted using DL are widely used in many fields, such as speech recognition, image classification, text processing, and many more. A CNN's in-built ability to identify more high-level semantic image retrieval features solves the problem of the semantic gap faced by SBIR. CNNs generate abstract high-level features by combining pixel of the images.

Features are extracted from within the CNN layers and then used to search for similar images to the query within the database by matching features using a distance metric function. Liu *et al.* [23] used the Corel dataset which contains 1,000

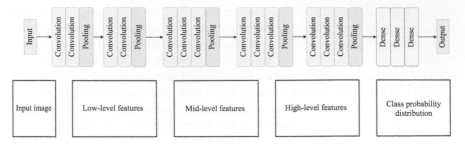

Figure 3.3   Architectural diagram for VGGNet. Adapted from [24]

images belonging to 10 classes along with AlexNet to propose an image retrieval algorithm that utilizes a CNN for image feature extraction. They use the average image retrieval accuracy as metrics to conclude that we find features that more accurately describe the query image in the last layers of a CNN.

Lin *et al.* proposed an approximate nearest neighbor search using binary hash codes for image retrieval from a large database in an efficient manner. They pre-trained a CNN on the ImageNet dataset consisting of approximately 14 million images categorized into 21,841 classes (referred to as synsets) to learn mid-level image features. A latent layer is then added to the CNN. This layer provides fine-tuning the CNN on the target domain dataset by learning hash-like features. The images are retrieved using a coarse-to-fine approach that employs the learnt hashes, such as binary codes and extracted features. The used approach has shown a 30% and 1% increase in precision for the CIFAR10 dataset and MNIST datasets, respectively.

Convolutional neural networks are responsible for success in the computer vision domain. Earlier the computer vision domain was struggling with the feature extraction process. The traditional feature extraction procedure is time-consuming and inefficient to solve many of the complex computer Vision tasks. Computer vision evolution with CNNs turned access to many applications in the domain with good efficiency and easy to implement. However, feature extraction is a fundamental component for CNN. The CNN architecture is mainly composed of a collection of convolutional layers, pooling layers, and fully connected layers. Collectively such architectures extract more robust and effective features from the images. Liu *et al.* [23] have proposed an image retrieval approach with a comparison between an improved LeNet-5 architecture and traditional AlexNet architecture. The authors have used the COREL dataset for experimentation. This dataset has 1000 images with 10 classes, each class has 100 images. In the COREL dataset, the image size is 384*256. Traditional LeNet-5 architecture is used with 32*32 image size; therefore, the last pooling layer will have 400 neurons further fully connected with 120 neurons [25]. However, dealing with 384*256 image size, the pooling layer will have 90,728 neurons and further fully connected to 120 neurons. This will lead to the loss of many important image features useful for further processing. To resolve this problem, authors have proposed a LeNet-L architecture and added a fully connected layer with K neurons between the last pooling layer and the fully connected layer. This LeNet-L architecture is specifically designed for image retrieval feature extraction and for further experimentations authors have used fully connected layer F6. AlexNet architecture won the ILSVRC 2012 competition as constructed by Krizhevsky *et al.* [20] The authors made a comparison of LeNet-L architecture with AlexNet architecture for image retrieval performance. The AlexNet architecture is deeper than LeNet-L and uses modern activation functions such as ReLu which provided a better convergence rate; with that deeper architecture, it needed a greater number of training parameters and thus more training time. In AlexNet, fully connected layer FC8 is used by the author for image retrieval. For evaluation of image retrieval performance of these architectures, authors have used precision, recall, and mean average precision metrics. Mean average precision (mAP) can be calculated using the formula:

$$mAP = \frac{\sum\limits_{q=1}^{Q} AveP(q)}{Q} \tag{3.1}$$

where Q is the number of queries in the set and $AveP(q)$ is the average precision for the query q. Average precision can be calculated using the expression:

$$\text{Average precision} = \frac{\sum\limits_{k=1}^{n} (P(k) * \text{rel}(k))}{\text{No of relevent queries}} \tag{3.2}$$

where $P(k)$ is the precision for k relevant query and rel(k) is the function equating to 1 for k relevant query.

During experimental analysis, the author has found the K=1400 neurons have a better mAP score than any other number of neurons in the added L layer of the LeNet-L architecture. The LeNet-L architecture has an output feature with 84 dimensions, whereas the AlexNet architecture has 1,000 output feature dimensions. Because of this, the AlexNet CNN achieves better image retrieval performance. The author has suggested that both the features FC8 and FC6, when fused into an important image feature information proposed as AL representation, must provide higher level feature extractions and eventually minimize the semantic gap (Table 3.1; Figure 3.4).

Table 3.1 mAP scores with respective feature vectors for top-k retrieved images. Adapted from [23]

Feature vectors	mAP (top-10)	mAP (top-20)	mAP (top-30)	mAP (top-40)	mAP (top-50)
AL	94.78	92.56	90.83	89.35	87.69
FC8	92.77	90.32	88.14	86.35	84.64
FC6	79.62	74.5	71.03	68.07	65.52

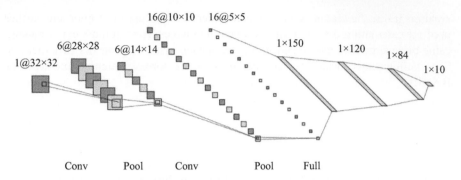

Figure 3.4   Architectural diagram for LeNet-L. Adapted from [23]

The fused feature representation between the LeNet-L and AlexNet CNN architecture has achieved better image retrieval performance than LeNet-L and AlexNet individually when evaluated using the mAP metric. Using this approach, authors have also discussed how CNN can effectively minimize the semantic gap, which was the prime reason for the failure of traditional image processing tools.

Kuo *et al.* in [26] proposed another research with an image retrieval system using a CNN. The feature extractions using CNN are more likely to reduce the semantic gap than the handcrafted descriptors and eventually produce better retrieval results. The dataset used for testing is CIFAR-10 and CIFAR-100. The methodology proposed can be considered into three parts including data pre-processing, training, and testing. Before passing the images to the CNN model for feature extraction, a sparse autoencoder (SAE) is used to pretraining the convolutional kernels. Data augmentations techniques were also performed later for enlarging the dataset and to avoid overfitting. To learn good feature representations, SAE is performed before the CNN model. SAE is an unsupervised learning algorithm that learns an approximation to the identity functions where patches with size 5 by 5 are sampled randomly and used as an input. Further ZCA whitening was done on the sampled patches as a part of normalization. The weights from SDE can be expressed as $W_{SAE} \in R^{64*25}$ and biases $b_{SAE} \in R^{64*1}$. These are very good feature representations from the data and used as initial weights to improve the CNN model responsible for extracting key features of the image. Data augmentation increased the data dimension to the fourth and fifth dimension by adding greyscale images from RGB images. The authors designed a 7-layer CNN model for training, composed of three pairs of convolutional and subsampling layers with 64 convolution kernel and 5×5 convolution filter. ReLU is applied to each sub-sampling layer to avoid vanishing gradient issue. ReLU is mathematically defined as:

$$f(x) = \max(0, x) \tag{3.3}$$

Finally, the fully connected layer was added with the 400-dimension feature vector. For the classification task, another fully connected layer can be added in the last with 100 or 10 feature vectors depending upon the number of classes. For retrieval tasks, the feature vectors are considered as feature descriptor and further used for calculating the similarity between the images. Here authors experimented using three similarity metric and sorted the images based on those distance metrics.

Euclidean distance: It is also known as the L2 norm and can be expressed as follows:

$$d_{\text{Euclidean}} \ (a, \ b) = \sqrt{\sum_{k=1}^{n} (x_{ak} - x_{bk})^2} \tag{3.4}$$

where x_{ak} and x_{bk} are two feature vectors of the images.

Manhattan distance: It is also known as the L1 norm and expressed as follows:

$$d_{\text{Manhattan}} \ (a, \ b) = \sum_{k=1}^{n} |x_{ak} - x_{bk}| \tag{3.5}$$

Cosine distance: It can be expressed as

$$\text{Similarity}(a, b) = \frac{\sum_{k=1}^{n} x_{ak} * x_{bk}}{\sqrt{\sum_{k=1}^{n} x_{ak}^2} \ \sqrt{\sum_{k=1}^{n} x_{bk}^2}} \tag{3.6}$$

$$d\text{cosine} \ (a, b) = 1 - \frac{\cos^{-1}(\text{similarity}(a, \ b))}{\pi} \tag{3.7}$$

This methodology is evaluated using mean average precision mAP (Table 3.2).

Results show that the cosine distance metric can be more effective for finding the similarity between the image feature descriptors extracted by CNN [27] (Figure 3.5).

Liu *et al.* [28] proposed a methodology including CNN and its application in retrieval for crime scene investigation (CSI). Multiple times the possibility of serial crime needs to be nullified from the crime scene investigation. The database is vast and would require human power and resources. An automatic and effective retrieval methodology which can retrieve images from similar crime scene investigation

Table 3.2 mAP and matching time for different datasets and different distance metrics. Adapted from [26]

Distance metrics	CIFAR-10		CIFAR-100	
	mAP	Matching time (s/query)	mAP	Matching time (s/query)
Euclidean	0.671	0.085	0.189	0.115
Manhattan	0.694	0.083	0.217	0.081
Cosine	0.707	0.262	0.244	0.229

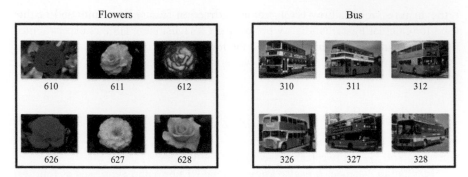

Figure 3.5   Images in Corel dataset. Adapted from [29]

will benefit the efficiency and come to some decision early. The author discussed two approaches for image retrieval such as using low-level features and high-level semantic. HSV color histogram, GIST features, Gabor features, and DCT wavelet are low-level features that have been extracted. Thus, the author proposed a methodology for image retrieval using three technologies such as CNN feature extraction, low-level features, and fusion features. The experimentation has been done using MatConvNet, a MATLAB® toolbox for CNN. The dataset used was of Crime Scene Investigation Image Database which has 10,500 images having 12 classes including biological evidence, tools, tires, bloodstains, cars, site plans, shoe prints, doors, fingerprints, skin tattoos, and windows. Another GHIM-10K database dataset has been used, which has 10 classes of images with 500 images in each class and a total of 10,000 images. To reduce the semantic gap using only the low-level features, the authors have merged two CNN models based on extracting CNN features and then fused them with the dataset's low-level features. This would increase the reliability of the model. A pre-trained CNN architecture known as VGGG-F was selected which was trained on the ImageNet dataset. VGG-VD16 (VGG Very Deep Convolutional Network) was another pre-trained architecture that was used for feature extraction. VGG-F has eight layers including five con-volutional layers and three fully connected layers. VGG-VD16 has 16 layers including 13 convolutional layers and 3 fully connected layers. Further, the CNN models were fine-tuned with resizing the images to 224*224 resolution and kept the same parameters till Conv-fc7 of the pre-trained network and modified the last layer from 1000 to the number of class and retrained it. The pre-trained network has three fully connected layers, for the retrieval task the second-last fully connected layer of dimension 4096 was used. Since the fusion of these two models will create a very high dimension space, principal components analysis (PCA) is done before fusion. The fusion feature F can be expressed as

$$F = [w_1 f_1, w_2 f_2] \tag{3.8}$$

where $f1$ represents features extracted from the fc7 layer of VG-VD16 and $f2$ represents features extracted from the fc7 layer of the VGG-F model, $w_f = [w_1, w_2]$

is the feature weight. Low-level feature extraction was done using HSV color histogram, Gabor Features, DCT wavelet, and GIST features. HSV color histogram can be calculated using the following equation:

$$H(k) = \frac{n(k)}{N} \qquad (3.9)$$

where N is the total number of image pixels, $n(k)$ is the number of pixels having the feature value k in the image, and $k = 0, 1, ..., L-1$, L is the number of possible feature values. Gabor filter is used for extracting texture information from the image. Initially, a Gabor filter is made with 4 scales and 6 directions consisting of 24 Gabor filters; further image is obtained from 24 filter outputs after being convolved from the Gabor filters. Finally mean and variance of each filter can be considered as a feature with 48 dimensions. Discrete cosine transform (DCT) wavelet is used to extract image texture filters using frequency domain information of the system. The final DCT wave F can be expressed as

$$[F] = [kw]d[kw]^T \qquad (3.10)$$

where d is the DCT transform coefficient and kw is the kekre wave matrix. The authors have divided the image into 4 blocks and 3 channels, R, G, and B, each block is DCT transformed. Finally, the feature vectors of each block are connected to form the texture features with 24 dimensions. GIST features quantify the image using statistical attributes. Initially, each image is divided into a grid of $n_a * n_b$ regions further, each region is convolved with Gabor filter of m-scale n direction. Finally, calculate the mean of the Gabor feature in each region and obtain the GIST feature after cascading them together.

The equation can obtain fusion feature expressed as

$$F = \{w_1 f_{CNN1}, w_2 f_{CNN2}, w_3 f_{GIST}, w_4 f_{HSV}, w_5 f_{Gabor}, w_6 f_{DCT-W}\} \qquad (3.11)$$

where f_{CNN1} denotes the feature extracted from the CGG-F CNN model, f_{CNN2} denotes the features extracted from VGG-VD16 CNN model, f_{GIST} denotes feature extracted from GIST features from HSV color histogram, f_{Gabor} denotes features extracted from Gabor features, and f_{DCT-W} denotes feature extracted from DCT wave features, and features weight vector can be expressed as

$$w_f = [w_1, w_2, w_3, w_4, w_5, w_6] \qquad (3.12)$$

Precision is used as an evaluation metric to measure retrieval performance (Tables 3.3 and 3.4).

For the GHIM-10K dataset, best results were achieved from a combination of CNN1, CNN2, HSV, Gabor, and GIST. For the CSID dataset, best results were achieved from a combination of CNN1, CNN2, GIST, and Gabor features. However, it can be concluded from the results table that the CNN2 architecture feature is individually sufficient for obtaining good retrieval performance.

Table 3.3 *Average precision for the different dataset and using traditional feature extraction methods. Adapted from [28]*

Methods	CSID				GHIM-10k [30]			
Single feature	Single feature	Average precision	Fusion feature	Average precision	Single feature	Average precision	Fusion feature	Average precision
HSV	HSV	0.55	HSV + GIST+ DCT-wave	0.63	HSV	0.43	HSV + GIST+ DCT-wave	0.57
Gabor	Gabor	0.63	GIST+DCT wave	0.66	Gabor	0.44	GIST+DCT wave	0.63
DCT wave	DCT wave	0.45	HSV+Gabor+GIST	0.67	DCT wave	0.29	HSV+Gabor+GIST	0.58
GIST	GIST	0.65	Gabor+GIST	0.70	GIST	0.52	Gabor+GIST	0.65

Table 3.4   CNN and fusion features with average precision for different datasets. Adapted from [28]

Features	CSID		GHIM-10K	
	Average precision	Average retrieval time/ image(s)	Average precision	Average retrieval time/ image(s)
GIST+Gabor	0.70	0.044	0.65	0.120
CNN1	0.87	0.024	0.94	0.020
CNN2	0.91	0.028	0.98	0.021
CNN1+CNN2	0.92	0.030	-	-
CNN1+CNN2+GIST+Gabor	0.93	0.065	0.98	0.191

3.5   Image retrieval using autoencoders

Autoencoder is a form of artificial neural network where the model learns the data representation then compresses it in a form of efficient data encoding in an unsupervised manner. By compressing into an efficient encoding, the autoencoder reduces the data dimensions while ignoring noise in the data. The autoencoder architecture has four fundamental components such as encoder, bottleneck, decoder, and reconstruction loss. The encoder first takes in the input data and learns to reduce the input dimensions, and then compress it in a form for data embedding representation. The bottleneck layer has efficient data encoding with minimal dimensions of the input data. Decoder aims to reconstruct the data from the compressed data encoding as closely similar as possible to the original data. The reconstruction loss measures the performance of the decoder and targets the result as similar as possible to the original data. The minimal the loss, the better the performance. Autoencoder is also used to solve many real-world problems due to autoencoder functionality to accept data with high dimension space, and then encode it into an efficient embedding that can be restored in the input. Autoencoder-based applications for image denoising and image compression are very popular. Recently autoencoder-based approach was used in recommendation systems where the encoder is used to catch users' interests and the decoder has to project the unseen content and the newly created content to the user. Convolutional autoencoder has shown excellent performance in many computer vision applications, because of which convolutional autoencoders are used for feature extraction tasks [31]. The key component in an autoencoder is the complete architecture's bottleneck where a latent space embedding is calculated using convolutional feature extraction. The image generated again using this latent space embedding is supposed to reduce the noise in the image, thus being used for image denoising applications. This latent space embedding is also applicable for image retrieval tasks where the similarity between these embedding is observed and K-best similar images are retrieved. Earlier autoencoder architectures were directly implemented using neurons and neural networks but as the number of images and their dimensions increased, this approach had to face the curse of dimensionality. Feature descriptors and image similarity criteria are very crucial in this case. Autoencoder architecture can provide an important application in image retrieval tasks (Figure 3.6).

Zhao *et al.* [6] proposed an autoencoder-based approach for image retrieval and showed a comparison with an already developed state-of-the-art methodology such as SIFT and PCA-SIFT using INRIA Holidays and ORL datasets. The INRIA Holiday dataset has 1491 images divided into 500 image groups, each group has roughly 10 images captures by a different point of view or different lighting conditions. In a group of ten images, one is used as a query image while the rest nine are used for observing retrieval performance. The ORL database has face images of 40 individuals and 10 face images of each individual. One image of each individual is used as a query image and retrieval performance is monitored for the remaining images. 92 × 112-pixel images with 256 grayscale levels per pixel were taken in different lighting conditions at a different duration of the day and with conditions such as smiling/not smiling, glasses/no glasses images with black homogenous background. The authors developed two frameworks for online image retrieval and offline image retrieval. The interest points in all the images in the database are extracted using SIFT detectors. A local gradient patch is generated based on the interest points and a gradient vector corresponding to each interest point is generated. A compressed feature representation is extracted from the generated gradient vector using a pre-trained autoencoder. The similarity between the query image and the images from the database is computed using Euclidean distance. If the distance between the feature vector of the query image and image in the database is less than the certain defined threshold then that image is picked. The similarity of the images is calculated based on the number of such correlated feature vectors. If the number

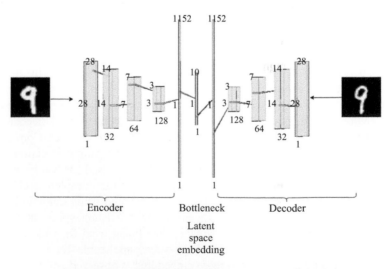

Figure 3.6   Architectural diagram of Autoencoder

of feature vectors matches is more than threshold zero in this case, then that image is returned as the best-matched image from the database. Finally, sorting is done to find the best-matched images from the database in descending order of a number of similarities with the query image. Precision and recall are used as evaluation metrics for evaluating the performance. Precision and recall are mathematically defined as follows:

$$\text{Precision} = \frac{\text{Number of true positives}}{\text{Total number of matches}} \tag{3.13}$$

$$\text{Recall} = \frac{\text{Number of true} - \text{positives}}{\text{Total number of positives}} \tag{3.14}$$

Precision is the ratio of the number of similar images retrieved to the total number of images retrieved. Recall is the ratio of the number of similar images retrieved to the total number of similar images. Precision measures the quality of the retrieved images while recall measures the ability to find similar images. Ideally higher the precision and higher the recall, the better the performance. Here the authors have compared the precision versus recall curve and concluded that the curve closest to the top of the chart represents better performance. The autoencoder-based methodology achieved better results than SIFT and PCA-SIFT, whereas SIFT showed better performance as compared to PCA-SIFT. The autoencoder-based methodology is also three times faster as compared to SIFT methodology [6].

Rupapara *et al.* [32] have proposed a methodology for the CBIR system using autoencoder where images can be retrieved using a query image without any label, names, or tags but only based on the visual inspection. In traditional CBIR methods, feature extraction was not well optimized for large database images since there would be thousands of pixels making it difficult to process the similarity between the images based on those pixels' information. Time complexity was also very large in the early methods making it convenient for users. Autoencoder is based on unsupervised learning techniques used in various computer vision applications. MNIST handwritten dataset is used for experimentation. Keras DL framework is used with the Python backend. The research's main idea is to put forward an approach for an image retrieval system using a convolutional autoencoder. In the convolutional autoencoder, the encoder component contains convolutional layers responsible for finding optimal feature representation and further compressing into a latent space encoding. The decoder also has convolutional layers where again the output will be generated from the compressed latent space encoding. The authors propose a methodology where image feature representations were extracted using a convolutional autoencoder in latent space representation. Similarly, the features of the query image were also extracted. The feature vectors between the images in the database in the form of latent space representation and the query image's feature vector are compared. The nearest neighbor technique is used to compare and find correlated images from the database to the query image by calculating the distance between them. The best-matched images from the database to the query image are sorted according to the nearest neighbor technique's similarity and the best images are retrieved. The nearest neighbor distance can be calculated using the following mathematical formula:

$$d(q, s) = \sqrt{(q1 - s1)^2 + (q2 - s2)^2 + .. + (qn - sn)^2} \qquad (3.15)$$

where $d(q, s)$ is the distance, q is the required image, s is the sample image, and n is the dimension.

The author has used handwritten digit 9 for testing and the proposed methodology has retrieved five best-matched images to the query image nine and thus validates that the process can be used with a large database efficiently.

Song J *et al.* [33] have proposed an approach for image retrieval system using binary generative adversarial network (BGAN) based on unsupervised learning. Hashing methods are compact and have efficient hashing distance calculation leading to applications in image retrieval. Binary vectors can be generated by embedding the data into binary format, that is, 0 and 1 into a vector having code length L. Binary codes can be expressed as

$$b = h(x) \in \{0, 1\}^L \qquad (3.16)$$

where b is the binary vector with code length L, $x \in R^{M \times 1}$ and $h(.)$ are the hashing functions.

While using hashing methodology with unsupervised learning majorly the similarity/distances between the similar features can be grouped and those important features are retained. This also creates a drawback where these methods fail to capture relevant features when used in different contexts. Whereas in supervised hashing methods, the predefined labels are given more importance and the hashing distance tries to approximate the similarity of the pairwise labels. However, the supervised hashing methods perform better since unsupervised hashing struggle with the less amount of labeled data and they are subjective. The combination of DL with such hashing methods has been very popular lately. Deep hashing algorithms with unsupervised learning still fail to produce satisfactory results. Generative adversarial network (GAN) has proved efficient in producing new similarity data from the representation in the latent space. Thus, the authors have proposed a methodology where GAN learns the binary representation of the image features and a similar image to the original one can be generated. The BGAN aims to learn the compact binary code b and generates the image IR when N training images are given, $I = \{I_i\}_{i=1}^N$. This was evaluated over three publicly available dataset CIFAR-10, NUS-WIDE, and Flickr. CIFAR10 dataset has 60,000 images divided into 10 distinct classes having 32*32 resolution and each class has 6,000 images. A subset of the NUS-WIDE dataset is used with 195,834 images with 21 most frequent semantic concepts and each concept consists of 5,000 images. A subset of Flickr data is used with 25,000 images containing 38 concepts, each image having 256*256 resolution. Further for using it for the image retrieval task in NUS-WISE and CIFAR-10, 100 randomly selected per class images were used as a query image test set and 1,000 images per class as the training dataset. In the Flickr dataset, 1,000 randomly selected images were used as a query image dataset and 4,000 images as the training dataset. The proposed BGAN architecture has fundamental components such as encoder, hash layer, generator, and discriminator. The encoder is used for feature extraction. The encoder consists of convolutional layers significantly used with CNN architectures such as VGG, RESNET, MOBILENET, etc. Here VGG19 like architecture is used for feature extraction which has five groups of convolutional layers with 64, 128, 256, 512, and 512 filters and similarly five convolutional max pool layers with 2*2 filter. Fully connected layers are used as output layers having 4,096 units. The hashing layer is calculated using the learned features from the fully connected layer of the encoder. An L-dimensional representation z from the FC layer is continuous and is further connected to the binary after passing it through a signum activation function. The standard signum function leads to a vanishing gradient issue and is infeasible for optimally training deep neural networks. To deal with this, the author has designed an *app ()* function for approximating the *sgn ()*. The *app()* function can be expressed as

$$
app(z) = \begin{cases} +1, & if \quad z \geq 1 \\ z, & if \ 1 \geq z \geq 1 \\ -1, & if \quad z < -1 \end{cases} \tag{3.17}
$$

This generated binary code is given as input to the generator. The work of the GAN is to generate images using this binary code. The generator network is formed when the binary code b is given as an input to the fully connected layer of size 8*8*256. Then four deconvolutional layers having 256, 128, 32, and 3 kernels with kernel size 5×5, 5×5, 5×5, and 1×1, respectively, are added. Finally, a batch-normalization layer with an eLU activation function is used. GAN is based on the adversarial learning concept where the generator produces new input. The discriminator has to discriminate between the generated images and those already available from the original training data, thus optimizing the generated results generated by the generator. The generator tries to minimize the error and simultaneously the discriminator tries to maximize the error. This is done using a loss function. The authors have formulated a loss function in a form of the weighted sum of neighbor structure loss, content loss, and adversarial loss. The combined BGAN loss can be expressed as

$$
L = l_N + l_C + l_A \tag{3.18}
$$

where l_N is the neighbor structure loss, l_C is the content loss, and l_A is the adversarial loss.

The neighbor structure loss can be expressed as where L is the length of the binary code, S is the similarity matrix, and Binary code is $B = \{b_i\}_{i=1}^{N}$. The neighbor structure loss has to optimize the similarity between the similar images. The content loss can be explained with MSE loss and perpetual loss:

$$
l_{\mathrm{MSE}} = \frac{1}{WH} \sum_{i=1}^{W} \sum_{j=1}^{H} \left(I_{ij} - I_{ij}^R \right)^2 \tag{3.19}
$$

$$l_{\text{Perceptual}} = \frac{1}{WH \sum_{i=1}^{W} \sum_{j=1}^{H} \left(\phi(I_{ij}) - \phi\left(I_{ij}^{R}\right)\right)^{2}} \tag{3.20}$$

$$l_C = l_{\text{MSE}} + l_{\text{perpetual}} \tag{3.21}$$

The content loss together aims to optimize the reconstructed images. The adversarial loss can be calculated as

$$l_A = \log(D(I)) + \log\left(1 - D\left(I^{R}\right)\right) \tag{3.22}$$

The adversarial loss aims to optimize the generator and discriminator by emphasizing the misclassifications between the discriminators. Further back-propagation is used for weight learning and stochastic gradient descent is used as an optimizer to minimize the loss. Mean average precision (mAP) and the precision two evaluation metrics are used for evaluation for k-best similar images and further precision-recall curve and precision@k is observed for each stage of retrieval. The following table achieved mAP scores for the proposed BGAN approach for the respective dataset and the number of bits hash codes used (Table 3.5).

Zhang *et al.* [34] proposed a novel framework ClothingOut which is an application of GAN for generating tiled clothing images used in the clothing sector and provided a methodology for clothing retrieval using images. Applications of GAN were very dominant in the clothing industry including applications such as FashionMnist and FashionGAN. Clothing feature extraction is possible using traditional image processing techniques and using DL. However, DL has shown a more efficient and easier implementation-based approach; thus, the authors used a DL-based CNN technique for feature extraction. Dataset was generated using Tianmo which is a clothing commercial in China. For this ClothingOut framework, a dataset containing 21,592 pairs of the wearer and its corresponding tiled clothing images were generated. A number of 2,192 images were used for training and 500 images were used for testing. The annotations were done manually for the image pairs. The frequently searched indexes of clothing such as tops, coats, jumpsuits, dresses, pants, and skirts are used as a category by manual annotations. This trained GAN model is also used for clothing retrieval tasks. The generator network works like an encoder–decoder and generates new images by learning the distribution of the dataset while the discriminator network has to discriminate between the generated images as real or

Table 3.5 CNN and fusion features with average precision for different datasets. Adapted from [33]

Methods	CIFAR-10 [35]				NUS-WIDE [27]				Flickr			
	12 bits	24 bits	32 bits	48 bits	12 bits	24 bits	32 bits	48 bits	12 bits	24 bits	32 bits	48 bits
BGAN	0.401	0.512	0.531	0.558	0.675	0.690	0.714	0.728	0.683	0.702	0.703	0.703

fake, specifically trying to identify the fake images. The generator has to keep on optimizing its performance to make the generated output as real as possible and fool the discriminator network. Since in this application the generated image must not only have similar attributes to the dataset distribution but should also be similar to the input image; hence, an L1 distance is added to the generator's objective. The model aims to generate a tiled clothing image using a wearer clothing image, thus the generated tiled images must have the same category of the wearer clothing. This is formulated using a classifier that produces each category's probabilities giving additional input to the generator model. Mini batch stochastic gradient descent and adam optimizer are used during training. The proposed methodology of CatGAN is compared with traditional GAN, cGAN and pix2pixGAN. L2 distance is used to determine retrieval performance. VGG19 CNN Network is trained using the clothing dataset created with IMAGENET weights is used for feature extraction of the query image. The third fully connected layer in the VGG19 extracted a 1,000-dimensional feature vector and further used to calculate the similarity between the query image and the images in the dataset; eventually, top n similar images were retrieved. Precision, recall and F1 performance metrics were used for further evaluation.

Yanagi *et al.* [36] proposed a novel approach for scene retrieval tasks from a video dataset and proposed a 'Query is GAN' framework. This framework is based on the text-to-image GAN. The authors discuss a very unique and significant research interest approach. Text-based image retrieval systems are used traditionally; however, they lack to map between the descriptor keywords and the semantic gaps from an image. Recent advances in GANs have made it possible to combine text-based descriptors with image generation models efficiently. For this query, GAN framework authors have used COCO dataset which contains 82,783 training images, each image with five descriptions, and MP-II MD dataset which has 68,000 scene images from 94 movies, each scene associated with one description. The goal of framework is to retrieve images of that particular scene from the movie scenes dataset using the description of that scene. In this proposed approach, instead of using a query image as input to the image retrieval system, the text-to-image generation model is used to generate query images from the text. Similarly, the user has to input a description text, the text-to-image generation model will further generate three query images which will be further used for the image-image retrieval task. AttnGAN based network is constructed and three query images are generated. This AttnGAN has three generators $Gr = (l,h,m)$; where l, h, and m represent low, high, and mid resolution image generation. These three generators also have three different hidden states and three different neural networks. To generate such query images of different resolutions, the AttnGAN model is used where text description is accepted as an input and based on that the trained model returns the images. The loss used for this is a combination of loss due to conditional and unconditional distributions and loss due to text-image matching. The second phase of the framework is directly related to the processing and retrieval of similar images to the query images. Visual features from all the scene images dataset as well as from the query images are to be extracted. The feature extraction is done using the third pooling layer of the Inception-V3 architecture. Furthermore,

Inception-V3 architecture is used in the text-image model for calculating text-image matching loss. Finally, a similarity metric such as cosine similarity is calculated from the query images and the database images. The query image of low-resolution Q_1 is dependent on the whole information of the input sentence. Thus the Q_1 query image is used to screen through the large database and rank them for the retrieval images. Similarly, Q_m and Q_h images are also used to screen through the database and find the k top similar images for retrieval. Since Q_h and Q_m focus mainly on important words in the sentences, the images retrieved by then also have an object relationship from the images. This method is considered a baseline method and a similar approach using DL was used for retrieval performance comparison. Recall metric is used for evaluation. The recall to the rank curve was the highest for this proposed framework when compared to other techniques. Furthermore, 25 individuals were invited to grade the retrieved images and this proposed approach achieved grade 4 out of 5. These types of methodology are very novel and involve a booming research interest. This methodology is directly applicable to retrieving the scenes from the video database very efficiently.

3.6   Image retrieval using generative adversarial networks (GAN)

Generative adversarial networks (GANs) are a DL-based methodology used for various computer vision applications, described by Goodfellow *et al.* [37] in 2014. In 2015, Alec *et al.* [38] proposed deep convolutional generative adversarial networks (DCGAN) model where an unsupervised learning-based GAN approach was studied in computer vision applications, particularly in the computer vision domain. GANs are capable of producing new data from the already existing trained data. This is possible because in GANs both the generator model and the discriminator model work together. The data generated by a GAN can even challenge human interpretations. In the traditional machine learning problem of image classification using supervised learning approach, the model takes up training data and outputs the label, this is a discriminative model where it discriminates and outputs a label for the given image. In GANs, the generative model is given the training data. The generative model has a random noise distribution data initially which after training learns the probability distribution from the training data and produces results based on that probability distribution. The discriminative model is a binary classification model that aims to discriminate between the real, actual training, and fake data produced from the generator model. Log loss error function is mostly used with GANs. When the generator is in the training phase, the discriminator is idle and when the discriminator is in the training phase, the generator is idle. The discriminator penalizes the generator for producing fake results thus the discriminator model accuracy increases when the generator models generate fake results. The generator model aims to generate results as real as possible and increase accuracy. In this way, the generator accuracy increases and discriminator accuracy decreases, and more real data results are produced from the GANs (Figure 3.7).

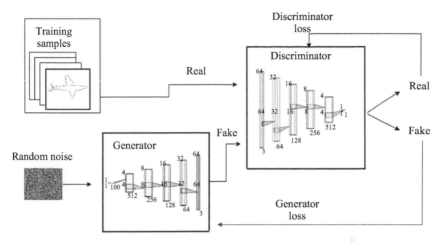

Figure 3.7   Architectural diagram of the generative adversarial network (GAN)

Pahariyya *et al.* [39] have proposed a multi-modal approach for CBIR system using sketch and color images. This approach is used with Cycle-GAN architecture further validated and trained over sketchy and TU-Berlin dataset. The sketchy dataset has 7,500 sketch images and 12,500 color real-world images. Additionally, 60,000 real work images from ImageNet have been added to this class. The TU-Berlin has 20,000 sketch images categorized into 250 categories. An 80:20 Training Testing slit has been used while training. Initially, the search query is passed through a domain classifier CNN model trained with five convolutional layers, two fully connected layers and the last layer with binary classification label of sketch or color. If the query image is a sketch, this sketched image is transformed into the color image using multi-class cycle generative adversarial network. A supervised deep domain adaptation (SDDA) technique is used to maintain the generated shared feature representations since a real-world image generated by Cycle-GAN can be noisy or blurry. This SDDA technique is used with contrastive semantic alignment loss (L_{CCSA}).

The contrastive semantic alignment (CCSA) loss is a combination of classification loss denoted as L_C for classification between sketch and real-world image and semantic alignment loss denoted as L_{SA} which targets images from a different domain but with similar labels. Next is the separation loss denoted as L_S which encourages images with different domains and with different labels. Together the CCSA loss can be considered as

$$L_{CCSA} = L_C(\hat{z}) + L_{SA}(g) + L_S(g) \qquad (3.23)$$

CCSA loss tries to maximize the distance between images of the same labels but with a different domain minimizes the distance between images of different labels and different domains and the classification loss tries to attain optimal classification accuracy. The images generated by M-cycle GAN using sketch images are considered target *(S)* and the real work images used for training the SDDA are considered source*(I)*. The goal is to learn a prediction function $\widehat{z}: I \rightarrow \widehat{S}$. In general, $\widehat{z}$ is a combination of function $g: I \rightarrow Z$, where Z is a feature space and the function $h: Z \rightarrow Y$ where Y would be the prediction or classification such as $\widehat{z}$ is an inner product of *h* and *g*. For evaluating the similarity between the representations in the embedding space, inverse of Euclidean distance with a classification score is used in all experiments. Mean average precision mAP is used for evaluating retrieval performance. The mAP can be given as follows.

The mAP score for retrieval rate with booth sketches and real-world image as a query from with TU-Berlin dataset is 0.68 and that with the Sketchy dataset is 0.73. Retrieval rate for only real-world images as the query has mAP values of 0.75 for the TU-Berlin dataset and 0.81 for the Sketchy dataset (Figures 3.8 and 3.9) (Table 3.6).

A novel unsupervised adversarial image retrieval (UAIR) framework for CBIR system is given by Huang *et al.* [40]. The authors have used MNIST and CIFAR10 datasets for experimentation. The MNIST dataset has 70,000 grayscale images with 28*28 dimensions belonging to 10 classes of handwritten digits from 0 to 9. Randomly selected 100 images from each class are used as a query image set and the rest images are used as the database set. CIFAR10 dataset has 60,000 color images belonging to 10 classes with 32*32 image dimensions and each class has 6,000 images. Randomly selected 100 images per class have been used as a query set and the remaining images as Gallery Images database. A pre-trained VGG model is used with ImageNet weights. This framework takes input as the query image's features and images in the Gallery Images database outputs top k-matched images. The input images are converted to feature representations after fine-tuning the CNN model further. The UAIR approach has two fundamental architectures: the generator model and the discriminative model. The newly designed generative

Figure 3.8   Images in the sketchy dataset. Adapted from [41]

Figure 3.9   Images in TU-Berlin database. Adapted from [42]

Table 3.6   mAP results for sketch and color input queries with the respective dataset. Adapted from [39]

Dataset	mAP (sketch and color)	mAP (sketch)
TU-Berlin [42]	0.68	0.75
Sketchy [41]	0.73	0.81

model tries to find the best similar images to the Gallery Images database's query image. The discriminative model judges similar images given by the generative model as the well-matched similar image to the query image thus optimizing to retrieve the best K-matched images to the query image from the database. For a given query image, the generative model finds the image features using a three-layer fully connected network. Finally, k-best-matched images are returned according to the similarity scores obtained by comparing image features. The discriminative model takes the generative model's images and again weighs the image features using three fully connected layers. Furthermore, the similarity score is calculated between the k-best-matched images from the generator model and the query image. The discriminative model regards the best-matched images according to the newly generated similarity scores and discards the remaining images. Discrimination is done within the best-matched images using their distances by the discriminator model. The threshold distance is set to zero so every image from the database with a distance more than zero is considered an unmatched image and needs to be optimized by the generative model. In this case, the generative model aims to find the best K-matched images from the database and the discriminator model aims to find the unmatched images from those images. This leads to a min–max game between the generative model and the discriminator model. The loss function in the GAN model can be considered as

$$fG, D = \min_{\theta} \max_{\varnothing} \sum_{n=1}^{N} E_{s \sim q\text{true}(s)} \left[\log D(s) \right] + E_{s' \sim q_{\text{select}} s'} \left[1 \log D\left(G\left(s' \right) \right) \right] \quad (3.24)$$

where the generative model is denoted as *D(s)* and the discriminative model is denoted as *G(s)*. $q_{\text{true}(s)}$ is the ideal condition of the generative model for image retrieval and $q_{\text{select}(s')}$ is the actual condition of the generative model.

The similarity score is defined using the cosine distance metric. The cosine distance can be calculated using expression (3.6).

The optimization function for the UAIR framework should be considered as

$$
\begin{aligned}
\theta_g &= \operatorname{argmin}_\theta \sum_{n=1}^{N} E_{s \sim q_{\text{select}}(s)}[1 - \log D(g_\theta(s|,q,r))] \\
&= \operatorname{argmax}_\theta \sum_{n=1}^{N} E_{s \sim q_{\text{select}}(s)}[\log(1 + g_\theta(s|,q,r))]
\end{aligned}
\tag{3.25}
$$

where $g_\theta(s/q,r)$ is the similarity function which mAPs between 0 and 1.

Mean average precision mAP is used as evaluating criteria for the retrieval performance and the actual ground truth images (Table 3.7).

Creswell *et al.* [43] proposed a generative adversarial network-based Sketch-GAN model for the retrieval of sketch images. The image retrieval performance of GAN has experimented for retrieval performance over Merchant Markers dataset. The Merchant Markers are only line drawing with the absence of texture and color features, making it difficult to use traditional CBIR methods. The authors have designed a GAN specifically for sketch retrieval. GAN has two models generator and discriminator. The generator's objective is to learn the distribution of the given data and generate new outcomes, whereas the discriminator tries to discriminate between the output of the generator as machine-generated or fake and human-generated or real. The generator has to make the machine-generated outcomes similar to human-generated and try to fool the discriminator. Thus, the generator aims to minimize and the discriminator aims to eventually maximize the loss function into a min–max game. Here authors have proposed the GAN model to be used as the encoder for the sketch retrieval task. The final layer for the trained GAN discriminator is removed to be used as an encoder. The encoder now outputs the

Table 3.7   mAP results with UAIR and other methods comparison. Adapted from [40]

Methodology	MNIST (mAP) [25]	CIFAR10 (mAP) [35]
CCA-ITQ [44]	0.62	0.65
UAIR	0.98	0.85
NDH [45]	0.96	0.69
ITQ [44]	0.45	0.16
QANIR [46]	0.95	0.67
Spherical [47]	0.34	0.15
DH [48]	0.46	0.49
UH-GAN [49]	0.93	0.32
SDH [50]	0.94	0.66

representations for the images passed through it such as query images and images from the database, further used for image retrieval. The GAN is trained over 2,000 samples of the Merchant Marker dataset. The Sketch-GAN network with 33k parameters and the thin-GAN network with 50k parameters have been used to compare retrieval tasks. The networks are evaluated using visual inspection. Sketch-GAN has shown better performance with rotation, scale, and shift as compared to thin-GAN. Concerning the retrieval performance, Sketch-GAN shows consistent and robust results as compared to thin-GAN.

References

[1] Minaev, A. Internet statistics 2021: Facts you need-to-know. Internet: FirstSiteGuide; 2021. Available from https://firstsiteguide.com/internet-stats/ [Accessed on January 27, 2021].

[2] Holst, A. Amount of information globally 2010-2024. Internet: Statista; 2021. Available from https://www.statista.com/statistics/871513/worldwide-data-created/ [Accessed on January 27, 2021].

[3] Webmaster. Google search statistics. Internet: Internet live stats; 202. Available from https://www.internetlivestats.com/google-search-statistics/ [Accessed on January 27, 2021].

[4] Carrington, D. How many photos will be taken in 2020. Internet: mylio.com; 2020. Available from https://focus.mylio.com/tech-today/how-many-photos-will-be-taken-in-2020 [Accessed on January 27, 2021].

[5] Qayyum, A., Anwar, S. M., Awais, M., and Majid, M. "Medical image retrieval using deep convolutional neural network." *Neurocomputing*. 2017; 266: 8–20.

[6] Zhao, C. "An autoencoder-based image descriptor for image matching and retrieval." Electronic Thesis or Dissertation. Wright State University, 2016. https://etd.ohiolink.edu/ [Accessed on January 27, 2021].

[7] Kato, T. "Database architecture for content-based image retrieval." image storage and retrieval systems. International Society for Optics and Photonics. 1992; 1662: 12.

[8] Alkhawlani, M., Elmogy, M, and El Bakry, H. "Text-based, content-based, and semantic-based image retrievals: A survey." International Journal of Computer Science and Information Technologies. 2015; 4(1): 58–66.

[9] Choraś, R. S. "Content-based image retrieval—A survey." In *Biometrics, computer security systems and artificial intelligence applications*, pp. 31–44. Boston, MA: Springer; 2006.

[10] Wang, H. H., Mohamad, D., and Ismail, N. A.. "Approaches, challenges and future direction of image retrieval." 2010. *arXiv preprint arXiv:1006.4568*.

[11] McCulloch, W. S., and Pitts, W.. "A logical calculus of the ideas immanent in nervous activity." *The Bulletin of Mathematical Biophysics*. 1943; 5(4): 115–133.

[12] Hopfield, J. J. "Neural networks and physical systems with emergent collective computational abilities." *Proceedings of the National Academy of Sciences*. 1982; 79(8): 2554–2558.

[13] Hinton, G. E., Osindero, S., and Teh, Y.-W. "A fast learning algorithm for deep belief nets." *Neural Computation.* 2006; 18(7): 1527–1554.

[14] Voulodimos, A., Doulamis, N., Doulamis, A., and Protopapadakis, E. "Deep learning for computer vision: A brief review." *Computational Intelligence and Neuroscience.* 2018 (2018).

[15] Chowdhary, C. L., Goyal, A., and Vasnani, B. K. "Experimental assessment of beam search algorithm for improvement in image caption generation." *Journal of Applied Science and Engineering.* 2019; 22(4): 691–698.

[16] RM, S. P., Reddy, P. K., Maddikunta, M. P., *et al.* "An effective feature engineering for DNN using hybrid PCA-GWO for intrusion detection in IoMT architecture." *Computer Communications.* 2020; 160: 139–149.

[17] Khare, N., Devan, P., Chowdhary, C. L., *et al.* "SMO-DNN: Spider monkey optimization and deep neural network hybrid classifier model for intrusion detection." *Electronics.* 2020; 9(4): 692.

[18] Jain, A. K., Mao, J., and Mohiuddin, K. M. "Artificial neural networks: A tutorial." *Computer.* 1996; 29(3): 31–44.

[19] Hu, X., Li, K., Han, J., Hua, X., Guo, L., and Liu, T. "Bridging the semantic gap via functional brain imaging." *IEEE Transactions on Multimedia.* 2011; 14(2), 314–325.

[20] Krizhevsky, A., Sutskever, I., and Hinton, G. E. "Imagenet classification with deep convolutional neural networks." *Advances in Neural Information Processing Systems.* 2012; 25: 1097–1105.

[21] Nair, V., and Hinton, G. E. "Rectified linear units improve restricted boltzmann machines." In ICML. 2010.

[22] Scherer, D., Müller, A., and Behnke, S. "Evaluation of pooling operations in convolutional architectures for object recognition." In International Conference on Artificial Neural Networks, pp. 92–101. Berlin, Heidelberg: Springer; 2010.

[23] Liu, H, Li, B., Lv, X., and Huang, Y. "Image retrieval using fused deep convolutional features." *Procedia Computer Science.* 2017; 107: 749–754.

[24] Simonyan, K., and Zisserman, A. "Very deep convolutional networks for large-scale image recognition." 2014. *arXiv preprint arXiv:1409.1556.*

[25] LeCun, Y., Bottou, L., Bengio, Y., and Haffner, P. "Gradient-based learning applied to document recognition." *Proceedings of the IEEE.* 1998; 86(11): 2278–2324.

[26] Kuo, C.-H., Chou, Y.-H., and Chang, P.-C.. "Using deep convolutional neural networks for image retrieval." *Electronic Imaging.* 2016; 2(2016): 1–6.

[27] Chua, T.-S., Tang, J., Hong, R., Li, H., Luo, Z., and Zheng, Y. "Nus-wide: A real-world web image database from national university of singapore." In Proceedings of the ACM international conference on image and video retrieval, pp. 1–9. 2009.

[28] Liu, Y., Peng, Y., Hu, D., Li, D., Lim, K. P., and Ling, N. "Image retrieval using CNN and low-level feature fusion for crime scene investigation image database." In *2018 IEEE Asia-Pacific Signal and Information Processing Association Annual Summit and Conference (APSIPA ASC)* (pp. 1208–1214). 2018.

[29]   Li, J., and Wang, J. Z. "Automatic linguistic indexing of pictures by a statistical modeling approach." *IEEE Transactions on Pattern Analysis and Machine Intelligence.* 2003; 25(9): 1075–1088.

[30]   Liu, G. H., Yang, J. Y., and Li, Z. "Content-based image retrieval using computational visual attention model." *Pattern Recognition.* 2015; 48(8): 2554–2566.

[31]   Masci, J., Meier, U., Cireşan, D., and Schmidhuber, J.. "Stacked convolutional auto-encoders for hierarchical feature extraction." In *International Conference on Artificial Neural Networks*, pp. 52–59. Berlin, Heidelberg: Springer; 2011.

[32]   Rupapara, V., Narra, M., Gonda, N. K., Thipparthy, K., and Gandhi, S. "Auto-encoders for content-based image retrieval with its implementation using handwritten dataset." In *2020 5th International Conference on Communication and Electronics Systems (ICCES)* (pp. 289–294). 2020.

[33]   Song, J. "Binary generative adversarial networks for image retrieval." 2017. *arXiv preprint arXiv:1708.04150.*

[34]   Zhang, H., Sun, Y., Liu, L., Wang, X., Li, L., and Liu, W. "ClothingOut: A category-supervised GAN model for clothing segmentation and retrieval." *Neural Computing and Applications.* 2020; 32(9): 4519–4530.

[35]   Krizhevsky, Alex, and Geoffrey Hinton. "Learning multiple layers of features from tiny images." (2009): 7.

[36]   Yanagi, R., Togo, R., Ogawa, T., and Haseyama, M. "Query is GAN: Scene retrieval with attentional text-to-image generative adversarial network." *IEEE Access* 2019; 7 : 153183–153193.

[37]   Goodfellow, I. J., Pouget-Abadie, J., Mirza, M., *et al.* "Generative adversarial networks." 2014. *arXiv preprint arXiv:1406.2661.*

[38]   Radford, A., Metz, L., and Chintala, S. "Unsupervised representation learning with deep convolutional generative adversarial networks." 2015. *arXiv preprint arXiv:1511.06434.*

[39]   Pahariya, G. "Bi-modal content based image retrieval using multi-class cycle-GAN." In Procedding of IEEE *2018 Digital Image Computing: Techniques and Applications (DICTA)* (pp. 1–7). 2018.

[40]   Huang, L., Bai, C., Lu, Y., Chen, S., and Tian, Q. "Adversarial learning for content-based image retrieval." In *2019 IEEE Conference on Multimedia Information Processing and Retrieval (MIPR).* (pp. 97–102). 2019.

[41]   Sangkloy, P., Burnell, N., Ham, C., and Hays, J. "The sketchy database: Learning to retrieve badly drawn bunnies." *ACM Transactions on Graphics (TOG).* 2016; 35(4): 1–12.

[42]   Eitz, M., Hays, J., and Alexa, M. "How do humans sketch objects?." *ACM Transactions on graphics (TOG).* 2012; 31(4): 1–10.

[43]   Creswell, A., and Bharath, A. A. "Adversarial training for sketch retrieval." In *European Conference on Computer Vision* (pp. 798–809). Cham: Springer; 2016.

[44]   Gong, Y., Lazebnik, S., Gordo, A., and Perronnin, F. "Iterative quantization: A procrustean approach to learning binary codes for large-scale image

retrieval." *IEEE Transactions on Pattern Analysis and Machine Intelligence*. 2012; 35(12): 2916–2929.

[45]   Chen, Z., Lu, J., Feng, J., and Zhou, J. "Nonlinear discrete hashing." *IEEE Transactions on Multimedia*. 2016; 19(1): 123–135.

[46]   Bai, C., Huang, L., Pan, X., Zheng, J., and Chen, S. "Optimization of deep convolutional neural network for large scale image retrieval." Neurocomputing. 2018; 303: 60–67.

[47]   Heo, J.-P., Lee, Y., He, J., Chang, S.-F., and Yoon, S.-E. "Spherical hashing: Binary code embedding with hyperspheres." *IEEE Transactions on Pattern Analysis and Machine Intelligence*. 2015; 37(11): 2304–2316.

[48]   Lu, J., Liong, V. E., and Zhou, J. "Deep hashing for scalable image search." *IEEE Transactions on Image Processing*. 2017; 26(5): 2352–2367.

[49]   Dizaji, K. G., Zheng, F., Sadoughi, N., Yang, Y., Deng, C., and Huang, H. "Unsupervised deep generative adversarial hashing network." In Proceedings of the IEEE Conference on Computer Vision and Pattern Recognition. pp. 3664–3673. 2018.

[50]   Shen, F., Shen, C., Liu, W., and Shen, H. T. "Supervised discrete hashing." In Proceedings of the IEEE Conference on Computer Vision and Pattern Recognition. pp. 37–45. 2015.

Chapter 4

Handwritten digits recognition using dictionary learning

Vahid Abolghasemi[1], Rasoul Ameri[2]
and Kianoush Nazarpour[3]

Abstract

Handwritten documents have been a valuable resource in human transactions for many years. Today, there is an immediate need for computer-based techniques to intelligently read and analyze such documents. Meanwhile, handwritten numerals are of particular importance due to their role in finance, business, post, etc. Although there exist many researches on English handwritten number recognition, the development of reliable recognition systems has been paid little attention for non-English scripts. In this chapter, an overview of the state-of-the-art on handwritten number recognition (with focus on non-English languages) is presented. Dictionary learning as a supervised learning technique, which has been recently shown great success in image classification problems, is introduced. We describe the ways one can design discriminative dictionaries for classification of handwritten numbers. The obtained dictionaries convey exclusive features of the associated numerals. In order to improve the classification performance of handwritten numbers using dictionary learning, two novel approaches are presented. First, an incoherence penalty is combined with the learning process to fine-tune the structure of the dictionaries learned for each class. Second, class label information is embedded into the learning process in order to produce class-specific weights which improve the discriminativity of the learned dictionaries. We further adopt a new feature space, that is, histogram of oriented gradients (HOG) to generate the dictionary atoms. HOG is a strong descriptor of most handwritten images especially those studied in this chapter. Four different handwritings, namely, Chinese, Persian, Arabic, as well as English are used to evaluate the performance of the proposed

[1]School of Computer Science and Electronic Engineering, University of Essex, Colchester, United Kingdom
[2]School of Computer Engineering, Shahrood University of Technology, Shahrood, Iran
[3]School of Informatics, University of Edinburgh, Edinburgh, United Kingdom

methods. We also present a convolutional neural network model to compare the performance of deep learning with that of dictionary learning for hand-written digits recognition. The obtained results and their comparisons with benchmark methods confirm the effectiveness and robustness of the proposed approaches for recognition of handwritten numbers.

Key Words: Histogram of oriented gradients (HOG); handwritten recognition; handwritten character recognition (HCR); handwritten numbers recognition (HNR); artificial neural network (ANN); multilayer perceptron (MLP)

4.1   Introduction

4.1.1   *Optical character recognition*

By definition, optical character recognition (OCR) is known as a computer vision technology that recognizes the printed or handwritten characters inside a piece of text which is available in form of digital images of a scanned document. OCR covers a broad domain of research in artificial intelligence, pattern recognition, and computer vision. It is considered as a popular replacement of handwritten or printed text with the flexibility to be electronically amended, stored, and searched more efficiently, quickly, and correctly. The importance of this technology in our daily lives is more revealing as nowadays we need to process almost all documents electronically. However, there are some challenges in obtaining a universal and perfect recognition system. For instance, since texts can be written in a variety of languages, fonts and styles, attaining a reliable OCR system is extremely challenging and needs a great amount of research and algorithmic design. In this regard, researchers have found that focusing on two categories, that is, character recognition and handwriting recognition are more beneficial. Also, the sub-categories of handwriting recognition are handwritten digits (or numbers) and handwritten characters.

Two main stages of a typical OCR system includes (1) character segmentation from the text and (2) interpreting/recognizing the characters by converting them into a computer processable code. A typical OCR pip-line is shown in Figure 4.1. The purpose of segmentation stage is to automatically separate and enhance the visual representation and quality of images of characters and prepare them for the recognition stage. There are many researches focused on this part as it is prone to many challenges depending on the application of interest, for example, car number plate detection [1], text detection from natural scenes [2], etc. The second stage, that is, character recognition is to interpret the image, recognize it, and convert it to a machine readable code, for example, ASCII. In this stage, computer vision and machine learning techniques are normally used depending on different languages and applications. The main focus of this chapter is on handwritten numbers recognition. Therefore, recent related methods and techniques will be reviewed in the sequel.

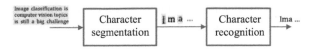

Figure 4.1   A generic OCR system

4.1.2   Handwritten recognition

Handwriting recognition, also called handwriting OCR, can be generally executed in two online and offline modes. In online methods, a digital pen/stylus is used with access to the stroke information and pen location while the text is being written. The recognition algorithm does not require a segmentation stage and encompasses a lot of information with regard to the flow of text being written. Therefore, it is anticipated to perform with very high accuracy and speed. In contrast, offline methods attempt to recognize a written text after it has been written down and hence no information of the strokes/directions involved during writing is utilized. Although online methods seem to be more accurate, they require specific hardware to work properly. On the other hand, offline techniques can be simply applied on any scanned images from an arbitrary text.

Handwritten text mainly involves alphabetical and numerical characters as well as some symbols. Handwritten character recognition (HCR) poses great challenges due to huge variability and unpredictability of handwritings, different handwriting styles, poor quality of source documents, cursive and connected words, and lack of enough available datasets with ground truth. A generic handwritten recognition system uses machine learning to interpret and recognize the received handwritten data from different sources, for example emails, bank cheque, exam papers, tests, images, etc. Traditional recognition systems comprise two major stages: feature extraction and classification. The first stage transforms the input data into a space to accurately describe the data while reducing the amount or dimensionality of data, and the second stage assigns the input data to the associated class. Various techniques have been proposed for handwritten classification where the main challenge is to learn efficient and comprehensive model capable of handling a diverse range of handwritten styles.

Due to importance of precise recognition of numbers and digits in various documents, some researchers prefer to consider a sub-group of methods with focus on recognition of numbers, the so-called handwritten numbers recognition (HNR). HNR has been paid less attention despite its importance in our daily lives. There exist scattered works in this regard [3], still requiring more study [4–6]. Particularly, much amount of research is to be carried out for building an effective HNR system for non-English texts. The main focus of this chapter is to address this gap by reporting existing methods and developments, followed by proposing novel techniques in HNR. Besides, lack of comprehensive "handwritten numbers" data-bases, particularly in non-English languages is another major issue. In this chapter, we will introduce existing databases in addition to the one published by the authors.

A brief overview of the handwritten number recognition literature with focus on two main learning-based methods, that is, deep learning and dictionary learning and HOG-related techniques will be also provided.

One good example of non-English HNR is Chinese numbers recognition. Chinese characters are cursive and complicated and so do the Chinese numbers, particularly when written by hand. In addition, they have a wealthy history behind them. For instance, the number 6 (六) (Pinyin: *lu*) which corresponds to six types of morality or the number 8 (八) (Pinyin: *bā*) is related to fortune since it sounds similar to the word 发 (Pinyin: *fā*) which means "make a fortune, to be rich". In China, two native numbering systems, namely simplified and traditional, are very popular for communicating numeral values. Traditional Chinese numbers, also called *banker's numerals*, are mainly utilized in business correspondences. The reason is that the complicated shapes of these characters make them robust against forgery. Two examples of simplified and traditional Chinese numbers and their decimal (also known as Hindu-Arabic) counterparts are illustrated in Figure 4.2.

Despite a huge amount of literature in pattern classification of Chinese characters, for example, refs. [7–9], there is little work conducted on the recognition of handwritten Chinese numbers [10]. This could be partly due to the lack of a user-friendly and compact database of Chinese numbers. In this chapter, we present two new databases of handwritten simplified and traditional Chinese numbers acquired from 100 Chinese nationals. In addition, several classification algorithms are introduced to classify these numbers.

Arabic and Persian numbers are among those non-English language numbers that have totally different shapes than those in English. It is worthwhile to note that Arabic and Persian handwritten numbers are very similar but not identical. Figure 4.3 gives an example of certain Arabic and Persian numbers. As observed from this figure, there exist significant similarities between the two sets.

The rest of this chapter is organized as follows. A comprehensive overview of the existing studies and approaches for handwritten number recognition is given in Section 4.2. In Section 4.3, dictionary learning as a cornerstone of image classification will be described. Section 4.4 is devoted to explicitly describe the details of two

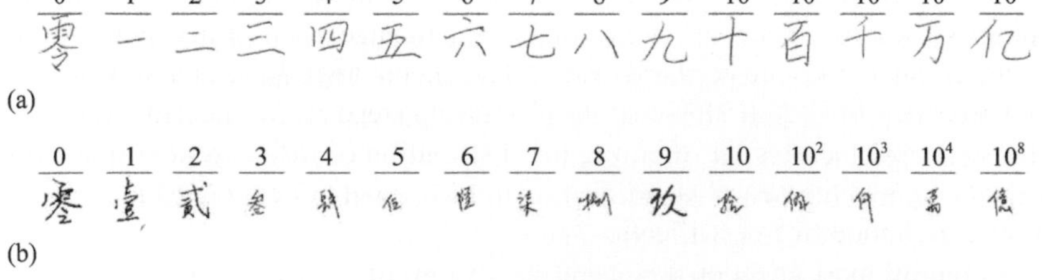

Figure 4.2   Examples of Chinese number images and their decimal counterparts: (a) simplified and (b) traditional

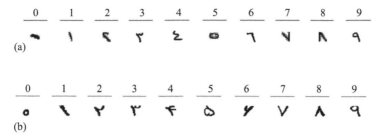

Figure 4.3   Examples of (a) Arabic and (b) Persian number images and their decimal counterparts

novel handwritten numbers recognition methods based on dictionary learning. The novel data preparation including image preprocessing and feature extraction based on HOG features will be described in Section 4.5. In Section 4.6, details of four related available databases are reviewed. The simulation details and experimental results are provided in Section 4.7. Finally, some concluding remarks are drawn in Section 4.8.

4.2   Related works

Since the main focus of this chapter is on handwritten number recognition, most related works we review here are in this category. However, due to the closeness of HNR and HCR, some relevant works in HCR will be also reviewed. In order to be consistent, we mainly refer to a general term "handwritten recognition" but will stress on HCR or HNR where necessary. Moreover, only off-line approaches will be reviewed as online techniques are out of the scope of this chapter.

Handwritten recognition in general is an established pattern recognition problem. Majority of conventional HCR and HNR systems operate based on train-and-test protocol. Meaning that first a labeled dataset is used to train the recognition algorithm. Then, the obtained model attempts to classify the alphabets and/or digits. Artificial neural networks (ANNs) are among those approaches that have been extensively used for this problem. One of the early implementations of the well-known multilayer perceptron (MLP) network in handwritten recognition has been proposed by Shamsher *et al.* for Urdu language [11]. Other neural network structures such as feed-forward MLP have been applied to Farsi and Bangla numerals [12]. In [12], first, some pre-processing steps are applied to input images, then, statistical features representing the distribution of local stroke orientation are used as inputs to the neural network. Finally, MLP with one hidden layer is used to training the model for classification.

Recently, most attention has been drawn toward convolutional neural networks (CNNs) and deep learning approaches for handwritten recognition. In [13], a transfer learning approach was introduced for off-line recognition of isolated handwritten

Arabic characters. A CNN model to learn strokes, radicals, and character features of Chinese characters was proposed in [14]. This method was tested on CAPTCHA (completely automated public turing test to tell computers and humans apart) which is increasingly used in many web applications. A single CNN has been proposed in [15] for Persian HCR based on simple LeNet-5 structure. The method performed over 97% accuracy on a local Persia characters dataset. A deep unsupervised network was proposed in [5] to learn invariant image representation from unlabeled data. The network architecture comprised a cascade of convolutional layers trained sequentially to represent multiple levels of features. In another work, a deep neural network classifier has been proposed in [6] for Farsi handwritten phone numbers recognition. Bengali handwritten number detection was addressed in [16] based on a deep structure called region proposal networks (RPN). One of the major limitations of deep learning-based approaches is their requirement for accessing to a large training dataset. Furthermore, in most conventional deep structures, a large number of parameters need to be adjusted.

Kernel methods, which can be categorized as classic techniques in this regard, have been widely used for many years. Support vector machine (SVM) as one of the most well-known kernel-based methods has been used for text classification. Cheng and Fujisawa in a study for Chinese character recognition found that discriminative classifiers such as ANN and SVM outperform statistical classifiers when the sample size is large [17]. Nevertheless, in this study, SVM demonstrated better accuracy than neural networks in many experiments. SVM has been also used for efficient recognition of Persian handwritten digits [18]. The feature set for SVM classifier was obtained based on intensity variations in the vertical and horizontal directions of a digit image combined with Freeman chain code. The main advantage of this approach is simplicity and low computational costs. Combination of SVM classifier with RBF (random basis function) kernel method has shown promising performance in the classification of handwritten Farsi digits [19]. A large-scale handwritten Chinese character database called HCL2000 was introduced in [20]. It contains 3,755 frequently used characters along with the information of its 1,000 different writers. Three different algorithms have been used to evaluate the HCR system on HCL200 [20]: linear discriminant analysis (LDA), locality preserving projection (LPP), and marginal fisher analysis (MFA). In this work, a nearest neighbor classifier applies initial character grouping prior to the main analysis. The experimental results indicate that MFA and LPP outperform LDA. k-nearest neighbor (kNN) as a statistical method has been used in many works [21]. The main advantage of statistical techniques, in general, is their low computational complexity and ability to operate on small-size datasets. Another statistical method used in this context is hidden Markov model (HMM). The authors in [22] use two sets of local and global features for the classification of Arabic handwritten characters. They utilize HMM for processing local features and providing the best feature selection procedure.

There exist other studies in the literature that use a combination of different approaches to improve the accuracy of classification. For instance, a handwritten number recognition is proposed in [23,24] based on LeNet-5 and support vector machine (SVM). In these works, the feature extraction task is performed through a neural network and then SVM is applied for classification. Obaidullah *et al*. [25]

addressed numeral text identification written in Bangla, Devanagari, Roman, and Urdu. They proposed a framework based on a combination of Daubechies wavelet decomposition and spatial domain features. Combination of CNN and SVM was also addressed by Elleuch *et al.* [26], where handwritten Arabic characters are to be recognized. While protecting their model against over-fitting, it automatically extracts appropriate features from raw images and then classifies the characters. Other relevant research such as Choudhury *et al.* [27] utilizes a combination of histogram of oriented gradients (HOG) and SVM for feature extraction and classification, respectively. In a recent study [28], HOG and Gabor filters were employed as feature descriptors for Arabic words, leading to promising results using a *k*NN classifier.

Since HOG descriptors extract the structure of the object of interest based on the gradient of edges in the image, it is anticipated to be useful for cursive characters too. HOG was first proposed for human detection, but later showed significant influence on handwritten characters [27]. Tian *et al.* [29] presented two extensions of HOG, called co-occurrence HOG (Co-HOG) and convolutional Co-HOG (ConvCo-HOG) features for the purpose of recognition of multilingual scene characters. They introduced a new offset-based approach to reduce the dimension of obtained features. The experimental results in [29] confirm the efficiency of this method for achieving higher recognition accuracy of multilingual scene texts. Despite promising performance of HOG descriptor for character recognition, not many works have thoroughly studied its capabilities in this context, particularly for handwritten numbers recognition.

4.3   Dictionary learning

Many researchers have been studying for years to find transform domains which can best represent the data of interest. Since no single predefined transform domain, for example, Fourier, Wavelet, etc. can guarantee appropriate extraction of hidden information in the data, the solution could be in the hand of "data-driven" techniques. Dictionary learning is an interesting solution which can find a near-optimal transform domain merely by using the data of interest. In fact, in dictionary learning methods the best possible transform domain is *learned* for the given dataset. This is in contrast to explicit methods, for example, Fourier, where only explicit analytical transformation is used. Data representation using dictionary learning has shown promising performances in various video, image, and signal processing applications, such as image denoising [30], Terahertz imaging [31], seismic data reconstruction [32], as well as image classification [33]. Dictionary learning originates from sparse coding where a sparse representation of the input data in form of a linear combination of some atoms (dictionary columns) are obtained. As the dictionary is normally chosen in form of an overcomplete matrix, the atoms are desired to be nearly orthogonal or as independent as possible. Under these conditions, the data can be represented sparsely in a higher dimension than the original data. Sparse data representation in a new subspace allows more accurate data separation and classification. This is the reason that dictionary learning has been extensively used for data classification. In fact, a dictionary that can appropriately sparsify samples of one particular class is not suitable for sparse representation of other classes. And this can be a good criterion for learning class-specific dictionaries from the training data. This idea has been utilized in the sparse representation classification (SRC) framework proposed in [34]. In this approach, sparse representation and learned dictionaries are used for the classification of face images in the pixel domain. SRC has been extended later in different forms for other applications. One of the exertions is [35], where a supervised dictionary learning algorithm is proposed for constructing image classes based on a shared dictionary but with discriminative atoms of each class model.

A typical dictionary learning problem can be mathematically represented as

$$\{\hat{\mathbf{D}},\hat{\mathbf{S}}\} = \arg\min_{\mathbf{D},\mathbf{S}}[||\mathbf{X} - \mathbf{DS}||_F^2 + \lambda||\mathbf{S}||_1] \tag{4.1}$$

where $\mathbf{X} = [\mathbf{x}_1, \mathbf{x}_2, \ldots, \mathbf{x}_K]$ represents the input data matirx, $\mathbf{D} = [\mathbf{d}_1, \mathbf{d}_2, \ldots, \mathbf{d}_K]$ denotes the dictionary, and $\mathbf{S} = [\mathbf{s}_1, \mathbf{s}_2, \ldots, \mathbf{s}_K]$ is the matrix containing sparse coefficients. In addition, $||.||_F^2$ and $||.||_1$ are the Frobenius and ℓ_1-norms, respectively. The parameter $\lambda > 0$ is a constant scalar which defines the contribution of sparsity penalty. Since (4.1) is a non-convex problem with respect to both $\mathbf{D}$ and $\mathbf{S}$, alternating minimization techniques can be used to solve it. Two major steps, that is, sparse coding and dictionary update, should be performed alternately while minimizing (4.1). In sparse coding (i.e., solving (4.1) with respect to $\mathbf{S}$), the aim is to find the sparse representation of the input data over a fixed dictionary. Numerous techniques such as basis pursuit (BP) [36] or orthogonal matching pursuit (OMP) [37] can be used for this purpose. The sparse coefficients obtained in this stage are used to update the dictionary atoms in the next stage where only data fidelity (i.e., $||\mathbf{X} - \mathbf{DS}||_F^2$) should be minimized. This two-stage process is repeated alternately until reaching a local minimum. K-singular value decomposition (K-SVD) method is one of the well-known dictionary learning methods that tackles (4.1) to find the dictionary for image denoising [38]. K-SVD applies singular value thresholding to the error associated with every single dictionary atom during the dictionary update stage. This method has been applied and extended for a various image processing problems, including inpainting, compression, and classification. Discriminative K-SVD (D-KSVD) [39] incorporates the classification error into the objective function to generate class-specific dictionaries. Li *et al.* [40] present a reference-based objective function combined with original K-SVD for classification of natural scene images. Label consistent KSVD (LC-KSVD) is also another extension of K-SVD that associates label information about the classes within the columns of the dictionary matrix during the learning process. The authors in [41] proposed a method for dictionary learning that jointly learns the classifier parameters and dictionary for face recognition.

One of the main limitations of traditional dictionary learning methods is their poor performance when applying to data with a large number of classes. In fact, by adding more classes to the model, the number of dictionaries to be learned is increased. Not only this situation increases the requirement for large memory storage, the dictionary discrimination performance is also declined. One of the solutions to mitigate this issue is learning one common dictionary for all classes but with sub-sets of atoms associated with every individual class. This can either be obtained from the scratch or by first learning class-specific dictionaries and then merging them by optimizing an appropriate objective function [42]. Besides mitigating the storage concerns, this technique can also reduce the mutual information between the dictionary atoms and the class labels [42]. However, despite the promising classification performance of these dictionaries, they tend to be computationally expensive due to the post-processing stage for merging the atoms. This problem has been addressed by adding a new constraint to the dictionary atoms during the learning process. As atoms of a learned dictionary are expected to be as incoherent as possible, various studies have improved the quality of learned dictionary by adding related penalties into the dictionary learning problem. For example, Mailhé *et al.* [43] and Abolghasemi *et al.* [44] constrained the K-SVD dictionary learning algorithm [45] to be incoherent. A joint dictionary learning-projection was proposed for the compressed sensing problem in [46]. However, very few works have addressed this issue for designing dictionaries aimed at classification problems. Also, different applications require distinct forms of incoherent penalties which have not been studied thoroughly in the literature.

Most traditional dictionary learning approaches provide *synthesis* dictionaries in which directly transform the input data into a sparse latent subspace. Synthesis dictionaries are great for representing and preserving the local structure of input data. Recently, *analysis* dictionaries were also introduced. These dictionaries are built based on the assumption that the input data, when multiplied by the corresponding dictionary, can be transformed into a sparse subspace [47]. One of the major advantages of analysis dictionaries is their ability to provide sparse data representation using a linear transformation without calculating costly ℓ_0/ℓ_1 minimization. In [48], a classification method based on discriminative analysis dictionary learning was proposed for the classification of gray-scale images. In this work, $\ell_{2,1}$-norm constraint was applied to the coding coefficients while achieving the dictionaries. In another work, a pair of dictionaries was learned to form analysis (for generating discriminative code by linear projection) and synthesis (for reconstructing the data) representation [49]. This way, the requirement of calculating cumbersome ℓ_0-norm or ℓ_1-norm minimization is relaxed. Dictionary pair learning (DPL) exhibits encouraging results for face image classification compared to other related methods. This technique has also been successfully utilized in other applications, for example, the classification of electroencephalogram (EEG) signals in a brain-computer interfacing application [50].

Recent magnificent growth of using deep learning for various applications has also shown successful deep learning-based works for HCR and HNR. Since this is not the scope of this chapter, we refer the reader to [51] for further reading. Our interest is in some recent works where dictionary learning and deep learning are combined for use in related classification problems. Most notably is deep dictionary learning, proposed in [52], for producing a deeper structure than those existing in traditional dictionaries. In [53], the authors consider most of the standard deep layers (e.g., pooling, fully, and connected) to propose a method called deep micro-dictionary learning and coding. The main novelty of this work is augmenting the deep network architecture by replacing fundamental convolutional layers with compound dictionary learning and coding layers. In [54], a convolutional dictionary learning technique was introduced based on auto-encoder. This network has been tested for analysis of natural exponential type distributions such as image denoising and neural spiking data. A deep dictionary learning technique was recently proposed for handwritten number recognition [55]. Their method, inspired by ConvNet, is a multilayer framework on the basis of K-SVD suitable for the recognition of English handwritten numbers.

In this chapter, a comprehensive set of dictionary learning methods for the HNR problem will be presented and evaluated. First, the integration of an incoherence constraint into the dictionary learning problem is proposed. The aim of this algorithm is to minimize dependencies among dictionary atoms related to different classes of handwritten numbers. Second, we propose a novel dictionary learning method that utilizes the class label information within the minimization process. In this method, a pair of synthesis and analysis dictionaries are learned from the input training images. We derive the solution to the minimization problem based on alternative minimization. The advantage of this scheme is reaching optimum trade-off between sparsity and classification performance without using ℓ_0/ℓ_1 regularizers. Third, we compare the algorithms' performance in the case of using raw pixel domain as well as a histogram of oriented gradient (HOG) features for designing the dictionaries. By relying on the great ability of HOG descriptors, we expect to boost the dictionary learning performance for HNR. This will be implemented by generating discriminative dictionaries from HOG-based features during the learning process. Finally, the performance of the proposed methods will be quantitatively evaluated using our extensive experiments. Various HNR databases have been considered for this purpose in which their details will be explained in the sequel. In addition, we present the performance of several deep learning methods in comparison with the dictionary learning techniques and discuss the pros and cons. It is worth mentioning that the backbone of the proposed methods presented in the sequel is the dictionary pair learning (DPL) method [56] which has shown promising performance in other settings in the past. Hence, we first go into details of DPL in Section 4.4 and then explain the proposed modifications for the HNR application.

4.4   DPL variants for HNR

This section is built upon expanding and repurposing dictionary pair learning (DPL) method for handwritten numbers classification. We first give a detailed mathematical description of DPL to demonstrate how this method learns sparsifying dictionaries for performing the desired classification task. Then, two extensions of DPL, that is, (1) incoherent DPL and (2) L-HOG-DPL will be presented with the required details.

4.4.1   Dictionary pair learning model

Let matrix $\mathbf{X}_i \in \mathbb{R}^{m \times n}$, $i = 1, \ldots, K$, contains all n training samples in class i and $\mathbf{X} = [\mathbf{X}_1, \mathbf{X}_2, \ldots, \mathbf{X}_K]$, where K is the total number of classes. If $\mathbf{D}_i \in \mathbb{R}^{m \times p}$ denotes a synthesis dictionary and $\mathbf{S}_i \in \mathbb{R}^{p \times n}$ is a sparse coefficient matrix, general dictionary learning classification problem [57] can be defined with

$$\{\hat{\mathbf{D}}, \hat{\mathbf{S}}\} = \arg\min_{\mathbf{D}, \mathbf{S}}[\|\mathbf{X} - \mathbf{D} \circ \mathbf{S}\|_F^2 + \lambda\|\mathbf{S}\|_1 + \psi(\mathbf{X}, \mathbf{D}, \mathbf{S})] \tag{4.2}$$

where $\lambda > 0$ is a constant regularization scalar, $\mathbf{D} = [\mathbf{D}_1, \mathbf{D}_2, \ldots, \mathbf{D}_K]$ is dictionary matrix, $\mathbf{S} = [\mathbf{S}_1, \mathbf{S}_2, \ldots, \mathbf{S}_K]$ is the sparse coefficients matrix, and $\mathbf{D} \circ \mathbf{S} = [\mathbf{D}_1\mathbf{S}_1, \mathbf{D}_2\mathbf{S}_2, \ldots, \mathbf{D}_K\mathbf{S}_K]$ denotes the block Hadamard product. Further, $\|.\|_F^2$ and $\|.\|_1$ are the Frobenius and ℓ_1-norms, respectively. The penalty term $\psi(\mathbf{X}, \mathbf{D}, \mathbf{S})$ is considered to be the most important part of this problem as it should be specifically designed for the classification task. One of the inspiring works on turning (4.2) into an effective classification problem was conducted by Gu *et al.* [56]. They proposed dictionary pair learning (DPL) model, where a linear combination of the sparse matrix as $\mathbf{S} = \mathbf{P} \circ \mathbf{X}$ with $\mathbf{P} \in \mathbb{R}^{m \times nK}$ as an *analysis* dictionary was added to (4.2). Then, they attempted to simultaneously learn $\mathbf{D}$ and $\mathbf{P}$, which advantageously can approximate the sparse coefficients in $\mathbf{S}$ without the need for applying cumbersome $\ell_{0,1}$-norm minimization. DPL is defined based on the following problem:

$$\{\hat{\mathbf{D}}, \hat{\mathbf{S}}, \hat{\mathbf{P}}\} = \arg\min_{\mathbf{D}, \mathbf{S}, \mathbf{P}} \sum_{i=1}^{K}[\|\mathbf{X}_i - \mathbf{D}_i\mathbf{S}_i\|_F^2 + \tau\|\mathbf{S}_i - \mathbf{P}_i\mathbf{X}_i\|_F^2 + \lambda\|\mathbf{P}_i\overline{\mathbf{X}}_i\|_F^2] \tag{4.3}$$

where $\tau, \lambda > 0$ are fixed regularization values and $\overline{\mathbf{X}}_i$ denotes a matrix containing samples of all classes but those of the ith class. In this settings, $\mathbf{P}_i \in \mathbf{P} = \{\mathbf{P}_1, \cdots \mathbf{P}_i, \cdots, \mathbf{P}_K\}$, which is called analysis sub-dictionary, best represents samples of the ith class and simultaneously least represents samples belonging to other classes. This property can be mathematically expressed via:

$$\mathbf{P}_i\overline{\mathbf{X}}_j \approx 0, \quad \forall i \neq j \quad \text{and} \quad 1 \leq i, j \leq K. \tag{4.4}$$

where $\mathbf{P}_i\overline{\mathbf{X}}_j \approx 0$ means that the analysis sub-dictionary $\mathbf{P}_i$ will project the samples from class i to a nearly null space. Since the Frobenious norm $\|\mathbf{P}_i\overline{\mathbf{X}}_i\|_F^2$ is included as a penalty in (4.3), it is expected that the obtained analysis sub-dictionaries be class-specific. Solving (4.4) leads to a nearly block diagonal coefficient matrix $\mathbf{P} \circ \mathbf{X}$, and thus, the DPL model enforces group sparsity on $\mathbf{P} \circ \mathbf{X}$ rather than a straightforward sparse representation. Although original DPL model can achieve competitive classification performance with those dictionary learning methods based on sparse coding, there are still possibilities to further improve its effectiveness by adding new constraints. These will be investigated next where we show how to extend DPL models for HNR problem.

4.4.2   Incoherent dictionary pair learning (InDPL)

An ideal dictionary has an approximately orthogonal structure. This means that the dictionary atoms are as independent as possible with minimum redundancy. This, however, cannot always be guaranteed in general dictionary learning algorithms. Therefore, imposing an appropriate constraint on the dictionary learning problem can provide dictionaries with desired structure. One of the relevant constraints is *incoherence* which enforces orthogonality among dictionary atoms. This constraint has already been tackled differently for general dictionary learning problem [43,44]. One of the feasible approaches to add such penalty to problem (4.4) is to calculate the inner product among distinct atoms between any sub-dictionary pair $\{\mathbf{D}_i, \mathbf{D}_j\}$ in $\mathbf{D}$, followed by introducing a measure to minimize it. This is a simple criterion that can lead to incoherent sub-dictionaries with small inner product among their columns. This concept can be achieved by introducing the following minimization problem:

$$\{\hat{\mathbf{D}},\hat{\mathbf{S}},\hat{\mathbf{P}}\} = \arg\min_{\mathbf{D},\mathbf{S},\mathbf{P}} \sum_{i=1}^{K} [||\mathbf{X}_i - \mathbf{D}_i\mathbf{S}_i||_F^2 + \tau||\mathbf{S}_i - \mathbf{P}_i\mathbf{X}_i||_F^2 + \lambda||\mathbf{P}_i\overline{\mathbf{X}}_i||_F^2] + \beta\sum_{j\neq i}||\mathbf{D}_j^T\mathbf{D}_i||_F^2$$

$$(4.5)$$

where $\beta > 0$ is a fixed scalar and $(.)^T$ stands for matrix transpose operation. This new penalty will enforce $\mathbf{D}_j^T\mathbf{D}_i \approx \mathbf{0}, \forall i \neq j$.

Solving (4.5) requires estimating $\mathbf{D}$, $\mathbf{P}$, and $\mathbf{S}$ which cannot be achieved, simultaneously. Hence, we use alternating minimization technique where two variables are kept constant at any time while the third is being calculated. We start by considering fixed $\mathbf{D}$ and $\mathbf{P}$, to solve (4.5) for $\mathbf{S}_i$. As (4.5) is convex and differentiable with respect to $\mathbf{S}_i$, we first calculate the gradient of (4.5), and then find $\mathbf{S}_i$ by zeroing the gradient:

$$\hat{\mathbf{S}}_i = [\mathbf{D}_i^T\mathbf{D}_i + \tau\mathbf{I}]^{-1}[\tau\mathbf{P}_i\mathbf{X}_i + \mathbf{D}_i^T\mathbf{X}_i], \ \forall \ i = 1, 2, \cdots, K \qquad (4.6)$$

where $\mathbf{I}$ is the identity matrix. In the next step, we follow the same procedure to obtain $\mathbf{P}_i$ through:

$$\hat{\mathbf{P}}_i = \tau\mathbf{S}_i\mathbf{X}_i^T[\tau\mathbf{X}_i\mathbf{X}_i^T + \lambda\overline{\mathbf{X}}_i\overline{\mathbf{X}}_i^T + \gamma\mathbf{I}]^{-1}, \ \forall \ i = 1, 2, \cdots, K \qquad (4.7)$$

where γ is added as a very small positive constant to avoid appearing a zero in the denominator. Finding $\mathbf{D}_i$'s is more challenging and cannot be achieved explicitly. We follow alternating direction method of multipliers (ADMM) [58] which is an iterative method suitable for this sort of problems. In order to be able to implement ADMM, we should first introduce an auxiliary matrix $\mathbf{T}$ which turns (4.5) into

$$\{\hat{\mathbf{D}},\hat{\mathbf{T}}\} = \arg\min_{\mathbf{D},\mathbf{T}} \sum_{i=1}^{K}||\mathbf{X}_i - \mathbf{D}_i\mathbf{S}_i||_F^2 + \beta\sum_{j\neq i}||\mathbf{D}_j^T\mathbf{D}_i||_F^2$$

$$s.t. \quad \mathbf{D} = \mathbf{T}, \ ||\mathbf{t}^k||_2^2 = 1 \qquad (4.8)$$

where $k \in \{1, 2, \cdots, p\}$ and $\mathbf{t}^k$ denotes the kth column of $\mathbf{T}$. The columns of $\mathbf{T}$ were normalized to avoid trivial solutions. Also, note that since the objective in this step is to estimate $\mathbf{D}$, any unrelated term with this matrix has been removed in (4.8). In order to solve (4.8), we adopt the following set of rules which should be executed within an iterative procedure:

$$\mathbf{D}^{(r+1)} = \arg\min_{\mathbf{D}} \sum_{i=1}^{K} \left[||\mathbf{X}_i - \mathbf{D}_i\mathbf{S}_i||_F^2 + \rho||\mathbf{D}_i - \mathbf{T}_i^{(r)} + \mathbf{U}_i^{(r)}||_F^2 \right] + \beta \sum_{j \neq i} ||\mathbf{D}_j^T \mathbf{D}_i||_F^2 \tag{4.9}$$

$$\mathbf{T}^{(r+1)} = \arg\min_{\mathbf{T}} \sum_{i=1}^{K} \rho||\mathbf{D}_i^{(r+1)} - \mathbf{T}_i + \mathbf{U}_i^{(r)}||_F^2 \, s.t. \ ||\mathbf{t}^k||_2^2 = 1 \tag{4.10}$$

$$\mathbf{U}^{(r+1)} = \mathbf{U}^{(r)} + \mathbf{D}^{(r+1)} - \mathbf{T}^{(r+1)}, \tag{4.11}$$

In the above set of rules, r is the iteration counter and $0 < \rho < 1$ is a progressive scalar which gradually increases with rate $\rho_{\text{rate}} \geq 1$. The first two rules require explicit expressions which can be found using closed-form solutions by taking the derivatives of sub-dictionaries and equating them to zero:

$$\mathbf{D}_i^{(r+1)} = [\rho(\mathbf{T}_i^{(r)} - \mathbf{U}_i^{(r)}) + \mathbf{X}_i\mathbf{S}_i^T] \left[\rho\mathbf{I} + \mathbf{S}_i\mathbf{S}_i^T + \beta \sum_{j \neq i} \mathbf{D}_j^T \mathbf{D}_j \right]^{-1} \tag{4.12}$$

$$\mathbf{T}_i^{(r+1)} = \mathbf{D}_i^{(r+1)} + \mathbf{U}_i^{(r)}. \tag{4.13}$$

The pseudo-code of the proposed approach is given in Algorithm 4.1.

Algorithm 4.1 Incoherent dictionary pair learning (InDPL)

    Input: $\mathbf{X}_1, \mathbf{X}_2, \ldots, \mathbf{X}_K$ and parameters $\lambda = 0.005, \tau = 1, \beta = 0.08, \gamma = 10^{-4}$, $\rho = 1, \rho_{rate} = 1.2$, and synthesis sub-dictionary size $p = 30$.
        Initialize $\mathbf{D}^{(0)}, r = 0$.
    Output: D, P, and S
        for $l \leftarrow 1, Iter$ **do**
            for $i \leftarrow 1, K$ **do**
                perform (4) for $\mathbf{S}_i$
            end for

        $\mathbf{S} \leftarrow [\mathbf{S}_1, \mathbf{S}_2, \ldots, \mathbf{S}_K]$

        for $i \leftarrow 1, K$ **do**
            perform (5) for $\mathbf{P}_i$
        end for

$$\mathbf{P} \leftarrow [\mathbf{P}_1, \mathbf{P}_2, \ldots, \mathbf{P}_K]$$

for $i \leftarrow 1, K$ **do**
    repeat
        perform (10) to solve for $\mathbf{D}_i$

        $\mathbf{T}_i \leftarrow \mathbf{D}_i + \mathbf{U}_i$

        Normalize columns of $\mathbf{T}_i$

        $\mathbf{U}_i \leftarrow \mathbf{U}_i + \mathbf{D}_i - \mathbf{T}_i$

        $\rho \leftarrow \rho \times \rho_{rate}$

        $r \leftarrow r + 1$

    until convergence
    end for

    $\mathbf{D} \leftarrow [\mathbf{D}_1, \mathbf{D}_2, \ldots, \mathbf{D}_K]$

end for

4.4.3   *Labeled projective dictionary pair learning*

One important missing part in the original DPL method is taking advantage of existing prior knowledge about class labels within the classification problem. This information exist for training data and its utilization can improve classification accuracy. This has already been shown in other dictionary learning methods for various applications [57,59]. In this section, we elaborate on this concept to impose an appropriate penalty into DPL for handwritten numbers recognition.

Recall from Section 4.4.1, the input training samples of all classes are collated in $\mathbf{X} = [\mathbf{X}_1, \mathbf{X}_2, \ldots, \mathbf{X}_K]$. We also defined analysis dictionary as $\mathbf{P} = \{\mathbf{P}_1, \mathbf{P}_2, \cdots, \mathbf{P}_K\}$. Then, the sparse coefficient matrix can be expressed as $\mathbf{A} = \mathbf{P} \circ \mathbf{X}$. Also, we developed synthesis dictionary $\mathbf{D} = \{\mathbf{D}_1, \mathbf{D}_2, \cdots, \mathbf{D}_K\}$ which contains structural information about different classes. In order to impose an appropriate penalty on (4.2), the following criteria should be considered. The proposed cost function should still be able to indirectly achieve sparse representation coefficients, that is, $\mathbf{P} \circ \mathbf{X}$. Furthermore, finding class-specific subdictionaries while minimizing the classification error should be a priority. The proposed approach in the sequel modifies the original DPL cost function to satisfy these objectives and at the same time adds the information about the class labels as a constraint into the optimization problem.

In (4.3), the synthesis dictionaries are forced to be discriminant, as summation over reconstruction errors at each individual class is to be minimized. However, no strong class-specific information is enforced on analysis dictionaries. We want to define and add a new term to (4.3) so that this condition is fulfilled. We first constitute a binary matrix $\mathbf{H}$ which contains classification labels associated to the training data of each class. Then, we balance the sparse coefficients using a weight matrix $\mathbf{W}$ which is bounded by $\mathbf{H}$. Since, we do not directly find the sparse coefficient matrix in DPL, $\mathbf{W}$ should be applied to $\mathbf{P}_i\mathbf{X}_i$ instead. This setting will effectively incorporate the classification error term $||\mathbf{H}_i - \mathbf{W}_i\mathbf{P}_i\mathbf{X}_i||_F^2$ in the objective function. Therefore, the modified DPL cost function can be expressed as

$$\underset{\mathbf{P},\mathbf{D},\mathbf{W}}{\arg\min} \sum_{i=1}^{K} ||\mathbf{X}_i - \mathbf{D}_i\mathbf{P}_i\mathbf{X}_i||_F^2 + \lambda_2||\mathbf{H}_i - \mathbf{W}_i\mathbf{P}_i\mathbf{X}_i||_F^2 + \lambda_1||\mathbf{P}_i\overline{\mathbf{X}}_i||_F^2 \quad (4.14)$$
$$s.t. ||\mathbf{d}_j||_2^2 \leq 1 \text{ for } j = 1, 2, \cdots, m$$

where $\mathbf{d}_j$ denotes jth column of the sub-dictionary $\mathbf{D}_i$. As an example on how the binary matrix is formed, one can generate the following $\mathbf{H}_1$ matrix for the simplified case of four training samples and three classes:

$$\mathbf{H}_1 = \begin{bmatrix} 1 & 1 & 1 & 1 \\ 0 & 0 & 0 & 0 \\ 0 & 0 & 0 & 0 \end{bmatrix}.$$

Equation (4.14) cannot be solved as simple as what explained in original DPL. Hence, we modify (4.14) to convert it to a solvable problem by embedding $\mathbf{A}_i = \mathbf{P}_i\mathbf{X}_i$ into the first and second terms. The resultant modified cost function can be expressed by (4.15), where $\mathbf{P}^*, \mathbf{D}^*, \mathbf{W}^*$, and $\mathbf{A}^*$ should be estimated:

$$\underset{\mathbf{P},\mathbf{D},\mathbf{W},\mathbf{A}}{\arg\min} \sum_{i=1}^{K} ||\mathbf{X}_i - \mathbf{D}_i\mathbf{A}_i||_F^2 + \lambda_1||\mathbf{P}_i\overline{\mathbf{X}}_i||_F^2 + \lambda_2||\mathbf{H}_i - \mathbf{W}_i\mathbf{A}_i||_F^2$$
$$+\lambda_3||\mathbf{P}_i\mathbf{X}_i - \mathbf{A}_i||_F^2 \, s.t. \, ||\mathbf{d}_j||_2^2 \leq 1 \quad (4.15)$$

In this equation, λ_1, λ_2, and λ_3 are positive scalars as regularization parameters which are set empirically. In order to solve (4.15) in all variables, ADMM method can be adopted where only one variable is found at a time, while other variables are kept unchanged. Such procedure is implemented alternatingly for all variables based on the following steps.

Step 1: In order to find $\mathbf{A}$ that satisfies (4.15), we only consider 1st, 3rd, and 4th terms, fixing $\mathbf{D}_i, \mathbf{W}_i, \mathbf{P}_i$, and minimize:

$$\mathbf{A}^* = \underset{\mathbf{A}}{\arg\min} \sum_{i=1}^{K} ||\mathbf{X}_i - \mathbf{D}_i\mathbf{A}_i||_F^2 + \lambda_2||\mathbf{H}_i - \mathbf{W}_i\mathbf{A}_i||_F^2 + \lambda_3||\mathbf{P}_i\mathbf{X}_i - \mathbf{A}_i||_F^2.$$

$$(4.16)$$

Since (4.16) only involves Frobenius norms, its gradient, with respect to $\mathbf{A}_i$, can be simply obtained. So, minimization of (4.16) is achieved by tending the gradient to zero and estimating:

$$\mathbf{A}_i^* = (\mathbf{D}_i^T \mathbf{A}_i + \mathbf{W}_i^T \mathbf{W}_i + \lambda_3 \mathbf{I})^{-1}(\mathbf{D}_i^T \mathbf{X}_i + \lambda_2 \mathbf{W}_i^T \mathbf{H}_i + \lambda_3 \mathbf{P}_i \mathbf{X}_i) \tag{4.17}$$

Step 2: The same settings, carried out in Step 1, is applied for $\mathbf{P}_i$ where all variables except $\mathbf{P}$ is considered fixed and only 2nd and 4th terms in (4.15) are included in the calculations:

$$\mathbf{P}^* = \arg\min_{\mathbf{P}} \sum_{i=1}^{K} \lambda_1 ||\mathbf{P}_i \overline{\mathbf{X}_i}||_F^2 + \lambda_3 ||\mathbf{P}_i \mathbf{X}_i - \mathbf{A}_i||_F^2. \tag{4.18}$$

And then by taking the gradient with respect to $\mathbf{P}_i$ and making it zero we get:

$$\mathbf{P}_i^* = (\lambda_3 \mathbf{X}_i \mathbf{X}_i^T + \lambda_1 \overline{\mathbf{X}_i}\,\overline{\mathbf{X}_i}^T + \gamma \mathbf{I})^{-1}(\lambda_3 \mathbf{A}_i \mathbf{X}_i^T) \tag{4.19}$$

where γ is a small number to prevent division by zero.

Step 3: Since $\mathbf{W}_i$ appears only in the 3rd term in (4.15), its value can be simply estimated using the following expression:

$$\mathbf{W}_i^* = (\mathbf{A}_i \mathbf{A}_i^T + \gamma \mathbf{I})^{-1}(\mathbf{H}_i \mathbf{A}_i^T). \tag{4.20}$$

Step 4: Finally, by fix $\mathbf{P}, \mathbf{A}, \mathbf{W}$ and applying the alternating direction method of multipliers (ADMM) algorithm [60], we can estimate dictionaries $\mathbf{D}$:

$$\mathbf{D}^{(r+1)} = \min_{\mathbf{D}} \sum_{i=1}^{K} ||\mathbf{X}_i - \mathbf{D}_i \mathbf{A}_i||_F^2 + \rho ||\mathbf{D}_i - \mathbf{S}_i^{(r)} + \mathbf{T}_i^{(r)}||_F^2$$

$$\mathbf{S}^{(r+1)} = \min_{\mathbf{S}} \sum_{i=1}^{K} \rho ||\mathbf{D}_i^{(r+1)} - \mathbf{S}_i^{(r)} + \mathbf{T}_i^{(r)}||_F^2 s.t. ||\mathbf{S}_i|| \leq 1$$

$$\mathbf{T}^{(r+1)} = \mathbf{T}^{(r)} + \mathbf{D}_i^{(r+1)} - \mathbf{S}_i^{(r+1)}. \tag{4.21}$$

The pseudo-code of the proposed method is summarized in Algorithm 4.2.

Algorithm 4.2 Pseudo-code of the proposed labeled-based DPL.

Input: Training samples for K classes $\mathbf{X}$, m, λ_1, λ_2, λ_3, γ
$\quad$ $\mathbf{D}_0$ and $\mathbf{P}_0$ as random matrix and calculate $\mathbf{A}_0$ in equation (4.17) and $\mathbf{W}_0$ in equation (4.20), $l = 0$

Output: P*, D*, W*, A*
while not converge **do**

$$l = l + 1$$

for $i = 1 : K$ ***do***

        Update $A_k^{(l)}$ by equation (4.17)

        Update $P_k^{(l)}$ by equation (4.19)

        Update $W_k^{(l)}$ by equation (4.20)

        Update $D_k^{(l)}$ by equation (4.21)

      end for
    end while

4.5   Input data preparation

In general, the raw images are given to the dictionary learning models introduced in Section 4.4. However, some works in other applications have shown that mapping data to other sub-spaces can provide even more promising dictionary learning performance [50]. In this section, we will examine both scenarios. First, raw images are preprocessing and given to the DPL model. Second, HOG descriptors of the raw images are used for learning class-specific dictionaries. In any case, though, some preprocessing steps are required which will be explained in Section 4.5.1.

4.5.1   Image preprocessing

To improve the classification performance and preserve consistency among all input images, several preprocessing operations are to be performed on raw images. The following hierarchy of steps are conducted for this purpose. The raw images are swept vertically and horizontally to determine the center and the bounding box of the number. Then, the background, which is dominantly dark but may involve some noisy pixels is removed. Then, global image threshold is determined based on well-known Otsu's method to convert the image into binary. Finally the images are resized to 25×25 pixels for reducing the computational complexity. The preprocessed handwritten images cannot be still given to the dictionary learning model as they are in two-dimensional format. Therefore, the vectorization operation is performed on the preprocessed images, that is, 25×25 image is converted to a 625-length vector. The obtained vectors in this way are then placed as one column of $\mathbf{X}_i$ associated to ith class. The entire procedure is depicted in Figure 4.4.

4.5.2   Histogram of oriented gradient

Histogram of oriented gradient (HOG) is a shape descriptor that counts occurrences of gradient orientations in an image. This descriptor has been widely used in computer vision applications, particularly for handwritten characters description. In using the proposed label-based DPL, we aim to feed the HOG features to the dictionary learning stage instead of raw images. Hence, the following procedure should be applied prior vectorization as depicted by dashed lines in Figure 4.4. The reprocessed images are divided into small square blocks of size 3×3. Then, the gradient directions on each small block is calculated based on the central differences. The histogram of these directions are recorded followed by normalization of the local histograms. The normalization is applied with regard to the extremums in image contrast. The aim of this step is to make the dictionaries (to be learned in the next stage) generalized and robust against different variation conditions. Figure 4.5 depicts exemplary images of of handwritten English digit "5" and Chinese digit "10" with associated extracted HOG features at all possible directions and orientations. It is clearly observed from this figure that fine details of the digit have been extracted. The encouraging aim in our proposed method is to obtain an exclusive

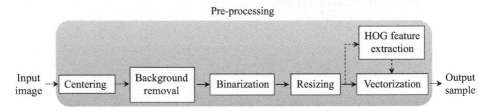

Figure 4.4   Preprocessing steps applied to raw handwritten images

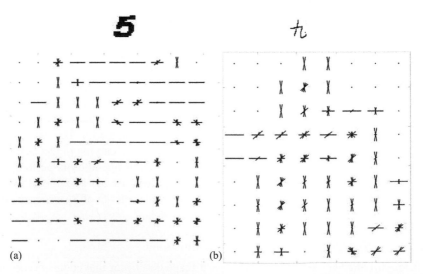

Figure 4.5   Handwritten images (top) and corresponding HOG features (bottom):
(a) English digit "5" and (b) Chinese digit "10"

dictionary for each character with the ability to model all these variations. On the other hand, this setting can improve the discrimination power of the dictionaries as they learn much deeper details than those existed in the raw images.

4.5.3 Classification stage

All the aforementioned procedures are implemented by using the training data, that is, images with known labels. This is to ensure that appropriate dictionaries capable of classifying an unlabeled input image are learned. After the completion of training stage using both proposed methods, that is, InDPL and L-HOG-DPL, two sets of dictionaries (synthesis $\mathbf{D}$ and analysis $\mathbf{P}$), in addition to the transformation matrix $\mathbf{W}$, associated to each class are obtained. The classification (or test) phase is to identify the label of an unseen input image (denoted by $\mathbf{y}$ in vectorized format). This process can be mathematically expressed as follows:

For InDPL:

$$\text{Class}(\mathbf{y}) = \operatorname*{argmin}_{i} ||\mathbf{y} - \mathbf{D}_i \mathbf{P}_i||_F^2 \tag{4.22}$$

For L-HOG-DPL:

$$\text{Class}(\mathbf{y}) = \operatorname*{argmin}_{i} ||\mathbf{y} - \mathbf{D}_i \mathbf{P}_i||_F^2 + ||\mathbf{H}_i - \mathbf{W}_i \mathbf{P}_i \mathbf{y}||_F^2 \tag{4.23}$$

4.6 HNR datasets

In general, there exist few handwritten numbers databases with enough images for evaluation, particularly in non-English languages. In an effort at the Newcastle University, a Chinese handwritten numbers database has been recently launched [61]. We use the images of this database to study and examine the effectiveness of our methods in the chapter. This database is composed of two subsets. First one contains 15,000 handwriting image numerals from 100 Chinese students at Newcastle University, UK. The participants were asked to write 10 times the 15 numbers illustrated in Figure 4.2. The second subset, which has been collected independently is written in traditional Chinese language. It consists of 5,100 hand-written numbers from 34 persons, was also used to analyse this method. Each person wrote 10 times the 15 numbers illustrated in Figure 4.2.

To cover handwritten styles in other languages, we have selected an Arabic and a Farsi handwritten numbers database too (MADBase [62] and HODA [19], respectively). MADBase consists of 70,000 digits written by 700 individuals who each one wrote 10 times each digit from 0 to 9. HODA is composed of about 12,000 images scanned at 200 dpi in 24 bit color format. Samples in this dataset are handwritten digits extracted from registration forms of university entrance examination in Iran. Also, a well-established English numbers database (USPS [63]) was included in our case studies. USPS database consists of 7291 training images and 2007 testing images of digits 0–9. Example images of these databases are illustrated in Figure 4.3.

4.7   Experimental results

Extensive experiments have been conducted to investigate the effectiveness of the proposed methods for handwritten numbers recognition. We compared the performance of the proposed algorithms with that of the DPL algorithm [56]. Further, the obtained results have been compared with the results obtained using other approaches not belonging to dictionary learning family. Notably, we report here the results of using k-nearest neighbor (kNN) classifier. kNN was applied directly to the vectorized images (Figure 4.4) along with the associated label information of each class. Since deep learning techniques have also been recently shown great performance on related HNR problems, we further evaluate and compare the results of our proposed methods with some deep models. In particular, three benchmarked deep neural network model, namely, GoogLeNet [64], MobileNetV2 [65], and SqueezeNet [66] have been considered.

4.7.1   Cross-validation

In order to perfectly evaluate the performance of the proposed methods, three types of cross-validations (CVs) were implemented. Let us consider the following notation on Chinese dataset: number of subjects $n_s = 100$, number of repetitions $n_r = 10$, and number of digits $n_c = 15$. The CV settings are as follows:

- *Conventional*: All n_r repetitions from all n_s subjects were pooled. Consequently, the training dataset involves $(n_s \times n_r)$ images associated to each of the n_c classes; total: $n_s \times n_r \times n_c = 15,000$. Then, to reduce variability, a conventional 10-fold cross-validation was implemented during training stage.
- *Between-subjects*: In each fold of the between-subject validation, the training set includes samples from $n_s - 1$ subjects, n_r repetitions, and n_c classes. On the other hand, the testing set comprised the remaining $n_s = 1$ subject, n_r repetitions, and n_c classes. Again, this procedure was repeated 100 times to improve consistency and reduce variability. Each time all 10×15 images from a distinct subject were left out for testing.
- *Within-subject*: In each fold of this cross-validation method, the training set encompasses data samples from n_s subjects, $n_r - 1$ repetitions, and n_c classes. The testing set consisted of the remaining n_s subjects, $n_r = 1$ repetition, and n_c classes. This process was repeated for 10 times, and each time all 100×15 images from an independent repetition were set aside for testing.

One of the important properties of dictionaries to be learned is the number of atoms per dictionary. Most dictionary learning methods empirically decide on the value of this parameter, that is, p. Here, we conducted an experiment to chose appropriate p depending on the overall classification performance. Hence, the classification accuracy is recorded against various number of atoms learned during dictionary learning process. Figure 4.6 illustrates a plot of this experiment for InDPL. This figure shows that as p reaches 30, maximum accuracy is achieved and stabled for $p > 30$. Therefore, it is reasonable to select $p = 30$ to avoid unnecessary computational complexity and preserving the high accuracy of the overall system.

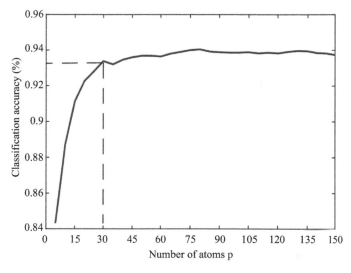

Figure 4.6   Classification accuracy of InDPL against varying number of atoms p in the synthesis dictionary

Table 4.1   Mutual coherence metrics between synthesis dictionaries at two different sizes

Method	$p = 30$			$p = 50$		
	μ_{min}	μ_{max}	μ_{mean}	μ_{min}	μ_{max}	μ_{mean}
DPL	3.34	7.19	5.30	3.53	7.28	5.50
InDPL	3.02	6.72	4.51	3.27	6.92	5.24

This is a very important experiment as it identifies the size of synthesis dictionary $\mathbf{D}_i$ as well as the analysis dictionary $\mathbf{P}_i$.

Mutual coherence between any two distinct dictionary atoms, which is defined as the inner product between two normalized atoms, is a great measure to observe the quality of learned dictionaries. It is desired that the mutual coherence to be minimized as it is an indicator of a well-structured dictionary. In the first proposed method in this chapter, that is, InDPL, the coherence of between-class dictionaries $\mathbf{D}_i$ and $\mathbf{D}_j$ were aimed to be minimized. Here, we consider three simple incoherence measures for this purpose which are expressed as $\mu_{mean} = \frac{1}{K}\sum_{i \neq j}\|\mathbf{D}_j^T\mathbf{D}_i\|_F^2$, $\mu_{max} = \max_{i \neq j}\|\mathbf{D}_j^T\mathbf{D}_i\|_F^2$, and $\mu_{min} = \min_{i \neq j}\|\mathbf{D}_j^T\mathbf{D}_i\|_F^2$. Smaller values of μ_{min}, μ_{max}, and μ_{mean} indicate that higher incoherence between dictionaries is achieved. In Table 4.1, the values of the calculated coherence metrics for the learned dictionaries over three experiments with different numbers of atoms are reported. As seen from this table, the obtained values for the dictionaries learned by the proposed

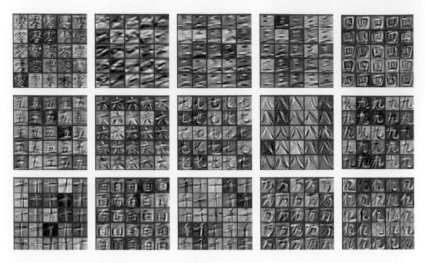

*Figure 4.7   An illustration of 25 learned atoms of synthesis dictionaries of all
15 classes (Chinese numbers). Adapted from [67]*

InDPL algorithm are invariably less than those obtained with the DPL algorithm. Moreover, as the number of atoms goes beyond $p = 30$ (as an optimum number found in previous experiment), the mutual coherence increases.

As a visual indication for the clarity of the learned dictionaries, we depict in Figure 4.7 a representation of dictionary atoms for all 15 classes. These images have been formed by including only 25 of the atoms in each sub-figure. The atoms are resized to two-dimensional cells where each cell represents some level of information on the associated number. Visual inspection of Figure 4.7 suggests obvious discrimination between the dictionaries learned for each class. This observation has been confirmed by the numerical results which will be represented in the sequel.

To ensure the robustness of the proposed algorithm, multiple running with random initialization of **D** and **P** were conducted. In fact, we observed the method is not sensitive to initialization step, based on the obtained results. In Figure 4.8, the convergence curve of objective function has shown for 30 epochs of running Algorithm 4.2. This figure clearly indicates steady decrease in the value of cost function after a few iterations.

An illustration of the confusion matrix, as a result of applying L-HOG-DPL algorithm on Chinese handwritten numbers are given in Figure 4.9. It is worth to note that conventional cross-validation is employed to generate Figure 4.9. It is observed that the recognition accuracy of all 15 classes are above 95% which is encouraging. Nevertheless, classification accuracy of classes 13 and 11 (Chinese numbers 10 and 1,000, respectively) is 94.3% which is not as high. This is obviously because of a very similar semantic structure between these two digits, i.e. 10 and 10^3, in Chinese language (Figure 4.2(a)). This drawback is expected to be mitigated once a larger set of data and subjects are available and used for training.

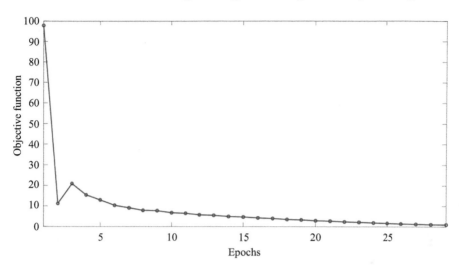

Figure 4.8   Convergence graph of L-HOG-DPL versus the number of iterations

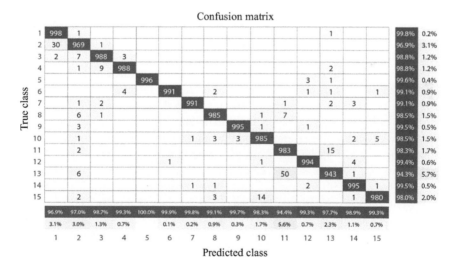

Figure 4.9   Confusion matrix representation when applying L-HOG-DPL on handwritten Chinese database. Horizontal and vertical axes respectively show the true and predicted classes. The diagonal values indicate the number of correctly classified images, and off-diagonal elements represent incorrectly classified images corresponding to each target class

4.7.2   Benchmarking results

4.7.2.1   Comparison with classic models

The results are compared with a well-know classic classifier, that is, *k*NN. In Table 4.2, average classification accuracy achieved using DPL, InDPL, L-HOG-DPL, and *k*NN algorithms are presented. These scores are tabulated with respect to three different cross-validation method explained above. As can be seen from this table, the InDPL algorithm outperforms the DPL and the *k*NN algorithms in both conventional and within-subject cross-validations. However, L-HOG-DPL exhibits the best performance among all which confirms the effectiveness of adding classification labels and HOG features for obtaining the dictionaries. For between-subjects cross-validation, the accuracies of all methods are comparable which suggests that when a large training dataset is available, the choice of algorithm is less important from the accuracy point of view. In order to assess the effects of using HOG features, we intentionally implemented the same experiment but without using the HOG features in L-HOG-DPL. We observed that the classification accuracy was dropped by ~11%. This experiment highlighted the significant impact of HOG features in the proposed method.

4.7.2.2   Comparison with deep learning

In this part of the experiments, a customized CNN architecture is considered for HNR problem. It includes a set of empirically selected combination of layers consisting of convolutional, max-pooling, and fully connected layers. The network architecture design is illustrated in Figure 4.10. The architecture of CNN consists of two parts: feature extraction and a soft-max layer. For feature extraction, we propose a set of convolution and max-pooling layers. In the convolution layer, features from previous layers are convolved with learnable kernel. The max-pooling layer performs the downsampled operation on the input layers. The fully connected layer computes the score of each class from extracted feature in the preceding steps. In the final softmax layer, a score vector that outputs a probability distribution is generated; the class with the highest score is used for classification. The first layer is a convolutional layer with kernel size 5×5 pixels and 8 output channels. The second layer is a max-pooling layer with 2×2 kernel size. The third layer is a convolutional layer with kernel size 5×5 pixels and 12 output channels. The fourth layer is a max-pooling layer with 2×2 kernel size.

Table 4.2   Classification accuracy (%) of different methods for Chinese HNR

Method	DPL	InDPL	-HOG-DPL	*k*NN
Conventional	91.25	93.00	98.53	87.52
Within-subject	92.74	93.13	98.56	90.58
Between-subject	97.28	97.53	98.07	97.36
Average	93.75	94.55	98.38	91.82

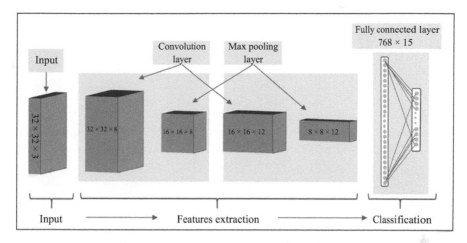

Figure 4.10   Visualization of the proposed CNN architecture

Table 4.3   Classification accuracy (%) of different methods for Chinese HNR

Method	GoogleNet	MobileNetV2	SqueezeNet	L-HOG-DPL	Proposed
Accuracy (%)	99.83	99.77	98.55	98.38	99.10

In order to provide a comprehensive evaluation, we compare the performance of the proposed dictionary learning-based methods with the customized CNN, as well as other well-known related deep models. We selected three well-established platforms for this purpose; GoogLeNet [64], MobileNetV2 [65], and SqueezeNet [66]. The accuracy difference between our proposed method and GoogleNet and MobileNetV2 is 0.73% and 0.67%, respectively. Despite the large size and number of parameters of these networks (i.e., 1.27, 7, and 3.5 million parameters in SqueezeNet, GoogleNet, and MobileNetV2, respectively), our proposed network provided competitive performance. On the other hand, the number of calculated parameters of the proposed model is much lower than GoogleNet and MobileNetV2. Also, we compare our proposed method with a lesser deep network, SqueezeNet, which is a well-known CNN architecture compatible with small computers. SqueezeNet produced an average classification accuracy of 98.55% over ten-folds cross validation, which makes our customized CNN fits nicely in the literature. These results are tabulated in Table 4.3. It is worth to note that the deep learning experiments were conducted on Ubuntu 18.04 with MATLAB® 2019b environment using NVIDIA GeForce RTX 2080 Ti.

4.7.2.3   Comparison with related dictionary learning methods

Apart from DPL-based methods, there exist other dictionary learning-based techniques for the classification tasks in the literature. Most of the related techniques have been already reviewed in Section 4.3. In this part of the experiments, we provide a comprehensive performance analysis on the results of applying related methods with different handwritten numbers datasets. The methods that we consider here are SRC (sparse representation classification) [34], DLSI (dictionary learning with structure incoherence) [68], LC-KSVD1 (label consistent K-SVD) [69], and LC-KSVD2 [69] under conventional cross-validation settings. We have used four handwritten numbers databases for this purpose; two independent Chinese, one English USPS, one Arabic MADBase, and one Farsi HODA handwritten databases as described in Section 4.6. Also, no significant changes in parameters of these dictionary learning methods were needed when applying to different datasets. The obtained classification for this experiment appears in Table 4.4. It is observed from this table that L-HOG-DPL outperforms other methods on all four databases. However, DLSI achieves comparable performance with our proposed L-HOG-DPL. It is also very encouraging to observe from the results of Table 4.4 that HOG features (utilized in L-HOG-DPL) have more tangible effects on Chinese numbers (than Arabic and English) which have complicated textures comprising many line orientations. This observation re-enforces the role of HOG descriptors during the dictionary learning process.

As stated in Section 4.1, the HNR methods proposed in this chapter are categorized as off-line techniques. Hence, processing time is not a major concern. However, investigating the running time of different methods could provide useful insight about the complexity of the methods. In Table 4.5, the running times of different dictionary learning methods are shown including the training time and testing time. This experiment was conducted with simplified Chinese numbers dabaset using different techniques. It is seen from Table 4.5 that SRC is the fastest

Table 4.4   Comparison of classification accuracy (%) for popular dictionary learning methods with different databases

Method	SRC	DLSI	LC-KSVD1	LC-KSVD2	L-HOG-DPL
Simplified Chinese	96.28	97.80	95.23	95.24	98.53
Traditional Chinese	93.47	97.57	90.65	90.67	97.82
USPS English	81.81	96.13	91.25	91.10	97.17
MADBase Arabic	97.13	–	–	–	98.75
HODA Persian	83.47	95.31	92.69	92.54	97.19

Table 4.5   Investigating the running times of the proposed method and other related methods

Method	SRC	DLSI	LC-KSVD1	LC-KSVD2	L-HOG-DPL
Training time (s)	3.89	55.77	127.01	128.40	33.49
Testing time (s)	0.0002	2.9067	0.0598	0.0363	0.3842

technique both in terms of training and testing times. The second most inexpensive method within the training phase is L-HOG-DPL. In addition, the proposed L-HOG-DPL method requires almost the same amount of time as LC-KSVD1 and LC-KSVD2 in testing phase, and it functions much faster than DLSI. Overall, the recommendation is that the proposed L-HOG-DPL can be considered a fast technique but it requires more elaboration to be able to compete faster methods such as SRC. All these experiments were conducted on a machine equipped with Intel core i7, 2.20 GHz processor, and 8 GB of memory.

In the final experiment, we evaluate the robustness of the proposed methods against variations of regularization parameters. In particular, we are interested in measuring sensitivity of Algorithm 4.1 against changing λ, τ, and β, and sensitivity of Algorithm 4.2 against λ_1, λ_2, λ_3, and γ. To do this, we conduct experiments to measure the classification accuracy at different selected values for these parameters. At each experiment, we vary the value of one parameter in a certain range, while keeping the values of other parameters unchanged. Figures 4.11 and 4.12 illustrate the classification accuracy of InDPL and L-HOG-DPL under the

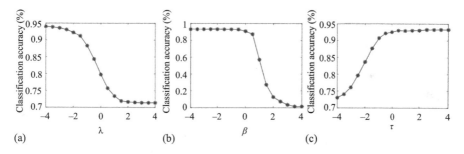

Figure 4.11 Performance of InDPL against changes of regularization parameters: (a) λ, (b) β, and (c) τ. The value of parameters varied within $[10^{-4}, 10^4]$

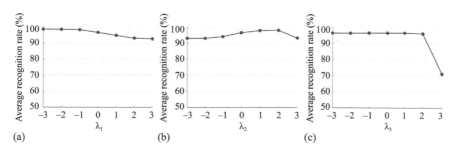

Figure 4.12 Performance of L-HOG-DPL against changes of regularization parameters: (a) λ_1, (b) λ_2, and (c) λ_3. The value of parameters varied within $[10^{-3}, 10^3]$

aforementioned experimental conditions with simplified Chinese handwritten numbers dataset. Figure 4.11(a) shows that as λ increases, the classification accuracy drops. This is due to the fact that the term associated to λ incurs a large value to the cost function. Similar behaviour can be seen for β from Figure 4.11(b) where increasing it to up around $\beta = 10^0$ still maintain the accuracy at the highest level. However, performance falls for β beyond this value. Finally, it is observed from Figure 4.11(c) that τ behaves differently. This regularization parameter which contributes to the analysis dictionary error should not be chosen very small as it shows a poor performance. This is due to important role of τ in reflecting the dictionaries into sparse codes. As observed, for $\tau > 10^0$, almost a steady yet maximized accuracy is achieved. It is observed from Figure 4.12(a) that as long as $\lambda_1 < 10^{-1}$, L-HOG-DPL performs at the maximum level. However, the accuracy reduces for large λ_1 due to overweighting the discrimination factor. Figure 4.12(b) shows that maximum accuracy occurs around $\lambda_2 = 10^2$ meaning that the contribution of class label information positively influences the performance. However, the accuracy decays when λ_2 gets larger. Figure 4.12(c) reveals that L-HOG-DPL is highly insensitive to selection of λ_3 as the accuracy is almost steady for all ranges of this parameter. However, for extremely large $\lambda_3 > 10^2$, the performance drop is significant. Overall, we observed that L-HOG-DPL is not sensitive to the parameters' variations within a broad range.

4.8   Conclusions

In this chapter, we introduced the handwritten number recognition problem followed by an overview of the existing works. The core of the chapter is devoted to describing dictionary learning approach and its role in the image classification problem. DPL as a well-established dictionary learning method, designed for image classification problem offering a pair of dictionaries for each class, has been introduced. We extended the DPL algorithm based on three main contributions: (1) adding dictionary incoherence penalty, (2) utilizing label information into the cost function, and (3) using HOG features as inputs of the dictionary learning procedure. Incoherence penalty is to ensure that dictionary columns are distinct enough as class representatives. Utilizing the class labels in the dictionary learning can increase the discriminability of the learned dictionaries. Finally, HOG features can generate brand new types of dictionaries which learned *shape* of the characters as a strong intrinsic feature. The proposed methods have been tested with several handwritten databases in English, Chinese, Arabic, and Persian languages. The results of our extensive experiments verified that the proposed approaches achieve promising classification performance which are superior to the previous methods. While deep learning techniques require high-power computers, our proposed methods are performed locally on machines equipped with ordinary processors. Most notably, the proposed model relies merely on eight parameters to be tuned, while one needs to tune 7, 3.5, and 1.24 million parameters in GoogLeNet, MobileNetV2, and SqueezeNet, respectively.

References

[1] Abolghasemi V, and Ahmadyfard A. "An edge-based color-aided method for license plate detection." Image and Vision Computing. 2009; 27(8):1134–1142.

[2] Jiang D. "Detecting dense text in natural images." IET Computer Vision. 2020; 14(7): 597–604.

[3] Diehl P, and Cook M. "Unsupervised learning of digit recognition using spike-timing-dependent plasticity." Frontiers in Computational Neuroscience. 2015; 9: 99.

[4] Qiao J, Wang G, Li W, *et al.* "An adaptive deep Q-learning strategy for handwritten digit recognition." Neural Networks. 2018; 107: 61–71.

[5] Aly S, and Almotairi S. "Deep convolutional self-organizing map network for robust handwritten digit recognition." IEEE Access. 2020; 8: 107035–107045.

[6] Akhlaghi, M., and Ghods, V. "Farsi handwritten phone number recognition using deep learning." SN Applied Sciences. 2020 2(3).

[7] Dai, R., Liu, C., and Xiao, B. "Chinese character recognition: history, status and prospects." Frontiers of Computer Science in China. 2007; 1(2): 126–136.

[8] Wang, S., Chen, L., Xu, L., *et al.* "Deep knowledge training and heterogeneous CNN for handwritten Chinese text recognition." In: Proceedings of the 15th International Conference on Frontiers in Handwriting Recognition (ICFHR). 2016. pp. 84–89.

[9] Shao, Y., Gao, G., and Wang, C. "A connection reduced network for similar handwritten chinese character discrimination." In: Proceedings of the 15th International Conference on Frontiers in Handwriting Recognition (ICFHR). 2016. pp. 54–59.

[10] Qiang, C., Yu-jun, S., and De-shen, X. "A novel segmentation method of handwritten Chinese number character strings." In: Proceedings of the 8th Control, Automation, Robotics and Vision Conference (ICARCV). Vol. 2; 2004. pp. 1123–1128.

[11] Shamsher, I, Ahmad, Z, and Orakzai, J. K., *et al.* "OCR for printed urdu script using feed forward neural network." World Academy of Science, Engineering and Technology. 2007; 1(10): 2986–2989.

[12] Liu, C.L., and Suen, C.Y. "A new benchmark on the recognition of handwritten Bangla and Farsi numeral characters." Pattern Recognition. 2009; 42(12): 3287–3295. New Frontiers in Handwriting Recognition.

[13] Boufenar, C., Kerboua, A., and Batouche, M. "Investigation on deep learning for off-line handwritten Arabic character recognition." Cognitive Systems Research. 2018; 50: 180–195.

[14] Lin, D., Lin, F., and Lv, Y., *et al.* "Chinese character CAPTCHA recognition and performance estimation via deep neural network." Neurocomputing. 2018; 288: 11–19. Learning System in Real-time Machine Vision.

[15] Alizadehashraf, B, and Roohi, S. "Persian handwritten character recognition using convolutional neural network." In: 2017 10th Iranian Conference on Machine Vision and Image Processing (MVIP). 2017. pp. 247–251.

[16]   Tajrean, S., and Abu Yousuf. M. "Handwritten Bengali number detection using region proposal network." In: 2019 International Conference on Bangla Speech and Language Processing (ICBSLP). 2019. pp. 1–6.

[17]   Liu, C.L., and Fujisawa, H. "Classification and learning methods for character recognition: Advances and remaining problems." In: Marinai, S., and Fujisawa H., editors. *Machine Learning in Document Analysis and Recognition*. Berlin, Heidelberg: Springer; 2008. pp. 139–161.

[18]   Boukharouba, A, and Bennia, A. "Novel feature extraction technique for the recognition of handwritten digits." Applied Computing and Informatics. 2017; 13(1): 19–26.

[19]   Khosravi, H., and Kabir, E. "Introducing a very large dataset of handwritten Farsi digits and a study on their varieties." Pattern Recognition Letters. 2007; 28(10): 1133–1141.

[20]   Zhang, H., Guo, J., Chen, G., *et al.* "HCL2000: A large-scale handwritten Chinese character database for handwritten character recognition." In: 2009 10th International Conference on Document Analysis and Recognition. 2009. pp. 286–290.

[21]   Liu, C.L., Nakashima. K., Sako. H., *et al.* "Handwritten digit recognition: benchmarking of state-of-the-art techniques." Pattern Recognition. 2003; 36 (10): 2271–2285.

[22]   Alma'adeed, S., Higgins, C., and Elliman, D. "Off-line recognition of handwritten Arabic words using multiple hidden Markov models." Knowledge-Based Systems. 2004; 17(2): 75–79. AI 2003, the Twenty-third SGAI International Conference on Innovative Techniques and Applications of Artificial Intelligence.

[23]   Yu, N., Jiao, P., and Zheng, Y. "Handwritten digits recognition base on improved LeNet5." In: The 27th Chinese Control and Decision Conference (2015 CCDC). IEEE; 2015. pp. 4871–4875.

[24]   Lauer, F., Suen, C.Y., and Bloch, G. "A trainable feature extractor for handwritten digit recognition." Pattern Recognition. 2007; 40(6): 1816–1824.

[25]   Obaidullah, S.M., Halder, C., Das, N., *et al.* "Numeral script identification from handwritten document images." Procedia Computer Science. 2015; 54: 585–594.

[26]   Elleuch, M., Maalej, R., and Kherallah, M.. "A new design based-SVM of the CNN classifier architecture with dropout for offline Arabic handwritten recognition." Procedia Computer Science. 2016; 80: 1712–1723. International Conference on Computational Science 2016, ICCS 2016, 6-8 June 2016, San Diego, California, USA.

[27]   Choudhury, A., Rana, H.S., and Bhowmik, T. "Handwritten bengali numeral recognition using HOG based feature extraction algorithm." In: 2018 5th International Conference on Signal Processing and Integrated Networks (SPIN). IEEE; 2018. pp. 687–690.

[28]   Hamida, S., Cherradi, B., and Ouajji, H. "Handwritten Arabic words recognition system based on HOG and Gabor filter descriptors." In: 2020 1st

International Conference on Innovative Research in Applied Science, Engineering and Technology (IRASET). 2020. pp. 1–4.

[29] Tian, S., Bhattacharya, U., Lu, S., *et al.* "Multilingual scene character recognition with co-occurrence of histogram of oriented gradients." Pattern Recognition. 2016; 51: 125–134.

[30] Aharon, M., Elad, M., and Bruckstein, A. "K-SVD: An algorithm for designing overcomplete dictionaries for sparse representation." IEEE Transactions on Signal Processing. 2006; 54(11): 4311–4322.

[31] Abolghasemi, V., Shen, H., Shen, Y., *et al.* "Subsampled terahertz data reconstruction based on spatio-temporal dictionary learning." Digital Signal Processing. 2015; 43: 1–7.

[32] Nazari Siahsar, M.A., Gholtashi, S., Abolghasemi, V., *et al.* "Simultaneous denoising and interpolation of 2D seismic data using data-driven non-negative dictionary learning." Signal Processing. 2017; 141: 309–321.

[33] Dumitrescu, B., and Irofti, P. Dictionary learning algorithms and applications. 1st ed. Springer Publishing Company, Incorporated; 2018.

[34] Wright, J., Yang, A.Y., Ganesh, A., *et al.* "Robust face recognition via sparse representation." IEEE Transactions on Pattern Analysis and Machine Intelligence. 2008; 31(2): 210–227.

[35] Mairal, J., Bach, F., Ponce, J., *et al.* "Supervised dictionary learning." In: Proceedings of the 21st International Conference on Neural Information Processing Systems. NIPS08. Red Hook, NY, USA: Curran Associates Inc.; 2008. pp. 10331040.

[36] Chen, S.S., Donoho, D.L., and Saunders, M.A. "Atomic decomposition by basis pursuit. SIAM Review. 2001; 43(1): 129159.

[37] Tropp, J.A., and Gilbert, A.C. "Signal recovery from random measurements via orthogonal matching pursuit." IEEE Transactions on Information Theory. 2007; 53(12): 46554666.

[38] Aharon, M., Elad, M., and Bruckstein, A. "K-SVD: An algorithm for designing overcomplete dictionaries for sparse representation." IEEE Transactions on Signal Processing. 2006; 54(11): 4311–4322.

[39] Zhang, Q., and Li, B. "Discriminative K-SVD for dictionary learning in face recognition." In: Proceedings of IEEE Conference on Computer Vision and Pattern Recognition (CVPR); 2010. pp. 2691–2698.

[40] Li, Q., Zhang, H., Guo, J., *et al.* "Reference-based scheme combined with K-SVD for scene image sategorization." IEEE Signal Processing Letters. 2013;20(1):67–70.

[41] Zhang, Q., and Li, B. "Discriminative K-SVD for dictionary learning in face recognition." In: 2010 IEEE Computer Society Conference on Computer Vision and Pattern Recognition. IEEE; 2010. pp. 2691–2698.

[42] Fulkerson, B., Vedaldi, A., and Soatto, S. "Localizing objects with smart dictionaries." In: European Conference on Computer Vision. Springer; 2008. pp. 179–192.

[43] Mailhé, B., Barchiesi, D., and Plumbley, M.D. "INK-SVD: Learning incoherent dictionaries for sparse representations." In: Proceedings of IEEE

International Conference on Acoustics, Speech, and Signal Processing (ICASSP). 2012. pp. 3573–3576.

[44]   Abolghasemi, V., Ferdowsi, S., and Sanei, S. "Fast and incoherent dictionary learning algorithms with application to fMRI." Signal, Image and Video Processing. 2015; 9(1): 147–158.

[45]   Aharon, M., Elad, M., and Bruckstein, A. "K-SVD: An algorithm for designing overcomplete dictionaries for sparse representation." IEEE Transactions on Signal Processing . 2006; 54(11): 4311–4322.

[46]   Chen, W., and Rodrigues, M.R.D. "Dictionary learning with optimized projection design for compressive sensing applications." IEEE Signal Processing Letters. 2013; 20(10): 992–995.

[47]   Tang, W., Panahi, A., Krim, H., *et al.* "Analysis dictionary learning based classification: Structure for robustness. IEEE Transactions on Image Processing. 2019; 28(12): 6035–6046.

[48]   Zhang, Z., Jiang, W., Qin, J., *et al.* "Jointly learning structured analysis discriminative dictionary and analysis multiclass classifier." IEEE Transactions on Neural Networks and Learning Systems. 2018; 29(8): 3798–3814.

[49]   Gu, S., Zhang, L., Zuo, W., *et al.* "Projective dictionary pair learning for pattern classification." In: Advances in Neural Information Processing Systems; 2014. p. 793–801.

[50]   Ameri, R., Pouyan, A., and Abolghasemi, V. "Projective dictionary pair learning for EEG signal classification in brain computer interface applications." Neurocomputing. 2016;218:382–389.

[51]   Memon, J., Sami, M., Khan, R.A., *et al.* "Handwritten optical character recognition (OCR): A comprehensive systematic literature review (SLR). IEEE Access. 2020; 8: 142642–142668.

[52]   Tariyal, S., Majumdar, A., Singh, R., *et al.* "Deep dictionary learning." IEEE Access. 2016; 4: 10096–10109.

[53]   Tang, H., Wei, H., Xiao, W., *et al.* "Deep micro-dictionary learning and coding network." In: 2019 IEEE Winter Conference on Applications of Computer Vision (WACV). 2019. pp. 386–395.

[54]   Tolooshams, B., Song, A.H., Temereanca, S., *et al.* "Convolutional dictionary learning based auto-encoders for natural exponential-family distributions." 2020. Available from: https://arxiv.org/abs/1907.03211. [Accessed: October 12, 2020].

[55]   Montazeri, A., Shamsi, M., and Dianat, R. "Using a new approach in deep dictionary learning to handwriting number classification." In: 2020 25th International Computer Conference, Computer Society of Iran (CSICC). 2020. pp. 1–8.

[56]   Gu, S., Zhang, L., Zuo, W., *et al.* "Projective dictionary pair learning for pattern classification." In: Advances in Neural Information Processing Systems 27 (NIPS 2014). 2014. pp. 793–801.

[57]   Jiang, Z., Lin, Z., and Davis, L.S. "Label consistent K-SVD: Learning a discriminative dictionary for recognition." IEEE Transactions on Pattern Analysis and Machine Intelligence. 2013; 35(11): 2651–2664.

[58]   Boyd, S., Parikh, N., Chu, E., *et al.* "Distributed optimization and statistical learning via the alternating direction method of multipliers." Foundations and Trends in Machine Learning. 2011; 3(1): 1–122.

[59]   Jiang, Z., Lin, Z., and Davis, L.S. "Learning a discriminative dictionary for sparse coding via label consistent K-SVD." In: CVPR 2011. IEEE; 2011. pp. 1697–1704.

[60]   Goldstein, T., O'Donoghue, B., Setzer, S., *et al.* Fast alternating direction optimization methods. SIAM Journal on Imaging Sciences. 2014; 7(3): 1588–1623.

[61]   Handwritten Chinese numbers. Available from https://data.ncl.ac.uk/articles/ Handwritten_Chinese_Numbers/10280831/1. [Accessed: November 29, 2019].

[62]   The Arabic handwritten digits databases. Available from http://datacenter. aucegypt.edu/shazeem/. [Accessed: September 10, 2020].

[63]   Hull, J.J. "A database for handwritten text recognition research." IEEE Transactions on Pattern Analysis and Machine Intelligence. 1994; 16: 550–554.

[64]   Sandler, M., Howard, A., Zhu, M., *et al.* "Mobilenetv2: Inverted residuals and linear bottlenecks." In: Proceedings of the IEEE conference on computer vision and pattern recognition. 2018. pp. 4510–4520.

[65]   Szegedy, C., Liu, W., Jia, Y., *et al.* "Going deeper with convolutions." In: Proceedings of the IEEE Conference on Computer Vision and Pattern Recognition. 2015. pp. 1–9.

[66]   Iandola, F.N., Moskewicz, M.W., Ashraf, K., *et al.* SqueezeNet: AlexNet-level accuracy with 50x fewer parameters and <1MB model size. CoRR. 2016. abs/1602.07360. Available from: http://arxiv.org/abs/1602.07360. [Accessed: March 10, 2020].

[67]   Abolghasemi, V., Chen, M., Alameer, A., *et al.* "Incoherent dictionary pair learning: Application to a novel open-source database of Chinese numbers." IEEE Signal Processing Letters. 2018; 25(4): 472–476.

[68]   Ramirez, I., Sprechmann, P., and Sapiro, G. "Classification and clustering via dictionary learning with structured incoherence and shared features." In: 2010 IEEE Computer Society Conference on Computer Vision and Pattern Recognition. IEEE; 2010. p. 3501–3508.

[69]   Jiang, Z., Lin, Z., and Davis, L.S. "Label consistent K-SVD: Learning a discriminative dictionary for recognition." IEEE Transactions on Pattern Analysis and Machine Intelligence. 2013; 35(11): 2651–2664.

Chapter 5

Handwriting recognition using CNN and its optimization approach

Phattharaphon Romphet[1], Supasit Kajkamhaeng[1] and Chantana Chantrapornchai[1]

Abstract

Handwriting recognition is a famous problem to convert the handwriting to text efficiently. The problem can be solved by utilizing a deep learning approach. A large data set is required to build an excellent model. This research uses the public data set on handwriting to train the neural network and to validate the model performance with our augmented dataset to prove that the model can run well with the unseen handwriting style.

This research investigates several state-of-the-art handwriting models, namely *Flôr*, *Bluche*, and *PuigCerver* models with the modified data set. The data set initially given by the Research Group on Computer Vision and Artificial Intelligence INF, University of Bern contains 112,746 words. The experiment methodology explores the extensions to improve accuracy. It considers modifications such as adding more depth in encoder and decoder, adding a skipped connection, changing the activation function, and adding state-of-the-art neural network architecture, that is, Squeeze and Excitation block and Bottleneck block from MobileNetV2 model. We also consider the model size, accuracy and inference time, along with each configuration. The results show that our refinement using the skipped connection performs the best with the unseen test data set among all other designs.

Key Words: Handwriting recognition; optical character recognition (OCR); deep learning; long-short term memory (LSTM); recurrent neural network (RNN); convolutional neural network (CNN)

[1]Department of Computer Engineering, Faculty of Engineering, Kasetsart University, Bangkok, Thailand

5.1   Introduction

Optical character recognition (OCR) is a process of transforming images of typed, handwriting, or printed into machine-encoded text by distinguishing characters inside images or scanned documents. The simple explanation task of OCR is to extract texts from possible images which can be in a standard printed page from a book or an image with graffiti found in daily life such as plated, captchas or street signs, etc. OCR is useful in many ways, such as data entry for a document, autonomous number plate recognition, and traffic sign recognition by using the image processing algorithm.

The OCR processes an image as an input. The image may be scanned from a document scanner and converted into black and white images. The white area can be identified as background, where the black space can be identified as text or character after splitting the text from the environment, the character has to be processed by one of two algorithms: pattern recognition and feature extraction. Pattern recognition is the process that uses the character example to compare with the input characters against the document image. Feature extraction is the process that applies rules of each character feature such as the straight line or the curve of each character. For example, the letter O does not have a straight line in the character. Finally, the analyzed character will be converted as a machine-encoded text such as ASCII code.

Computer vision techniques cannot process messages written by humans effectively because conventional computer vision techniques have to apply the filters to extract the characters from the background, then apply contour detection to recognize each character and use the image classification to identify the characters. The complexity is how to select the filter that can apply to the handwriting which can be diverse due to various writing styles, and the contour detection algorithm is hard to define the character due to the light condition or the color of text and background. Thus, deep learning technology becomes an exciting technology for this type of problem.

Deep learning is one of the approaches in machine learning used to construct the recognition model. The deep learning model is a neural network that contains many layers. It is a computational model to understand the underlying relationships between a set of data like the neural network inside the human brain that can adapt to various inputs. A neural network typically contains two to three layers and a fixed number of hidden nodes in each layer. Every two consecutive layers are fully connected with the nonlinear function. For the deep neural network, there are many more layers that require lots of computation for forwarding pass and backward pass. Due to the advance of computing power, the deep neural network can be trained faster than in the past. The deep neural network allows learning features from extensive training data.

Two types of deep neural networks structure mostly used in handwriting recognition problem is the convolutional neural network (CNN) and recurrent neural network. The CNN is also known as ConvNet. It is a class of neural network that is used for image recognition tasks. The CNN is proficient in processing the grid-like data, such as an image. An image in a computer is the array of a pixel that is stored like a grid. Each pixel contains the value that denotes the color, brightness or saturation in images. The second network is a recurrent neural network (also called RNN) which is specialized in processing the sequence data. Basically, they are ordered data in which related ones follow another. Examples are the financial data or the relationship between pixels. RNN has the ability to remember an essential feature of input in a sequence it receives. The recurrent neural network can predict the trends or the next sequence element. For the handwriting recognition task, it is a combination of image and sequence data. In our work, CNN is used to extract features from the image. Then, since each character is drawn next to each other in sequence, the features are fed into the RNN to encode inputs and decode the prediction output.

In this work, we consider the three basic models, namely *Puigcerver* model [1] that contains five layers of convolution and max-pooling to extract features and five layers of bi-directional Long-Short Term Memory (LSTM) to learn the sequence of the features, *Bluche* model [2] that inserts Gated-Convolution [3] by applied the technique from Language modeling with gated convolutional networks [4]. By adding GCNN between the convolutional layer to increase the model's performance and reduce the depth of bi-directional LSTM to two layers, and *Flôr* model developed by Arthur Flor. Flor model uses bi-directional gated recurrent instead of bi-directional LSTM that can make handwriting recognition more efficient. Since we concern with the sequence data, the loss function, Connectionist Temporal Classification (CTC) [5], is considered. We also explore the network structure add-on to increase accuracy while monitoring the size of weights.

The contribution of the work is listed as follows:

1. We experiment a methodology to improve the existing handwriting recognition model: (1) *Small Encoder Flor* by decreasing the depth of encoder on the hypothesis that too many encoders can hide the feature.

   We remove CNN-Gated CNN layers in the encoder; (2) For *Extend Encoder Flor*, the increase of encoder's depth allows receiving more features by adding more CNN-Gated CNN layers in the encoder. We learn that decreasing the encoder layer results in the reduction in accuracy by 2% in character error rate while increasing the encoder layer results in the increment of accuracy by 0.2%. Making the network deeper by adding more CNN layer in the encoder part does not improve significant accuracy.

2. We experiment a methodology to improve by reducing the depth of decoder due to bi-directional GRU using much computation, reducing the depth of decoder by removing a bi-directional GRU which can decrease the computation cost and reduce the inference time. *Extend Decoder Flor* is modified to increase the depth of decoder. This is to measure the worthiness of increasing accuracy while increasing the inference time. In other words, we try to make the decoder layer deeper. The results show that the accuracy is also not improved in both cases.

3. We experiment a methodology to improve *ResFlor* model by adding skipped connection [6] in Flor model. We demonstrate the experiments with possible connection additions. The results show that the effective way is to add the skipped connections when the skipped layer is not essential. The weights on that layer will be close to 0, and the connection takes the input from the previous layer. The accuracy is improved by 2%, in character error rate and 7% in word error rate. However, adding too many skipped connections will not be helpful while increasing the number of parameters.

4. We experiment a methodology to improve handwriting recognition. We add Squeeze and Excited (SE) block to the vanilla ResFlor model, called *ResSEFlor*. The SE block is used to improve channel dependency [7]. The SE block was connected before the connection point (add operation) in *ResSeFlor* and connected in the middle of the residual in *ResSeFlor2*. The results show that connecting the squeeze and excitation network cannot further improve this case's accuracy.

5. We experiment a methodology to improve the vanilla ResFlor model, by adding the bottleneck network, called *ResBNFlor*. This new connection can decrease the error 3%; however, this solution increases the inference time around two times of Flor HTR (from 1.4 milliseconds to 2.89 milliseconds).

The chapter is organized as follows: Section 5.2 presents the important related works and Section 5.3 describes the backgrounds of theories related to handwriting recognition. Then, our methodology of experiment exploration and model building is described in Section 5.4. In Section 5.5, the experimental results are reported and Section 5.6 presents a summary of the chapter. Finally, Section 5.7 concludes the finding and suggests future work.

5.2 Related works

Handwriting recognition has been classified into online and offline types. Offline handwriting recognition is the task of recognizing text once it has written down. Hence, it will not have information on the strokes/directions involved during writing different from online handwriting recognition that uses stoke direction.

Handwriting recognition has been a well-founded problem for many years. The challenges of such a problem are the variation of writing styles, colors, contrast, and resolutions of the characters and the document backgrounds' noises.

Several approaches have been investigated to solve handwriting recognition. The approaches include image processing, template matching, and machine learning. Recently, due to the advances in high-performance computing, deep learning network is popularly applied to create models. With the deep neural network, it can learn features by itself. Here, we are interested in using deep learning to perform handwriting recognition tasks.

Alex and Jürgen introduced multidimensional LSTM with connectionist temporal classification (CTC) [8]. This model can achieve the handwriting recognition task by applying the multidimensional LSTM to extract Arabic handwriting image features. This research uses the IFN/ENIT database of handwritten Arabic words for this work. This work contains three main parts: the first is multidimensional LSTM (MDLSTM), the second is connectionist temporal classification, and the third is the hierarchical structure. Using MDLSTM instead of a regular recurrent neural network (RNN), we can scan the surrounding context in all directions that can extract more features than the regular RNN. The problem of MDLSTM is that it has a lot of computation costs.

Paul, Patrick, and Hermann introduced a new model that uses CNN combined with MDLSTM as an encoder and uses CTC as the decoder on the English dataset [9]. This model uses the CNN block connected to the MDLSTM to extract the feature and use average pooling connected to the CTC decoder. This research purposed that this model could release an efficient GPU-based implementation which significantly reduces training times. Furthermore, Zenghui Sun and his colleague purposed a model that uses CNN block called CDRN and MDLSTM. This model used the shortcut connection of MDLSTM and proposed that it can accelerate the training procedure.

Puigcerver purposed that MDLSTM is not necessary for the handwriting recognition task due to the expensive computation cost [1]. In Puigcerver model, MDLSTM was replaced by Bi-directional LSTM, which has a lower computation cost. Puigcerver model used five convolutional blocks to encode the handwriting image. Each block contains a two-dimensional CNN layer with the dropout layer [10] to reduce overfitting and uses batch normalization [11] to normalize the input. This model uses leaky rectifier linear units (LeakyReLU) [12] and uses max pooling to reduce the input images' dimensions. In the decoder part, it contains five recurrent blocks that contain bi-directional 1D-LSTM with dropout layers. In the final layer, the model uses a linear layer to map the output to the character label. Puigcerver model that uses bidirectional 1D LSTM can achieve better accuracy than others.

Next, Bluche purposed the model that uses Bidirectional LSTM in the same way as Puigcerver but with a smaller size [2]. The Bluche model can reduce the model size by more than 10 times than the Puigcerver model. Bluche model uses the Gated CNN [3] with residual connection connected to the two layers of BDLSTM which can reduce the model size.

Recently, in 2020, Arthur Flôr purposed the model that inspired by Puigcerver and Bluche models [13]. Flor model can achieve better accuracy than the original one. Using the combination of CNN and his modification Gated-CNN block, HTRFlor model uses the Gated-CNN like in the Bluche model to extract the relevant features in images. However, HTRFlor's Gated-CNN is slightly different from Gated-CNN of HTRFlor model. The half of input of Gated CNN was applied sigmoid activation while the other half does not. HTRFlor model has been added with batch normalized [14] layer and PReLU (Parametric Rectified Linear Unit) [15] to increase the performance of the model. Flor introduces methods for image processing by enhancing the contrast of the image [16] and reducing the tilt of characters [17] to improve the efficiency of the handwriting-to-text recognition model. There were no attempts to improve the network accuracy by adding microblocks. In this chapter, the residual operation [6], *Squeeze and Excited block and Bottleneck Network* are considered to enhance the performance of the vanilla Flor model.

5.3   Background

In this section, we present the background on theories which are related to our work.

5.3.1   *Convolutional neural network*

CNN is a deep neural network that contains many layers. Between layers, the connection may not be a fully connected type. CNN is usually used for image recognition tasks. It takes image pixels as inputs, and the output is a vector of classes. Each layer processes portion of the inputs (not all) by using some filter. This simulates humans' vision as it looks at sub-areas and tries to visual features in the sub-areas. For an image problem type, the features are such as the lines, curves, pattern, and texture. The CNN filter compute in the small area to extract the feature. Each sub-feature of the image is applied to the filter for the following computation in the next layer. The early layers in CNN process image feature directly while the later layers gather the features into abstracted features, called high-level features. The high-level features are used for classification at last.

In the offline handwriting recognition task, CNN is an excellent method to extract the handwriting features since the offline handwriting is an image that is the array of pixels in a two-dimensional grid. Also, it does not require the computing feature extraction such as traditional image processing feature extraction. However, CNN is more computationally expensive, requiring extensive training data and graphical processing units (GPUs) to train a model. Convolution is a specialized type of linear operation used for feature extraction, where a small array of numbers, called a kernel, is applied across the array of pixels. The outputs of each CNN layer are feature maps obtained by a product between inputs and kernels.

5.3.2   *Gated convolutional neural network*

Gated convolutional neural network (GCNN) is commonly used in language processing [3]. Using the GCNN layer, one can select the feature from previous layers by determining the feature values at a given position and the neighbor position and computes the probability to keep or not select them by using the sigmoid of input with zero paddings, to compute the probability. The output of the sigmoid function was multiplied with the input value as shown in (5.1):

$$\text{GatedCNN}(x) = \text{linear}(x) * \text{sigmoid}(x) \tag{5.1}$$

The value of gating weights is usually between 0 and 1. This value is used to restrict the amount of information that can pass into the gates. With well-designed gating mechanisms, GCNN can reduce the vanishing gradient problem for deep architectures. GCNN utilizes half of the abstract features as the gating weights to control the other half abstract features.

Gated CNN in HTRFlor model is slightly different from the traditional one. Flor Gated CNN uses only half of the input features h_1 to perform Sigmoid activation (s), while the other half does not use h_2. The multiplication between two halves is done in (5.2):

$$GatedCNN(x) = linear(h_1) * sigmoid(h_2) \tag{5.2}$$

Flor proposed that this method is a better use of gated mechanism in term of the number of parameters [18].

5.3.3   Gated recurrent unit (GRU)

Gated recurrent neural network (RNN) has shown benefits in several applications involving sequential or temporal data such as speech recognition, natural language processing, and machine translation. Gating network signals measure how the present input and previous memory are used to update the current activation and produce the current state. These gates have weights that are adaptively updated in the learning phase.

Gated recurrent unit (GRU) aims to solve the vanishing gradient problem, which is the typical problem of a standard recurrent neural network. Although the workflow of GRU is same as RNN but the difference in the operation inside their unit. There are the update gate and reset gate in GRU can be trained to keep information from the past. The update gate and reset gate use sigmoid function that represents the probability of keeping the information or not, and the memory of the gate unit uses *tanh* activation function to weight the stored data in the memory.

5.3.4   Connectionist temporal classification (CTC)

CTC is a well-known algorithm that is used in speech recognition or handwriting recognition task. The offline handwriting recognition of an input image can be spitted into sub-images as shown as an example in Figure 5.1. Each sub-image can represent some part of a character. The single image can be read as a-a-r-r-e. The CTC algorithm uses the character—between the same character and repeated character in the input sequence. For example, the word "Hello", the output can be HH-e-lll-ll-ooo, and the CTC decoder is used to decode it as "Hello". In the loss

Figure 5.1   Sequence of character

function, we use CTC to compute the probability of each character position as shown in (5.3):

$$p(\pi|x) = \prod_{t=a}^{T} y_{\pi_t}^t, \forall \pi \tag{5.3}$$

where x is the input sequence and π is the probability of the output, and $y_{\pi_t}^t$ is the probability of identifying labels when there is more than one input sequence. The probability of the final output is as shown in (5.4):

$$p(l|x) = \sum_{\beta(\pi)=l}^{N} p(\pi|x) \tag{5.4}$$

In (5.4), x is the input and l is the order of the output sequence. The final output is equal to $p(l|x)$. CTC is the loss function to improve the performance of the model. It can be applied to the handwriting recognition problem.

5.3.5   Residual operation

The purpose of a residual connection is to send the information between the layers. It makes the shortcut path by using the add operation between the output from the previous layer and the input of the previous layer [19]. Parametric ReLU (PReLU) [15] has been used as the activation function to avoid the dying ReLU problem.

In particular, the mapping $F(x) + x$, called *identity mapping* is created, and the feature output from previous layers can be transferred. $F(x)$ is called *residual learning* operation which may be some convolution layers. During the learning, $F(x) + x$ is approximate as well as $F(x)$. The operation is used to solve the problem of accuracy degrading when increasing the depth of the network. The shortcut edge is called *skipped connection*. Making the network deeper, this way can lead to more accuracy than in the original model.

5.3.6   Bi-directional gated recurrent unit (BiGRU)

BiGRU network is the sequence of GRU cells connected in both directions, that is, feeding sequence data two ways, that is, forward sequence and the reverse of the sequence data. Both connections make the model learn from previous GRU cells and GRU cells simultaneously increase performance and accuracy.

5.3.7   Squeeze and excited network (SENet)

SENet (as shown in Figure 5.2(a)) is a building block that can improve the accuracy of CNNs model with no computation cost. From the imageNet competition, SENet can improve accuracy by 25%. SENet contains SE block that can easily be added to an existing architecture [7].

SE block excites feature maps which help classification and suppress some feature maps. The concept underlying the SENet is that the feature map in each channel is unequal. Some channel has an essential feature, while some channel does not. Squeeze and Excitation network can be adaptive by adjusting the weighting of each feature map. Thus, it can emphasize some features and suppress less useful features.

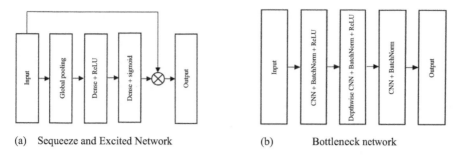

   (a)   Sequeeze and Excited Network   (b)   Bottleneck network

Figure 5.2   Implemented network structure in our research

SE block contains two main parts. The first is Squeeze and the second is Excitation. The squeeze operation can be called global information embedding. The purpose of this part is to find the representation of each channel in the convolutional layer. The global average pooling was applied to the convolutional network to calculate the embedded of each channel. Excitation operation can also be called adaptive recalibration. The purpose of this part is to adjust the weights in each embedded convolutional channel. In the excitation part, the bottleneck was formed by two fully connected (FC) networks and was used as a dimension reduction layer with a reduction ratio of r. The first FC layer scales down the dimension to select the essential feature and then scales up for calibrating the weights. ReLU activation function was used for selecting the information, and sigmoid activation function was used as a gating mechanism by multiplying the product of sigmoid function to each embedded channel.

5.3.8   Linear bottleneck network

From the MobileNetV2 model [20], the state-of-the-art model achieves the optimal balance between the accuracy and the inference time. MobileNetV2 architecture contains the block of invert residual with linear bottleneck convolution architecture. The linear bottleneck neural network is the layer that can embed the input and filter the essential feature to the next layer. The linear bottleneck network, which is used in our research, is shown in Figure 5.2(b).

The linear bottleneck contains depth-wise separable convolution that is the factorized standard convolution. The basic idea is to replace a full convolution with the factorized version that splits convolution into two separate parts. The first part is depth-wise separable and the second layer is pointwise separable, that is, 1×1 convolution builds a new feature by computing a linear combination of the input channel. Applying depth-wise separable operation, it can reduce the computation cost compared to using the regular convolutional layers.

5.3.9   Encoder and decoder model

The encoder–decoder model contains two main parts: first is an encoder. The concept of the encoder model concept is to transform or compress information into a new state. In the decoder part, it gives the transformed or compressed information to the new valuable state. For example, the encoder model reads the image of the word "Hello" and then sends the word as the sound of "Hello". The decoder receives the sound from an encoder and transforms it to the word "Hello" or text of "Hello". In this research, the encoder transforms the word's image to encapsulate the whole information of an image, and the decoder transforms the encapsulated information into text.

5.4   Methodology

We first present the whole methodology of experiments, starting from data gathering, preprocessing, and then model refinement.

5.4.1   Data gathering

The dataset for the training the model is obtained from FKI, the research group on computer vision and artificial intelligence INF, University of Bern [21]. It consists of images and labels. It is a compilation of 115,320 words from 657 authors by scanning books and using automatic word interpretation and validation programs by researchers. The example word in the dataset is shown in Figure 5.3(a). The distribution of each character in the dataset is shown in Figure 5.3(b). In the data set, the number of each character is not the same.

5.4.2   Preprocessing

The preprocessing for each character image is done traditionally. We consider the IAM-word dataset in the experiments. First, we perform the data cleansing and augmentation.

5.4.2.1   Data removal

From IAM-word dataset, it consists of 95 characters which are A-Z, a-z, 0-9, and special characters. In this research, we use the letters A-Z, a-z, 0-9, and special characters, e.g., [?!,.'] and spaces, in a total of 67 characters. Thus, we remove the words which contain characters that we do not consider.

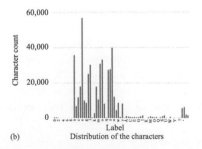

(a) Example of image in the dataset   (b)   Distribution of the characters

Figure 5.3   Example of the dataset and their distribution: (a) example of an image in the dataset and (b) distribution of the characters

5.4.2.2   Image augmentation

We perform the data augmentation to experiment and create a variety of writing. Figure 5.4 presents examples of handwriting augmentation. The augmentation methods for the handwriting text are the following:

- Image dilation: By changing the font size using kernel metric to calculate the image, the character lines become thicker.
- Image erosion: By changing the font size by using kernel metric to calculate the image, it results in the reduced font thickness.
- Height shift, width shift and image rotation: This is to move the character and rotate the characters.
- Image scaling: The purpose is for enlarging and reducing image size.
- Image de-slant: This is to adjust the tilt of characters.

5.4.3   *Model overview*

Flor model was developed from two model Puigcerver model and Bluche model as shown in Figure 5.5(a) and (b). The Flor model is divided into two parts. The first part is the encoder which uses CNN as feature extraction and the decoder, which uses bi-directional LSTM network. The features derived from the encoder layer are processed in the decoder layer.

The encoder of the input image made up of convolutional layers. It processes the representations of a 2D-handwriting image and creates features to send to the decoder. CNN is computationally efficient because it can make full use of the parallelism of Graphics Processing Units (GPUs) and use fewer parameters (around 20 % of the model). In the encoder part, the input image is fed to the first CNN layer.

The decoder section is a bidirectional Gated Recurrent Unit (GRU) network that takes the feature sequences from the encoder block to predict sequences of characters. The decoder from Flor model is used by using two bi-directional GRUs. We do not alter this part of Flor model.

We create the skipped connection between layers of CNN and GCNN. The size of skips may be one layer or two layers. In particular, the skipped connection is between two layers to pass the output of the previous layer to the next layers. If the dimension of the previous layers and the destination layers is the same, the output from the skipped connection is added to the last layer's output. If the dimension of the previous layers is not the same, the output from the previous layer has to be transformed using the 1×1 convolution layer and max-pooling to retain the dimensionality.

| Original image | Image erosion | Image dilation | Image de-slant |

Figure 5.4   Example of data augmentation

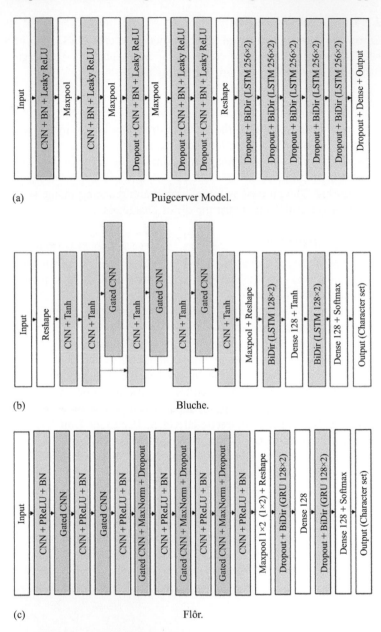

(a)   Puigcerver Model.

(b)   Bluche.

(c)   Flôr.

Figure 5.5   Puigcerver, Bluche, and Flor model structure

The Flor model is shown in Figure 5.5(c). The model consists of the CNN block (blue box in Figure 5.5(c)) and GCNN block (orange box Figure 5.5(c)) to extract the features. In the CNN block, the activation function is PReLU (Parametric Rectified Linear Unit) to prevent dying ReLU. Next, the output is fed into the bi-directional GRU block [22] (green box in Figure 5.5(c)). At last, it is followed by the dense layer decoder and softmax activation to get a probability of each character.

The following describes the variations of the skipped connections and depth increasing we apply. https://github.com/terng03412/ResFlor stores the code for each step, models, as well as the dataset.

5.4.3.1 Small encoder Flor (SmallFlor) and extend encoder Flor (ExtendFlor)

We explore the relationship between a number of CNN-gated CNN blocks versus the accuracy. These two models were creative to prove that the number of CNN-Gated CNN blocks is not too many or too few to extract the essential features. In these two models, we find how the depth of the encoder part affects the model's performance. SmallFlor model removes 56 filters CNN and GCNN layer, and ExtendFlor adds 64 GCNN layers and 72 CNN layers; both models are shown in Figure 5.6(a) and (b).

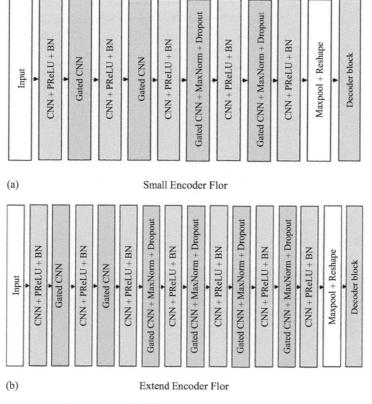

(a) Small Encoder Flor

(b) Extend Encoder Flor

Figure 5.6 Modified encoder model structure

5.4.3.2 Small decoder Flor (SmallDecFlor) and extend decoder Flor (ExtendDecFlor)

From the previous model, small encoder (SmallDecFlor) and extend encoder (ExtendDecFlor) explore the layer's depth in the encoder block; in this section, we explore the decoder block. Both models would like to find the relation between the depth of the decoder and the accuracy. SmallDecFlor removes the bidirectional GRU layer and time distribution dense layer. ExtendDecFlor adds more bidirectional GRU layer and time distribution dense layer.

5.4.3.3 ResFlor

There is some unnecessary layer that removes essential information from the previous layer. The skipped connection is applied to these new models. ResFlor model uses the skipped connection across the layer to use the information that the previous layer would remove. There are four types of layers: CNN layer, Gated-CNN layer, CNN-Gated CNN block, and Gated CNN-CNN block in the encoder block of Flor model. In this research, we experiment with four models. ResFlor CNN (shown in Figure 5.7(a)) uses the skipped connection across CNN layers (from GatedCNN to GatedCNN). ResFlor GCNN (shown in Figure 5.7(b)) uses the skipped connection across GCNN layers (from CNN to CNN). ResFlor(CNN-GCNN) uses the skipped connection across CNN-GatedCNN block (shown in Figure 5.7(c)) and ResFlor (GCNN-CNN) uses the skipped connection across Gated CNN to CNN block

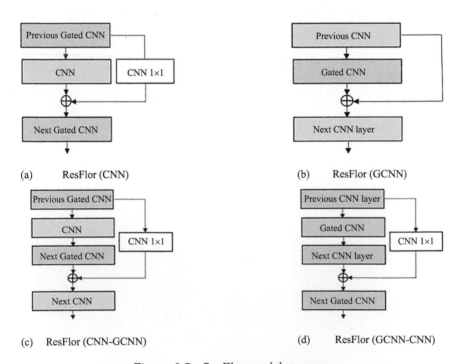

(a)   ResFlor (CNN)   (b)   ResFlor (GCNN)

(c)   ResFlor (CNN-GCNN)   (d)   ResFlor (GCNN-CNN)

Figure 5.7   ResFlor model structure

(shown in Figure 5.7(d)). In ResFlor model, the skipped connection has to use CNN 1×1 to change the dimension since the previous layer's dimension and destination layer is not equal except for ResFlor (GCNN).

5.4.3.4   ResSEFlor model

ResFlor model uses the skipped connection across the layer. The model performs better and more accurate than the vanilla Flor model. We would like to improve the performance of the skipped connection. Squeeze and excitation block is applied in the new model.

This model use Squeeze and Excited (SE) network connection to the ResFlor model in the encoder block. ResSeFlor has two sub-models: ResSeFlor and ResSeFlor2. The difference between the two models is the position where SE is connected. ResSeFlor and ResSeFlor2 are shown in Figure 5.8(a) and Figure 5.8(b).

5.4.3.5   ResBNFlor model

ResSeFlor and ResSeFlor2 that utilize Squeeze and Excitation network to improve the performance of the skipped connection. These models use the bottleneck network implemented to ResFlor network in the encoder block. ResBNFlor has two submodels, namely ResBNFlor and ResBNFlor2 which are shown in Figure 5.8(c) and Figure 5.8(d).

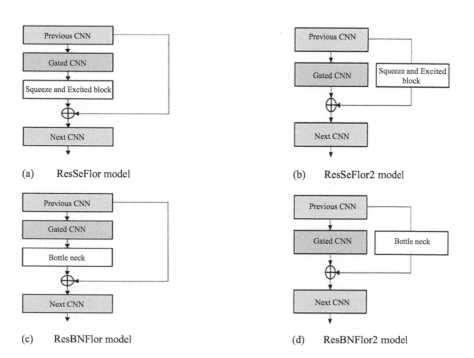

(a)   ResSeFlor model

(b)   ResSeFlor2 model

(c)   ResBNFlor model

(d)   ResBNFlor2 model

Figure 5.8   Implemented SE and bottleneck model structure

5.4.4   Metrics

The metrics that are used in this evaluation are character error rate (CER) and word error rate (WER). CER is measured by comparing the prediction from the model and ground truth character by character. WER is measured by comparing the predicted word and ground truth word using edit distance (or aka Levenshtein distance) that counts the number of operations: insert, delete and modify to make the same word as that of the ground truth. For example, distance (geek, gesek) = 1 since it can insert 's' in one operation.

5.4.5   Training configurations

Connectionist temporal classification (CTC) [5] is used as a loss function and decoder. RMSprop [23] is used for optimization. We assume batch size is 16, learning rate is 0.0001, and total number of training epoch is 100. The experiments were run on the Kasetsart University AI Server with 4 Nvidia v100 GPUs, 256 GB memory.

5.4.6   Unseen testing

The unseen testing is constructed using handwriting fonts and words from the IAM dataset to create images and ran the model to measure CER and WER. The fonts that we used in the experiments are Butter cake, Sardinia Demo, A Sensible Armadillo and alphabetized CassetteTapes. The fonts are shown in Figure 5.9. We have approximately 101,544 images for evaluating the error of the models. The test set is fed into the models, and the results will be decoded into text. This font is chosen because they are more cursive than normal handwriting.

5.4.7   Inference time testing

Due to the machine learning application, we want the model to run as fast as possible, although the model size is large to handle in real-time to interact with the user. In this research, there are three datasets generated by our program with three different sizes by using the words from IAM word database. The size of the dataset is shown in Table 5.1. We measure the total running time divided by the number of images. Finally, we average the obtained value for three datasets.

Figure 5.9   Example of fonts

Table 5.1   Dataset size

Dataset	Number of images
Small dataset	18,473
Medium dataset	91,248
Large dataset	101,544

5.4.8   Visualize inside the model

We determine how model architecture affects the image after passing through the model layer by layer. If we can visualize what is inside the black box model, we can understand how good or bad the model architecture is.

To visualize inside of the model, the dimension is the problem because the dimension in the neural network layer is not two dimensions but three dimensions. We have to change the feature map's dimension. In our research, the 1×1 convolution is applied to map the feature from three dimensions to two dimensions.

We separate the model into encoder and decoder for visualizing. In the encoder section, the model is split into CNN block. One single block contains CNN and gated CNN using the same size filter. For example, in Small Encoder Flor (Figure 5.6(a)), the encoder in this model contains CNN and Gated CNN (the blue block and orange block). By grouping the same-size convolution block, there are four blocks of CNN-Gated CNN. In ResFlor model, the encoder contains the skipped connection across the block. ResFlor model is separated at the connected position. For example, in Figure 5.7(a), the connection position is a plus sign. For the decoder section, the visualization can be done after the output layer.

To use the trained model weight, transfer learning is applied to this section; our program copies the model architecture and cuts the model out at the layer that we want to visualize. Then, we copy the model weights from the trained model. After that, the 1×1 convolution is applied to convert to the output dimension to be visualized as an image.

5.5   Experiments

In this section, we demonstrate six experiments as mentioned in Section 5.4.

5.5.1   Experiment 1: Bluche versus Puigcerver versus Flor model

In the first experiment, we compare the results between three models: Flor model, Bluche model and Puigcerver model. In this experiment, we train against IAM word dataset. The results are shown in Table 5.2. These experiments show that Flor performs better compared to the other two models: Puigcerver and Bluche.

Table 5.2 shows that Flor model has better accuracy in word error rate and character error rate significantly. From the WER and CER of Flor model's in

Table 5.2   Experiment 1: Bluche versus Puigcerver versus Flor

Model	Parameter	Word error rate	Character error rate	Average times (ms)
Bluche	721,998	0.547	0.276	0.739
PuigCerver	9,577,558	0.489	0.222	2.524
Flor	685,654	0.435	0.179	1.488

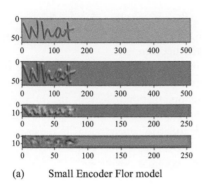

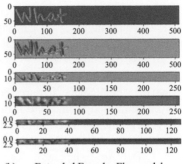

(a)   Small Encoder Flor model   (b)   Extended Encoder Flor model

Figure 5.10   Visualization inside the model

Table 5.2, the error is less than Bluche 10% in character error rate and 5% less than Puigcerver. Table 5.2 shows the average inference time per image in a millisecond. Although the Flor model parameter is less than other models, it takes more time to inference compare with Bluche model because Flor model having more CNN layer that causes the model inference slower.

5.5.2   *Experiment 2: performance comparison of the encoder*

In experiment 1, Flor model performs the best performance in terms of accuracy. In this experiment, we investigate how the depth of the models, varying the encoder size, affects the accuracy. The model SmallFlorHTR and ExtendFlorHTR are created for this purpose. SmallFlorHTR (Figure 5.6(a)) removes the 56 filters Gated CNN and 64 filters from Flor model because the pattern of encoder of Flor model contains the repeat of Gated CNN and CNN block. SmallFlorHTR removes the last block in the encoder. On the other hand, in ExtendedFlor, we increase the model's depth by adding Gated CNN and CNN block.

From the visualization in Figure 5.10(a), Figure 5.10(b), and Figure 5.11, the visualization shows the text region that each model found. By comparing the fourth layer (from the top) of Figure 5.10(b) with Figure 5.11, the image can show the feature of word "What" correctly (the yellow color in the image) clearer than Flor model and Small Encoder Flor model (Figure 5.10(a)).

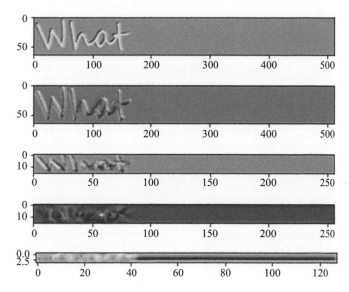

Figure 5.11   Visualization inside the HTRFlor model (baseline model)

Table 5.3   Experiment 2: performance comparison of the encoder

Model	Parameter	Word error rate	Character error rate	Average times (ms)
SmallFlorHTR	583,974	0.451	0.192	1.361
ExtendFlorHTR	754,014	0.427	0.177	2.524
FlorHTR	685,654	0.435	0.179	1.488

5.5.3   Experiment 3: performance comparison of the decoder

From Table 5.3, the result shows that the ExtendedFlor performs the better result than FlorHTR model and SmallFlorModel. This means the encoder block can be improved in some way. Encoder of ExtendedFlor is almost CNN architecture with downsampling. The output of each layer in deeper layer is smaller than the upper layer and more saturated that causes the performance better, and from the decoder block are recurrent layer if the input sequence is small, the inference time can be faster than others.

From Experiment 2 (Section 5.5.2), the encoder block in the main objective to improve. In this experiment, the decoder block is improved by adding more decoder layers. SmallDec has one block of bidirectional GRU-Dense, and ExtendedDec has three blocks of bidirectional GRU-Dense. The results in Table 5.4 show that the word error rate and the character error rate do not differ significantly. The hypothesis that more decoder layer can improve the performance but increase in the

Table 5.4   Experiment 3: compare the performance of the
different depth decoder

Model	Parameter	Word error rate	Character error rate	Average times (ms)
SmallDec	454,614	0.437	0.173	1.172
FlorHTR	685,654	0.435	0.179	1.485
ExtendedDec	916,694	0.436	0.177	1.720

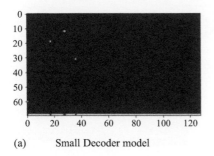

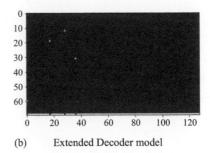

(a)   Small Decoder model   (b)   Extended Decoder model

Figure 5.12   The output of small decoder and extended decoder model

depth of Decoder is not worthy due to the parameter increase around 200,000 parameter per decoder block and from the inference time increase around 0.3 millisecond that is 20% of overall inference time.

From the visualization in Figure 5.12(a) and (b), the probability of each character will be shown as a yellow point. Look at the highest yellow point between the two figures. The results show that Small decoder Flor performs worse than Extended decoder Flor because the probability point in Small Decoder Flor is larger than Extended decoder Flor. It means Small decoder Flor cannot clearly decide this character.

5.5.4   Experiment 4: performance comparison of the skipped connection

In this experiment, the residual connection (skipped connection) is implemented in the Flor model in the encoder block between the convolutional layers. The encoder of Flor model contains two main structures convolution and gated convolution. This research designs four different models: ResFlor (CNN), ResFlor(GCNN), ResFlor(Gate-CNN) and ResFlor(CNN-Gate).

From Table 5.5, ResFlor(GCNN) performs the best performance among other models. The difference between ResFlor (GCNN) model and other models is that ResFlor (GCNN) does not have CNN 1×1 transformation layer because the dimension of the input of CNN and the output of the next GCNN are equal. Identity

Table 5.5 Experiment 4: performance comparison of the skipped connection

Model	Parameter	Word error rate	Character error rate	Average times (ms)
ResFlor (GCNN)	685,846	0.404	0.165	1.525
ResFlor(CNN-Gate)	692,454	0.482	0.195	1.740
ResFlor(Gate-CNN)	696,118	0.450	0.192	1.642
ResFlor(CNN)	790,758	0.414	0.170	1.748

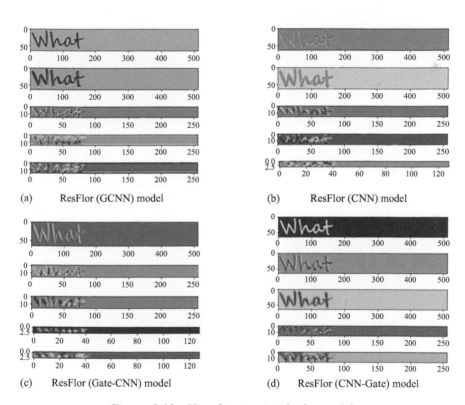

(a)   ResFlor (GCNN) model

(b)   ResFlor (CNN) model

(c)   ResFlor (Gate-CNN) model

(d)   ResFlor (CNN-Gate) model

Figure 5.13   Visualization inside the models

mapping can increase the accuracy just like the case of ResNet [24]. From Table 5.5, ResFlor(GCNN) also performs fastest since ResFlor(GCNN) does not have 1×1 CNN layer.

From the visualization in Figure 5.13, it shows the feature map of each model. By comparing at the fifth layer, the yellow highlights of ResFlor(GCNN) model visualization show the region more clear than other models it can prove that why the character error rate of ResFlor(GCNN) is lower than ResFlor(CNN).

5.5.5   Experiment 5: performance comparison of other ResFlor model

In this experiment, ResFlor (GCNN)* is ResFlor(GCNN) model that uses PReLU activation after skipped connection (from Figure 5.7(b) adding PReLU activation in the plus sign). In Table 5.6, ResFlor(GCNN)* can perform the best accuracy since PReLU activation can handle the cursive writing style more than other models. CER of ResFlor(GCNN)* is lower than the baseline FlorHTR model by 2% and 5% in word error rate. By adding the PReLU activation, the inference time increases only 0.2 milliseconds from FlorHTR model, but the error decreases significantly. From the visualization in Figure 5.14, the visualization shows the effect of the activation on the feature map. This image is the third layer of Figure 5.13(a), Figure 5.15(a), and Figure 5.15(b), respectively.

In Figure 5.14, in the yellow highlights, the ResFlor(GCNN) yellow highlights are not connected due to the missing activation function. This explains why the

Table 5.6   Experiment 5: performance comparison of other ResFlor model

Model	Parameter	Word error rate	Character error rate	Average times (ms)
FlorHTR	685,654	0.435	0.179	1.485
ResFlor (GCNN)	685,846	0.404	0.165	1.525
ResFlor (GCNN)*	685,846	0.368	0.150	1.642
ResFlor (GCNN) ReLU	685,654	0.456	0.188	1.448

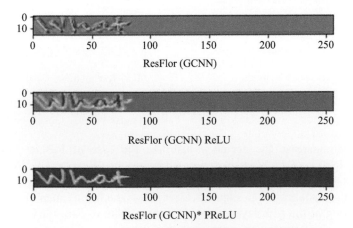

Figure 5.14   Visualization effect of activation function

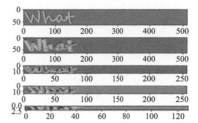

(a) ResFlor (GCNN)* model (PReLU)   (b) ResFlor (GCNN)* ReLU model

Figure 5.15 Visualization inside the models with a different activation function

Table 5.7   Experiment 6: performance of ResFlor with SE

Model	Parameter	Word error rate	Character error rate	Average times (ms)
ResFlor (GCNN)	685,846	0.368	0.150	1.606
ResSEFlor	694,166	0.390	0.163	2.770
ResSEFlor2	694,166	0.435	0.180	2.713

validate loss of ResFlor(GCNN) is the lowest, but the error is not the lowest. The training dataset is human handwriting, but the unseen testing dataset is the combination of human handwriting and cursive handwriting generated by the program. Since the yellow highlights of ResFlor(GCNN) are not connected smoothly, the performance on cursive handwriting is decreased. From the ReLU activation, the function of ReLU (Equation 5.5) is between zero and infinity, so ReLU filters out the negative value feature that causes the feature as connected as ResFlor(GCNN)*:

$$ReLU(x) = \max(0, x) \tag{5.5}$$

5.5.6   Experiment 6: ResFlor residual with SE network

Experiment 5 shows that the ResFlor(GCNN)* can perform the best performance in terms of accuracy due to the skipped connection across Gated CNN network. In this experiment, Squeeze and Excited network is connected to our ResFlor(GCNN)* model. The model in this experiment is ResFlorSE and ResFlorSE2 (Figure 5.8(a) and Figure 5.8(b)). From Table 5.7, with SE connection, we cannot increase the performance of ResFlor model since the number feature of handwriting image is not large enough. From the visualization in Figure 5.16(a) and Figure 5.16(b), it shows that Squeeze and Exited Network connection does not improve the performance in terms of accuracy and error rate. By comparing the fourth layer, it shows that the fired result is not clear.

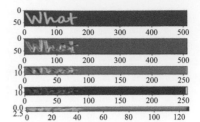

(a)   Visualisation inside the ResSEFlor model   (b)   Visualisation inside the ResSEFlor2 model

Figure 5.16   Visualization inside the models with SE network

Table 5.8   Experiment 7: connect the ResFlor residual with bottleneck network

Model	Parameter	Word error rate	Character error rate	Average times (ms)
ResBNFlor	804,454	0.403	0.148	2.818
ResBNFlor2	804,454	0.379	0.155	2.775
ResFlor (GCNN)*	685,846	0.368	0.150	1.596

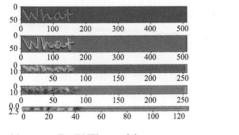
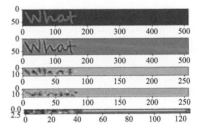

(a)   ResBNFlor model   (b)   ResBNFlor2 model

Figure 5.17   Visualization inside the models with bottleneck network

5.5.7   Experiment 7: ResFlor with residual and bottleneck network

From Table 5.8, the character error rate of ResBNFlor is lower than ResFlor (GCNN)*. However, from Figure 5.8, the inference time shows that the inference time increases nearly two times from ResFlor(GCNN*), although the accuracy of ResBNFlor is better than ResFlor(GCNN)*, it is not worth.

From the visualization in Figures 5.17(a) and 5.17(b), we cannot indicate why ResBNFlor performs better than ResFlor (GCNN)* in the character error rate. The visualization shows the reason why the word error rate of ResFlor(GCNN)* is

Table 5.9   Precision, recall, and F1-score compared with baseline

Model	F1_score	Precision	Recall
Flor (baseline)	0.717	0.868	0.659
ResFlor (GCNN)*	**0.723**	0.855	**0.674**

predict   :   and
ground truth :   and

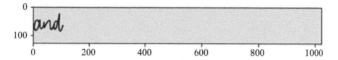

predict   :   save
ground truth :   save

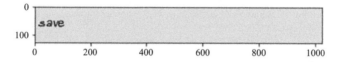

predict   :   proposals
ground truth :   proposals

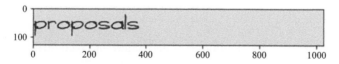

Figure 5.18   Example of the model good prediction

lower than ResBNFlor and ResBNFlor2. From the last layer of encoder in the visualization, the feature map of each character is overlapped, then it makes the word error rate is higher than ResFlor(GCNN)*.

5.6 Summary

Table 5.9 compares ground truth words and predicted words at the character level. The table compares the precision, recall, and F1-score between Flor model(baseline) and ResFlor(GCNN) model. F1-score is the harmonic mean between precision and recall. From Table 5.9, ResFlor(GCNN) model has a higher F1-score more than that of the Flor model. The examples of prediction from ResFlor(GCNN) are shown in Figure 5.18.

5.7   Conclusion and future work

We explore the variety of optimizing the CNN for the handwriting recognition task. The optimization approaches are putting the skipped connections between Flor model layers for handwriting to text recognition, adding/decreasing depth of encoder/decoder, adding the SE block, and Bottleneck block. The experiments show that simply adding convolutional layers may not yield the improvement due to the overfitting and may not worth since it may increase the inference time significantly. The results show that using the skipped connection performs the best in this case. Particularly, putting the skipped connection between layers with the same size can yield the smaller CER and WER. 1×1 convolution can be added to transform the size and then add skipped connection results in the model with more errors. In the future, we will use another visualization method to analyze the model to find how to improve the model performance by using other neural network layers. In the future by using the image registration for ensemble image [25], using some dimension reduction algorithm such as Spider Monkey Optimization (SMO) [26] and use of some linear feature extraction [27] can improve the accuracy and reduce the model sizes.

Acknowledgments

The authors are grateful to Asst. Prof. Putchong Uthayopas who facilitated the usage of HPC cluster for this project and the Faculty of Engineering who provided the budget for the researchers.

References

[1]   Puigcerver, J. "Are multidimensional recurrent layers really necessary for-handwritten text recognition?" In: 2017 14th IAPR International Conference on Document Analysis and Recognition (ICDAR). vol. 1. IEEE; 2017. pp. 67–72.

[2]   Bluche, T., and Messina, R. "Gated convolutional recurrent neural networks for multilingual handwriting recognition." In: 2017 14th IAPR International Conference on Document Analysis and Recognition (ICDAR). vol. 1. IEEE; 2017. pp. 646–651.

[3]   Liu, Y., Ji, L., Huang, R., *et al.* "An attention-gated convolutional neural network for sentence classification." Intelligent Data Analysis. 2019; 23(5): 1091–1107.

[4]   Dauphin, Y.N., Fan, A., Auli, M., *et al.* "Language modeling with gated convo-lutional networks." In: Proceedings of the 34th International Conference onMachine Learning. Volume 70. JMLR. org. 2017. pp. 933–941.

[5]   Graves, A., Fernandez, S., Gomez, F., *et al.* "Connectionist temporal clas-sification: Labelling unsegmented sequence data with recurrent neural

networks." In: Proceedings of the 23rd International Conference on Machine Learning. ICML '06. New York, NY, USA: Association for Computing Machinery; 2006. pp. 369–376. Available from: https://doi.org/10.1145/1143844.1143891.

[6]   He, K., Zhang, X., Ren, S., *et al.* "Deep residual learning for image recognition." In: Proceedings of the IEEE Conference on Computer Vision and Pattern Recognition. 2016. pp. 770–778.

[7]   Hu, J., Shen, L., and Sun, G. "Squeeze-and-excitation networks." In: 2018 IEEE/CVF Conference on Computer Vision and Pattern Recognition. 2018. pp. 7132–7141.

[8]   Graves, A., and Schmidhuber, J. "Offline handwriting recognition with multidimensional recurrent neural networks." In: Proceedings of the 21st International Conference on Neural Information Processing Systems. NIPS'08. RedHook, NY, USA: Curran Associates Inc.; 2008. pp. 545–552.

[9]   Sun, Z., Jin, L., Xie, Z., *et al.* "Convolutional multi-directional recurrent network for offline handwritten text recognition." In: 2016 15th InternationalConference on Frontiers in Handwriting Recognition (ICFHR). 2016. pp. 240–245.

[10] Srivastava, N., Hinton, G., Krizhevsky, A., *et al.* "Dropout: A simple way to prevent neural networks from overfitting." Journal of Machine LearningResearch. 2014; 15(06): 1929–1958.

[11] Ioffe, S., and Szegedy, C.. "Batch normalization: accelerating deep network train-ing by reducing internal covariate shift." In: Proceedings of the 32nd In-ternational Conference on International Conference on Machine Learning. Volume 37. ICML'15. JMLR.org. 2015. pp. 448–456.

[12] Maas, A.L., Hannun, A.Y., and Ng, A.Y. "Rectifier nonlinearities improve neural net-work acoustic models." In: Proceedings of the International Conference onMachine Learning. Atlanta, Georgia. 2013. p. 3.

[13] Neto, A.F.S., Bezerra, B.L.D., Toselli, A.H., *et al.* "HTR-Flor: A deep learningsystem for offline handwritten text recognition." In: 2020 33rd SIBGRAPIConference on Graphics, Patterns and Images (SIBGRAPI). SIBGRAPI' 33. Los Alamitos, CA, USA: IEEE Computer Society; 2020. pp. 54–61. Available from: https://doi.org/10.1109/SIBGRAPI51738.2020.00016.

[14] Ioffe, S. "Batch renormalization: Towards reducing minibatch dependence inbatch-normalized models." In: Advances in neural information processingsystems; 2017. pp. 1945–1953.

[15] He, K., Zhang, X., Ren, S., *et al.* "Delving deep into rectifiers: Surpassing human-level performance on ImageNet classification." In: Proceedings of the IEEE International Conference on Computer Vision. 2015. pp. 1026–1034.

[16] Chen, K.N., Chen, C.H., and Chang, C.H. "Efficient illumination compensation techniques for text images." Digital Signal Processing. 2012; 22 (09):726–733.

[17] Vinciarelli, A., and Luettin, J. "A new normalization technique for cursive handwrit-ten words." Pattern Recognition Letters. 2001 07; 22(9):1043–1050.

[18] de Sousa Neto, A.F., Bezerra, B.L.D., Toselli, A., *et al.* "HTR-Flor++: A handwrit-ten text recognition system based on a pipeline of optical and languagemodels." Proceedings of the ACM Symposium on Document Engineering 2020. 2020.

[19] He, K., Zhang, X., Ren, S., *et al.* "Deep residual learning for image recognition." 2015. arXiv:151203385.

[20] Sandler, M., Howard, A., Zhu, M., *et al.* "Mobilenetv2: Inverted residuals and linear bottlenecks." In: Proceedings of the IEEE Conference on Cputer Vision and Pattern Recognition. 2018. pp. 4510–4520.

[21] Marti, U.V., and Bunke, H. "The IAM-database: An English sentence database for offline handwriting recognition." International Journal on Document Analysis and Recognition. 2002; 5(1): 39–46.

[22] Nallapati, R., Xiang, B., and Zhou, B. "Sequence-to-sequence RNNs for text summarization." ArXiv. 2016; abs/1602.06023.

[23] Dauphin, Y., Vries, H., Chung, J., *et al.* "RMSProp and equilibrated adaptivelearning rates for non-convex optimization. arXiv. 2015; 02; 35.

[24] He, K., Zhang, X., and Ren, S., *et al.* "Identity mappings in deep residual networks." In: Leibe, B., Matas, J., Sebe, N., *et al.*, editors. Computer Vision – ECCV 2016. Cham: Springer International Publishing; 2016. pp. 630–645.

[25] Chowdhary, C.L., and Mouli, P.C. "Image registration with new system for ensemble of images of multi-sensor registration." World Applied Sciences Journal. 2013; 26(1): 45–50.

[26] Khare, N., Devan P., Chowdhary, C. L., *et al.* "Smo-dnn: Spider monkey optimization and deep neural network hybrid classifier model for intrusion detection." Electronics. 2020; 9(4): 692.

[27] Chowdhary, C. L. "Linear feature extraction techniques for object recognition: study of PCA and ICA." Journal of the Serbian Society for Computational Mechanics. 2011; 5(1), 19–26.

Chapter 6

Real-time face mask detection on edge IoT devices

Aditya Dinesh Oke[1], Saumya Verma[1],
Ayush Sinha[1] and K. Deepa[1]

Abstract

Real-time object detection is a task that involves the detection of one or more objects with high precision and very low latency. It is a longstanding problem in the field of computer vision. Various methods and algorithms have tried to make this task faster and efficient. Earlier real-time object detection involved traditional image processing algorithms and techniques. The traditional techniques had good speed but very low accuracy. Also, with the advent of deep learning and graphic processing unit (GPU) compute availability, deep learning methods became very popular for real-time detection tasks. Real-time object detection needs to process a stream of images or videos. Traditionally high compute was not available on Internet of things (IoT) devices and hence traditional client–server architecture techniques were popular. In the client–server architecture technique, people would process the webcam or sensor data to remote servers. These caused heavy latency and hence real-time detection was very difficult. Edge IoT devices solved the latency issue by creating a compute environment close to sensors. These devices made it possible to create real-time object detection with low latency.

Key Words: Real-time object detection; IoT; generic detection algorithm; feature extraction; histogram of oriented gradients (HOG); support vector machine (SVM)

6.1 IoT devices and object detection

6.1.1 IoT devices and object detection

Internet of things (IoT) devices such as Raspberry Pi, NVIDIA Jetson Platform, Google Coral, etc. have become immensely popular today. These devices can be categorized as edge IoT devices. All have good amounts of compute power available

[1]Department of Computer Science and Engineering, SCOPE, Vellore Institute of Technology, Vellore, India

and can process a high volume of data. These devices are compact, do not cause any intrusion, and can be easily maintained. Some of these devices such as Raspberry Pi are CPU-based, while some like NVIDIA Jetson, NVIDIA TX2, and AGX Xavier have GPU available. These devices can process deep learning-based methods. These usually take input from a webcam and process in place. Also, it is possible to use these devices securely and send only relevant data to a storage system or server. Hence, we can preserve the privacy of users as well as use relevant data.

6.1.2   *Real-time object detection on edge IoT devices*

Implementation of real-time object detection is possible with edge IoT devices. Algorithms can be optimized so that computation is reduced and parameters are decreased. Hence, they are efficient to run on such edge devices. These devices offer lower latency and better response times. Real-time object detection requires a service to store and process the bulk of data. Here we use MongoDB with NodeJS server. Since Node.js is an asynchronous and fast JavaScript runtime, it makes the processing of detected objects faster. The accuracy of real-time object detection is usually measured in mean average precision (mAP). Mean average precision (mAP) corresponds to how close the estimation of predicted boxes to target boxes is. In real-time detection, equal importance is given to the frame per seconds (FPS) of processing. A higher frame per second means better and faster real-time processing. Many optimization strategies often reduce the mAP of detection while increasing the FPS. These also require faster data pipelining, lower latency, and modeling specific use cases. These are possible with edge IoT devices, and hence they play a significant role in real-time object detection.

6.1.3   *A generic detection algorithm*

A generic detection algorithm usually has two stages. In the first stage, it tries to learn features from a given image. This stage is often called the feature extraction stage or also referred to as obtaining regions of interest (ROI). In this stage, the detection algorithm tries to learn the unique features of an image. It does not associate any features associated with a given label or class. There are various techniques for obtaining features. Traditionally, these involved various image processing techniques. The image processing techniques relied on factors such as gradients, corners, and reference images. In recent times, deep convolutional networks are used to obtain regions of interest. These neural networks learn from the datasets about possible regions where features can be learnt to detect objects uniquely.

The second stage contains two tasks: classification and localization. Classification involves identifying the label or type of object, while localization involves locating the position of the object in an image. These two tasks involve a classification algorithm and a regression algorithm. These algorithms take features derived from the first stage of detection and learn to classify and localize the object. These tasks were earlier done with simpler algorithms such as SVMs or logistic regression. Nowadays simple networks such as multilayered perceptron or classifiers can be used for the same.

6.2   Literature survey

We analyzed various object detection and face detection studies. These studies described various techniques and methods to achieve real-time detection [1]. Viola–Jones is the eldest but efficient method for face detection. But these techniques used Haar-like features that extracted features from faces. It will not work on mask-covered faces as most of these features targeting face-like features are covered by the mask. A research [2] dataset called WIDERFace showed how a face mask detection dataset was created. Faster RCNN [3] is one of the most accurate and extensively used algorithms for object detection. Multiple techniques such as negative sampling, background elimination, and non-maximum suppression and region of interest proposal make this algorithm very robust as well as efficient. We could customize this algorithm with a feature extracting convolutional neural network (CNN) of our choice. Other techniques such as Feature Pyramid Networks [4] too are very useful and can be additionally used to enhance the speed of detection. We also studied a few studies that showed how face detection works. This showed us that such techniques are popular and quite successful in real-time applications. RetinaFace was one of the popular techniques to introduce novel loss to analyze faces. Also, face detection algorithms work quite well for occluded faces [2,5] as well. This makes it possible to create mask detectors using deep neural networks. Further analyzing the works, it is found that very few were used on edge IoT devices [6]. These techniques are massively popular in client–server architecture and GPU-based environments.

After finding the appropriate studies for our algorithms for occluded face detection, we turned our attention to that studies that had done some work that can be helpful for our study too, one such study we found was using Raspberry pi for a smart security system [7–16]. We found the study very helpful as it had laid the work for us on how to use the Raspberry pi environment to capture data and feed it to our algorithm [8]. The studies pointed out how edge IoT devices can be used with object detection techniques that can work in real-time. Using these above ideas we will formulate how real-time face mask detection. Such an implementation will help in security and surveillance. Also, amidst the coronavirus 2019 (COVID-19) pandemic, such systems are extremely crucial. These can promote the safety of people.

Many reference studies regarding object detection, basic CNN architectures and training deep neural networks are listed in the references section [10–17]. These will provide a broad idea about these topics. Also, referring to any deep learning library such as PyTorch or Tensorflow is beneficial. Torchvision also provides models for classification and detection. We have used torchvision and PyTorch to train the Faster RCNN model. A slight modification is done in the architecture using the mobile net backbone.

6.3   Traditional feature extraction techniques

As we know now, an object detection algorithm involves two steps, such as feature extraction and detection. Traditional object detection techniques used feature extraction-based approaches. These approaches usually did not involve any deep neural networks or CNNs. Feature extraction approaches involved using edge detection or properties such as localization. These are less robust but were primarily used as the first stage for object detection.

6.3.1   Histogram of oriented gradients (HOG)

Histogram of oriented gradients (HOG) [18] (Figure 6.1) is a popular feature extraction method that originated from edge detection. The main objective of HOG is to calculate an image histogram. An image histogram is a histogram of distribution pixels in an image. Similar to edge detection suitable kernels can be used to calculate Oriented Gradients. Oriented Gradients for pixels are arranged in an image histogram. This gives us an abstract representation of the image which contains a few key features. Histogram of oriented gradients is fast, involves very little mathematical computation, and is available in many libraries such as OpenCV.

6.3.2   Scale invariant feature transform (SIFT)

Scale invariant feature transform (SIFT) [2] is another technique used to describe features in an image. We use a set of reference images. We wish to find out features that are similar to the features present in the reference images. SIFT calculates key points from the reference images. To create a feature from every key point, it creates a "descriptor". Each descriptor contains a description of a key point. Usually, such 128 descriptors are written for a key point. These descriptions are features of key points, and hence using these descriptors, we obtain features in the image. These key points along with their description are stored in the database. For every new image, to detect features and objects, we can search for these key points using the feature descriptions.

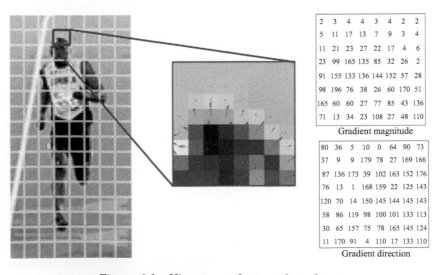

Figure 6.1   Histogram of oriented gradients

6.3.3   *Speeded up robust features (SURF)*

Speeded up robust features (SURF) [5] is a modification of the SIFT algorithm. This algorithm is faster and more robust than SIFT. It involves similar steps as in SIFT. Here we use a set of reference images. These reference images are passed to compute points of interest. Here the feature extraction and descriptors are more robust. This is because instead of images, we use a Gaussian or laplacian pyramid of images to compute features. It makes the algorithm more robust to various sizes of images. Same way as in SIFT, the descriptors and points of interest are stored in the database. For a new image, we match the stored features and descriptors.

6.4   Traditional detection methods

Traditional detection methods involved training a regression algorithm to estimate the location of obtained key points. Traditional detection methods include algorithms such as support vector machines (SVM) or logistic regression. These algorithms rely on training a classification algorithm on features obtained from feature extraction. The classifier learns to detect or localize a certain region to predict the location of an object.

6.4.1   *Histogram of oriented gradients with support vector machines (HOG + SVM)*

This algorithm consists of several steps. We will just walkthrough over them
   Step 1:
   Sample P positive samples from your training data of the object you want to detect and extract HOG descriptors from these samples.
   Step 2:
   Sample N negative samples from a negative training set that does not contain any of the objects you want to detect and extract HOG descriptors from these samples. In practice N >> P.
   Step 3:
   Train a Linear Support Vector Machine on your positive and negative samples.
   Step 4:
   Apply hard-negative mining. For each image and each possible scale of each image in your negative training set, apply the sliding window technique and slide your window across the image. At each window, compute your HOG descriptors and apply your classifier. If your classifier (incorrectly) classifies a given window as an object (and it will, there will be false positives), record the feature vector associated with the false-positive patch along with the probability of the classification. This approach is called hard-negative mining.
   Step 5:
   Take the false-positive samples found during the hard-negative mining stage, sort them by their confidence (i.e. probability), and re-train your classifier using these hard-negative samples.

Step 6:

The classifier is now trained and can be applied to your test dataset. Again, just like in Step 4, for each image in your test set, and each scale of the image, apply the sliding window technique. At each window extract HOG descriptors and apply your classifier. If your classifier detects an object with a sufficiently large probability, record the bounding box of the window. After you have finished scanning the image, apply nonmaximum suppression to remove redundant and overlapping bounding boxes.

6.5   Traditional face detection techniques

Although face detection is achieved with deep learning techniques in the real world, not many use deep learning to detect faces. Some algorithms were developed in 2002 and are used even today. Due to the lack of computing power, deep learning methods were not used earlier. But with the advent of technologies and GPUs, it is possible now to use deep learning for such tasks. Also, at that time, we only had a small set of deep learning techniques. A study in the field of face detection research usually revolved around hand-tuning the parameters.

6.5.1   *Viola–Jones Haar cascade method*
6.5.1.1   Problems with face detection
This method is efficient in its way of tackling the common problems of face detection than most of the other techniques of face detection. A major problem in face detection is face size of image. Sometimes the image contains only the top half of the face or sometimes only the bottom half. These images can occur in various resolutions and hence make the model training process very difficult. Also, if the face is covered by some object then it becomes even more difficult to detect it. These problems can be solved if a dataset contains images which are located at a fixed distance from the camera and have an unobstructed image of the face. Another problem with other face detection algorithms is that we do not know if the image sent to the algorithm will be of a defined resolution, and this is a problem especially if you have to detect faces in a very high-resolution image as the time and space complexity of the algorithms will make the face detection process extremely slow due to a large number of compare operations or increased number of parameters to evaluate by the machine learning algorithm. This happens as we cannot look at very tiny parts of the pictures multiple times. One other difficulty faced by the other algorithms is the difference in age, ethnicity, sex and accessories worn (spectacles, turban, mustache, beard, etc.). These attributes of a face cause the faces to lead to partiality in the dataset to detect one kind of face and may them be of one race or sex or age. Training an algorithm with a narrow ethnicity or age will result in a higher level of accuracy for that same ethnic face but will result in a significant decrease in the accuracy for people of different age and ethnicity.

6.5.1.2   Tradeoff between speed and accuracy

To increase the speed of processing we need to lower the computation which in turn creates a lower accuracy. This leads to a trade-off between speed and accuracy. If we compress the picture so that we do not have to deal with an image with very high resolution, this will cause the algorithm to become less accurate as of the number of workable pixels and reduced number of features to detect a face. This will instead lead to an increased number of false positives and false negatives.

6.5.1.3   Working principle of Viola–Jones method

This method came up with a classifier that uses very simple features. It can quickly find the differences between the two images.

Unlike deep learning techniques identifying facial features like nose or eyes, this algorithm contrasts between two parts of a face/image. For example, if we contrast a portion of our eye and our forehead, the portion in our forehead will result in lighter pixel values as compared to the eye that will have the darker pupil most of the time (Figure 6.2).

Although only using one feature will result in a very high number of false positives, to tackle it they introduced two types of features that will help in identifying the approximate location of the image. After gathering all the feature information from the image, we can use machine learning methods to create a face classification model. The algorithm can predict if the image contains a face. It runs all the feature tests on the image and finds the most promising areas of the image.

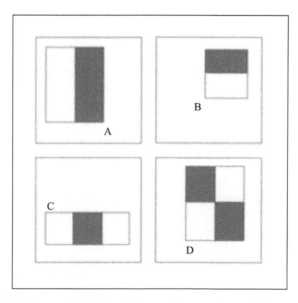

Figure 6.2   Viola–Jones algorithm features. Two portions of images are compared to identify the face

Figure 6.3   Contrasting the two portions of the image will help us identify the possibility of a face in a grayscale image

In these areas, the probability of the face being present is high. For the main areas, deeper and more complex features are tested (Figure 6.3).

6.6   Face mask detection

Face mask detection can be considered as an application of object detection. In face mask detection, we need to identify and localize faces that are covered by masks. There are multiple approaches to it. Here, we will illustrate one such method that can work in real-time on edge IoT devices.

6.7   Deep learning for object detection

6.7.1   Convolutional neural networks (CNNs)

With the rise of deep learning techniques, detection tasks have become faster, accurate and even possible on edge IoT devices. Deep learning techniques involve CNNs that automatically learn features. Convolutional neural networks are specialized networks that involve multiple convolution layers and connections. These layers perform operations and introduce nonlinearities that extract features. These features are then passed to a simple fully connected layer that learns and recognizes the images. Convolutional neural networks also have standard architectures. These architectures are baselined over large datasets such as Imagenet. By training deep neural networks on such a large dataset, it becomes possible to learn a variety of

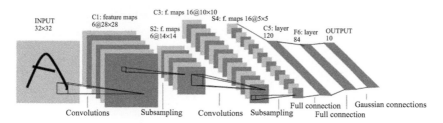

INPUT 32×32   C1: feature maps 6@28×28   C3: f. maps 16@10×10   S4: f. maps 16@5×5   S2: f. maps 6@14×14   C5: layer 120   F6: layer 84   OUTPUT 10

Convolutions   Subsampling   Convolutions   Subsampling   Full connection   Gaussian connections   Full connection

Figure 6.4   LeNet architecture. Each plane is a feature map set of units whose weights are identical

features. Hence a single CNN can detect many classes. The neural networks trained on certain features are used to train on other specialized datasets. This process is called "transfer learning". It involves fine-tuning specific blocks of a CNN. With transfer learning, the same network can relearn a few parameters and be used to classify or detect a new set of images.

To train a deep CNN, a loss function is required to create an optimization problem. This optimization problem is solved by a backpropagation algorithm that updates the parameters of the neural network. Once an optimal set of parameters is achieved, the loss is significantly small; we stop our backpropagation algorithm. Training a CNN is usually done over multiple GPUs and involves fine-tuning many hyperparameters. These include batch size, learning rate, number of iterations initialization parameters, etc. There are a few default values and recipes that have been tried and tested. These are commonly used for training.

Convolutional neural networks are then specialized to do different tasks. A few tasks are object detection, semantic segmentation, instance segmentation and key-point detection. Object detection involves identifying and location of a specific object by drawing boxes around it. Semantic segmentation involves classifying every pixel in an image. Instance segmentation is a combination of both. It consists of both drawing boxes around a specific object and classifying every pixel in the given bounding box. Here for face mask detection, we will be illustrating a simple object detection model called Faster RCNN (Figure 6.4).

6.7.2   Object detection using deep learning

Object detection is one of the major tasks in deep learning. There are two popular approaches to solve an object detection task. The first is a two-stage algorithm as we described earlier and the other is a single-stage detector that infers directly from features. An object detection task involves us predicting bounding boxes around a specific object in a given image. At the training time, we have both the image as well as boxes around the object. During the prediction time, we are given only images and we need to predict the boxes. We measure the mean average precision of predictions (mAP) to analyze the quality of detection. Higher the mean average detection, the better the model. As a rule of thumb, a mean average precision above

Classification   Object detection

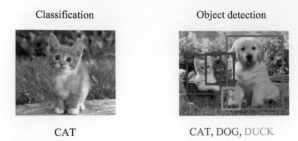

CAT   CAT, DOG, DUCK

Figure 6.5   Application of CNN as classification and detection

35 is good and above 45 is excellent. Mean average precision describes how close the boxes were to original predictions. It is computing only on training data where we have actual boxes in an image. During the inference time, the speed of the model matters. This speed is computed by frames per second (FPS) processed by the model. The higher the FPS the faster the model is. Real-time object detection requires a minimum of 4–5 frames per second processing. Usually, there is a tradeoff in balancing frames per second (FPS) against mean average precision (mAP). This is because a faster model will be a little less accurate and vice versa. Hence real-time object detection involves balancing both the parts; faster inference as well as accurate detection. Here we will describe a widely used two-stage object detector called Faster RCNN. Also, to make detection faster and towards a more real-time scenario, we will be using MobileNet. It is an efficient CNNs architecture (Figure 6.5).

6.7.3   Faster RCNN for object detection

Faster RCNN is a popular model as well as one of the first models that could make real-time object detection possible. It is a two-stage detector and hence involves two stages. The first stage is the feature extraction stage. This involves proposing region of interests (ROIs). The second stage is the detection phase, which involves a classification as well as a regression task to learn bounding boxes.

The feature extraction stage has multiple parameters. To propose the ROIs, we first make a well-educated guess. This guess is made using the shape of an object that we would need to detect. This shape is called the "anchor" of the object. Using such anchor boxes, we create the ROIs. As we train the model to learn about objects (face masks in this case), the ROIs learn the features of the object. After a few training steps, the loss between the region of interests and actual boxes reduces. This leads to stable predictions and we reach a stage where the network has learnt about the objects. To postprocess the ROIs, we perform a step called nonmaximum suppression. Here we remove an overlapping region of interests based on their intersection threshold. If the intersection threshold between two boxes predicted by ROIs for the same object is high we eliminate the boxes. Thus we train a faster RCNN for detection (Figure 6.6).

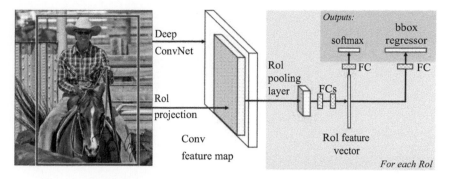

Figure 6.6   Working of faster RCNN architecture

6.7.4   Enhancing faster RCNN with MobileNet

Faster RCNN is trained with a very deep CNN called ResNet. A typical ResNet architecture involves more than 50 layers of convolutional blocks. These are computationally very expensive and hence training, as well as inference, is very slow. ResNets provide better accuracy due to their deep representational capacity and residual connections. For real-time inference, ResNets consume a lot of memory. Typically a ResNet 50 (50 layers deep) architecture consumes around 4 GBs of RAM. Edge IoT devices do not have a huge capacity, and hence we need to optimize the algorithm. The ResNet feature extraction is a bottleneck that causes very slow and heavy inference time. It is difficult to obtain a real-time object detection model on low power edge IoT devices with such heavy computation. To solve this problem, we use a different architecture of feature extraction.

MobileNet is a family of deep CNNs aimed at performing efficient computations. These architectures use a smaller network, which is not very deep. Also, the computations such as activation functions and convolution blocks are optimized to perform lower calculations. These techniques make it possible to lower the computation cost and hence reduce the memory footprint of neural networks. As a side effect, these techniques reduce the mean average precision (mAP) of the model. But due to efficient computation, we get a high throughput and a lower latency. The overall memory footprint of mobilenet v2 architecture is around 1GB RAM. It achieved around 4 frames per second speed in our experiments.

These minor enhancements such as changing the architecture of the network, make edge IoT detection possible. It is possible to get Raspberry pi or equivalent devices having 2-3 GBs of RAM. The object detection algorithm can be trained to detect face masks, and hence a real-time edge IoT solution is possible. We also need a very sophisticated architecture to store and process results produced by our model. Because of an efficient model, the process can occur within the device, hence, can eliminate the need of having a traditional client–server architecture (Figure 6.7).

Figure 6.7   Faster RCNN for face mask detection

6.8   Internet and deep learning

Today the entire world is dependent on the Internet. From healthcare to defence and from schools to socializing, it is affecting every aspect of our life. Even when we are not noticing it is working behind the scenes. The Internet works on certain fixed things. There are the protocols and the architectures involved. Although better versions keep coming and we slowly migrate from the old one to the better one. The Internet of things (IoT) facilitates the use of the Internet to edge devices. IoT devices are located near users and send directly connected over the Internet. Some examples of edge IoT devices are Raspberry Pi, Arduino boards, etc. Earlier it was very hard to make deep learning possible on servers or edge IoT devices. Now with efficient architectures and system designs, it is possible to provide low latency and high throughput deep learning applications. Two possible architectures made these possible namely are client–server and edge IoT. Each has its own merits and demerits. We will describe the working of both and illustrate a simple edge IoT architecture for real-time face mask detection.

6.8.1   Client–server architecture

Client–server architecture is one of the most important and widely used computing models on the Internet. It comprises several components that need to work together for successful functioning. This architecture is also known as the networking computing model. In a client–server architecture, there are many client computers connected to the central server of the architecture. The job of a server is to store all the resources that a client computer can ask. In this architecture, the client acts as the consumer (as it is asking for the resources to be consumed), and the server has the role of a producer (as it produces the content being asked by the client). The client can request many items for a single page for the storage or file-sharing permissions. The client–server is activated when a client requests a certain server with some resources. Also, the client can instead send some information to the server for processing the data. In return, the server responds with the appropriate result for the request.

Let us understand the structure and working of the client–server architecture using Figure 6.8. As you can see from the figure that the IoT device is a client that takes the input from its respective environment. After the collection of the information, it needs to be processed and hence is sent over the network to a server. Here it is processed for further operation on the data. After the server is done processing the data, it is stored in the database. If required by the client it is sent back to the client. This is one of the examples of how the client–server architecture is used. Another example that is always working when on the Internet is the average use of the browser to access a certain website. Now how this works is that the user enters the URL of the website platform that they want to visit in the browser. After the user presses enter, the domain name system (DNS) comes into play. The DNS server looks up the IP-address of the web server which is responsible for responding to the request coming from this website/platform. When that server is located, the DNS gives the corresponding address to the browser. The browser then sends the HTTP or HTTPS request to the given IP address. Finally, the server which is also the producer sends back the requested files to the browser which then displays them to the client.

There are a few drawbacks with the client–server architecture that made it necessary to develop a new architecture which is a peer-to-peer model. Since the scaling of the client–server models is done vertically so it makes them a little bit tough to handle unpredictable workloads. Another major drawback is the handling of the distributed denial of service (DDoS) attack. Since this is a central server model where the central server is responsible for handling all the requests coming

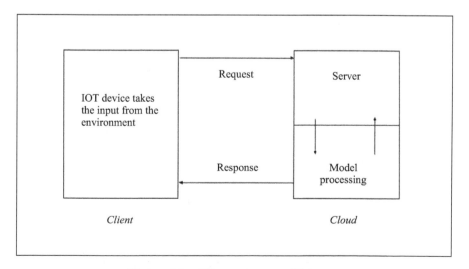

Figure 6.8   Client–server architecture

in from the clients so it makes it very easy to have a DDoS attack on that server and take the whole platform down because of the very high load which the server cannot handle. One other issue with this architecture is the latency. The latency comes into play when the data are being transferred between the client and the server. As when the processing is being done on the server-side, the client system is sitting idle waiting for the response. And then the processed data has to be transferred back to the client. So this results in a big latency time.

6.9   Edge IoT architecture

In an edge IoT system, the processing takes place at the client-side on an edge IoT device. First, we need to understand what we mean by edge IoT devices. An edge IoT device is a device located near the end-user where all the processing occurs. Whereas in the client–server architecture, the computing needed to be done over the cloud or server. Because of the local processing in edge IoT devices, it results in fewer security issues and less delay in giving the response back. The processed data can be stored in the cloud for further use (Figure 6.9).

6.10   Implementing an edge IoT architecture

6.10.1   Dynamic web pages

There are two types of websites residing on the Internet. They are (1) static sites and (2) dynamic sites. Depending upon the use of the company or the individual, they decide to go with either one of them. Let us look into what we mean when we

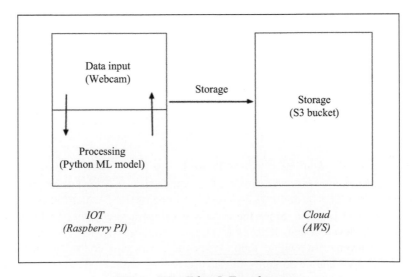

Figure 6.9   Edge IoT architecture

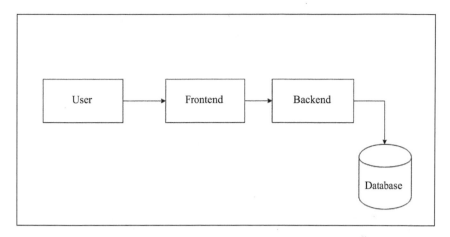

Figure 6.10   Connections from frontend to backend

say that this site is static or dynamic. If a particular site is static then that platform involves no processing of the data. Most of the work is to display some static data from the platform. On the other side if a site is said to be dynamic then it involves a lot of things other than displaying the data to the client. These other things have to establish a connection with the server behind the scenes. It can be anything from authentication of the incoming user to data processing. But all these happening behind the scenes are kept abstract from the client. The client only sees what happens on the front of the site. They do not know what is going behind the scene. Now the dynamic sites also have two parts. What the client sees is Frontend and the other is what is behind the scene which is Backend. The frontend is where the HTML files are displayed to the client and. The Backend is where things such as authentication, authorization, data processing, and storage take place.

Now every platform serves a different purpose. The user might be using a particular platform for chatting purposes and another platform for gaming purposes. There are a lot of different types of backend frameworks. Each framework specializes in a certain aspect. A framework might be good for the platform allowing users to chat in real-time. Similarly, there might be a platform for training their models for machine learning. There are a lot of backend frameworks such as Node. js, Django, Golang. Java, etc. One of them is NodeJS (Figure 6.10).

6.10.2   Backend using Node.js

Node.js was created by Ryan Dahl in 2009. Node.js is a JavaScript runtime written in JavaScript, C, C++ and CoffeeScript. It is open-source which means that the source code is accessible. Since the node.js is open-source, many developers contribute to its development. It leads to huge community support. Node.js is built upon the Chrome V8 engine that makes the JavaScript code run outside the browser. The V8 engine compiles the JavaScript code to convert them to machine level code using the just in time (JIT) compiler. It makes the process till the compilation much faster because the compilation is done at the run-time. It is when the code is getting executed instead of doing the compilation before the execution. Node.js has an event-driven architecture which makes the I/O asynchronous. By having an event-driven architecture, it becomes possible to handle and act on the event and the actions happening in real-time on the platform. Because of this event-driven architecture, the input-output on the platform becomes asynchronous. In synchronous mode, the system waits for the I/O to get completed before moving to the next I/O operation. Whereas in the asynchronous mode, the system does not wait for the I/O to get completed, it moves to the next operation. When that particular I/O is completed, the execution returns acknowledgement (ACK) to continue after the input/output part (Figures 6.11 and 6.12).

Figure 6.11   Creating simple POST request using Hoppscotch

```
1  {
2      "image_id":1,
3      "box": [[131,212,333,413]],
4      "labels": [1],
5      "confidence":[0.5]
6  }



    < >


rameters   Authentication   Headers   Pre-request Script   Tests

ameters  v


ponse  ^

atus

00


SON   Raw   Headers · 12

sponse

1  {
2      "code": 1,
3      "message": "Data uploaded successfully"
4  }
```

Figure 6.12   Verifying response of POST request using Hopscotch

6.10.3 MongoDB as database

Now when all this processing is happening on the dynamic site, a lot of data are being generated. To have this data persistent or stored for a long time we make use of storage called a database. The database is not physical storage. It is stored on hardware having some storage space such as disks. There are two types of database types present: (1). SQL and (2). NoSQL. SQL means structured query language. It is designed for managing the data in a relational database management system (RDBMS). It is used for the creation, storage and managing of data. The other form is NoSQL that is not a structured query language. It is not relational. NoSQL has a dynamic schema while SQL has a predefined schema. MongoDB is a type of NoSQL database. It is a cross-platform database. MongoDB makes use of collections and documents. Collections are what tables are in MySQL. They consist of documents. Documents are like different data collected from the users. It has got a flexible schema when compared to MySQL. It works by making use of JSON type data. It makes it easy to transfer data between the Node.js backend and MongoDB database.

6.11 Discussion

In this study, we decided to tackle the problem of real-time detection of faces that are occluded with masks or helmets to help in the enforcement of the organization's policy and help the company's management to quickly know when and where the violation took place. For our project, we have used Raspberry Pi which is the most widely used and supported mini computer that can be attached with the existing CCTV cameras and help increase their function from just passively recording the area to actively monitoring the premises for possible policy violations like not wearing masks or helmets and in future iterations, we are planning to include other features as well that will not only help in detection of face masks and helmets but also identify a nonemployee of the organization in their premises and help prevent corporate espionage. For this, we trained an AI model to identify faces with or without masks and optimized it enough so that it can run on a Raspberry Pi without overheating or overflowing the system memory available to the device. We then developed the backend of the system with the use of NodeJs to deliver the results to AWS Cloud infrastructure for the data to be stored for further organization usage for investigation and audits.

6.12 Conclusion

This chapter aims to present a simple view of how these components can be arranged and made to work in real-time. It focuses on a simple demonstration of how such implementation can occur as well as optimizing for real-time environments. In this chapter we present a minimalist IoT based solution that can achieve low latency. We were able to achieve this by using the processing power of onboard computing capabilities of the Raspberry Pi and using the power of cloud architecture to store our final results for further analysis and identification of the person who has violated the company policy of wearing a mask or helmet. We plan to include systems that will encrypt the data on the cloud so that the images and the names of the employees can be safeguarded from hackers or accidental data leak, and this can be useful in real-life scenarios where privacy and latency are very crucial for example in virology labs where masks are crucial to prevent any type of disease spreading and the management needs quick identifications of persons violating the rule. This application can be extended further where it is possible to do much more tasks such as intrusion detection, vulnerability detection, hazard detection to name a few. This is due to the inherent flexibility of the model where the AI can be trained to detect faces with or without masks and even identify the employees of the organization. Hence, the model is highly adaptable for a wide range of applications involving quick detection and analysis. Hence, with our project, we were able to achieve our goal of identification of faces without masks with the image coming from the CCTV cameras of an organization.

References

[1]   Wang, Z., Wang, G., and Huang, B. *et al.* "Masked face recognition dataset and application" 2020.

[2]   Lowe, D. G. "Distinctive image features from scale-invariant keypoints." 2004. University of British Columbia Vancouver, Canada.

[3]   Meenpal, T., Balakrishnan, A. and Verma, A. "Facial mask detection using semantic segmentation." 2019 4th International Conference on Computing, Communications and Security (ICCCS), Rome, Italy, 2019, pp. 1–5. doi: 10.1109/CCCS.2019.8888092.

[4]   Ren, S., He, K., Girshick, R. and Sun, J. "Faster R-CNN: Towards real-time object detection with region proposal networks." Advances in Neural Information Processing Systems (NeurIPS), 2015, pp 91–99, vol. 28.

[5]   Bay. H., Tuytelaars. T., and Van Gool, L. SURF: Speeded up robust features. In: A., Leonardis, H., Bischof, and A., Pinz (eds), Computer Vision – ECCV 2006. ECCV 2006. Lecture Notes in Computer Science, vol 3951. Berlin, Heidelberg; Springer; 2006.

[6]   Deng, J., Guo, J., Zhou, Y, Yu, J., Kotsia, I., and Zafeiriou, S. "RetinaFace: Single-stage dense face localisation in the wild."

[7]   Wu, C., Brooks, D., Chen, K., and Chen, D., *et al.* "Machine learning at Facebook: Understanding inference at the edge." In 2019 IEEE International Symposium on High Performance Computer Architecture (HPCA). pp. 331–344. 2019.

[8]   Zhang, X., Zhou, X., Lin, M., and Sun, J. "Shufflenet: An extremely efficient convolutional neural network for mobile devices." In 2018 IEEE/CVF Conference on Computer Vision and Pattern Recognition. pp. 6848–6856. 2018.

[9]   Redmon, J. and Farhadi, A. "Yolov3: An incremental improvement." 2018. arXiv preprint arXiv:1804.02767.

[10] Chowdhary, C. L. "3D object recognition system based on local shape descriptors and depth data analysis." Recent Patents on Computer Science. 2019; 12(1), 18-24.

[11] Iandola, F. N, Han, S., Moskewicz, M. W., Ashraf, K., Dally, W. J., and Keutzer, K. "Squeezenet: Alexnet-level accuracy with 50x fewer parameters and < 0.5 MB model size." 2016. arXiv preprint arXiv:1602.07360.

[12] Bhattacharya, S., Maddikunta, P. K. R., Pham, Q. V., *et al.* Deep learning and medical image processing for coronavirus (COVID-19) pandemic: A survey. Sustainable cities and society. 2020; 65: 102589.

[13] Goar, V., Yadav, N. S., Chowdhary, C. L., Kumaresan, P., Mittal, M. "An IoT and artificial intelligence based patient care system focused on COVID-19 pandemic." International Journal of Networking and Virtual Organisations. Preprint, 2021.

[14] Chowdhary, C. L., Sai, G. V. K., and Acharjya, D. P. "Decreasing false assumption for improved breast cancer detection." Journal of Science and Arts. 2016; 35(2): 157–176.

[15] Chowdhary, C. L., Patel, P. V., Kathrotia, K. J., Attique, M., Perumal, K., and Ijaz, M. F. "Analytical study of hybrid techniques for image encryption and decryption." *Sensors.* 2020; 20(18): 5162.

[16] Chowdhary, C. L., Mittal, M., Pattanaik, P. A., and Marszalek, Z. "An efficient segmentation and classification system in medical images using intuitionist possibilistic fuzzy C-mean clustering and fuzzy SVM algorithm." Sensors. 2020; 20(14): 3903.

[17] Tripathy, A. K., Das, T. K., and Chowdhary, C. L. "Monitoring quality of tap water in cities using IoT." In Emerging Technologies for Agriculture and Environment (pp. 107–113). Singapore: Springer; 2020.

[18] Dalal, N. and Triggs, B. "Histograms of oriented gradients for human detection," 2005 IEEE Computer Society Conference on Computer Vision and Pattern Recognition (CVPR'05), San Diego, CA, USA, 2005, pp. 886–893, vol. 1. doi: 10.1109/CVPR.2005.177.

Chapter 7

Current challenges and applications of DeepFake systems

Sandeep Bhat[1], Zeel Naman Shah[1] and G.M. Siddesh[1]

Abstract

Synthetic audio and video content are enormously growing in the Internet world today, creating many problems in recent years. The use of techniques such as artificial intelligence over multimedia to create fake content is known as DeepFake. It challenges the reality and genuineness of the created high-quality audio and video content. The synthetic media created is almost similar to the real media, and with bare eyes, it is almost impossible to differentiate them. Though the DeepFake has also been a boon in many multimedia fields such as film making, advertising, and animation industry to create magnetic media, it has also become a threat to society. There is software available across the Internet that can be used even by a novice to create fake multimedia contents that look very realistic and used for various criminal activities. The applications such as Snapchat, Instagram, Facebook, Twitter, and TikTok use multimedia as its contents. Social media applications can be easily falsified and can cause severe threats both personally and psychologically using DeepFake technology. Hence, there is a need for tools to detect the forged contents in the media to check and authenticate the data's genuineness and integrity.

This chapter highlights the various challenges the human race faces because of the DeepFake technology and the limitation of different forensic tools available to analyze and forecast the challenging future and understand the solutions incorporated to secure the current data situation.

Key Words: DeepFake; forensics; artificial intelligence; machine learning; cybercrime

7.1 Introduction to DeepFake

In recent years, the use of technology to manipulate or generate audio/visual false content is seen. The border has become very thin between real and synthetic media.

[1]Department of Information Science and Engineering, Ramaiah Institute of Technology (affiliated to VTU), Bangalore, India

On the one hand, it creates software opportunities in various domains such as cinematic production, creative arts, advertising, video games, and many more. Nevertheless, it also poses an enormous security threat as it can create illusions of the presence of the person and scenarios that has not happened in real, which leads to significant social, political, legal, and financial implications. The possible risks range from faking the people's faces and victimize them for fake pornography where the face is synthesized and morphed into realistically looking videos to making fake allegations of the political people/parties to tarnish their image. They make it look as if they were making an offensive remark; they never really made it. A high-level executive may be depicted as reporting on the success of her company that could affect the sales of the stock market, or as an Internet bully claiming to be a known person or part of the family itself. DeepFakes are synthetic media in which a human replaces someone else's likeness in an actual picture or video.

Deep learning and training of generative neural network architectures, such as generative adversarial networks (GANs) or autoencoders, are the critical machine learning approaches used to build DeepFakes. To paste/graft the image of the person's face onto someone else's digital, DeepFakes use artificial intelligence (AI), which seems like that person said things and acted the way they never actually did. Most of the DeepFakes are outlandish and funny for now; a few have also appeared in innovative advertisements.

For instance, many videos or photos floating on social media platforms have DeepFake manipulations wherein the faces of the actual people are swapped to that of some well-known personality.

7.1.1   Scenario

Through Kaggle (a Google-owned coding contest platform), Facebook's DeepFake Detection Challenge is carried out. It gives an endless aggregation of face-swap recordings: 100,000 DeepFake photos made by Facebook utilizing on-screen characters which are paid, on which participants have tried executing their image detection algorithms. The projects pulled in over 2,000 members from industry and academics, and it created surpassing 35,000 DeepFake image detection models and methodologies.

Multimedia forensics research has been in demand for the past 15 years [1,2]. It received significant attention from the academy and significant information technology companies and funding agencies such as United States' Defence Advanced Development Projects Agency (DARPA). In 2016, the extensive Media Forensic initiative (MediFor) was initiated by the Department of Defence to facilitate research on media legitimacy with substantial results in methodology and reference datasets.

7.2   Various DeepFake detection methods available and their limitations

A person's image can be manipulated based on attributes or the face, expressions, and identity, or a completely new face can be grafted over the original image.

There are three major types of fake video characterization:

1. **Head puppetry** entails editing a video of a target person's whole head and upper shoulder using a video of the source person's head until the altered target seems to act in the same way as the source.
2. **Face flipping** means making a screenshot of the target with the faces substituted by the source's edited faces while retaining the same facial expressions.
3. **Lip synchronization** is to create a falsified video by only adjusting the area of the lip such that anything that is not said appears to talk to the goal.

Electronic media corroboration must search for physical authenticity, semantic authenticity, and digital authenticity, following the MediFor taxonomy. Many strategies suggest revealing physical contradictions, such as shadows, lighting, or perspective. However, modern, sophisticated manipulations are increasingly successful in avoiding such traps, and automated integrity testing techniques are much more common and reflect the current state of the art. Every multimedia is characterized by various characteristics, which rely on the various stages of its digital history, that is, image acquisition to internal camera processing and processing of the images external to the model and image editing operations as well. Manipulating the image digitally aims to change such characteristics, leaves a trail of hint that pixel-level analysis methods can manipulate while invisible to the eye. Instead, when the media commodity under review transmits details that are not consistent with the factors or with reality originating from correlated sources, semantic credibility is violated. For instance, when artifacts are animated, duplicated, or created out of pictures, it is very straightforward to identify the copies and locate some of them, proposing manipulation possibilities. It is possible to create manipulation history by identifying connections among the same resource renditions. The best DeepFake detector captures just about two-thirds of them to arise from a significant Facebook-led attempt to battle the updated images.

7.2.1 Traditional detection methods

This section reviews the key study directions of multimedia forensics previous to the detection of DeepFakes and deep learning. A common approach to locate searchable details is to look at how the program processes photos and look further at something that exists in the context (editing instructions) [3]. Figure 7.1 shows that the essential components of the image acquisition process which includes an array of filters, color interpolation, compression mechanism, and editing.

7.2.1.1 Blind methods

These methods do not use external source data for teaching or different types of preprocessing. It relies solely on the analyzed media property and tries to uncover any differences that suggest multimedia manipulation. They look for a specific piece of art created by a camera or process outside of the camera. The process of creating an image within the camera requires multiple operations (hardware and software) for the individual camera to have specific and unique markings on the captured image. For instance, different demosaicing algorithms usually have

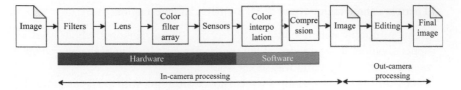

Figure 7.1   The essential components of the image acquisition process are represented in the figure

different camera models. It is clear that most identities are extremely sensitive and cannot be understood in visual inspection. However, if enough focus has been placed on them, they are the key source of evidence to create digital credibility.

Distortion of the lens

Cameras have a complicated optical method that cannot entirely focus light on all wavelengths. It can be utilized for forensic purposes. The proposed process uses lateral chromatic decompositions of light components at different wavelengths, off-axis displacement, which gives rise to colored channel mismatch [4].

The second proposed method is based on disruptions arising from the lens and sensor interaction [5]. Wide-angle lenses, which cause radial distortion, are commonly used for outdoor as well as indoor video surveillance [6].

CFA artifacts

Color filter arrays (CFA) are used for most modern cameras in order to make it possible for each image sensor element to discern light within a particular color spectrum (RGB). Demosaicing process interpolates all the missing color information from the surrounding pixels. All of these captured images represent patterns of all acquired images. When the image is manipulated, the patterns are disturbed from time to time.

As the interpolation algorithms and CFA configurations are unique for every camera model, when an area is combined with a photograph taken by a different camera model, its structure appears abnormal [7,8]. In 2005, Popescu and Farid [9] allow the use of inscribed artifacts based on a basic linear model (to fix periodic correlations).

In the Fourier domain, the periodic signal produces firm peaks. It can be used to differentiate between natural and computer-generated images (to extract more useful features), specifically after high-pass filtering.

In the Bayesian framework [10], fine-grained image tampering localization is enabled by the probability map in output. It can also be extended across color channels to consider pixel correlation.

Noise frequency and noise pattern

Noise in an image can be induced by a variety of reasons. One of them is that noise can be added during the acquisition. Since different cameras have different internal noise, local noise level analysis helps identify the residuals [11]. This analysis can perform using statistical imaging tools or wavelet domains. At the center of error level analysis (ELA), this approach is used.

Only noise intensity may provide wrong indications and is not very informative. Rich features to characterize local neighbors better can be extracted by using high-pass noise residual [12]. The expectation-maximization algorithm clusters these rich features and exposes every possible anomaly present in the image.

Agnostic approaches [3] to imaging use noise residual, and another technique uses noise residual to predict the imaging model and identify the intrinsic finger-print of the device. The anomalies of the sample are used to suggest alternative manipulations to the model. These images are considered motion-compensated videos since the audio is processed and frame-by-frame subtracted of the noise to create an output video of no motion displaying noise residuals in the audio. [13]

Compression artifacts

The misuse of the compression pattern was a workhorse in image forensics. Exploiting the lock artifact grid (BAG) is a popular approach. Because the processing block blocks the JPEG, conflicts occur within the compressed image block's boundaries, creating a specific and easily detectable grid pattern [14].

The BAGs of the host image and the inserted image do not match in the case of copy-move manipulations or splicing, which enables validation. Another integral approach is based on double compression. When a JPEG compressed image [15] is locally edited and re-compressed, double compression artifacts appear in the full image, except for the spoofed area. These sculptures vary depending on whether the two tight spaces are compatible. However, effective detection methods [16] and localization methods [17] have been suggested in both cases.

One other method is based on JPEG ghosts [18]. In this method, compression of the picture against three separate stages of QFS is used to evaluate what it appears like as it is shrunk into the smallest dimension that is aligned with the surrounding pixels (QF).

Other approaches search for variations in the statistical distribution of the initial DCT samples, believed to conform with the Benford regulations. Model-specific implementation of JPEG involves postprocessing measures and personalized quantification tables. Chroma subsampling also presents hints of manipulation due to integer rounding.

It is also possible to detect video manipulation with a compression sample, but this is more complicated due to the video coding algorithm's complexity. One approach to boost the double compression calculation is to take into account the variations in macroblock prediction forms in re-encoded P-frames. This pattern [19] is further used to detect tampering in interframes and deal with two-dimensional framework video settings.

Editing artifacts

An expected fact that is created indirectly by the method of manipulation is a trail of traces that are called precious. It is when an item is moved into a new background that different postprocessing measures can be added prior to writing the final image. They include geometric transformations, such as rotation or scaling, contrast adjustment or blurring, etc. Nothing at all like this is involved in this modality or method. Some methods [11,20] try to identify traces of resampling required when rotating or resizing using artifacts. Several other approaches focus on blurring anomalies [21] and inconsistencies at objects' boundaries when performing compositions.

The copy and move operation duplicates or hides objects in the image. The same area's presence is a strong indication of counterfeiting, but duplicates are often altered to hide traces, and there are also nearly identical natural artifacts that confuse forensic analysis. Currently, powerful and reliable solutions are possible to track copy movements including in the presence of resizing, rotation and other geometric distortions [22]. Extending this to video is very difficult due to its complexity. Changes between frames may be detected depending on how quickly frames seem to travel [23].

7.2.1.2   One-class and model-based time series approaches

The camera's sensor would have new details regarding the crime scene. As a consequence of manufacturing defects, pressure sensor components display slightly nonuniform readings—these slightly nonuniform readings are classified as photoresponse nonuniformity noise (PRNU). The captured image will have traces of the camera's PRNU pattern used to capture it, considering a camera fingerprint. If the image is altered, the equivalent PRNU noise pattern is interrupted/removed, allowing us to identify the manipulation.

PRNU based manipulation detection [24] is based mainly on two steps:

1. Camera PRNU design is judged by the large number of images taken with this camera.
2. The selected image PRNU estimated during the noise reduction filter examination is compared with the reference.

This method relies on essential prior knowledge collected from the device itself or images taken by the source device. It is also a compelling method to identify all attacks reasonably well, regardless of their nature. A limitation of the method is that a single image is estimated at test time. The PRNU pattern will quickly be overrun by an imperfectly omitted picture material since the PRNU pattern is a poor signal.

The predictor is designed [25] to eliminate disturbing nonunique objects, change the decision threshold to local picture statistics, and minimize false alarms. Intense spatial dependences are generated by Markov random field to render collective decisions and not only independent decisions.

This method can be unrolled in blind scenarios that classify photos that share the same PRNU noise pattern without previous camera awareness providing an effective clustering procedure. [26,27].

Instead of the PRNU noise pattern, the analysis can also be based on the camera model's local characteristics. The same model's cameras share the same hardware and software design options, so the captured image has similar traces. The sliding window modality extracts the same descriptor compared to the test time and reference. Large deviations indicate image manipulation. However, model-related outcomes are far more potent than device-related PRNU trends and have more accurate identification.

Latest DeepFakes often display certain obvious asymmetries, such as distinct colored eyes or badly patterned teeth. However, such artifacts are likely to disappear in the near future.

7.2.1.3 Supervised approaches with changed functionality

These are machine learning-based methods. The attributes required to help distinguish between ancient and manipulative images are described first. Classifiers are trained in both types of large datasets. Based on the experience of target manipulation, the features described by the forensic analyst are modified. Some features were developed to detect specific features, most notably from the publication of JPEG compression [28] or camera response function (CRF) [29]. Universal attributes based on accurate image statistics that authorize the detection of various manipulation types are precious.

Good statistical models help in selecting attributes that assure the highest discriminative power. The most valuable features are derived in the spatial or transform domain from the noise residuals. Such statistical anomalies caused by manipulations are categorized as noise.

The opportunities for attributes dependent on top-order picture statistics were shown by Farid and Lyu in 2003 [30]. These characteristics catch subtle distinctions in photo microtechnologies and have shown their usefulness in many environments, such as digital graphics, biometrics, and steganalysis.

One of the blind approaches' main attractions is that no additional detail is needed outside of the tested image/video. However, based on specific details, methods rely significantly on their statistical model and most often collapse when the assumptions are not correct. Copy-move detectors perform much better in postprocessing than they do during camera capture, but they cannot identify cloning or several forms of colors. On the other hand, noise-based models are more generic and stable for posttreatment since they often do not rely on explicit statistics but instead examine anomalies in residual noise. Noise modeling techniques can be used in a supervised modality to improve reliability.

The machine learning model's performance depends significantly on the test dataset's calibration and the training dataset [31]. Independent datasets would make it easier for our team to do higher, by as little as 50% (that is a random guess). Because of the lack of robustness of the system, the applicability of their method is restricted to unique cases only.

7.2.2 Methods based on deep learning

A considerable amount of research has been committed to methods that rely on deep learning, where attributes are explicitly learned from the results. Deep learning techniques have been proved to be victorious in several computer vision applications. This part deals with deep learning-based methods proposed to detect manipulations in multimedia.

7.2.2.1 Supervised CNNs looking at specific clues

Double JPEG compression provides vital clues for authenticity verification. Localization can be enabled by using a histogram of discrete cosine transform coefficients [32] as an input to the convolution neural network architecture and statistical blocks correlated with histograms. There are several approaches to operate on noise fragments rather than image pixels which use CNN layers to extract histogram-related functions to allow effective use of CNN learning capabilities. Better outcome can be gained by compressing the test images by a QF never seen in the training set. To improve the performance further, use a multi-domain method based on the frequency and spatial domain inputs.

Detection using double compression can be extended video analysis using H.264 [33], which proposes a separate analysis of two-stream neural network, predictive and intra-coded frames. The semi network has identified the first coarse-grained matches between the candidates' clones built on ResNet architecture, which indicates an adequate level of correspondence [34].

When splicing of the material from various sources is done, at the boundaries the results arise, as observed in Section 7.2.1. A fully convolutionary multitask network [35] is built, which includes a particular branch to detect boundaries between added regions and context, and it is possible to use another branch for the manipulation surface.

This method is also used to detect copy-move manipulation. A complete CNN-based method [36] implements the three-step solution: matching the features, extracting the data, and postprocessing to reduce the false alarms. This, in turn, helps in optimizing the different modules together and gives the expected manipulation localization map as output.

Overall, deep learning approaches work well on low-resolution pictures than traditional approaches where the parameters are adapted to high-resolution images. There are source and target mismatch issues [37]. The Copy move method maps the original object and its clones and does not establish duplicate fields but focuses on manipulating objects with interpolation and boundary inconsistencies.

A CNN-based solution [38] has been developed to detect artifacts introduced by some manipulation tools. The model is trained on automatically generated duplicate images using the same tool. Data expansion includes resizing, JPEG compression, and different forms of modification of histograms to increase robustness.

7.2.2.2   Generic supervised CNNs

Regular CNN detectors cannot detect certain types of operations or artifacts. Training on such networks is difficult due to the diversity of available networks and data history.

The first group of approaches were inspired by the characteristics of the modified model and is used effectively in image forensics. A CNN with a restricted first layer is proposed that implements high-pass filtering of the film, suppresses the content of the scene, and enables it to operate on residuals. SVM is liable for global decision-making [39,40] and the device is used for removing features only. Methods enable limited batch detection. The positioning is possible with the use of sliding window analysis over the entire image. This solution is heavily focused on lower-level features, believing that manipulation does not help detect higher-level features.

Poor image editing may leave indications such as artificial tampered boundaries or strong contrast. A two-stream network is used to search for high-level traces. In order to remove low-level functionality, in the first path—a rich model filter is used and the second path is based on RGB data. To obtain a binary position map as an output, a fully linked network is used to define the image stage. The effects of pixel shrewd are obtained by incorporating transposing convolution. There is a much smaller region of the regulated locus than the first untouched pixels and a focus loss is achieved to overcome the distortion of the class which allocates the balancing factor to the trans-entropy term.

The shifts in the clean and fabricated blocks in the frequency domain, and the modulation of the encoder–decoder segments through the usage of the long short-term memory (LSTM) cells are demonstrated. Inconsistencies can be caught by using the resampling features [41]. A different network is used such that boundary objects are forced to look at the algorithm.

However, the patch level analysis does not make it possible to consider local simultaneously (texture analysis) and global (context analysis) information. This is not simple, as CNN allows input patches that are far smaller than the specifications of the entire image. This issue is resolved in computer vision by resizing the background, which masks essential traces of counterfeiting. The gradient break-point [42] offers end-to-end preparation for aggregation and extraction of attributes, allowing co-optimization without resizing, helping to evaluate the whole image with texture-sensitive characteristics and highlighting irregularities that do not occur at the level of the patch.

7.2.2.3 One-class training

In one-class training, look for discrepancies against internalized internal data models. Any manipulation is an inconsistency and must be detectable.

Expressive attributes are eliminated from residual noise by an autoencoder in a single-asset (blind) [43] one class process, and iterative attribute labeling divides two classes. The pristine data model is defined by the largest class. We should take the approach to video and expand it to account for transient situations. GANs are used to learn new images correctly, after which a one-class SVM is educated on their dataset to discern distortion and ultimately distinguish whether a picture was altered or not.

In the presence of splicing, powerful forensic hints are given by the fact that different camera models obtain different image pieces. A CNN [44] is used to track variations from a sequence, and then cluster the deviations together to categorize images. First, only a restricted network is used to allow high-level camera-model functionality, and then, another network is trained on the previously learned relationships between the extracted functions. A Siamese network is also qualified to determine whether matching metadata is available for the two image patches. The network can be used on any image until it has been conditioned on new images with the EXIF header. These principles are used to extract a fingerprint model of the camera, called Noseprint. A CNN denoiser is equipped to separate pairs of patches in the Siamese modality. The network can extract the image-size Noseprint once it is trained to emphasize artifacts related to the camera model. Noseprint [45] can be used to detect splicing along with many other manipulations due to their spatial sensitivity. It can also be extended to videos [46].

7.3   Applications used to forge the multimedia

There are several ways of manipulating multimedia, and new techniques are being developed by the day. Adding, replicating, or deleting objects are normal operations. You may insert new objects into the multimedia by copying them from separate images (splicing) or from the same file (copy-move). A current object may also be removed by stretching it to cover it. With widespread image processing software, both of these functions can be quickly achieved. Any postprocessing requirements, such as resizing, rotation, or color changes may be required to properly align the object to the scene in order to improve the visual appearance as shown in Figure 7.2 which shows the image before and after postprocessing functions such as color adjustments, resizing, and rotation.

Comparative results are obtained by sophisticated computer graphics (CG) techniques and profound learning strategies for greater semantic accuracy. "Cheap fakes" are identified as forgeries that do not need sophisticated AI software, but have major manipulating effects on reality.

Deep learning and computer graphics strategies often include a modern range of methods helpful in this manipulation. A media resource may be fully synthesized from scratch. Autoencoders and generative adversarial networks have made it possible to create effective solutions for this purpose, in particular for face synthesis, where a high level of photo-realism has been achieved. You may also construct a completely synthetic image or video using the segmentation map as data. A picture synthesis is also feasible using either a drawing or a text description. Similarly, a person's face may be animated on the basis of an audio input sequence. Most specifically, alteration modifies original images or videos. For example, the transition of styles such as revisions, shifts in the motif of a painting, improvements in the

Figure 7.2   Image before and after postprocessing functions such as color adjustments, resizing, and rotation

presentation of an entity, and a reproduction of a picture in a different season which are well known. A variety of different studies have been performed to try to access knowledge from faces, including those with high semantic sense (Faces, Faces Target, and Entertain, 99Faces, HTK, etc.). There has been a method suggested for modifying the expression of a face to move the expression from a source to a target actor or to on-face turn faces.

Lastly, it has also recently been seen that successful facial alteration is feasible without the use of a sequence of images of the targeted person. No matter the movie's genre, a still portrait's expression can also be animated and a multitude of emotions can be expressed. Several recent experiments have attempted to explore the human reaction to the way that someone moves and are attempting to incorporate that to machine hardware for the video game industry. How realistic the deep fakes look and the potential automatic editing capabilities available can be easily observed.

Few of the prominent applications to manipulate multimedia are as follows:

Picasa: It is an exceptional multimedia-related method for displaying, arranging, and manipulating photographs on a laptop.

Adobe Photoshop: It was designed for Windows and Mac OS raster graphics editing. The multimedia program supports and has its file format in different graphics file formats (PSB and PSD).

Inkscape: Inkscape is software to create as well as edit vector images. The special aspect of Inkscape is that it can accept images in many formats, but image editing takes place in the scalable vector graphics format (SVG).

GIMP: It is Adobe Photoshop's alternative open-source tool. The [GIMP] is an acronym for GNU image manipulation program. It is used mostly for photo retouching, the composition of photographs, and the authoring of images.

Krita: It is a graphics editor that is free and open source, specifically for visual painting and animations.

Blender: It is a 3D development suite that, along with video editing, 3D pipeline modelling, rigging, animation, modelling, visualization, layout, and motion monitoring are provided.

A few of the most trending applications for "face swap" in recent times have been REFACE, Face Swap Live, Snapchat, Face Stealer, Face Swap Booth, MSQRD, Cupace, Reflect: Realistic Face Swap, and several other applications.

7.4 Current challenges and future of the technology

Although there has been impressive progress in working with the DeepFake detection methods, there are many concerns about existing search methods that suggest caution.

7.4.1 Quality of DeepFake dataset

The accessibility of vast DeepFake databases enables DeepFake recognition techniques to be developed. In any case, current datasets show a few good graphic quality comparisons to the real DeepFake videos on the site. Low-quality synthesized images, visible splicing thresholds, color bungles, visible portions of the initial mask, and contradictory synthesized face orientations are typical visual anomalies that can be experienced. High detection performance on the datasets may not be fitting to identify imitation when the strategies are conveyed within the wild [47].

7.4.2   Performance evaluation

DeepFake dispute, on the other side, is evaluated as a definition, remedy, and binary classification issue about manipulated footage. In supervised studies, it is simple to set up such a classification. However, as the analysis approach is employed in the modern world, the scene gets more unpredictable. For example, videos other than DeepFake may be produced or modified. So if it does not seem like a profound video, it does not imply that it's a genuine video. DeepfFake video may be subject to other forms of exploitation, and not one mark is enough to represent such manipulation. It is necessary to expand the binary classification to identify multiple classes, multiple labels, and local data to handle the actual data manipulation complexity.

7.4.3   Explainability of detection results

Current techniques for identification are meant to conduct batch processing of video databases, but only a limited percentage of images are reviewed by journalist/law enforcement authorities. Useful numerical analyses of videos cannot prove that videos would be generated using computer networks. These situations are important in order to demonstrate the essential essence of the job. Due to the black-box design of the DNN model, several DF detection techniques (data-driven) focused on deep neural networks are not clarified.

7.4.4   Temporal aggregation

Current DeepFake detection strategies depend on twofold classification at the frame level. They decide whether an individual frame is genuine or manipulated.

This method has two main issues:

Firstly, the transient consistency among frames is not explicitly considered as numerous manipulated videos display transient artifacts and real/DeepFake frames tend to appear in continuous intervals.

Secondly, it requires an additional step when a video-level integrity score is required (scores over individual frames need to be aggregated to compute such integrity score at video level).

7.4.5   Social media laundering

Most images are currently shared through social networks such as Facebook, WhatsApp, Retweet, and Instagram. To conserve network space and maintain consumer anonymity, these videos are stripped of meta-data, compressed, and downsized before being posted to a website called social networking laundering. These are negative for the recovery of the traces of the required manipulations. It also classifies a number of actual videos as manipulated videos owing to this kind of laundering.

A practical measure to improve the robustness of social media laundering DeepFake detection strategies is to efficiently coordinate simulations of such impacts into training information and create assessment datasets to incorporate genuinely and synthesized social media laundered images.

In the past few years, intense research and significant progress were observed in multimedia forensics. However, there are still many difficulties, each day new obstacles are arising and it still continues to be a long path. The emergence of deep learning has brought extraordinary impetus to media manipulation and forensic tools, generating new fields of study. The presence of professional criminals means that there will still be no resources to secure multimedia, and innovative strategies will be required to comply with the attacks. Thus, the most important fields for potential study are as follows.

7.4.5.1   *Fusion*

As operations become increasingly intelligent, detection tools are becoming less effective against various attacks. Hence, numerous discovery tools, multiple networks, and numerous approaches ought to be practiced together, and the best combination of all available information must be the goal of a more sustainable investigation. Individual media possessions ought to be analyzed with all correlated evidence. For instance, images/videos utilized to convey fake news should not be investigated exclusively but ought to be analyzed with accompanying text, sound, and all accessible, relevant data [48]. Based on additional data accessible, the methodology may be updated. Finally, as envisaged by DARPA's Semantics Forensics project, certain semantic analyses could be conducted.

7.4.5.2   *Interpretability*

The black-box design of deep learning makes it impossible to explain why an individual strategy choice is taken. For particular forensic applications, this is a genuine concern. For illustration, a judge can barely base choices on measurable bases alone. More broadly, checking the thinking of a deep network will permit its design and training process to be progressed and give more prominent robustness concerning malicious attacks.

Digital watermarking has been under considerable study in recent years [49]. Blockchain technology [50] and cryptography [51] have now gone on to be important and even modern methods to digital media credibility or to protect the victims of AI attacks are proposed [52]. As already stated, considering its long background and strong requirements from the industry and from society, multimedia forensics continue to be established and a significant volume of input still remains.

7.5   Conclusion

Multimedia forensics was a specialty field of strategic significance only for a small group of law enforcement, intelligence, and private investigators 15 years ago. Both attacks and defenses had a handcrafted flavor and demanded consideration and dedication. The laws have been significantly changed by deep learning. High-grade counterfeiters now appear to arise from a line that calls for extraordinary efforts from scientists and policymakers. In reality, today's multimedia forensics are witnessing total development, major institutions fund large research programs, and scientists from many places participate actively, with rapid progress in ideas and tools. A large variety of instruments are currently being created, and awareness of certain methods and principles on which they rely and their scope of application is a prerequisite for the security of institutions and ordinary citizens.

References

[1]   Farid, H. "Image forgery detection." IEEE Signal Processing Magazine. 2009; 26(2): 16–25.

[2]   Farid, H. *Photo forensics*. Cambridge, MA: MIT Press; 2016.

[3]   Swaminathan, A., Wu, M., and Liu, K. R. "Digital image forensics via intrinsic fingerprints." IEEE Transactions on Information Forensics and Security. 2008; 3(1), 101–117.

[4]   Johnson, M. K., and Farid, H. "Exposing digital forgeries through chromatic aberration." In *Proceedings of the 8th Workshop on Multimedia and Security* (pp. 48–55). 2006.

[5]   Yerushalmy, I., and Hel-Or, H. "Digital image forgery detection based on lens and sensor aberration." International Journal of Computer Vision. 2011; 92(1): 71–91.

[6]   Fu, H., and Cao, X. "Forgery authentication in extreme wide-angle lens using distortion cue and fake saliency map." IEEE Transactions on Information Forensics and Security. 2012; 7(4), 1301–1314.

[7]   Bayram, S., Sencar, H., Memon, N., and Avcibas, I. "Source camera identification based on CFA interpolation." In IEEE International Conference on Image Processing 2005 (Vol. 3, pp. III-69). IEEE; 2005.

[8]   Cao, H., and Kot, A. C. "Accurate detection of demosaicing regularity for digital image forensics." IEEE Transactions on Information Forensics and Security. 2009; 4(4): 899–910.

[9]   Popescu, A. C., and Farid, H. "Exposing digital forgeries in color filter array interpolated images." IEEE Transactions on Signal Processing. 2005; 53 (10): 3948–3959.

[10]   Ferrara, P., Bianchi, T., De Rosa, A., and Piva, A. "Image forgery localization via fine-grained analysis of CFA artifacts." IEEE Transactions on Information Forensics and Security. 2012; 7(5): 1566–1577.

[11]   Popescu, A. C., and Farid, H. "Statistical tools for digital forensics." In *International Workshop on Information Hiding* (pp. 128–147). Berlin, Heidelberg; Springer; 2004.

[12]   Cozzolino, D., Poggi, G., and Verdoliva, L. "Splicebuster: A new blind image splicing detector." In 2015 IEEE International Workshop on Information Forensics and Security (WIFS) (pp. 1–6). IEEE; 2015.

[13]   Ding, X., Yang, G., Li, R., Zhang, L., Li, Y., and Sun, X. "Identification of motion-compensated frame rate up-conversion based on residual signals."

IEEE Transactions on Circuits and Systems for Video Technology. 2017; 28(7): 1497–1512.

[14] Fan, Z., and De Queiroz, R. L. "Identification of bitmap compression history: JPEG detection and quantizer estimation." IEEE Transactions on Image Processing. 2003; 12(2), 230–235.

[15] Chen, Y. L., and Hsu, C. T. "Detecting recompression of JPEG images via periodicity analysis of compression artifacts for tampering detection." IEEE Transactions on Information Forensics and Security. 2011; 6(2): 396–406.

[16] Barni, M., Costanzo, A., and Sabatini, L. "Identification of cut and paste tampering by means of double-JPEG detection and image segmentation." In Proceedings of 2010 IEEE International Symposium on Circuits and Systems (pp. 1687–1690). IEEE; 2010.

[17] Farid, H. "Exposing digital forgeries from JPEG ghosts." IEEE Transactions on Information Forensics and Security. 2009; 4(1): 154–160.

[18] Gironi, A., Fontani, M., Bianchi, T., Piva, A., and Barni, M. "A video forensic technique for detecting frame deletion and insertion." In 2014 IEEE International Conference on Acoustics, Speech and Signal Processing (ICASSP) (pp. 6226–6230). IEEE; 2014.

[19] Kirchner, M. "Fast and reliable resampling detection by spectral analysis of fixed linear predictor residue." In Proceedings of the 10th ACM Workshop on Multimedia and Security (pp. 11–20). 2008.

[20] Dong, J., Wang, W., Tan, T., and Shi, Y. Q. "Run-length and edge statistics based approach for image splicing detection." In *International Workshop on Digital Watermarking* (pp. 76–87). Berlin, Heidelberg: Springer; 2008.

[21] Christlein, V., Riess, C., Jordan, J., Riess, C., and Angelopoulou, E. "An evaluation of popular copy-move forgery detection approaches." IEEE Transactions on Information Forensics and Security. 2012; 7(6): 1841–1854.

[22] Wu, Y., Jiang, X., Sun, T., and Wang, W. "Exposing video inter-frame forgery based on velocity field consistency." In *2014 IEEE International Conference on Acoustics, Speech and Signal Processing (ICASSP)* (pp. 2674–2678). IEEE; 2014.

[23] Lukáš, J., Fridrich, J., and Goljan, M. "Detecting digital image forgeries using sensor pattern noise." In Security, Steganography, and Watermarking of Multimedia Contents VIII (Vol. 6072, p. 60720Y). International Society for Optics and Photonics. 2006.

[24] Chen, M., Fridrich, J., Lukáš, J., and Goljan, M. "Imaging sensor noise as digital x-ray for revealing forgeries." In International Workshop on Information Hiding (pp. 342–358). Berlin, Heidelberg: Springer; 2007.

[25] Cozzolino, D., Gragnaniello, D., and Verdoliva, L. "Image forgery localization through the fusion of camera-based, feature-based and pixel-based techniques." In 2014 IEEE International Conference on Image Processing (ICIP) (pp. 5302–5306). IEEE; 2014.

[26] Cozzolino, D., Marra, F., Poggi, G., Sansone, C., and Verdoliva, L. "PRNU-based forgery localization in a blind scenario." In *International Conference on Image Analysis and Processing* (pp. 569–579). Cham: Springer; 2017.

[27] He, J., Lin, Z., Wang, L., and Tang, X. "Detecting doctored JPEG images via DCT coefficient analysis." In European Conference on Computer Vision (pp. 423–435). Berlin, Heidelberg; Springer; 2006.

[28] Ng, T. T., and Tsui, M. P. "Camera response function signature for digital forensics-part I: theory and data selection." In 2009 First IEEE International Workshop on Information Forensics and Security (WIFS) (pp. 156–160). IEEE; 2009.

[29] Farid, H., and Lyu, S. "Higher-order wavelet statistics and their application to digital forensics." In 2003 Conference on computer vision and pattern recognition workshop (Vol. 8, pp. 94–94). IEEE; 2003.

[30] Cozzolino, D., Gragnaniello, D., and Verdoliva, L. "Image forgery detection through residual-based local descriptors and block-matching." In 2014 IEEE International Conference on Image Processing (ICIP) (pp. 5297–5301). IEEE; 2014.

[31] Wang, Q., and Zhang, R. "Double JPEG compression forensics based on a convolutional neural network." EURASIP Journal on Information Security. 2016; 2016(1): 1–12.

[32] Nam, S. H., Park, J., Kim, D., Yu, I. J., Kim, T. Y., and Lee, H. K. "Two-stream network for detecting double compression of H. 264 videos." In 2019 IEEE International Conference on Image Processing (ICIP) (pp. 111–115). IEEE; 2019.

[33] He, K., Zhang, X., Ren, S., and Sun, J. "Deep residual learning for image recognition." In Proceedings of the IEEE Conference on Computer Vision and Pattern Recognition (pp. 770–778). 2016.

[34] Salloum, R., Ren, Y., and Kuo, C. C. J. "Image splicing localization using a multi-task fully convolutional network (MFCN)." Journal of Visual Communication and Image Representation. 2018; 51: 201–209.

[35] Wu, Y., Abd-Almageed, W., and Natarajan, P. "Image copy-move forgery detection via an end-to-end deep neural network." In 2018 IEEE Winter Conference on Applications of Computer Vision (WACV) (pp. 1907–1915). IEEE; 2018.

[36] Barni, M., Phan, Q. T., and Tondi, B. "Copy move source-target disambiguation through multi-branch CNNs." IEEE Transactions on Information Forensics and Security. 2020.

[37] Wang, S. Y., Wang, O., Owens, A., Zhang, R., and Efros, A. A. "Detecting photoshopped faces by scripting photoshop." In Proceedings of the IEEE/CVF International Conference on Computer Vision (pp. 10072–10081). 2019.

[38] Fridrich, J., and Kodovsky, J. "Rich models for steganalysis of digital images." IEEE Transactions on Information Forensics and Security. 2012; 7(3): 868–882.

[39] Rao, Y., and Ni, J. "A deep learning approach to detection of splicing and copy-move forgeries in images." In 2016 IEEE International Workshop on Information Forensics and Security (WIFS) (pp. 1–6). IEEE; 2016.

[40] Zhou, P., Chen, B. C., Han, X., Najibi, M., Shrivastava, A., Lim, S. N., and Davis, L. "Generate, segment, and refine: Towards generic manipulation segmentation." In *Proceedings of the AAAI Conference on Artificial Intelligence* (Vol. 34, No. 07, pp. 13058–13065). 2020.

[41] Marra, F., Gragnaniello, D., Verdoliva, L., and Poggi, G. "A full-image full-resolution end-to-end-trainable CNN framework for image forgery detection." *IEEE Access*. 2020; 8, 133488–133502.

[42] Cozzolino, D., and Verdoliva, L. "Single-image splicing localization through autoencoder-based anomaly detection." In 2016 IEEE international workshop on information forensics and security (WIFS) (pp. 1–6). IEEE; 2016.

[43] D'Avino, D., Cozzolino, D., Poggi, G., and Verdoliva, L. "Autoencoder with recurrent neural networks for video forgery detection." Electronic Imaging. 2017; 2017(7): 92–99.

[44] Cozzolino, D., and Verdoliva, L. "Noiseprint: A CNN-based camera model fingerprint." 2018. arXiv preprint arXiv:1808.08396.

[45] Verdoliva, D. C. G. P. L. "Extracting camera-based fingerprints for video forensics." In Proceedings of the IEEE/CVF Conference on Computer Vision and Pattern Recognition (CVPR) Workshops. 2019.

[46] Li, Y., Yang, X., Sun, P., Qi, H., and Lyu, S. "Celeb-DF: A large-scale challenging dataset for DeepFake forensics." In Proceedings of the IEEE/CVF Conference on Computer Vision and Pattern Recognition (pp. 3207–3216). 2020.

[47] Khattar, D., Goud, J. S., Gupta, M., and Varma, V. "MVAE: Multimodal variational autoencoder for fake news detection." In *The World Wide Web Conference* (pp. 2915–2921). 2019.

[48] Cox, I., Miller, M., Bloom, J., Fridrich, J., and Kalker, T. *Digital watermarking and steganography*. San Francisco, CA: Morgan Kaufmann; 2007.

[49] Boneh, D., Grotto, A. J., McDaniel, P., and Papernot, N. "How relevant is the turing test in the age of sophisbots?." IEEE Security & Privacy. 2019; 17(6): 64–71.

[50] Li, Y., Yang, X., Wu, B., and Lyu, S. "Hiding faces in plain sight: Disrupting ai face synthesis with adversarial perturbations." 2019. arXiv preprint arXiv:1906.09288.

[51] Hasan, H. R., and Salah, K. "Combating DeepFake videos using blockchain and smart contracts." IEEE Access. 2019; 7: 41596–41606.

[52] Barnes, C., Shechtman, E., Finkelstein, A., and Goldman, D. B. "PatchMatch: A randomized correspondence algorithm for structural image editing." ACM Transactions on Graphics. 2009' 28(3): 24.

Chapter 8

Vehicle control system based on eye, iris, and gesture recognition with eye tracking

Harpreet Kaur[1] and Chiranji Lal Chowdhary[2]

Abstract

In recent years, eye-gaze detection and monitoring has been an active area of research as it provides convenience to a range of applications. It is considered to be an effective nontraditional human computer interaction form. Detection of head movement has also gained the attention and interest of researchers as it has been found to be an easy and efficient form of interaction. The simplest alternative device approaches are considered by both technologies. They represent a significant number of chronically handicapped people with limited motor skills. Several different methods have been proposed and used for both eye tracking and head movement detection to incorporate various algorithms for these technologies. Researchers are also trying to find robust approaches to be used efficiently in different applications, considering the amount of research performed on both technologies. This chapter provides a study of the eye tracking and head motion identification approaches. Examples of various implementation areas are also discussed in both innovations, such as cooperation with the person and computer systems, driver assistance systems, and assistive technology.

Key Words: Detection; monitoring; human computer; handicapped; driver assistance

8.1 Introduction

Eye tracking is quickly gaining commercial popularity and soon will be a reality for things we see, use, and consume daily. Driving, gaming, and marketing are all on the verge of (if not already) incorporating this technology into their processes and tools. The concept of eye tracking technology was introduced years ago but it is finally

[1]Electrical Engineering Department, Chandigarh University, Mohali, India
[2]School of Information Technology and Engineering, VIT University, Vellore, India

gaining to the stamina through attractive start-ups, big funding, and innovative designs. In expressing a person's feelings, requirements and psychological declarations, eyes, and their movement are important [1]. It is certainly recognized the role of eye gestures in the understanding and exposure of the visual environment since it is the mechanism by which the information necessary to recognize the features of the visual world is processed in order to be used in the human brain. Good visual recognition and monitoring are therefore seen as critical to the advancement of interaction between person and machine, to the design of near user interfaces, and to the study of human mental states. Head movement is also a normal, quick, and efficacious way to point to objects, relationships, and contact. In recent studies, identification of head movement has also gained substantial interest. The consumer is allowed to communicate with a computer for the identification and monitoring of the head movement [2]. It also allows several instruments to be operated by mapping the head location in control signals. Face monitoring and identification of head movement as possible interface techniques are commonly discussed. It is easier to use than other approaches like speech recognition or EEG/ECG signals. Their precision and efficiency have also been improved. Furthermore, it benefits a vast spectrum of profoundly disabled individuals with limited abilities to conduct cooperative movement using the tracing of their eyes or heads as alternate device, control, or contact mechanisms. Face and head action are the least impaired since, for instance, damage to the spinal cord do not influence the ability to monitor them, because they are controlled directly by the brain. A greater range of potential control instructions can be used in assistive devices such as a wheel chair by integrating eye recognition and head motions identification. There are a variety of approaches to eye tracking introduced by different authors in the literature [3,4]. They can be used as the basis for designing a device for eye monitoring that achieves optimum precision, highest efficiency, and lowest costs. The identification of head movement has also gained heightened attention. Due to the flexibility of the algorithm used, some methods can be used with low computer hardware such as a microcontroller. A study of various eye monitoring and head motion recognition strategies has published in literature and examples of different implementations that use these technologies are provided in this article.

8.2 Eye tracking

Face tracking is either the point of sight (where you look) or the rotation of the eye in relation to the head. The eye tracker is an instrument to calculate the location of the eye and the motion of the eye. The eye trackers are used as an input device for human computer interaction and product creation for visual system testing, psychological research, psycholinguistic research, and marketing. Face tracking systems (in particular wheel chairs, robot arms, and protheses) are now increasingly used for rehabilitative and assisting applications [5]. Many tools are used to assess eye expression. Video clips from which the eye angle is derived are used with the most common version. Other techniques are based on the electrooculogram which uses search coils.

Eye Tracking is a sensing technology that lets you know where you are searching for a machine or other gadget. An eye tracker can sense the user's presence, concentration, and interest. It delivers unique knowledge on human activity and includes a wide variety of devices with natural user interfaces. The ability to manipulate a machine with the eyes is also important to people who cannot talk or use their hands. The geometric and motion properties of the eyes are uniquely important for measurement and control of the gazes, for example, for human attention analysis, human emotional state analysis, immersive software platforms, and human elements. In a wide variety of uses, there are several common methods for integrating vision recognition and monitoring technologies [6].

Three basic elements of an efficient eye monitoring device are described as follows:

- Specially designed sensors—The hardware is a high-performance detector and not built to take decent images. It requires specialized projection systems, custom image sensors, optics, and digital processing with integrated algorithms.
- Progressive algorithms—Algorithms are the machine brain, which interprets the sensors' image stream.
- User-oriented applications—The use of different methods of technology is allowed by an intelligent implementation layer.

8.2.1 How eye tracker works

The basic idea is to use an illumination source to illuminate the eye, which produces incredibly visible reflexes and a camera to record the picture of the eye that displays those reflections. Eye tracking is a way of studying the visual interest of people. The picture taken by the camera is then used for the reflection of the corneal (glint) and pupil of the light source. Near infrared light is directed to the middle of the eye (pupil). The pupil and cornea are seen to be reflective (the outermost optical element of the eye). The infrared camera monitors these reflexes—the vector between the cornea and the pupil [7,8]. This is the visual monitoring of corneal reflection, named the pupil center corneal reflection (PCCR).

An infrared source of light (and hence detection method) is required since the precision of the calculation of gaze direction depends both on a simple demarcation (and detection) of the pupil and on a detection of the corneal reflection. Regular light sources (with ordinary cameras) cannot produce as much contrast, which means a suitable amount of accuracy without infrared light is much harder to achieve. To guarantee your eye monitoring is as exact as possible, you must be mindful of your eyes as Figure 8.1 indicates. This is why the calibration is important. The eye sensor tests how the lights represent your eyes during the calibration process. A point, a film, or another graphically moving feature across the screen would be used to calibrate it [9]. These calibration data are then paired with our special 3D human eye model to provide you with an optimum eye tracking experience together.

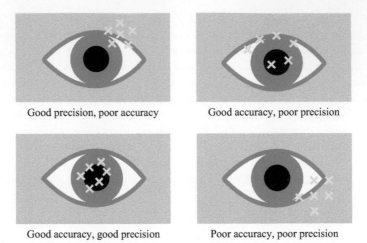

Good precision, poor accuracy   Good accuracy, poor precision

Good accuracy, good precision   Poor accuracy, poor precision

Figure 8.1   Calibration for better accuracy. Adapted from [9]

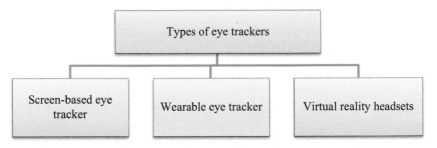

Figure 8.2   Classification of eye trackers

When using the gaze interaction, three methods to press are possible and the form available depends on the use. You also rely on your capability for the way you want to press.

- Blink—Blinking can be used as a click, but it is not the safest way to do so since you are losing attention.
- Dwell—A predefined number of milliseconds would center the attention on a certain region and then a clicking is carried out.
- Switch—It is also the easiest and most effective way to press if you can manage the turn. To pick the position you would like to click, use your eyes and then push the button to click.

Three major types of eye trackers are available: screen-based tracker (also called a remote or desktop), eye lenses or eye tracker, also known as handheld eye tracker, and VR headsets, as seen in Figure 8.2 [10]. Webcam-based eye-tracking was considered to be an alternative, but inherently not as good as infrared eye tracking technology.

8.2.1.1 Screen-based eye tracker

Screen-based devices enable participants to sit before a computer to communicate with show contents. Although these instruments measure the eyes only within certain limits (the so-called headbox), the movement is still reasonably broad for respondents (at least in terms of a normal range of movement while watching screen-based stimuli). The photo on the left of Figure 8.3 illustrates how an eye tracker based on a screen operates [10]. The main components for eye tracking are illuminators, cameras and the vision recognition, the 3D-eye model, and the view mapping algorithms in the treatment kit. Screen-based eye sensor captures visual data up to 1200 Hz. It delivers excellent data consistency and is equipped for detailed study of action and eye activity—from fixation experiments to micro saccades.

8.2.1.2 Wearable eye tracker

Figure 8.4 illustrates how an eye tracker works. Much as the equivalents on the screen, a wearable eye tracker consists of the same critical eye tracking elements: illuminators, sensors and the vision recognition processing unit, 3D eye pattern, and optical algorithms [10].

8.2.1.3 Virtual reality headset

A headset is a head-mounted system that gives the wearer augmented reality. In video games, virtual reality (VR) headsets are commonly used, but they also are used in other applications, including simulators and coaches. They have a stereoscopic head-mounted monitor, stereo sound, head-movement sensors which can include gyroscopes, accelerometers, magnetometers, organized light systems, etc, as seen in Figure 8.5, and eye tracking sensor and game controllers [11]. Some VR headsets also include eye tracking sensors.

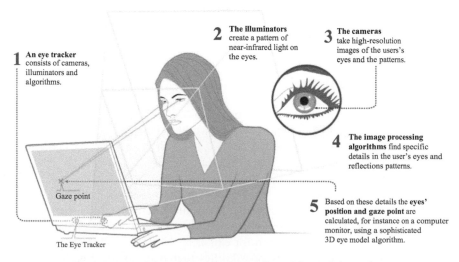

Figure 8.3   Screen-based eye tracker. Adapted from [10]

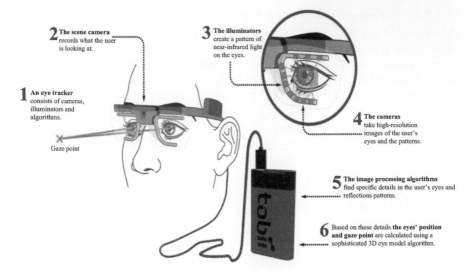

Figure 8.4   Wearable eye tracker. Adapted from [10]

Figure 8.5   Virtual reality headset. Adapted from [11]

8.3   Human gesture

Humans use gestures to interact with the environment. Gestures such as touching, grabbing, and dragging are used in the real world. Using this to control computers could make for a more natural interaction than what is currently used. Gestures and eye tracking have been used in many projects to enable a new sort of interaction, although it is often as separate inputs. Creating a multimodal interaction by combining eye tracking and gestures is an area which remains mostly unexplored.

While eye tracking and gestures have been separately developed and sold commercially, there has not been much research into combining the two in a commercial product. There is room for exploring whether combining eye tracking and gestures could lead to new possibilities that may not be possible by using gestures or eye tracking separately [12,13].

Gestures exist in many different forms. Some gestures are complex, such as sign language gestures. Other gestures are simpler, such as dragging the hand left, right, or closing the hand to select.

Looking at something on a computer screen may signal selection, but it is difficult to do activation using only the eyes without accidental activation [14]. With gestures, the problem somewhat lies in how the gestures should be interpreted. It is possible to have complex gestures which are location independent, or the gestures may be more general but instead depend on the location relative to the screen.

Eye gestures are a form of body language in which the eye movements and the pupil dilation are studied to understand the nonverbal communication. Taking note of eye gestures is a natural and important part of communication process. While evaluating body language close attention to eye gaze, eye movement, blinking, and pupil size can help better understand messages. Just like other forms of gestures, they allow individuals to communicate their feelings and thoughts nonverbally. They can be accompanied with other body language and words as well [15]. Eyes are a form of body language, in which nonverbal contact is studied by the action of the eye and the dilation of the pupils. Face movements are an essential and normal part of the communication process. When assessing the language of the body, closer exposure to the eye will help to better interpret signals through eye expression, twitch, and pupil sizes. Similar to other types of gestures, they encourage people to nonverbally express their thoughts and feelings. It may also be followed by other vocabulary and body language (Figure 8.6) [15].

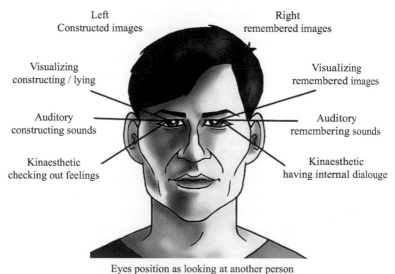

Left
Constructed images

Right
remembered images

Visualizing
constructing / lying

Visualizing
remembered images

Auditory
constructing sounds

Auditory
remembering sounds

Kinaesthetic
checking out feelings

Kinaesthetic
having internal dialouge

Eyes position as looking at another person

Figure 8.6   Eye position. Adapted from [15]

Based on the research and observation of people from different cultures and races all over the world, the patterns of eye movement are defined as follows during the different cognitive tasks (in relation to the person):

- Eyes up and left: visual remembered, that is, remembered imagery (Vr).
- Eyes up and right: visual constructed, that is, constructed imagery and visual fantasy (Vc).
- Eyes lateral left: auditory remembered, that is, remembered sounds, words, and "tape loops" (Ar) and tonal discrimination.

Combining gestures and eye tracking, the technologies can complement each other. The eye can signal where the user wants to interact, and the gesture can then signal what the user wants to do. By doing this, the separate parts can be simple—looking at a button and tapping with a finger to activate it.

Eyes lateral right: auditory constructed, that is, constructed sounds and words (Ac).

Eyes down and left: internal dialogue, or inner self-talk (Ad).

Eyes down and right: feelings, both tactile, and visceral (K).

Eyes straight ahead, but chromatic aberration or dilated: easy access to nearly all sensory information, but mostly visual. So upward gestures in the eye are dreaming, and so it is retrieving or creating words and pictures when viewed upwards. Whereas looking down is about emotion, respect, internal dialog, and so on. The analysis of the eye will help to explain whether or not the individual is concerned [16]. For example, immediate eye contact during the interaction may be of attention, while protracted eye connections can feel challenged and eye contacts may also break away. Too often blink may indicate pain or irritation, while uncommon blinkage may indicate a person willingly tries to regulate the eye movements. The student dilation can also be observed to understand the emotions of an individual.

In expressing a personal interest, desires, and emotional status, the eyes and their motions are critical. The relevance of the visual world's eye motions is known as the way to classify the features of a visual world for the purpose of processing the human brain [17]. The usefulness of eye motions for the visual world is definitely recognized. Therefore, robust eye recognition and control play a key role in the advancement of human-computer interaction, in the design of near user interfaces, and in the study of human affective conditions.

8.3.1   Head movement

Head movement is also a natural, transparent, and productive way to point at objects, contact, and conversation. In recent studies, the identification of head movement has gained considerable interest. One of the different uses of head tracking and identification is to allow the user to communicate with a computer [18]. This also allows several instruments to be operated by mapping the head location into control signals.

Head movement is a natural function to sensitize environmental events in our world. Head movement is of special significance in determining the location of a

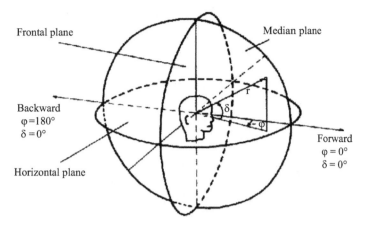

Frontal plane

Median plane

Backward
φ=180°
δ = 0°

Horizontal plane

Forward
φ = 0°
δ = 0°

Figure 8.7   Head coordinate system. Adapted from [19]

blind rear-facing target in order to deter danger or harm by way of listening. The horizontal plane is a plane that is cross to the head and parallel to the ground. The frontal plane is parallel to the face and perpendicular to the ground, and the median plane is nose sliced through. The coordinate system used in this analysis is shown in Figure 8.7.

The identification of eye tracks and head motion as alternate interface approaches was commonly studied. It is seen as easier to use than other approaches such as speech reconnaissance or EEG/ECG signals. They have also increased precision and performance. In addition, it allows for a wide variety of seriously handicapped individuals with minimum ability to willingly move by using eye monitoring or head motion recognition as an alternate interface, control, or contact strategies. Because eyes and head motions are directly governed by the brain, being less injured by them has no effect on their capacity to follow spinal cord injuries [19]. A greater range of potential control instructions can be used with assistive devices such as a roller chair by integrating eye monitoring with head movement recognition.

8.4   Applications of eye tracking

In 1947, the American air force made the first use of eye trackers to find the best control locations on an aircraft hood. It is easy to see where the look is going in expectation to find power while providing a new gadget for someone whose eyes are monitored. to solve the challenge. In the fields such as vision-based communication and human computers (HCI) and video games, recovery, simulation of drives, exhaustion recognition, cognitive sciences, communications analysis and advertisement monitoring, accessibility research, medical research, and car assistant devices, eye tracking technology advancements encourage you to make use of eye-based interfaces. An eye-gazing interface seems to be a promising candidate for a new application for an interface. Traditionally, individuals with disabilities who have no expression nor eyes have interactions with the body. The systems are configured solely for the eye to guide your computer. Such devices are useful for those who need them but they are bulky and less effective than keys and mouse for some. But it is nowadays possible for a person to use tracking based connections because of improvements in the architecture of eye tracking systems and high processing speed. The usability, interaction speed, maintenance free, hygienic interface, remote control, safer interaction, more information on user's behavior, and so forth make eye-tracking systems more common every day. The interaction could speed up via visual tracking interfaces as the eyes are fast. Video eye tracking operates without touching, so no maintenance is needed. An eye view GUI would be helpful in areas with high hygiene demands, such as a surgical operating room, as it permits interfaces without touching.

Eye monitoring provides an optical recording of the location and the movement of the eye based on corneal reflexes, allowing for an examination of the eye and focus in both 2D and 3D space. Early eye trackers were massive and burdensome—eye trackers are today as compact as a pencil case and expanding the future use cases to provide a more flexible appliance. It allows to evaluate human processing of visual evidence for immersive and medical applications. Any sector of science will benefit significantly from the gathering of quantitative data using a tool that does not discomfort participants [20]. Audio analysis is an effective method for every form of human behavior study applied in a number of fields including psychology, medicine, marketing, architecture, education and gaming as well as for optimizing human computer interaction by using the eyes for navigation and power, as seen in Figure 8.8 and discussed below. Eye tracking tracks focus, curiosity, and enthusiasm.

- Academic and scientific research

    There is no doubt that the academic and scientific fields are making the most of eye-tracking applications in psychology, neuroscience, growth, experiment, and media.
- Market research

    In recent years, eye monitoring has been particularly relevant for market analysis. Often major businesses use this instrument to analyze their goods, styles, advertisements, and even their consumers' purchasing habits to improve customer overall experience. By measuring the vision, attention to brands, products, and their main messaging can be assessed and store navigation is simple or challenging.
- Psychology research

    In this region, visual focus can be assessed and connected to other actions like the workings of the brain. Visual emphasis should be achieved on normal people as well as particular sub-populations with visible personality behaviors or varying forms of mental health issues.
- Medical research

    Face monitoring paired with traditional testing techniques or other biosensors can also help to detect disorders including attention deficit hyperactivity disorder (ADHD), autism spectra disorder (ASD), obsessive compulsive disorder (OCD), schizophrenia, Parkinson's, and Alzheimer's.

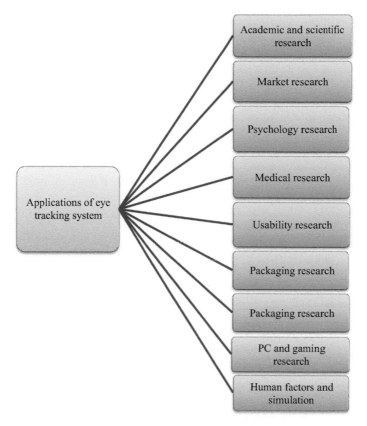

Figure 8.8   Applications of eye tracking system

- Usability research

    The use of these methodologies is an emerging area for eye monitoring and user experience. Website checking is a classic example. In this regard, the concern can be calculated for property, contact, and call to action (CTA).
- Packaging research

    In addition, a lot of money is spent in developing a goods kit before they are put on the market. In particular, this is the case for quickly moving consumer products because competition is very difficult. It is important to ensure that a product package receives ample visual exposure on the shelf, thereby separating it from other products. The key aim of eye monitoring is to develop packages and consider customers' tastes.
- PC and gaming research

    In the area of interaction and play, eye tracking has now been introduced, which today, for example, enables game makers to develop a deeper understanding of the game world, so that it is possible to influence the environment and develop features that further stretch the boundaries of reality.

- Human factors and simulation

  Automotive testing has long been using eye-tracking glasses to test drivers' visual focus—both in navigation and in a dashboard style. In the near future, cars can respond to their driver's eyes, eye movements, or the pupil's expansion. The above-mentioned applications are only the most widely used in surveys. Eye tracking is not limited, however, and can be much more effective in combination with additional biometric sensors [21–23].

  – **ADAS:** Advanced driver-assistance systems (ADAS) are an automated system that assists drivers in driving and parking functions. ADAS improves vehicle and road safety by a safe human-machine interface. Automated technologies such as sensors and cameras are used by ADAS systems to detect and respond to nearby barriers or driver errors [23].

Because of human negligence, most traffic accidents occur. Advanced driver assistance systems are systems intended to simplify, adjust, and expand automotive safety and driving systems. Automated ADAS devices have been shown to minimize road fatality by reducing human error. Protection features help to deter injuries and crashes by providing technology to advise drivers of problems, apply precautions and, if necessary, gain control of a car. Adaptive characteristics are capable of automating lighting, adaptive cruise maintenance, assisting in preventing colloids, including Sat Nav/traffic alerting, providing protection for barriers and lane centering, providing mobile steering assistance, and offering even more features [24].

Advanced driver assistance systems (ADAS) are capable of dramatically improving road safety. They can warn or help drivers avoid or minimize accidents. These devices are fitted with additional vehicles every year and sold. The Annual Engine Accident Report, carried out by the National Highway Safety Board showed that driver negligence in 94% of accidents was critical. The main part of these concerns are drivers who struggle to recognize threats and distractions. Many of the most popular ADAS technologies are designed to recognize possible hazards and respond to them more rapidly than a human driver [25].

Essential safety-critical ADAS applications include:

- Blind spot detection
- Pedestrian detection/avoidance
- Traffic sign recognition
- Lane departure warning/correction
- Automatic emergency braking.

These life-saving systems are critical to the performance of ADAS applications with the new interface requirements and the operation of several vision-based algorithms to enable multimedia, vision co-processing, and fusion of sensor subsystems in real-time. ADAS apps' "smart phonezation" are the first steps in the development of autonomous cars. Automobiles form the basis for the next generation of mobile devices with fast advancement in autonomous vehicles [26]. Autonomous technologies are split into chips called SoCs (systems on a chip).

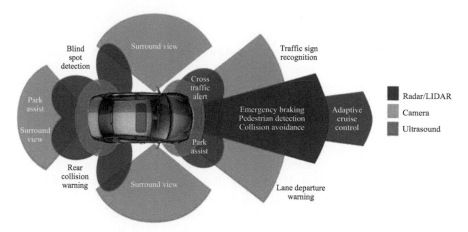

Figure 8.9   Advanced driver assistance systems. Adapted from [28]

These chips connect sensors via interfaces and high-power ECUs (electronic controller units) to actuators.

Self-driving vehicles use a range of these applications and technologies to create a 360° view, near and far. This means that hardware designs use advanced process nodes not only to achieve performance goals that are even higher but also to reduce power and footprint demands (Figure 8.9) [27,28].

8.5   Top eye tracking hardware companies

Face monitoring is becoming more indispensable in 2020. Eye monitoring technology in too many situations is a crucial improvement, regardless of whether psychology research, consumer research, usability testing, or other human care research was carried out. By integrating eye tracking with iMotions, it is quick and clear to map visual focus to any of the above-listed regions. Below are the top-ranked eye tracking companies [29]:

- **Tobii:** It was established in 2001 in Stockholm and has been a pioneer in eye tracking with an overwhelming number of publications that use its software. It has proven to be a flexible and enormous organization by offering eye monitoring units for testing, assistive devices, and gaming. They manufacture screen-based eye-tracking units and eye-tracking units with glasses and eye-tracking headsets
- **SMI** (senso motoric instruments): For over 26 years, SMI was evaluated as an experienced manufacturer of eye monitoring devices. SMI was bought by Apple and till today over 6,000 units are sold and this is featured in many newspapers. They have provided both glass and VR eye monitoring.
- **Eye Link:** Eye Connect eye trackers are produced by SR research that offers various solutions, including handheld and head-mounted devices. Its equipment

was used in thousands of journals, which makes it an incredibly effective eye tracking competitor.

- **Smart Eye:** Smart Eye started in 1999 and now comprises eye monitoring systems as well as head tracking units. Smart Eye is an organization that partners with vehicle makers and in the area of flight simulators to help develop travel.
- **LC technologies:** This was established in 1986 and soon the Eye gaze device has been developed (in the basement of Virginia). With their computer-based settings, binocular and even monocular eye monitoring is available.
- **Gazepoint:** For 10 years, Gaze point has been designing eye trackers and is headquartered in Canada offering testing, UX design, and usability test equipment.
- **The Eye Tribe:** The Eye Tribe was founded as an eye monitoring firm in 2007 in Copenhagen. The systems have been built to be usable with the intention of improving the productivity of ordinary users' experiences with the technology.
- **Pupil Labs:** It is an open source technology and hackable visibility monitoring company that provides very modern Berlin-based solutions. The company has relatively inexpensive and personalizable eye monitoring units focused on architecture and esthetics, as can be seen by Pupil Labs Invisible, their newest offering.
- **Mirametrix**: In 2011, Mirametrix began to offer small USB-connected visual monitoring units in Montréal but it has now developed a proprietary app framework that focuses on the user interface.
- **Ergoneers:** Established in Munich in 2005, Ergoneers now offers portable eye monitoring tools as well as broad-based simulation driving systems for vehicles. The business promotes real-world driving and benchmarking research.
- **Eyetech:** For over two decades, Eyetech Automated Solutions has been delivering testing eye detection and assistive technologies. Centered in Arizona, the organization was the first to build a USB eye monitoring unit and it has operated more than 10,000 facilities globally.
- **Argus Science LLC:** It was founded just across Boston, USA, by an engineering company devoted to improving eye-tracking equipment of the next generation. Their glasses are used in fields ranging from scholarly and business research to sports performance [30,31].

8.6 Case studies

Below are some of the important case studies [32,33]:

- **Smashbox and beauty recommendations**

    The increased realism in the beauty industry is becoming commonplace as multiple brands introduce AR focused applications to create a more engaging user interface. As a useful AR technology feature, eye-tracking technology is being launched too. The firm behind the successful AR application, Mascara, collaborated in 2017 with Smashbox Modiface. The goods of Smashbox were the first to be publicly used in the Make-up app and also the company has tested eye monitoring apps through Modiface to identify users' interests. Essentially, Smashbox helps you to decide where the focus is and allows the brand to promote or suggest special items. For instance, if a customer lingers with an eye-shadow or a mascara but takes action, the company will then in subsequent marketing campaigns actively bring its focus back to this product. Smashbox also uses the technology to test and evaluate the placing of call-to-action buttons in addition to identifying the most common items. To demonstrate the influence of technology, the marketing teams divided 889 app users into two categories: One of them has a call-to-action button positioned permanently at the top of the page; the second only saw the effect after engaging with the device. Results showed that the conversion rate for the second category rose from 6.2% to 7.9% justifying the use of this technology and shows that this can lead to driving sales in real-time.

- **Palace resorts and personalized marketing**

    Eye-Tracking technology is very recent but has been used for some time with webcams (particularly for UX research). Palace Resorts, however, integrates a camera tech into its new online marketing strategy, offering a tailored interface for the customer focused on their eyes. The campaign includes a microsite where tourists will take part in a questionnaire: dubbed "Never Raise a finger" (a nod to brand's high-end luxury standing). By flipping on the camera of your machine, you can pick your favorite type of Palace getaway by selecting the categories you like (for instance, "upscale" restaurants, or "lodge-restaurants").

- **GSK and product development**

    GSK, a global pioneer in customer health care, has meanwhile used eye surveillance technologies for a much more operational and traditional purpose. A 'Sensory Consumer Laboratory' has been launched to research the products using eye tracking and monitoring systems. The "Shopper Science Lab" looks and sounds like an actual store, which helps real customers to search and shop under study. The technology for eye monitoring allows the brand to observe how customers communicate with shelving items and what packaging (or pieces of it) attracts most. Based on this experience, the organization will prepare and improve new goods (or make improvements to the existing ones). For example, if anyone exhibits a high degree of fixation or repeats a fixation, copying the product might be tougher to process or overly difficult. Market monitoring is without a doubt one of the most common ways in which businesses use technology, but GSK reveals how many invest in it on a broad footing.

- **Toyota and its in-store experience**

    Just as retail arrangements, car showrooms will have a major effect on customer purchasing. Toyota has worked with eye monitoring specialists Tobii Pro in the effort to learn and develop their own showroom to figure out how guests communicate during the surf. Before visiting the immersive showroom, the 92 attendees were split into two categories—millennials and others. Of course, two key points have been protected by the Eye Tracking Technologies. First of all, younger shoppers spent more time on digitally interactive elements, while older shoppers concentrated on textual content. But ultimately it was found that immersive digital displays created the most effort to prove that this is an efficient way to take customers down the road. Eye-tracking technology not only gives general knowledge but may have a direct impact on revenue for car brands such as Toyota. The explanation being the use of showrooms by car shoppers for a single order, so it is crucial for brands to recognize the most important features.

8.7   Conclusion

Detection of eye and head expression is known to be efficient and accurate contact between human machine and alternative communication methods. Therefore, several academic activities have been ongoing. In the literature, many applications will profit from the use of efficient methods of eye monitoring and/or head movement sensing. Many applications are documented for these technologies. The inquiry is however already faced with difficulties in providing robust methods to reliably identify and trace movements of the eye or head in applications. Methods of eye tracking seldom research the CPU time required. In real-time implementations, however, the performance specifications must be analyzed and optimized. Furthermore, most experiments do not use a known image archive to assess eye tracking that includes differing photographs of various participants under different conditions, including lighting conditions, noise, distance, etc. As it may be influenced by various test conditions, the stated exact approach is less accurate.

Detection of head movement requires high hardware computing. A microcontroller known to be low computing hardware cannot use algorithms reported in the literature to incorporate head movement detection. Further work and analysis are required to provide accurate and useful eye monitoring and head motion detection methods for true applications.

Eye motion is guided both by visual world properties and processes in the mind of an individual. Face gestures are an invaluable technique for psychology and are specific between vision and cognition. The eye motions of a subject will provide a complex, diverse database for the temporal processes and psycho-processing contributing to response in contrast with the single point given by the button-press reaction time. These characteristics are also very useful for designers and engineers because they allow accurate evaluation of how a user communicates with a system. With the highly efficient technologies, such information can now be returned in real-time to computers and the action of the eye of users is used for commands or personalized computing processes. While the most basic of all human activities can be found in these systems, they can offer the fluidest and most expressive interface between people and machines.

In the future, the use of eye-patterning technology can be influenced in several respects. Obviously, the areas listed above are not the only areas that are influenced by observing eye movements. However, they have shown great potential to make the most of ever more available technologies. Expanded awareness about their use is being made more common in areas where eye monitoring is more common (psychology, promotion, human factors, etc.) The number of publications using these devices is increasing year after year within each sector.

References

[1]   Carter, B. T., and Luke, S. G. "Best practices in eye tracking research". *International Journal of Psychophysiology*. 2020; 155: 49–62.

[2]   Sharafi, Z., Sharif, B., Guéhéneuc, Y. G., Begel, A., Bednarik, R., and Crosby, M. "A practical guide on conducting eye tracking studies in software engineering." *Empirical Software Engineering*. 2020; 25(5): 3128–3174.

[3]   Pérez-Edgar, K., MacNeill, L. A., and Fu, X. "Navigating through the experienced environment: Insights from mobile eye tracking." *Current Directions in Psychological Science*. 2020; 29(3): 286–292.

[4]   Dolcos, F., Bogdan, P. C., O'Brien, M., *et al.* "The impact of focused attention on emotional evaluation: An eye-tracking investigation." *Emotion*. 2020.

[5]   Lim, Jia Zheng, James Mountstephens, and Jason Teo. "Emotion recognition using eye-tracking: Taxonomy, review and current challenges." *Sensors*. 2020; 20(8): 2384.

[6]   Jacob, R. J. "Eye tracking in advanced interface design." *Virtual Environments and Advanced Interface Design*. 1995; 258: 288.

[7]   Poole, A., and Ball, L. J. "Eye tracking in HCI and usability research." *In Encyclopedia of human computer interaction* (pp. 211–219). IGI Global; 2006.

[8]   Wedel, M., and Pieters, R. "A review of eye-tracking research in marketing." *Review of Marketing Research*. 2008.

[9]   See https://www.tobiidynavox.com/support-training/eye-tracker-calibration/

[10] See https://www.bitbrain.com/blog/eye-tracking-devices

[11] Harezlak, K., and Kasprowski, P. "Application of eye tracking in medicine: A survey, research issues and challenges." *Computerized Medical Imaging and Graphics*. 2018; 65: 176–190.

[12] Venugopal, D., Amudha, J., and Jyotsna, C. "Developing an application using eye tracker." In *2016 IEEE International Conference on Recent Trends in Electronics, Information & Communication Technology (RTEICT)* (pp. 1518-1522). IEEE; 2016.

[13] Jacob, R. J. K., and Karn, K. S. "Commentary on Section 4 - Eye tracking in human-computer interaction and usability research: Ready to deliver the

promises." In *The Mind's Eye*, Hyönä, J., Radach, R., and Deubel, H., editors (pp. 573–605). Amsterdam: North-Holland; 2003.

[14]   Zheng, S., Chen, Y., and Wang, C. "Application of eye-tracking technology in humanities, social sciences and geospatial cognition." In *Spatial synthesis* (pp. 431–448). Cham: Springer; 2020.

[15]   See https://www.sustainableevolution.com/blog-1/2015/8/13/neuro-linguistic-programming-part-5-calibration

[16]   Tono, Y. "Application of eye-tracking in EFL learners' dictionary look-up process research." *International Journal of Lexicography*. 2011; 24(1): 124–153.

[17]   Punde, P. A., Jadhav, M. E., and Manza, R. R. "A study of eye tracking technology and its applications." *2017 1st International Conference on Intelligent Systems and Information Management (ICISIM), Aurangabad*, 2017, pp. 86–90. doi: 10.1109/ICISIM.2017.8122153.

[18]   Vass, C., Rigby, D., Tate, K., Stewart, A., and Payne, K. "An exploratory application of eye-tracking methods in a discrete choice experiment." *Medical Decision Making*. 2018; 38(6): 658–672.

[19]   See https://iobridger.wordpress.com/spatial-sonification-of-data-2/sound-synthesis-sonification-and-spatialization/spatialization/acoustics/coordinate-system/

[20]   Blascheck, T., Kurzhals, K., Raschke, M., Burch, M., Weiskopf, D., and Ertl, T. "State-of-the-art of visualization for eye tracking data." In *EuroVis (STARs)*. 2014.

[21]   Fink, L. K., Lange, E. B., and Groner, R. "The application of eye-tracking in music research." *Journal of Eye Movement Research*. 2018; 11(2).

[22]   Zheng, S., Chen, Y., and Wang, C. "Application of eye-tracking technology in humanities, social sciences and geospatial cognition." In *Spatial synthesis* (pp. 431–448). Cham: Springer; 2020.

[23]   Holmqvist, K., Nyström, M., Andersson, R., Dewhurst, R., Jarodzka, H., and Van de Weijer, J. "Eye tracking: A comprehensive guide to methods and measures." OUP Oxford; 2011.

[24]   Cutrell, E., and Guan, Z. "What are you looking for? An eye-tracking study of information usage in web search." In *Proceedings of the SIGCHI Conference on Human Factors in Computing Systems* (pp. 407–416). 2007.

[25]   Goldberg, J. H., and Wichansky, A. M. "Eye tracking in usability evaluation: A practitioner's guide." In *The Mind's Eye*, Hyönä, J., Radach, R., and Deubel, H., editors (pp. 493–516). Amsterdam: North-Holland; 2003.

[26]   Wedel, M. "Attention research in marketing: A review of eye-tracking studies." In Fawcett, J. M., Risko, E. F., and Kingstone, A., editors. The Handbook of Attention, (pp. 569–588). Boston Review; 2015.

[27]   Corbetta, D., Guan, Y., and Williams, J. L. "Infant eye-tracking in the context of goal-directed actions." *Infancy*. 2012; 17(1): 102–125.

[28]   See https://www.synopsys.com/automotive/what-is-adas.html

[29]   See https://imotions.com/blog/top-eye-tracking-hardware-companies/

[30]   Peker, S., Menekse Dalveren, G. G., and İnal, Y. "The effects of the content elements of online banner ads on visual attention: Evidence from an-eye-tracking study." *Future Internet*. 2021; 13(1): 18.

[31]   Asplund, C., Barkman, P., Dahl, A., Danielsson, O., Martini, T., and Nilsson, M. (2021). U.S. patent application no. 16/834,153.

[32]   See https://www.tobiipro.com/applications/scientific-research/case-studies/

[33]   See https://www.open.ac.uk/about/campus/jennie-lee-research-labs/exemplars/eye-tracker-case-studies

Chapter 9

Sentiment analysis using deep learning

Parul Gandhi[1], Surbhi Bhatia[2] and Norah Alkhaldi[2]

Abstract

Analyzing sentiments using computational techniques is one of the prominent areas of research these days. Both research domains, sentiment analysis and deep learning, are promising technologies of AI which has widely been used to solve complex real-life problems. In this modern era of E-commerce, decisions are immensely dependent on sharing and posting opinions, reviews, and sentiments on world wide web. Text classification was performed manually and engineering tasks applied on the text were accomplished using handcrafted features. This was achieved by labeling the text through some predefined knowledge-based techniques, taking use of dictionaries or using ontologies by joining hierarchical components seen in texts using graph data structures. Humans mainly did all these tasks with no automation. In the fast-developing phase, need is to develop some automatic procedure of classifying the text with least or no intervention of humans, taking machines as a whole using artificial intelligence techniques and algorithms for such kind of feature engineering tasks. The chapter includes concepts of deep learning and its algorithms, mainly convolutional neural networks for classifying sentiments. Deep learning is one of the important subsets of machine learning used to work with images, text, sound, etc.; the most attractive feature of deep learning is relevant feature extraction and transformation.

The elementary block for deep learning is neural network which combines with deep learning to form a deep neural network. The terminology deep in deep learning refers to the total number of layers present in the network. The more the number of layers in the network, the more deeper the network will be. A deep neural network as compared to the traditional neural network can have hundreds of layers to get more accurate results. It is the combination of various processing layers controlled by various biological nervous systems. There are basically one input layer, multiple hidden layers, and one output layer. All these

[1]Department of Computer Applications, Manav Rachna International Institute of Research and Studies, Faridabad, India
[2]College of Computer Sciences and Information Technology, King Faisal University, Al-Ahsa, Saudi Arabia

layers are connected with each other through neurons, where the output of one hidden layer becomes the input for other layer. The multilayer concept of deep learning gives fruitful results especially in the field of speech and image recognition. Various neural networks architectures exist for deep learning:

- Multilayer perceptrons, which are the oldest and simplest ones
- Convolutional neural networks (CNN), especially for image processing and text classification.

This chapter will propose the novel method of classifying the opinions by automatically training the classifier. The details of the layers and other parameters will be discussed in the chapter highlighting on the learning is achieved through word representations. The accuracy achieved using several information retrieval metrics will be illustrated using visualization tools.

Key Words: Machine learning; deep learning; opinion mining; sentiments; convolutional neural networks; deep belief network

9.1   Sentiment analysis: an interesting problem

The creation of social media has provided a platform for people to publicly share their views. Sentiment analysis is also referred to as opinion mining; however, there is little difference between these two: the opinion mining extracts and analyzes people's views about an entity while sentiment analysis searches for the sentiment words/expression in a text and then analyzes it. It is a field that encompasses natural language processing that constructs systems that try to find out and extract different opinions within the text. Generally, besides extracting opinions, these also help to extract various aspects of the given expression such as (Figure 9.1)

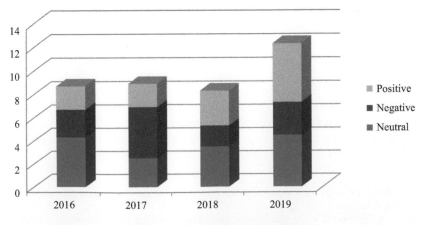

Figure 9.1   Sentiment trends

- Whether the speaker is expressing a positive opinion or a negative opinion
- The message that has been passed on by the speaker
- The speaker or the person who had expressed the opinion

Recently sentiment analysis is becoming a topic of huge interest as it encompasses various practical operations. As the publicly and even privately accessible information on the Internet is growing at a fast pace, so there is an availability of a huge number of texts expressing different opinions in various mediums such as review sites, blogs, etc. Sentiment analysis-based systems help to automatically convert unstructured information into structured information depicting various public opinions about any product, brand, service, or the current topic. This structured data can be used for various commercial applications such as analysis of marketing, reviews about products, feedback of any product, etc. Sentiment analysis can be used in various fields such as

- It is used in monitoring social media as it helps in gaining public opinions.
- It is also used to analyze various insights about social information which is being currently adopted by various organizations all over the world.
- In 2012, Obama's authorities used this technique to study opinions of the public to various announcements related to their policies.
- This could be a very crucial element related to your market research.
- This helps you to know quickly about the public opinions for your products as well as services provided by you.
- This also helps to quickly know about the overall experiences of your customers.

9.2 Sentiment and opinions

Opinion mining is a field in which emotional tone is determined within a sequence of words in order to get a better understanding of emotions as well as opinions expressed through these words [1]. Data analysts use sentiment analysis within large companies to analyze the opinions of the public to conduct market research about brands and product's reputations as well as to know about the experiences of their customers [2,3]. These companies incorporate sentiment analysis APIs from third parties into their own management of customer's experiences and monitoring of social media platforms so as to carry meaningful insights to their end customers (Figure 9.2).

Textual information can be divided into two types: facts and opinions. Objective expressions related to something are known as fact, whereas subjective expressions describing sentiments of different persons and their views for any topic is known as opinion.

9.3 Components of opinion

Opinion comprises various components that play an important role while optimization (Figure 9.3).

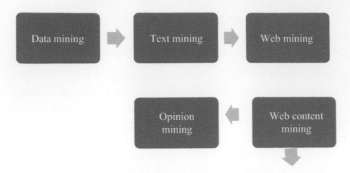

Figure 9.2   Opinion mining hierarchy

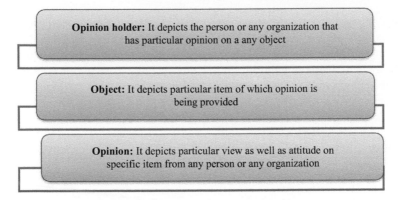

Figure 9.3   Opinion components

9.3.1   Levels in sentiment analysis

Sentiment analysis has been studied in three levels. These levels are as follows.

9.3.1.1   Document level

In this level, opinion about the entire document is classified into various sentiments of any product or any service. This level helps to classify the document into positive, negative as well as neutral sentiments. This technique is not suitable if a document contains various opinions for different entities like in blogs. There are two approaches: supervised and unsupervised machine learning approach.

9.3.1.2   Sentence level

This level determines that whether the particular sentence is expressed positively, negatively, or neutrally. It is generally used for reviews and even for a comment that is expressed by the users. It is also known as fine-grained approach of the document. It contains two tasks: subjectivity classification and sentiment classification.

9.3.1.3 Entity and aspect level

This level classifies the document on the basis of a feature. This level identifies as well as extracts the features of a particular product from various source data. This approach is best when we want to extract sentiments of desired features in a particular review.

9.3.2 Classification techniques

Sentiment analysis deals with two approaches related to classification.

9.3.2.1 Supervised approach

In this approach, the classifier is trained according to the labeled examples which are similar to test examples.

9.3.2.2 Unsupervised approach

In this approach, labels are assigned on basis of internal differences among data points only.

9.3.3 Classification types

9.3.3.1 Machine learning algorithms

These algorithms deal with the artificial intelligence branch. It is used to build those models that have the capability to learn from given data. The supervised approach learns to do mapping between inputs to expected targets [4]. These algorithms must be able to do a generalization of training data after the proper implementation of the training procedure. It has the ability to map new data accurately.

9.3.3.2 Naive Bayes

This is a simple as well as a probabilistic model that depends on the feature independent's assumption so as to classify the given data. This approach is useful for text classification also.

It is very simple to implement, low cost, and has high accuracy. In this algorithm, every word in the given training set is considered and then the probability of the particular word in each class is calculated. Then this algorithm gets ready for classifying new data. The new sentence is then classified and spitted into a single word. The advantage provided by this algorithm is that it makes full utilization of all the available pieces of evidence to make a classification.

9.3.3.3 Support vector machine

This is the nonprobabilistic model that works on the principle of plotting training data into the multidimensional space and then separate classes along the hyperplane. If the classes are not linearly separable, then the algorithm would add on a new dimension so as to separate different classes [5]. The major disadvantage of this approach is that size of feature space increases due to the addition of extra dimensions to the feature space.

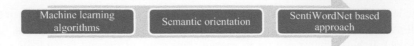

Figure 9.4   Classification techniques

9.3.3.4   Decision tree

This is the most widely used algorithms that can be applied to any kind of data. It segregates training data into smaller portions so as to identify patterns for applying classification. After this, the knowledge is depicted in a logical structure similar to flowcharts.

9.3.3.5   Semantic orientation

This approach is unsupervised because prior training is not required for mining the data. This measures whether the word is inclined more toward positive or negative.

There are two approaches: corpus-based approach and dictionary or lexicon-based approach.

SentiWordNet approach

It is a lexical source of opinion mining. This assigns three numerical scores to each synset. These scores are: Obj,Pos,Neg (Objective, Positive, and Negative). These scores range between 0.0 and 1.0. This approach initially extracts required terms and then searches for their scores. The standard performance metrics depicting accuracy-measure and entropy is being computed in order to evaluate the accuracy as well as the performance of various variants of this approach. SentiWordNet is a library that is available publicly containing scores of each and every word based on their scores (Figure 9.4).

9.4   Deep learning

Deep learning is a subset of machine learning research and is the state-of-the-art for artificial intelligence. Artificial intelligence is the capability of a machine to behave intelligently and it is not easy to implement without deep learning (Figure 9.5).

The elementary block for deep learning is a neural network which combines with deep learning to form a deep neural network. The terminology deep in deep learning refers to the total number of layers present in the network. The more the number of layers in the network, the more deeper the network will be. A deep neural network as compared to the traditional neural network can have hundreds of layers to get more accurate results [6]. It is the combination of various processing layers controlled by various biological nervous systems. There are basically one input layer, multiple hidden layers, and one output layer. All these layers are connected with each other through neurons, where the output of one hidden layer becomes the input for other layer. The multilayer concept of deep learning gives

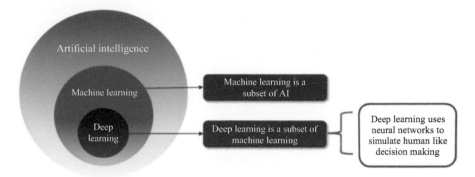

Figure 9.5   Relationship of deep learning, machine learning, and artificial intelligence

fruitful results especially in the field of speech and image recognition. Various neural networks architectures exist for deep learning:

- Multilayer perceptrons are the oldest and simplest ones.
- Convolutional neural networks (CNN), especially for image processing and text classification.

9.5   Machine learning

Machine Learning is the subset of artificial intelligence that comprises various techniques to parse the data, analyze the data, and use that data to make a wise decision. There are various machine learning algorithms that are designed and analyzed with the objective to make the computers "learn" automatically without being explicitly programmed. There are various areas these days in which there is extensive use of machine learning such as Amazon is using machine learning algorithm that helps to give better product choice recommendations to their customers based on their preferences and Netflix is using machine learning approaches to give better suggestions to their users of the TV series or movie or shows that they would like to watch.

Machine learning is a buzzword floating around and having a broad range of applications. It is doing a tremendous job in various real-time applications such as health care, online shopping, face recognition, etc. The task which has been performed by the human being in few days can be done with machine learning in a fraction of seconds, the only requirement is a high computation machine, a large amount of good quality image data, and machine learning algorithms (Figure 9.6).

From last many years, machine learning has been used to solve complex problems but applying machine learning in human society encounters some challenges. The evolution of artificial intelligence and deep learning supports machine learning and causes considerable impacts to the field. Deep learning overcomes the limitation of machine learning by incorporating various features like feature engineering and gives outstanding performance in a number of extremely complex applications.

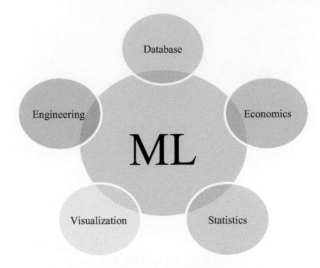

Figure 9.6   Machine learning applications

Figure 9.7   Traditional learning versus machine learning

9.6   Traditional learning

In traditional programming, both the data and program are fed as an input to run on the machine and get output while in machine learning, we feed both input and output simultaneously to run it on a machine during training and the machine creates its own logic based on experience, which can be further evaluated while testing [7]. Machine learning is a better approach as compared to traditional learning but it is still is not able to handle a huge amount of data having high dimensions (Figure 9.7).

9.7   Hybrid learning approaches

In today's competitive world the main focus is to develop a system that combines the capabilities of different approaches. Artificial intelligence and subfields are deployed to a great extent in our day-to-day activities. The objective is to produce a more flexible and versatile hybrid system that combines the best aspects of different approaches. Many different artificial intelligence and machine learning architectures and algorithms exist which have their own strengths and weaknesses. There are various hybrid approaches developed for sentiment analysis that makes the use of

- Sentiment lexicons and polarity shifting devices
- Naive Bayes and support vector machine of machine learning
- NLP essential techniques SentiWordNet and fuzzy sets
- Semantic rules, fuzzy sets, unsupervised machine learning techniques, and sentiment lexicon.

9.8   Deep neural networks

In fact, you would be surprised to hear that the idea behind deep neural networks is not new but dates back to the 1950s. However, it became possible to practically implement it because of the high-end resource capability available nowadays. Deep artificial neural networks have given outstanding performance in the field of sentiment analysis. They have the capability of designing modeling and processing nonlinear relationships. Most deep learning methods make use of neural networks. There are various deep learning neural networks available. Some of them are as follows.

9.8.1   Deep belief network

This is one of the deep neural networks that works on the principle of multilayer belief to learn a layer of features from visible units using the contrastive divergence algorithm. It treats activations of previously trained features as visible units and then learns features of features. Finally, the whole DBN is trained when the learning for the final hidden layer is achieved.

9.8.2   Convolutional neural networks

This is one of the approaches that give an advancement vision to deep learning. It is specially designed for image processing. Traditional neural networks are not best suited for image processing [8]. The neuron connectivity pattern in CNN is much analogous to that of the human brain. The best feature of CNN is its preprocessing which is much better as compared to other algorithms.

9.8.3   Stacked autoencoders

Stacked autoencoder is an unsupervised learning structure neural network that consists of three layers: input layer, hidden layer, and output layer. The whole process of an autoencoder training is implemented in two phases: encoder and decoder. An encoder is used for mapping the input data into hidden representation, and a decoder is referred to as reconstructing input data from the hidden representation. We can say that the encoding step for the stacked autoencoder is given by running the encoding step of each layer in forward order and the decoding step is given by running the decoding stack of each autoencoder in reverse order.

9.9   Convolutional neural networks

The hottest topic in the area of artificial intelligence [9] and machine learning is "deep learning." Deep learning refers to the set of techniques used for learning in neural networks (NN) with many layers. However, it is based on the previous ideas that appeared over the 1960s. The most important concepts behind deep learning are explained. Deep learning is a powerful set of techniques for learning in NN [10].

NLP applications and other tasks are easily done using deep learning techniques. Many tasks that can be achieved using the power of NLP by using computational techniques, mainly machine learning and deep learning are states as topic recognition, chunking, named entity recognition, semantic role labeling, parsing, paraphrasing, question-answering, and word-sense disambiguation [11]. Deep learning (DL) was born as a subfield of machine learning. This was inspired by the advent of even more powerful computers and much quicker ways to access larger volumes of data.

This indicates that the major difference between deep learning and machine learning is that deep learning is all about scaling up the capabilities of machine learning models. The objective of this subfield is to effectively work around the overfitting issues of other machine learning methods. So, by using larger artificial neural networks and more capable computers for training these models with larger quantities of data, the performance of these networks is known to continue to increase over time.

Clearly, a traditional machine learning algorithm can be designed using deep learning but not necessarily vice versa [12]. This is because deep NNs are capable of capturing very complex characteristics of data. There are various deep learning models [13,14] which have shown good accuracy in text classification such as CNN, LSTM, RNN, etc.

Other learning algorithms or models can also be used for text classification. However, CNN has emerged as the model of choice for multiple reasons. These include the multiple uses of the convolution operator in text processing. The CNN architecture implicitly combines the benefits obtained by a standard neural network training with the convolution operation to efficiently classify text. Further, being a neural network, CNN (and its variants) are also scalable for large datasets, which is often the case when texts are to be classified.

9.9.1   Word embeddings

Deep learning models take the text by using word embedding, taking features instead of text, the learning of the features is achieved thereafter. The vectors are constructed using vector-based models considering term frequency, and inverse document frequency into account for capturing the characteristics and semantic of the words [15]. Several approaches are widely adopted for word embedding. Some of them are explained below.

9.9.2   Bag of words (BOW)

Generally, a sparse bag of words representation is used for documents or sentences. The text contains words (broken into tokens). For example, two sentences as shown below:

Sentence 1: Python is interesting to learn.
Sentence 2: Machine learning models are built in python.

Weighting features need to be integrated with bag of words as not all the words should be taken for consideration. Figure 9.8 shows the matrix constructed using the above example.

The inverse document frequency (idf) of a term *t* is defined as follows:

$$\text{idf} = \log \frac{N}{df} \tag{9.1}$$

Dimensionality reduction is important and can be achieved by involving matrices and using singular value

$$tf - \text{idf} = tf * \log \frac{N}{df} \tag{9.2}$$

decomposition (SVD), LSA, or deep learning word embedding [16].

9.9.3   ConvNet structure

The CNN model consists of one convolution layer. The experimentation uses 301 feature maps of varied length filter heights. The vectors undergo concatenation by using word2vec embedding and by using SentiWordNet lexicon. Either of the two convolutions can be used as suggested by Chowdhary and Acharjya [17]. Wide convolution is preferred as it ensures that all weights in the filters reach all the words/sentences in the input document. The basic model used in the proposed work is displayed in Figure 9.9 as proposed by Kim (2014).

Sentence 1	Term	Sentence 1	Sentence 2		Stop word list
Python is interesting to learn.	Python	1	1		
	interesting	1	0		
	learn	1	1		is
	Machine	0	1		to
					are
Sentence 2 Machine learning models are built in python.	models	1	0		in
	built	0	1		

Figure 9.8   Example of bag of words (BOW)

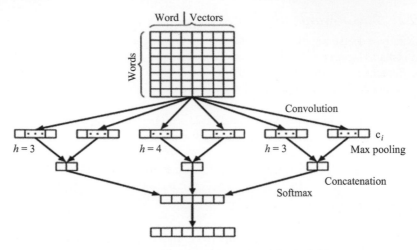

Figure 9.9   Kim model. Adapted from [18]

The proposed technique is built on the idea that features that might be important and that occur at the edge of the document should not be missed out. The max pooling layer gives the best feature representation as it maximizes the value. This local feature identified is then applied to the classifiers for the binary classification task. The scalable extension of the model can be done by changing the parameters. Careful selection of the loss function for learning can also help in optimizing the results. The experiments are also conducted with different machine learning classifiers and the accuracy is compared with the softmax classifier.

9.10   Proposed model

Input: I = Opinions with explicitly mentioned aspect
   Output: O = Classified opinions
   The following are the steps for generating a summary.
   Step 1: Constructing univariate vector
   Univariate vector is constructed by concatenating the two values obtained from Word2Vec embedding and SentiWordNet score. The semantically rich vector is obtained which will help in giving better results for classification. Figure 9.10 shows the construction of the vector.
   Step 2: Zero padding
   The average sentence length taken is 11 words. So, to make the matrix size compliable, the zeros are added to the words in order to feed them into the CNN model.
   Step 3: Train with CNN
   The important features are detected by feeding the vectors and training the CNN model for further classification. The three layers (convolution, max pooling, and softmax) are used for training it with the CNN model. Every layer performs its task and few neurons are dropped at the rate of 0.5 for better results. Other classifiers like SVM, NB, and ME are also employed and their accuracy is compared with the softmax classifier (Figure 9.10).
   The algorithm is given in Table 9.1.

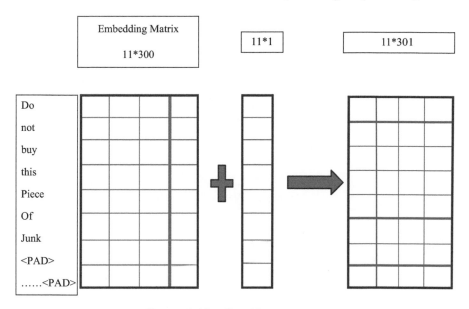

Figure 9.10   ConvNet structure

Table 9.1   Proposed CNN algorithm

Input: Sentence Matrix (S*d), F filters Output: Classified Opinions
  For each filter [....], do
  wj= xj+ xj+1+ .....xj+k-1
  cj= Tanh (wjx +b)
  c= (c1+ c2+ ....+cj)
EndFor

The input given is the univariate vector formed from each token of a sentence in the form of a matrix. The size of the matrix is taken to be 11*301. The filters slide over full rows of the matrix (words) to identify the most important feature in the sentence. The experimentation is done with 128, 256 and 512 filters. The "width" of the filters is usually the same as the width of the input matrix. The window size w is taken to be (2,3,4), (3,4,5), and (4,5,6).

1-max pooling is applied on the feature maps attained for each region size after the activation function. Finally, the softmax function is used to classify the sentence into either positive or negative classes. Putting all the above together, a CNN is presented in Figure 9.11.

9.10.1   Datasets and experimental setup

Experiments were performed on two datasets as follow:
  MR dataset: Pang-Lee MR dataset [19]:
  Extracted dataset: The reviews crawled for query "iPhone 7s" using Opinion Retriever consists of total 3,042 review sentences.

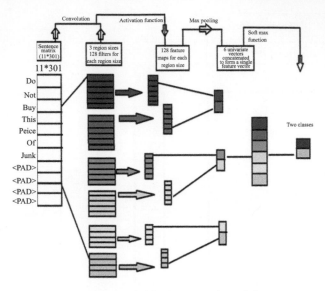

Figure 9.11   Proposed model

The implementation details include the use of Python 2.0 API on the Ubuntu 16.04.2 platform that was installed using Oracle VM Virtual Box 5.1.18. The mean accuracy is calculated via 10 fold cross validation $(CV)^1$, that is, the batch is divided into 10 parts and average accuracy is calculated.

All the experiments were carried for 10 epochs (epoch is a single pass through the whole dataset). The average sentence length is taken to be 11 words and varied batch sizes are considered.

The filter size of (2,3,4), (3,4,5), and (4,5,6) are considered for the creation of feature maps and a different number of filters (128, 256, and 512) with a dropout of 0.1 are experimented. For error optimization, the gradient descent method with Adadelta update rule [20] is used with the learning rate of 0.002 taken initially, then lowered to 0.0005 after 8 epochs and to 0.00005 after 16 epochs. The final softmax layer applies the Sigmoid function that gives the probability of output label. Also, the comparison of other traditional classifiers such as LR and SVM has also been done in place of the softmax layer to judge the accuracy level. For the creation of static and random word vectors, Google's Word2Vec is used that is trained on 100 billion words from Google news [21,22]. These word embeddings have a dimension of 300. Table 9.2 shows the list of parameters and specifications that were used for experiments.

The results for both the dataset are recorded for static and random word vectors.

9.10.2   Results

The performance of the baseline CNN configuration is used for comparison with the proposed approach. Specifically, it starts with the architectural decisions and hyper-parameters used in the previous work of Kim (2014) as described in Table 9.3.

Table 9.2   Initial parameter for CNN

Parameter	Value
Dataset	MR
Classes	2
Sentence length	11
Dataset size	10,662
Words present in the set of pretrained word vectors	3 Billion
Test set size	Cross validation CV (10)
Filter size	3,4,5
No. of Filters	256
Dropout	0.1
Activation function	Sigmoid
Epochs	10

Table 9.3   Description of hyperparameters used for classification

Filter region size	1. (2,3,4)
	2. (3,4,5)
	3. (4,5,6)
No. of filters	1. 128
	2. 256
	3. 512
Classifiers	1. Softmax classifier
	2. Logistic regression
	3. Support vector machines

The values of average precision, recall, and F-measure are recorded for each replication and observed accuracy is reported. This is accomplished for both random and static methods. For all experiments, the same preprocessing steps are used for the data as performed by Kim [18]. After establishing the baseline performance for CNNs, the effect of different architecture decisions and hyperparameter settings are considered. Table 9.3 describes the effect of varying parameters.

9.10.3   Effect of filter region size

The effect of filter region size is explored by using only one region size and the number of feature maps for this region size is set to be 7*296 (for filter region size 3). We consider region sizes of 2, 3, 4, 5, and 6.

9.10.4   Effect of number of filters

The different numbers of filters are experimented. Filters are like kernels which when applied on complete rows of words extract the most important feature by itself.

9.10.5   Effect of different classifiers

Three different types of classifiers are experimented. The results for probability distribution over labels is found better with the softmax classifier as it gives good results with a window of (3,4,5) and filters 256. LR gives good results with a window of (3,4,5) and 128 filters, and SVM gives good results with a window of (2,3,4) and filters (128 and 256).

The accuracy results of this variation with MR dataset (CNN-static) are illustrated in Table 9.4.

With the constant initial parameters as shown in Table 9.2, Table 9.4 analyzes the effect on the accuracy of proposed CNN with the number of filters equal to 128, 256, and 512 (Table 9.5).

Table 9.6 shows the effect of regularization with a dropout rate of 0.2 giving the best accuracy. The following parameters were derived from the experiments performed in Tables 9.2–9.6 and results are shown in Table 9.7.

The results clearly show that the proposed model outperforms the softmax classifier in the Kim model (2014) with an increase in accuracy in the case of the

Table 9.4   Results of three classifiers (softmax, LR, and SVM)

Classifiers	Softmax			LR			SVM		
Filter Region size No. of filters	128	256	512	128	256	512	128	256	512
2,3,4	0.793	0.800	0.796	0.796	0.793	0.796	0.802	0.802	0.794
3,4,5	0.795	0.829	0.813	0.801	0.799	0.795	0.799	0.799	0.800
4,5,6	0.793	0.797	0.796	0.800	0.797	0.796	0.799	0.797	0.800

Table 9.5   Effect of number of filters

No. of filters	Accuracy
128	0.795
256	0.829
512	0.813

Table 9.6   Effect of dropout rate

Dropout	Accuracy
0.1	0.807
0.2	0.829
0.3	0.819
0.4	0.813
0.5	0.829

Table 9.7　Results (accuracy) with proposed model variations

Model	MR dataset		Extracted dataset
	Original	**Proposed**	
CNN-random	76.10	78.52	74.89
CNN-static	81.00	82.97	78.32

MR dataset. Accuracy is only good for symmetric data sets. The accuracy results in the case of an Extracted dataset are marginally less due to the nature of the used datasets. Reviews are written in an unstructured format; therefore, there are some spelling mistakes, which will directly result in not getting good results.

The performance of a model is imperative to undergo variation with other choices of configuration.

The accuracy of the system is found better on performing experiments with activation function *ReLU* and a stronger regularization, that is, dropout out rate larger than 0.5. CNN-Static gives an accuracy of 84.79% with the MR dataset and 82.92% with the Extracted dataset.

9.11　Conclusions and future scope

Sentiment analysis using deep learning is a prominent area of research these days. Both research domains such as sentiment analysis and deep learning are promising technologies of AI which has widely been used to solve complex real-life problems.

The chapter includes concepts of deep learning for classifying sentiments that follow the least intervention of humans. Deep learning is one of the important subsets of machine learning used to work with images, text; sound, etc.; the most attractive feature of deep learning is relevant feature extraction and transformation.

Convolutional neural networks are the best performing algorithm in sentiment analysis. These networks provide promising results in various fields. They overcome the limitations of the traditional machine learning algorithm. Sentiment analysis is one of the emergent research areas with the development of social media. Today, there are a lot of opinions on the Internet but mining these opinions and sentiments is the need of today's competitive world. To achieve this objective, we proposed a convolutional neural network for sentiment analysis in this chapter. We experiment with our model on two datasets MR dataset and Extracted dataset. The implementation details include the use of Python 3.0 API on the Ubuntu 16.04.2 platform that was installed using Oracle VM Virtual Box 5.1.18. The performance of the proposed CNN was considered by carrying out experiments with various configurations. We also compared the proposed model with the existing one and the results obtained show that the proposed model gives the best results as compared to the traditional approaches.

References

[1] Yeole, A. V., Chavan, P. V., and Nikose, M. C. "Opinion mining for emotions determination." In *2015 International Conference on Innovations in Information, Embedded and Communication Systems (ICIIECS)* (pp. 1-5). IEEE; 2015.

[2] Bhatia, S., Sharma, M., Bhatia, K. K., and Das, P. "Opinion target extraction with sentiment analysis. International Journal of Computing." 2018; 17(3), 136–142.

[3] Bhatia, S. "A comparative study of opinion summarization techniques." *IEEE Transactions on Computational Social Systems*. 2020.

[4] Bhatia, S., Sharma, M., and Bhatia, K. K. "A novel approach for crawling the opinions from world wide web." *International Journal of Information Retrieval Research (IJIRR)*. 2016; 6(2), 1–23.

[5] Joachims, T. "Text categorization with support vector machines: Learning with many relevant features." In *European conference on machine learning* (pp. 137–142). Berlin, Heidelberg: Springer; 1998.

[6] Al Sallab, A., Hajj, H., Badaro, G., Baly, R., El-Hajj, W., and Shaban, K. "Deep learning models for sentiment analysis in Arabic. In *Proceedings of the Second Workshop on Arabic Natural Language processing* (pp. 9–17). 2015.

[7] Zhang, Y., and Wallace, B. "A sensitivity analysis of (and practitioners' guide to) convolutional neural networks for sentence classification." 2015. arXiv preprint arXiv:1510.03820.

[8] Shen, Y., He, X., Gao, J., Deng, L., and Mesnil, G. "Learning semantic representations using convolutional neural networks for web search." In *Proceedings of the 23rd International Conference on World Wide Web* (pp. 373–374). 2014.

[9] Kumar, N., Kharkwal, N., Kohli, R., and Choudhary, S. "Ethical aspects and future of artificial intelligence." In *2016 International Conference on Innovation and Challenges in Cyber Security (ICICCS-INBUSH)* (pp. 111-114). IEEE; 2016.

[10] Reddy, T., RM, S. P., Parimala, M., Chowdhary, C. L., Hakak, S., and Khan, W. Z. "A deep neural networks based model for uninterrupted marine environment monitoring." *Computer Communications*. 2020; 157, 64–75.

[11] Chandra, K., Kapoor, G., Kohli, R., and Gupta, A. "Improving software quality using machine learning." In *2016 International Conference on Innovation and Challenges in Cyber Security (ICICCS-INBUSH)* (pp. 115–118). IEEE; 2016.

[12] Bhatia, S., Chaudhary, P., and Dey, N. "Introduction to opinion mining." In *Opinion mining in information retrieval* (pp. 1–22). Singapore: Springer; 2020.

[13] Sharma, R. K., and Ghandi, P. "Reliability estimation and optimization: A neuro fuzzy based approach." International Journal of Computer Science and Information Security (IJCSIS). 2018. 16(12).

[14] Kaur, B., and Singh, V. "Business intelligence: Need and usage in Indian corporate sector." Journal of Critical Reviews, 2020; 7(11): 2486–2498.

[15] Mikolov, T., Deoras, A., Povey, D., Burget, L., and Černocký, J. "Strategies for training large scale neural network language models." In 2011 IEEE Workshop on Automatic Speech Recognition & Understanding (pp. 196–201). IEEE; 2011.

[16] Bengio, Y., Ducharme, R., Vincent, P., and Janvin, C. "A neural probabilistic language model." The Journal of Machine Learning Research. 2003; 3: 1137–1155.

[17] Chowdhary, C. L., and Acharjya, D. P. "Singular value decomposition: Principal component analysis-based object recognition approach." Bio-Inspired Computing for Image and Video Processing. 2018; 323.

[18] Kim, Y. "Convolutional neural networks for sentence classification." 2014. arXiv preprint arXiv:1408.5882

[19] Pang, B., and Lee, L. "A sentimental education: Sentiment analysis using subjectivity summarization based on minimum cuts." 2004. *arXiv preprint cs/0409058.*

[20] Mikolov, T., Chen, K., Corrado, G., and Dean, J. "Efficient estimation of word representations in vector space." 2013. arXiv preprint arXiv:1301.3781.

[21] Zeiler, M. D. "Adadelta: An adaptive learning rate method." 2012. *arXiv preprint arXiv:1212.5701.*

[22] RM, S. P., Maddikunta, P. K. R., Parimala, M., *et al.* "An effective feature engineering for DNN using hybrid PCA-GWO for intrusion detection in IoMT architecture." Computer Communications. 2020; 160: 139–149.

Chapter 10

Classification of prefeature extracted images with deep convolutional neural network in facial emotion recognition of vehicle driver

Ganesan Kaliyaperumal[1] and Manikandan N.S.[2]

Abstract

In several pattern recognition and classification problems, the prefeature extraction technique and deep learning methods have shown outstanding precision. This chapter presents a study on prefeature extraction with different models of convolution neural networks (CNN) and demonstrates its benefits through the use of face emotion classification problems. Gaussian filters with Canny edge detection, most significant bit (MSB) plane slicing, and Gabor filter with element-wise maximum feature extraction are the prefeature extraction techniques. We have considered and evaluated the efficiency of various prefeature extraction techniques with respect to three CNN techniques, such as LeNet, Alexnet, and VGG16 architectures. In our experiments, all CNN techniques implemented using CPU-based systems, along with Gabor filter with element-wise maximum feature extraction technique have high state-of-the-art accuracy and less execution time for the face emotion classification problems of vehicle drivers.

Key Words: Classification; convolutional neural networks (CNNs); feature extraction; deep learning; face emotion classification

10.1 Introduction and related work

The most widely used nonverbal communication for communicating internal feelings and aims is facial expressions. Six facial expressions (anger, disgust, fear, happiness, sadness, and surprise) [1] have been defined by Ekman *et al.* as basic emotional expressions of human beings in the universe. Driver emotion recognition

[1]School of Information Technology and Engineering, Vellore Institute of Technology, Vellore, India
[2]TIFAC-CORE in Automotive Infotronics, Vellore Institute of Technology, Vellore, India

should detect whether the driver is in emotion [2], such as frustration during stressful driving or sadness, so that a warning alarm can be generated or a fragrance/perfume can be sprayed to change the driver's mood. Various feature extraction and machine learning algorithms have been developed when designing the driver-computer interaction system. Most of these are hand-made extraction features with a classifier, such as support vector machine (SVM) categorized local binary pattern [3], Haar [4], SIFT [5], Gabor fisher linear discriminant filters [6], and local phase quantization (LPQ) [7].

In recent years, the problem of recognition of facial expression has been extended to deep learning using convolutional neural networks (CNNs) [8] for feature extraction and classification (neural network) of images.

For the automatic recognition of facial expression, Mayya *et al.* have suggested a deep convolutional neural network (DCNN) [9]. Their model implemented the extraction from a single image of an individual's facial expressions. Using a graphic processing unit (GPU) and using DCNN features, the feature extraction time has been reduced; a high recognition rate was also achieved. The different state-of-the-art facial expression recognition algorithms [10] using CNNs were reviewed by Pramerdorfer *et al.* They tested several preprocessing techniques for image training and tested the design of different CNN layers. They used the FER2013 [11] facial database and obtained 75.2% test accuracy by building an ensemble of CNNs. A combination of CNN and unique image preprocessing measures for facial expression recognition has been proposed by Lopes *et al.* [12]. The test-bed mostly used databases that were open to the public. They used preprocessing methods and extracted features from the image of the face. In the JAFFE [13], the Japanese female facial expression database, they achieved 82.10% accuracy and reached 96.76% accuracy in the CK+ [14] database. Al-Shabi *et al.* also focused on achieving good accuracy by only using a limited sample of training data [15]. Scale-invariant feature transform (SIFT) [15] features have been used to boost small data output as SIFT does not require detailed training knowledge to develop the compelling features. By integrating with CNN features, both dense SIFT and normal SIFT have been analyzed and compared. On the FER2013 and CK+ datasets, the proposed method has been checked. The findings showed that CNN with dense SIFT was superior to conventional CNN and CNN with SIFT. When all models were combined, accuracy also improved, which provided sophisticated results in the FER-2013 and CK + datasets, where 73.4% accuracy was achieved in FER-2013 and 99.1% accuracy was obtained in CK +. Alizadeh *et al.*, based on raw pixel data, focused on network performance [16]. Their study used a hybrid feature approach to combine raw pixel data and histogram of oriented gradient (HOG) [16] features, which were then trained using a CNN model. They used dropout and batch normalization in the CNN model to minimize over-fitting. The CNN model for facial expression recognition [17] has been used by Laranjeira *et al.* Instead of the overlapping approach for building the augmented dataset, they experimented with CK+ datasets; they suggested random disturbances from an extensive collection including skew, translation, scale, and horizontal flip to improve the quality of performance. Three important components were implemented recursively [18] by Li *et al.*: facial dataset generation, model building of facial expression recognition, and interactive research interfaces and new data collection. First, they created candid images for facial expression using CIFE [18] dataset. Second, to develop the CNN model, they applied CNN to CIFE and also fine-tuned the CNN model. They developed a facial expression game engine system on the basis of the fine-tuned CNN model; they obtained a new and more balanced dataset.

We propose the prefeature extracted images as CNN's training images in our study. We use the Gaussian Canny edge detection, bit plane slicing method, and Gabor filter in this prefeature extraction technique and compare them.

Shah *et al.* focused on images with different illumination conditions [19], used feature extraction using Canny edge detection technique, and categorized them with the Euclidian distance classifier and neural network classifier. The datasets used were JAFFE and IFE (Indian Facial Expression). The Euclidian distance classifier has shown 50% precision, while 75% accuracy has been shown by the neural network classifier. Anatomical information on facial features were used by Kumar *et al.* and they were extracted using the Canny edge detection algorithm [20]. Support vector machine for multiple classes was used for classification (happy, sad, disgust, anger, and surprise). Saeed *et al.* have investigated different methods [21] such as automatic expression recognition system (AERS) [21], graph-preserving sparse non-negative matrix factorization (GSNMF) [21] algorithm, two-phase test sample representation (TPTSR) [21], performance-based character animation [21], temporal template method [21], feature extractions using Gabor filter [22], and image sequencing-based methods [21]. They found that when using the Canny edge detection algorithm, the highest accuracy was achieved.

The principal component analysis (PCA) [22] has been used by Srinivas *et al.* on bit plane slices to decrease the complexity and time of computation. They used ORL [23] as their database of faces. For image decomposition, the bit-plane slice was used, and principal components analysis (PCA) was used to extract the features of the decomposed image. Using a thermal infra-red camera [24], Seal *et al.* have suggested a new model and captured the thermogram. To extract the features from the captured thermogram [24], the bit-plan slicing method was used to refer to these extracted features from blood perfusion data. For every human being, the extracted minutiae points from the data on blood perfusion of a human face were special. On a single face, there are many tiny points. The entire face image is divided into equal blocks, and the total number of minute points from each block is determined to create the final vector. This vector, which serves as a classifier, is fed as an input to the five-layer feed-forward backpropagation network. With a block size of 16×16, they obtained a maximum success of 95.24% recognition. The Gabor wavelet transformation [25] was proposed by Zhou *et al.* to extract the facial features, and the non-negative matrix factorization process (NMF) [25] reduced the high dimensional data [25]. Finally, by using a two-layer classifier (TLC) [25], they classified their data. Experiments on the JAFFE database of facial expressions gave a 98.1% precision by their proposed model. A new approach to facial emotion recognition using eye and mouth temporal features [26] with a high rate of recognition has been proposed by Rani *et al.* Feature extraction from every frame using Gabor wavelet was passed on to an ensemble classifier to detect the location of the facial field. To detect the eye and mouth regions, the Gabor face image signature was passed on to an ensemble classifier. In the consecutive frames, the blocks of temporal features were later derived from the signature of the eye and mouth regions. The eye and mouth Gabor signature temporal features were normalized using the Z-score normalization technique [26] in each block and were encoded as binary pattern features. To produce the enhanced temporal function, these normalized eye and mouth features were concatenated and passed on to a multiclass Adaboost classifier [26] to identify the facial emotions. In RML databases, this proposed method achieved 96% accuracy and 98% accuracy in CK+ databases.

10.2   Proposed models

In this work, using CNN, we propose few feature extraction techniques and classification of seven basic emotions, namely angry, happy, disgust, fear, sad, surprise, and neutral. We apply the techniques of prefeature extraction, namely Gaussian filter with detection of Canny edge, bit plan slicing, and Gabor filter techniques in our CNN. The block diagram of the proposed model is illustrated in Figure 10.1. Each input image is prefeature extracted and passed on to the CNN. The CNN model consists of several layers of convolution, Max-pooling layers accompanied by fully connected layers to identify the facial emotions.

10.2.1   Datasets

We have used JAFFE and FER2013 datasets in our experiments. As shown in Figure 10.2, each of these datasets consists of seven emotions.

In the ICML 2013 Challenges in Representation Learning, the Facial Expression Recognition 2013 (FER-2013) database was presented. The database was created using the Google image search API and seven types of emotion labels were used to mark the faces. A number of 35,887 images are found in the database. In addition, for 10 Japanese women, the Japanese Female Facial Expression (JAFFE) database has 213 images that were named using seven emotions. In each image, a 48 × 48 pixel resolution dataset set is used.

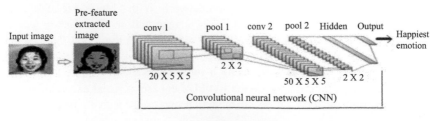

Figure 10.1   Proposed model

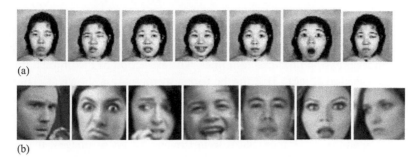

(a)

(b)

Figure 10.2   Seven emotions (anger, disgust, fear, happiness, neutral, surprise, and sad)

Figure 10.3   Preprocessing methods used in our proposed method

10.2.2   Preprocessing

Most of the face of the person is angled or cluttered with the background image in the FER2013 dataset; three preprocessing steps [27] were applied to resolve that: face detection, cropping, and resizing. Face detection techniques use the Haar-like feature [22] algorithm in our work. It seeks to delete the areas of context and non-face and then crop the region of the face. The next step used for preprocessing was down-sampling (resizing) the resolution to ensure that the image is 48×48 in size. The outcomes are shown in Figure 10.3.

10.2.3   Prefeature extraction

10.2.3.1   Gaussian Canny filter

The Canny edge detection algorithm [22] is commonly used in image processing for edge detection. For Canny edge detection, the following steps are followed.

By applying the Gaussian filter in step one, we clean up the noise in the image.

Step two is to figure out the power of the edge by taking the image's gradient. For this reason, a Sobel mask or a Robert mask can be added. For calculating the gradient, (10.1) is used:

$$|G| = \sqrt{Gx^2 + Gy^2} \approx |Gx| + |Gy| \tag{10.1}$$

In step three, (10.2) is used for finding the edge direction by using the gradient in x- and y-directions. We decide the edge direction along the horizontal, positive, vertical, and negative diagonal degrees after finding the edge direction:

$$\theta = \tan^{-1}\left(\frac{Gy}{Gx}\right) \tag{10.2}$$

The edge is traced in the final step, and the edge direction for the pixels for which the value is zero is suppressed (not considered as an edge). This method is called nonmaximum suppression. In the output edge image, the outcome of non-maximum suppression produces thin lines. The extraction of the original image by the Canny function (Figure 10.2 for the happiest emotion) is shown in Figure 10.4.

10.2.3.2 Bit plan slicing method

If users slice an X-bit per pixel image into different planes, it is called bit-plane slicing [22], and it plays a crucial role in the processing of images. It is used in applications such as data compression, transformation, and extraction of features. First, the grey level image is to be decomposed into bit planes: each pixel in the image is represented by 8 bits. The image is then broken down into eight 1-bit planes, starting from the least significant bits (LSB), 1st bit plane to the most significant bits (8th bit) plane (MSB). Figure 10.5 shows the decomposition of an

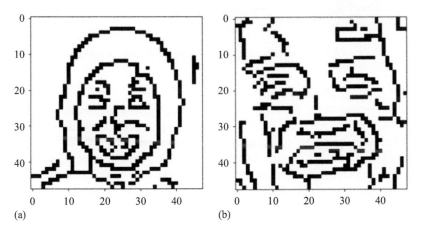

(a)   (b)

Figure 10.4   Gaussian Canny filter results (happiest emotion) of (a) JAFFE and (b) FER2013 dataset

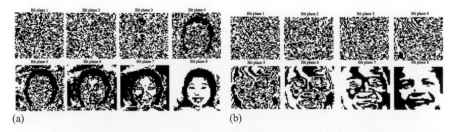

(a)   (b)

Figure 10.5   Bit plane slicing results (happiest emotion) of (a) JAFFE and (b) FER2013

image from the JAFFE and FER2013 datasets into 8-bit planes. The plane sliced image of the 8th bit (MSB) is taken as an extracted image of the MSB function.

10.2.3.3   Gabor filter as a feature extractor

The Gabor filter [22] is a linear filter used in spatial image processing for edge detection. A two-dimensional Gabor filter is a sinusoidal wave multiplied by the Gaussian function. There is a real and an imaginary part representing the orthogonal directions in the Gabor filter. The two components can be mixed into a complicated number or can be used separately. The Gabor filter's real and imaginary parts are shown in (10.3) and (10.4) as follows:

$$\text{Real } g(x, y; \lambda, \theta, \psi, \sigma, \gamma) = \exp\left(-\frac{x'^2 + \gamma^2 y'^2}{2\sigma^2}\right) \cos\left(2\pi\frac{x'}{\lambda} + \psi\right) \tag{10.3}$$

$$\text{Imaginary } g(x, y; \lambda, \theta, \psi, \sigma, \gamma) = \exp\left(-\frac{x'^2 + \gamma^2 y'^2}{2\sigma^2}\right) \sin\left(2\pi\frac{x'}{\lambda} + \psi\right) \tag{10.4}$$

where $x' = x\cos\theta + y\sin\theta$ and

$$y' = -x\sin\theta + y\cos\theta$$

In this equation, λ describes the sinusoidal factor wavelength, θ refers to the normal orientation of the Gabor function to parallel lines, ψ is the phase offset, σ is the standard deviation of the Gaussian envelope, and γ is the spatial aspect ratio and defines the Gabor function ellipticity. The entire frequency spectrum and amplitude and phase, as shown in Figure 10.6, are captured by combining the input image with the sophisticated version of the Gabor filter with five spatial frequencies and eight orientations.

The element-wise maximum of array elements technique uses feature extraction from between 40 kernels of filtered result images. We compare two or more arrays of images and return a new array of images containing an element-wise maximum, as described in (10.5):

$$E^{in}(i,j) = \max(F_1(i,j), F_2(i,j), F_3(i,j), .., F_L(i,j)) \tag{10.5}$$

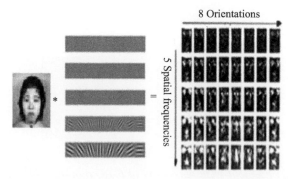

Figure 10.6   Gabor filter for Gabor feature extraction (sad emotion as input)

where $E^{in}(i,j)$ is an element-wise image result limit (10.5). Here i,j is the pixel position of the $n \times m$ matrix. Here F is the Gabor function that has extracted 40 filtered image kernels and $L=40$ here. Figure 10.7(a) gives an example of an element-wise maximum of elements in an array. Here, (i), (ii), and (iii) are images whose maximum element is selected as the maximum image on the right side. Figure 10.7(b) and (c) displays the element-wise maximum technique for the resulting image of 40 kernels filtered. The abbreviation of this Gabor filtered image with element-wise maximum feature extraction is known as Gabor-EM.

10.2.4 Convolutional neural networks

Convolutional neural network-based facial expression recognition is performed by feeding the prefeature extracted images to the first convolution layer with a kernel size of 5 × 5 and a stride of 1. It attempts to extract features such as borders, shapes, corners, and aligned edges. We consider input images of size 48 × 48 and 20 filters were applied. Thus, the performance of the first convolution layer is 20 times 44 × 44 scaled feature maps and is passed on to the activation function rectified linear unit (ReLU) [3], which aims to retain the properties of each output. A maximum value which is greater than or equal to zero is known as ReLU. The 44 × 44 output of the triggered ReLU image is then passed on to a 2 × 2 kernel max-pooling layer with a stride of 2 for each dimension, and the image size is then reduced to 22 × 22. Max pooling is attempted in each dimension to find the underlying features of the image. In Figure 10.8, the effects of the activation of ReLU and max-pooling layers are shown for the JAFFE and FER2013 datasets. The feature maps resulting from the original JAFFE and FER2013 images are shown in Figure 10.8(a) and (e). The Gaussian filter feature maps with the detected Canny edge image (Figure 10.4) for JAFFE and FER2013 dataset images are shown in Figure 10.8(b) and (f), respectively. Figure 10.8(c) and (g) displays MSB

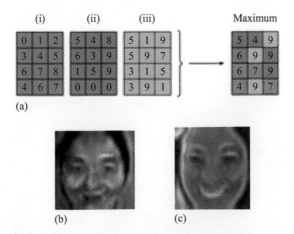

Figure 10.7   *(a) Element-wise maximum of (b) Gabor-EM JAFFE and*
(c) Gabor-EM FER2013 dataset

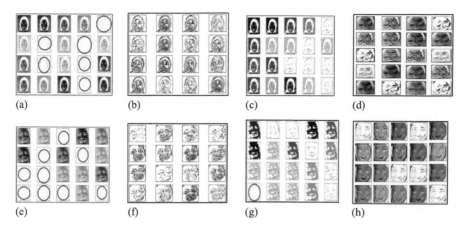

(a) (b) (c) (d)

(e) (f) (g) (h)

*Figure 10.8   First convolutional and maxpool layer feature map over normal
images ((a) and (e)), Gaussian Canny ((b) and (f)), bit plane sliced
images ((c) and (g)), and Gabor-EM ((d) and (h)) feature
extracted images*

sliced image (Figure 10.5) feature maps resulting from the JAFFE and FER2013 datasets. In Figure 10.8(d) and (h), we show the Gabor-EM image feature maps (Figure 10.7(b) and (c)) of the JAFFE and FER2013 datasets. Figure 10.8(a) and (e) clearly show about 30%–40% of losses in feature maps (red circled) from the study of the above visualization feature maps, but there is a loss of about 5% when we compare to Figure 10.8(c) and (g). But there is not much loss in Figure 10.8(b), (f), (d), and (h) in their function maps. The results of the previous step were convoluted by a second convolution layer with 5×5 kernel size, stride of 1, and 50 filters. Finally, we obtained images of size 20×20 pixels and passed them on to a ReLU activation function. In the fourth layer, we have also implemented max-pooling to minimize the image size to 10×10, and it is accompanied by a fully connected layer with 500 neurons.

In Figure 10.9, the visualization of second convolutional and max pooled layer feature maps is shown. We notice a loss of 25%–35% of feature maps (red circled) in Figure 10.9(a) and (e). When compared with Figure 10.9(c), (g), (d), and (h), we have a loss of just 1%. But there are no losses on their feature maps in Figure 10.9(b) and (f).

Finally, the output of this layer is linked to the seven output nodes of the output layer, representing seven basic emotions. Using the Adam [8] optimizer, the CNN model is trained because the method calculates individual adaptive learning rates for different parameters from estimates of first and second gradient moments. For the error function, cross-entropy [8] is used. A commonly used alternative to square error is the cross-entropy test. It is used when node functions are interpreted as representing the likelihood that each hypothesis will be valid. This architecture for CNN is known as Lenet [28]. In our testbed, the Alexne [29] and VGG16 [30] were also included.

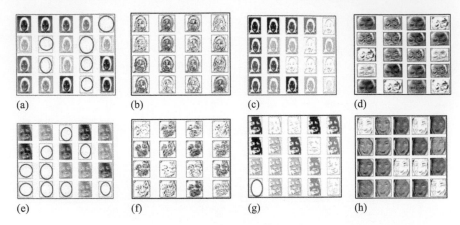

Figure 10.9   First convolutional and maxpool layer feature map over normal images ((a) and (e)), Gaussian canny ((b) and (f)), bit plane sliced images ((c) and (g)), and Gabor-EM ((d) and (h)) feature extracted images

10.2.5   Model design

The block diagram of a CNN model with a Gaussian Canny filter is shown in Figure 10.10. Depending on three different models, all prefeature extracted images are passed on to the CNN model, which has convolution, ReLU activation, and max pool, and are replicated. Softmax obtains the outcomes of the emotion classification. Algorithm 10.1 illustrates the Gabor-EM pseudo-code with the CNN model.

Algorithm 10.1 Algorithm for recognizing facial expressions using Gabor-EM with CNN

    Input: Input of facial image
    Output: facial expression recognition
    1: **Function** RECOGNIZE-FACIAL- EXPRESSIONS(images)
    2: **for all** image (i), depicting facial expressions ∈ face dataset **do**
    3: convert the image (i) to gray-scale
    4: detect frontal face in (i) and crop only the face
    5: apply pre-feature extraction with Gabor filter with 40 kernel
    6: apply Element-wise maximum to generate extracted image
    7: convolution 2D (size 5×5 with 20 kernel size)
    8: maxpool (size 2×2)
    9: convolution 2D (size 5×5 with 30 kernel size)
    10: maxpool (size 2×2)
    11: with softmax recognize facial expression
    12: **end Function**

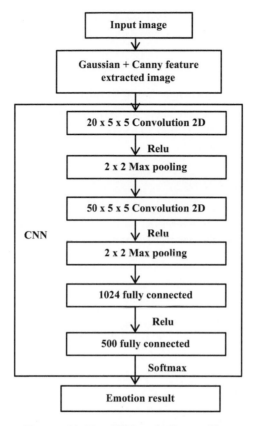

Figure 10.10   CNN with Canny filter

The CNN model analysis with bit plane slicing is discussed below.

The greyscale image X is defined as follows:

$X \in \{X(m,n),\ m \in \{1,\ldots,M\},\ n \in \{1,\ldots,N\}\}$, and M, N are the maximum dimensions of an image, where $X(m,n) \in \{0,\ldots 255\}$ is the total number of grey levels. We decompose the original image into 8-bit planes:

$$X(m,n) = X_{b1}(m,n) + X_{b2}(m,n) + \ldots + X_{b7}(m,n) + X_{b8}(m,n) \qquad (10.6)$$

Simply we can extract the 8th (MSB) bit from all pixels to generate the feature extracted image and pass it on to the convolution layer:

$$Z_{ij}^{(k)} = \sum_{c} \sum_{s=0}^{m-1} \sum_{t=0}^{n-1} w_{st}^{(k,c)} x_{(i+s)(j+t)}^{(c)} \qquad (10.7)$$

where, w is the weight of the kernel and c denotes the channel of the image. If the number of kernels is k and the number of channels is c, we have $W \in \mathbb{R}^{k \times c \times m \times n}$. Then, we can see from the equation that the size of the convolved image is $(M - m + 1) \times (N - n + 1)$.

After the convolution, all the convolved values are activated by the activation function. We have implemented the CNN with the ReLU. With the activation, we have

$$a_{ij}^{(k)} = h\left(z_{ij}^{(k)} + b^{(k)}\right) = \max\left(0, z_{ij}^{(k)} + b^{(k)}\right) \tag{10.8}$$

where b denotes the bias and it does not have subscripts of i and j, that is, we have $b \in \mathbb{R}^k$, a one-dimensional array. Then, we have to forward-propagate the values of the convolutional layer. Next comes the max-pooling layer. The propagation can simply be written as follows:

$$y_{ij}^{(k)} = \max\left(a_{(l_1 i + s)(l_2 j + t)}^{(k)}\right) \tag{10.9}$$

where l_1 and l_2 are the size of pooling filter and $s \in [0, l_1], t \in [0, l_2]$. Each unit in the feed-forward network is expressed as the sum of the weight of the network connected to the unit. So the generalized term is given as follows:

$$a_j = \sum_i w_{ji} x_i + b_j \tag{10.10}$$

$$z_j = h\left(a_j\right) \tag{10.11}$$

where x_i is the value of the input layer and h is the nonlinear activation function.
The softmax function is defined as

$$\sigma(z)_j = \frac{e^{z_j}}{\sum_{k=1}^{k} e^{z_k}} \; for \; j = 1, \ldots, k \tag{10.12}$$

In probability theory, the output of the function of the softmax is used to denote a derivative distribution, that is, the probability distribution over k represents different possible outcomes.

10.2.6   Metrics

10.2.6.1   Accuracy

$$\text{Accuracy} = \frac{TP + TN}{TP + FN + FP + TN} \tag{10.13}$$

The consistency of training is typically the accuracy when the model is applied to training data. But when the model is implemented over validation data, the validation accuracy is obtained. If the accuracy of validation is lower than the accuracy of training, it is called overfitting. The best model is known to be any model that provides low overfit. In testing accuracy, the accuracy is tested using the formula for every emotion.

Each emotion accuracy $=$

$$\frac{\text{Each emotion TP} + \text{each emotion TN}}{\text{Each emotion TP} + \text{each emotion FN} + \text{each emotion FP} + \text{each emotion TN}} \tag{10.14}$$

Summation of each emotion accuracy divided by the number of emotions is called mean testing accuracy.

10.2.6.2   Cross-entropy loss

The cross-entropy is a (minus) log-likelihood of data y_i', under a model y_i. If there is a fixed model, which predicts for n classes $\{1,2,\ldots,n\}$ their hypothetical existence probabilities $y_1, y_2, \ldots, y_n$. Assume that k_1 instances of class 1, k_2 instances of class 2, k_n instances of class n, etc. According to the model likelihood of this happening is

$$P[\text{data}|\text{model}] := y_1^{k1} y_2^{k2} \cdots y_n^{kn} \tag{10.15}$$

By taking the logarithm and changing the sign we get

$$-\log P[\text{data}|\text{model}] = -[k_1 \log y_1 + k_2 \log y_2 + \cdots + k_n \log y_n] = -\sum_i k_i \log y_i \tag{10.16}$$

If we divide the right-hand sum by the number of observations $N = k_1 + k_2 + \cdots + k_n$ and denote the observed probabilities as $y'_I = k_i/N$, then the result is cross-entropy:

$$-\frac{1}{N} \log P[\text{data}|, \text{model}] = -\frac{1}{N} \sum_i k_i \log y_i = -\sum_i y'_i \log y_i \tag{10.17}$$

Training loss is usually the cross-entropy loss when the model is applied to training data. The validation loss also like training loss is the model applied over validation data.

10.2.7   System configuration

Prefeature extraction steps and CNNs were performed using OpenCV and TensorFlow python libraries running on a CPU machine using an Intel i5 processor with an 8 GB RAM memory and an Ubuntu 14.02 operating system. Based on this configuration, we conclude that Lenet, Alexnet, and VGG16 of the CNN model work better than GoogleNet. In CPU-based systems, Inception V3 and Resnet do not perform well because these models are well built for GPU-based systems to run. The bad performance of GoogleNet and Resnet in the CPU system in terms of accuracy and loss is clearly shown in Figure 10.11.

10.3   Experiments and results

We have used the JAFFE and FER2013 datasets in the current analysis. For training and validation, we split the dataset into a 90:10 ratio. 40% of the data were chosen randomly and were used for testing. For each emotion, we obtained a single image of the subject from all datasets (JAFFE and FER2013). With a batch size of 50, the JAFFE dataset provided 191 training data and 22 validation data. There is poor

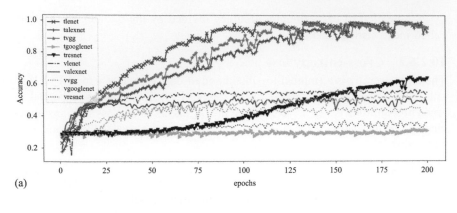

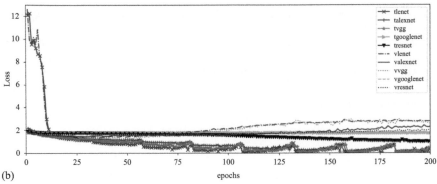

Figure 10.11   CNN models performance in CPU-based system: (a) accuracy and
(b) loss

precision and greater overfitting when the training data was too low, as is clearly seen in Figure 10.12. With all three prefeature extraction techniques, training, validation accuracy, and loss were tested, but the standard image and Canny feature extracted images displayed low accuracy and highest loss when compared to the MSB sliced and Gabor EM ones; the method of data augmentation is used to avoid overfitting. For each JAFEE image, 25 types of data augmentation were used.

An affine transformation [22] (Figure 10.13) maps image variables (e.g., an input image) by applying a linear combination of translation, rotation, scaling, and/ or shearing to new image variables (e.g., an output image).

In perspective transformation [22] (Figure 10.13), we project an image from a different point of view that should be understood in advance to apply this position of the object.

The translation of the original image [22] (Figure 10.14) transfers it to a different location on the screen. We add a translation coordinate (tx, ty) to convert a point into a 2D image with the original coordinate (X, Y) to get the new coordinate (X', Y').

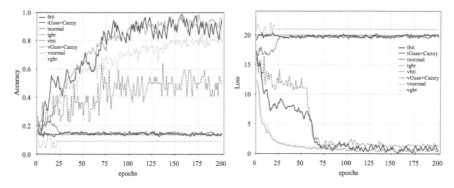

Figure 10.12 Lenet with JAFFE dataset

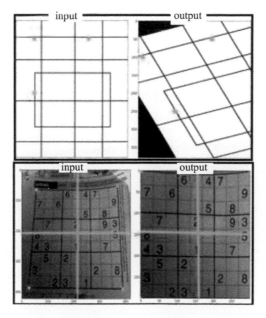

Figure 10.13 Affine transform and perspective transform

Scaling transformation [22] is used in order to adjust the size of an object. Here, a scaling factor multiplies the original coordinate to get the desired result (Figure 10.14). The transformation matrix shown in (18) achieves rotation [22] (Figure 10.14) of an image using an angle θ.

$$M = \begin{pmatrix} \cos\theta & -\sin\theta \\ \sin\theta & \cos\theta \end{pmatrix} \tag{10.18}$$

By rotating at multiples of 90°, flipping generates various image sets (Figure 10.14).

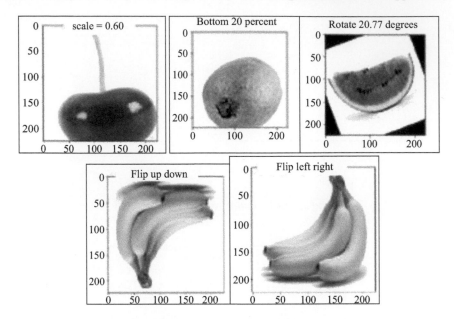

Figure 10.14   2D transform

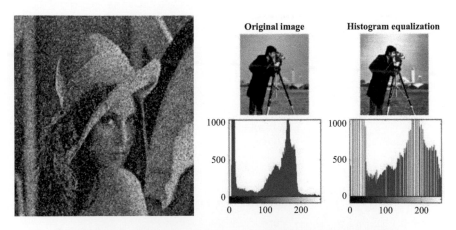

Figure 10.15   Slat and pepper noise and histogram equalization

White and black pixels were created by the addition of salt-and-pepper noise [22] (Figure 10.15) to the images. It is often called the noise of impulses. A sharp and unexpected disruption in the image signal can produce this noise. One of the well-known techniques in image processing is histogram equalization [22]. The image's contrast adjustment is rendered by using the histogram of the image (Figure 10.15).

The mean filter [22] (Figure 10.16) is a simple spatial filter that uses a sliding window technique to substitute the window's center value with the mean of all the

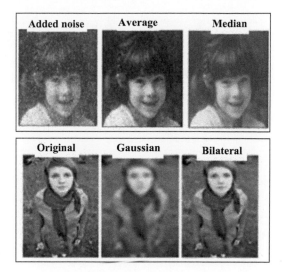

Figure 10.16   Mean, median, Gaussian, and bilateral filter

pixels present in the window selected. In general, the window or kernel is a square one and can be of any dimension.

The median filter [22] (Figure 10.16) is similar to the mean filter, but the sliding window that replaces the window's center value is the median of all the window pixel values picked.

Gaussian filter [22] (Figure 10.16) is a filter whose impulse response is shown in (10.19), is a Gaussian function

$$G(x, y) = \frac{1}{2\pi\sigma^2} e^{-\frac{x^2+y^2}{2\sigma^2}}$$

(10.19)

where x represents the distance from the origin in the horizontal axis, y represents the distance from the origin in the vertical axis, and σ is the standard deviation of the Gaussian distribution.

Bilateral filtering [22] (Figure 10.16) is a filter for nonlinear, edge filtering, and noise reduction technique applied to the image. This adjusts the intensity of each pixel to the surrounding pixels' weighted average intensity value. The Gaussian distribution can be centered on this weight:

$$BF\,[I]_p = \frac{1}{W_p} \sum_{q\in S} G_{\sigma_s}(\|p - q\|)\, G_{\sigma_r}\left(I_p - I_q\right) I_q$$

(10.20)

where W_p is a normalization factor:

$$W_p = \sum_{q\in S} G_{\sigma_s}(\|p - q\|)\, G_{\sigma_r}\left(I_p - I_q\right)$$

(10.21)

where the parameters σ_s and σ_r measure the amount of filtering for the image I. Equation (10.20) is a normalized weighted average one where G_{σ_s} is a spatial

Figure 10.17   Data augmentation

Gaussian that decreases the influence of distant pixels, G_{σ_r} is a range Gaussian that decreases the influence of pixels q with an intensity value different from I_p.

The augmentation technique applied for the JAFFE dataset is shown in Figure 10.17. The original image, affine transform, average filter, Gaussian filter, cropping, mean filter, median filter, bilateral filter, histogram equalization, horizontal flip, perspective transform, $(90°, 180°, 270°, -16°, -46°, -76°, 46°, 16°)$ rotation, $(0.01, 0.02, 0.05)$ noise degree levels, translation, and vertical flip are shown here in the JAFFE dataset.

We have taken 11770 images for training and 1308 images for validation with a batch size of 500 in the FER2013 dataset. For testing, 40% of randomly chosen images were used. Three CNN models namely Lenet, Alexnet, and VGG16 were used to test both datasets.

To boost the efficiency of CNN, we used three prefeature extraction steps: (a) Gaussian filter with Canny edge detection, (b) MSB plane slicing, and (c) Gabor-EM filtering. The results were checked using four steps after applying the enhancement steps in CNN, namely training accuracy, validation accuracy, training error, and validation loss. These are shown in Figures 10.18–10.21. The study of the outcomes achieved is discussed below.

Testbed 1:

In the case of the CNN model using LeNet with JAFFE dataset, we note that at the 50th epoch itself, MSB plane slicing as well as Canny feature extraction training images achieved 90% training accuracy compared with the normal unprocessed and Gabor-EM images that only obtained 90% accuracy at 100th epoch. In comparison to the Gabor-EM image, which has very little overfitting, the validation accuracy clearly shows that the Canny filtered image is strongly overfitting, as shown in Figure 10.18(a). In the case of MSB plane slicing, when using the Canny and Gabor-EM feature extraction method, the loss rate quickly decreased within the 20th epoch when compared to the typical image, which takes more than 25 epochs, as far as the loss is concerned. But the loss of validation clearly shows that even after the 25th epoch, the Canny filtered images do not show up any decrease in the loss rate, as shown in Figure 10.19(a). The Gabor-EM method completes the training epoch in less than 13.7 s in terms of the average training epoch (Table 10.1). During the training and validation phase, the Gabor-EM method has better accuracy and loss in this test-bed, and it takes less training time.

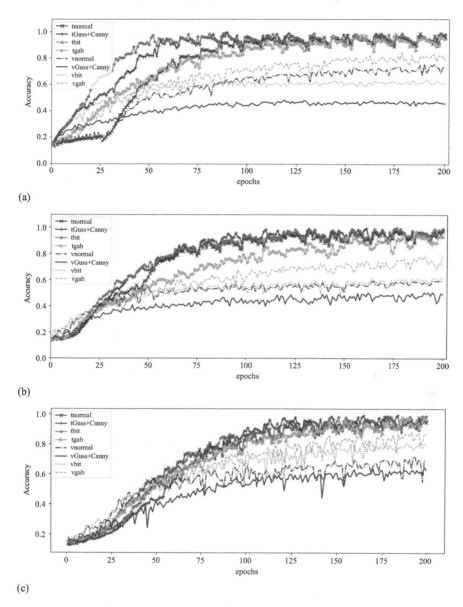

(a)

(b)

(c)

Figure 10.18 Training and validation accuracy for (a) Lenet, (b) Alexnet, and (c) VGG models in JAFFE dataset using bit plane slicing, Gaussian Canny, Gabor-EM, and normal image

Testbed 2:
The Alexnet CNN model with the JAFFE dataset is used here. The normal unprocessed image, MSB plane slicing method, and Canny filtered image reached 90% of training accuracy before the 100th epoch but the Gabor-EM method

achieved training accuracy at 175th epoch. The Gabor-EM approach is marginally overfitting relative to others during validation accuracy (Figure 10.18(b)). As far as loss is concerned (Figure 10.19 (b)), in both training loss and validation loss, the Gabor-EM system has achieved a loss rate of less than 0.5. The Gabor-EM system has thus performed well in terms of accuracy and loss in this test-bed. For the Gabor-EM with 53.2 s, the average training time was higher (Table 10.1).

Testbed 3:

The VGG16 CNN model with the JAFFE dataset is used here. All techniques generated almost similar results during training accuracy. But validation accuracy of the Canny filter and normal unprocessed image produced heavy overfitting when compared to the Gabor-EM method, whose validation accuracy has very little overfitting (Figure 10.18 (c)). But the Canny filtered image did not reach a loss rate of less than 1.5 (Figure 10.19(c)) in the validation loss. Among others, the Gabor-EM approach takes less training time, but due to a large number of VGG16 layers, it took 339.3 s (Table 10.1).

Testbed 4:

Here the LeNet CNN model with the FER2013 dataset is used as a testbed. Here, before the 50th epoch, the MSB plane slicing and Canny feature extracted training images achieved 90% training accuracy when compared to the normal unprocessed image and Gabor-EM method, which reached 90% at the 100th epoch. All of them showed good overfitting for validation accuracy, but among them, the Gabor-EM method is better (Figure 10.20 (a)). The MSB plane slicing, canny filter, and normal unprocessed image achieved an error rate of 2.5 when compared to the Gabor-EM system with a loss rate of less than 2.5 (Figure 10.21(a)) for validation loss. For the Gabor-EM system, the average training time was less, namely 31.8 s (Table 10.1).

Testbed 5:

The CNN model Alexnet with dataset FER2013 is used here. The MSB plane slice and Canny filtered image achieved 90% training accuracy before the 100th epoch. Validation accuracy showed high overfitting, but among them, the Gabor-EM method is better in performance (Figure 10.20(b)). Compared to the normal unprocessed image and Gabor-EM method, loss rate is less than 2.5 (Figure 10.21 (a)), and the MSB plane slice and Canny filter have crossed the 2.5 error rate due to validation loss. For the Gabor EM method, the average training time is less than 129 s (Table 10.1).

Testbed 6:

The VGG16 CNN model with the FER2013 dataset is used here. All methods obtained almost the same results during training accuracy. But for validation accuracy, the Gabor-EM method gave better (Figure 10.20(c)) results. In comparison to the Gabor-EM method whose loss rate is less than 2.5 (Figure 10.21(c)), the MSB plane slicing, Canny filter, and typical image crossed more than 2.5 error rate for validation loss. Among other things, the Gabor-EM approach takes less training time, but because of a large number of VGG16 layers present, it takes 871.4 s (Table 10.1).

For all three models using both datasets, the research accuracy results are shown in Table 10.2 and we compared them for seven forms of A, D, F, H, N, S, and U emotions and estimated the average accuracy.

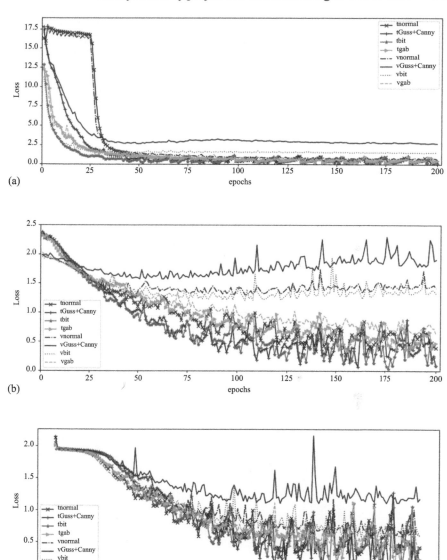

Figure 10.19 *Training and validation loss for (a) Lenet, (b) Alexnet, and (c) VGG*
models in JAFFE dataset using bit plane slicing, Gaussian Canny,
Gabor-EM, and normal image

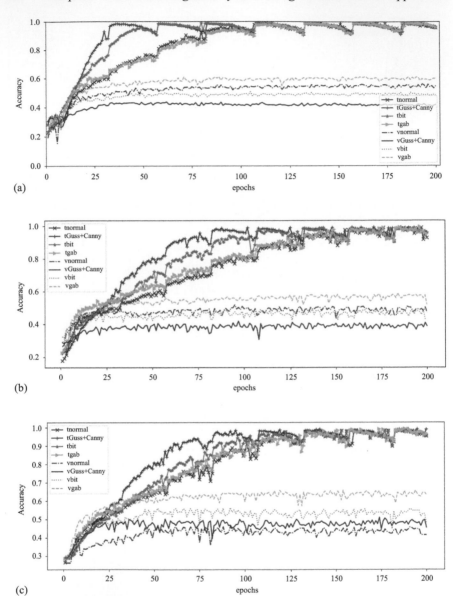

Figure 10.20   Training and validation accuracy for (a) Lenet, (b) Alexnet, and (c) VGG models in FER2013 dataset using bit plane slicing, Gaussian Canny, Gabor-EM, and normal image

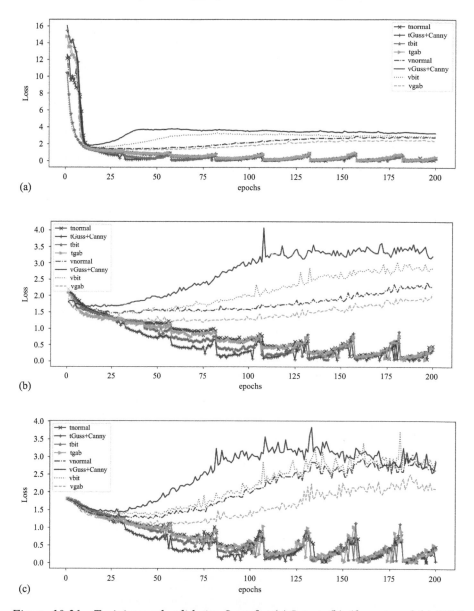

Figure 10.21 Training and validation Loss for (a) Lenet, (b) Alexnet, and (c) VGG models in FER2013 dataset using bit plane slicing, Gaussian Canny, Gabor-EM and normageal image

Table 10.1   Average time (seconds) taken to complete an epoch

	Normal	**Canny**	**MSB**	**Gabor_EM**
Lenet (JAFFE)	13.8	13.9	13.9	13.7
Alexnet (JAFFE)	53.5	53.5	53.4	53.2
VGG16 (JAFFE)	357.5	361.4	341.8	339.3
Lenet (FER2013)	33.4	33.2	34.1	31.8
Alexnet (FER2013)	132.4	132.9	132.3	129
Vgg16 (FER2013)	896.2	901.6	894.9	871.4

Table 10.2   Accuracy for all seven emotions and mean accuracy

	A	**D**	**F**	**H**	**N**	**S**	**U**	**Avrg**
Lenet (JAFFE) normal	95	97	**98**	94	94	95	92	95
Lenet (JAFFE) Canny	96	94	94	94	96	94	94	94.6
Lenet (JAFFE) MSB	96	96	**98**	94	**97**	95	93	95.6
Lenet (JAFFE) Gabor_EM	**99**	**98**	**98**	**98**	94	**99**	**98**	**97.7**
	A	**D**	**F**	**H**	**N**	**S**	**U**	**Avrg**
Alexnet (JAFFE) normal	94	94	98	95	97	95	92	95
Alexnet (JAFFE) Canny	96	95	96	94	94	94	95	94.8
Alexnet (JAFFE) MSB	**98**	**96**	95	96	97	97	94	96
Alexnet (JAFFE) Gabor_EM	**98**	95	**99**	**98**	**98**	**99**	**96**	**97.5**
	A	**D**	**F**	**H**	**N**	**S**	**U**	**Avrg**
VGG16 (JAFFE) normal	**99**	**99**	97	**99**	**99**	98	95	98
VGG16 (JAFFE) Canny	96	96	98	94	97	95	93	95.5
VGG16 (JAFFE) MSB	97	98	**99**	**99**	**99**	98	97	98
VGG16 (JAFFE) Gabor_EM	**99**	**99**	**99**	**100**	**99**	**100**	**99**	**99.3**
	A	**D**	**F**	**H**	**N**	**S**	**U**	**Avrg**
Lenet (FER2013) normal	**95**	92	**97**	93	94	92	89	93
Lenet (FER2013) Canny	92	**98**	90	95	91	95	90	93
Lenet (FER2013) MSB	91	92	93	95	94	96	91	93
Lenet (FER2013) Gabor_EM	**95**	96	96	**98**	**95**	**98**	**92**	**95.7**
	A	**D**	**F**	**H**	**N**	**S**	**U**	**Avrg**
Alexnet (FER2013) normal	91	96	**93**	95	**94**	96	93	94
Alexnet (FER2013) Canny	92	**98**	91	96	**94**	96	**94**	94
Alexnet (FER2013) MSB	**97**	96	92	96	93	95	93	**94.5**
Alexnet (FER2013) Gabor_EM	92	92	92	**97**	93	**98**	92	93.7
	A	**D**	**F**	**H**	**N**	**S**	**U**	**Avrg**
VGG16 (FER2013) normal	90	92	93	96	94	92	95	93
VGG16 (FER2013) Canny	92	**98**	95	95	90	90	91	93
VGG16 (FER2013) MSB	**96**	91	93	94	**95**	91	92	93
VGG16 (FER2013) Gabor_EM	94	94	**96**	**97**	**95**	**98**	**98**	**96**

Here A is angry, D is disgust, F is fear, H is happy, N is neutral, S is surprised, U is sadness, and Avrg is the mean accuracy. The extracted image dataset of the Gabor-EM feature achieves the highest precision in all models. But in all seven emotions, the Gabor-EM process did not achieve the highest accuracy. Much of the emotions generated by the Gabor EM had the highest accuracy (bold), but in some emotions, the MSB plane slicing and Canny filter (bold) also compete with Gabor EM with distinct CNN models and datasets. Disgust, happiness, and surprise are the most unequal feelings that CNN can remember. Sadness, as many of them misclassified sorrow into anger and fear, is the most difficult emotion to identify. This suggests that it is difficult for CNN to differentiate sadness since it appears close to anger and fear.

10.4 Vehicle driver emotion recognition experimental setup, results, and discussion

In this section, we set up an experimental setup and check the findings obtained from different models of recognition of facial emotions that are suggested in Section 10.3. We used a vehicle with one webcam, one speaker, and one i5 laptop in our experimental setup. The webcam was fixed on the windshield of the car (front) and was centered to face the driver (1-m range), linked to the laptop almost with a speaker system. On the laptop, three kinds of facial expression recognition models discussed before are loaded. Three types of models, namely MSB + Lenet, Canny + Lenet, and Gabor EM + Lenet, have been checked. The webcam's streaming video was transformed into frames of 120 × 90 resolutions at 24 fps. Using the face detection technique, each frame face is identified using the Haar-like feature. The detected face is cropped and, using feature extraction techniques (MSB/Canny/Gabor-EM), per-feature extraction is carried out. The extracted prefeature image is then transferred to the Lenet model (which is already generated and loaded). The output of the classification method produced any one of seven emotions. Finally, the system plays the music or warning on the basis of the emotion result. This configuration is demonstrated in Figure 10.22.

Figure 10.22   Real-time testing

Four Indians participated in this experiment: three of them were male and one of them was female, ranging in age from 30 years to 50 years and whose height varied from 157 cm to 170 cm. The experiment was conducted under sunny lighting conditions on the road. The participants sat inside the vehicle and were driving. The system was able to identify the emotions of the participant while driving and play the alarm or music appropriately. Depending on the prefeature extraction technique used, the accuracy of the device varied, and the results are shown in Table 10.3, and the different prefeature extraction process of detected face images is shown in Figure 10.23.

With the Lenet model, the MSP prefeature extraction technique showed poor results in experiments (Figure 10.24(b) and Table 10.3) because the MSP method was unable to extract features in inadequate lighting conditions. Then the race was between the methods of extraction due to Canny and Gabor EM methods. The Canny method produced the extraction of the edge feature (Figure 10.23(c)) and was fed to the Lenet model, and then it produced good precision, but surprisingly it misclassified angry and neutral emotions as sad (Table 10.3). The Gabor EM extracts useful features of the image with the element-wise maximum feature extraction technique (Figure 10.23(d)) and generates excellent Lenet model classification results. But for Participant M3, neutral emotion was misclassified by the

Table 10.3   overall classification results

Participant	MSB + Lenet		Canny + Lenet		Gabor_EM + Lenet	
	Emotion	Label	Emotion	Label	Emotion	Label
Participant M1	Neutral	Sad	Neutral	Neutral	Neutral	Neutral
Participant M2	Surprise	Neutral	Surprise	Angry	Surprise	Surprise
Participant M3	Neutral	Happy	Neutral	Sad	Neutral	Sad
Participant F1	Neutral	Neutral	Neutral	Neutral	Neutral	Neutral
Accuracy	¼		2/4		3/4	

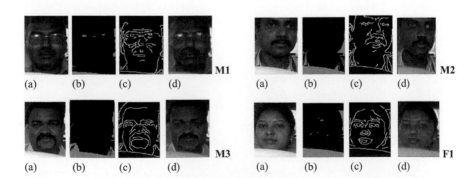

Figure 10.23   Prefeature extracted MSB (b), Canny (c), and Gabor_EM (d) image of original image (a)

Gabor-EM model because the edge of the facial features showed it as sad. Based on the above analysis, we have seen that proper feature extraction and excellent classification are provided by the Gabor EM with CNN models. In the sunny light conditions, the experiment was carried out. Often the lighting inside the car was not adequate, so the MSB model has failed. Head movement and facial orientation are other studies in this experiment. Often, because of some extraordinary circumstance, the participant has not shown a straight face to the camera (Participant M2 in Figure 10.23). In our future enhancements, we need to consider this situation.

10.5 Conclusion

We have considered the effects and performance of various prefeature extraction techniques with a CNN model. We have studied our performance with respect to three networks namely LeNet, Alexnet, and VGG16. As a case study, we considered the facial emotion recognition and evaluated the person we used two datasets namely JAFFE and FER2013. Our findings show that the extraction of the Gabor-EM feature method yielded accuracy with respect to the three networks of 97%. The extraction using the MSB slicing method increases precision up to 95%. The extraction of the Gaussian Canny function gave an accuracy of up to 94%. And in CPU-based systems, Gabor-EM's execution time is lower than others.

Acknowledgments

The proposed work was carried out at the TIFAC-CORE in Automotive Infotronics Research Centre at VIT, Vellore. The authors would like to thank DST, Government of India, for the support given to the center.

References

[1] Ekman, P. and Friesen, W. V. "Constants across cultures in the face and emotion." *Journal of Personality and Social Psychology*. 1971; 17(2):124.

[2] Zhang, Y., and Hua, C. "Driver fatigue recognition based on facial expression analysis using local binary patterns." *Optik – International Journal for Light and Electron Optics*. 2015; 126(23): 4501–4505.

[3] Shan, C. "Facial expression recognition based on local binary patterns: A comprehensive study." *Image and Vision Computing*. 2009; 27(6): 803–816.

[4] Whitehill, J., and Omlin, C. W. "Haar features for FACS AU recognition." In *7th In-ternational Conference on Automatic Face and Gesture Recognition (FGR06)*. pp. 5–101. 2006.

[5] Berretti, S. "A set of selected SIFT features for 3D facial expression recognition." In: 2010 *20th International Conference on Pattern Recognition (ICPR)*. pp. 4125–4128. 2010.

[6]   Liu, C., and Wechsler, H. "Gabor feature based classification using the enhanced Fisher linear discriminant model for face recognition." *IEEE Transactions on Image Processing.* 2002; 11(4): 467–476.

[7]   Wang, Z., and Ying, Z. "Facial expression recognition based on local phase quanti-zation and sparse representation." In 2012 *Eighth International Conference on Natural Computation* (ICNC). pp. 222–225. 2012.

[8]   He, K., Zhang, X., Ren, H., and Sun, J. "Deep residual learning for image recognition." *Computer Vision and Pattern Recognition.* 2015; 1512. arXiv:1512.03385.

[9]   Mayya, V., Pai, R. M., and Manohara Pai, M. M. "Automatic facial expression recognition using DCNN." *6th International Conference on Advances in Computing & Communications, ICACC 2016,* 6–8 September 2016, Cochin, India. pp. 453–461. Elsevier; 2016.

[10]   Pramerdorfer, C., and Kampel, M. "Facial expression recognition using convolutional neural networks: State of the art." *Computer Vision and Pattern Recognition,* 2016. arXiv:1612.02903v1.

[11]   Challenges in representation learning: Facial expression recognition challenge. Available from http://www.kaggle.com/c/challengesin-representation-learning-facial-expression-recognitionchallenge [Accessed September 18, 2020].

[12]   Lopes A. T., de Aguiar E., De Souza A. F, and Oliveira-Santos T. "Facial expression recognition with convolutional neural networks: Coping with few data and the training sample order." *Pattern Recognition.* 2017; 61: 610–628.

[13]   JAFFE (Japanese Female Facial Expression Dataset). Available from http://www.kasrl.org/jaffe.html [Accessed October 20, 2020].

[14]   Lucey, P., Cohn, J., Kanade, T., Saragih, J., Ambadar, Z., and Matthews, I. "The extended Cohn–Kanade dataset (CK+): A complete dataset for action unit and emotion- specified expression." In *2010 IEEE Computer Society Conference on Computer Vision and Pattern Recognition Workshops* (CVPRW). 2010, pp. 94–101.

[15]   Connie, T., Al-Shabi, M., Cheah, W. P., and Goh, M. "Facial expression recognition using a hybrid CNN–SIFT aggregator." *Multi-disciplinary trends in artificial intelligence.* Cham: Springer; 2017; 39–149. https://doi.org/10.1007/978-3-319-69456-6_12

[16]   Alizadeh, S., and Fazel, A. "Convolutional neural networks for facial expression recognition." *Computer Vision and Pattern Recognition.* 2017. arXiv:1704.06756v1.

[17]   Laranjeira A., Frazão X., Pimentel A., and Ribeiro B. 'How deep can we rely on emotion recognition." *Progress in Pattern Recognition, Image Analysis, Computer Vision, and Applications. CIARP* 2016. Lecture Notes in Computer Science, vol 10125. Springer; 2017.

[18]   Li, W., Tsangouri, C., and Abtahi, F. "A recursive framework for expression recognition: From web images to deep models to game dataset." *Machine Vision and Applications.* 2018; 29: 489. https://doi.org/10.1007/s00138-017-0904-9

[19] Shah, Z. H. and Kaushik, V. "Performance analysis of Canny edge detection for illumination invariant Facial Expression recognition." *Industrial Instrumentation and Control (ICIC), International Conference.* IEEE; 2015. doi: 10.1109/IIC.2015.7150809.

[20] Kumar, A., and Agarwal, A. "Emotion recognition using anatomical information in facial expressions." *Industrial and Information Systems (ICIIS) 2014. 9th IEEE International Conference.* 2015.

[21] Saeed, S. "An exposition of facial expression recognition techniques." *Neural Computing and Applications.* 2016; 29:425–443. https://doi.org/10.1007/s00521-016-2522-2

[22] Jayaraman, S., Esakkirajan, S., and Veerakumar, T. *Digital image processing.* Indian Edition: Tata McGraw Hill Publication; 2015.

[23] Srinivas, T., Sandeep Mohan, P., Shiva Shankar, R., Surender Reddy, C., and Naganjaneyulu P.V. "Face recognition using PCA and bit-plane slicing." In *Proceedings of the Third International Conference on Trends in Information, Telecommunication and Computing.* Lecture Notes in Electrical Engineering, vol 150. New York, NY: Springer; 2013.

[24] Seal, A. "Minutiae from bit-plane sliced thermal images for human face recognition." *International Conference on SocProS 2011.* AISC 131, pp. 113–124, Springer India; 2012.

[25] Zhou, J., Zhang, S., Mei, H., and Wang, D. "A method of facial expression recognition based on Gabor and NMF." *Pattern Recognition and Image Analysis.* 2016; 26: 119.

[26] Rani, P.I. and Muneeswaran, K. "Recognize the facial emotion in video sequences using eye and mouth temporal Gabor features." *Multimedia Tools Application.* 2017; 76: 10017. https://doi.org/10.1007/s11042-016-3592-y

[27] Pitaloka, D. A., Wulandari, A., Basaruddin, T., and YantiLilianaa, D. "Enhancing CNN with preprocessing stage in automatic emotion recognition." Procedia Computer Science. 2017; 116: 523–529.

[28] LeCun, Y., Bottou, L., Bengio, Y., and Haffner, P. 'Gradient-based learning applied to document recognition'. *Proceedings of the IEEE.* 1998; 86(11): 2278–2324.

[29] Swarna Priya, R.M., Maddikunta, P. K. R., Parimala, M., *et al.* "An effective feature engineering for DNN using hybrid PCA-GWO for intrusion detection in IoMT architecture." *Computer Communications.* 2021; 160: 139–149.

[30] Simonyan, K., and Zisserman, A. 'Very deep convolutional networks for large-scale image recognition'. *Computer Vision and Pattern Recognition.* arXiv:1409.1556, 2014.

Chapter 11

MobileNet architecture and its application to computer vision

Rupa Patel[1] and Anita Chaware[1]

Abstract

With the advancement in technologies, computer vision aims to imitate the potential capacities of human vision. Many computer vision applications are finding place in our lives. Deep convolutional neural network (DCNN) is a driving force behind these applications. It first extracts low-level features such as lines and edges, then progressively extracts higher and complex features from the data to give the desired output. More the number of layers in the network, higher the accuracy of the network. No doubt a large network gives better results but it will use too much power and becomes a heavy network.

Nowadays, smartphones have become an integral part of day-to-day life. If computer vision applications can be used in smartphones then the user can use them anywhere and anytime. The increasing adoption of edge devices has motivated researchers to focus on the network that will work with these resource-restricted edge devices.

A large family of deep convolutional neural network (DCNN) works with floating point precision format (float32). This makes the network heavy thereby increasing the computation and inference time. These heavy weight networks are not suitable to be deployed directly on resource-constrained devices. The resource-restricted devices have limited computational speed, power, and storage capabilities. With mobiles, if cloud services are used for processing and analyzing the visual information then not only system inference time will increase but it will also require good Internet connectivity and good bandwidth. Apart from this, there are certain domains where the confidentiality of data is of utmost importance. If we are dealing with the healthcare domain, then the privacy of data needs to be preserved. This leads to the need for on-device machine learning models.

For mobile and embedded devices, light weight models are required. These Mobile Net architectures are efficient models for mobile and embedded applications. The expected desirable properties of such network are small

---

[1]P.G. Department of Computer Science, S.N.D.T. Women's University, Juhu Campus, Mumbai, India

model size, low latency, low power consumption, and sufficiently high accuracy. To deploy large DCNN on mobile devices, one needs to optimize them. Quantization techniques are used to compress the models. Vgg16, Inceptionv3, MobileNetV1, MobileNetV2, and NASNet Mobile models are first fine-tuned. Then quantization aware training is used to optimize these fine-tuned networks. These optimized models can be used for any computer vision application.

In this study, the diabetic retinopathy dataset is used for experimental purpose. The model complexity is analyzed by counting the number of learnable parameters. Experimental result shows that the optimized fine-tuned model size is reduced since the number of trainable parameters is less as compared to their counterpart fine-tuned models. There is a marginal difference in accuracy between fine-tuned and quantized models. InceptionV3 is better than VGG16. NASNETmobile architecture outperforms MobileNetv1 and MobileNetv2.

This chapter reveals the Mobile Net architecture that is built especially for its use on mobile devices.

Key Words: Deep convolutional neural network (DCNN); artificial neural network (ANN); convolutional neural network (CNN); quantized deep convolutional neural network

---

11.1   Introduction

One of the basic definitions of artificial intelligence that we often come across is to make computers do things which at the moment people do better. Believe it or not, researchers dreamed of imparting human intelligence in a machine, a machine that can think like humans and act like humans. One of the enthralling ideas is to make machines capture, analyze, and interpret visual information the way the human visual system works. The human visual system includes the eye that acquires information (image) about the environment and the brain that processes this information and interprets it. Computer vision, often abbreviated as CV, is a subfield of artificial intelligence. It aims at developing methods and algorithms that can help computers process visual data (usually digital images and videos), retrieve information from it, analyzes and interprets it. The importance of computer vision is growing since several real-life domains are benefitting from this technology. Healthcare, agriculture, security domain, and gaming to name a few.

Over a decade, deep convolution neural network (DCNN) has become an effective approach for solving a wide variety of computer vision problems. With deep learning (DL), many computer vision applications such as image classification (medical image classification and image style classification), object detection (face detection and recognition, and self-driving car), and semantic segmentation (text detection from images) have been introduced and are becoming a part of everyday lives. These applications can be provided for Internet-connected systems with high computational speed, power, and large storage capabilities. Most of the machine vision systems require cloud computing also. In cloud computing, the visual information is sent into the cloud for computation and analysis, which then provide an appropriate response to the devices.

In this era of digital technology, it is observed that everyone is so dependent on mobile smart devices and embedded devices that they have become an essential and inseparable part of day-to-day life. Imagine if the same device can be used for computer vision tasks then it would make life better and help society at large. But mobile devices are resource-constrained devices. They have limited storage and processing capabilities and often run on batteries. In general, the large deep neural network model such as LeNet, AlexNet, VGG16, VGG19, and Inceptionv3 gives better accuracy but at the cost of execution speed. If the same architecture is used on mobile phones, it will not only make the smartphones hot but will also drain its battery. Therefore computer vision task on mobile devices generally uses cloud services for processing information and providing predictions to the users for further actions. This can lead to increased latencies in system response time. With the cloud-based, application developers have to ensure that the complete process (data transferred, process, and returned) should be at the speeds according to application requirements.

A small DCNN that matches the requirement of resource-constrained devices is the need of an hour. An architecture with low latency, low power consumption, small model size, and good accuracy will make it suitable for computer vision tasks on Mobile devices. This will enable users of the devices to use computer vision applications anywhere, anytime regardless of Internet connections. Model compression techniques such as quantization, pruning, and distillation can be applied on pretrained deep neural networks. This approach reduces the model size as well as computational and inference time. This makes them easy to deploy on resource-constrained devices. Thus optimization technique is an effective and efficient approach for deploying DCNN to smartphones.

11.2 Preliminaries

This section provides the background necessary for understanding MobileNet architecture. A brief overview of the artificial neural network (ANN), CNN, and DCNN is given.

11.2.1 Artificial neural network

Artificial neural networks are conceptually inspired by human brains. The network consists of neurons arranged in layers. The input layer receives all the input, the hidden layer does all the processing, and an output layer gives the output of the computation [1]. A simple ANN is depicted in Figure 11.1.

Each neuron in a network is connected with adjacent layers of neurons through a connection. Each connection has a particular weight. It decides how much

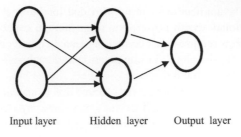

Input layer   Hidden layer   Output layer

Figure 11.1   A simple ANN

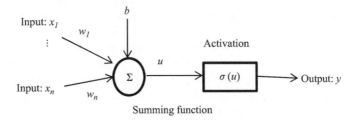

Figure 11.2   A single neuron. Adapted from [1]

influence the input will have on the output. A single neuron may take the input from the previous layer multiplied by the weight and then add a bias before passing the data to the next layer. Bias is the constant value, it guarantees that there will be activation in a neuron even when all the inputs are zero. Weights and bias are the learnable parameters of the neural network. The activation function (σ) normalizes the weighted sum of the neuron before it passes to the next layer. Activation function can be linear, sigmoid, Tanh, ReLu, or any other function. Figure 11.2 shows a single neuron with input $X_1, \ldots, X_n$, weights $W_1, \ldots, W_n$, and a bias b [1]:

$$y = \sigma(W_1 X_1 + W_2 X_2 + \ldots + W_n X_n + b) \tag{11.1}$$

11.2.1.1   How artificial neural network works?

Consider a digital image of size 28×28. The image is composed of pixels (picture element), the smallest addressable unit on the screen. Each pixel has an intensity value, a number representing the brightness and magnitude of a pixel. The internal representation of an image is stored as a grid (two-dimensional array). Let us see how neural network works.

- Input layer: Total number of pixels in a digital image is 784 (28 multiplied by 28). Each one of these 784 pixels holds a grayscale value between zero and one. This number in a neuron is called an activation value. When activation of a neuron is high then that neuron is lived up. For all these 784 pixels of the image, there will be 784 neurons in the first input layer of the network.

- Hidden layer: The number of neurons in these layers is the arbitrary choice. Recognizing the image involves identifying the edges that make it up. Each neuron in the first hidden layer corresponds to the various little edges of the image which in turn up the neurons in the next upper layers. All the activation is considered and the weighted sum is calculated as shown in Figure 11.2. The bias is also added. Since the activation should be between zero and one, the activation function is applied.
- Output layer: The number of neurons in the last layer depends upon the classes/ labels in which we have to classify the image. If the input image consists of a handwritten number, then the task is to identify it. As the numbers are from zero to nine, the last output layer of the network will have ten neurons indicating which digit a network is choosing. If there are five classes/labels to which our image may belong then there will be five neurons in the output layer. Therefore, depending on the problem domain, the number of neurons will be present in the output layer. The activation in these neurons represents how much the system thinks the give image corresponds to the particular class or to a particular label.

For example:

- Task: to recognize handwritten digit. Input image size: 28×28—total 784 pixels.
- Expected output: one of the digits (from 0 to 9).
- Artificial neural network: first layer (input layer): 784 neurons, second layer (first hidden layer), and third layer (second hidden layer): 16 neurons each, and last layer (output layer): ten neurons.
- Learnable parameters (weights and bias): The first connection is between the first and second layer of the network. Sixteen neurons in the second layer are connected to 784 neurons of the first layer along with 16 biases, let the bias value be 10:

$$\text{weights} = 784 \times 16 + 16 \times 16 + 10 \times 16 \text{ and bias} = 16+16+10.$$

In this way, weight and bias are calculated for all the connected neurons in the subsequent layers. Each neuron in the output layer will have the activation value. This process is called feed-forward propagation to determine the output.

If the desired (actual) output is 4 but the activation value (predicted output) of the corresponding neuron is different than there is an error in the output. Error is calculated between the correct value and the predicted value using some calculus. It is back propagated to the network so that accordingly weights and bias are changed to achieve the higher activation for the correct output. This is done for each output neuron. The process is called backpropagation. This is how the neural network learns.

Broadly speaking, supervised, unsupervised, semisupervised, and reinforcement learning are the learning strategies for using ANNs in solving a particular problem. Supervised learning is also referred to as learning with the teacher. Along with the input data, the target data are provided. The predetermined class labels are provided and the network is trained based on the labeled training dataset. In unsupervised learning, during training, only input data are provided. The network learns itself depending on some structure in the input data. During training, labeled and nonlabeled data are used in semisupervised learning. In reinforcement learning, the input data are provided and activation is propagated forward but it will just convey whether the network has produced target output or not [2].

11.2.2 Convolution neural network

Convolution neural network (CNN) also referred to as ConvNet is a multilayer ANN. This network is designed especially for pattern recognition and image classification task. To solve the computer vision problem, it is important to understand how to extract the information from the image pixels and interpret it.

The structure of a simple convolutional neural network as shown in Figure 11.3 consists of the input layer, the convolution layer, the pooling layer, the fully connected layer, and the output layer. The functionality of the input layer is the same as that of ANN. When convolution layers, pooling layers, and fully connected layers are stacked, a CNN architecture is formed.

11.2.2.1 Convolution layer

The convolution layer is used to extract the features from the input image, that is, to detect the patterns in the image. The first convolution layer in any network is generally used to detect the edges of the image. The convolution layer as the name indicates is based on the mathematical function of convolution [2]. This is the backbone of CNN.

The input vector is generally padded with zero. If $P=1$, then the input matrix is padded with zero from all the sides as shown in Figure 11.4(a). This allows the kernel to uniformly move over the input vector and the resultant feature map will have the desired dimension. Through zero padding [2], the spatial dimensionality of the convolutional layer output can be altered:

Suppose input image size $(V) = D_F \times D_F \times M$

where D_F is the height of the image and D_F is the width of the image and M is the depth of the image (number of channels, in case of the color image (RGB) = 3, grayscale = 1)

Kernel/filter $= D_K \times D_K \times N$

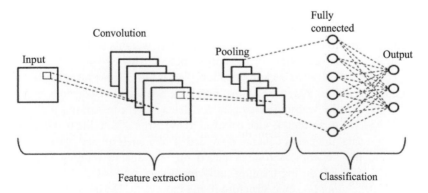

Figure 11.3   A simple CNN. Adapted from [2]

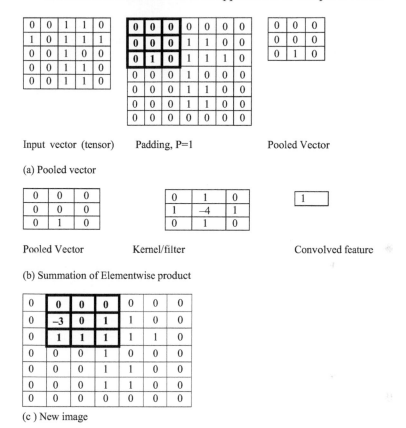

Input vector (tensor)   Padding, P=1   Pooled Vector

(a) Pooled vector

Pooled Vector   Kernel/filter   Convolved feature

(b) Summation of Elementwise product

(c) New image

Figure 11.4   Representation of convolution layer operation

where D_K is the height and width of the kernel, N is the number of kernel,
 Zero padding $= Z$, the amount of padding
 Stride $= S$, kernel moves over the image S pixel at the time
 Feature map size:

$$R = ((V - R) + 2Z)/(S + 1) \tag{11.2}$$

If the result of (11.2) is not an integer, then it indicates that stride is not correctly set [2].

The kernel size can be either 1×1 or 3×3 or 5×5, or 7×7. In Figure 11.4(b), convolution of the image with an edge detection filter is applied. The convolution operation is performed between the tensor and a kernel. The summation of the element-wise product is taken between the part of the input vector and the kernel by sliding the filter over the image. The computed value is then placed into the image as shown in Figure 11.4(c). The filter slides over the image. If the kernel moves over the image 1 pixel at a time, then it is said to have a stride equal to 1. The process is

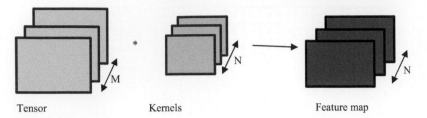

Figure 11.5   *Convolution layer operation with more than one channel and with more than one filter*

repeated to get the feature map. In an example, to an input image of size $5 \times 5 \times 1$, only one filter of size $3 \times 3 \times 1$ is applied with bias zero.

If the depth of the image $M > 1$ and the depth of the kernel $N > 1$, then the above-explained convolution operation is repeated for each of the channels (Figure 11.5) and then they are added up along with the bias of the respective filter. This convolved value corresponds to the value in the corresponding position of the feature map as depicted in Figure 11.6.

Kernels can be considered as feature extractors. Different kernels extract different characteristics of the input tensor. Maximum features can be extracted from the image if the number of filters is increased. The network will be able to recognize patterns more accurately.

For standard convolution operation (Figure 11.7), the output dimensions can be calculated using formula (11.3):

$$(D_F - D_K + 1) \times (D_F - D_K + 1) \times N \tag{11.3}$$

Total computation cost can be obtained using formula (11.4) [3]:

$$\text{Total computation} = D_K \times D_K \times D_F \times D_F \times M \times N \tag{11.4}$$

11.2.2.2   Activation function

The activation function helps to normalize the output of each neuron. It introduces nonlinearity into the neuron output. It determines which neurons should be activated based on the input relevant to the model's prediction. The softmax activation function is used to handle the classification problem and is generally used in the output layer. ReLu is a widely used activation function and is usually implemented in hidden layers.

11.2.2.3   Pooling layer

It is performed to reduce the dimensionality of the convolved feature. This decreases the computational power required for processing the data and also helps to extract dominant features. Max pooling, average pooling, and sum pooling are the different types of pooling. Max pooling returns the maximum value of the part of the image covered by the kernel [2,5]. Average pooling takes the average of all the values while sum pooling returns the summation of all elements in the feature map covered by the kernel.

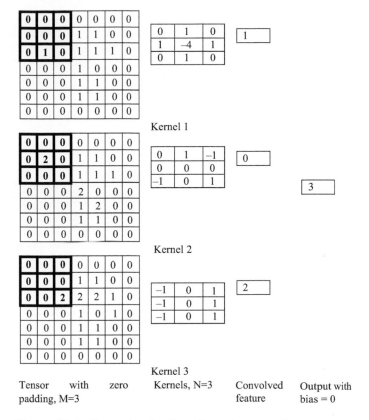

Figure 11.6   Steps showing how input is mapped to an output

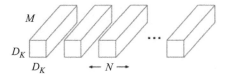

Figure 11.7   Standard convolution. Adapted from [3]

11.2.2.4   Fully connected layer

Every neuron in a fully connected network is connected to every other neuron of the next layer. It is often referred to as a feed-forward network. The output from the pooling layer is a three-dimensional matrix. These data are flattened and are converted into one dimension vector. It is then fed into a fully connected layer or ANN. The feed-forward propagation is used to obtain the output vector from input vector. While backpropagation is used to improve the neural network performance. Feed-forward and backpropagation together are considered as one complete pass for one epoch. Since training dataset is used to train the neural network. In one epoch the network will work through entire dataset. Over the succession of epochs, the neural network model is able to differentiate between dominating and low level features in images. Images are classified using softmax classification approach [4,5].

11.2.3 Deep convolution neural network

A deep CNN is a multilayer neural network with DL capability. An important characteristic of the network is that it progressively extracts higher and complex features from the data at each layer to provide the desired output. It is supervised by single feedback. Whenever a network adjusts internal features, all other features depending on it automatically adapt to the change. This allows more complex and abstract information to be learned by intermediate layers. Due to these properties, DL is gaining importance [5] and have become an effective approach for solving a wide variety of computer vision problems

11.3 Benchmarked convolutional neural network

11.3.1 VGG16

VGGNet was born out of the necessity to reduce the number of parameters in the CONV layers and improve on training time. There are several variants of VGGNet (VGG16, VGG19, etc.) which differ only in the total number of layers in the network [7]. VGG16 has a total of 138 million parameters [8]. All the conv kernels are of size 3×3 and max pool kernels are of size 2×2 with a stride of two [7]. It contains 140 million parameters and is expensive.

11.3.2 Inception v3

Inception-v3 is a classical deep network. The network is composed of 11 inception modules of five kinds in total. Each module is designed by experts with a convolutional layer, activation layer, pooling layer, and batch normalization layer. In the Inception-v3 model, these modules are concatenated to achieve maximal feature extraction [9].

11.4 MobileNet architecture

MobileNet architecture refers to the class of efficient models for mobile and embedded vision applications.

11.4.1 MobileNetv1

In the year 2017, Google researchers proposed MobileNetv1 architecture. The basic goal of MobileNetV1 is to use a fewer number of parameters indirectly smaller network and the second goal was to use a lesser multiplication and addition computation. MobileNetV1 is a low power, low latency, and open-source architecture

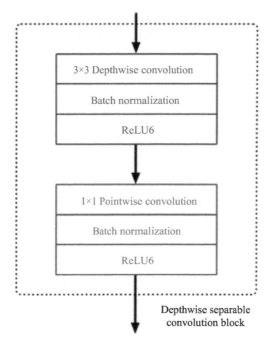

Depthwise separable
convolution block

Figure 11.8   Depthwise separable convolution block diagram. Adapted from [11]

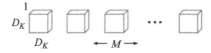

(a) Depthwise Convolutional Filters

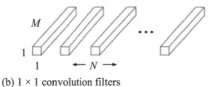

(b) 1 × 1 convolution filters

Figure 11.9   Depthwise separable convolution filters. Adapted from [3,11]

for efficient on-device vision designed to maximize accuracy keeping in mind the resource constraints of edge devices [3,10].

MobileNetv1 is 28 layers of streamlined architecture. The key ingredient of this architecture is depthwise separable convolution and a set of two hyperparameters—width and resolution multiplier. The architecture consists of a 3×3 convolution layer as a first layer followed by 13 times of depthwise separable convolution block. Depthwise separable convolution block is depicted in Figures 11.8 and 11.9. Each block is followed by batch normalization followed by the activation function ReLU6. It is observed that ReLU6 is more robust with low precision computation.

Depthwise separable convolution: It helps to build a lightweight deep neural network. It is a combination of two convolution operations—depthwise convolution followed by pointwise convolution. Depthwise convolution operates channel-wise. First, it convolutes only on each channel. That is, in depthwise convolution, each channel of a kernel is used to produce a feature map. To create a new feature, pointwise convolution combines the output channels of depthwise convolution (filtered values to create new features).

Let the input size of the image: $D_F \times D_F \times M$

where D_F is the width, D_F is the height, and M is the number of input channels.

Filter/Kernel size : $D_K \times D_K \times N$

where D_K is the width, D_K is the height of the kernel, and N is the number of filters.

In depthwise convolution, each channel of a kernel is used to produce a feature map. In depth-wise convolution, a filter of shape $D_F \times D_F \times 1$ is applied to each input channel to produce an output $D_G \times D_G \times M$.

The cost of computation in the first step $= D_K \times D_K \times M \times N \times D_F \times D_F$

In point-wise convolution, the filter of shape $1 \times 1 \times N$ is applied on the output of the first step to produce an output of shape $DG \times DG \times N$.

The cost of computation in the second step $= M \times N \times D_F \times D_F$.

Combining the cost of computation from both steps in depth-wise separable convolution, we get the

$$\text{Total cost} = D_K \times D_K \times M \times N \times D_F \times D_F + M \times N \times D_F \times D_F \quad (11.5)$$

Hyperparameters: The width multiplier and resolution multiplier can be used to build the small and fast architecture. Width multiplier can take the value {0.25, 0.5, 0.75, and 1}. This uniformly thins a network at each layer thereby reducing the number of parameter and computational cost. The resolution multiplier takes the values {224,192,160,128}, thereby reducing the input size.

11.4.2   MobileNetv2

MobileNetv2 is the second version of MobileNet architecture unveiled in 2018. It is a 53 layer architecture with an input size of 224 × 224. It uses previous architecture depthwise separable convolution. The main building block of MobileNetv2 is depicted in Figure 11.10.

The bottleneck is used to obtain a representation of input data with reduced dimensionality. Residual block is often referred to as identity block (see Figure 11.11).

Where I is the input, $H(I)$ is the expected output, and $R(I)$ is the residual connection. One can skip the training of few layers using skip connection or residual connection. The activation from the previous layer is being fast-forwarded to the activation of a deeper neural network.

On a similar ground in MobileNetv2, the bottleneck residual block task is to reduce the amount of data flows through the network. The advantage of doing this

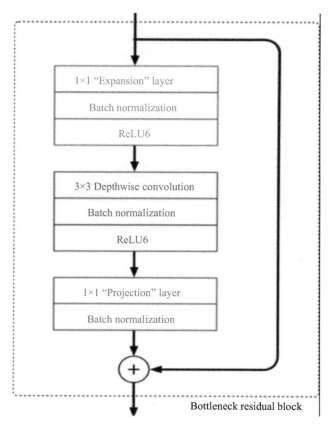

Figure 11.10   Bottleneck residual block diagram. Adapted from [11]

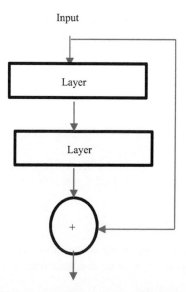

Figure 11.11   Bottleneck residual layers

is to reduce the number of computation, that is, lesser multiplication at the convolution layer. The input tensor and output tensor of the block has a low dimension while inside the block, the tensor has a high dimension. The low dimension tensor requires less multiplication thereby reducing the number of computation. But with low dimensional tensors, it is difficult to extract maximum information. So the expansion layer decompresses the data. Depthwise filter then performs the filtering and the projection layer compresses the data.

Three convolution layers are present. The 1×1 expansion layer whose purpose is to expand the number of channels in the data before it goes into the depthwise convolution. The expansion layer has more output channels than input channels. Data are expanded using expansion factor 6 and this is the default value. Depthwise convolution applies its filter to expanded input. The projection layer/bottleneck layer compresses the data to make its size the same as that of input size. This layer project data into tensor with low dimension. The expansion and projection layer uses learnable parameters so that architecture can learn at each stage in the network. Except for the projection layer, every other layer has batch normalization and activation function [11,12].

11.4.3   MobileNetv3

MobileNetv3 relies on AutoMLMobileNetv3. It was introduced to optimize Mobilenetv2. It is a combination of depthwise separable convolution, inverted residual with linear bottleneck, and squeeze and excitation structure of MnasNet. It combines the advantage of MobileNetv1, MobileNetv2, and MnasNet architecture.

In MobileNetv2 expansion, the layer is used so that maximum features can be extracted. It involves overhead and delays. To reduce this, author [13] introduced the h-swish activation function and effectively improve the accuracy of the network:

$$\text{h-swish}\,[x] = x\frac{\text{ReLU6}(x+3)}{6} \tag{11.6}$$

To work in different conditions without compromising on the performance, google researchers introduced two new MobileNet models for high and low resources MobileNetV3-Large and MobileNetV3-Small. The main contribution of MobileNetV3 is the use of AutoML to find the best possible neural network architecture for a given problem.

On mobile CPUs, MobileNetV3 is twice as fast as MobileNetV2 with equivalent accuracy and advances the state-of-the-art for mobile computer vision networks.

MobileNetV3 is still the best performing network when using mobile CPU as the deployment target.

The combination of swish nonlinearity, squeeze-and-excitation layers, depthwise and pointwise convolutions are used in MobilNetV 3 as the building blocks to build the most effective models.

11.4.4   NASNet mobile

The process of designing a neural network for a particular domain specially for a large dataset requires expertise. It is time-consuming and expensive also. NasNet addressed this problem. Neural architecture search (NAS) developed by Google Brain is a technique that automates the designing of architecture to give good performance for a certain task on a small dataset. Then the same architectural design to transfer to a larger dataset.

NasNet search space is used in the NAsNet model. In this search space, all the convolutional networks have identical convolutional layer structures but with different weights [14]. The best convolutional layer (cell) is searched by the reinforcement learning search method on the small dataset of interest (CIFAR-10). Normal cells and reduction cells are the two types of convolutional cells used in the NasNet model. The input to the cells is a feature map. The input and output feature map dimension (height and width) is the same for a normal cell while the dimension of the output feature map returned by the reduction cell is reduced by a factor of 2. For the CIFAR-10 dataset, the best convolutional layer was designed and then the copies of these cells are stacked, each with its parameters to be applied to the ImageNet dataset. To optimize CNN for different sizes, NAS can be used. NASNETMobile is the reduced version.

11.5   Model optimization techniques

To deploy heavyweight CNN models on a resource-constrained mobile device, we need to apply model optimization strategies. Quantization, pruning, and clustering are the strategies that can be applied to the models to make them lightweight models. In pruning, the parameters that have less significance on model prediction are pruned. Using quantization technique models with low precision and computing can be created [15–17,19].

11.5.1   Quantization technique

Most of the DCNN models are heavyweight. One of the reasons for this is the models operate with floating-point precision format (float 32). The model's parameters are stored in this format. The speed of the network inference is directly correlated with the parameters' precision format. If the precision format is reduced (float16 or int8), the size of the model will be compressed and the prediction speed will be improved. There are two approaches.

- Post-training quantization: Post-training quantization is applied to the trained models.
- Quantization aware training: Due to quantization, some information is lost. In quantization aware training, model is trained in a way that it would learn to compensate the loss of information. Literature study reveals that the quantization aware technique outperforms the post-training quantization approach in terms of model accuracy [17].

11.6   Quantized deep convolutional neural network

VGG16, Inceptionv3, MobileNetv1, MobileNetv2, and NASNET-mobile architecture are compressed using the quantization aware technique. Quantized models

Table 11.1   The number of parameters in the networks

Models	Trainable	Nontrainable
VGG16	14,717,253	0
Quantized VGG16	14,713,029	12,728
Inceptionv3	21,778,597	432
Quantized Inceptionv3	21,761,381	86,542
MobileNetv1	3,272,901	21,888
Quantized MobileNetv1	2,19,322	88,388
MobileNetv2	2,306,181	34,112
Quantized mobileNetv2	2,272,069	88,394

use 8-bit precision. Thereby compressing the models. The latency is also reduced. The model size is generally shrunk by 4×.

11.6.1   Methodology

The following steps are involved:

1. Load predefined model
   Excluding the top classification layers, the predefined model is loaded. The model is customized by adding our stacked classifier.
2. Train the fine-tuned network
   The predefined network is freezed so that it should not forget what it has learned with a large dataset. Thereby the weights will not get updated during network training. Only the classifier which is stacked over the predefined network is trained.
3. Quantize the model
   The models are very heavy due to the precision it uses. There is a direct correlation between the heaviness of the model and the speed with which it makes predictions. So if the model precision is reduced, automatically prediction time will also decrease. The models are quantized to reduce their size. This often results in loss of information. To compensate for it, quantization aware training is used [19].
4. Train the quantize fine-tuned model
5. Evaluate the quantize fine-tuned model

The accuracy of the quantized model may be degraded. But the drop in accuracy is acceptable.

Using this approach a lightweight architecture can be built and that can be deployed on resource-constrained mobile devices.

Weights and bias are considered as parameters of trainable parameters that are optimized during the learning phase while nontrainable parameters are not optimized during the training phase. Table 11.1 shows the parameters of eight networks.

11.7   Case study: healthcare domain

The healthcare domain mostly relies on different types of images and screening for diagnosis and patient treatment, and this is where computer vision in healthcare comes into the picture. Although technology cannot replace medical professionals, yes it can simplify their task by assisting them.

One of the major health issues that are raising alarm worldwide is diabetes. According to IDF Diabetes Atlas Ninth edition 2019 almost half a million people are diabetic and it will rise to 578 million by 2030 [18].

Automatic screening of retinal fundus images can provide vital information and can speed up the detection of the severity of disease thereby identifying the potential patients.

In this study, VGG16, Inceptionv3, MobileNetv1, MobileNetv2, and NAsNetmobile architecture are evaluated to identify how useful they are as feature extractors. Feature extractor is the heart of any model on which the rest of the model is built.

Quantized VGG16, Quantized Inceptionv3, Quantized MobileNetv1, Quantized MobileNetv2, and Quantized NAsNetmobile architecture are also evaluated to identify which quantized model can become the heart of the mobile phone operating system.

11.7.1   Diabetic retinopathy

Diabetic retinopathy (DR) is an eye disease, if not treated timely it can lead to loss of vision. It is caused due to damage in the blood vessel of the retina. There are mainly two stages of DR. Nonproliferative diabetic retinopathy is an early stage of DR (mild, moderate, and severe) and proliferative diabetic retinopathy is an advanced stage of DR. It generally affects the vision [10].

11.7.2   Kaggle diabetic retinopathy image datasets

Data collection is one of the important steps in a health care domain since the privacy and security of the information are of utmost importance. Most of the researchers generally use easily available public datasets for study purposes. For this study, the dataset of diabetic retinopathy images is taken from Kaggle. It consists of a large set of retina images taken under different conditions using fundus photography. Each image is rated according to the severity of diabetic disease on a scale of 0–4 [10,20] (Table 11.2).

Table 11.2   Types of diabetic retinopathy

Scale	Types of DR
0	No DR
1	Mild
2	Moderate
3	Severe
4	Proliferative diabetic retinopathy

11.7.3   Approach

1. Collect fundus retinal images
2. Preprocess the data
   (i) All the images are resized to 224 × 224. Then they are converted to an RGB color image. 80% of the data is considered for training purposes while the remaining 20% of data is used for validation purposes. To build the model, the training dataset is used while the validation dataset is used to check the efficiency of the network.
3. Train the fine-tuned models
4. Train the quantized fine-tuned models
5. Evaluate the models

11.7.4   Experiment results and discussion

The experiments are performed with all the five fine-tuned models and with all the five quantized fine-tuned models. All the models are trained for 40 iterations (epoch), with a batch size of 32, with an initial learning rate of 0.00002. GPU hardware accelerator is used to perform the experiments. We compared the classification results of a total of ten networks. There are 3662 retina fundus images in a Kaggle dataset. To train the models, 2,992 images were used. While 733 images are used for validation. These images belong to one of the classes [10,20]

The comparison between normal fine-tuned models and quantized fine-tuned models is shown in Table 11.3.

11.7.5   Conclusion

The models are optimized for mobile vision applications. The number of trainable parameters in quantized models has been reduced as compared to their counterparts. The testing accuracy achieved by the models shows that there is a marginal difference between fine-tuned and quantized fine-tuned networks and this is acceptable.

Table 11.3   The performance (%) of the networks on the clinical dataset: diabetic retinopathy

Fine-tuned baseline models	Accuracy	Quantized fine-tuned model	Accuracy
VGG16	97%	Quantized VGG16	90%
Inceptionv3	98%	Quantized Inceptionv3	93%
MobileNetv1	94%	Quantized MobileNetv1	80%
MobileNetv2	96%	Quantized mobileNetv2	81%
NasNetMobile	97%	Quantized NasNetMobile	85%

11.8   Selected MobileNet application

Computer vision technology has opened opportunities in many real-life domains such as the industry field, healthcare, transportation, agriculture, and security system to make human lives more efficient and safer. The most popular computer vision application involves image classification, object detection, and segmentation.

11.8.1   Image classification

Image classification involves extracting features (attributes) from the images to observe similar patterns in the dataset. Based on the extracted features images are assigned to different classes/labels. To classify the images into different categories the relationship between the data and the classes in which they are classified is given utmost importance. The role of an image classifier is to discriminate one class against another. Generally, it is high for one class and low for other classes.

11.8.1.1   Healthcare

There are many areas where computer vision is used for assisting healthcare such as timely detection of the early symptoms of fatal illness such as cancer, medical image classification, and analysis through which medical professionals can gain a comprehensive understanding of a patient's health condition.

Diseases such as cancer if diagnosed at an early stage then it will help doctors to save human lives. Computer vision serves as an assistant for healthcare professionals by excluding the possibilities of human error (false-negative/false-positive results as it may lead to delay in treatment) to some degree.

Breast cancer detection
The early detection and diagnosis of cancer progression is an efficient approach for controlling and treating the disease. Mammography is medical imaging (specialized X-ray) used to examine the human breast for screening breast abnormalities and diagnosis. Mammography helps in the early detection of cancer. Mass classification in mammograms plays a vital role in helping radiologists inaccurate diagnosis. Smartphones based breast cancer detection system [21] can provide an inexpensive and friendly way to detect cancer. For early breast cancer detection, MobileNet based architecture can be used to classify mass into malignant and benign. This can relieve radiologists from some of the burdens that screening impose and might reduce the number of cancer cases that would have slipped through the screening programs. MobileNetv1 architecture gives a better result. But Mobilenetv2 architecture with fewer parameters also gives almost similar results [22–24].

Skin cancer detection
Skin cancer means the abnormal growth of skin cells. It is categorized as Actinic Keratosis and Melanoma depending on the cells involved. Actinic Keratosis develops when the skin gets exposed to the sun and Melanoma develops when melanocyte cells are involved. The cause of Melanoma is due to exposure to UV light and genetic factors also. Through smartphones, it is possible to detect skin cancer.

Images can be captures by smartphone cameras and can be processed to detect abnormalities. This can tell the user whether it needs immediate attention (to visit a dermatologist) or not. It is possible to run the MobilenetV2 model on smartphones for image analysis of skin cancer detection and classification. The MobilenetV2 has 95% accuracy for object detection and 70% for classification [23].

Detection of Covid-19 from chest X-ray images
COVID-19 is a communicable disease caused by a newly discovered coronavirus. Most people infected with the COVID-19 virus experience mild to moderate respiratory disease and require special treatment. To save lives, it is necessary to detect COVID-19 at its initial stages. Infection caused due to COVID-19 can develop into pneumonia and it can be detected by examining chest X-ray images. To verify the lung conditions automated image analysis based on MobileNetv2 architecture has been developed to detect and monitor COVID-19 infections as well as healthy lungs.

Another lightweight DL model, LightCovidNet, for mobile phones is proposed to automate the X-ray screening process for potential carriers of Covid19 [25].

11.8.1.2   Other image classification example
Garbage classification
In every walk of life, there are unwanted materials that are generally considered waste. Household waste such as vegetable peeling leftover foods, industrial waste such as scrap metal, chemicals, wood, etc., and healthcare waste such as soiled dressing, needles, syringes, diagnostic samples, blood, etc. are generated. Grouping these waste materials into different categories is referred to as waste segregation. Classification of the garbage into plastic, paper, metal, and other trash is an important step in waste segregation, reuse, and recycle.

MobileNet architecture can be used to generate a model that can classify common trash according to different categories of waste materials. Stephen L. Rabano has developed a model that can successfully identify a cardboard container with the cardboard material in an image [26].

11.8.2   Object detection
Object detection is one of the computer vision technique that identifies and recognize an object within an image or video. In this technique, the bounding box is drawn around the object of interest, this helps to find the object and label it.

The input image is first divided into different regions. Each region is then treated as a separate image. Each separate image is classified by a CNN. It involves the extraction of statistical features from the images to find and label objects. Once the objects are detected, then the prediction of bounding boxes and labels for each object is done.

11.8.2.1   Object/human detection in surveillance videos
Surveillance systems often connected with a recording system are generally used to monitor critical areas such as government organizations, banks, etc. They help organizations to prevent crime. Studies reveal that watching and analyzing video surveillance is possible only after a few minutes. So automated surveillance system

that detects the presence of humans is needed. Such a system is developed using Mobilenetv2 [27].

11.8.3 Segmentation

Image segmentation is to classify images at the pixel level, determine the category of each point, and divide the image area.

11.8.3.1 Natural scene text detection

Scene text detection can be considered as a pixel-level text/nontext classification. It is the process of detecting the text in a scene image. Extracting the semantic information from scene images plays a significant role in understanding image content. Identifying the vehicles by reading their license plates, recognizing signs in driver-assisted systems, and providing scene information to visually impaired people are some of the applications of scene text detection. Since in daily activities text information in scene images are useful, it can be applied to mobile phones. MobileNet v2 and U-Net model can be used in semantic segmentation for images captured by mobiles with good quality cameras.

Scene text detection and reading play an important role in several applications, such as indexing multimedia archives and identifying vehicles by reading their license plates. With the explosion and widespread diffusion of low-priced digital cameras and mobile phones endowed with good quality cameras, text extraction from camera-captured scenes has gained renewed attention in computer vision research [28]

11.9 Future direction

There is tremendous progress in the field of computer vision. Several heavyweights of CNN architecture are available for computer vision tasks. Optimization techniques can be applied to compress the heavyweight models to make them deployable on mobiles. But this is at the cost of accuracy.

While deploying the models on edge devices, model size and inference efficiency are the major concerns. However, computer vision on the mobile device is still a challenge. For the healthcare domain, accuracy is important along with the inference time. A small architecture that satisfies the resource-constrained needs, as well as healthcare requirements, can be build using pretrained models along with optimization techniques or directly from scratch.

References

[1] Zurade, J. M. *Introduction to Artificial Neural Systems*, St. Paul, MN: West Publishing Co.; 1992.

[2] Binary Image Classifier CNN using Tensorflow. Online. 2020. Available from https://medium.com/techiepedia/binary-image-classifier-cnn-using-tensorflow-a3f5d6746697 [Accessed: July 17, 2021].

[3] Howard, A. G., Zhu, M., Chen, *et al.* "Mobilenets: Efficient convolutional neural networks for mobile vision applications." 2017. *arXiv preprint arXiv:1704.04861.7o.*

[4] O'Shea, K. and Nash, R. "An introduction to convolutional neural networks." 2015. *arXiv preprint arXiv:1511.08458.*

[5] Comprehensive Guide to Convolutional Neural Network. Online. 2018. Available from https://towardsdatascience.com/a-comprehensive-guide-to-convolutional-neural-networks-the-eli5-way-3bd2b1164a53 [Accessed: July 15, 2021].

[6] Elgendy, M. "Deep Learning for Vision Systems, Manning Publication," Shelter Island, NY. Online. 2019. Available from https://livebook.manning.com/book/grokking-deep-learning-for-computer-vision/welcome/v-7/ [Accessed: July 13, 2021].

[7] Simonyan, K. and Zisserman, A. "Very deep convolutional networks for large-scale image recognition." *Int. Conf. on Learning Representations,* 2015. *arXiv preprint arXiv:1409.1556.*

[8] Difference between AlexNet, VGGNET, ResNET and Inception. Online. 2019. Available from https://towardsdatascience.com/the-w3h-of-alexnet-vggnet-resnet-and-inception-7baaaecccc96 [Accessed: July 13, 2021].

[9] Szegedy, C., Liu, W, Jia, Y., *et al.* "Going deeper with convolutions." *Proceedings of the IEEE Conference on Computer Vision and Pattern Recognition.* 2015, pp. 1–9.

[10] Patel, R., and Chaware, A. "Transfer learning with fine-tuned MobileNetV2 for diabetic retinopathy." *2020 International Conference for Emerging Technology (INCET).* IEEE; 2020.

[11] MobileNet Version2. Online. 2018. Available from https://machinethink.net/blog/mobilenet-v2/ [Accessed: October 17, 2020].

[12] Sandler, M., Howard, A., Zhu, M., Zhmoginov, A., and Chen, L.-C. "MobileNetV2: inverted residuals and linear bottlenecks." *Proceedings of the IEEE Conference on Computer Vision and Pattern Recognition.* 2018, pp. 4510–4520.

[13] Howard, A., Sandler, M., Chu, G., *et al.* "Searching for mobilenetv3." *Proceedings of the IEEE/CVF International Conference on Computer Vision.* 2019, pp. 1314–1324.

[14] Zoph, B., Vasudevan, V., Shlens, J., and Le, Q. V. "Learning transferable architectures for scalable image recognition." *Proceedings of the IEEE Conference on Computer Vision and Pattern Recognition.* 2018.

[15] Raghuraman, K. "Quantizing deep convolutional networks for efficient inference: A whitepaper." 2018. *arXiv preprint arXiv:1806.08342.*

[16] https://www.tensorflow.org/lite/performance/model_optimization [Accessed: June 5, 2020].

[17] https://www.tensorflow.org/model_optimization/guide/quantization/training_comprehensive_guide [Accessed: June 5, 2020].

[18] Saeedi, P., Petersohn, I., Salpea, P., *et al.* "Global and regional diabetes prevalence estimates for 2019 and projections for 2030 and 2045: Results

from the International Diabetes Federation Diabetes Atlas." *Diabetes Research and Clinical Practice.* 2019;157:107843.

[19] Patel, R. and Chaware, A. "Quantizing MobileNet models for classification problems." INDIACom-2021. *8th International Conference on Computing for Sustainable Global Development.* IEEE; March 17–19, 2021.

[20] APTOS 2019 Blindness detection. Online. 2019. Available from https://www.kaggle.com/c/aptos2019-blindness-detection/data [Accessed: June 2, 2019].

[21] Wibowo, A., Hartanto, C. A., and Wirawan, P. W. "Android skin cancer detection and classification based on MobileNet v2 model." *International Journal of Advances in Intelligent Informatics.* 2020;6(2):135–148. doi:10.26555/ijain.v6i2.492.

[22] AI rivals human radiologists at breast-cancer detection. Online. 2020. Available from https://physicsworld.com/a/ai-rivals-human-radiologists-at-breast-cancer-detection/ [Accessed: November 5, 2020].

[23] Ansar, W., Shahid, A. R., Raza, B., and Dar, A. H. "Breast cancer detection and localization using mobilenet based transfer learning for mammograms." *International Symposium on Intelligent Computing Systems.* Cham: Springer; 2020, pp. 11–21.

[24] Falconí, L. G., Pérez, M., and Aguilar, W. G. "Transfer learning in breast mammogram abnormalities classification with Mobilenet and Nasnet." *International Conference on Systems, Signals and Image Processing (IWSSIP).* Osijek, Croatia; 2019, pp. 109–114. doi:10.1109/IWSSIP.2019.8787295.

[25] Zulkifley, M. A., Abdani, S. R., and Zulkifley, N. H. "COVID-19 screening using a lightweight convolutional neural network with generative adversarial network data augmentation." *Symmetry.* 2020;12(9):1530.

[26] Rabano, S. L., Cabatuan, M. K., Sybingco, E., Dadios, E. P., and Calilung, E. J. "Common garbage classification using MobileNet." *2018 IEEE 10th International Conference on Humanoid, Nanotechnology, Information Technology, Communication and Control, Environment and Management (HNICEM),* Baguio City, Philippines; 2018, pp. 1–4. doi:10.1109/HNICEM.2018.8666300.

[27] Yassine, B., Larbi, G., and Hicham, L. "Human detection in surveillance videos using MobileNet." *2020 2nd International Conference on Computer and Information Sciences (ICCIS),* Sakaka, Saudi Arabia; 2020, pp. 1–5. doi:10.1109/ICCIS49240.2020.9257662.

[28] Cao, D., Zhong, Y., Wang, L., He, Y., and Dang, J. "Scene text detection in natural images: A review." *Symmetry.* 2020;12(12):1956.

Chapter 12

Study on traffic enforcement cameras monitoring to detect the wrong-way movement of vehicles using deep convolutional neural network

S.R. Mani Sekhar[1], Sainya Goyal[1],
Lakshya Aditi Sinha[1] and G.M. Siddesh[1]

Abstract

To ensure the imposition of traffic rules, the most essential yet difficult task is to identify the traffic rule violators. One of these tasks comprises the finding of wrong-way drive of vehicles. In this chapter, traffic enforcement camera monitoring techniques are demonstrated to spot the wrong-way movement of automobiles using a deep convolution neural network. The idea behind this is to recognize such vehicles when they enter a region covered by a closed-circuit television camera and alert the driver. Different case studies are presented using various vehicle detection and monitoring techniques to perform various operations such as counting vehicles, detecting vehicles, and wrong-direction detection.

Key Words: Convolutional neural network; Deep convolutional network; Cameras; Traffic enforcement; Vehicle movement; Monitoring

12.1 Introduction

An intelligent transportation system (ITS) is a high-level approach that means offering innovative services of assistance involving various methods of transport and traffic administration. It allows users to be more educated and make secure, organized, and 'smarter' utilization of transport networks [1]. To ensure the efficiency and safety of drivers, the ITS plays an important role. The main aim of a vision-based ITS is to utilize the surveillance technologies most efficiently and extract precise and useful traffic data. With an immense population, metropolitan

[1]Department of Information Science and Engineering, M S Ramaiah Institute of Technology, Bangalore, India

areas worldwide are encountering issues in decreasing traffic violations and enforcing traffic rules. One such violation is the wrong-way movement of vehicles. Generally, the wrong-way movement of vehicles occurs because of the following reasons: the driver did not pay attention to the traffic signs or pavement markings, the driver is confused or diverted, the driver purposely violates the rules, the driver is under the influence of alcohol, and so on. Although it is practically difficult to control the human driving mechanism, it is essential to categorize and comprehend irregular activities in regular traffic scenarios to avoid serious car accidents.

Today, the task of identification of such activities is manually performed by the workers. However, with the fair increase in the camera devices on the road, the requirement for the automatic smart system is even more. The technologies for wrong-direction detection can be categorized into three parts: video imaging-based detection, sensor-based detection, and radar-based detection. The main focus of this study is to automate the process of recognizing violations of moving vehicles, hence requiring as little human interaction as possible, and also to detect vehicles moving in the wrong direction using cameras.

12.2   Background

Traffic offences could be misdeeds, according to the type of infringement that a person conducts. The movement of vehicles in the wrong direction continues to be a progressing subject of traffic supervision as it enhances the possibility of deadly accidents and leads altogether to traffic jam. Given that in this chapter an attempt to discover an objective to automate the detection of the movement of vehicles in the wrong direction with the assistance of computer vision is made, the detection of an object is a major piece of this study.

The detection of the object is an emerging matter in the discipline of computer vision. Vision-based vehicle (object) detection algorithms can be categorized into three parts: hand-crafted feature-based algorithms, motion-based algorithms, and convolutional neural network (CNN)-based algorithms. Hand-crafted feature-based algorithms include scale invariant feature transform (SIFT) [2] and histogram of oriented gradients [3]. These approaches have a lower feature representation. Motion-based algorithms consist of optical flow [4], background subtraction [5], and frame subtraction. Optical flow computes the motion vector of every pixel and then monitors these pixels. However, the technique is time-consuming and complex. Background subtraction detects the vehicle by designing the distribution of the foreground and the background. Frame subtraction detects the motion of the object by calculating the difference between three or four consecutive frame sequences. However, it is not ideal for too slow or too fast motion. CNN-based approaches include R-CNN, fast-R-CNN, faster-R-CNN, YOLO (You Only Look Once), and SSD.

CNN is a strategy that has a well-built ability to retrieve features from the images. The two primary object detection algorithms derived from CNN are the regional proposal algorithm and the regression algorithm. The regional proposal algorithms extract important features from the image that occurs by analyzing the candidate portions which decides the position and class of the output, for examples, R-FCN [6], fast R-CNN [7], R-CNN [8], faster R-CNN [9], and SPP-NET [10]. The regression algorithms do not require applicant frames to give an anticipated position of the target with actual coordinates and identifies its class, for example, SSD [11] and YOLO [12].

Object detection techniques based on the deep neural network can be categorized into the following parts: the one-stage approach and the two-stage approach. In the two-stage approach, a network of region proposal or selective search is used to produce a set of candidate object boxes, and later, they are categorized and regressed. This includes R-CNN, R-FCN, Fast R-CNN, Faster R-CNN, and SPP-Net. R-CNN uses a selective search algorithm to generate object proposals, which trains the CNN model for detection tasks, but it has low efficiency. Fast R-CNN and SPP-Net speed up the process by producing region proposals on the feature map. Faster R-CNN increases the accuracy and speed of the network by using the region proposal network instead of selective search. R-FCN uses position-sensitive score maps, which decreases the computation time.

Whereas in the one-stage approach, dense samples are generated by the network over various locations, aspect ratios, and scales, and simultaneously, they are categorized and regressed. This includes SSD and YOLO. YOLO utilizes a single feed-forward convolution network to directly anticipate object location, as well as classes that are tremendously fast. SSD extracts scales on various feature maps and anchors of various aspect ratios. The principal benefit of the one-stage approach is its real-time application, even though the accuracy of detection of the two-stage approach is better.

12.3   Techniques for data collection

The purpose of this model is to spot the wrong-way vehicles movement; therefore, we need a large data set comprising different vehicle specifics. The data can be collected in the following two ways: CCTV cameras and manual videos.

12.3.1   Closed-circuit television

Traffic cameras are an inventive and enormously practical utilization of video surveillance technology. They are placed on traffic lights and set along occupied roads and at busy crossing points of highways. Using cameras and intelligent units, the video turnstile vehicle traffic reckoning system attains over 98% accuracy in all conditions of day and night [13]. The traffic surveillance footage from roads and highways is used to train this model. Algorithms can be used to obtain data essential for the detection of vehicles.

12.3.2   Manual videos

The most traditional way of assembling traffic flow data is the manual way. In this, a person is allocated to document the traffic during different stages of the day. This technique of data collection can be costly in terms of the workforce; however, it is nevertheless mandatory in utmost cases where vehicles need to be categorized with numerous movements recorded distinctly, for example, at intersections. The road traffic on individual arms ought to be counted and recorded distinctly for each movement at intersection sites.

The data set consists of manually taken videos of vehicles from different roads and highways as the principal data to make this model acquainted with real-life situations.

12.4   Purpose and benefit of the cameras monitoring system

- *Traffic measurement and planning*: Congestion on roads is hard to control due to several reasons such as bad weather, accidents, and the road under construction which results in lane closings. According to a study done by IIT Madras, traffic bottleneck on Delhi roads costs about Rs. 60,000 crore annually. This is on the interpretation of fuel lost, owing to the idealness of vehicles. As the vehicular number rapidly grows in the capital, the study shows that by 2030, congestion cost would rise to the tune of around Rs. 98,000 crore [14]. Traffic cameras are important resources when challenged with these encounters of recurring and one-time congestion. For starters, a video of a congested roadway gives valuable insight into the count of a vehicle and how traffic flows grow throughout the day and in specific events such as an extended roadwork or a heavy rainstorm. Further, plans about lane allotments, exit openings, and closings to optimize the congestion and to make choices regarding long-term construction development and construction projects can be drawn by this video.
- *Safer driving*: Driving is a risky means of transportation compared to a train or a plane. Million public die every day due to road traffic crashes. More than half of all deaths due to road traffic are among helpless road users: bicyclists, walkers, and motorcyclists [15]. Activities such as not following traffic regulations at night and speeding through a red/yellow traffic light which makes driving dangerous have been prevented via such video-based solutions. Traffic cameras along the highway are also useful for detecting illegal vehicles and pedestrians in restricted movement areas. It is impossible to completely prevent an accident from happening, but we can narrow down the chances of the accident.
- *Detect criminal activities*: This is one of the biggest benefits of installing CCTV cameras on the roads. They are an adequate deterrent for burglars and protect parked vehicles. Hence, it can be a profitable means to document, deter, and lessen crime.
- *Enable remote monitoring*: This is one of the most unnoticed advantages of a camera monitoring system. Using a highly integrated video surveillance system, a person can monitor the action on the surveillance feeds from anyplace in the world, provided he/she is connected to the Internet. Mobile devices,

laptops, and tablets are all fair game. A person can log in to his/her security system from any device such as mobile, laptops, tablets, and watch live streams or access recorded footage.

- *Law enforcement*: Traffic cameras are used to impose traffic rules and speed limits. The movement of vehicles in the wrong direction is one of the most common violations of traffic rules and regulations to prevent U-turn, avoid traffic, *etc*. Traffic cameras issue tickets for violating rules and hence limit the amount of workforce required for issuing such citations.
- *Increase productivity*: Traffic cameras can monitor the intersections more effectively and efficiently than humans. Since officers cannot be present everywhere, traffic cameras at the roads and intersection can take their place, resulting in more officers available for additional duties. Traffic cameras grant 24/7 traffic monitoring at a much lower cost than police officers. Also, traffic cameras are considered much safer than officers as they do not have to trail down the criminals.

12.5 Techniques used in the monitoring of vehicles

The first step in determining the wrong-way movement of a vehicle is the identification of the vehicle itself. This step includes the use of a well-known deep learning algorithm CNN to identify the objects in an image.

12.5.1 Convolution neural network

A convolutional neural network (ConvNet/CNN) is a deep learning process that takes input in the form of an image frame, assigns learnable biases and weights to several objects in the image frame, and distinguishes them from one another. In general, CNN extracts the feature of the image and converts it into a lower dimension without losing its features.

At present, CNN is the greatest and most powerful technique for automated processing of images with vast learning capacity mostly due to the use of many hidden layers, i.e., feature extraction phases which can automatically be trained from representations of the data.

A basic CNN structure comprises the following six layers: input layer, convolution layer, rectified linear units (ReLU) layer, pooling layer, fully connected or dense layer, Softmax/logistic layer, and output layer. Figure 12.1 illustrates the layers of CNN.

12.5.1.1 Input layer

An input layer takes images as input and performs normalization of data. A frame or image data proposed by a three-dimensional matrix is used to represent the input layer. It is a pixel value matrix that needs to be converted into a single column before feeding into the input. For example, to convert an image of dimension $25 \times 25 = 625$, we need to reshape it into 625×1. Suppose we have "n" training examples, then the dimension of the input matrix will be $(625, n)$. Also, the number of input layers should be a multiple of 2, for example, 16, 32, 64, 128.

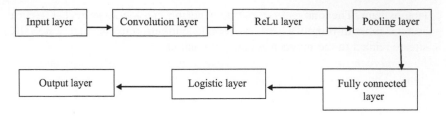

Figure 12.1   Layers of CNN

12.5.1.2   Convolution layer

The convolution layer is also known as the feature extractor layer since it helps to learn the characteristics and features of the image given as input. Convolution is a mathematical term that is used to explain the procedure of joining two features to generate another feature. This new feature is known as a feature map. The result of the first layer becomes the input for the next layer when it passes through the convolution layer. This layer permits the data onto the next layer by employing a convolution function to the input. The convolutional layer comprises several components [16, 17].

Filters and stride

A convolutional layer comprises neurons that join regions of the outputs of the previous input layer or the input images. The filterSize input arguments to specify the size of such regions.

For every region, a method calculates a dot product of the weights (information about the input image which is represented as a matrix) and the input, followed by adding a bias (another weight) term.

This produces an integer quantity for every cell in the feature map. A filter is a group of weights that is addressed to a particular area in the given input image. The same computation is repeated for each region by moving the filter horizontally and vertically. Stride is the size of the step by which the movement of the filter occurs across the different regions.

The amount of weights in a filter is $w * h * c$, where w is the width, h is the height of the filter, and c is the number of channels in the input, respectively. For example, one channel for grey-scale images and three channels for a colour image.

Dilated convolution

A dilated convolution is required to expand the filter by inserting spaces between its elements which enhances the receptive field of the layer without changing the amount of parameters. The expansion of filters is performed by entering zeros among every filter component.

Feature maps

A feature map is generated by moving filters along the input using the same bias and the same set of weights for the convolution.

Such convolution, which uses a different bias and a different group of weights, generates a new feature map. Therefore, the amount of filters is equal to the number of feature maps. The total number of arguments in a convolutional layer is (($h * w * c + 1$) * number of filters), where 1 is the bias. Furthermore, the feature map size is inversely related to the number of convolutional layers.

Output size
The output size of the whole image should be an integer that fully covers it. If the output value is not able to fully cover the image, then the system itself ignores the remaining portion of the image.

Zero padding
Columns or rows of zeroes inserted to the edges of an image are called padding. This technique is used to maintain the output size of the layer such that border data do not get missed.

Number of neurons
In a feature map, the total amount of neurons is given by calculating the product of the output width and height, known as Map Size. The full quantity of neurons in a convolutional layer is given by Map_Size * Number_of_Filters. Some non-linear functions such as ReLu can be used to pass the output from these neurons.

Learning parameters
These are the coefficients that are chosen by the neural network itself. While learning, the algorithm is used to optimize these parameters in a way to reduce the error.

Number of layers
The number of convolutional layers in a CNN can be one or more than one, depending on the complexity and size of data.

12.5.1.3 ReLu layer

It is also known as rectified linear units that apply non-linear activation function which normalizes the feature map values acquired from the preceding convolution layer. This layer performs a threshold operation to an individual element by removing negative values and setting them to zero, which is mathematically defined as follows:

$$f(x1) = x1; \text{ for } x1 \geq 0 \text{ and } f(x1) = 0; \text{ for } x1 < 0 \tag{12.1}$$

The volume size of input remains the same in this layer.

12.5.1.4 Pooling layer

This layer is also known as the downsampling layer. It is used to lessen the size of the input image, hence minimizing the computational complexity of the model. Overfitting can be avoided by such reduction as it extracts essential features. Some process for such operations include average, max, and sum pooling. Max pooling is widely used in a convolution neural network. In this layer, the input is divided into rectangular regions to compute the maximum of every region.

12.5.1.5   Fully connected layer

This layer is also known as a dense layer. It connects each neuron in one layer to each neuron in another layer. It uses neurons, weight, and bias. It is used to categorize images between different classes by the training dataset.

12.5.1.6   Softmax/logistic layer

It is the last fully connected layer in a convolution neural network which uses the softmax function to classify the images. It is used to represent numbers into probabilities. This function gives a vector as output which contains the list of probability distributions of potential outcomes. For binary classification, a logistic layer is used, whereas a softmax layer is used for multi-classification.

12.5.1.7   Output layer

After numerous layers of convolution, the output is generated in the form of one-hot encoded. The pooling and convolution layers would be able to reduce the size of images and extract important features. However, we need the output in the form of classes for which we have to apply an entirely linked layer. The layer has a loss function to compute the inconsistency between the actual label and the predicted value.

12.5.2   R-CNN

There are four stages in R-CNN, also known as region-based convolution neural networks. The objective of R-CNN is to process an input image and generate several bounding boxes where every bounding box comprises an object and also the class of the object. The four stages are given in the following.

12.5.2.1   Selective search for region proposal

This method uses selective search to extract only a fixed number of regions from the image, thereby called region proposal. The selective search procedure [18] operates by producing sub-divisions of the image which could refer to one object concerning different texture, colour, shape, and size—and iteratively joining comparable regions to frame objects. This results in 'object proposals' of various scales. Region proposals are simply smaller portions of the actual input image, which consists of the objects to be searched. Hence, instead of working with the whole image, the given function can be performed on the selected region which is very efficient in comparison to the brute-force sliding window approach.

12.5.2.2   CNN for feature extraction

In this step, with each region proposal, a feature vector is created which represents the input image in a smaller dimension using CNN. The AlexNet is used as a feature extractor. The issue with this system is that the whole system cannot be trained in one go. Each part needs to be trained independently that signifies before the classification task AlextNet needs to train.

12.5.2.3 Support vector machine for object classification

In this step, the feature vectors created from the image proposals are classified using support vector machine (SVM) classificatory. This phase involves learning a separate linear SVM classifier for each class that detects the presence or absence of an object belonging to a particular class. For each object class, there is one SVM which means for each feature vector, and there are n outputs, where n represents the number of various objects to be detected. This output is a confidence score. The greedy non-maximum suppression (NMS) is used to combine all the image proposals classified on each object class into one image.

12.5.2.4 Bounding box regression

To improve the bounding box, corrections are performed in the size and location of the predicted box. After this step, an accurate and corrected bounding box is formed around every object, for all positive regional proposals of every class anticipated from the SVM.

The problems with R-CNN are that it takes a large amount of time for training the network. Almost 47 s are required to process each test image; therefore, it cannot be practiced in real-time. Learning cannot happen during a selective search algorithm as it is a fixed algorithm which could result in the creation of bad region proposals.

12.5.3 Fast region-based convolution neural network

The disadvantages of R-CNN were solved by building a quicker object detection algorithm known as a fast region-based convolution neural network. This works in a similar manner as the R-CNN algorithm. Here, the input image is fed to CNN to generate a convolutional feature map. The region of proposals is identified from the convolutional feature map and wrapped into different squares. An RoI pooling layer is used to reshape the boxes into a constant size and later fed into the fully connected layer.

To predict the category of the proposed region from the RoI feature vector and the bounding boxes' offset values, the softmax layer is used. The reason "Fast R-CNN" is faster than R-CNN is as there is no need to region proposals to CNN every time. Instead, the operation is performed only once per input image and a feature map is produced from it. Both R-CNN and Fast R-CNN use the CPU-based region proposal algorithm, the selective search algorithm for object classification. This algorithm is time-consuming which affects the overall performance of the network.

12.5.4 Faster R-CNN

This is the most widely used version of the R-CNN family. The evolution in the different versions of this family was in terms of performance improvement, computational efficiency, and reduction in test time. In this technique, the selective search algorithm is eliminated so that the network can learn the region proposals by itself. A separate regional proposal network is used to anticipate the regional proposals in place of a selective search algorithm. The anticipated region proposals are then reformed employing an RoI pooling layer which is further used to categorize the input image in the proposed region and anticipate the offset values for the candidate bounding boxes. This decreases the number of proposed regions created while confirming precise article discovery.

12.5.5   *Single-shot MultiBoxDetector*

SSD stands for Single-shot MultiBoxDetector [19], which is a technique for sensing objects in input images using a single deep neural network. Single shot means that jobs of object classification and localization are performed in a single forward pass of the neural network. MultiBox is the name of the technique used for bounding box regression. Detector refers to the network as an object detector which also categorizes the detected objects. This technique consists of two steps: convolutional filter applications and feature map extraction. VGG16 [20] is used to extract feature maps, and then object detection is performed with the help of the Conv4_3 layer.

The bounding box production considers the application of matching pre-calculated, fixed-size boxes known as priors with the actual allocation of ground truth boxes. The intersection over union (IOU) ratio is kept greater than or equal to 0.5 with the help of priors. To improve the accuracy and precision, SSD uses small convolutional filters for the prediction of object classes, multi-scale feature maps for the detection of objects, and individual filters for separate default boxes in order to manage the variation in aspect ratios. Thus, SSD has better exposure to aspect ratios, location, and scale and makes more accurate predictions.

12.5.6   *You Only Look Once*

YOLO is one of the most widely used object detection algorithms. Although it does not give 100% accuracy, it is a preferable choice for real-time detection. The YOLO model enables real-time speed and end-to-end training while sustaining high average precision. The input image is splitted into a T × T grid. The grid cell in which the centre of an object lies is responsible to detect that object. A fixed number (N) of bounding boxes is predicted by each grid cell. A bounding box describes the square/rectangle that encloses an object. Then, a confidence score is calculated for each bounding box which implies how confident it is that the bounding box really encloses the expected object. Equation (12.2) illustrates the same

$$
\begin{aligned}
\text{Confidence} = & (\text{Probability\_of\_Object}) \\
& *(\text{intersection\_over\_union (IOU) between the truth and the predicted box})
\end{aligned}
\tag{12.2}
$$

If there is no item in a particular cell, the confidence score of that cell is zero. Otherwise, a confidence score is IOU between the truth and the predicted box.

Every bounding box contains five parameters: a, b, c, d, and confidence. The first two parameters (a, b) coordinates denote the centre of the bounding box. The next two parameters c and d are the width and height of the image, respectively. Lastly, confidence represents the IOU between the truth and the predicted box.

Conditional class probability is predicted for each grid cell, Prob (Classj| Object). For each grid cell single set of conditional class probabilities are predicted, irrespective of the number of bounding boxes N. During test time, the class probabilities are multiplied with each box confidence prediction, which results in class-specific confidence scores for the individual box. These scores calculate how well the anticipated box fits the object. There are six main versions of YOLO to date they are YOLOv1(2016), YOLOv2(2017), YOLOv3(2018), YOLOv4(2020), YOLOv5(2020), and PP-YOLO(2020).

YOLOv1: Darknet framework (an open-source neural network framework written in CUDA and C) is used in YOLOv1 which is trained on the ImageNet-1000 dataset. It has many limitations such as distinguishing small objects that appeared as a cluster. This version also found issues in the speculation of objects if the dimensions of the input image are different from the trained image. The significant problem here is the localization of the given object in the image.

The YOLOv2 is named YOLO9000. It refined the design and improved the bounding box proposal by making use of anchor boxes. The major improvements in YOLOv2 from YOLOv1 are batch normalization, anchor boxes, fine-grained features, higher resolution classifier, multi-scale training, Darknet 19 which makes YOLOv2 faster, better, and stronger as said by [21].

YOLOv3 further refined the architecture of the model and training process by providing improvements in real-time object detection with accuracy and classification of objects by using logistic regression. Such improvements are known as an incremental improvement by [22]. It includes class predictions, bounding box predictions, feature pyramid networks, and Darknet-53.

YOLOv4 is also based on Darknet and is considered the most accurate and fastest real-time architecture for object detection. It takes the effect of state of art bag of freebies (BoF), which enhances the detector's accuracy without affecting the reference time. Also, many bag of specials (BoS) is used for improving the correctness of object detection by a small increase in inference cost.

YOLOv5 is not quite the same as the previous version as it uses PyTorch instead of Darknet. The main improvements comprise auto-learning bounding box anchors and mosaic data augmentation.

PP-YOLO is based on PaddlePaddle, which is an open-source deep learning framework. It is mainly based on the YOLOv3 model, but notable changes are observed using ResNet in place of Darknet53 and enlarge the training batch size from 64 to 192.

12.6   Case study

This section provides a brief discuss on the various techniques used in the detection of wrong-way movement of vehicles

12.6.1   *The detection of wrong-way drive of automobiles based on appearance using deep convolutional neural network*

In this case study, a deep convolution neural network is used to detect the back and front sides of vehicles on the road or highway. This is an appearance-based method that finds the wrong-way movement of vehicles based on the expectation of the user to look at a particular side (back or front) of an automobile on every way of the highway by implementing a handmade region-divider algorithm.

The initial step to detect the wrong-way movement of a vehicle is recognizing the vehicle itself and for that data set of vehicles is required. This data set was collected by three means. First, the Stanford Car data set [23] was utilized to train the model of the back and front sides of various cars. Next, manually taken pictures of cars were used to make the model acquainted with real-life situations. Additionally, a large number of traffic surveillance videos from many crowded highways of Dhaka City were used as a test data set. After the collection of data, the data set was filtered to get rid of unnecessary details from those images and extract the images which consist of the front and back sides of the vehicles only. To further enhance the data set, data augmentation is done by making slight changes in images such as scaling, rotation, and so on. Then, with the above data set, the images from highways of Dhaka City were added and each car on the highway was enclosed in a bounding box and marked correspondingly (front_car or back_car).

After this, several batches of data set were formed and the complete data set was passed numerous times through the same convolution neural network. With the increase in the number of epochs, the weights in the neural networks keep updating and the resulting curves give different outcomes such as underfitting, ideal curve, and later overfitting.

YOLO was used for image detection (front_car or back_car) by dividing the input image into a 13×13 matrix. Each cell of this matrix was in charge of predicting five bounding boxes, which further calculates a certainty score. A class was predicted by each cell for every bounding box. It gives an appropriate assumption over all the expected classes and works essentially like a classifier. The class prediction of the bounding box and the certainty score are combined to form another score that reveals the likelihood of this bounding box comprising a specific kind of object. In this model, the value of the threshold was maintained at 20% or 0.2 because most of the crates had particularly low certainty scores. A large number of ROIs were detected by the model due to the low threshold value.

Prior to the detection operation, the system operator was requested to split the images of the highway into different areas and position the particular side (front_car or back_car) of vehicles that the user expected to view on each of the specific areas, as shown in (12.3) and (12.4). Let r be the coordinate value and highway divider value be nr:

$$\text{For}(nr - r) > 0, \text{Vehicles}(r, s, w, h) \text{ in the left region} \qquad (12.3)$$

$$\text{For}(nr - r) < 0, \text{Vehicles}(r, s, w, h) \text{ in the right region} \qquad (12.4)$$

This calculation examines if a car in a specific area matches the side of the car (front or back) as it was anticipated by the camera. Thus, the wrong-way movement was detected by marking the vehicles with the correct match by green colour and rest by red colour.

This model is much better as compared to the model proposed in the paper by Monteiro *et al.* [24]. The latter model requires two validation systems to prevent false detection of the wrong-way movement of the vehicle. First, a validation based on the appearance was needed to activate the alarm particularly for vehicles, and second, a temporal validation was used to prevent the activation of alarm by noise. Clearly, these two validations were not required in the above-proposed model owing to the idea of a convolution neural network. This model initially performs object detection and finds the object of interest then based on the decision-making function chooses to activate an alarm or not. So distinctly, this model gives better performance as it requires fewer advances.

The major future improvements of this model are using an automatic region-divider algorithm instead of doing it manually. The present model was trained only with car-like vehicles which is why it cannot detect other vehicles; therefore, the model must be introduced to all kinds of vehicles. Ideally, the model should apply the algorithm only to moving vehicles, but the present model does not consider the classification of vehicles based on movement.

12.6.2   Real-time wrong-direction detection based on deep learning

In this case study, an ITS was developed to detect the movement of vehicles in the wrong direction. The system was categorized into three aspects: vehicle detection, tracking of the vehicle using a unique ID, and the validation of direction. For detection of a vehicle, a deep learning model named YOLOv3 was used and Kalman filtering was utilized for tracking the vehicle. Lastly, an "entry–exit" algorithm was implemented for the validation of the direction of movement of vehicles.

There are many techniques for vehicle detection such as background subtraction, optical flow, YOLOv3. In the background subtraction technique, the foreground mask was applied on static cameras and moving objects were detected by subtracting the foreground mask from the stationary portion of the scene. However, this technique gave the wrong result when vehicles in the input image are closely located. Also, it is not suitable during night time. The optical flow technique supposes that the intensity or colour of a pixel should not vary under movement from one frame to another. In general, it is unacceptable in action where object occlusions happen or brightness intensity varies. To overcome the issues stated above, a CNN-based approach known as YOLOv3 was used due to its speed efficiency.

Vehicle tracking involves identifying the detected cars and assigning unique IDs to track them as long as they are present in the frame. One such method known as Kalman filtering is used in this proposed model. It is based on linear quadratic estimation (LQE) which is a sequence of measurements observed over a while. This technique involves two major steps: prediction and update. In the initial step, the current state was predicted with the help of previous states. In the second step, the predicted state was corrected by using current measurements. YOLOv3 detection method was combined with Kalman filter tracking estimation as it improves accuracy, robustness in different weather conditions, and time of detection.

The proposed system contains three steps: detection and tracking, direction estimation, and direction validation. In the first step, YOLOv3 was used for object detection by extracting a vehicle's bounding box, which is further applied in tracking algorithms and direction identification. The vehicle's bounding box information was obtained by sending incessant frames to the trained model. With the help of centroid tracking, unique IDs were assigned to each of the bounding boxes. Then, the cost between the detected car and its prediction was calculated. A tracker was assigned to each of the detected cars if there were numerous detections. IOU was determined between the detection bounding box and tracker bounding box as a metric. Further, the Hungarian algorithm [25] was used to deduce and assign correct ID's to each detected object by maximizing the sum of IOU. The existing tracks are maintained and the unassigned track predictions and detections are handled simultaneously. Kalman filter was applied to predict several objects from a frame [26]. At last, tracking lines were drawn on every detected car using OpenCV libraries.

After detecting the objects and assigning unique IDs and tracks to them, the next step was Direction Estimation. In this method, vehicle trajectory was estimated by computing the variation in the pixels in the different frames range. Initially, in frame zero centroid was calculated from one of the detected vehicle's bounding boxes and set as initial points. The centroid's position changes as the vehicle move from one frame to another. Thus, we calculated the centroid for each frame and found the difference between the last frame and the second frame as discussed in (12.5).

Difference for direction estimation (D)

$$= \text{Last frame centroid} - \text{Second frame centroid} \qquad (12.5)$$

This was because the first frame was used for ID assignment and detection. For example, assume that there were eight frames for tracking the vehicle. Then, the pixel position difference value would be calculated between the second frame and the eighth frame. To determine the direction of the vehicle, the polarity of D was checked. If it was positive, that is the last frame centroid was greater than the second frame centroid, then the vehicle was moving from left to right and vice versa. After determining the direction in which the vehicle was moving, we need to check whether it is going in the correct way. The entry–exit algorithm was created for direction validation. In this algorithm, imaginary entry lines were created on the video frame. Suppose any vehicle crossed those entry lines, then the corresponding unique ID of that vehicle was saved in a list, and the ID was removed when it crossed the exit area. If the vehicle enters through the exit area or leaves through the entry area then wrong-way movement was detected and an alert signal was sent.

The above-proposed model works well under various lighting conditions and presents outstanding speed performance. However, the model did not consider the pedestrians walking on the road. So, the next update in the model may include violation recognition of jaywalking.

12.6.3   A vehicle finding and counting system based on vision using deep learning

In this case study, a vision-based vehicle detection system was proposed for all sizes of vehicles which results in the counting of vehicles and multi-object tracking.

Vehicle detection using vision-based techniques was categorized into two methods: deep learning methods and conventional machine vision methods. Conventional machine vision techniques utilize the movement of vehicles to distinguish them from a stable background image. The technique was categorized into three groups: the process of applying optical flow [27], the process of applying video frame difference [28], and the process of applying background subtraction [29].

The deep convolutional networks were categorized into two methods: one-stage and two-stage methods. In the two-stage method, a candidate box of the input object was generated by different algorithms and later CNN was used to classify the object, whereas in a one-stage method, no such candidate box was generated. In this method, the positioning issue of the input object bounding box was directly converted into a regression issue for processing. The most widely used two-stage method are Region-CNN (R-CNN) [30], SPP-NET [31] and one-stage method are YOLO [32], single-shot multibox detector (SSD) [33]. The conventional machine vision method detects the vehicles with high speed but gave an inappropriate result in real-time and to overcome this shortcoming CNN methods were developed.

The most common multi-object tracking techniques utilize detection-free tracking (DFT) and detection-based tracking (DBT) for the initialization of objects. The DBT strategy utilizes background modelling to recognize the non-stationary objects in the input video frames prior to vehicle tracking. It was required to initialize the object of the tracking in the DFT strategy, but it cannot deal with the removal of old objects and the insertion of new objects. The algorithms for multiple objects tracking system needs to examine the resemblance of intra-frame objects and their related issue. The comparability of intra-frame objects can utilize NCC. With inter-frame objects, it was mandatory to check that one track contains only one object and an object shows up only on one track. The ORB multiple objects tracking algorithm satisfies the above requirements and hence was used in the proposed system.

The vehicle dataset for the proposed model consists of several datasets from all over the world which were categorized into three groups: images from a surveillance camera, images from non-monitoring cameras, and images from a car camera.

There were three methods used in the proposed system: Road surface segmentation, vehicle detection using YOLOv3, and multi-object tracking using ORB. The first method explains the process of highway road extraction and segmentation. Gaussian mixture modelling, an image processing method, was implemented for road surface extraction and segmentation. The ROI in the input image was the area with highway road and the centre of attention was the vehicle. The pixel value in the input image was Gaussian about a middle value in a particular range of time, and every pixel in every image frame was calculated. Foreground pixels are those which were far away from the centre and background pixels are those where point of pixel differs from the middle quantity by a particular variance. Then, a Gaussian filter was used to smooth the background image.

The meanShift calculation was utilized to smoothen the shade of the background image, balance the shading with a comparable colour dispersion, and also disintegrate the coloured region with a more reduced region. This way the flooding filling algorithm was implemented to segregate the surface region of the road. At last, the morphological expansion and hole filling operations were performed to thoroughly extract that region of the road. A minimum confined rectangle was developed for the extracted highway road surface image without any rotation. Then, the image was split into five equal portions; the one-fifth area near the coordinate axis origin was called as near remote region and the lasting four-fifth area was called as the near proximal region. Column-wise search was performed on pixel quantities of the near remote region and the near proximal region. When all the pixel quantities in a particular column are zero, the picture belonging to that column becomes fully black which indicates that the surface area was not a road and so it was erased. Then, after the exclusion of not-road-surface areas, reserved areas have remained and they are called proximal and remote areas of the road.

The second method describes the detection of a vehicle using the CNN technique, YOLOv3. The CNN method detects the object by extracting the features of the input image. YOLOV3 divides each input image into $n * n$ grid according to the feature map size. The grid unit centre was used to anticipating the object. To detect the various size of one object, each grid unit had three bounding boxes. The final prediction outcome from the above three bounding boxes was which had a maximum overlapping area with the marked box. To determine large objects, deep features were used, whereas to determine small objects, shallow features were used, and hence the network was successfully capable of detecting an object of different sizes. The output of the CNN network was confidence, category, and coordinates of the object. This model was used to detect three kinds of vehicles: trucks, buses, and cars.

The last method was used to track multiple vehicles using the ORB algorithm. This algorithm used features from accelerated segment test (FAST) for the detection of feature points and to detect the corners Harris operator was implemented. The BRIEF algorithm was used to calculate the descriptor that had rotation consistency. Then, the XOR operation was used for matching the feature points. The point was said to be successfully matched when the quantity of matching feature points is higher than the threshold. Then, the object's matching box was drawn and the prediction box was calculated with the help of the RANSAC algorithm which performs feature point purification and also eliminates the wrong noise points of the comparable faults. Then, the homography matrix was calculated.

A perspective transformation is executed according to the location of the actual object detection box and the homography matrix to acquire a prediction box. In the proposed model, ORB was used for extracting feature points from the detection box which was acquired by the algorithm for vehicle detection. The threshold was set which is defined as the largest pixel displacement of the detected centre point of the vehicle box that travels amidst two adjoining frames. If the pixel distance of the centre point of the vehicle is lower, then the match was successful which means vehicles in both frames were the same. In this case, the object's features were updated and tracks were drawn. If the tracks were updated for more than ten consecutive frames, then tracking continued else the track was deleted. However, if the object did not match, then the next ten frames were checked. If the object did not match in the last ten frames, then the object was deleted else object's features were updated, tracks were drawn and further tracking continues.

The trajectory analysis was also performed along with the counting of numerous object traffic data. The majority of the highways were run in two different directions, and those roadways were isolated by boundaries. In the world coordinate system, the direction of the vehicle was distinguished into the two following parts: Direction 1 as the one going towards the cameras and direction 2 as the one driving away from the cameras. For vehicle classification statistics, an undeviating line was set in the traffic images at the 1/2 position on the higher side as a means for statistics for vehicle characterization. The road traffic flow was simultaneously counted in both directions 1 and 2. The data of the object was recorded when its trajectory intersected the detection line. At last, the number of objects in various categories and various directions in a specific period could be obtained.

Initially, the data of the traffic in the form of video were inserted in the proposed model. Next, the highway road surface was retrieved from the input via road surface segmentation and then it was partitioned into a proximal region and a remote region by a recently suggested segmentation technique. The strategy is essential for enhancing vehicle detection for small objects and the multi-scale deviation of the object. At that point, the two regions are set into the YOLOv3 structure to detect the vehicles in each area. At last, the trajectories of the vehicle are acquired with the help of ORB calculation that can be utilized to pass judgment on the driving course of the vehicle and get the count of various vehicles. According to the research in this case study, the speed of the vehicle can be determined by the calibration outcome of cameras. The proposed model in the case study had practicability and great performance.

12.6.4   *A highway automobile discovery algorithm based on CNN*

In this case study, an effective and efficient model for vehicle classification and detection from traffic surveillance footage is proposed. Initially, the aspect ratios and vehicle scales were clustered in the vehicle dataset. Next, convolution neural network (CNN) was used to detect the vehicle. The different feature combination techniques were utilized to conjugate low-level features and high-level features to detect various scales of vehicles on various features. Further, fully convolution architecture was adopted in place of fully connected layers to increase the speed. The above method integrates the advantages of the one-stage and two-stage approaches of CNN.

First, the data was prepared using the k-means algorithm. The conventional algorithms for object detection implemented a sliding window technique to create a candidate box, but those processes were time-consuming. This problem was overcome by using detectors based on CNN such as SSD and Faster R-CNN, but they still had certain issues. The first problem was that the aspect ratios were chosen manually. Good detections could be easily predicted by the CNN network if better priors of the dataset were picked. The second problem was that the aspect ratios were modelled to detect a general object such as COCO [34] and PASCAL VOC [35] dataset. It was not very appropriate for the detection of a vehicle. In order to resolve these problems, the k-means clustering algorithm was used instead of hand-picked aspect ratios. The cluster centroids were remarkably different from manually chosen anchor boxes which were quite suitable for the detection of a vehicle. The k-means algorithm could be mathematically formulated as follows:

$$C = k \sum j = 1 \sum y \epsilon Ej \|y - \mu j\|2 \qquad (12.6)$$

where y is the sample, μj is the mean vector of Ej, and k is the clustering centre.

The VGG-16 pre-trained with ImageNet [36] dataset was used as the baseline network. It had 3 fully connected layers and 13 convolutional layers. Convolutional layer helps to learn the characteristics and feature of the image given as input and fully connected layer help to connect neuron of one layer to other. The convolutional layer was used instead of three fully connected layers to reduce the parameters and increase detection speed.

Earlier, faster R-CNN used the concluding feature map to create a candidate box, but it was not satisfactory for detecting the vehicle because the vehicle scale varies. Therefore, the high-level and low-level features were concatenated. The low-level features were used for object localization as they were near to the unprocessed image. The high-level features had more linguistic data for the classification of an object. The feature pyramid was adopted to detect multilayers. The feature pyramid could detect an object on various feature layers and improve the feature presentation. This approach was appropriate for detecting vehicles of various sizes on various feature layers. The above method also improved the accuracy of detection.

The candidate box was generated on various feature maps to detect vehicles of various sizes. All feature maps have various sizes of the receptive field. A high-level feature map has a larger size of receptive field as compared to the low-level feature map. The k-means algorithm was running on the JSHD dataset to get three aspect ratios and five vehicle sizes. The height and width of each box were evaluated concerning the aspect ratio. At every feature map location, there were three aspect ratios and two scales in total. Lastly, both were combined, and NMS was used to refine the outcome.

New technologies such as batch normalization and inception were included to improve the results of vehicle detection. The simplest inception module known as inceptionV1 was used to improve the detection accuracy and feature presentation. Batch normalization directed to substantial improvements in convergence during training. It also helped in standardizing the model.

After vehicle detection, training and testing of the network were performed using hard negative mining, data augmentation, and loss function. Since labelling data is expensive, there was a shortage of labelled data. Data augmentation was used to prevent overfitting during training the network. Two data augmentation methods were used: one was randomly sampling a patch, and the other was utilizing the flipping input image [37]. Hard negative mining was used to diminish the severe class imbalance as most of the default boxes were negative after performing the matching step. A multi-task loss method was used to instruct the CNN network back-to-back. It contains two parts, bounding box regression and the loss of classification.

The baseline of the above-proposed model was SSD and Faster R-CNN, which was improved by feature concatenation, k-means algorithm, and detection of various features. The model succeeded in the detection of vehicles with different scales, different appearances, and heavy occlusion. The network attained the finest trade-off between speed and accuracy and could be employed in real-time ITS.

12.6.5   Comparison of case studies

Table 12.1 provides a set of evaluations drawn among the case studies formerly presented. It is clear that there is a general trend of collecting data through traffic surveillance cameras present on the road and highways. After collection of data, detection of the vehicle is performed using YOLOv3 in three of the above case studies and using CNN-based detectors such as SSD and R-CNN in the last one.

The wrong-way movement of the vehicle is detected in the first case by using an appearance-based approach that categorizes the movement of the vehicles as right or wrong based on the front and back images of the vehicle. In the second case, a real-time deep learning-based method is used, which tracks the vehicle using a unique ID and validates the direction of the vehicle by using Kalman filtering, Hungarian algorithm, and OpenCV libraries. The third case study proposes a vision-based vehicle detection and counting system using the deep learning model YOLO. In comparison, the last one presents an effective and efficient model for vehicle classification and detection from traffic surveillance cameras. Table 12.1 shows a comparison of various case studies related to vehicle monitoring.

12.7   Conclusion

In this chapter, the main objective was to spot the wrong-way movement of automobiles using a deep convolution neural network via traffic enforcement cameras. The author discussed the various methods used to detect the wrong-way movement of vehicles and its process. The most widely used technique for data collection includes CCTV cameras and manual videos. Data collection via CCTV has many advantages such as traffic measurement and planning becomes simpler, driving becomes safer, reduces criminal activities, enables remote monitoring, helps in enforcing the laws hence increases productivity. For the identification of vehicles, object (vehicle) detection is also required, which could be performed with the help of CNN. There are many CNN-based approaches for object detection, such as R-CNN, Fast R-CNN, Faster R-CNN, YOLO, and SSD.

Table 12.1 Comparison of various case studies

Case study	Basis	Data collection techniques	Vehicle detection and monitoring Techniques	Purpose	Future work
7.1	Appearance based	Stanford car-dataset, manually taken pictures, and traffic surveillance footage	YOLOv3, CNN	Detection of wrong-way movement of vehicles	Introduce automatic region-divider algorithm, detect all kinds of vehicles, and classify vehicles based on movement
7.2	Deep learning based	CCTV camera	YOLOv3, CNN, LQE, Kalman filtering, entry–exit algorithm, Hungarian algorithm	Wrong direction detection	Include violation recognition of jaywalking.
7.3	Vision-based	Images taken by surveillance cameras, by monitoring cameras and by car cameras	YOLOv3, CNN, ORB algorithm, mean shift algorithm, BRIEF algorithm, RANSAC algorithm	Vehicle detection and counting system	Introduce to all kind of vehicles
7.4	CNN-based	Highway surveillance video	K-means algorithm, CNN, SSD, Faster R-CNN	Highway-vehicle detection	Research in urban with complex scene and occlusion

This chapter discusses the case studies in a wide range of fields show the importance and emergence of CNN in the detection of movement of vehicles in the wrong direction. Subsequently, four case studies were discussed in this work. The first case study is an appearance-based approach that finds the wrong-way movement of vehicles based on the expectation of the user to look at a particular side (back or front) of a vehicle on every way of the highway by implementing a handwritten region-divider algorithm. In the second case study, an ITS system was created to detect the wrong-way movement of vehicles. The system was categorized into three aspects: vehicle detection, tracking of the vehicle using a unique ID, and the validation of direction. The third case study is a vision-based approach for all sizes of vehicles which results in the counting of vehicles and multi-object tracking. In the fourth case study, an effective and efficient model for vehicle classification and detection from traffic surveillance cameras is proposed. Further, a comparison between all these case studies is listed in Table 12.1.

In summary, this chapter discusses the various techniques for data collection, which are further used by different CNN approaches to detect vehicles. The CNN layers were also discussed in detail in this chapter. After the detection of vehicles, various techniques were discussed in different case studies for the wrong-way movement of vehicles.

References

[1] Wikipedia. Intelligent transportation system [online]. 2020. Available from https://en.wikipedia.org/wiki/Intelligent_transportation_system [Accessed 20 Dec 2020].

[2] D.G. Lowe, "Distinctive image features from scale-invariant keypoints." International Journal of Computer Vision, 60(2), 91–110 (2014).

[3] N. Dalal, B. Triggs. "Histograms of oriented gradients for human detection." In IEEE Computer Society Conference on Computer Vision & Pattern Recognition. (2005), pp. 886–893.

[4] Z. Sun, G. Bebis, R. Miller. "On-road vehicle detection using optical sensors: a review." In International IEEE Conference on Intelligent Transportation Systems, 2004. (2004), pp. 585–590.

[5] C. Stauffer and W. E. L. Grimson, "Adaptive background mixture models for real-time tracking." In IEEEComputer Society Conference on Computer Vision and Pattern Recognition, 1999., Fort Collins, 1999, p. 252 Vol. 2.

[6] J. Dai, Y. Li, K. He, and J. Sun. "R-FCN: object detection via regionbased fully convolutional networks." In Advances in Neural Information Processing Systems, pp. 379–387, 2016.

[7] R. Girshick. "Fast R-CNN." In 2015 IEEE International Conference on Computer Vision (ICCV), pp. 1440–1448, Dec 2015.

[8] R Girshick, J. Donahue, T. Darrell, and J. Malik. "Rich feature hierarchies for accurate object detection and semantic segmentation." In Proceedings of the IEEE Conference on Computer Vision and Pattern Recognition, pp. 580–587, 2014.

[9]   S. Ren, K. He, R. Girshick, and J. Sun. "Faster R-CNN: towards real-time object detection with region proposal networks." In Advances in Neural Information Processing Systems, pp. 91–99, 2015.

[10] K. He, X. Zhang, S. Ren, and J. Sun. Spatial pyramid pooling in deep convolutional networks for visual recognition. IEEE Transactions on Pattern Analysis and Machine Intelligence, 37(9):1904–1916, 2015.

[11] W. Liu, D. Anguelov, D. Erhan, C. Szegedy, S. Reed, C.-Y. Fu, and A. C. Berg. "SSD: single shot multibox detector." In European Conference on Computer Vision, pp. 21–37. Springer, 2016.

[12] J. Redmon, S. Divvala, R. Girshick, and A. Farhadi. "You only look once: unified, real-time object detection." In Proceedings of the IEEE Conference on Computer Vision and Pattern Recognition, pp. 779–788, 2016.

[13] Retail sensing. Vehicle traffic counting using CCTV or IP-Cameras. [online]. Available from https://www.retailsensing.com/vehicle-traffic-counting.html [Accessed 22 Dec 2020].

[14] D. K. Dash. Fuel Worth Rs 60,000 Crore Wasted Annually due to Heavy Traffic Congestion in Delhi [online]. https://www.indiatimes.com/news/india/fuel-worth-rs-60-000-crore-wasted-annually-due-to-heavy-traffic-congestion-in-delhi-270915.html [Accessed 22 Dec 2020].

[15] WHO. Road traffic injuries [online]. Available from https://www.who.int/news-room/fact- sheets/detail/road-traffic-injuries [Accessed 22 Dec 2020]

[16] K. P. Murphy, Machine Learning: A Probabilistic Perspective. Cambridge, Massachusetts: The MIT Press, 2012.

[17] T. Reddy , S. P. RM, M. Parimala, C. L. Chowdhary, S. Hakak, and W. Z. Khan, "A deep neural networks based model for uninterrupted marine environment monitoring." Computer Communications. 2020 pp. 64–75.

[18] J. R. Uijlings, K. E. Van De Sande, T. Gevers and Smeulders. "Selective search for object recognition." International Journal of Computer Vision. 2013; 104.2.

[19] W. Liu, D. Anguelov, D. Erhan, C. Szegedy, S. Reed, C. Y. Fu and A. C. Berg, "SSD: single shot multibox detector." In European Conference on Computer Vision. Cham: Springer; 2016. pp. 21–37.

[20] K. Simonyan, and A. Zisserman. "Very deep convolutional networks for large-scale image recognition." arXiv preprint arXiv:1409.1556; 2014.

[21] J. Redmon, and A. Farhadi. "YOLO9000: better, faster, stronger." In Proceedings of the IEEE Conference on Computer Vision and Pattern Recognition. 2017 pp. 7263–7271.

[22] J. Redmon, and A. Farhadi. "Yolov3: an incremental improvement." arXiv preprint arXiv:1804.02767. 2018.

[23] J. Krause, M. Stark, J. Deng, and L. Fei-Fei. "3d object representations for fine-grained categorization." In Proceedings of the IEEE International Conference on Computer Vision Workshops. 2013, pp. 554–561.

[24] G. Monteiro, M. Ribeiro, J. Marcos, and J. Batista. "Wrongwaydrivers detection based on optical flow." In 2007 IEEE International Conference on Image Processing. IEEE. 2007 vol 5.

[25] H.W. Kuhn "The Hungarian method for the assignment problem". Naval research logistics quarterly. 1955, 2, 83–97.

[26] G. Bishop, and G. Welch. "An introduction to the kalman filter." In Proceedings of SIGGRAPH, Course 8, no. 27599-23175. 2001: 41.

[27] Y. Liu, Y. Lu, Q. Shi, and J. Ding. "Optical flow based urban road vehicle tracking." In 2013 Ninth International Conference on Computational Intelligence and Security. IEEE, 2013. pp. 391–395.

[28] Q.-L. Li, and J.-F. He. "Vehicles detection based on three-frame-difference method and cross-entropy threshold method." Computer Engineering 37. 2011, 4 pp. 172–174.

[29] R. Manikandan, and R. Ramakrishnan. "Video object extraction by using background subtraction techniques for sports applications." Digital Image Processing 5. 2013, 9 pp. 435–440.

[30] R. Girshick, J. Donahue, T. Darrell, and J. Malik. "Rich feature hierarchies for accurate object detection and semantic segmentation." In Proceedings of the IEEE Conference on Computer Vision and Pattern Recognition. 2014 pp. 580–587.

[31] H. Kaiming, Z. Xiangyu, R. Shaoqing, and S. Jian "Spatial pyramid pooling in deep convolutional networks for visual recognition". IEEE Transactions on Pattern Analysis & Machine Intelligence, 2014 37(9), pp. 1904–16.

[32] J. Redmon, S. Divvala, R. Girshick, and A. Farhadi "You only look once: unified, real-time object detection." In 2016 IEEE Conference on Computer Vision and Pattern Recognition. IEEE, 2016 pp. 779–788.

[33] W. Liu, D. Anguelov, D. Erhan, C. Szegedy, S. Reed, C. Y. Fu, and A. C. Berg "SSD: single shot multibox detector." In 2016 European Conference on Computer Vision. Springer, 2016, pp. 21–37.

[34] T.-Y. Lin, M. Maire, S. Belongie, J. Hays, P. Perona, D. Ramanan, P. Dollár, and C. L. Zitnick. "Microsoft COCO: common objects in context." In European Conference on Computer Vision, pp. 740–755. Springer, Cham, 2014.

[35] L. Wen, D. Du, Z. Cai, Z. Lei, M. Chang, H. Qi, J. Lim, M. Yang, and S. Lyu. "DETRAC: a new benchmark and protocol for multi-object tracking." arXiv preprint arXiv:1511.04136 2, no. 4 (2015): 7.

[36] O. Russakovsky, J. Deng, H. Su, J. Krause, S. Satheesh, S. Ma, Z. Huang *et al.* "Imagenet large scale visual recognition challenge." International Journal of Computer Vision, 2015, 115, no. 3, pp. 211–252.

[37] W. Liu, D. Anguelov, D. Erhan, C. Szegedy, S. Reed, C.-Y. Fu, and A. C. Berg. "SSD: single shot multibox detector." In European Conference on Computer Vision, Springer, Cham, 2016, pp. 21–37.

Chapter 13

Glasses for smart tourism applications

Soorya Ram Shimgekar[1], Pathi Preetham Reddy[1],
Praveen Kumar Reddy Maddikunta[2] and
Giridhar Reddy Bojja[3]

Abstract

In this modern and associated world, the travel industry is one of the quickest developing industries and is actually a central point in deciding the economy of some countries such as the UAE and Singapore. 'Tourism' alludes to the movement of individuals from their original place of living to somewhere else with the intention of returning after a brief timeframe. As per insights, around 1.4 billion individuals travelled in the year 2018 and the amount it generated is roughly USD 250 billion around the world. In any case, numerous travelers experience issues when they travel to foreign nations like not understanding the language, issues in understanding the routes and lack of fundamental knowledge. Because of this, the traveler needs to suffer from immense loss of cash and time. Therefore, we have compared and analyzed various features that are essential for helping a traveler, alongside proposing a proficient method to incorporate all these fundamental features and other advanced options to support a vacationer, which is based on Kaldi called Kaldi-based speech interaction system (KBSIS) and OpenCV for performing image analysis. Alongside this, we have used Android Packages (APKs) of leading developers in numerous fields with the goal that we do not rely on onboard high processing powers. We have, for the present, included highlights such as navigation, interpreting text from images, plant and animal identification, face recognition and other essential highlights such as note-taking, time, weather forecast and playing music. All these functions are included on a glass frame which can project the necessary information images onto the glasses. All controls depend on speech recognition and the output is on either visual or sound.

[1]School of Computer Science Engineering, Vellore Institute of Technology, Vellore, India
[2]School of Information Technology and Engineering, Vellore Institute of Technology, Vellore, India
[3]College of Business and Information Systems, Dakota State University, Madison, SD, USA

Key Words: Smart glasses; tourism; Kaldi; speech recognition; augmented reality; OpenCV; APKs; face recognition; optical character recognition; language translation; navigation; image classification

13.1 Introduction

Tourism around the world is increasing at an unbelievably fast rate with the development of technology. The trend in the number of people traveling is increasing at an exponential scale every year. Tourism has an important role in developing countries such as India, China and other Asian countries as it is the biggest and fastest-growing industries globally which increases the economy of a country in a dramatic way.

Benefits of tourism/traveling: There are many benefits of tourism and traveling to both the country and the person. Tourism helps in improving the country's economy by developing and strengthening the country's infrastructure such as roads, transportation, accommodation, wildlife, arts and entertainment and also generates new job opportunities, such as foreign exchange, investments and payments of goods and services provided. It allows local people to learn and understand different cultures and also creates opportunities for economic and educational growth [1], and tourism can also induce more consumption of local goods and services, thereby acts as a boost for local industries [2]. Tourism generates extra revenue for the government that can be used for the nation's development [3]. Traveling can improve a person's health and can have a tremendous impact on your mental well-being by getting disconnected from one's regular life. Traveling can also make a person smarter by understanding different cultures, traditions and food [4].

Risks and problems associated with traveling: There are many risks and common problems that are caused while traveling where llanguage barriers is one of the most common problems that is often associated with traveling to foreign countries. This issue can easily frustrate a traveler and the tourist might even get lost [5]. Many countries do not show clear route marks and therefore a person who is completely unfamiliar with the routes can easily get lost. Sometimes there are many animal and plant species that can harm the tourist if they do not have any information about it. It might cause various diseases and illnesses [6]. Many times, the tourist might forget the names of a few important people such as the guide, driver, or hotel manager. This might waste a lot of time as the tourist has to remember the name and face of the person which is generally difficult if the place is new.

Types of Travelers [7]: Numerous kinds of travelers exists who make a trip because of an assorted arrangement of reasons. Many travel because of business reasons, where these tourists frequently carry with them professional and sophisticated stuff which are required for their profession or work. Then, there are numerous travelers who travel alone and invest a lot of time alone after reaching their destination. Few people travel with their companions where they need to hang out and experience new perspectives of view of the world, while others want to go with their families, and few others make a large group that share regular interests and have similar mentalities like all need to visit a religious spot. Numerous individuals travel to enjoy absolute best degrees of individual and mindful help, luxurious and lavish convenience, choice and unparalleled degrees of gastronomy and informative and educational guides, while others want to visit far off or outlandish areas so as to participate in physically testing outside exercises. Those individuals who venture out so as to get benefits for clinical issues go on a medical trip which by and large incorporates going to places having less clinical expense, or to get other wellbeing-related advantages. Figure 13.1 shows different types of travellers.

Manually performing tasks while traveling: Table 13.1 shows a brief glimpse of various tasks that are to be performed manually while traveling along with providing its limitations and other.

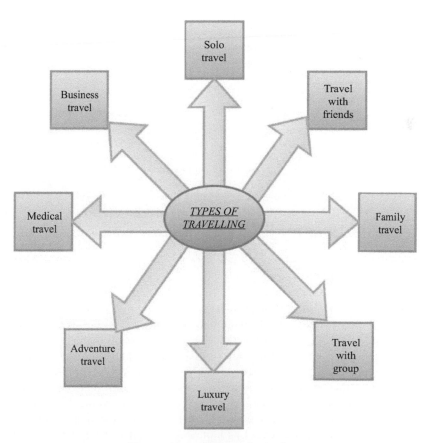

Figure 13.1   Types of travelers

Table 13.1   List of manual operations that are performed during traveling

S. no	Case	Common practices
1.	Identifying animals and plants	In order to identify a plant, you need to recognize characteristics such as size, form, leaf shape, flower color, or fragrance [8]. The following are the characteristics to be used for in-depth evaluation: broad vs. narrow leaves, leaf attachment, simple and compound leaves, leaf lobes, leaf margin, shape of the base, pattern of venation, the odor of the leaves when crushed, overall shape, surface properties [9]. You will have to go through a lot of books and websites to analyse the characteristics of the plant you found which in turn is not a comfortable thing to do.
2.	Translating text on boards	Most of the text on billboards, informative boards are written in the local language of the country. So when you are in a foreign country you might want to have some knowledge about the language there and also carry a translation book. If you do have a smartphone you will have to point the camera at the text to translate it [10].
3.	Navigation	While driving or walking you can use your phone for navigation but that is said to be dangerous as it causes the driver to get distracted from the driving [11]. The more traditional way of navigation is asking people on the roads for directions but as the case here is of being in a foreign country, that is not a thing to consider.
4.	Remembering Names	The human mind can only remember so many faces and how many times have we forgotten the person's name just after they tell it. Studies show that people forget names quickly due to lack of interest in the other person, but the other person's name and information may be useful later on [12]. Humans need some time to remember a person as a human brain just stores the information temporarily and it may not retrieve the data later. People use pocket notes to note information such as phone numbers and names in a manual manner.

13.1.1   Motivation

The main motivation of this project is to help the tourists to get more comfortable with their travel. It is commonly seen that tour guides and workers take more money than normal from foreigners taking advantage of their lack of knowledge about the local language. This not only is a loss of money to the tourists but also, they may not be getting the best experience with the workers due to the language barrier. Many people dream of visiting to foreign countries, but their main concern is that they do not know the language. Along with these, many tourists have zero or minimal knowledge about the local flora and fauna which can be a serious problem as one might not be able to differentiate between a harmless and a harmful organism, leading to diseases and other related problems. Many tourists usually are unaware of routes or directions to freely roam and enjoy the place.

Although there are many other ways to know the direction, a few methods are available that are both reliable and interactive. This is an attempt to make tourism to foreign nations a little more accessible and easier by including all these features in a simple, easy-to-use glasses that the tourist can wear and *get all* the information right in front of them.

13.1.2   *Contribution of our work*

The smart glasses proposed in this paper include a voice recognition system that runs on Kaldi and can convert speech to text locally on a device, thus eliminating the additional overhead of API requests to recognize speech. Due to this reason, our smart glasses purely run on voice recognition and therefore can eliminate any inconveniences caused by gestures in air or depending on any external device to operate the various options. The main difficulties caused due to air gestures is that it is not accurate enough and by using an external device there might be always a risk of losing it and therefore making the whole device useless. Along with this, the smart glasses contain various options and features in it making it a very versatile device capable of functioning perfectly for any application being navigation to plant and animal identification. All these features rely on external APIs along with few which are executed on a local processor giving a perfect balance between functionality and processing load.

13.2   Article structure

The whole paper consists of eight main sections including introduction, Article Structure, Existing Technologies related to Smart Glasses, System Assumptions, Functional Architecture, Proposed System, Results and Conclusion. Under the introduction, we discuss about various benefits of traveling, risks that are associated with traveling, types of travelers, a brief information about manually performing tasks, our motivation and, finally, the contribution of our work. Under existing technologies, we discuss about various applications of smart glasses, smart glasses technologies that are present in the market and a brief review of various papers that are associated with using smart glasses in real-case scenarios. In system assumptions, we discuss about all the parameters and conditions that were assumed in creating this system. Under Functional architecture and relevant technologies, we discuss about our systems functional architecture and various solutions and algorithms that were proposed by various other authors regarding each of the features that we are implementing in our proposed system for smart glasses. Under proposed system, we discuss about a brief information about the KALDI engine, the dataset and models that were considered in training the KALDI engine, the inputs that are possible, what processing and inference can be made from the input and finally the various possible outputs. Under Results, we discuss about our proposed system and also provide few screenshots of the system performing its tasks. Finally, we end with a conclusion. Figure 13.2 illustrates the highlight of this structure.

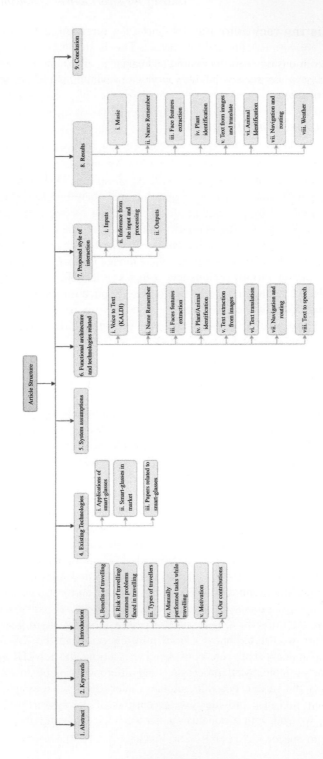

Figure 13.2   Article structure

13.3 Existing technologies related to smart glasses

Various innovations are identified with the smart glasses that are now present in the market. A smart glass is a type of eyewear that has additional features such as interfacing with the web and furthermore processing the data to some extent. It is essentially utilized for augmenting the user's knowledge on his environmental factors by actively presenting relevant information. These features are achieved through presenting the relevant information directly onto the glass lenses in front of eyes using transparent heads up display or optical head mounted display, which makes a pseudo-real-world, otherwise called augmented reality (AR). This technology heavily depends on wireless advancements such as Wi-Fi, GPS and Bluetooth for almost the entirety of its features.

13.3.1 Applications of smart glasses

In [13], we can observe that the author has compared and analyzed various applications of the smart glasses in different domains. Along with this, the author has also discussed the various reasons for its efficacy and the limitations and challenges that are present which hamper the use of AR in that respective domain. Table 13.2 provides various applications of smart glasses in different domains.

13.3.2 Smart glasses technology in the market

A wide range and variety is available in the market for various smart glasses for different applications. Many of these glasses rely on different methods of interaction and different processors for performing their various operations. Table 13.3 displays few features, methods of interaction and on-board processor. Along with this, we have also compared various limitations that are present in each smart glasses that might cause any inefficiency in its performance.

13.3.3 Smart glasses solutions papers

Various smart glasses-related technologies and systems are proposed by various authors and researchers for a wide range of applications. These papers that discuss smart glasses technology are reviewed in the following, finding their field of application and methodology used. A smart glasses system is proposed in [16] that specifically focuses on Alzheimer's patients that can help them recognize their relatives and friends and also where they might have placed the objects they need. The glasses are equipped with AR, which shows them the information without completely blocking their vision. Artificial intelligence-based smart glasses are proposed in [17] that help in enhancing AR technology. Today we have news that all major tech companies are working on some kind of smart glasses and they may be the next big market leading product. A solution for the visually impaired children is proposed in [18] where the smart glasses can help people who are visually impaired 'read' by processing the camera on their glasses data and applying optical character recognition (OCR) to it. The text recognized by OCR can be given to Google text to speech (gTTS) to be pronounced out for the person. Reading and

Table 13.2 Applications of Smart Glasses

S. No.	Application	Benefits	Methodologies	Challenges
1.	Medicine	• It merges the gap between the patient and patient data by over-lapping necessary information with the actual environment. • Anatomical and functional data can be a support in surgery as well as in diagnostic of preoperative and intra-operative data or in training tasks.	• Accurate tracking systems provide the required precision. • To improve perception stereoscopic visualization devices are used. • Multi-modal interfaces such as touch, gesture.	• Require precise positioning up-to the degree of 1 mm. • It involves very complex setups and accurate calibrations. • Overcome three main issues, tracking precision, misperception and interaction with synthetic data.
2.	Repair/main-tenance	• Reduces cognitive and memory load from workers. • User manuals are very complicated and generally require expert understanding. • Operations can be performed by telepresence too.	• Assets are overlaid and correctly aligned with the object to be repaired. • All the procedure is managed as a set of sequential states.	• The present procedures have to be changed, created or modified to suit the AR application.
3.	Collaborative visualiza-tion space	• Improving visualization by using virtual objects within a physical space. • Very useful for collaborative visualization. • Bridge the gap between physical and virtual space. • Provide the users with custom visualizations.	• Communicate by using speech, gaze, gesture and other nonverbal cues. • Migrate both objects and users (represented by avatars) in a cyberspace. • Organizing data to be displayed on layers which should contain computer generated objects, which share attributes and each layer can be activated or deactivated. • Features are virtuality, augmentation, cooperation, independence, individuality.	• Tracking system of the AR application must be able to track both users' heads and artifacts selected as alter egos of virtual Objects. • See-through glasses are more efficient. • Provide stereoscopic visualization for objects.

	Domain	Applications	Challenges
4.	Tourism	• Improve user experience by multimedia and customized contents.	• Augmented guides, find information from the internet. • Merging the real space with the contents collected from cyberspace. • Tourism with layers that act as a multi-level game. • Augmented tourism tourist where useful information is shown.	• Having a proper inter-operability among applications.
5.	Architecture and Construction	• It improves the spatial communication by providing the architects and designers with information like appearance, scale and features.	• Represent buildings virtually in the real world from initial stage to final stage. • Act as an X-ray display to show structural supports, pipes, etc. • Virtual meetings between architect and designer to model, analyze and assess CAD models. • Can be used for maintenance tasks.	• An increased and proper implementation of AR in the actual construction phases. • Have a proper standard to integrate CAD with AR.
6.	Education	• Engage the students in a more efficient manner and proactive way. • Develop cooperative and collaborative learning. • Visualize and represent many phenomena in biology, geography, etc.	• Concepts similar to maintenance AR to train beginners • Interactive courses using interactive pages and stickers.	• Making a correct and appropriate AR content that can be quickly deployed. • Make the content flexible for teachers and students.
7.	Military	• Gives a complete feel to the soldier in the real-world scenarios. • Mitigates the risks of training injuries caused by real objects. • Does not require specialized setup rooms.	• Create synthetic battlefields by placing virtual objects in the real world which is navigable. • Overlapping the information on the real world.	• Actively tracking the head position and gun aim position of the soldier. • Information conveyed to soldiers has to be carefully managed. • Not to visually overload the soldier.

(Continues)

Table 13.2 (*Continued*)

S. No.	Application	Benefits	Methodologies	Challenges
			• Collaboration between the soldiers to communicate their information.	• Examine soldiers' stress levels.
8.	Entertainment	• The players can completely immerse themselves in the game and feel more connected. • Can be used to augment live broadcast of sport events.	• Use the real world as scenario and characters and assets are virtual. • Stickers which depict an individual asset in virtual space. • Assets have to be overlapped to raw images in real time.	• Identify and track a given object in the scene in a very performing way.

Table 13.3 Different smart glasses in the market

S. No.	Company	Features	Interface	Onboard-computer	Limitations
1	Google Glass Enterprise Edition	An enterprise focused device which helps employees work smarter. Main use cases in manufacturing factories.	• Main interface: Touchpad on the frame of glass. • Secondary interface: Cloud-based voice assistant	Qualcomm Quad Core, 1.7 GHz, 10 nm	• As the main method of interfacing in it is by swiping on the glass frame it cannot give a lot of functionality as it can only have functions such as up, down, left, right, enter. • Need a bit of practice to get used to.
2	Vuzix Blade	• Autofocus HD camera • Integrated stereo speakers in temples • Noise cancelling mics • Full color display (right-eye only) • Wireless Wi-Fi and Bluetooth • Full UV protection lenses with safety certifications	• Main interface: touchpad on the frame of glass. • Secondary interface: cloud-based voice assistant	Quad Core ARM CPU	The case is the same as the Google Glass from above as these use the same touchpad-based and cloud-based voice control. Cloud-based voice control is not preferable as it does not work in the absence of the internet.

(Continues)

Table 13.3 (*Continued*)

S. No.	Company	Features	Interface	Onboard-computer	Limitations
3	Everysight Raptor	• Touchpad: to activate different functionalities, users may tap and swipe over the integrated touchpad. • Built-in audio: these smart glasses feature an internal speaker as well as two microphones. • Front camera: the 13.2 MP camera enables users to capture HD videos and photos. • Memory and storage: Raptor glasses feature 2 GB of RAM and either 16 or 32 GB of internal memory. • Controller (optional): users may attach the Everysight controller to their bicycle handlebar for easier control. Furthermore, the controller features large buttons for use even with cycling gloves.	Main interface: touch-pad on the frame of glass.	Qualcomm® Snapdra-gon™ 410E	The case is the same as the Google Glass from above as these use the same touchpad based. Here, the problem goes even further as there is no voice based control in here.

then displaying the text in front of view can be extremely helpful when you want to read the statement closer, or one might use this text to perform additional operations such as translation. Instead of covering the whole visual space with content like in the case of virtual reality (VR). A method is proposed in [19] where AR augments itself in the real world without causing a lot of distraction using a system called Peritext which uses rapid serial visual presentation (RSVP) which helps in determining the placements and presentation of the text. Another use of smart glasses is in the case of blind people to navigate. For people with low vision AR can make a big difference by supporting their vision by adding needed information. For these kinds of people, AR can supply them directions and instructions in transit and therefore smart glasses that use dual stereo cameras are proposed in [20] to calculate the depth of the object near them and gives the blind person signals by vibrations and sounds. Various ways in which smart glasses technology can help blind people by making navigation a bit easier for them are proposed in [21]. Smart glasses have countless applications in the field of crime control where the Smart glasses can be used to detect criminals by using face recognition techniques. a facial recognition system for the smart glasses is proposed in [6] that aims at identifying the criminal faces. The author [22] investigates the various visitors' requirements that must be present in a smart glass technology that aims at making museums and art-galleries more informative and interactive. The use of smart glasses in the case of task assistance applications where deep learning models are used in smart glasses technology is discussed in [23]. Deep learning-based task assistance can help users in daily work and it can deliver guidance in an effective way. They can be used in basic use cases such as navigation and task guidance. The smart glasses technology cannot become the mainstream with all the issues plaguing it and all those issues need to be solved. Most of the issues were user interface (UI) related and will help in building the UI for future smart glasses.

13.4 System assumptions

In this section, we are discussing the various assumptions that were made in our proposed smart glasses solution, specific for tourism-related applications. Various assumptions are considered in developing this system because it is the first prototype of the final smart glasses. Few of the assumptions that have been made are having an external processing unit, the main reason for it being that the proposed system is a first-level prototype and therefore does not focuses on making the system compact. Another assumption that was considered in this paper is that all the features that are present in the smart glasses are to be executed in a sequential manner. Being only a presentation of the concept to be developed the present system does not focus on parallelization of the software. Many features that are considered and used in this system are from external and third-party vendors that provide their APIs. Development of self-designed APIs for carrying out the operation is yet to be worked on and have therefore been considered as a development in future developments. Because of relying on external vendors there has to be a stable and reliable internet

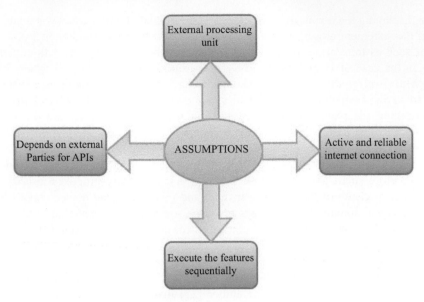

Figure 13.3   Assumptions

connection. Figure 13.3 summarizes the various assumptions that are considered in the development of this system.

13.5   Functional architecture and technologies relevant

In this paper, we have proposed a simple system to aid a traveller to make his trip more efficient and simple. A Kaldi-based speech recognition way of interaction was proposed along with integrating various functions and features that helps a traveller. Few of these features include face recognition and name remembering system, navigation system, animal and plant recognition, translation system, note taking from speech, music search and play, current and next-day weather and lastly, date and time. The whole system presently works on python for executing all of its features along with APIs provided by third-party vendors. In this proposed system, a voice recognition-based interaction system was used to perform all the functionalities, which runs on KALDI as its back-end. Figure 13.4 illustrates the functional architecture of the proposed smart glasses.

Below, we present various papers and algorithms which are useful in making a functional system including all the features that are proposed in this paper. Various methods were compared in this paper that could constitute in the making of this smart glasses.

13.5.1   *Voice to text conversion-KALDI*

In this paper, a voice-based approach of system was proposed that relies on KALDI and VOSK for voice recognition and signal processing. KALDI is a neural network

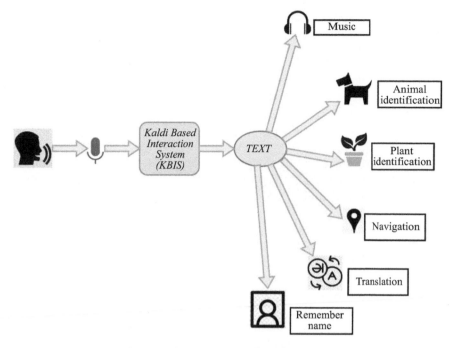

Figure 13.4   Functional architecture

model that is specifically used for processing and recognizing voice and converting it into text. It was first using subspace Gaussian mixture models (SGMMs) but is being shifted to deep neural networks (DNNs) for most of the use cases. The toolkit is being updated from time to time [24]. As Kaldi is primarily written in C++, python is a more flexible, and now popular language pytorch made a wrapper for kaldi as a library in python. So python users can use kaldi toolkit with the PyKaldi library. The whole toolkit is also modernised to develop the state-of-the-art speech recognizers in python [25]. However, we do not use the PyTorch wrapped python version of kaldi. We used the original Kaldi in C++. Before we decided to go with Kaldi, we were considering other alternatives and the following are the concepts of those concepts. The recent developments in speech recognition with deep learning. DNN can be used to create and use speech recognition techniques including multi-band DNNs which can be used to recognize multiple bands of speech and multi-language DNNs which have common layers [26]. Normal neural networks can only be trained up to a certain level of accuracy and giving context to the neural network can greatly improve the level of accuracy that can be reached. The context-dependent deep neural network hidden Markov models (CD-DNN-HMM) have been proven to be better at speech recognition than the more traditional Gaussian mixture model (GMM) by giving 2%–30% more accuracy. The CD-DNN-HMM can also be used with simple mics, whereas GMM can only be used with high-quality mic [27]. The context-dependent deep belief network hidden Markov models (CD-CBN-HMM) are tested and have proven to have promising results on phone-based recognition applications. They particularly specialize in spontaneous speech recognition and recognition models with large vocabulary sets [28]. Different research are taking place in the speech recognition with neural networks area and the other alternatives to context- based neural networks other types of neural networks such as deep belief networks (DBN). The differentiating element in the DBN is that instead of the input being filtered in each layer in a traditional neural network here all the input is given to each layer. They are worse in efficiency but maybe better at producing results. Deep convex networks were observed to be better than the previous DBNs in semantic utterance understanding (SUN). SUN is the understanding of the meaning of the words on the basis of the group of semantics. However, the downside is that the number of features that are needed is very big [29].

Below, we discuss various features that are essential in making this smart glasses system. Various papers are compared which focuses on each feature individually and we discuss various methods used along with their limitations.

13.5.2 Name remember

The proposed system can recognise faces with the built-in cameras. Although we used face recognition APIs to do the underlying work, we referred to some other research papers and the following are our findings. The two most popular algorithms that are used in face detection and recognition are local binary patterns histogram algorithm and convolution neural networks. A comparison between these two approaches was conducted based on different datasets such as ORL dataset, FEI dataset and author's dataset created by 12 individuals each of 100 images. The result was that CNN works better for face detection and identification [30]. Another paper where the authors propose a face recognition and verification algorithm for criminal identification-related applications uses the facenet (FN) model for face detection directly from live videos. This system utilizes a deep coevolutionary network that learns the Euclidean embedding of each image to be able to identify faces accurately from both still images, and as well as from live video [31]. We have referred to some papers where the authors compared different face recognition algorithms and laid out the statistics of their findings. They compare various algorithms and techniques that are extensively used in face recognition such as Eigen-faces, Fisher-faces and local binary patterns histograms (LBPH). The author compares these algorithms based on their accuracy, efficiency along with other 17 popular algorithms [32]. Filtering the data can be very useful in face recognition as we only need to differentiate between certain features of different faces instead of processing the whole image data every time. The author of the paper we referred for pre-filtering algorithms compares advantages and disadvantages of popular face recognition and identification algorithms based on their pre-filtering techniques and edge detection methods which can be further improved for higher efficiency and accuracy [33]. Another research paper we have referred to where the author of this paper proposes an efficient and robust model which can identify, detect and associate faces directly from videos, which works by localizing faces in the live video by using multi-scale single-shot face detectors, which are then grouped together by using face association techniques. The faces are then identified by using face matching algorithms which are based on an unsupervised subspace learning approach and a subspace-to-subspace similarity metric [34].

13.5.3 Facial features extraction

We have implemented identification of different features on the face of people such as age, emotions and gender. Various papers were compared that specifically aimed at finding these features by analyzing a person's facial features. This technology of emotion detection is necessary for understanding the feelings of the person with whom the traveller is communicating with. Many times the way in which the person's face affects the meaning of what the person is trying to communicate. An algorithm to analyze facial emotions was proposed in [35] using neural networks of texture features where the face is first localized and identified using facial landmarks, after which texture features are found out by face features vector using the linear binary pattern, where then these features are passed into the neural network for finding the emotion. The author proposes An algorithm to find basic human emotions from a face by utilizing the GLCM approach is proposed [36] which gives the texture characteristics of by using second-order statistical measurements. Nearest neighbours alongside with fuzzy Euclidean distance are used for classifying and predicting accurate age, and a novel algorithm for finding the emotion of a face by using advanced maximally stable extremal regions was proposed in [37]. This model extracts the features of the faces which is then utilized by the artificial neural networks for classification and predicting the emotion of the face. An approximate age of the person could affect the veracity of the statements that he/ she is trying to convey. This trifle but yet important information about a person could affect the trustworthiness of the person. Therefore, an intelligent and efficient algorithm that can identify the age of a person by using facial features was proposed [38]. These features are then used by the deep learning model employing convoluted neural networks to find an estimated age of the person. A different approach was proposed in [39] to estimate the age of a person by using active appearance models which finds the traits vector of the face along with classification algorithms such as support vector machine (SVM), K-nearest neighbor (KNN) and support vector regression (SVR) to predict an accurate age of the person [13,40]. We can also use three-dimensional data for finding patterns in images which results in object/face recognition more accurate and efficient as we can apply similarity based algorithms to identify [41] or even use shape index identification to identify from the features extracted with the SIFT/SURF descriptors [42].

13.5.4 Object (plant and animal) identification

Another feature that is needed for a traveller while he is traveling is to classify and identify the various local flora and fauna. This information might be useful for people who trek when they encounter with a new organism be it a plant or animal which might very well be harmful to the traveller. A multi-view saliency guided deep neural network (MVSG-DNN) was proposed in [43], which is used for classification and identification using three key modules that comprise of model projection rendering for capturing multiple views of 3D objects, visual context learning using CNN for feature extraction and LSTM for selecting representative view and multi-view representation learning for object retrieval and identification and we can observe a novel method in [44] to detect and identify moving objects using DNNs for the classification of the object using the keras environment that was proposed by the author. By the means of the paper [45], the author compares and analyzes various algorithms that are being presently used for object detection and also object tracking. The author compares various features such as accuracy, time and limitations of using the particular algorithm keeping in mind the effect of it on power constrained device's battery life and performance. Identifying an object and classifying is an important trait and in [46], the author has compared and analyzed various object detection algorithms based on various trends, features, open issues and future directions based on two widely used techniques which includes optical/vision based identification or electronically identifying the object. Finding the tag that are related to a specific object in the smallest possible time is a crucial factor for a traveller. In [47], the author has built a wine label retrieval system using CNN-SURF and consecutive filtering and matching (CSCFM) framework where CNN is used filtering the main brands and then speeded up robust features (SURF) matching along with random sample consensus (RANSAC) mechanism and the modified term frequency-inverse document frequency (TF-IDF) distance is used for finding the sub-brands.

13.5.5   Text detection

Extracting text from the images be it live or from saved images is a crucial step that is necessary for performing any further operations [44]. This text extracted from the images is called OCR. Once the text is extracted this string can be used for advanced operations translation. This extraction must be quick as well as efficient. In [48], the author has proposed a light-weight, fast and accurate text detection algorithm that can detect multilingual languages in live scenes using feature fusion mechanism and self-attention mechanism and similarly in [49] the author has improved the EAST algorithm for it to be able to detect and identify the text on the utility pole plate which uses VGG-16 for speeding up the process. Since this is one of the crucial steps that is needed for further operation, the text recognition system must be robust and therefore in paper [50] the author has proposed a robust model for detecting text in live scenarios using a simple and fast pipeline of only one neural network which can detect text present in any orientation and any color. Performing this OCR in real time scenarios could improve the overall time for computation and therefore in paper [51] the author has proposed a light algorithm for text detection in live scenarios where a very small dataset is used for training using a multi-scale text feature extraction network with feature pyramid based on Faster R-CNN and in paper [52] the author has proposed an effective algorithm that can detect text directly on a live video stream where Sobel operator is used to perform edge detection, K-means clustering used to extract text from the background and maximum stable external region (MSER) is used for text detection.

13.5.6 Text-translation

Translation is one key feature that is needed for any traveller that is traveling to a foreign country. Translating the text in an efficient and quick manner is crucial for a traveller since wrong translation can cause many problems which can also cause wastage of money. Performing this translation in the fastest method is the key in this case. In [53], the author has proposed a light-weight and effective web application that can be used for text recognition and translation using a natural language processing system that can understand the context using a semantic approach. Similarly, in [54], the author has developed an application that can translate text from images directly and also compared various techniques and approaches to do the same. The application relies on OCR for extracting the text from an image and then translates it instantaneously. The main challenge that is faced while translating a text is not able to understand the correct context of the text. In paper [55] the author has proposed a method to cope with the data paucity that is generally encountered while performing Spoken Language Translation using transfer learning which performs machine translation using target-language embedding to shift the input representations in different portions of the space according to the language.

13.5.7 Navigation

For a traveller that is totally unaware of the neighborhood streets and routes finding the fastest course between his source and destination is one of the significant factors that troubles any traveller. For finding the correct and shortest course between any two points, different algorithms are proposed; for instance, in [56], the creator expresses that Modern Robots need to have some sort of automated motion control system for mobility. Motion planning is done using various types of algorithms such as A*, genetic algorithms, probability-based roadmap and therefore the reviews these algorithms in this paper along with testing them using simulations. In [57], the author puts forth his words by saying that movement control framework for robots utilizes way arranging calculations which are thus grouped into analytical, enumerative, evolutionary and meta-heuristic techniques for which analytical methods become extremely complex with regards to immaterial applications. Till now meta-heuristic strategies have indicated critical outcomes which is currently being utilized by the majority of robot creators. By the methods for paper [58], the author states that one of the forces to be reckoned with for most research ahead is collision free path planning (CFPP). Collision avoidance is one of the key parts of the movement control framework. The main comparison between the papers being published is the presentation of the calculations in them. There are certain favorable circumstances and impediments to all the calculations.

13.5.8   Text to speech conversion

The main method of interaction from the glasses to its user is by speech, and for this, a robust, accurate and lively text to speech conversion system is necessary. In [14], the author has proposed an efficient method to translate the text into an expressive speech in one flow which has improved the disentanglement capabilities of sequence to sequence system using variational autoencoder (VAE) and a householder flow, and in [59], an efficient and accurate model for text to speech system by using Tacotron-based acoustic models where Tacotron decoder and phoneme duration are used with phoneme alignment instead of relying on attention is proposed by the author, where the phoneme duration are calculated using HMM-based forced alignment and the duration model is a simple bidirectional LSTM-based network. By means of [60], the author has proposed a solution to the existing sequence-to-sequence by using multitask learning with text-to-speech (TTS) which can now linguistic information and preserve the training stability without worrying about tedious alignments. For the interaction to be as lively and natural as possible time for it to respond must be as small as possible. In [61], the author has proposed a way to lessen the time that is required for training the model compared to conventional Tacotron-based models by introducing a transformer-based acoustic model with weighted forced attention obtained from phoneme durations. In [62], the author proposed an expressive and intelligent text to speech translator which relies on DNNs which uses a style-dependent shared hidden layer model. The author compares and analyzes various other DNN-based TTS systems, and in [63], a method to expressively differentiate between a pair of heteronym words where the pronunciation of the word is crucial for understanding the context of the sentence is put forth. The author also compares various techniques and approaches that are present for heteronym words where the data is generally not tagged for a particular target language.

13.6   Proposed style of interaction (KBSIS)

13.6.1   KALDI

For the voice recognition feature, Kaldi toolkit was used. Kaldi is a voice recognition toolkit which was written in C++. It uses finite-state transducers (FSTs) using OpenFst library for lexical analysis of the words. This toolkit was developed using subspace Gaussian mixture models (SGMMs) for feature extraction from speech data. As Kaldi is an FST-based speech recognition toolkit, it is in theory possible to use any language that can be given in FST form. Although Kaldi was used in English in this project, Kaldi was used to recognise Kannada (an Indian language) by different projects [64].

Figure 13.5 illustrates basic architecture of KALDI. The developers of Kaldi intended Kaldi to support traditional speech recognition models such as GMMs and Subspace GMMs and, at the same time, can be extended to upcoming types of models. This helped the toolkit to be upgraded over time to neural network-based models.

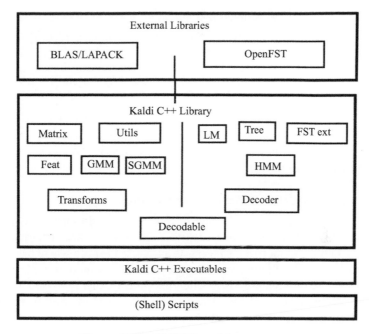

Figure 13.5   KALDI architecture map

The toolkit is compatible with maximum likelihood linear regression (MLLR) for feature extraction from the speech data and also supports feature-space adaptation using feature-space MLLR and speaker normalization using vocal tract length normalization (VTLN) to adapt to different speakers as the training data may not be of the same person.

The reason for choosing Kaldi over a cloud-based speech recognition tool is latency. As latency is critical for the user experience, Kaldi has been chosen. Kaldi toolkit had impressive accuracy running on the testing computer.

13.6.2   Dataset and model used

For running the script, we have utilized vosk-model-en-us-aspire 0.2 model that is given by the VOSK. The used model had a precision of 13.64 (librispeech test-clean) and 12.89 (tedlium). The model was prepared on Fisher data which is one of the latest LM that is accessible. The lexicon that was utilized in preparing this model is US English. All the discussion is translated by the Linguistic Data Consortium at the University of Pennsylvania [65]. The information is a piece of conversational phone discourse (CTS) where it contains 5,850 complete discussions, each enduring as long as 10 min. The information likewise contains a table that describes the speakers, the properties of the calls, and the set of topics that were utilized to start the discussions. The transcribed information contains expression end-focuses on the two channels of every discussion which goes about as a timestamp. The transcribed information record contains start-time, end-time, speaker/channel-ID and transcripted text and there were no changes in the content and are actually equivalent to that, that were spoken by the speakers. At a couple of spots where the words were not satisfactory – ((...)) – was utilized as a substitution. You can see an example of the data from [66].

13.6.3   Inputs

The input that is passed into the framework is the user's speech. The user talks his/her command using a microphone. This speech is broken down by the KALDI framework and after processing it changes over the speech into a string. The string is a fairly precise transcription of the speech that was spoken by the speaker.

13.6.4   Inference from input and processing

The string that is found by the KALDI engine is fed as an input that triggers a specific feature. The string is compared with a set of predefined strings and string that matches with the input string triggers its associated feature where basic python functions where used for finding this match. Each of this condition is a separate 'if' statement and once the condition is fulfilled the function that is written under each of these 'if' statement is executed. There were APIs used by third-party vendors which are discussed below.

13.6.4.1   Face-characterisation (SightCorp Face API)

We have used the F.A.C.E. API by the SightCorp to classify various faces. The API makes use of infused AI-based face analysis functionalities to detect faces, analyse the emotions, and also find the crowd demographics. All these functionalities are executed in the cloud and therefore the need to utilise powerful hardware is lessened. The API return these information in a simple and easy-to-access JSON format. We can also implement temperature sensors to detect COVID-19 [67] in the faces detected by the glasses which can be an important feature to have as traveling after the pandemic is still going to be doubtful and fearful.

13.6.4.2   Navigation (Geoapify API)

We have used Geoapify API to find the route between two points on a geographic plane. The API helps us to find the shortest path between the source to destination. The routing API provided by geoapify provides cross-platform and flexible service where it is accessible by HTTP GET request which makes it very easy and efficient. The API returns the information in a GeoJSON response which follows universal standards. The API can also give the shortest fastest and shortest path based on the way of traveling, i.e., car, bike, truck, walk, etc.

13.6.4.3   Plant identify (Plant.id API)

By using Plant.id API we are able to classify and identify various plants. This API is successfully able to identify over 10,675 Identifiable plant species with a success rate of 85% and that too under 2 seconds. The API provides the matching plants name in a JSON format. The API is also highly scalable and can also provide additional information about the identified plant. We can use 3D object recognition techniques to detect the desired object in the frame which is then sent to the API as sending all the frames can be inefficient for both network and processor on the server [68]. The object detector uses feature descriptors like SIFT and SURF to extract features and detect objects. As this method does not involve neural networks they will not add an overhead for the local processor.

13.6.4.4 Translate (Google Translate API)

By using Google's Translate API, we have included a feature of translating the foreign language into a language that could be understood by the tourist. The Google Translate API can dynamically translate text between thousands of language pairs. All this processing and translation is executed in Google's cloud platforms that releases the load from local processors.

13.6.4.5 Image to text (Cloudmersive OCR API)

Cloudmersive OCR API is being used in our glasses to extract the textual content from the image that can be further used for translation. We have made use of Cloudmersive OCR API that can automatically pre-process the captured image and then find the text in it by making use of Machine Learning models.

13.6.4.6 General/animal identification (IBM Watson Developer Cloud's VisualRecognitionV3)

To identify the various objects and animals that might be encountered by the traveller we have made use of IBM watson developer cloud's VisualRecognitionV3 API to identify and label an image efficiently. Visual recognition understands the contents of images, analyse images for scenes, objects, faces, colors, food and other subjects that can give you insights into your visual content which makes use of deep learning algorithms to do the same.

13.6.4.7 Weather (openweathermap API)

To keep the tourist up-to-date with the weather condition of the place and also an approximate forecast of weather we have used openweathermap API. openweathermap API provides Hourly forecast for 4 days with higher geographic accuracy. The results are displayed in the form of JSON and XML formats.

13.6.5 Outputs

After the processing of input by various associated APIs and functions, there are two main categories of outputs that are possible:

13.6.5.1 Visual output

This type of output is used in the case of navigation where the directions are directly shown to the user in front of the user's eyes. The directions include straight, left, right, back and U-turn. This form of output is apt for navigation because it gives real-time feedback of the traveller's path and therefore is much more convenient to use.

13.6.5.2 Speech narration

This form of output is the majority in our proposed smart glasses and is used in almost the entirety of the system. It includes providing additional information, asking for commands and also providing guidelines to use the proposed smart glasses. It is also used to interact with the user and therefore provide any information that is requested by the user. Figure 13.6 shows various types of outputs and which feature is under which specific category of output.

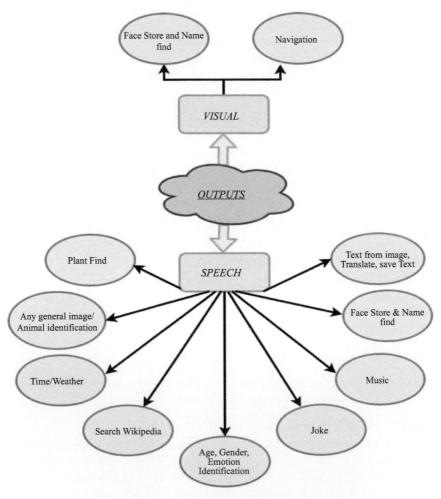

Figure 13.6   Types of outputs

13.7   Results and discussion

This proposed system was tested on a computer that runs on Intel i5 eighth generation processor and 16 GB RAM. The CPU clock is around 2.4 GHz. The operating system used to run this system is Ubuntu 16.04 LTS. The Python interpreter used is python 3.6.

13.7.1   Navigation

Using the Navigation feature, the user can speak his destination, and the API calculates the routes and returns the various checkpoints in the form of GPS coordinates. The function then checks the current GPS coordinates of the traveller and checks whether he/she is walking based on the checkpoints that were provided. Constant feedback of the route is projected in front of the user in the form of direction arrows. The rate of updating the GPS coordinates of the user is 2 s, i.e. after 2 s the coordinate of the user is updated and then compared with its nearest checkpoint. Based on this, a feedback is given to the traveller regarding his next moves. We can see an example of the feedback given in Figure 13.7 where they are projected in front of user's eyes.

13.7.2   Music

The user commands the system to play a music. The system asks the user about what song does the user wants to listen to. The user has to tell his song name and this is name is fed into YouTube-dl where the song is searched on YouTube and a link is returned. This link is now used to play the song directly to the user without actually having to search and open any app.

13.7.3   Text from image and Translate

In this feature, the user scans the text which he wants to analyse and translate. In this example, we have considered a handwritten piece of text which is scanned by the system's camera, as can be seen in Figure 13.8(a). After choosing the best snap of the text, it is sent to the OCR API which analyses the image and extract its textual data and returns the text string. This text can be seen in the first half of Figure 13.8(b). Now this text in English is sent to Translating API which translates the text in English into Hindi (An Indian Language). This can be seen as the second half of Figure 13.8(b). All this spoken by a text to speech converter that speaks this to the user.

13.7.4   Remembering face and naming

Using this feature, the user can store a face by analysing the facial features and encoding it into machine understandable form. This encoded format is now referenced to compare with live video feed and display the name of person by analysing and comparing it with encoded features. This takes two steps and the user has to first store the person's face by commanding the system to do so and storing it by a

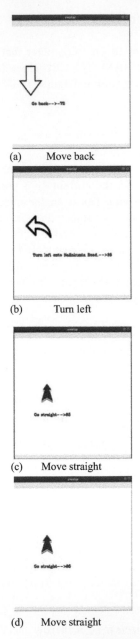

(a)   Move back

(b)   Turn left

(c)   Move straight

(d)   Move straight

Figure 13.7   Navigation

particular name. After this, the system analyses and encodes the face. Now whenever the user wants to know that particular person's name he can again command the system to display the name. The system then analyses the live video feed from the camera and then compares it with the encoded information that is present. After

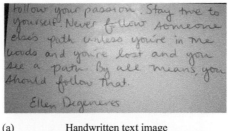

(a)   Handwritten text image

(b)   Extracted text and translated text

*Figure 13.8   Images of output given by extract and translate feature: (a)
handwritten text image and (b) extracted text and translated text*

Figure 13.9   Name from saved face

this, the name of the person is displayed in front of the user by drawing a name box
around the person's face, as shown in Figure 13.9.

13.7.5   Face characteristics

This feature is used to analyse basic face features such as age, gender and emotion.
The user can command the system to show the facial features of the person. The
system then analyses the face by using the camera. It first captures the best image and
then sends it to the facial features finding API. This information about age, gender
and emotions is returned by the API in JSON format and then this is spoken to the
user by using the text to speech converter. We can observe an example of this feature
in Figure 13.10. We can also add other features like intrusion detection for knowing
when to detect faces to save energy of the glasses as they run on batteries [13].

(a)   Original face

(b)   Features that are extracted

*Figure 13.10   Images of output given by extract and translate feature: (a) original
face and (b) features that are extracted*

Without intrusion detection, the glasses will be continuously trying to detect faces
which might become a problem for efficiency of the glasses.

13.7.6   Weather

Whenever the user wants to know about the current or next day's weather condition, he/she can speak to the system and query about the weather. The system then
contacts the weather API which returns the weather information in the form of
JSON format which is then converted into an array of arrays, as shown in
Figure 13.11. This information is then converted into speech by the text to speech
converter.

13.7.7   Plant identification and search

This feature is used when the user wants to analyse and get some information about
a particular plant. The user can scan a plant, as seen in Figure 13.12(a), and the
image is sent to be processed to the plant identification API. The API returns the
plant name and this name is searched on Wikipedia to get basic information about
the plant, as shown in Figure 13.12(b). The information is spoken by the text to
speech converter and speaks it the information about the plant to the user.

13.7.8   Animal identification and search

This feature is used when the user wants to analyse and get some information about
a particular animal. The user can scan an animal, as seen in Figure 13.13(a), and the
image is sent to be processed to the animal identification API. The API returns the
animal name and this name is searched on Wikipedia to get the basic information
about the animal, as shown in Figure 13.13(b). The information is fed into the text
to speech converter and speaks it the information about the plant to the user.

[[53, 27.6, 11.84, 'scattered clouds'], [47, 28.37, 13.28, 'scattered clouds']]

Process finished with exit code 0

Figure 13.11 Current and next day's weather

(a)   Plant image

(b)   Information about the plant

Figure 13.12 Images of output given by plant identification feature: (a) plant image and (b) information about the plant

(a)   Animal image

(b)   Information about the animal

Figure 13.13 Images of output given by animal identification feature: (a) animal image and (b) information about the animal

13.8   Conclusion

The paper has proposed a smart glasses system for tourism purposes using the Kaldi speech recognition toolkit. There have been many attempts at making proper interaction systems between users and their smart glasses. The interaction system was made mainly based on speech for input and output. This project was made focusing on the tourism aspect. The features proposed to cater to tourists include Plant recognition, animal recognition, handwriting detection and translation, navigation, face recognition and music playback. Plant and animal recognition can be helpful as tourists will not be needing a guide for explaining as finding a proper guide can be quite difficult in places you do not know. Handwriting recognition and translation can be very helpful as the user may not know the local language in a foreign place. Navigation can be quite important as asking for directions in a foreign country where the user does not know the local language might be very helpful. Music playback without an offline library gives the user quite some flexibility to listen to all kinds of music without being limited to a small library.

References

[1]   Benefits of tourism. http://www.auburn.edu/academic/classes/ geog/chanepl.
[2]   Kshitiz Thakur. Importance of tourism and its economic value. http://www. market-width.com/blogs/Importance-Tourism-Industry-Economic-Value.htm.
[3]   Dr Hayley Stainton. Economic impacts of tourism. https://tourismteacher. com/economic-impacts-of-tourism/,year=2020.
[4]   Thomas Busson. Benefits of travelling. 2019. https://www. claimcompass. eu/blog/benefits-of-travelling/.
[5]   Georgina Lawton. 6 common travel problems that will affect you at some point (and how to keep going). 2017. https://www.liligo.com/ travel-edition/l.
[6]   AVMA(American Veterinary Medical Association). Disease precautions for outdoor enthusiasts and their companion animals. 2020. https://www.avma. org/resources-tools/veterinarians-and-public-health/disease-precautions-outdoor-companion-animals.
[7]   7 types of travel for different types of travelers. https://www.urby.in/blog/ types_of_travel/#Travel_With_Friends.
[8]   Teo Spengler. Plant leaf identification: how to tell plant leaves apart. 2020. https://www.gardeningknowhow.com/garden-how-to/ info/plant-leaf-identification.htm.
[9]   Patrick Breen. Plant identification: examining leaves. 2020. https://landscapeplants.oregonstate.edu/ plant-identification-examining-leaves.
[10]   Kane Williamson. 6 best online translation tools. 2020. https://omniglot. com/language/articles/translationtools.htm.
[11]   Can using navigational apps be as dangerous as texting and driving? https:// www.cbsnews.com/news.

[12] Lauren Schumacker. There's a reason you forget someone's name immediately after meeting them. 2018. Available from https://www.insider.com/why-do-i-forget-peoples-names-2018-9.

[13] Swarna Priya RM, Praveen Kumar Reddy Maddikunta, M Parimala, Srinivas Koppu, Thippa Reddy, Chiranji Lal Chowdhary, and Mamoun Alazab. An effective feature engineering for DNN using hybrid PCA-GWO for intrusion detection in IOMT architecture. Computer Communications, 2020.

[14] Vatsal Aggarwal, Marius Cotescu, Nishant Prateek, Jaime Lorenzo-Trueba, and Roberto Barra-Chicote. Using vaes and normalizing flows for one-shot text-to-speech synthesis of expressive speech. In ICASSP 2020-2020 IEEE International Conference on Acoustics, Speech and Signal Processing (ICASSP), pp. 6179–6183. IEEE, 2020.

[15] https://www.geoapify.com/routing-api/.

[16] Mohamed Ait Gacem, Saifeddin Alghlayini, Wessam Shehieb, Muaid Saeed, Ahmed Ghazal, and Mustahsan Mir. Smart assistive glasses for alzheimer's patients. In 2019 IEEE International Symposium on Signal Processing and Information Technology (ISSPIT), pp. 1–5. IEEE, 2019.

[17] Naman Sharma and Ruchika Bathla. Coalescing artificial intelligence with augmented reality to vitalize smart-glasses. In 2019 4th International Conference on Information Systems and Computer Networks (ISCON), pp. 149–154. IEEE, 2019.

[18] Hawra AlSaid, Lina AlKhatib, Aqeela AlOraidh, Shoaa AlHaidar, and Abul Bashar. Deep learning assisted smart glasses as educational aid for visually challenged students. In 2019 2nd International Conference on new Trends in Computing Sciences (ICTCS), pp. 1–6. IEEE, 2019.

[19] Yu-Chih Lin, Jun-You Liu, Yu-Chian Wu, Pin-Sung Ku, Katherine Chen, Te-Yen Wu, Yu-An Chen, and Mike Y Chen. Peritext+ utilizing peripheral vision for reading text on augmented reality smart glasses. In Proceedings of the 23rd ACM Symposium on Virtual Reality Software and Technology, pp. 1–3, 2017.

[20] Jung-Hwna Kim, Sun-Kyu Kim, Tea-Min Lee, Yong-Jin Lim, and Joonhong Lim. Smart glasses using deep learning and stereo camera. In 2019 IEEE 8th Global Conference on Consumer Electronics (GCCE), pp. 294–295. IEEE, 2019.

[21] Hein Min Htike. Utilizing ar glasses as mobility aid for people with low vision. In 2020 IEEE Conference on Virtual Reality and 3D User Interfaces Abstracts and Workshops (VRW), pp. 541–542. IEEE, 2020.

[22] M Claudia tom Dieck, Timothy Jung, and Dai-In Han. Mapping requirements for the wearable smart glasses augmented reality museum application. Journal of Hospitality and Tourism Technology, 2016.

[23] Kyeong-Beom Park, Minseok Kim, Sung Ho Choi, and Jae Yeol Lee. Deep learning-based smart task assistance in wearable augmented reality. Robotics and Computer-Integrated Manufacturing, 63:101887, 2020.

[24] Daniel Povey, Arnab Ghoshal, Gilles Boulianne, Lukas Burget, Ondrej Glembek, Nagendra Goel, Mirko Hannemann, Petr Motlicek, Yanmin Qian,

Petr Schwarz, *et al.* The kaldi speech recognition toolkit. In IEEE 2011 workshop on automatic speech recognition and understanding, number CONF. IEEE Signal Processing Society, 2011.

[25]   Mirco Ravanelli, Titouan Parcollet, and Yoshua Bengio. The Pytorch-Kaldi speech recognition toolkit. In ICASSP 2019-2019 IEEE International Conference on Acoustics, Speech and Signal Processing (ICASSP), pp. 6465–6469. IEEE, 2019.

[26]   Li Deng, Jinyu Li, Jui-Ting Huang, *et al.* Recent advances in deep learning for speech research at microsoft. In 2013 IEEE International Conference on Acoustics, Speech and Signal Processing, pp. 8604–8608. IEEE, 2013.

[27]   Dong Yu, Kaisheng Yao, Hang Su, Gang Li, and Frank Seide. Kl-divergence regularized deep neural network adaptation for improved large vocabulary speech recognition. In 2013 IEEE International Conference on Acoustics, Speech and Signal Processing, pp. 7893–7897. IEEE, 2013.

[28]   George E. Dahl, Dong Yu, Li Deng, and Alex Acero. Large vocabulary continuous speech recognition with context-dependent DBN-HMMS. In 2011 IEEE international conference on acoustics, speech and signal processing (ICASSP), pages 4688–4691. IEEE, 2011.

[29]   Gokhan Tur, Li Deng, Dilek Hakkani-Tür, and Xiaodong He. Towards deeper understanding: Deep convex networks for semantic utterance classification. In 2012 IEEE international conference on acoustics, speech and signal processing (ICASSP), pp. 5045–5048. IEEE, 2012.

[30]   Agnihotram Venkata Sripriya, Mungi Geethika, and Vaddi Radhesyam. Real time detection and recognition of human faces. In 2020 4th International Conference on Intelligent Computing and Control Systems (ICICCS), pp. 703–708. IEEE, 2020.

[31]   Saibal Manna, Sushil Ghildiyal, and Kishankumar Bhimani. Face recognition from video using deep learning. In 2020 5th International Conference on Communication and Electronics Systems (ICCES), pp. 1101–1106. IEEE, 2020.

[32]   Nawaf Alsrehin and Mu'tasem A. Al-Taamneh. Face recognition techniques using statistical and artificial neural network: A comparative study. In 2020 3rd International Conference on Information and Computer Technologies (ICICT), pp. 154–159. IEEE, 2020.

[33]   S Pavithra, R Ramesh, and B Sundrambal. Survey on face recognition with pre filtering techniques and their comparative study. In 2020 6th International Conference on Advanced Computing and Communication Systems (ICACCS), pp. 1089–1096. IEEE, 2020.

[34]   Jingxiao Zheng, Rajeev Ranjan, Ching-Hui Chen, Jun-Cheng Chen, Carlos D Castillo, and Rama Chellappa. An automatic system for unconstrained video-based face recognition. IEEE Transactions on Biometrics, Behavior, and Identity Science, 2(3):194–209, 2020.

[35]   Alpna Singh, Mohd Aamir Khan, and Neeraj Baghel. Face emotion identification by fusing neural network and texture features: facial expression. In 2020

International Conference on Contemporary Computing and Applications (IC3A), pp. 187–190. IEEE, 2020.

[36] Maryam Imani and Gholam Ali Montazer. Glcm features and fuzzy nearest neighbor classifier for emotion recognition from face. In 2017 7th International Conference on Computer and Knowledge Engineering (ICCKE), pp. 8–13. IEEE, 2017.

[37] M Kalpana Devi and K Prabhu. Face emotion classification using amser with artificial neural networks. In 2020 6th International Conference on Advanced Computing and Communication Systems (ICACCS), pp. 148–154. IEEE, 2020.

[38] Thippa Reddy Gadekallu, Neelu Khare, Sweta Bhattacharya, Saurabh Singh, Praveen Kumar Reddy Maddikunta, and Gautam Srivastava. Deep neural networks to predict diabetic retinopathy. J. Ambient Intell. Humaniz. Comput, 2020.

[39] Thippa Reddy Gadckallu, Dharmendra Singh Rajput, M Praveen Kumar Reddy, et al. A novel PCA–whale optimization-based deep neural network model for classification of tomato plant diseases using GPU. Journal of Real-Time Image Processing, pp. 1–14, 2020.

[40] Mamoun Alazab, Suleman Khan, Somayaji Siva Rama Krishnan, Quoc-Viet Pham, M Praveen Kumar Reddy, and Thippa Reddy Gadekallu. A multidirectional LSTM model for predicting the stability of a smart grid. IEEE Access, 8:85454–85463, 2020.

[41] Muatjitjeja K. Jat D. S. Chowdhary, C. L. Athree-dimensional object recognition based intelligence system for identification. In 2015 International Conference on Emerging Trends in Networks and Computer Communications (ETNCC), pp. 162–166. IEEE, 2015.

[42] C. L. Chowdhary. Application of object recognition with shape-index identification and 2d scale invariant feature transform for key-point detection. In Feature Dimension Reduction for Content-Based Image Identification, pp. 218–231. IGI Global, 2018.

[43] He-Yu Zhou, An-An Liu, Wei-Zhi Nie, and Jie Nie. Multi-view saliency guided deep neural network for 3-d object retrieval and classification. IEEE Transactions on Multimedia, 22(6):1496–1506, 2019.

[44] Thippa Reddy, Swarna Priya RM, M Parimala, Chiranji Lal Chowdhary, Saqib Hakak, Wazir Zada Khan, et al. A deep neural networks based model for uninterrupted marine environment monitoring. Computer Communications, 2020.

[45] Shreyas Anil Talokar, Gajrajsingh Narde, and Mohit Chaudhari. Analysis of object classification and detection methods to mitigate power utilization. In 2019 2nd International Conference on Intelligent Communication and Computational Techniques (ICCT), pp. 170–173. IEEE, 2019.

[46] Xavier Williams and Nihar Mahapatra. Analysis of recent trends in automatic object identification. In 2019 International Conference on Computational Science and Computational Intelligence (CSCI), pp. 425–428. IEEE, 2019.

[47] Xiaoqing Li, Jiansheng Yang, and Jinwen Ma. Large scale category-structured image retrieval for object identification through supervised learning of CNN and surf-based matching. IEEE Access, 8:57796–57809, 2020.

[48] Liang Zhang, Yufei Liu, Hang Xiao, Lu Yang, Guangming Zhu, Syed Afaq Shah, Mohammed Bennamoun, and Peiyi Shen. Efficient scene text detection with textual attention tower. In ICASSP 2020-2020 IEEE International Conference on Acoustics, Speech and Signal Processing (ICASSP), pp. 4272–4276. IEEE, 2020.

[49] Shaofu Lin and Qianwen Wei. Study on text detection and positioning method of utility pole identification plate based on improved east. In 2020 IEEE 4th Information Technology, Networking, Electronic and Automation Control Conference (ITNEC), volume 1, pp. 2374–2379. IEEE, 2020.

[50] Mukhriddin Mukhiddinov. Scene text detection and localization using fully convolutional network. In 2019 International Conference on Information Science and Communications Technologies (ICISCT), pp. 1–5. IEEE, 2019.

[51] Yan-Feng Lu, Ai-Xuan Zhang, Yi Li, Qian-Hui Yu, and Hong Qiao. Multi-scale scene text detection based on convolutional neural network. In 2019 Chinese Automation Congress (CAC), pp. 583–587. IEEE, 2019.

[52] Rakadetyo AP Putro, Farica Perdana Putri, and Maria Irmina Prasetiyowati. A combined edge detection analysis and clustering based approach for real time text detection. In 2019 5th International Conference on New Media Studies (CONMEDIA), pp. 59–62. IEEE, 2019.

[53] Minal Acharya, Priti Chouhan, and Asmita Deshmukh. Scan. it-text recognition, translation and conversion. In 2019 International Conference on Advances in Computing, Communication and Control (ICAC3), pp. 1–5. IEEE, 2019.

[54] Ajmal Muhammad, Farooq Ahmad, AM Martinez-Enriquez, Mudasser Naseer, Aslam Muhammad, and Mohsin Ashraf. Image to multilingual text conversion for literacy education. In 2018 17th IEEE International Conference on Machine Learning and Applications (ICMLA), pp. 1328–1332. IEEE, 2018.

[55] Mattia A Di Gangi, Matteo Negri, and Marco Turchi. One-to-many multi-lingual end-to-end speech translation. In 2019 IEEE Automatic Speech Recognition and Understanding Workshop (ASRU), pp. 585–592. IEEE, 2019.

[56] Byron Hernández and Eduardo Giraldo. A review of path planning and control for autonomous robots. In 2018 IEEE 2nd Colombian Conference on Robotics and Automation (CCRA), pp. 1–6. IEEE, 2018.

[57] Mohd Nayab Zafar and JC Mohanta. Methodology for path planning and optimization of mobile robots: a review. Procedia Computer Science, 133:141–152, 2018.

[58] Hyunwoo Shin and Junjae Chae. A performance review of collision-free path planning algorithms. Electronics, 9(2):316, 2020.

[59] Takuma Okamoto, Tomoki Toda, Yoshinori Shiga, and Hisashi Kawai. Tacotron-based acoustic model using phoneme alignment for practical neural text-to-speech systems. In 2019 IEEE Automatic Speech Recognition and Understanding Workshop (ASRU), pp. 214–221. IEEE, 2019.

[60] Tae-Ho Kim, Sungjae Cho, Shinkook Choi, Sejik Park, and Soo-Young Lee. Emotional voice conversion using multitask learning with text-to-speech. In ICASSP 2020-2020 IEEE International Conference on Acoustics, Speech and Signal Processing (ICASSP), pp. 7774–7778. IEEE, 2020.

[61] Takuma Okamoto, Tomoki Toda, Yoshinori Shiga, and Hisashi Kawai. Transformer-based text-to-speech with weighted forced attention. In ICASSP 2020-2020 IEEE International Conference on Acoustics, Speech and Signal Processing (ICASSP), pp. 6729–6733. IEEE, 2020.

[62] Siniša Suzié, Tijana Nosek, Milan Secˇujski, Darko Pekar, and Vlado Delié. dnn based expressive text-to-speech with limited training data. In 2019 27th TelecommunicationsForum (TELFOR), pp. 1–6. IEEE, 2019.

[63] Nur-Hana Samsudin and Lukman Nurhaqim Rahim. Rapid heteronym disambiguation for text-to-speech system. In 2019 4th International Conference and Workshops on Recent Advances and Innovations in Engineering (ICRAIE), pp. 1–6. IEEE, 2019.

[64] Thimmaraja Yadava and HS Jayanna. Automatic isolated kannada speech recognition system under degraded conditions. In 2019 4th International Conference on Electrical, Electronics, Communication, Computer Technologies and Optimization Techniques (ICEECCOT), pp. 146–150. IEEE, 2019.

[65] Christopher Cieri, David Graff, Owen Kimball, Dave Miller, and Kevin Walker. Fisher English training speech part 1 transcripts. Philadelphia: Linguistic Data Consortium, 2004.

[66] Christopher Cieri, David Graff, Owen Kimball, Dave Miller, and Kevin Walker. Fisher English training speech part 1 transcripts. 2004. https://catalog.ldc.upenn.edu/desc/addenda/LDC2004T19.txt.

[67] Maddikunta P. K. R. Pham Q. V. Gadekallu T. R. Chowdhary C. L. Alazab M. Piran M. J. Bhattacharya, S. Deep learning and medical image processing for coronavirus (covid-19) pandemic: a survey. Sustainable cities and society, 2020.

[68] C. L. Chowdhary. 3d object recognition system based on local shape descriptors and depth data analysis. Recent Patents on Computer Science, 12:1 pp. 18–24, 2019.

[69] https://face-api.sightcorp.com/.

[70] https://web.plant.id/.

[71] https://cloud.google.com/translate/docs.

[72] https://cloudmersive.com/ocr-api.

[73] https://www.ibm.com/in-en/cloud/watson-visual-recognition.

[74] https://openweathermap.org/api.

Chapter 14

Renal calculi detection using modified grey wolf optimization

Isha Sharma[1] and Vijay Kumar[1]

Abstract

In this chapter, the grey wolf optimizer-based support vector machine method is proposed to detect renal calculi. The proposed method utilizes the pre-processing step, which consists of two main sub-processes, such as filtering and histogram equalization. These methods are used to enhance the image quality by removing speckle noise and normalizing the images. The extracted features are applied on a support vector machine for the classification of renal calculi. The proposed technique shows better conduct when evaluated in comparison with the already existing techniques. The proposed technique attained an accuracy of 96% during classification. This method is expected to aid medical image diagnosis systems with better speed and reliability.

Key Words: Renal calculi; grey wolf optimization; support vector machine; classification; ultrasound images

14.1 Introduction

The spontaneous detection and segmentation of kidney stones using ultrasonographic images is a co-operative procedure in medical image processing. As in many areas, doctors manually go through 2D and 3D ultrasound (US) images to detect the presence of disorders in the human body. Advancement in the visualization of medical images will be beneficial for doctors. Image processing plays a vital role in the early prediction, detection, and diagnosis of calculi present in the patient. Patients rarely realize the development and presence of calculi in their body, which may lead to severe pain [1,2]. Therefore, the early prediction and detection of calculi are required to relieve the patients from severe pain.

[1]Department of Computer Science and Engineering, National Institute of Technology, Hamirpur, India

The kidney, ureter, and urinary bladder are the three major areas for the presence of calculi in the human body. Various calculis are made up of amalgamation of substances such as phosphate, oxalate, or calcium. These substances are responsible for the development of different physical characteristics in calculi. The intensity of calculi shadows varies for the stones of different compositions. US imaging techniques are widely used in medical imaging. The US imaging technique is highly preferred over computed tomography, magnetic resonance imaging, and X-rays. The main advantages of this technique are radiation free, economically cheaper, non-invasive, and computational efficient.

The US imaging technique uses a lubricating gel for the smooth transmission of sound waves. The waves transmit easily inside the body by creating echo waves on hitting a dense object such as an organ or bone. The demerit of this technique is very high interference of speckle noise with sound waves. The segmentation of stone is very difficult due to this disturbance. The presence of speckle noise in US images makes it uphill work to detect the presence of varying structures, compositions, sizes, and different positions of stones. The foremost aim of the already present segmentation techniques is to detect the renal calculi with precise accuracy. In this chapter, a novel image segmentation technique is developed to achieve the chief aim of detecting the presence of calculi in the US-kidney images. The developed technique consists of median–Wiener filtering, histogram equalization, and modified grey wolf optimizer-based classification. This chapter isorganized as follows. Section 14.2 lays the background consisting of the preliminaries of basic definitions and related works after reviewing the basic concept of the grey wolf optimizer (GWO) algorithm; Section 14.3 discusses about the challenges and proposed approach used in renal calculi detection; followed by experimentation and discussion in Section 14.4; at last, concluding the work with guidelines for possible future improvements in the mentioned approach has been discussed in Section 14.5.

14.2 Background

In this section, the preliminary concepts of segmentation, a brief description of grey wolf optimization algorithm and related work done in the direction of renal calculi detection are presented.

14.2.1 Image segmentation

The chief objective of image segmentation is to discover the objects of an image such as contours, lines, edges, etc. Image segmentation is about disintegrating an image into different regions or a set of pixels. Pixels are the smallest unit of an image, which contains a lot of information in itself. These pixels are similar within a segment of an image. Image segmentation can be performed by applying any of the three major techniques, that is, clustering, edge detection, and region extraction [3].

The mathematical formulation of segmentation is given below [4]. Let S be the grid of a set of pairs (x, y)

$$x = 1, 2, \ldots, N \text{ and } y = 1, 2, \ldots, M$$

where N and M denote the quantity of pixels in the x-axis and y-axis, respectively. Y is the non-empty subsets of S having contiguous points. Thereafter, $P(Y)$ assigns the brightness matrix for the point Y.

The segmentation should be applied for each and every point and regions must consist of contiguous points [5,6]. Image segmentation plays a key role in diagnosing and reckoning the presence of stone, blockage of urine, cysts, cancer, and other irregular behaviors.

14.2.2   Grey wolf optimization

Grey wolves, also known as Canis Lupus, plays a very crucial role in the maintenance of a healthy ecosystem and are considered at the top of the food chain. They are seen to be one of the wildest predators and highly social animals living in close nuclear packs. These animals develop close social bonds forming hierarchical bonds living in a pack of about 5–12 wolves on an average. Grey wolves are called key predators as they are responsible for maintaining a balanced ecosystem. The pack of grey wolves follows a strict hierarchy among their packs which helps them in maintaining order, where alpha wolves also known as leader wolves are a dominant male and a female wolf. Alpha wolves are responsible for guiding activities of the group by taking important decisions about hunting and forging, where a female alpha is decisive in activities like taking care of their offsprings. The hierarchical structure is strictly followed in the wolves.

The other level in the pack of grey wolves is beta wolves; they are behind every decision of alpha wolves, they can either male or female; in the absence of alpha wolves, they make sure that the pack is well organized and in discipline. In the absence of alpha wolves, they are considered to be the best among all candidates from the pack. They strictly follow commands from alpha wolves and ensure that alpha's commands are being followed by their packmates too.

Another level in the hierarchy is delta wolves; they follow commands from alpha and beta wolves, most of the hunters who are responsible for predation, watching boundaries and protecting the pack are done by the wolves of this level. Last in the hierarchy of grey wolves are omega wolves, all other wolves are considered as omega wolves who are usually ones living on the outskirts and get last to eat the food being attacked by other dominating wolves.

A mathematical model of the social relations and hunting behavior of grey wolves has been proposed in [7] for representing the optimization based on the behavior of grey wolves while searching for prey and hunting for it. The following subsection will mathematically represent the social hierarchy and foraging behavior of grey wolves.

14.2.2.1   Social positioning

In the mathematical model, the fittest of all the solution is considered to be the alpha solution, the second fittest is called the beta solution and the third fittest is known as the delta solution, rest all other solutions are called omega solutions. However, foraging process positions of all omega wolves are updated according to the positions of alpha, beta, and delta solutions, representing the decision-making ability of alpha, beta, and delta wolves, and slave behavior of omega wolves.

14.2.2.2   Foraging behavior

The foraging process consists of three steps: (1) encircling of prey, (2) hunting, and (3) attacking prey, where (14.1) and (14.2) depict the encircling behavior of the grey wolves:

$$\vec{S} = |\vec{C}.\vec{Y}_p(t) - \vec{Y}(t)| \tag{14.1}$$

$$\vec{Y}(t+1) = \vec{Y}_p(t) - \vec{A}.\vec{S} \tag{14.2}$$

Here, t shows the iteration number, $\vec{A}, \vec{C}$ depict the coefficient vectors, $\vec{Y}_p$ represents position vector of the prey, and $\vec{Y}$ represents the position vector of all the grey wolves.

Coefficient vectors are calculated as follows:

$$\vec{A} = 2\vec{u}.\vec{v}_1 - \vec{u} \tag{14.3}$$

$$\vec{C} = 2.\vec{v}_2 \tag{14.4}$$

where $\vec{u}$ is decreasing factor within an interval of [2,0] and $\vec{v}_1$ and $\vec{v}_2$ are random vector in interval [0,1]. The positions of grey wolves are updated according to the position of the best solution, which can further be modulated by updating the values of random vectors $\vec{v}_1$ and $\vec{v}_2$.

Another step in the foraging process is of hunting the best solution obtained so far (prey); here, we proceed with the assumption about the location of the prey, which is assumed to be best estimated by alpha, beta, and delta wolves. Further other omega wolves update their positions according to the best three positions of the search agents. The mathematical depiction of this step is as follows.

Distance between the position of the search agent with respect to the position of the alpha, beta, and delta wolves

$$\vec{S}_\alpha = |\vec{C}_1.\vec{Y}_\alpha - \vec{Y}| \tag{14.5}$$

$$\vec{S}_\beta = |\vec{C}_2.\vec{Y}_\beta - \vec{Y}| \tag{14.6}$$

$$\vec{S}_\gamma = |\vec{C}_3.\vec{Y}_\gamma - \vec{Y}| \tag{14.7}$$

The position of the search agent after updating the old position according to the distances calculated in (14.5)–(14.7)

$$\vec{Y}_1 = \vec{Y}_\alpha - \vec{A}_1.\left(\vec{S}_\alpha\right) \tag{14.8}$$

$$\vec{Y}_2 = \vec{Y}_\beta - \vec{A}_2.\left(\vec{S}_\beta\right) \tag{14.9}$$

$$\vec{Y}_3 = \vec{Y}_\gamma - \vec{A}_3 \cdot \left(\vec{S}_\gamma\right) \tag{14.10}$$

$$\vec{Y}(t+1) = \frac{\vec{Y}_1 + \vec{Y}_2 + \vec{Y}_3}{3} \tag{14.11}$$

Equation (14.11) shows the final position of the search agent around the best solution (prey). This mathematical model handles the two main phases of optimization with great efficiency, that is, exploration and exploitation, in the exploration phase, the search agents search guided by the position of the three best solutions in the search space, the two main components controlling the divergence of the position of search agent from prey is handled by modulating the values of $\vec{A}$ greater than 1 and less than -1. In addition, $\vec{C}$ impacts the search process by emphasizing the best solution with its value >1 and deemphasizing by modulating its value <1. During the exploitation or hunting phase, values of $\vec{A}$ are in range $[-1,1]$, leading to the position of the search agent anywhere between its current position and position of the prey.

14.2.3 Previous work

Sridhar and Kumaravel [8] developed a computerized model for the detection of renal calculi using the physical traits of the stone. The work showed failure in analyzing the accuracy during the segmentation process. Sridhar *et al.* [9] extended their work by incorporating the pyramidal seeded region growing and morphology-based segmentation algorithm. The proposed approach showed the accuracy of 95%. In [10], artificial neural networks were explored for classification in medical analysis for diagnosing. They used three neural network algorithms such as Learning vector quantization (LVQ), backpropagation training algorithm, and radial basis function (RBF) having different architecture and analyzed on the basis of accuracy, time, and data size. Real-world dataset consists of 1,000 instances and 8 attributes.

In [11], an automated system was developed for kidney segmentation. They used the Gabor filter in the pre-processing stage followed by histogram equalization. After a comparison of performances of region-based segmentation technique and cell-based segmentation technique, they have used region-based segmentation on their dataset followed by plucking region of interest as a final result. In [12], intensity histogram feature, invariant moments, gray level co-occurrence matrices (GLCM), gray level run-length matrices were extracted feature set of 48 features per image were calculated. Selected optimal feature using Waikato Environment for Knowledge Analysis tool wase used for the classification of kidney images as normal and abnormal. They showed using COMBINED features has resulted in better performance in classification of normal and abnormal kidneys.

In [13], median and wavelet filter were used in the seed region growth algorithm for renal calculi segmentation. If segmentation does not provide any region, it indicates the absence of the calculi then further region properties are not extracted for such images. It shows the area of the calculi and time of evaluation of the process. In [14], an automatic system was proposed for performing the classification of kidney diseases using US images. Dataset used by them had four classes: normal, cyst, renal failure and angiomiolipoma where extraction of statistical features and another set of multi-scale wavelet-based features was performed from the region of interest (ROI) of every image and they were reduced using the principal component analysis. The features were used to design and train a neural network classifier showing a 92% correct classification rate.

In [15], a semiautomatic system is developed where selection of region is done by operator, features are extracted like Contrast, Entropy and Correlation, KNN classification is done on the training image dataset. The overall accuracy of the classification system is around 91%. In [16], the gradient descent-based image segmentation was used for classification. They extracted the features such as energy, mean, variance, entropy, correlation, skewness and kurtosis, from the segmented image. Thereafter, these features were used to train the neural networks and perform classification task.

In [17], improvised seeded region growing method has been used followed by intensity threshold variation classification on the basis of sizes of stones which will help in identification of multiple classes as normal, stone and early stone stages, and for this purpose, image granularity features were used. In [18], an automated system for detection of kidney stones was developed. They used median and Wiener filter to reduce the noise. The texture analysis was done by using the local entropy. It is observed from experimental results that the proposed approach performed better than the classical techniques in terms of ROI. Table 14.1 shows the comparative analysis of the existing techniques.

In [19], adaptive mean median filtering was used for getting rid of the speckle noises. Segmentation using conventional K-means is performed and extraction of GLCM features has been done for classification by using a meta-heuristic support vector machine (SVM) classifier. The proposed method was used over 250 clinical US kidney images; of which 150 are having calculi and the rest are healthy, showing an accuracy rate of 98.8% with a false acceptance rate (FAR) of 1.8 for a false recognition rate as high as 3.3. In [20], the image segmentation method over various image analysis techniques. The effective method using region growing method for segmenting the affected part from the renal image showing Peak-SNR value to be 14.7225 and the SNR value is 3.2217.

In [21], Spider monkey based DNN hybrid classifier model was proposed. The proposed classifier model was evaluated on NSL-KDD and KDD Cup 99 dataset. Results revealed that the proposed classifier was effectively used in dimensionality reduction. The accuracy and precision obtained from the proposed classifier were 99.5% and 92.7%, respectively [22–28].

14.3 Proposed approach for renal calculi detection

In this section, the challenges faced in the field of renal calculi detection followed by the motivation behind the developed technique is presented. Thereafter, the proposed grey wolf-inspired SVM technique is discussed.

Table 14.1   *Comparative analysis of the existing techniques*

Ref.	Technique used	Images used	Performance measures
S. Sridhar *et al.* (2001)	Pyramidal seeded region growing algorithm	37 Kidney images	Detection accuracy of 95%
V. Velmurugan and P. Gnanasivam	Region growing algorithm.	NA	Peak-SNR value of 14.7225 and the SNR value of 3.2217.
Karthik Kalyan *et al.*	Artificial neural network	47 Normal and 47 abnormal US images	87.5% Accuracy over the testing dataset and 100% accuracy over the training dataset
Prema T. Akkasalgar Shruti S. Karakalmani	Seed region growth algorithm	40 US images	95% Accuracy in the normal images and 90% accuracy for renal calculi US images
S. Manjunath *et al.*	Multilayer perceptron, radial basis function, and linear vector quantization.	160 US kidney images	98% Accuracy obtained from the proposed technique.
S. Selvarani, P. Rajenan	Conventional K-Means	250 Clinical US kidney images	98.8% Accuracy with minimal FAR and FRR.

14.3.1   Challenges in renal calculi detection

There are many techniques available for image segmentation. But, these techniques suffer from various challenges such as the presence of noise, no standard structure of calculi, no specific position or composition of renal calculi. The optimal selection of renal calculi and non-calculi tissues is a major challenge. Besides this, the optimal hyper-parameter margin in the SVM is another challenge. To handle these issues, a methodology is developed, which plays a significant role in the detection of renal calculi.

14.3.2   Proposed approach

The proposed approach uses the combination of median and Wiener filters to remove noise from the given image. The GLCM feature extraction technique is used to extract the features from the noise-free image. These features are applied to the SVM for the classification of calculi. The hyper-parameters of SVM are optimized through a grey wolf optimizer. The basic steps of the proposed approach are given below:

    Step 1: Median–Wiener filtering is applied to the image dataset to remove the noise.

    Step 2: Histogram equalization is applied to the noise-free image to maintain the uniform intensity of pixels.

    Step 3: Grey-level spatial dependence matrix is used to extract the features.

    Step 4: GWO is opted for finding the optimal hyper-plane for SVM classification.

    Step 5: The selected features are applied on SVM for the detection of stone.

Figure 14.1 depicts the proposed renal calculi detection method. The details of these steps are mentioned in the succeeding subsections.

14.3.2.1   Pre-processing

The intention behind the pre-processing process is to lessen the effect of speckle noise. The noise affects the performance of the proposed method. In the proposed approach, the median and Wiener filters are used to remove the speckle noise. Median filtering is performed by replacing the pixels in a mask with the middle value of the sorted pixel of neighbors. This filter does not create new values when filter straddles an edge. It is better in the preservation of sharp-edged than the mean filter. It has a better capability to separate the range noise from significant features. Weiner filtering is done with the help of prior knowledge about the noise. It has the capability of behaving as a bandpass filter. The histogram equalization process is applied for further enhancement of the image contrast by redistributing the intensity.

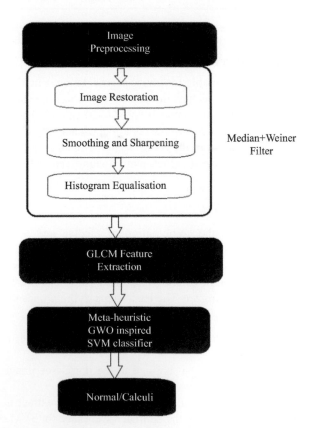

Figure 14.1   Proposed renal calculi detection technique

14.3.2.2   GWO-inspired SVM

SVM performs mapping through the function where the training dataset is plotted to a high dimensional feature space by separating maximal margin. The basic idea behind SVM is to create a margin for separating the decision function values of classification problems. The hyper-plane of SVM is optimized through the GWO, which is used for the separation of high-dimensional feature space.

GWO is a popular meta-heuristic technique motivated by the social hierarchy and attacking mechanism of grey wolves [23]. The positions of the three best solutions are considered during the updating of grey wolves' positions. They guide the population to find the best prey over the landscape. Radial-kernel SVM is used. The values of the tuning parameters are set as $\gamma = 0.023$ and $C = 27$. The population of grey wolves direct their positions according to the leader's positions in the search space, which is used in finding the optimal solution for the given problem. The position of α, β, and δ wolves arc the best possible values of wolves. These are used to evaluate the hyper-parameter of SVM. The parameter of SVM is controlled through the values of control parameters (a, A, and C) of GWO. The grey wolves will be able to investigate the most optimal search space.

Due to this, a suitable hyper-plane computing cost function is developed. The top three fitness values are considered for leading the pack of wolves in the adjustment of their positions using alpha, beta, and delta wolves. The exploration and exploitation is controlled using the estimated values of a and A. Figure 14.2 shows the parameter tuning of SVM through GWO.

Algorithm:

Initialization of the parameters such as: a, A, C

Input: data generated from the trained linear-SVM using radial-kernel

Initialization of positions of the grey-wolves population

For iteration = 0

    For all wolves

        Update position of the search agents

        Find result of SVM using new obtained positions

        Update positions of α, β and δ

    End for

    Update a, A, C

    iteration = iteration + 1

End For

return position of α wolf

Figure 14.2   Grey wolf optimizer inspired classification technique

14.4   Experiment and results

14.4.1   Dataset

Fifty US kidney images have been collected from the local medical center. The dataset consists of 80 healthy kidney and 70 unhealthy kidney images. The images have been resized into 512×512 pixel dimension. Accuracy (ACC), false acceptance rate (FAR), and false rejection rate (FRR) are used for performance analysis of the proposed approach. The formulation of ACC, FAR, and FRR is given as follows:

$$ACC = \frac{(TP + TN)}{(P + n)} \tag{14.12}$$

$$FAR = \frac{FP}{(FP + TN)} \tag{14.13}$$

$$FRR = \frac{FN}{(FN + TP)} \tag{14.14}$$

where TP and TN represent the true positive and true negative, respectively, and FP and FN represent the false positive and false negative, respectively.

14.4.2   Performance analysis

In this context, the GWO-based SVM classifier has been developed in order to deal with the classification among two class problems to determine the presence or absence of kidney stones. The accuracy of the meta-heuristic SVM model proposed by Selvarani and Rajendran [19] has been used to analyze the performance of the proposed GWO–SVM model along with accuracy. The proposed method has been analyzed in comparison with Selvarani and Rajendran's method and the conventional SVM method. The features are extracted from 150 kidney images. The images are classified into 80 healthy and 70 unhealthy images, which were first pre-processed using the combination of median and Wiener filter. Figure 14.3 shows the calculi captured from the given image using the proposed approach. Table 14.2 shows the peak signal-to-noise ratio (PSNR) and the mean square error (MSE) obtained from the proposed approach. These filtered images are further pre-processed using the histogram equalization technique; these processed and normalized images have been used for the extraction of GLCM features, which were further utilized for training of the GWO-based SVM model by training more than 90 image set and tested more than 60 image set. The proposed technique shows the diminished error between the manually calculi detection and the proposed method.

Table 14.3 shows the results obtained from the proposed method, SVM and AMM-PSO-SVM method. It is observed from Table 14.3 and Figure 14.4 that the proposed technique inspired by GWO has shown better performance than AMM-PSO-SVM with an accuracy of 96%. It also depicts that the proposed approach has a low FAR rate compared to the existing methods over the kidney image dataset (see Figure 14.5).

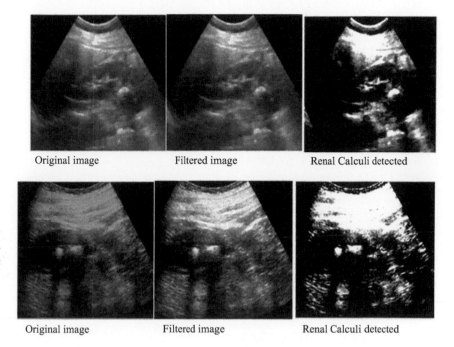

| Original image | Filtered image | Renal Calculi detected |

Figure 14.3   Two images with calculi of different numbers and sizes: (i) original image, (ii) pre-processed image, and (iii) calculi-detected image

Table 14.2   Performance analysis after filtering using the proposed approach

Images	Selvarani and Rajendran's method (AMM-filtering)		Proposed method (median–Wiener filter)	
	MSE	PSNR	MSE	PSNR
150	0.07	110.5	**0.06**	**112.7**

Table 14.3   Performance measures obtained from the proposed and existing techniques over kidney dataset

Methods	FAR (%)	FRR (%)	ACC (%)
Simple SVM	5.34	13.8	86
AMM-PSO-SVM	3.3	9.81	95
MW-GWO-SVM	3.14	9.10	96

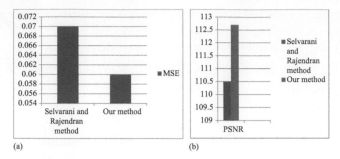

(a)   (b)

Figure 14.4   Comparison in performance of Selvarani's method and proposed method in terms of (a) mean square error (MSE) and (b) peak signal-to-noise ratio (PSNR)

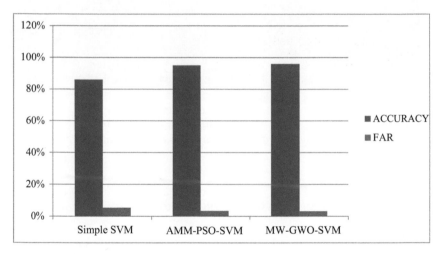

Figure 14.5   Performance of MW-GWO-SVM, AMM-PSO-SVM, and simple SVM in terms of accuracy and FAR

14.5   Conclusions and future scope

This chapter proposes the segmentation method to detect calculi in the US kidney images. The proposed approach used median and Weiner filter to remove the speckle noises from kidney images. The feature extraction technique was used to extract the features and applied the SVM. The hyper-parameters of SVM were optimized through GWO. The performance of the proposed approach was compared with the existing technique in terms of the peak signal-to-noise ratio and the mean square error. The results reveal that the proposed approach outperforms the existing technique. The effect of optimal parameter on the SVM was also analyzed. The proposed approach is able to detect multiple calculi of different sizes and different positions in the kidney images.

In future, the proposed work can be extended by utilizing the statistical features from the given image. In real-time detection, the feature set can further be classified using neural network methods or fuzzy approaches. The other meta-heuristic approaches can also be used in the proposed approach.

References

[1] Pal N. K., and Pal S. K. 'A review on image segmentation techniques', vol. 26, no. 9, 1993, pp. 1277–1294.

[2] Zaitoun N. M., and Aqel M. J. 'Survey on Image Segmentation Techniques', *Procedia Computer Science*, vol. 65, 2015, pp. 797–806.

[3] Horowitz S. L., and Pavlidis T. 'Picture segmentation by a directed split-and-merge procedure', *Proc. 2nd Int. Joint Conf. Pattern Recognition*. 1974, pp. 424–433.

[4] Fu K. S., and Mui J. K. 'A survey on image segmentation'. *Pattern Recognition*. vol. 13, no. 1, 1981, pp. 3–16.

[5] Pavlidis T. 'Structural Pattern Recognition'. New York, NY: Springer; 1977.

[6] Shapiro L. G., and Stockman G. C. 'Computer Vision'. Upper Saddle River, NJ: Prentice-Hall; 2001.

[7] Seyedali M., Mohammad M. S., and Andrew L. 'Grey wolf optimizer'. *Advances in Engineering Software*, vol. 69, 2014, pp. 46–61.

[8] Sridhar S., and Kumaravel N. 'Automatic segmentation of medical images for renal calculi and analysis', *Biomedical Sciences Instrumentation*. vol. 37, 2001, pp. 405–409.

[9] Sridhar S., Kumaravel N., and Easwarakumar K. S. 'Segmentation of renal calculi in ultrasound images', *Medical Informatics and Internet Medicine*. vol. 27, no. 4, 2002, pp. 229–236.

[10] Kumar K., and Abhishek, 'Artificial Neural Networks for Diagnosis of Kidney Stones Disease', *International Journal of Information Technology and Computer Science(IJITCS)*. vol. 4, no. 7, 2012, pp. 20–25.

[11] Rahman T., Uddin M. S. 'Speckle noise reduction and segmentation of kidney regions from ultrasound image', International Conference on Informatics, Electronics and Vision (ICIEV), IEEE; 2013. pp. 1–5.

[12] Kalyan K., Jain S., Lele R. D., Joshi M., and Chowdhary A. 'Application of artificial neural networks towards the determination of presence of disease conditions in ultrasound images of kidney', *International Journal of Computer Engineering & Technology*. vol. 4, 2013, pp. 232–243.

[13] Akkasalgar P. T., and Karakalmani S. S. 'Abnormality detection in kidney ultrasound imaging', *International Journal of Engineering and Computer Science*. vol. 4, no. 7, 2018, pp. 13151–13155.

[14] Soumya N., and Narayanan P. P. 'Classification of kidney disorders from ultrasound images using adaptive neuro-fuzzy inference system', *International Journal of Scientific Engineering and Applied Science (IJSEAS)*. vol. 1, no. 3, 2015, pp. 298–305.

[15]   Pathak M., Sadawarti H., and Singh S. 'Features extraction and classification for detection of kidney stone region in ultrasound images', *International Journal of Multidisciplinary Research and Development*, vol. 3, no. 5, 2016, pp. 81–83.

[16]   Manjunath S., Pande S., and Raveesh B. N. 'Computer aided system for diagnosis of kidney stones using neural networks', *International Journal of Current Engineering And Scientific Research (IJCESR)*, vol. 4, 2017, pp. 22–27.

[17]   Tamilselvi P. R., and Thangaraj P. 'Computer aided diagnosis system for stone detection and early detection of kidney stones', *Journal of Computer Science*, vol. 7, no. 2, 2013, pp. 250–254.

[18]   Raja R. A., and Ranjani J. J. 'Segment based detection and quantification of kidney stones and its symmetric analysis using texture properties based on logical operators with ultra sound scanning', *International Journal of Computer Applications*, vol. 997, 2013, pp. 8–15.

[19]   Selvarani S. and Rajendran P. 'Detection of renal calculi in ultrasound image using meta-heuristic support vector machine', *Journal of Medical Systems*, vol. 43, no. 9, 2019.

[20]   Velmurugan V. and Gnanasivam P. 'A segmentation approach of the ultrasound image to detect renal calculi', *International Journal of Latest Trends in Engineering and Technology*, vol. 9, no. 1, pp. 1–5.

[21]   Khare N., Devan P., Chowdhary C. L. *et al.* 'SMO-DNN: Spider Monkey Optimization and Deep Neural Network Hybrid Classifier Model for Intrusion Detection'. *Electronics*, vol. 9, no. 4, 2020.

[22]   Chowdhary C. L. '3D object recognition system based on local shape descriptors and depth data analysis', *Recent Patents on Computer Science*, vol. 12, no. 1, 2019, pp. 18–24.

[23]   Tippa Reddy, G., Swarna Priya R. M. Parimala M., *et al.* 'A deep neural networks-based model for uninterrupted marine environment monitoring'. *Computer Communications*, vol. 157, 2020, pp. 64–75.

[24]   Kaur G., Singh S. and Singh S. 'A Review on Automatic Detection of Kidney Abnormalities in Ultrasound Images', Proceedings of the International Conference on Innovative Computing & Communications (ICICC), 2020.

[25]   Maity A., Pattanaik A., Sagnika S. and Pani S. 'A Comparative Study on Approaches to Speckle Noise Reduction in Images', 2015 International Conference on Computational Intelligence and Networks, Bhubaneshwar, 2015, pp. 148–155.

[26]   Al-Ghaib H. and Adhami R. 'On the digital image additive white Gaussian noise estimation', 2014 International Conference on Industrial Automation, Information and Communications Technology, Bali, 2014, pp. 90–96.

[27]   Swarna Priya, R. M., Maddikunta, P. K. R., Parimala, M., *et al.* 'An effective feature engineering for DNN using hybrid PCA-GWO for intrusion detection in IoMT architecture', *Computer Communications*, vol. 160, 2020, pp. 139–149.

[28]   Reddy, T., Swarna Priya, R. M. Parimala, M., Chowdhary, C. L., Hakak, S., and Khan, W. Z. A deep neural networks based model for uninterrupted marine environment monitoring. *Computer Communications*, vol. 157, 2020, pp. 64–75.

Chapter 15

On multi-class aerial image classification using learning machines

Qurban A. Memon[1] and Najiya Valappil[1]

Abstract

Computer vision and image processing are excelling in the field of segmentation, feature extraction and object detection from image data. In this decade, machine learning, especially deep learning, has brought about significant breakthroughs in vision systems, notably in object detection and recognition area. The major challenging problem in object detection is locating a specific object from within multiple objects. There has been a sustained increase in research in industry and academia related to machine learning in general and deep learning in particular for objection detection and recognition using drones or unmanned aerial vehicles (UAVs) for crop and forest analysis, traffic monitoring, robotics, aerial surveillance, etc. Unlike stationary surveillance, the camera platform of UAVs is in constant motion and makes object extraction difficult. Recent research involving transfer learning and re-use methods for multi-class image classification tested on large-scale datasets has built trust to explore further to optimize algorithms with respect to accuracy, speed, reduction in parameters, etc. The objectives in this chapter are set to benefit readers, who are interested in abreast themselves of recent research in the area of object detection and classification from aerial images using deep learning methods and their efficiency. The challenges faced, respective training issues and testing metrics, available databases and development platforms with useful applications are also discussed in this research.

Key Words: Unmanned aerial vehicles (UAV); deep learning networks; recursive neural network (RNN); backpropagation through structure (BTS); convolutional neural network (CNN); generative adversarial network (GAN); variational autoencoder (VAE)

[1]Electrical Engineering, College of Engineering, UAE University, Al Ain, UAE

15.1   Introduction

Most recent works in object detection, except works like [1–3], are still prevalent by the use of handcrafted and shallow learning-based [4,5]. The traditional non-learning methods deployed for signal or object detection [6–8] and some machine learning techniques with human extracted features have shown remarkable success for object detection tasks. The involvement of human imagination in feature design or shallow structure to extract feature maps significantly affects the generalization ability and feasibility for object detection. For vision applications, the description capability of handcrafted features becomes limited or even undetermined, thus making way for deep learning architectures which show stronger feature representation power in computer vision applications. The deep learning features are directly extracted from data on unmanned aerial vehicle (UAV) platforms using neural networks of deep architecture. Deep learning improves object detection by enhancing the quality of feature maps, thus reducing the error of human ingenuity. It describes a hierarchy of learning algorithms rather than a single method to learn complex prediction models.

Recently, deep learning has been profitably applied to several real-world applications, like the classification of handwritten digits of the Modified National Institute of Standards and Technology (MNIST) dataset with an error rate of 0.21 [9]. Further areas in which deep learning has made considerable progress include natural language understanding [10], acoustic modeling [11], natural computational biology [12–14], target detection [15,16], emotion recognition and classification [17–19]. This chapter is structured as follows. In the next section, different types of deep learning approaches and networks are discussed, along with current challenges to deep learning, especially in the area of aerial imagery. Section 15.3 presents learning approaches and binary and multi-class classification techniques in the context of aerial imagery obtained through UAVs. In Section 15.4, training of data is discussed in detail along with various datasets available to facilitate network training.

15.2   Learning approaches

The most commonly used technique in machine learning is supervised learning. Let us consider a scenario where an object detection system can classify buildings, pedestrians, vehicles, or trees from aerial images. Once each category is labelled in the dataset of images containing each of the objects, the next stage is training, where the machine is made to administrate an image and produces an output in the form of a vector, one for each category. The aim is to have the highest score for the desired class among all classes. Later, an objective function is computed that measures the error between the output scores and the desired scores. The machine then reworks its internal adjustable parameters to reduce the error. In a typical deep-supervised learning system, there may be a huge number of labelled examples with which the machine is trained, and many more adjustable weights. The advantage of deep-supervised networks is noted when there is no human inter-vention in the extraction of features, thus combining the positives of supervised learning as well as deep networks. The higher the number of labelled inputs, the greater the efficiency of the deep-supervised system.

The large number and variability of the dataset available for training make the desired labelling difficult. Viewing from the scenario of multi-class detection from UAV images, the presence of variable objects in the background and the variety of objects to be detected is huge. Manual labelling of images in likewise situations is time demanding, labor intensive and cumbersome. This demands for the use of unsupervised deep learning, which derives intuitions directly from the data, and works as feature extraction or grouping it, so that the machine can reach on data-driven decisions. The accuracy of unsupervised learning is low when compared with supervised learning. Also, dealing with the number of groups formed by the algorithms poses a potential risk to the inaccuracy of such systems.

Between supervised and unsupervised learning is semi-supervised learning, which allows the machine to have the advantage of both. The algorithm learns from a set of data that includes both labeled and unlabeled data, in which the latter forms the majority part. Limited labelled data and the restriction of resources in acquiring them make semi-supervised learning an upcoming area of study. These learning methods focus on discovering and propagating labels to samples in the unsupervised category by adding the sample to the correct class in the training set and thus improving the classification performance.

Deep reinforcement learning is another sub-field of machine learning that utilizes reinforcement learning and deep learning together and enables the machine to learn the best possible actions in a virtual environment in order to attain the best decisions. Reinforcement learning is about an operator interacting with its environment and learning an optimal policy by trial and error or by the method of reward and penalty. In the scenario of UAV navigation [20,21], these techniques have proven to provide an accurate object detection for collision-free movement. Figure 15.1 illustrates the classification of learning methods.

15.2.1 Deep learning networks

In this section, a brief overview of deep learning networks is presented. Although the list is exhaustive, we restrict ourselves to key points of well-known deep learning networks.

15.2.1.1 Recursive neural network

Adaptive and non-linear models that learn in-depth and structured in arbitrary shapes such as graphs or trees are called recursive neural networks (RvNNs). This network is more of a hierarchy, where the input data are without time aspects but are hierarchically interpreted in a tree-type manner. The backpropagation through structure (BTS) algorithm [22] supports a tree-like structure and is typically used to train the network. The tree-like structure allows branching of connections and hierarchy. The output or structured prediction is dependent on the number of neurons in each layer and the number of connections between them. Each layer has a loop that allows transferring the results of previous neurons from another layer. Because of their

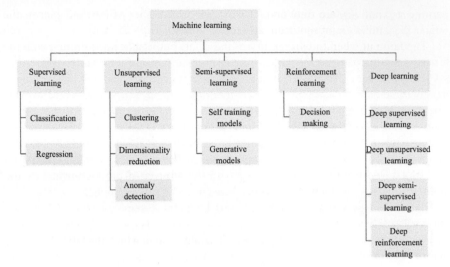

Figure 15.1   Types of machine learning

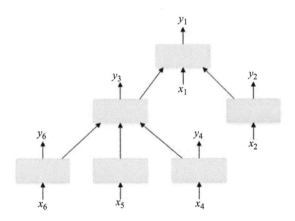

Figure 15.2   Recursive neural network

recursive nature, these networks are inherently complex and, therefore, are not yet accepted broadly and that they are quite computationally expensive at the learning phase. Figure 15.2 illustrates the example of the RvNN structure, where x_s are the children representations at each intermediate node and y_s are the output. The governing equations for each intermediate and corresponding output are given as follows:

$$x_\eta = f\left(W_L x_{l(\eta)} + W_R x_{r(\eta)} + b\right) \qquad (15.1)$$

$$y_\eta = g\left(U x_\eta + c\right) \qquad (15.2)$$

where $r(\eta)$ and $l(\eta)$ are right and left children of η, b is the bias at the intermediate node, W_R and W_L represent right and left weight matrices connecting to the parent, U is the output weight matrix, c is the bias at the output node and f and g being the mapping functions.

15.2.1.2 Recurrent neural network

Another well-known deep learning network is recurrent neural network (RNN). This network recurs over time and utilizes information in sequential order and time-series data. That is why, it is widely used in speech processing, stock market prediction and natural language processing (NLP). In other words, a recursive network is just a generalization of a recurrent neural network. The RNN contains short-term memory units that include input layer, hidden (state) layer and output layer. The network maintains two types of data: current and previous (recent) to generate outcome for new data. The backpropagation through time is used to train RNN. The structure of the RNN unit is illustrated in Figure 15.3, and functions that govern computation are also stated

$$A_t = g(w_{ax}x_t + w_{aa}A_{t-1} + b_a) \tag{15.3}$$

$$H_t = g(w_{ay}A_t + b_y) \tag{15.4}$$

where W is the weight matrix, A is the hidden layer output, $g\,()$ is the activation function, x is the input, H is the output at a time step and b is the bias.

15.2.1.3 Convolutional neural network

In convolutional neural networks, the algorithm passes the input data through distinct layers where each layer is capable of extracting features progressively and passes them to the next layer, as shown in Figure 15.4. Initial layers extract low-level features, and succeeding layers combine features to form a complete representation. The most common deep learning architecture used in computer vision architectures is the convolutional neural network (CNN). A typical ConvNet is a special case of feed-forward neural network which is structured as a series of layers. Units in a

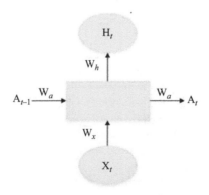

Figure 15.3   The structure of the RNN unit

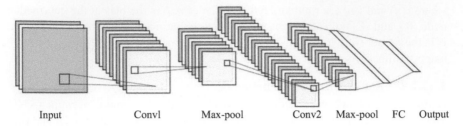

Input   Conv1   Max-pool   Conv2   Max-pool   FC   Output

Figure 15.4   Two-layer convolutional neural network

convolutional layer are grouped in feature maps, in which each layer uses a local connectivity to perform the computation between input and the hidden neurons through a set of weights called a kernel, and the results are stored in an activation map. The size of the activation map is an important parameter and can be calculated if the hyperparameters such as size of kernels (N), stride (S) and zero-padding (P) are known. For an input of dimension $W_{input} \times H_{input} \times D_{input}$ and the above parameters, the output volume $W_{out} \times H_{out} \times D_{out}$ can be estimated by [23]:

$$W_{out} = \frac{W_{input} - N + 2P}{S + 1} \tag{15.5}$$

$$H_{out} = \frac{H_{input} - N + 2P}{S + 1} \tag{15.6}$$

$$D_{out} = D_{input} \tag{15.7}$$

Local connectivity can significantly reduce the total number of parameters in the network. The pooling layers are usually placed between a convolutional layer and the next layer, aiming to reduce the dimension of the input by sustaining as much information available. Different pooling methods include min-pooling, average pooling and some advanced pooling methods, such as fractional stochastic pooling and max-pooling. The most commonly used method is max-pooling, which extracts the maximum value within each specified sub-window across the activation map and can be formulated as follows:

$$A_{i,j,k} = \max\left(C_{i-n \,:\, i+n, j-n \,:\, j+n, k}\right) \tag{15.8}$$

where $A_{i,j,k}$ denotes the maximum activation value in the matrix C of size $n \times n$ centered at index i, j in the k-th activation map, with n being the window size. The resulting weighted sum is then carried through a non-linear function such as ReLU, tanh, sigmoid, etc. A fully connected layer is often added before the output layer to further design non-linear relationships of the input features map. The output layer is usually a classifier entitled for providing the labels of the class of targets. The reason for robustness of the architecture is fairly straightforward. The local statistics of images and other signals are invariant to location. If a pattern can appear in one part of the input image, then it could appear anywhere. Thus, different locations sharing the same weights can detect the same pattern in different parts of the image.

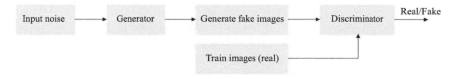

Figure 15.5   Training GAN

Table 15.1   Learning networks with key points

Deep learning network	Key points
Recursive neural network (RvNN)	Uses a tree-like structure, preferred for NLP
Recurrent neural network (RNN)	Good for sequential information, preferred for NLP and speech processing
Convolutional neural network (CNN)	Originally for image recognition, extended for NLP, speech processing and computer vision
Variational autoencoders (VAEs)	Unsupervised learning, probabilistic graphical model
Generative adversarial networks (GANs)	Unsupervised learning, game-theoretical framework

15.2.1.4   Deep generative networks

It is considered possible nowadays to learn a powerful generative model that resembles the true data distribution with useful data representations in an unsupervised way. Recently, there has been much progress toward deep generative networks. Examples in these networks include variational autoencoders (VAEs), generative adversarial networks (GANs) and auto-regressive networks along with many of their variants that have led to remarkable results in a variety of applications such as image synthesis, semantic image editing, image-to-image translation to low-level image processing. A unified view tells that whereas GANs tend to generate low diversity but sharp images, the images by VAEs tend to be blurrier. One important point to note is that these networks can be trained even with small training data. Furthermore, the results from GANs are promising, but the training procedure is not easy when it comes to setup hyperparameters of the network. The objective of GAN is to find equilibrium between generator and discriminator. A sample from a simple distribution is taken and then this noise is transformed to data distribution using learning such as neural networks. This approach is illustrated in Figure 15.5. For analysis, the evaluation metric such as the log-likelihood metric or classification performance is generally used to evaluate generated contents via generative models [24].

To summarize, the descriptive key points of above-mentioned deep learning networks are provided in Table 15.1.

15.2.2   Feature learning

The difference between deep learning and traditional machine learning is how features are extracted. In deep learning, features are extracted in multiple levels and in hierarchy. The steps in learning include initial extraction of simple features, followed by complex features in the next hierarchy and then these features are mapped to get output. In fact, deep learning has effectively reduced the number of challenges to UAVs in addition to enhancing its capabilities along with opening the door to its widespread adoption in different sectors. Feature extraction here refers to the extraction of valuable features from sensors on-board UAVs. The task of most deep learning algorithms is to learn these data features extracted from raw measurements. Typical sensors range from monocular RGB camera, RGB-D sensors, infrared, etc., and most of the deep learning feature extractors are based on a layered architecture, for example, CNNs. For object recognition, recent literature [25] suggests the use of bounding box and object classification embedded in the same CNN model. The authors in [26] focus on global image representations from pre-trained CNNs with fully connected layers to extract representative features and generalize them for classification purposes in another environment such as aerial imagery. In a detailed experimental setup, a multi-layer CNN was employed to classify images taken by a quadrotor drone [27]. Such a UAV platform has its own constraints such as weight, payload, etc., which require specific software to be embedded on specific hardware on-board a UAV. These constraints enable the use of graphical processing units (GPUs), where detection, localization and classification of targets are addressed by using a platform that holds a camera mounted on-board a UAV.

15.2.3 Challenges for deep learning

A number of challenges have been reported in deep learning approaches. Most notable are scalability, ability to generate data in the absence of data needed for learning, energy-efficient algorithms for devices such as UAV's, multi-tasking, transfer learning, data security, etc. The scale of each of these challenges is problem dependent. Various research works in the literature have already addressed most of these issues. For scalability, as it is understood, a large number of machine learning algorithms involves feeding data to an algorithm to do computations iteratively, so the right choice of the central processing unit (CPU) is important. This issue becomes serious when the environment involves UAVs. So, the selection of hardware may preferably choose GPUs or ASICs for the increase in performance compared to CPUs. A number of vendors such as Google, Huawei, Microsoft, Facebook and Apple are working on designing ASICs for machine learning. The second challenge mentioned above is generating data for the problem. For this, generative models such as GAN generate data with the same distribution [28]. The energy efficiency in deep learning requires optimization between hardware, architecture and algorithm selection and is very critical on UAV platforms. During training, deep learning models often have access to user information and thus expose privacy and security. This aspect has not been addressed by the research community as well as an industry while developing algorithms and architectures for deep learning. Recent work [29] has highlighted this issue and proposed some countermeasures.

15.2.4 Challenges related to aerial video classification

The analysis of images collected from UAV poses many challenges due to the rapid motion of the camera, instability of image perspectives and limited size of the captured object. The complication involved in the aerial surveillance from a UAV motion is due to panning, rotation and tilting. Similarly, the height at which the UAV is flying also largely affects object detection results. In addition to a couple of practical entanglements such as short battery life and privacy trouble, the most important technical issue in programmed UAV-based object detection is the ego-motion issue, that is generated either deliberately (e.g., control at base station) or accidently (e.g., by wind). The background motion, caused by UAV ego-motion, makes the customary object detection and stream estimation techniques intended for fixed reconnaissance methods not to function admirably. Thus, blob detection and background subtraction [30,31] cannot be applied for UAV-based videos. Compared with other challenges such as occlusion, shadows and reflections, ego-motion is the most challenging issue in aerial video processing.

The object detection task becomes challenging with varying illumination conditions, complicated scenes and different density conditions. Furthermore, the UAV images are often of varying scales, perspectives and appearances due to UAV speed, its multiple viewpoints and altitudes. Thus, the viewpoint, the shape and size of an object vary as the camera position and orientation change with the UAV approach angle. As pointed out in previous sections, the images captured by a drone usually are different from those available for training, which are often taken by a stationary camera. Thus, conventional object detection algorithms which are intended for images from stationary cameras do not perform well on images captured by UAVs.

15.2.5 Applications

Regarding UAV imagery, a lot of work has been done in application areas, such as food crop identification for the purpose of food security. The authors in [32] use a model based on transfer learning for pretraining using a publicly accessible ImageNet dataset. The RGB images were collected through UAV. The classification required from this system was bananas, legumes and maize. Another research work [33] related to the monitoring of trees for growth, pest control and fruit production for long-term management is also of importance to farm owners. The UAVs have also found application in disaster management and emergency response systems as UAVs can easily be operated in difficult areas for real-time alert in the case of floods, fire and collapsed buildings. The authors in [34] discuss the use of aerial scene classification on-board a UAV system for disaster management. Locating and tracking wildlife using UAVs has been an important aspect of wildlife management and research. The authors in [35] use the aerial VHF tracking on-board a UAV for a wide range of wildlife to extend the search range and minimize this effort compared to other tracking systems. UAVs have also been explored for next-generation communication networks for spectral efficiency and to extend coverage, even though this may bring new challenges as well. In [36], the authors use a machine-based framework to address problems (such as resource management, positioning, security and channel modeling) that have already been identified in UAV-based communication environment.

15.3   Learning architecture and classification

15.3.1   Supervised learning architectures

The core methodologies of deep learning techniques include AEs, deep feed-forward neural networks, CNNs, deep belief networks (DBNs) and long short-term memory networks. Deep learning methods have exploited CNNst with various depths, and some important variants are well appreciated for its architecture and performance. AlexNet [37] was formulated with eight layers that consist of five convolutional layers and three fully connected layers. The method exhibited reduced top-1 and top-5 error rates of 37.5% and 17.0%, respectively. The game-changing innovation introduced in the paper was the replacement of Tanh by ReLU, which accelerated the speed by six times at the same accuracy. It also adopted dropout instead of regularization to deal with overfitting and overlap pooling to reduce the size of the network.

VGGNet proposed by Simonyan and Zisserman [38] in 2014 extended the size of the network from 8 weight layers as proposed by AlexNet to 16–19 layers depending on the VGG variant. According to the reported research results, the error rate dropped from 29.6 to 25.5 regarding top-1 error and from 10.4 to 8.0 regarding top-5 error. The architecture was built using a stack of multiple 3×3 convolutional layers without a pooling layer in-between convolutional layer instead of large filter sizes, such as 7×7 or 11×11, with reduced parameters and increased non-linearity. The results gave way to the realization that a deeper CNN architecture carries the ability to perform better compared to shallower networks.

GoogLeNet [39] was introduced in 2014, making the architecture deeper by stacking of layers that increased the number of parameters to overfitting and the model became hard to train. It contained 22 layers with bottleneck architecture which considerably reduced the number of parameters; hence, it is much more efficient. The inception module is a block of parallel convolutional layers with different filters sized 1×1, 3×3 and 5×5 and a 1×1 and 3×3 max-pooling layer. The results of which are then concatenated. The method gave a top-5 error as low as 6.67% on both the validation and testing data.

ResNet [40] was introduced in 2016 with a deep residual learning framework consisting of multiple residual blocks formulated to overcome the degradation issue of CNN. Residual blocks are built using identity mapping which are direct connections from the input node to the output node. The implementation results of ResNet helped to increase layers of CNNs to 152 by building stacked blocks along with the network.

Representation learning is the common property followed by all deep learning techniques. Deep learning models learn the representation with multiple steps corresponding to multilevel representation transformations between hidden layers. Moreover, as individual representations are not architected by human intervention but are learned through training input data, the deep learning techniques are

Table 15.2   Comparison between different CNN models [37–40]

Models	AlexNet	VGGNet	GoogLeNet	ResNet
Input size	227 × 227	224 × 224	224 × 224	224 × 224
Filter size	3, 5, 11	3	1, 3, 5, 7	1, 3, 7
Convolution layers	5	16	21	50
Feature maps	3-256	3-512	3-1024	3-1024
Stride	1, 4	1	1, 2	1, 2
Weights	2.3M	14.7M	6.0M	23.5M
MACs	666M	15.3G	1.43G	3.86G
FC layers	3	3	1	1
Weights	58.6M	124M	1M	1M
MACs	58.6M	124M	1M	1M
Weights total	61M	138M	7M	25.5M
MACs total	724M	15.5G	1.43G	3.9G
Top-5 errors	16.4	7.4	6.7	5.3

considered to be very flexible. All these discussed models can be compared using network parameters, as shown in Table 15.2.

15.3.2   Unsupervised learning

Unsupervised learning involves a model to extract relationships within data. The relevant algorithms use techniques on the input to detect patterns and rules, and group data points in deriving useful insights and describe the data for better use. Technically speaking, it has a lot of potentials to unlock most of the unsolved problems, that is why it is gaining attention from the machine learning and deep learning community. There are many real-world unsupervised deep learning applications. The notable applications include remote sensing, mini-UAV for naval capability, mini-UAV for seeing through forest, storm or foggy weather, early tumor detection and futurist robots.

The aerial scene data provided by UAVs or drones provide an opportunity to understand spatial and structural formations. The object and pixel-based classification techniques use these data in a limited way. The authors in [41] investigate the unsupervised feature learning technique as a detection system by learning a set of basis functions to extract local spatial features. The ORNL-I dataset, UCMERCED dataset and ORNL-II dataset are used to determine classification accuracy in [41].

Some research studies have attempted visual simultaneous localization mapping and visual odometry to understand the new environment. In [42], the authors combine traditional methods with machine learning on RGB images to understand unknown images and later use the YOLO (you only look once) detection method on the smartphone platform to classify objects with high computational speed. In the absence of labelled training data and due to the relatively high cost for capturing and labelling videos from UAVs, people tend to turn towards unsupervised and semi-supervised learning techniques for flow estimation, as an example. The authors in [43] investigate optical flow using image warping to minimize photometric consistency using unsupervised learning from end-to-end and show that corresponding results are close to what were achieved through full supervised learning. For action recognition, a study has been conducted in [44] for action recognition on 5,250 drone-based videos by employing adaptation methods together with a classifier for knowledge transfer from the source to the target.

15.3.3   Deep learning for planning and situational awareness

A number of research works have appeared in the literature that discuss planning for UAV tasks that require solutions to complex problems with unstructured, dynamic environment or the scope of the task is diverse. The examples of such situations include navigation and path planning for collaborative search and rescue missions, etc. Similar applications also exist for unmanned ships that require automatic path planning, navigation strategies and then build control action plans during sea exploration, emergency navigation and rescue, water quality monitoring, self-localization, etc. In [45], for example, the authors discuss CNN architecture for on-site and on-demand classification instead of pre-trained classifier for terrain classification and mapping for a ground-based robot. Similarly, for a delivery robot to reach a new location with little prior information, the research in [46] addresses a two-layer hierarchical approach that combines model-based planning with deep learning. At a high level, a map computes a path from the current location to the destination, whereas, at a low level, a machine learning-based controller is trained end-to-end for navigation.

The other type of task involves self-localization and mapping, state estimation, etc. Deep learning methods may also be used for such a type of task as well. For example, in [47], the authors use deep learning for cross-view localization of images based on the nearest neighbor visual features or landmarks and then subsequent matching with features extracted through the input query run on the reference database of aerial images. In a similar work [48], the authors propose deep learning architecture to produce position-dependent control actions based on aerial images captured on-board together with a motion plan. The architecture effectively learns mapping from the images. The works [45–48], though slow in implementation, provide insight into the use of deep learning approaches in path planning and situational awareness.

15.3.4   Deep learning for motion control

In the literature, a lot of research works can be found for classical control to help solve various control issues in an analytical way. For easy adaptable control, deep learning can be explored further to manage challenging control situations when UAV or drone finds itself in hostile environment like excessive wind gusts, heavy rain, a mechanical failure, or location of obstacles such as birds or other UAVs in the field of view. These situations can be managed by inference based on images or patterns received and thus labelled as input data. As an example, certain control actions such as turn left/right, go straight, or rotate left/right can be generated from raw images mapped to behavior action [49] in CNN-like architecture. In a similar work [27], the authors use raw images in a model that is pre-trained end-to-end to generate action probabilities for obstacle-free trajectory in a hostile natural environment like dense forests. Although theoretically time-consuming and lacking real-time response in such critical missions, the approach, however, provides an insight into how such a situation can be managed once a high-performance computational device becomes available on-board a UAV. In another work [50], the authors use a hierarchical approach where supervised learning is used for raw images and deep reinforcement learning is used for self-play games for situations such as following a tracked target with a safety-critical constraint. Deep learning has also been explored in areas such as UAV cooperation and navigation with tasks such as pursuit and evasion [51]. For tracking, a deep object detector for distant objects and search area proposal are used to predict the position of the target UAV in the next frame, whereas deep reinforcement learning is used to predict action as a follower UAV.

15.3.5   Object detection

Emerging machine learning techniques for powerful feature representations consider object detection as a classification problem. Object detection is done by a classifier learning the difference in appearances and textures from a dataset. Learning through the dataset can either be supervised or unsupervised or semi-supervised. Feature extraction and classifier play a huge role in the accuracy of machine learning algorithms. Feature fusion and dimension reduction are some steps applied to the extracted features to further improve the performance. After feature extraction, a classifier is trained to minimize the misclassification error on the training dataset. A large number of research works can be found in the literature that discuss object detection using machine learning. Below, we summarize well-known and recent research.

Yang *et al.* [52] proposed a network to detect sparsely clustered targets unifying object clustering and detection in an end-to-end framework. Three sub-networks are part of the work: ClusDet comprises a cluster proposal sub-network; a scale estimation sub-network (ScaleNet); a dedicated detection network (DetecNet) with experiments conducted on publicly available datasets VisDrone, UAVDT and DOTA. In another work [53], a novel double focal loss convolutional neural network (DFLCNN) framework is proposed that uses the skip connection in the CNN structure to enhance the feature learning. The performance of model is evaluated on the German Aerospace Center (DLR) 3K dataset and the ITCVD dataset. A deep neural network named feature fusion deep networks (FFDNs) is proposed in [54]. It combines convolutional restricted Boltzmann machines with conditional random fields. The authors claim that the structural learning in the model provides more robust spatial information. The experiments are carried out on UAV123 and UAVDT datasets. For extraction of small object features, the authors in [55] propose a vehicle detection algorithm based on Faster R-CNN with fusing of a hyperactive feature map network with Eltwise model and Concat model and claim effectiveness of the model.

Table 15.3   Learning algorithms versus Aerial systems

Learning algorithms	Sensing technologies	Aerial systems
Supervised	Image, Acoustic. LIDAR, Radar	Feature extraction
	Image	Planning
	Image	Situational awareness
	Image	Motion control
Unsupervised	Image, Radar	Feature extraction
Reinforcement	LiDAR	Motion control

Support vector machine (SVM) is also investigated in the form of the con-volutional support vector machine (CSVM) vehicle detection system [56] for UAV imagery. The convolutional layers in CSVM rely on a set of linear SVMs as filter banks for feature map generation and use a forward supervised learning strategy for computing the weights of these filters. The authors in [57] propose CNN together with unsupervised training dataset collection for weeds detection from UAV images. The unsupervised labelling is formulated by a combination of Hough transform and simple linear iterative clustering algorithm. These data are then processed by deep learning technique, ResNet being the backbone, for weed detection. In [58], the authors adopted deep residual network and feature pyramids network in the back-bone stage for utilizing low-level features and high-level features simultaneously. The feature extraction is carried out by ResNet, bounding boxes proposed by a region proposal network and classification by Faster R-CNN. The experiments of the pro-posed method were carried out on the DOTA, VEDAI and VisDrone datasets. Finally, the authors in [59] conduct a survey on object detection using deep learning techniques including one-shot and two-shot detectors, Viola–Jones (VJ), histogram of oriented gradient (HOG), etc. benchmark datasets, evaluation matrices, speedup techniques, etc. Various applications involving object detection are investigated by corresponding authors in areas such as crowd and pedestrian environment. To better understand, learning architectures along with sensing technologies targeting various applications are tabulated as in Table 15.3.

15.3.6   Classification

15.3.6.1   Binary classification

Once object detection is done, the data heads for classification. Much research has been conducted in this area. The recent work [60], for example, presents a deep learning framework for online moving object recognition in videos in contrast to approaches that exploit pixel-wise segmentation of frames. The authors use current frames and past history to learn spatial and temporal features by employing labeling of axis aligned bounding boxes for moving objects and generating feature pyramids to determine classification.

In another work [61], the authors propose a method to detect oil palm trees from UAV images. It is a hierarchy of SVM classifiers, one for classifying vegetative areas at a pixel level and the other for detecting palm trees at an image patch level. A feature descriptor based on the HOG is incorporated. The author claims overall accuracy rates of 99.21% for the training site and 99.39%, 99.06%, 99.90% and 94.63% for the four testing sites, respectively. The SVM is also explored in a framework [62] that uses HOG to detect cars in the road maps possibly available from geographic information system. Filtering operations are performed in the horizontal and vertical directions to extract HOF features. However, the overall accuracy of the system obtained is limited to 80.94%. The authors [63] proposed a hybrid vehicle detection scheme by combining the Viola–Jones (V–J) and linear SVM classifier with the HOG feature. The method focuses on rotating the UAV image so as to align the road in the horizontal direction, which can increase the accuracy of vehicle detection, with a success rate of 82.32%.

In another research [64], the authors proposed a framework to automatically detect wind-turbine blade surface cracks based on images taken by UAV. Based on extracted Haar-like features, an extended cascading classifier is formulated from a set of base models such as the LogitBoost, Decision Tree and SVM to detect the presence of cracks on the blade surface.

15.3.6.2 Multi-class classification

As field view of UAV changes from one position to another, the object size and location may change in images, hence detection and classification accuracy may be affected. Multi-class image classification is a hot research topic with broader prospects in artificial intelligence field. Much research work has been reported in the literature for multi-class classification methods. For example, in [65], the authors analyze softmax and logistic regression functions for multi-class classification using CNNs and develop two objective functions that emerge to be alternative to softmax regression in single-label classification. The authors claim superior performance of the proposed function using comparative evaluations conducted on clothing attribute classifications. In food image classification, the authors [66] propose a framework to extract features from a dataset of 100 food ingredient images of 41 classes to improve the accuracy of multi-class classification using transfer learning (ResNet) applied on the deep feature set. The authors in [67] use tensor flow package to compare linear SVM and non-linear CNN for image classification accuracy band on feature selection and extraction. The study verifies the superior performance of SVM for binary classification and CNN performance for binary as well as multi-class classification. The CNN is also investigated in [68] for multi-class object recognition. The implementation uses the Python tensor flow framework with nine different object categories and sample test images from a widely varied dataset for initialization and training and resulting feature vectors are classified. Another multi-class application for UAV-based object detection has been reported in [69], where SVM is applied on selected UAV images to perform cotton field classification. The aerial images were processed to obtain the stitched image of the study area, and the SVM and maximum likelihood classification method were used to differentiate the cotton plants within the stitched image. With an accuracy of 96.65% compared to 87.85% of the maximum likelihood classification technique, the SVM performed better. Lastly, but not least, the authors in [70] propose a vehicle detection framework called rotation-invariant cascade forest to train the Auto-context cascaded forests classification model. The method is tested on two benchmark datasets: the DLR Munich vehicle dataset and the UAVDT dataset.

15.4   Training

To ensure best performance in machine learning systems, the datasets are typically divided into different sets: training, cross validation and testing. The training set, usually the large portion, is used to make the system learn or to fit the model from the input data. The validation set allows fine-tuning of hyperparameters of the model fit by the training dataset, thus used for parameter selection and to avoid overfitting. Models that require substantial data to fit the model are expected to have a larger training dataset. Similarly, models with few hyperparameters, which are easier to validate, also tend to have a larger portion of the dataset for training. Alternatively, a larger number of hyperparameters need a comparatively larger validation set or consider cross validation. Common method in the category is k-fold cross validation [71]. The training dataset is randomly partitioned into complementary subsets. The model is trained against different combinations of these subsets and validated against the remaining parts. The method provides a clever manipulation for the extensive use of the whole dataset, whereas the test dataset provides unbiased model evaluation.

15.4.1   Weight initialization

Initial weights are one among different parameters to tune, incredibly important as it affects the speed and probability of convergence, and the generalization in neural network methods. Thus, the weight initialization allows the networks to decide how quickly to converge or whether to converge at all. The effectiveness of the training largely depends on the gradients based on the distribution of weights. Network initialization aims to inhibit layer activations from vanishing or exploding during forward pass in the network, which will lead to a longer time for convergence. Random initialization is the usual method in CNN. Weight initialization is generally divided into two categories. Random initialization [72] sets all weights to random numbers, usually with values from a uniform or normal distribution. In zeroes and ones initialization [73], all weights are initialized to zeroes or ones, making all weights and the activation in all neurons same. Another factor that greatly affects the training time and accuracy is normalization. It makes the network unbiased to high-value features and reduces internal covariant shift. In deep learning, the regularly used method is batch normalization [74], which standardizes the inputs as a mini-batch for a layer. It computes mean, standard deviation and variance of each feature in a mini-batch. Inaccurate estimation of batch statistics with small batch size increases the error in the model. Layer normalization [75] calculates mean and variance from all summed inputs to the neurons in a layer on a single training case. Weight normalization [76] is another method that normalizes weights of a layer instead of activations. Group normalization [77] is a similar method but independent of batch size.

15.4.2 Convolutional methods

The key role of feature extraction in CNN takes place in convolution layers, which is composed of a stack of mathematical operations called convolution. Repeated convolutions between kernels and tensors give feature maps which is the representation of input tensors. Size, number of kernels, stride and zero-padding are some of the hyperparameters that define the convolutional layer. The size is denoted using *nxn*, where *n* usually takes the values 3, 5, 7, or 11. Recent works utilized different types of convolution methods from the structure of state-of-art CNN architecture. Dilated convolutions [78], also known as atrous convolutions, introduce spacing between the values in a kernel. The new term called dilation rate comes into existence that delivers a wider field of view at the same computational cost. Transpose dilations [79] or deconvolutions tempt to do inverse convolutions on the raw input pixels to produce the same spatial resolution a hypothetical deconvolutional layer would. It carries out regular convolution but inverts the spatial transformation. In separable convolution [80], the kernel operation is split into multiple steps. The dot product of different steps gives lesser parameters than normal convolutions. Spatially separable convolutions and depth-wise separable convolutions [81] are commonly used variants.

15.4.3 Activation functions

Activation functions as mathematical representations determine accuracy and computational efficiency of training. The function works in combination with each neuron in the network, determining whether the neuron is to be activated or not. The activation functions are broadly classified into three: binary step, linear activation and non-linear activation functions. A binary step function is threshold based, where the neuron is activated if the input value is above a certain threshold. This activation function does not support multi-class classification. Linear activation functions [82] create an output signal proportional to the input. However, linear activation functions do not allow backpropagation in training, thus reducing the efficiency. Recent deep neural networks use non-linear activation [82] functions that offer complex mappings between network inputs and outputs. Sigmoid, TanH, ReLU, SoftMax and Swish are the commonly used non-linear activation functions. Sigmoid [83] functions are usually used to predict probability as the range lies between 0 and 1. TanH is also a sigmoid function but allows negative values, thus differentiating between negative and zero inputs. ReLU [84] is the most used activation function and is used in almost all the convolutional neural networks, and is given by the function:

$$R(z) = \max(0, z)$$

The issue in ReLU arises when dealing with negative values, which become zero all of a sudden. This dying problem is solved by Leaky ReLU [85] in the range from negative infinity to infinity, and is given by

$$R(z) = \max(az, z) \tag{15.9}$$

Parametric ReLU provides more consistent predictions for negative inputs. SoftMax is used for multi-classification in logistic regression models, whose output falls in the range [0,1] with a total sum of 1, thus forming a probability distribution and is defined by [85]

$$\sigma(z)_j = \frac{e^{z_j}}{\sum\limits_{k=1}^{K} e^{z_j}} \tag{15.10}$$

where z is a vector of inputs to output layer and j indexes the output units from 1,2, 3, ..., k.

15.4.4 Subsampling or pooling layer

A pooling layer is periodically placed between successive convolutional layers in a CNN architecture to provide downsampling operation. The layer reduces the dimensionality of the feature maps, introduces a translation invariance to small shifts and distortions, and decreases the number of subsequent learnable parameters. It also helps in reducing overfitting. The layer as a whole does not participate in the learning process but contributes greatly to the efficiency of the architecture. Similar to convolutional layers, filter size, padding and stride are hyperparameters in pooling operations. Different pooling methods include min-pooling, average pooling and some other methods, such as fractional stochastic pooling, max-pooling, etc. The max-pooling function, the most favorite choice in CNN architectures, generates a single value for each filter operation as $A_{i,j,k} = \max\left(C_{i-n\,:\,i+n,j-n\,:\,j+n,k}\right)$, where $A_{i,j,k}$ denotes the maximum activation value in the matrix C of size $n \times n$ centered at index i, j in the k-th activation map, with n being the window size. Similar operation occurs in minimum pooling, which gives the minimum value in the $n x n$ kernel, formulated by $A_{i,j,k} = \min\left(C_{i-n\,:\,i+n,j-n\,:\,j+n,k}\right)$. Average pooling or mean pooling is also a commonly used pooling layer variant, in which the operation computes the average of each filter values: $A_{i,j,k} = \text{mean}\left(C_{i-n\,:\,i+n,j-n\,:\,j+n,k}\right)$. Stochastic pooling samples based on the probability distribution based on activations. The method is parameter free and can be combined with dropout and data augmentation.

15.4.5 Optimization techniques

Optimization techniques are incorporated so as to reduce losses and provide the most accurate results as possible. The basic optimizer used in deep learning is gradient descent [86]. The variables are updated iteratively in the direction that is opposite to the objective function gradients, gradually converging to the optimal value. The goal of the optimizer is to reduce the loss function $L(\theta)$, where θ is the parameter that needs optimization, and $f_\theta(x)$ [86]:

$$L(\theta) = \frac{1}{2N} \sum_{i=1}^{N} \left(y^i - f_\theta(x^i) \right)^2 \tag{15.11}$$

$$f_\theta(x) = \sum_{j=1}^{D} \theta_j x_j \tag{15.12}$$

where D is the number of input features, N is the number of samples in the training dataset, x^i is an independent variable and y^i is the output target. The update of θ_j is carried out by [86]

$$\theta'_j = \theta_j + \eta \cdot \frac{1}{N} \sum_{i=1}^{N} \left(y^i - f_\theta(x^i) \right)^2 \tag{15.13}$$

Once large-scale data are dealt, the cost is hard to estimate. The stochastic gradient descent (SGD) [87] method reduces the computational complexity per each iteration of large-scale data. This method uses one random sample while updating the gradient in each iteration. The loss function can be updated as [87]

$$L(\theta) = \frac{1}{N} \sum_{i=1}^{N} \cos t\left(\theta, (x^i, y^i) \right) \tag{15.14}$$

where $\cos t(\theta, (x^i, y^i)) = \frac{1}{2} (y^i - f_\theta(x^i))^2$ for a random sample i, and the gradient update takes place as [87]

$$\theta' = \theta + \eta (y^i - f_\theta(x^i)) x^i \tag{15.15}$$

When SGD is compared with other batch methods, it can reduce computational complexity considerably and can speed up convergence. The mini-batch gradient descent method [88] is a compromise between gradient-decent methods and SGD by using independent and identically distributed samples. A much lesser learning time is obtained by the Nesterov accelerated gradient descent [89] method, which is a momentum-based algorithm and introduces speed v, representing the direction and rate of the parameter's movement in its space. Considering momentum factor m and previous speed v^{old}, the speed can be formulated as follows:

$$v = \eta \cdot \left(-\frac{\partial L(\theta)}{\partial \theta} \right) + v^{\text{old}} \cdot m \tag{15.16}$$

and the update takes place as $\theta' = \theta + v$.

The problem to select an appropriate value of learning rate η was administrated by the adaptive learning rate method. The AdaGrad [90] approach adjusts the learning rate in a dynamic way that is based on the historical gradient in previous iterations.

15.4.6   Benchmark datasets

There are numerous datasets publicly available for object detection and classification from UAVs data. Each dataset possesses the criteria required for accomplishing the purpose of modelling with it. Most of these datasets were created in the last ten years and consist of videos or images for buildings, roads, vehicles, people, face, human behavior, etc., recognition. Table 15.4 lists the publicly available datasets.

15.5   Energy efficiency in learning approaches

The long-term operation of UAVs generally requires less power as well as less memory use. There can be different directions for building UAV systems that will have energy-efficient computational cost without lowering accuracy or better network structures. The first approach targets a design for a hardware-efficient network, and the second targets the network structure with an optimal operational cost like, for example, low-dimensional convolutional filter to keep a fewer number of parameters.

Whereas algorithm should reduce computational as well as storage complexity during training, the hardware part should have an efficient field-programmable gate array for reconfiguration, deep pipelining and resource re-using [104]. Recent works, for example [105], discuss different models for multi-task learning, where models share knowledge in hidden layers across different but similar tasks. In another research [106], the approach learns across different application domains to save time for retraining for a different domain. The efficiency is also discussed in [107] as an alternative to a deep learning network for efficiency. The network develops itself into a data-driven tree-like structure starting from the root node that splits the data into two classes to be handled by expert networks. The network is tested on CIFAR-10 and CIFAR-100 datasets.

For the efficient hardware platform, the authors in [108] propose the CNN architecture for vehicle detection with a frame rate of 5–18 fps and an accuracy of about 95% using a low-power embedded processor deployed on UAVs. In another application in the domain of aerial scene classification for disaster events [109], the authors introduce lightweight CNN for the embedded platform with minimum memory requirements on-board a UAV that provides three times higher performance than existing models. To reduce energy consumption and improve accuracy and speed on-board a UAV platform, the authors in [110] address energy-efficient real-time UAV visual object detection with performance parameters of 28.5 fps and 2.7 fps/W on the dataset. These types of efforts open the door to real-time classification using on-board UAV platforms.

15.6   Performance metrics

Performance metrics can be defined as data and figures that represent a model's performance, accuracy and overall quality. It serves to quantify how good the model works on a given task. The robustness of the object detection and

Table 15.4 *Well-known datasets created from aerial images and videos*

	Name	Year	Image/video		Resolution	Comments
			Images	Videos		
1	CICTE-People Detection [91]	2017	430,0200		704×480	Detecting pedestrians
2	Drone Face [92]	2017	2,057		$3,680 \times 2,760$	Face recognition
3	DroneSURF [93]	2019		200	$1,280 \times 720$	Face recognition
4	UAV123 [94]	2016		123	$1,280 \times 720$	Pedestrians and vehicles
5	VisDrone [95]		8,599		$1,920 \times 1,080$	Multiple objects tracking
6	UAVDT [96]		80K		$1,080 \times 540$	Object detection
7	Swimmers [97]	2019	9,000		$1,920 \times 1,080$	People detection
8	AU-AIR [98]		32,823		$1,920 \times 1,080$	People, vehicle detection
9	MOD20 [99]		503,086		720×720	Human action recognition
10	DOTA [100]	2018	2,806		$800 \times 800 - 4,000 \times 4,000$	Object detection
11	DLR-3K-Munich [101]		20		$5,616 \times 3,744$	Vehicle detection
12	DIOR [102]		23,463		800×800	Seasons, weathers
13	Urban [103]		1,222		$1,500 \times 1,500$	Buildings and roads

classification algorithm can be quantitatively evaluated by certain frame-based metrics. The most basic ones in object detection tasks include true positive (TP), false positive (FP), false negative (FN) and true negative (TN). True positive implies a correct detection, or the model correctly labels or categorizes an object. False positive dictates an incorrect detection of an absent object or a mislaid bounding box of an existing object. False negative implies undetected, or the model that does not label or categorize an object. True negative describes the cases where the regions with no objects are correctly identified. True negatives are of the least importance in object detection tasks. The assessment of object detection methods mostly uses concepts that mostly rule out the use of true negatives, such as Precision (P) and Recall (R). The ability of the model to identify relevant objects exactly is termed precision, given by the percentage of positive predictions.

$$\text{Precision} = \frac{\text{TP}}{\text{TP} + \text{FP}} \qquad (15.17)$$

Recall is the percentage of correct predictions representing the ability of a model to find all cases. It is also referred to as sensitivity, given by the equation:

$$\text{Recall} = \frac{\text{TP}}{\text{TP} + \text{FN}} \qquad (15.18)$$

Precision–Recall curves give the trade-off between the true positive rate and the positive values predicted by the detector model using different probability thresholds and confidence levels. A high precision is achieved with low FP; however, this can also lead to high FN and thus a low recall. Adjusting the model to increase positives can lead to the increase in FP, thus reducing the precision. A good detector is expected to detect all ground truth with high recall with FN equals to zero and high precision with FP equals to zero. Thus, for a good object detector with varying confidence levels, the precision and recall should always remain high. The area under precision–recall curve, also known as average precision (AP), is high for both high precision and recall, but difficult to determine in practical cases due to zig-zag-like shapes. Interpolation techniques like 11-point interpolation and all-point interpolation are often used to calculate the accuracy of the detector, which can bypass the effect of the random curve. The curve is shaped by calculating the mean of the maximum precision values at a set of 11 equally spaced recall levels ordered 0, 0.1, 0.2, ... ,1 in 11-point interpolation [111] and is given by

$$\text{AP}_{11} = \frac{1}{11} \sum_{R} P_{\text{interp}}(R) \qquad (15.19)$$

where $P_{\text{interp}} = \max_{\tilde{R}:\tilde{R} \geq R} P(\tilde{R})$, obtained by considering maximum precision values with values larger than R. In all-point interpolation [105], the method is carried out through all points, visualized by

$$\text{AP}_{\text{all}} = \sum_n (R_{n+1} - R_n) P_{\text{interp}}(R_{n+1}) \tag{15.20}$$

where $P_{\text{interp}}(R_{n+1}) = \max_{\tilde{R}:\tilde{R} \geq R_{n+1}} P(\tilde{R})$. The AP, in this case, is obtained by interpolating the precision at all points, taking the maximum precision with a recall value that is equal or greater than R_{n+1}. The mean average precision (mAP) is the metric used when the system has multiple categories, averages all APs, given by the equation

$$\text{mAP} = \frac{1}{N} \sum_{i=1}^{N} \text{AP}_i \tag{15.21}$$

where AP_i is the AP of the ith class out of N classes. F1 score is another performance metric in the object detection task, which is the harmonic mean of precision and recall. The overall accuracy of the model based on FP, FN, TP and TN is calculated as per the equation:

$$\text{Accuracy} = \frac{\text{TP} + \text{FN}}{\text{TP} + \text{TN} + \text{FP} + \text{FN}} \tag{15.22}$$

In the object detection task, it is crucial to learn the bounding box parameters. Intersection over union (IOU) [112] is the common way to evaluate the accuracy of the object detection based on bounding boxes used on a particular data. This metric requires both true bounding boxes and predicted bounding boxes by the model to evaluate the performance. The IOU is the ratio of intersecting area between the predicted bounding box and the ground-truth bounding box to the area of their union. Considering the area of the predicted bounding box to be A_p and the ground-truth bounding box as A_{gt}, IOU can be formulated as follows:

$$\text{IOU} = \frac{\text{area}(A_p \cap A_{gt})}{\text{area}(A_p \cup A_{gt})} \tag{15.23}$$

Obtaining the value of IOU and comparing it with a threshold 't' specifies whether the detection is correct or incorrect. A correct detection is acknowledged with an IOU $\geq t$ and an IOU $< t$ is considered as incorrect detection. Considering the scenario of multi-class classification of objects from UAV, a good model with an implicatively best object detector is required. A better detection gives a good label prediction. In practical cases, due to varying parameters of the model such as image pyramid scale, detection framework, sliding window size, and so on, an equivalency between predicted and ground-truth bounding boxes is seemingly unrealistic. Thus, the system works with giving rewards such that the predicted bounding boxes that overlap ground-truth bounding boxes have scores that are higher than those with less overlap. This shows that IoU is an excellent metric to evaluate custom object detectors.

15.7   Development kits and frameworks

With the wide applications of deep learning in various fields, the researchers have been motivated to develop unique and independent frameworks to implement deep learning. A deep learning framework is a library or an interface that permits to construct deep learning models effectively and rapidly, without getting into fundamental algorithms. They offer building blocks for designing, training and validating deep neural networks through a high-level programming interface. They provide a concise way of characterizing models using optimized and pre-defined components. The most popular deep learning frameworks include Keras, TensorFlow, PyTorch, Caffe, etc.

Keras [113], released in 2015, is the most popular framework that provides a Python interface to facilitate the rapid modeling of different deep neural networks, such as CNNs and RNNs. The design focuses to be extensible, user-friendly and modular. Keras is widely accepted as it possesses the advantages of broad adoption, integration with different back-end engines, support for a wide range of production deployment options and strong support to work with multiple GPUs and distributed training. It is an optimal option for deep learning applications. Keras library also provides the interface to other deep learning frameworks such as TensorFlow and Theano. The simplicity and modularity of the framework make it less flexible, not optimal in some applications.

TensorFlow [114], also released in 2015, is another most popular framework with flexible and scalable features, created for numerical computations using dataflow graphs. The core algorithms are written and optimized in C++ and CUDA. The framework supports a large number of languages such as Python, C++, Java, JavaScript etc., for implementing different deep learning models. It is supported and promoted by Google and a large group of developers by providing various documentations, guides and tutorials. The feature that makes TensorFlow is that it is completely open source. The popular applications include text-based detection, image recognition, sound recognition, video analysis and time-series analysis. In a practical scenario, the interface becomes a bit challenging and difficult to implement for beginners.

Caffe [115], released in 2013, is a library written in C++ which includes a Python, C, C++ and MATLAB® interface. The framework stands out for its speed in processing and learning of images, thus specialized in the development of convolutional neural networks. It provides an expressive architecture with extensible code and high speed. The developers claim that the framework is capable of processing 60M images on a NIVIDA K40 GPU on a single day. Caffe Zoo models have large applications such as simple regression, large-scale visual classification, Siamese networks for image similarity, speech and robotics applications. The biggest advantage is that the framework enables the ability for implementations apart from the zoo model.

PyTorch [116] provides a replacement for NumPy to use the power of GPUs and other accelerators. It also aims in providing an automatic differentiation

Table 15.5 Popular deep learning frameworks

Framework	Core language	Learning network supported
Keras [107]	Python	CNN, RNN, DBN
TensorFlow [108]	C++, Python	CNN, RNN, DBN
Caffe [109]	C++	CNN, RNN
PyTorch [110]	C++, Python, CUDA	CNN, RNN, DBN
Theano [111]	Python, CUDA	CNN, RNN
MXNet [112]	C++	CNN, RNN

library, for NumPy and SciPy, which are useful in implementing neural networks. The popularity of the framework is gained due to the quality that allows complex architectures to be built effortlessly. The framework is extremely powerful for creating computational graphs. The graph in PyTorch can be dynamically defined with the inputs during runtime, the process referred to as eager execution. The techniques used for this realization is called reverse-mode auto-differentiation. Even though considerable advancement has happened on the framework, it still lacks a mobile solution.

Theano [117] is a Python library that allows you to define, optimize and efficiently evaluate mathematical expressions involving multi-dimensional arrays. It is a low-level library supporting both CPU and transparent use of GPU computation. The framework features tight integration with NumPy, speed and stability optimizations and self-verification tools. It is a lower-level API, thus being difficult to create deep learning models directly. This framework is no longer under development.

MXNet [118] is a deep learning framework that allows mixing symbolic and imperative programming that aims to maximize efficiency and productivity. It is lightweight and portable, scaling effectively to be implemented on multiple GPUs. It also supports the efficient placement of trained models in low-end devices. The framework supports a flexible programming model with multiple languages such as C++, Python, MATLAB, JavaScript, R, etc. The key points of these frameworks are summarized in Table 15.5.

15.8 Discussions and future directions

A detailed survey of models and networks based on machine learning in general and deep learning in particular was presented with reference to UAV platforms. First, the CNN was briefly discussed along with other networks. The pertinent problems and challenges when such network(s) are deployed on-board UAV were also highlighted. Later in a separate section, supervised algorithms and corresponding developed models were presented in detail along with their performance parameters. Unsupervised algorithms were also investigated for situations and applications involving UAVs. This followed a detailed discussion on object detection and classification as a part of learning and how and what different approaches can be used for situations such as monitoring forests, streets, roads and other aerial applications including path planning, disaster management and machine control in case of UAV motion control failures. However, there are challenges reported in this direction since UAV autonomous operations suffer from limitations such as restricted weight, size and power consumption on-board a UAV—caused mainly by the current sensor and battery technology. Another limitation is caused by communication ability (or limited bandwidth) to transmit large amounts of data.

Training parameters and issues were discussed in detail. How weights are initialized in deep learning approaches, which convolution methods pertinent to feature extraction are possible, and which activation functions and pooling methods are available for such learning approaches. The variation depends on simplicity, speed and depth of training. How this scenario can be optimized to improve accuracy was also discussed. A number of benchmark datasets that can be used for the training of different deep learning networks were highlighted for purposes such as object (i.e., face, people, vehicle, buildings, roads) detection, human action recognition, multiple object tracking, etc. Various frameworks that have been developed to implement deep learning algorithms on different platforms for training and learning were also discussed in detail.

In order to determine the robustness and compare the performance of various learning approaches, different quantitative metrics such as accuracy, precision, recall and overall quality were discussed that employ values such as true positive, true negative, false positive, and false negative. Trade-off, random and interpolation curves were also highlighted to determine accuracy.

Lack of theoretical understanding exists to explain why some deep learning architecture perform better than others. Some efforts in the literature have been reported that investigate unsupervised learning since unlabeled data are becoming increasingly economical and technologically less expensive. Other problems exist in real-world applications that involve high-dimensional state spaces that turn problems intractable using current approaches. This area still remains a challenge.

The applications that involve UAV supervision and planning require complex representations, require a labelled dataset. The combination of UAV platform and deep learning techniques that involve extraction of useful information on-board UAV platforms still present a challenge as resources needed are hard to manage using the current state of technology. This challenge limits building reactive behavior embedded systems. More work needs to be done to develop efficient learning architecture.

References

[1] J. Han, D. Zhang, G. Cheng, L. Guo, and J. Ren, "Object detection in optical remote sensing images based on weakly supervised learning and high-level feature learning," *IEEE Trans. Geosci. Remote Sens.*, 53, 3325–3337, 2015.
[2] J. Tang, C. Deng, G.-B. Huang, and B. Zhao, "Compressed-domain ship detection on spaceborne optical image using deep neural network and extreme learning machine," *IEEE Trans. Geosci. Remote Sens.*, 53, 1174–1185, 2015.

[3]   J. Wang, J. Song, M. Chen, and Z. Yang, "Road network extraction: a neural-dynamic framework based on deep learning and a finite state machine," *Int. J. Remote Sens.*, 36, 3144–3169, 2015.

[4]   A. Krizhevsky, I. Sutskever, and G. E. Hinton, *ImageNet Classification with Deep Convolutional Neural Networks.* Curran Associates, Inc.; 2012.

[5]   Y. LeCun, Y. Bengio, and G. Hinton, "Deep learning", *Nature*, 521, 436, 2015.

[6]   Q. Memon, and S. Khoja, "RFID–based Patient Tracking for Regional Collaborative Healthcare," *Int. J. Comput. Appl. Technol.*, 45(4), 231–244, 2012.

[7]   Z. Ali, and Q. Memon, "Time delay tracking for multiuser synchronization in CDMA networks," *J. Networks*, 8(9), 1929–1935, 2013.

[8]   Q. Memon, Smarter health-care collaborative network, *Building Next-Generation Converged Networks: Theory and Practice*, 451–476, 2013.

[9]   A. Graves, "Generating sequences with recurrent neural networks," arXiv [Preprint]. arXiv:1308.0850, 2013.

[10]   R. Sarikaya, G. E. Hinton, and A. Deoras, "Application of deep belief networks for natural language understanding," *IEEE/ACM Trans. Audio Speech Lang. Process.*, 22, 778–784, 2014, doi: 10.1109/TASLP.2014.230 3296.

[11]   A.-R. Mohamed, G. E. Dahl, and G. Hinton, "Acoustic modeling using deep belief networks," *IEEE Trans. Audio Speech Lang. Process.*, 20, 14–22. 2011, doi: 10.1109/TASL.2011.2109382.

[12]   M. K. K. Leung, H. Y. Xiong, L. J. Lee, and B. J. Frey, "Deep learning of the tissue-regulated splicing code," *Bioinformatics*, 30, 121–129, 2014, doi: 10.1093/bioinformatics/btu277.

[13]   B. Alipanahi, A. Delong, M. T. Weirauch, and B. J. Frey, "Predicting the sequence specificities of DNA-and RNA-binding proteins by deep learning," *Nat. Biotechnol.*, 33, 831–838, 2015, doi: 10.1038/n bt.3300.

[14]   S. Zhang, J. Zhou, H. Hu, *et al.*, "A deep learning framework for modeling structural features of rna-binding protein targets," *Nucleic Acids Res.*, 43, e32, 2015. doi:10.1093/nar/gkv1025.

[15]   W. Zhang, X. Sun, H. Wang, and K. Fu, "A generic discriminative part-based model for geospatial object detection in optical remote sensing images". *ISPRS J. Photogramm. Remote Sens.*, 99, 30–44, 2015.

[16]   Y. Zhang, B. Du, and L. Zhang, "A sparse representation-based binary hypothesis model for target detection in hyperspectral images". *IEEE Trans. Geosci. Remote Sens.*, 53, 1346–1354, 2015.

[17]   R. Kumar, and M. Geetha, "Deep learning model: emotion recognition from continuous action video," In *Data Science: Theory, Analysis, and Applications*, 305–322, 2019.

[18]   S. Pal, S. Shaw, T. Saurabh, Y. Kumar, and S. Chakraborty, "A Study and Analysis of an Emotion Classification and State Transition System in Brain Computer Interfacing," In *Data Science: Theory, Analysis, and Applications*, 225–248, 2019.

[19]   A. Abubakar, H. Ugail, A. M. Bukar, and K. M. Smith, "Discrimination of healthy skin, superficial epidermal burns, and full-thickness burns from 2D-colored images using machine learning," In *Data Science: Theory, Analysis, and Applications*, 201–223, 2019.

[20]   Y. Chen, N. González-Prelcic, and R. W. Heath, "Collision-Free UAV Navigation with a Monocular Camera Using Deep Reinforcement Learning," *IEEE 30th International Workshop on Machine Learning for Signal Processing*, Espoo, Finland, 2020, pp. 1–6, doi:10.1109/MLSP49062.2020. 9231577.

[21]   L. He, N. Aouf, J. F. Whidborne, and B. Song, "Integrated moment-based LGMD and deep reinforcement learning for UAV obstacle avoidance," *IEEE International Conference on Robotics and Automation*, Paris, France, 2020, pp. 7491–7497, doi: 10.1109/ICRA40945.2020.9197152.

[22]   G. Christoph, and A. Kuchler, "Learning task-dependent distributed representations by backpropagation through structure," *IEEE International Conference on Neural Networks*, 1, 347–352, 1996.

[23]   Goodfellow, I. Bengio, Y. and Courville, A., *Deep Learning*, The MIT Press, 2016.

[24]   C. G. Turhan, and H. S. Bilge, "Recent trends in deep generative models: A review," in International Conference on Computer Science and Engineering (UBMK); 2018, pp. 574–579.

[25]   S. Ren, K. He, R. Girshick, and J. Sun, "Faster R-CNN: towards real-time object detection with region proposal networks," *Advances in Neural Information Processing Systems*, 28, 91–99, 2015.

[26]   F. Hu, G.-S. Xia, J. Hu, and L. Zhang, "Transferring deep convolutional neural networks for the scene classification of high-resolution remote sensing imagery," *Remote Sensing*, 7(11), 14680–14707, 2015.

[27]   A. Giusti, J. Guzzi, D. C. Ciresan, *et al.*, "A machine learning approach to visual perception of forest trails for mobile robots," *IEEE Robotics and Automation Letters*, 1(2), 661–667, 2016.

[28]   I. J. Goodfellow, J. Pouget-Abadie, M. Mirza, *et al.*, Generative adversarial nets. *Advances in Neural Information Processing Systems*; The MIT Press: Cambridge, MA, USA, 2014, pp. 2672–2680.

[29]   M. I. Tariq, N. A. Memon, S. Ahmed, *et al.*, "A Review of Deep Learning Security and Privacy Defensive Techniques", *Mobile Information Systems*, 2020, Article ID: 6535834, https://doi.org/10.1155/2020/6535834.

[30]   H. Yang and S. Qu, "Real-time vehicle detection and counting in complex traffic scenes using background subtraction model with low-rank decomposition," *IET Intelligent Transport Systems*, 12(1), 75–85, 2018, doi: 10.1049/iet-its.2017.0047.

[31]   N.A. Mandellos, I. Keramitsoglou, and C.T. KiranoudisA "Background subtraction algorithm for detecting and tracking vehicles" *Expert Systems with Applications*, 38(3), 1619–1631, 2011.

[32]   R. Chew, J. Rineer, R. Beach, *et al.*, "Deep Neural Networks and Transfer Learning for Food Crop Identification in UAV Images," *Drones*, 4(1), 7, 2020. https://doi.org/10.3390/drones4010007.

[33] O. Csillik, J. Cherbini, R. Johnson, A. Lyons, and M. Kelly, "Identification of Citrus Trees from Unmanned Aerial Vehicle Imagery Using Convolutional Neural Networks," *Drones*, 2(4), 39, 2018. https://doi.org/10.3390/drones2040039.

[34] C. Kyrkou and T. Theocharides, "Deep-Learning-Based Aerial Image Classification for Emergency Response Applications Using Unmanned Aerial Vehicles," IEEE/CVF Conference on Computer Vision and Pattern Recognition Workshops, Long Beach, CA, 2019, pp. 517–525.

[35] C. G. Muller, L. Chilvers, Z. Barker, *et al.*, "Aerial VHF tracking of wildlife using an unmanned aerial vehicle (UAV): comparing efficiency of yellow-eyed penguin (Megadyptes antipodes) nest location methods," *Wildlife Research*, 46(2), 145–153, 2019, https://doi.org/10.1071/WR17147.

[36] P. S. Bithas, E. T. Michailidis, N. Nomikos, D. Vouyioukas, A. G. Kanatas, "A Survey on Machine-Learning Techniques for UAV-Based Communications," *Sensors (Basel)*. 2019; 19(23):5170, http://doi:10.3390/s19235170.

[37] A. Krizhevsky, I. Sutskever, and G. E. Hinton, "Imagenet classification with deep convolutional neural networks," in *Advances in Neural Information Processing Systems*, 1097–1105, 2012b.

[38] K. Simonyan, and A. Zisserman, "Very deep convolutional networks for large-scale image recognition, " arXiv [Preprint]. arXiv:1409.1556, 2014.

[39] C. Szegedy, W. Liu, Y. Jia, *et al.*, "Going deeper with convolutions," in 2015 IEEE Conference on Computer Vision and Pattern Recognition (CVPR). IEEE; 2015, 1–9.

[40] K. He, X. Zhang, S. Ren, and J. Sun, "Deep residual learning for image recognition," in Proceedings of the IEEE Conference on Computer Vision and Pattern Recognition, 2016, 770–778.

[41] A. M. Cheriyadat, "Unsupervised Feature Learning for Aerial Scene Classification," *IEEE Transactions on Geoscience and Remote Sensing*, 52(1), 439–451, 2014, doi:10.1109/TGRS.2013.2241444.

[42] Zhang T, Hu X, Xiao J, and Zhang G, "A Machine Learning Method for Vision-Based Unmanned Aerial Vehicle Systems to Understand Unknown Environments," *Sensors (Basel)*, 20(11), 3245, 2020, doi:10.3390/s20113245.

[43] Z. Ren, J. Yan, B. Ni, B. Liu, X. Yang, and H. Zha, "Unsupervised deep learning for optical flow estimation," Proceedings of the Thirty First AAAI Conference on Artificial Intelligence, February 2017, pp. 1495–1501.

[44] J. Choi, G. Sharma, M. Chandraker, and J. B. Huang: Unsupervised and semi-supervised domain Adaptation for Action Recognition from Drones," IEEE/CVF Winter Conference on Applications of Computer Vision, 2020, pp. 1717–1726.

[45] J. Delmerico, E. Mueggler, J. Nitsch, and D. Scaramuzza, "Active autonomous aerial exploration for ground robot path planning," *IEEE Robotics and Automation Letters*, 2(2), 664–671, 2017.

[46] W. Gao, D. Hsu, W. S. Lee, S. Shen, and K. Subramanian, "Intention-net: Integrating planning and deep learning for goal-directed autonomous navigation," 1st Annual Conference. Robot Learn., 2017.

[47] T. Taisho, L. Enfu, T. Kanji, and S. Naotoshi, "Mining visual experience for fast cross-view UAV localization," Annual IEEE/SICE International Symposium on System Integration, 2015, pp. 375–380.

[48] F. Aznar, M. Pujol, and R. Rizo, "Visual navigation for UAV with map references using ConvNets," Advances in Artificial Intelligence, vol. 9868, Lecture Notes in Computer Science, Springer; 2016, pp. 13–22.

[49] F. Sadeghi, and S. Levine, "Real single-image flight without a single real image," arXiv [Preprint]. arXiv:1611.04201, 2017.

[50] S. Li, T. Liu, C. Zhang, D.-Y. Yeung, and S. Shen, "Learning unmanned aerial vehicle control for autonomous target following", *Twenty-Seventh International Joint Conference on Artificial Intelligence*, 2017, pp. 4936–4942.

[51] M. Akhloufi, S. Arola, and A. Bonnet, "Drones chasing drones: Reinforcement learning and deep search area proposal", *Drones*, 3(3), 58, 2019.

[52] F. Yang, H. Fan, P. Chu, E. Blasch, and H. Ling, "Clustered object detection in aerial images," in *Proceedings of the IEEE/CVF International Conference on Computer Vision (ICCV)*, 2019, pp. 8311–8320.

[53] M. Y. Yang, W. Liao, X. Li, Y. Cao, and B. Rosenhahn, "Vehicle detection in aerial images," *Photogramm. Eng. Remote Sensing*, 85(4), 297–304, 2019.

[54] H. Long, Y. Chung, Z. Liu, and S. Bu, "Object detection in aerial images using feature fusion deep networks," *IEEE Access*, 7, 30980–30990, 2019, doi:10.1109/ACCESS.2019.2903422.

[55] J. Shen, N. Liu, H. Sun, X. Tao, and Q. Li, "Vehicle detection in aerial images based on hyper feature map in deep convolutional network," *Multimedia Tools and Applications*, 76(20), 21651–21663, 2017.

[56] Y. Bazi, and F. Melgani, "Convolutional SVM networks for object detection in UAV imagery," *IEEE Trans. Geosci. Remote Sensing*, 56(6), 3107–3118, 2018, doi:10.1109/TGRS.2018.2790926.

[57] M. D. Bah, A. Hafiane, and R. Canals, "Deep learning with unsupervised data labeling for weeds detection on UAV images", arXiv [Preprint]. arXiv:1805.12395, 2018.

[58] J. Xiao, S. Zhang, Y. Dai, Z. Jiang, B. Yi, and C. Xu, "Multiclass object detection in UAV images based on rotation region network," *IEEE J. Miniaturization Air Space Syst.*, 1(3), 188–196, 2020, doi:10.1109/JMASS.2020.3025970.

[59] C. Murthy, M. Hashmi, N. Bokde, and Z. Geem, "Investigations of object detection in images/videos using various deep learning techniques and embedded platforms—a comprehensive review," *Appl. Sci.*, 10, 3280, 2020.

[60] M. Mandal, L. K. Kumar, M. Singh Saran and S. K. Vipparthi, "MotionRec: a unified deep framework for moving object recognition," *IEEE Winter Conference on Applications of Computer Vision*, CO, USA, 2020, pp. 2723–2732, doi: 10.1109/WACV45572.2020.9093324.

[61] Y. Wang, X. Zhu, and B. Wu, "Automatic detection of individual oil palm trees from UAV images using HOG features and an SVM classifier," *Int. J. Remote Sensing*, 40:19, 7356–7370, 2019, doi: 10.1080/01431161.2018.1513669.

[62] T. Moranduzzo and F. Melgani, "Detecting Cars in UAV Images with a Catalog-Based Approach," *IEEE Trans. Geoscience Remote Sensing*, 52(10), 6356–6367, 2014, doi:10.1109/TGRS.2013.2296351.

[63] Y. Xu, G. Yu, Y. Wang, X. Wu, and Y. Ma, "A hybrid vehicle detection method based on Viola-Jones and HOG + SVM from UAV images," *Sensors*, 16(8), 1325, 2016.

[64] L. Wang and Z. Zhang, "Automatic detection of wind turbine blade surface cracks based on UAV-taken images," *IEEE Trans. Ind. Electronics*, 64(9), 7293–7303, 2017, doi:10.1109/TIE.2017.2682037.

[65] Q. Dong, X. Zhu, and S. Gong, "Single-label multi-class image classification by deep logistic regression," *Proceedings of the AAAI Conference on Artificial Intelligence*, 2019, pp. 3486–3493. https://doi.org/10.1609/aaai.v33i01.33013486.

[66] L. Pan, S. Pouyanfar, H. Chen, J. Qin, and S. Chen, "DeepFood: automatic multi-class classification of food ingredients using deep learning," *2017 IEEE 3rd International Conference on Collaboration and Internet Computing (CIC)*, San Jose, CA, 2017, pp. 181–189, doi: 10.1109/CIC.2017.00033.

[67] A. Jawale, "Comparison of image classification techniques: binary and multiclass using convolutional neural network and support vector machines", *INFOCOMP J. Comput. Sci.*, 18(2), 28–35, 2019.

[68] S. Hayat, S. Kun, Z. Tengtao, Y. Yu, T. Tu, and Y. Du, "A deep learning framework using convolutional neural network for multi-class object recognition," *IEEE 3rd International Conference on Image, Vision and Computing, Chongqing*, 2018, pp. 194–198, doi: 10.1109/ICIVC.2018.8492777.

[69] L. Xia, R. Zhang, L. Chen, *et al.*, "Monitor cotton budding using SVM and UAV images," *Appl. Sci.*, 9(20), 4312, 2019.

[70] B. Ma, Z. Liu, F. Jiang, Y. Yan, J. Yuan, and S. Bu, "Vehicle detection in aerial images using rotation-invariant cascaded forest," *IEEE Access*, 7, 59613–59623, 2019, doi:10.1109/ACCESS.2019.2915368.

[71] P. Refaeilzadeh, L. Tang, and H. Liu, "Cross-validation," Liu L., Özsu M.T. (eds) *Encyclopedia of Database Systems*. Springer, Boston, MA; 2009. https://doi.org/10.1007/978-0-387-39940-9_565.

[72] A. M. Saxe, P. W. Koh, Z. Chen, M. Bhand, B. Suresh, and A. Y. Ng, "On random weights and unsupervised feature learning", *28th International Conference on Machine Learning*, 2011, pp. 1089–1096.

[73] Veenu, and P. Chandra, "Training of sigmoidal FFANN using zero weight initialization and gaussian learning rates", *International Conference on Computer Technology and Science*, 2012, pp. 29–33.

[74] S. Ioffe and C. Szegedy "Batch Normalization: Accelerating Deep Network Training by Reducing Internal Covariate Shift", *32nd International Conference on Machine Learning*, 2015, pp. 448–456.

[75] J. L. Ba, J. R. Kiros, and G. E. Hinton, "Layer normalization," arXiv [Preprint]. arXiv:1607.06450, 2016.

[76] T. Salimans, and D. P. Kingma, "Weight normalization: a simple reparameterization to accelerate training of deep neural networks," arXiv [Preprint]. arXiv:1602.07868, 2016.

[77]   Y. Wu, and K. He "Group normalization," *Int. J. Comput. Vis.*, 128, 742–755, 2020. https://doi.org/10.1007/s11263-019-01198-w.

[78]   F. Yu, and V. Koltun, "Multi-scale context aggregation by dilated convolutions," arXiv [Preprint]. arXiv:1511.07122, 2015.

[79]   V. Dumoulin, and F. Visin "A guide to convolution arithmetic for deep learning," arXiv [Preprint]. arXiv:1603.07285, 2016.

[80]   H. W. F. Yeung, J. Hou, X. Chen, J. Chen, Z. Chen, and Y. Y. Chung, "Light field spatial super-resolution using deep efficient spatial-angular separable convolution," *IEEE Trans. Image Process.*, 28(5), 2319–2330, 2019.

[81]   F. Chollet, "Xception: deep learning with depth wise separable convolutions," *IEEE Conference on Computer Vision and Pattern Recognition*, Honolulu, 2017, pp. 1800–1807, doi: 10.1109/CVPR.2017.195.

[82]   N. Chigozie, I. Winifred, G. Anthony, and M. Stephen. "Activation functions: comparison of trends in practice and research for deep learning," arXiv [Preprint]. arXiv:1811.03378, 2020.

[83]   S. Narayan, "The generalized sigmoid activation function: competitive supervised learning", *Inf. Sci.*, 99(1–2), 69–82, 1997. https://doi.org/10.1016/S0020-0255(96)00200-9.

[84]   H. Ide, and T. Kurita, "Improvement of learning for CNN with ReLU activation by sparse regularization," 2017 International Joint Conference on Neural Networks (IJCNN), 2017, pp. 2684–2691, doi: 10.1109/IJCNN.2017.7966185.

[85]   L. Nanni, A. Lumini, S. Ghidoni, and G. Maguolo, "Stochastic selection of activation layers for convolutional neural networks," *Sensors (Basel, Switzerland)*, 20(6), 1626, 2020, doi:10.3390/s20061626.

[86]   S. Ruder, "An overview of gradient descent optimization algorithms," arXiv [Preprint]. arXiv:1609.04747, 2016.

[87]   L. Bottou, "Stochastic gradient descent tricks." *Neural networks: Tricks of the trade*. Springer, Berlin, Heidelberg, 2012, pp. 421–436.

[88]   H. Robbins and S. Monro, "A stochastic approximation method," *Ann. Math. Statist.*, 22(3), 400–407, 1951.

[89]   A. Botev, L. Guy, and B. David, "Nesterov's accelerated gradient and momentum as approximations to regularized update descent." *IEEE International Joint Conference on Neural Networks*, 2017, pp. 1899–1903.

[90]   J. Duchi, E. Hazan, and Y. Singer, "Adaptive subgradient methods for online learning and stochastic optimization," *J. Machine Learn. Res.*, 12, 2121–2159, 2011.

[91]   W. Aguilar, M. Luna, J. Moya, V. Abad, H. Parra, and H. Ruiz, "Pedestrian detection for UAVs using cascade classifiers with mean shift," *IEEE 11th International Conference on Semantic Computing (ICSC)*, San Diego, January 2017, pp. 509–514.

[92]   H. Hsu, and K. Chen, "DroneFace: an open dataset for drone research," *8th ACM on Multimedia Systems Conference*, Taipei, 20–23 June 2017; 187–192.

[93]   I. Kalra, M. Singh, S. Nagpal, R. Singh, M. Vatsa, and P. Sujit, "DroneSURF: Benchmark dataset for drone-based face recognition," *14th IEEE International Conference on Automatic Face & Gesture Recognition*, Lille, 2019, pp. 1–7.

[94] M. Mueller, N. Smith, and B. Ghanem, "A benchmark and simulator for UAV tracking," *Proceedings of the European Conference on Computer Vision*, Amsterdam, 2016, pp. 445–461.

[95] D. Du, P. Zhu, L. Wen, *et al.,* "VisDrone-DET2019: The vision meets drone object detection in image challenge results," *IEEE International Conference on Computer Vision Workshops*, Long Beach, June 2019.

[96] D. Du, Y. Qi, H.Yu, *et al.,* "The unmanned aerial vehicle benchmark: object detection and tracking," *European Conference on Computer Vision*. Springer, Cham; 2018; pp. 375–391.

[97] E. Lygouras, N. Santavas, A. Taitzoglou, K. Tarchanidis, A. Mitropoulos, and A. Gasteratos "Unsupervised human detection with an embedded vision system on a fully autonomous UAV for search and rescue operations," *Sensors*, 19(16), 3542, 2019.

[98] I. Bozcan, and E. Kayacan, "AU-AIR: a multi-modal unmanned aerial vehicle dataset for low altitude traffic surveillance," *IEEE International Conference on Robotics and Automation*, 2020, pp. 8504–8510.

[99] A. G. Perera, Y. W. Law, T. T. Ogunwa, and J. Chahl, "A multiview point outdoor dataset for human action recognition," *IEEE Trans. Hum. Mach. Syst.,* 2020.

[100] G. S. Xia, X. Bai, J. Ding, *et al.,* "DOTA: A large-scale dataset for object detection in aerial images," *IEEE Conference on Computer Vision and Pattern Recognition*, 18–22 June 2018, pp. 3974–3983.

[101] M. M. Cheng, Z. Zhang, W. Y. Lin, and P. Torr, "BING: Binarized normed gradients for objectness estimation at 300fps," *IEEE Conference on Computer Vision and Pattern Recognition*, Columbus, OH, 24–27 June 2014, pp. 3286–3293.

[102] K. Li, G. Wan, G. Cheng, L. Meng, and J. Han, "Object detection in optical remote sensing images: a survey and a new benchmark." *ISPRS J. Photogramm. Remote Sens.,* 159, 296–307, 2020.

[103] V. Mnih, and G.E. Hinton, "Learning to detect roads in high-resolution aerial images," *Proceedings of the European Conference on Computer Vision*, Crete, 5–11 September 2010, pp. 210–223.

[104] Y. Wang, C. Ding, Z. Li, *et al.,* "Towards ultra-high performance and energy efficiency of deep learning systems: an algorithm-hardware co-optimization framework," *Thirty-Second AAAI Conference on Artificial Intelligence*, 2018, pp. 4235–4243.

[105] Y. Zhang, and Q. Yang, "An overview of multi-task learning," *National Science Review*, 5, 30–43, 2018.

[106] L. Kaiser, A. N. Gomez, N. Shazeer, *et al.,* "One model to learn them all," arXiv [Preprint]. arXiv:1706.05137, 2017.

[107] V. N. Murthy, V. Singh, T. Chen, R. Manmatha, and D. Comaniciu, "Deep decision network for multi-class image classification," *IEEE Conference on Computer Vision and Pattern Recognition*, Las Vegas, 2016, pp. 2240–2248, doi: 10.1109/CVPR.2016.246.

[108] C. Kyrkou, G. Plastiras, T. Theocharides, S. I. Venieris, and C. Bouganis, "DroNet: Efficient convolutional neural network detector for real-time UAV applications," *Design, Automation & Test in Europe Conference & Exhibition (DATE)*, Dresden, 2018, pp. 967–972, doi: 10.23919/DATE.2018.8342149.

[109] C. Kyrkou and T. Theocharides, "Deep-learning-based aerial image classification for emergency response applications using unmanned aerial vehicles," *IEEE/CVF Conference on Computer Vision and Pattern Recognition Workshops*, Long Beach, 2019, pp. 517–525, doi: 10.1109/CVPRW.2019.00077.

[110] J. Deng, Z. Shi, and C. Zhuo, "Energy-efficient real-time uav object detection on embedded platforms," *IEEE Trans. Computer-Aided Design Integr. Circ. Syst.*, vol. 39, no. 10, pp. 3123–3127, Oct. 2020, doi: 10.1109/TCAD.2019.2957724.

[111] E. Zhang, and Y. Zhang, "Eleven point precision–recall curve." In: Liu L., Özsu M.T. (eds) *Encyclopedia of Database Systems*. Springer, Boston; 2009. https://doi.org/10.1007/978-0-387-39940-9_481.

[112] R. Padilla, S. L. Netto, and E. A. B. da Silva, "A survey on performance metrics for object-detection algorithms," *International Conference on Systems, Signals and Image Processing*, Niterói, 2020, pp. 237–242, http://doi: 10.1109/IWSSIP48289.2020.9145130.

[113] F. Chollet. "Keras: Deep learning library for theano and tensorflow," https://keras.io/k, vol. 7, no. 8, T1.

[114] TensorFlow—an open-source software library for machine intelligence. https://www.tensorflow.org/.

[115] Caffe—deep learning framework by Berkeley Artificial Intelligence Research, http://caffe.berkeleyvision.org/.

[116] PyTorch—deep learning framework that puts python first. http://pytorch.org/.

[117] Theano. http://deeplearning.net/software/theano.

[118] Apache MXNet—a flexible and efficient library for deep learning. https://mxnet.apache.org/.

Chapter 16

Machine learning methodology toward identification of mature citrus fruits

Veena Nayak[1], Sushma P. Holla[1], K.M. Akshayakumar[1] and C. Gururaj[1]

Abstract

The citrus fruits cultivation is done throughout the world in a large quantity. The market requires good quality of fruits. However, harvesting using manual methods can be time-consuming, inefficient and also labor-intense process. The labor cost is increasing day by day. People are working to find an efficient method of agriculture where the investment is less and the profit is more. Many research studies have been carried out on both software and hardware part of this automatic mature fruit identification. We are trying to give a software solution in our project with the approach of machine learning.

Due to changes in sunlight exposure, weather condition, position randomness of fruits and many other conditions, the images are changed dramatically. In this project, we capture the images of citrus trees. Our objective of covering many natural variant conditions was achieved by collecting images of citrus fruits for all the possible conditions. Using image processing techniques and with the use of multi-class support vector machine, the fruits are segmented the feed-forward neural network is used to locate the fruit in three dimensions. The result of this would be the detection of fruits and clusters of fruits on the images.

Key Words: Machine learning; support vector machine; feed-forward neural network; shape features; color extraction; graphical user interface.

16.1 Introduction

The research work starts with an introduction chapter wherein the basics of farming are covered. The next chapter deals with the relevant literature survey. The third

[1]Department of Electronics and Telecommunication Engineering, BMS College of Engineering, Visvesvaraya Technological University, Bengaluru, India

chapter deals with the implementation aspects of the research. The next chapter includes a detailed result analysis followed by the conclusion chapter.

16.1.1   Harvesting

Harvesting is the process of removing a ripe crop from where it was growing and moving that crop to a secure location for processing, consumption or storage. The widely used techniques for harvesting are

- Manual harvesting: This is a time-consuming and a laborious process.
- Mechanical harvesting: This causes damage to fruits,
- Robotic harvesting: This gives more production with less labor.

Harvesting can be a labor-intensive process when done with minimum mechanization, especially in small farms. Thus, by using farm automation techniques, the efficiency of seeding and harvesting is improved.

16.1.2   Farm automation

It can also be called as "Smart Farming." It is nothing but the usage of robotics in the farm. The main advantages are increased efficiency as it reduces time consumption when compared with the traditional farming, reduced environmental footprint and more productivity. It also proves to be cost-effective in the long run even though initially we may have to invest a large amount of money.

16.1.3   Fruit detection

Fruits detection means detecting each fruit from the images. There are changes in their location and size of each of the instances of fruits in the image, as seen in Figure 16.1.

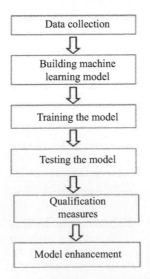

Figure 16.1   Flow chart of the proposed method

In the image, the fruit location identification is the main issue. We have taken up the citrus fruits for the same. The other issues include the change in illumination due to different camera positions, image digitization, etc. Color and shape of the fruit in the image play an important role in this process.

16.1.4   Proposed method

Figure 16.1 shows the flow chart of the method adopted.

16.1.4.1   Data collection

Data collection is the process of gathering and measuring information from countless different sources. In our project, we have collected images of matured citrus fruit which consists of orange and lemon fruit. This is the most important and primary step of the project. Various kinds of data set are collected using different means. The pictures clicked from various angles are taken for the project. It also involves the picture taken during the different times of the day.

16.1.4.2   Building the machine learning model

Machine learning models are nothing but the mathematical representation of real-world processes. Building the model takes the real-world data before the training which is nothing but the images of matured citrus fruit. This training is explained in the next step. There are mainly two model types: (1) classification model and (2) regression model.

There are many algorithms to build a model by the approach of machine learning.

1. Neural network: This algorithm resembles the way the human brain works, thus the name neural. It adapts itself to the changing input.
2. K-neighbor network (KNN): It is mainly used for classification.
3. Support vector machine (SVM): It is an ML model that uses the classification algorithm.

16.1.4.3   Training the model

Training the model means passing the algorithm with the real-world data. In this process, the algorithm learns the pattern of the data. The output of the model is used to make predictions. This process is also called "learning." Training is done only after we set parameters and define the model. We train the system by feeding the desired data. Training is a very crucial stage as the further steps are dependent on this. Artificial neural networks are nothing but simple electronic networks which are proposed based on the actual neural system of the human body. This works by recording one at a time and learning takes place through comparing the classification of record every time, which is arbitrary, with the actual classification.

16.1.4.4   Testing the model

Once the network is trained, it can be tested with new images which will be stored in the testing folder called citrus. It is done to check the system's precision or accuracy. We test the system for various conditions, thus ensuring that the system is compatible with any kind of data. The testing is done by knowing the limitations of the algorithm and requirements of the results to be obtained.

16.1.4.5   Qualification measures

These are some of the parameters which are determined to find out the efficiency of the system. In this process, if the model is not able to find the results properly, then by using trial-and-error method or another method is used to find the result accurately. Also, this process helps in improving efficiency execution time. Some of the parameters are accuracy, efficiency, sensitivity and specificity.

16.1.4.6   Model enhancement

It is the analysis of the entire process. The main purpose is to optimize the model built. The models must be optimized for efficient working. Hence, this process plays an important role. This includes performance measures, cross-validation of the model. Performance measures include the reasons for a specific problem and how to overcome problems. Cross-validation is an advanced approach with separating the dataset as training as well as testing dataset.

16.2   Literature survey

The survey on many related technical papers is given below and the same when implemented leads to an efficient system.

Green citrus fruit identification in different light conditions are discussed in [1]. They have explained the procedure of extracting circular objects using circular Hough transform (CHT) and removing false positives using SVM classification and text features. The system was built using MATLAB® and OpenCV, and data was collected manually by using a digital camera. Around 81.7% efficiency was achieved after removing false positives.

This research indicates the efficacy of using robots for identification of citrus fruits and branches under natural scene using various machine learning algorithms such as Support Vector Machine. Using this methodology, an efficient system was implemented which consisted of a color CCD camera and a PC. Researchers [2] had used color cameras due to the advancement of sensor and computer technology; also, a global thresholding approach was used to separate objects from the background. The multi-class support vector machine (SVM) is used to segment the images of citrus, branches, leaves and other background. From the 87 images, the performance of this algorithm was 92.4% as well as the branches whose diameter are more than 5 pixels are identified.

The paper on plant detection of intact tomato fruits [3] using image analysis and machine learning methods is all about intact tomato fruit using IP and machine learning. The experiment was conducted using a conventional RGB digital camera by the approach of machine learning. It consists of three steps. The method did not require any threshold value adjustment. It involved part-by-part fruit detection.

The work maturity indicators [4] and citrus fruit quality determine the maturity stage of citrus fruit based on acid content, juice content, etc. The authors conducted maturity indices in some parts of the world for sweet orange, lemon and grapefruit.

The paper detection of red tomato on plants [5] using image processing techniques is mainly about feeding the information to robots to pick up the red, ripened tomatoes from the plants. Under normal lighting conditions, pictures of tomatoes were captured. To distinguish red tomatoes from non-red ones, four steps were taken into consideration. The four steps of this algorithm are removing image background, removing noise of the image captured, separation of tomatoes touching one another using watershed algorithm and finally detecting red ones using the concept of region growing. It was found that the parts exposed to the sunlight as close to white color so, these parts of the fruit were taken separately. Later these extracted parts and the main area obtained after the removal of background were compared, the tomatoes were concluded as red if the extracted area was more than 90% of the main area of the tomato. The accuracy was around 82%.

A system for feature extraction using computer vision which is fast and more accurate is proposed in [6]. The author worked on reducing errors caused due to positioning, scaling and orientation and developing new machine learning classifiers. The feature extractors such as SMB feature extractor and MAM feature extractor were used. Food shape classification model consists of feature extractor and the classifier. The algorithm was tested on corn kernels, almonds and animal crackers. The results showed that accuracy and speed were at its best when the MAM feature extractor was used.

The images used in paper [7] are of particular citrus variety, taken manually from a farm using a particular camera, during different duration of day, different weather conditions and at different light ambiance. The system implemented uses cross correlation-based fruit position detection, filtering fruit detection using color analysis and CHT and false-positive removal using texture and the number of fruits is determined as the final output. The image resizing technique of bilinear interpolation is used to increase system efficiency. The combined algorithm was able to achieve around 84.4% accuracy.

The pomegranate fruit grading overview is given in [8]. The paper gives a brief about different pomegranate varieties, different possible classifiers like SVM, fuzzy logic and ANN. It explains the importance of contrast stretching and histogram equalization in pre-processing stage and also about the color and shape features extraction. The paper also gives review on around 7 more papers related automatic fruit grading.

The work [9] talks about orange fruit quality assessment using GLCM feature extraction and SVM classifier. The system discussed in the paper uses the GLCM algorithm for feature extraction and threshold-based segmentation for fruit and leaf separation. The system has taken consideration of many cases such as uneven brightness, fruit covered with barriers likes twigs, leaves and other fruits and also the irregular shading. It also compares result from naive Bayes and SVM classifier using accuracy, execution, and sensitivity and specification analysis and proves that SVM improves result about by 8%–10%.

The paper [10] mainly focuses on the quality evaluation of orange fruit. Some of the steps involved in segmentation are pre-processing, description and procedure, texture features. The gray level co-occurrence matrix (GLCM) algorithm is used for texture features of image. Also, a bilateral filter is used to remove noise from the image. The parameters such as accuracy, execution time, sensitivity and specificity are compared. Overall there is an 8%–10% improvement in this classifier.

In [11], the method artificial intelligence is used to classify the diseases and pattern matching. The steps like segmentation, feature extraction is also included.

In [12], the author has written about the use of IOT in agriculture. Wireless sensor networks and its uses are also discussed here. An idea has been proposed where the smartphones are used to monitor the farm.

In [13], authors gave given detailed explanation for feature extraction in the process of detecting brain abnormalities. The MRI images are pre-processed and then segmented using K-means clustering. Around nine GLCM or texture features and three shape features are extracted to differentiate between malignant tumor, benign tumor and normal brain MRI.

The work on [14,15] content-based image retrieval to retrieve the required images is implemented. The algorithm combines effort of color and texture feature extractions. The color features such as mean, standard deviation and skewness, texture features such as energy and entropy and precision of algorithm are calculated. The proposed system was able to achieve 98.% accuracy in image retrieval.

The paper [16] gives the image matching techniques using segmentation and different feature extraction techniques. The paper [17] gives the basic image organization that help to encrypt or decrypt the images using hybrid techniques.

The paper [18] describes the shape features of multi-dimensional objects which is used in the shape feature extraction for machine learning model training.

16.3   Implementation

Automation of mature citrus fruit detection is done using MATLAB software. The citrus fruits are detected automatically from the digital images. The images stored in folder named dataset are used for training machine learning model separately for fruit and leaf. The model is built on two layers, using support vector machine (SVM) on one layer and feed-forward neural network (FFNN) [19] on another layer. The two-layer SVM is used to separate fruit and leaf and also to separate fruit from the background. The FFNN is used to locate a single or bunch of citrus fruit in the image. The algorithms were built separately and combined together to have a single working model.

The model was built step by step and efficient autonomous system was built. Each stage of the program was tried with the trial-and-error method to have more accurate model for fruit detection. We have tried to cover many cases from the natural scenes of the fruit farm. For example, single or multiple fruits in a frame, different parts of a day, different weather conditions, different sun light ambiance and different color variations in the matured citrus fruit. The cases were fruits are covered by twigs, leaves, other fruits, and shades from different objects are also considered.

The implementation of the discussed system can be explained using a flow or block diagram. Any machine learning project general includes stages like data collection, data segmentation into test and training set, building the machine learning model, training the model, testing the model and finally model enhancement after qualification measures. These stages are already explained in the introduction part. Now we shall discuss the implementation of these steps in a more detailed manner and more specific to the project of automating mature citrus fruit.

The block diagram of the implementation shown in Figure 16.2 includes stages such as image acquisition, pre-processing, feature extraction [20], trained database

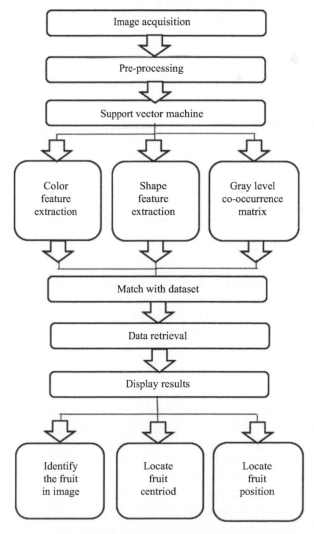

Figure 16.2   Block diagram of project implementation

creation, matching with the trained database, retrieving of training database and finally displaying the required result. The below block diagram can be referred for more understanding of the flow of these steps in the implementation.

16.3.1   *Image acquisition and data collection*

An image is usually defined as a two-dimensional function $f(x,y)$, where (x,y) is a co-ordinate in a 2D space and intensity is given by I. The co-ordinate position is nothing but pixel. Pixel is the smallest unit of an image that can also be called a pel or picture element. The main aim of image acquisition is to convert an optical image or real-world data into an array of numerical data which can be manipulated later in a computer.

The image captured will be in RGB format, later it is converted to grayscale image followed by the binary image. The former method is also called image acquisition where an image is retrieved from source mostly from the hardware-based source. The image obtained in this step is completely unprocessed. Image acquisition plays an important role as further processes are dependent on the same.

16.3.2   *Pre-processing*

This step is for the improvement of the image for the further process. Pre-processing involves many steps, such as converting the RGB image into grayscale, determining the threshold value of the image, converting the grayscaled image into the binary image, noise removal or removal of the lower pixels, background removal, morphological operations and many more. These pre-processing steps have a major role in the whole project as it determines the efficient identification of mature citrus fruit.

16.3.2.1   Resizing the image

It is the first step in the pre-processing stage. The main requirement is that image should have the uniform aspect ratio. Thus, we resize the image to the dimension 256 * 256 maintaining the desired aspect ratio. The resizing of the image will not alter any visual effect of the image instead the size will become small. One of the main reasons of resizing is for reducing efforts in processing.

16.3.2.2   RGB to gray conversion

The image in the RGB model is represented as the $M \times N \times 3$ matrix of color pixels, where the third dimensions refer to the color component, namely, red, green and blue. Similarly, the grayscale image is represented as only $M \times N$ matrix. Conversion from RGB to grayscale as shown from Figures 16.3 through 16.6 is done by eliminating the color component values and saturation information retaining only luminance values. In our project this conversion takes place in the function called "coloredToGray," which takes $M \times N \times 3$ RGB image and returns M $\times$ N grayscale image.

The algorithm for grayscale conversion involves the following steps:

- The image is read in RGB format.
- Extracting the color component values of red, green and blue color into three different two-dimensional matrices.

Original RGB image

Figure 16.3   RGB image

Grayscale image

Figure 16.4   Grayscale image

Original RGB image

Figure 16.5   RGB image

Grayscale image

Figure 16.6 Grayscale image

- Create a new matrix with the same number of rows and columns as RGB image, containing all zeroes.
- Each pixel of the RGB model is replaced by grayscale values by using the below formula:

$$\text{Grayscale value at } (i,j) = .2989 * \text{R}(i,j) + .5870 * \text{G}(i,j) + .1140 * \text{B}(i,j); \quad (16.1)$$

16.3.2.3 Median filtering

The gray level image used to carry out 2D median filtering. The median filtering is an example of non-linear operation. This is used to reduce noise basically. This is way more effective than convolution. This function is used to pad the image with 0 s in the edges. In the median filtering, a window of predetermined slides throughout the image and each time the all the pixel values under the window replaced by the median value of all those pixels. We have tried three level of median filtering and adopted the one which gives the best result with respect to noise removal, as shown in Figure 16.7.

Even though median filtering is carried out on the grayscale image, the effect of filtering can be clearly seen in the binary level image seen in Figure 16.8.

As we can observe in Figure 16.8, the [1,1] adds up the noise to the image instead of removing. The [3,3] window removes some amount of noise, whereas [5,5] window removes most of the noise. Hence, we have adopted two-dimensional median filtering with [5,5] window size.

16.3.2.4 Background separation

This is a step where the background is differentiated from the actual fruits. The training we did in the previous steps will make the system to identify only the fruits, thus removing the background which included leaves, stems or other unnecessary part. The same is depicted in Figures 16.9 through 16.12.

Before filtering   Using [1,1] window

Using [3,3] window   Using [5,5] window

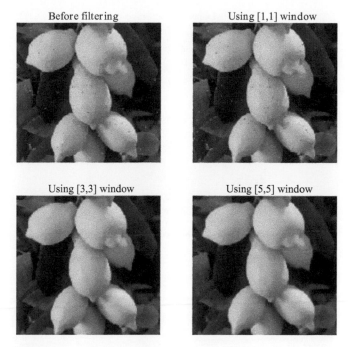

Figure 16.7   Grayscale images showing median filtering levels

Before filtering   Using [1,1] window

Using [3,3] window   Using [5,5] window

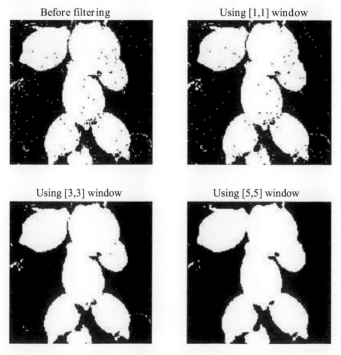

Figure 16.8   Binary images showing median filtering level

Median filtered image

Figure 16.9   Input median filtered image

Background   Fruit area

Figure 16.10   Separated background and fruit area

Median filtered image

Figure 16.11   Input median filtered image

Background   Fruit area

Figure 16.12   Separated background and fruit area

16.3.2.5   Finding the threshold of the grayscale image

We have used global image thresholding using Ostu's method. We compute threshold and that value is used to convert an intensity image to binary image. Threshold is a normalized value with values ranging from 0 to 1. To minimize the intra-class variance of the thresholded black and white pixels, the threshold can be selected using Ostu's method.

The function "graythresh" takes gray image as the input and returns the threshold value. The algorithm involves the following steps:

- The two-dimensional median filtered grayscale image is resized into single dimension.
- The histogram of the number plate image is found.
- The matrix values are initialized with 0–255.
- Weight mean and the variance for background and foreground is found using RF toolbox of MATLAB.
- Calculate (Weight of background * variance of background + Weight of foreground * variance of foreground).
- Find the minimum value which is nothing but the global threshold value of the grayscale image.

16.3.2.6   Binarization

Image binarization is the method of converting all the pixel values of the image to align between the only two values, that is [0,1]. We use the threshold value obtained by the Ostu's method as discussed. The function "imgbinarisatn" takes grayscale image and threshold value as the input and returns the binary image as the output. It involves the following steps:

- Create an image array having same number of rows and columns as the grayscale image.
- Initialize all the elements of image array to zero. Iterate over all the pixels of Grayscale image and assign 0 to image array of (i, j) if gray level value is greater than or equal to threshold value, else assign 1 to image array (i,j).
- These operations are shown in Figures 16.13–16.16.

Median filtered image

Figure 16.13   Median filtered image

Binarised image

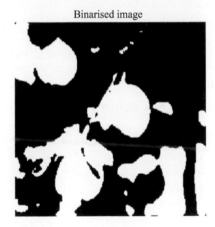

Figure 16.14   Binarized image of Figure 16.13

16.3.2.7   Morphological operations

Binary images will still contain noise and distortion even after the median filtering. The simple thresholding and binarization will not remove all the noise. Morphological operations are carried out to remove this noise. The same are depicted in Figures 16.17 and 16.18.

Erosion

It is one of the steps in image morphology. Initially it was implemented only for binary images later it was applied to grayscale images. This method erodes the white pixel that means white pixels are reduced and black pixels are increased.

Binary opening

It is also a step in the process of morphology. This method is used to find shaped in an image. This works similar to erosion removing the bright pixels from the image.

Median filtered image

Figure 16.15 Median filtered image

Binarised image

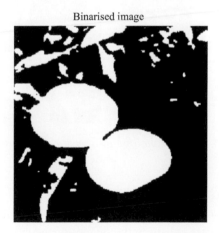

Figure 16.16 Binarized image of Figure 16.15

16.3.2.8 Obtaining a standard format

Whenever needed the image is either resized to 256*256 or 128*128 pixels, an array of data is padded with zeroes. The vector sizes are matched using MATLAB functions. These steps are carried out to maintain the same dimension of data for processing and storing.

This is required so as to maintain the proper database. Padding results in better filtering process. The padarray function of MATLAB helps us to pad the image with mirrored pixels. Vector size matching is required if there is any operation between them.

Before morphological operation   After morphological operation

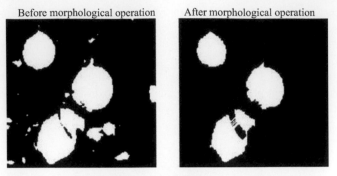

Figure 16.17   Morphological operation in Figure 16.13

Before morphological operation   After morphological operation

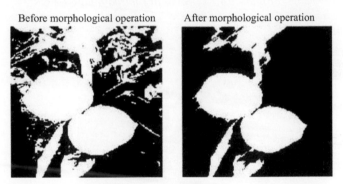

Figure 16.18   Morphological operation in Figure 16.18

16.3.2.9   Storing as training data

In this step, every time we test the model, the data obtained as result is stored as training data. This process enhances the quality of the system. The system stores the data every time we train the model, thus more were test the model the more we get trained data.

16.3.3   Feature extraction

Any machine learning model needs data in order to learn and perform required task. For our task of identification of matured citrus fruits, the inputs to the machine learning model will be set of images. We must feed many of these pre-processed images to make the model more efficient. Each pre-processed image is of 256*256 pixels. Considering single pixel is an 8-bit information, single pre-processed image gives lot of information. This makes the learning task hectic for the computer. Therefore, we must carefully select the information in each image which is specific to our task. The task of extracting region of interest which is nothing but the citrus fruit. This process of tuning our image information measurements into a lower dimension can be referred as feature extraction.

There are many features involved with an image. The three main global features have been considered in the project. Namely, color feature, shape feature and texture feature. The color feature is extracted using color moments, shape features are extracted using morphological operations and texture features using GLCM matrix. These features are helpful in matured fruit identification. The detailed description of these features is discussed below. All three features are extracted for all the training images.

16.3.3.1 Color moments

Color moments are used differentiate the images based on color feature. The calculated moments of color for the images gives the color similarity between them. The basis for these calculations is based on an assumption that the Red, Green and Blue color distribution in the image is same as probability distribution. There are three color features defined by Stricker and Orengo in 1995, namely Mean, Standard deviation and Skewness. In our project skewness will not help to differentiate between fruit and leaf in a gray level image. Thus, we have calculated Mean and Standard deviation for Red, Green and Blue colors.

Mean is nothing but the value of corresponding color and is given by,

$$\text{Mean, } E_i = \Sigma_{j=1}^{N} \frac{1}{N} p_{ij} \tag{16.2}$$

Standard deviation is same as the one defined in probability distribution, which is square root of variance. The variance here is the variance found between color pixels. It is given by

$$\text{Standard deviation, } \sigma_i = \sqrt{\left(\frac{1}{N}\Sigma_{j=1}^{N}\left(p_{ij} - E_i\right)^2\right)} \tag{16.3}$$

where
(i, j) – pixel at co-ordinate (i, j) N – total number of pixels

The color moments are shown in Figures 16.18–16.22. All the color moments for a single image is stored as,

ColorMoments = [meanRed stdRed meanGreen stdGreen meanBlue stdBlue]

Fruit
color_moments = [185.7911 78.6480 164.4843 70.8671 63.8484 25.9567]
color_moments = [200.0822 74.9586 125.6393 48.6843 25.7734 29.2103]

Leaf
color_moments = [73.9642 26.0051 101.0255 26.0616 35.4395 18.6335]
color_moments = [97.2977 39.8042 120.0385 39.6271 54.1029 22.1100]

We can see the significant variation in the values of color moments for the leaf as compared to that of fruit.

Fruit

Figure 16.19   Input image of fruit

Fruit

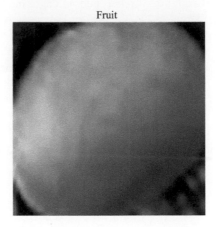

Figure 16.20   Input image of fruit

16.3.3.2   Shape features

The features that differentiate the image based on its visuality are called as shape features. There are shape features such as roundness, triangularity, area, perimeter, centroid and many more. In this project, the shape features extracted are area, centroid and bounding box for the image. These features are usually calculated on the gray level images, but the results are plotted on RGB images. The features are calculated for testing images and by analyzing these features through trial and error, the test images are classified.

Bounding box in image is a rectangular shape that surrounds the region of fruits. The bounding box will help us to visually locate the fruit on the farm image. Area is the total surface area of the connected component. The connected component is found from the binary image. The area feature is used to differentiate between single and bunch of citrus fruit. Centroid is the point of the object where

Leaf

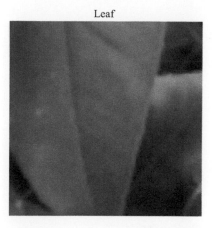

Figure 16.21   Input image of Leaf

Leaf

Figure 16.22   Input image of Leaf

its mass is centralized. Here the centroid of the connected component is found, which is the value of x and y scale from the origin.

These shape features are not specific to a shape such as circle, rectangle, triangle etc. As the shape of the fruit is not always circular and it cannot be defined as specific shape. All these aspects are represented in Figures 16.23–16.26.

Feature values for the corresponding
figure. Area: 3068
Centroid: [120.4472 197.7125]
Bounding Box: [93.5000 158.5000 54 74]
Feature values for the corresponding
figure. Area: [6581
            1018
            7991]

Original RGB image

Figure 16.23   Original image

Detected fruit with centroid   Detected fruit with centroid

Figure 16.24   Shape features plotted on processed and original image

Original RGB image

Figure 16.25   Original image

Detected fruit with centroid   Detected fruit with centroid

Figure 16.26   Shape features plotted on processed and original image

Centroid: [66.0837 161.0184

110.0265 46.3910
163.5965 183.6637]

Bounding Box: [24.5000 95.5000 83.0000 130.0000
82.5000 14.5000 47.0000 74.0000
114.5000 124.5000 123.0000 118.0000]

16.3.3.3   Gray-level co-occurrence matrix

Texture feature plays a very important role in identification of matured citrus fruit. Texture in image is the spatial arrangement of color intensities in the image. As the color intensities of fruit and background leaf or twigs vary at a larger scale, this feature is considered for extraction. We use the gray-level co-occurrence matrix (GLCM) to extract the texture feature from each pre-processed image.

In a GLCM matrix, the number of rows and columns is equal to the number of grey levels in the grayscaled image. Each element in the matrix is the relative frequency difference in the image pixels. The matrix element can be calculated as

$$P(i,j\,|\,\Delta x, \Delta y) = WQ(i,j\,|\,\Delta x, \Delta y) \tag{16.4}$$

$$W = \frac{1}{(M - \Delta x)(N - \Delta y)} \tag{16.5}$$

where

M, N – pixel length and width of grayscaled image $\Delta x, \Delta y$ – pixel difference of two pixels i, j

$Q\,(i, j|\, \Delta x, \Delta y)$ – number of pixel pairs

The GLCM for each image is constructed by using the pre-processed gray level images. The GLCM is formed for every training image by placing the sum of same pattern pixel from the original image matrix. There are many image texture features that can comes under GLCM feature. There are many features under GLCM, but the features considered here are contrast, correlation, dissimilarity, energy, entropy, maximum probability, and homogeneity. The calculated features for each test image are stored in a database using feature vector. The formulas for calculating these features were first given by Haralick in 1973. All the features describe the similarity and difference between the pixel patterns of an image.

Contrast is the color or grayscale difference that helps us to differentiate between multiple objects in an image. It refers to local variations in image pixel in GLCM. In GLCM we measure the color intensity between a pixel and its neighboring pixel. It the difference between highest and lowest pixel value. It can also be referred as difference moment. This is shown in Figure 16.27.

$$\text{Contrast} = \Sigma_{i,j=0}^{N_g-1} P_{(i,j)}(i-j)^2 \tag{16.6}$$

Correlation between any two images or pixels measures how closely they are related to each other. In GLCM it is the measure of how linearly the current pixel and its neighbor pixel are depended. It can be calculated as,

$$\text{Correlation} = \Sigma_{i,j=0}^{N_g-1} P(i,j)\left[\frac{(i-\mu_i)(j-\mu_j)}{\sqrt{(\sigma_i^2)(\sigma_j^2)}}\right] \tag{16.7}$$

$$\text{Mean } \mu_i = \Sigma_{i,j=0}^{N_g-1} i\left(P_{(i,j)}\right), \mu_j = \Sigma_{i,j=0}^{N_g-1} j\left(P_{(i,j)}\right) \tag{16.8}$$

$$\text{Variance } \sigma_i^2 = \Sigma_{i,j=0}^{N_g-1} P_{(i,j)}(i-\mu_i)^2, \sigma_j^2 = \Sigma_{i,j=0}^{N_g-1} P_{(i,j)}\left(j-\mu_j\right)^2 \tag{16.9}$$

Energy in image processing has a wide range of definition and it changes according to the related task. Here energy is the orderings or uniformity between gray level pixels. Less the number of gray pixels, more the energy. It can reach the

Figure 16.27   Set of images to show the contrast difference

maximum value equal to one and has the range normalized. Energy is calculated as angular second momentum using the formula below.

$$ASM = \Sigma_{t,j=0}^{N_g-1} P_{(i,j)}^2 \tag{16.10}$$

Entropy in image is the corresponding states of intensity levels that is adapted by its pixels. In GLCM terms it is the measure of disorder between image pixels. Entropy and energy are inversely related to each other. It is calculated as,

$$Entropy = \Sigma_{i,j=0}^{N_g-1} P_{(i,j)} \left(- \ln P_{(i,j)} \right) \tag{16.11}$$

Homogeneity is nothing but the similarity between pixels of an image. In GLCM it is referred as inverse difference moment (IDM) because it is highly but inversely related to the contrast. Homogeneity attains a maximum value when all pixels in the image are same. Hence it is measure of smoothness in the image. The formula for IDM is given by,

$$Homogeneity = \Sigma_{i,j=0}^{N_g-1} \frac{P_{(i,j)}}{1 + (i-j)^2} \tag{16.12}$$

Maximum probability is the measure of maximum likelihood that produces the pixels region of interest.

$$Max. \, Probability = max\left(P_{(i,j)}\right) for all (i,j) \tag{16.13}$$

The value of all feature discussed above are calculated for gray level images of both fruit and leaf.

Fruit

The specifications for Figure 16.28 are:

Max_probability = 0.1809 0.1857
Energy = 0.1107 0.1147
Entropy = 2.5640 2.5347
Contrast = 0.3284 0.2885
Dissimilarity = 0.2056 0.1862
Correlation = 0.9116 0.9215
Homogeneity = 0.9953 0.9958

The specifications for Figure 16.29 are:

Max_probability = 0.2936 0.2906
Energy = 0.1562 0.1531
Entropy = 2.2535 2.2955
Contrast = 0.1493 0.1815
Dissimilarity = 0.1390 0.1608
Correlation = 0.9322 0.9230
Homogeneity = 0.9977 0.9972

Fruit

Figure 16.28   Input gray level image of fruit

Fruit

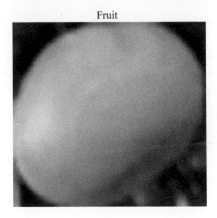

Figure 16.29   Input gray level image of fruit

Leaf

The specifications for Figure 16.30 are:

Max_probability = 0.3899 0.3803
Energy = 0.2651 0.2591
Entropy = 1.6611 1.6220
Contrast = 0.1342 0.0805
Dissimilarity = 0.1014 0.0804
Correlation = 0.9541 0.9598
Homogeneity = 0.9980 0.9988

The specifications for Figure 16.31 are:

Max_probability = 0.2985 0.3118
Energy = 0.1761 0.1900

Leaf

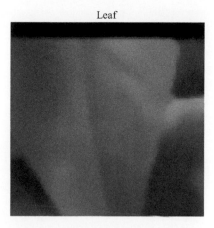

Figure 16.30   Input gray level image of Leaf

Leaf

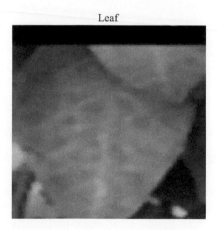

Figure 16.31   Input gray level image of Leaf

Entropy $= 2.1223$ 2.0278
Contrast $= 0.2740$ 0.1681
Dissimilarity $= 0.1991$ 0.1487
Correlation $= 0.9104$ 0.9287
Homogeneity $= 0.9960$ 0.9974
We can see a significant variation between the values of features for fruit and leaf.

16.3.4   Machine learning model and database formation

16.3.4.1   Feed-forward neural network

The feed-forward back propagation neural network (FFNN) is used for measuring three- dimensional location of fruit. Any neural network will have minimum three layers, namely input layer, hidden layer and output layer.

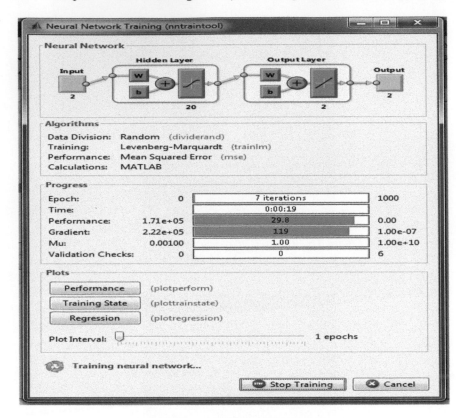

Figure 16.32   FFNN model in MATLAB

The FFNN is stands on the principle of learning from mistakes. Network feed the input and corresponding output in forwarding manner that is from input to output layer, calculate mean square error, back propagates the error and thereby modify the network weights to minimize that error. The training will continue until the minimum possible error is attained. After the system is trained with the correct classification, it can be tested for second set of samples.

The FFNN requires three parameters. These three parameters are considered to be the default reference point for the calculation of angle and distance of each centroids. The reference point is (128,256), which is the middle pixel of last line in any test image. As discussed in pre-processing stage, the standard test image size is 256*256. Xc contains the distance of the fruit from the reference point and the angle to be deviated from the reference point to reach the fruit. The network is trained to calculate the angle and the length to any point from the reference point. This training data is stored in database named "Netdata.mat." Given a point with x and y scale, the model will efficiently calculate the length and angle from the reference point at which the given point is located in 3-dimension. This is noticed in Figure 16.32.

16.3.4.2   Support vector machine

SVM is one of the supervised machine learning algorithms which can be used for classification problems. SVM works on the principle of separating data into

Figure 16.33   Plane separating two different classes

separate classes based on their features. Given the supervised or labelled data to the SVM it learns from the data and classifies the future test data into respective classes as shown in Figure 16.33.

In the SVM is used to perform two operation. First to separate the background and fruit area. Second is to separate the leaves which are incorrectly detected as fruit, this can be referred as removing false positives.

For background separation the training is given using set of pre-processed images from a folder called "images." The folder contains all RGB images, the images are pre-processed, background is separated, and the edges are stored. These stored edges act as training data for background separation of testing data.

For discarding wrongly classified leaves, the pre-processed images of fruit and leaf is separately stored in a folder named "dataset." The color and texture features are calculated for all the images and stored as feature vector. The corresponding group or output is mapped to the feature vector for every single image in the dataset. This mapping is saved in a database named "Training.mat." The dataset comprises of input and its corresponding target or output.

16.3.5   Data retrieval

Data retrieval is the process of retaining the stored data, which is obtained after the training. This data is already stored in variable. These variables are either the part of database or simply standalone variables.

The data required by the FFNN is stored in the database called Netdata.mat as discussed. The database is loaded when the length and angle of centroid of fruit needs to be calculated for a test image.

The data required SVM for separating fruit or edge from the background is stored in a set of two variables. These variables are loaded when the background separation needs to be done for a test image.

The data required for discarding the false positives or misclassified leaves is stored in a database called Training.mat as discussed. This database is loaded after the identification and separation of isolated fruits from the farm image.

16.3.6   Match with dataset or testing the model

This step is all about testing. Any system that is built and trained undergoes the testing process. Testing must be done carefully and slowly because it is very important to note if the system fails at any corner case. If any time the system fails to yield the required result, we must go back to very beginning of the whole process. After examining the system from the beginning, we must find the cause of failure, find solution and adapt that solution in the system. Sometimes it happens that solution demands a change that might want the system to compromise on efficiency, in that case we must carefully make decisions. Thus, it consumes lot of time.

The model is tested for variety of cases in order to determine the efficiency of the model. The testing image is an RGB image. The RGB image selected by the user is resized, processed and its features are extracted. The extracted features are matched with the data retrieved from the training and the required results are obtained.

16.3.7   Display result

The results of any process or system are the proof for its completion. When the system can yield the predetermined results, the process of implementation comes to an end. The main objective of identification of matures citrus fruit can be met when these three results are obtained for a test image.

16.3.7.1   Identify the fruit in image

This is about identification of fruit by separating the background from the image. The background is partially separated using pre-processing and partly using the SVM algorithm. The isolated or bunch of fruit is extracted from the image as seen in Figures 16.34–16.37.

Original RGB image

Figure 16.34   Input test image (isolated fruits)

Background   Fruit area

Figure 16.35   Background and fruit area separated

Original RGB image

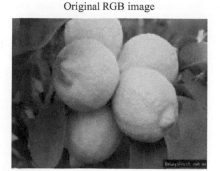

Figure 16.36 Input test image (BUNCH of fruit)

Background   Fruit area

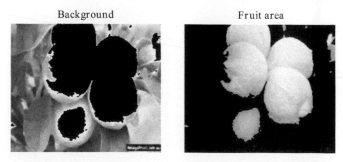

Figure 16.37 Background and fruit area separated

16.3.7.2 Locate fruit centroid

The centroid of fruit is located by finding the centroid of the connected region as discussed in the feature extraction. The bounding box surrounding the fruit and centroid is found and is plotted on the pre-processed or original image. If the fruits are not isolated, one single centroid is plotted for a bunch of fruit, as shown in Figures 16.38 and 16.39.

16.3.7.3 Locate fruit position

The process of locating fruit position or positioning in fruit in 3-dimension is done using FFNN. Given the centroid as the input the network calculates the length and angle of it from the reference point. This length and angle values are displayed in the command prompt. If more than one fruit is identified all the fruit positions are calculated from the reference point and displaced. This is seen in Figures 16.40 and 16.41. Another example for input test image and its corresponding positions are shown in Figures 16.42 and 16.43, respectively.

16.3.8 Application design

The only thing that matters to an end user is the ease of using the product. Thus, we have built a GUI for the project. The user gets the option like train SVM, train

Detected fruit with centroid   Detected fruit with centroid

(i)   (ii)

*Figure 16.38   Fruit center and bounding box plotted on (i) pre-processed and (ii)
original image (isolated fruit)*

Detected fruit with centroid   Detected fruit with centroid

(i)   (ii)

*Figure 16.39   Fruit center and bounding box plotted on (i) pre-processed (ii)
original image (bunch of fruit)*

Original RGB image

Figure 16.40   Input test image

neural network, browse test image, display many intermediate stages, displaying
final results and qualification measures like accuracy, execution time, sensitivity
and specificity both on individual and system level as shown in Figure 16.44.

```
Fruit--1  Location= 31.14572      120.1281  Go front      Length = 225.6618   Angle= 139.259
Fruit--2  Location= 133.3197      123.7541  Go front      Length = 123.0134   Angle= 134.9419
Fruit--3  Location= 186.8699      90.44495  Length = 79.4471   Angle= 94.2476
```

Figure 16.41   Fruit positions

Original RGB image

Figure 16.42   Input test image

```
Fruit--1  Location= 135.0377      117.3232   Length = 121.9872   Angle= 132.1182
```

Figure 16.43   Fruit positions

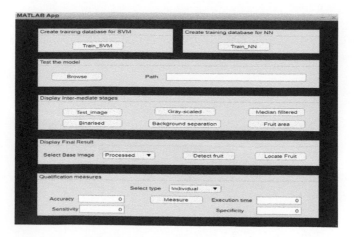

Figure 16.44   Application design

16.4   Experiments and result

16.4.1   Qualification measures

Qualification measurement is the important stage in any product development as it verifies and validates the product under the test, whether it works as expected or not. It is also necessary to test the system before deployment. In any classifier model, a confusion matrix is drawn in order to measure system performance.

16.4.1.1   Confusion matrix

It is basically a table drawn with different combinations of actual and predicted value. In the project the actual value refers to the fruit. The confusion matrix defines four terms which are true positive (TP), false positive (FP), true negative (TN), and false negative (FN), as seen in Table 16.1.

True positive is the condition where the actual value is predicted and is true. In our case, it is when the fruit is correctly detected. False positive in the condition where the actual value is detected, but it is false. In our case, it is when the leaf is detected as fruit. True negative is the condition when the actual value is not detected and is true. Here, it is the case when the classifier discards the detected leaf (during processing). Lastly, false negative is the condition where the actual value is not detected, but it is false. In our case, it is the unpredicted fruit.

Out of total 40 images in the database, we have 3 TN, 5 FP, 2 FN and 30 TP cases. We define some of the parameters are accuracy, specificity and sensitivity based on these values. The definition and formulas for the same can be explained as follows.

16.4.1.2   Accuracy

Accuracy is defined as the percentage of the correct predictions for the test data. It can be easily calculated by dividing the number of correct predicted output to the total number of predictions.

$$\text{Accuracy} = \left(\frac{TP + TN}{TP + TN + FP + FN} \right) * 100$$

16.4.1.3   Sensitivity

Sensitivity is defined as the portion of applicable instances along with the recovered instances. Sensitivity is also called recall. It can be calculated using below formula,

$$\text{Sensitivity} = \frac{TP}{TP + FN}$$

Table 16.1   Confusion matrix

	Prediction Yes	Prediction No
Actual Yes	TN 4	FP 4
Actual No	FN 2	TP 30

16.4.1.4 Specificity

Specificity is defined as the portion of applicable instances that have been retrieved above the sum amount of applicable instances. Specificity is also called precision. It can be calculated using below formula,

$$\text{Specificity} = \frac{\text{TP}}{\text{TP} + \text{FP}}$$

16.4.1.5 Execution time

Execution time is defined as the difference between the end time and start time of the algorithm.

$$\text{Executiontime} = \text{End time of algorithm} - \text{start time of algorithm}$$

16.4.1.6 Qualification results

We have calculated the qualification results both on system and individual level. The predetermined values for TP, TN, FP and FN are stored in an excel sheet for individual test image, and the same is retrieved later during calculation. System execution time is the average time taken for the execution of all test images in the dataset given in Table 16.2. The qualification results at individual level is given in Table 16.3.

16.4.2 Training result

16.4.2.1 Training SVM

SVM is trained to remove the leaves which are detected as fruit after the pre-processing. SVM is trained for fruit and leaf classes and the database is obtained, namely, Trained.mat. After the completion of training a message box will be displayed and we can plot the scatter plot of values in the database, as shown in Figure 16.45.

In the legend of the scatter plot, red dots show the fruit and green dots show leaf, as shown in Figure 16.46.

16.4.2.2 Training FFNN

The FFNN is trained for calculating the distance and angle from a reference point, as discussed earlier. The network training will stop either after six validation checks are completed or after 1000 iteration. The message box for the same will be displayed. The performance plot, training state plot and the regression plot for FFNN also plotted. The same can be seen in Figures 16.47 through 16.50.

Table 16.2 Qualification results at system level

Accuracy	Execution time (s)	Sensitivity	Specificity
85	16.09	.9375	.8823

Table 16.3   *Qualification results at individual level*

Image file	Accuracy	Execution time (s)	Sensitivity	Specificity
1.jpg	100	15.44	1	1
2.jpg	100	15.7	1	1
3.jpg	100	15.19	1	1
4.jpg	100	16.34	1	1
5.jpg	50	15.44	1	.5
6.jpg	100	14.28	1	1
7.jpg	100	15.47	1	1
8.jpg	100	16.19	1	1
9.jpg	100	16.09	1	1
10.jpg	100	16.18	1	1
11.jpg	100	15.28	1	1
12.jpg	100	16.98	1	1
13.jpg	100	16.8	1	1
14.jpg	100	16.62	1	1
15.jpg	100	15.42	1	1
16.jpg	100	15.04	1	1
17.jpg	100	14.98	1	1
18.jpg	100	15.12	1	1
19.jpg	100	14.24	1	1
20.jpg	100	15.12	1	1
21.jpg	60	20.68	1	.6
22.jpg	100	16.34	1	1
23.jpg	100	16.32	1	1
24.jpg	100	15.48	1	1
25.jpg	100	15.47	1	1
26.jpg	100	16.56	1	1
27.jpg	100	16.97	1	1
28.jpg	100	16.43	1	1
29.jpg	100	14.67	1	1
30.jpg	100	16.79	1	1
31.jpg	100	14.91	1	1
32.jpg	100	15.74	1	1
33.jpg	100	16.5	1	1
34.jpg	100	16.31	1	1
35.jpg	100	16.63	1	1
36.jpg	83.33	17.87	.8333	1
37.jpg	75	18.66	.667	1
38.jpg	100	14.99	1	1
39.jpg	100	15.47	1	1
40.jpg	100	18.71	1	1

Figure 16.45   Message box for SVM

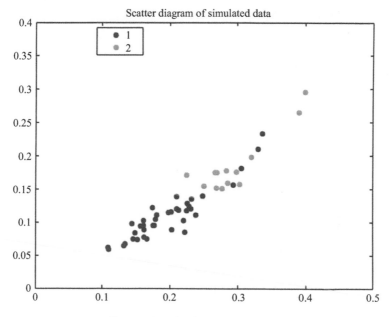

Figure 16.46   SVM scatter plot

Figure 16.47   Message box for FFNN

As is shown in the above figure, the training stops after all six validation checks are passed. In the above trail the training has stopped after 772 iterations or epochs. The total time taken for training was 3.30 minutes.

The FFNN network works the principle of attaining minimum mean square error. In each iteration, the network calculates the mean square error, back propagates the error and changes the weights of hidden layer accordingly. As the above performance plot depicts, the mean square error is reduced to a minimum possible value at the end of training. The change in the square error throughout the training is plotted for training and validation checking.

The above training state plot gives the gradient and control parameter (Mu) values at the 772 iteration and plots these values throughout the training. Also, we can conclude that the validation is stopped when the validation fail is nil, that is at the 772 iteration.

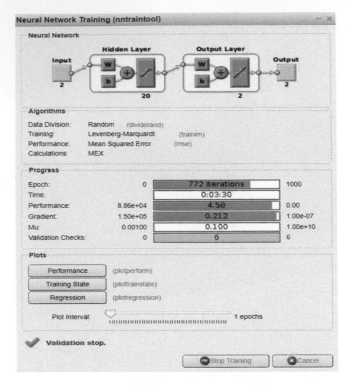

Figure 16.48   The FFNN model after training stopped

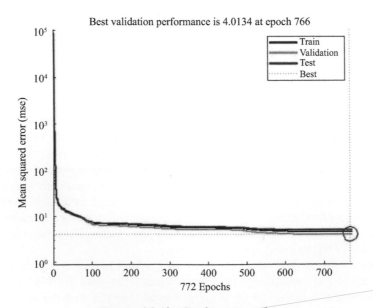

Figure 16.49   Performance plot

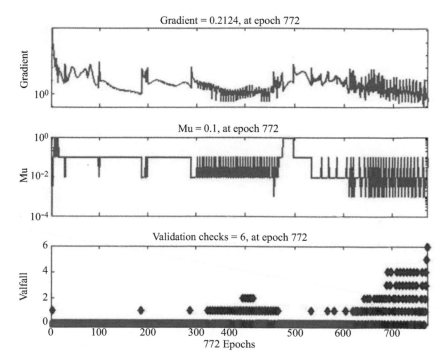

Figure 16.50   Training state plot

The regression plot shows the scatter plot of FFNN for training, testing, validation and average of all.

16.4.3   Testing result

16.4.3.1   Class 1: one fruit

This is the example for single isolated fruit. All the intermediate stages like original RGB test image, grayscaled image, median filtered image, binary image, background separation and fruit area after morphological operation is shown by below figures. The bounding box and centroid are plotted both on processed and original image. The three-dimensional location of fruit is also given. The same can be verified in Figures 16.52–16.60. The regression plot for the above class is shown in Figure 16.51.

Results

Reading the images.....

2 fruits detected before SVM Training the Data....

k =
   1
k =
   2

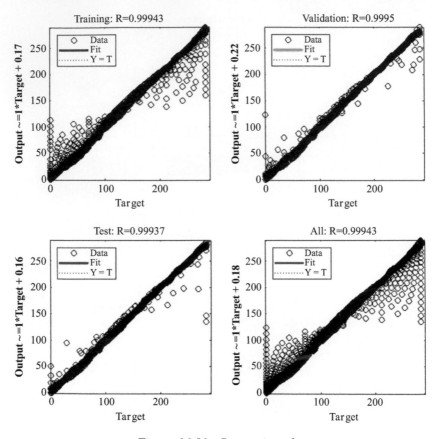

Figure 16.51   Regression plot

Figure 16.52   Test image

Grayscale image

Figure 16.53   Grayscaled test image

Median filtered image

Figure 16.54   Median filtered test image

Binarised image

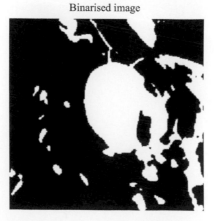

Figure 16.55   Binarized test image

Background   Fruit area

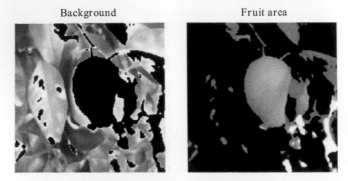

Figure 16.56   Separated background and fruit image

Fruit area after processing

Figure 16.57   Fruit area after morphological operation

Cropped fruit image

Figure 16.58   Cropped fruits from test image

Detected fruit with centroid

Figure 16.59   Centroid and bounding box plotted on processed and original image

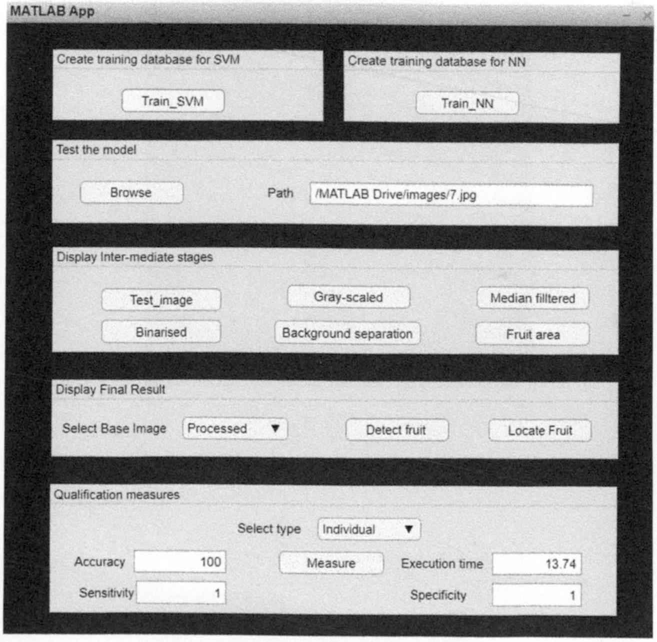

MATLAB App

Create training database for SVM

Train_SVM

Create training database for NN

Train_NN

Test the model

Browse   Path   /MATLAB Drive/images/7.jpg

Display Inter-mediate stages

Test_image   Gray-scaled   Median filltered

Binarised   Background separation   Fruit area

Display Final Result

Select Base Image   Processed ▼   Detect fruit   Locate Fruit

Qualification measures

Select type   Individual ▼

Accuracy   100   Measure   Execution time   13.74

Sensitivity   1   Specificity   1

Figure 16.60   MATLAB app showing path and qualification results

Testing the Data....
Training the Data....
k =
    1
k =
    2
Testing the Data....
Fruit–1 Location = 135.7534 119.029 Length = 121.0648 Angle = 132.7005

The leaf which was detected as the fruit after segmentation is discarded by the SVM classifier. Hence, the above image is identified to have a single isolated fruit. The bounding box, centroid and three-dimensional location of fruit are the result of fruit identification.

The particular test gives 100% accuracy, 13.74 s of execution time, specificity and sensitivity values equal to 1, as shown by the application.

16.4.3.2   Class 2: two fruit

This class represents the set where there are two or more isolated fruits present in an image. The same can be verified in Figures 16.61–16.69.

Original RGB image

Figure 16.61   Test image

Grayscale image

Figure 16.62   Grayscaled test image

Median filtered image

Figure 16.63   Median filtered test image

Binarised image

Figure 16.64   Binarized test image

Background   Fruit area

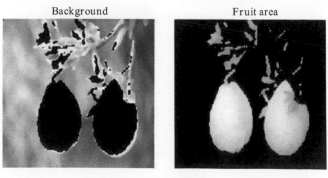

Figure 16.65   Separated background and fruit image

Fruit area after processing

Figure 16.66   Fruit area after morphological operation

Cropped fruit image   Cropped fruit image

Figure 16.67   Cropped fruits from test image

Detected fruit with centroid   Detected fruit with centroid

Figure 16.68   Centroid and bounding box plotted on processed and original image

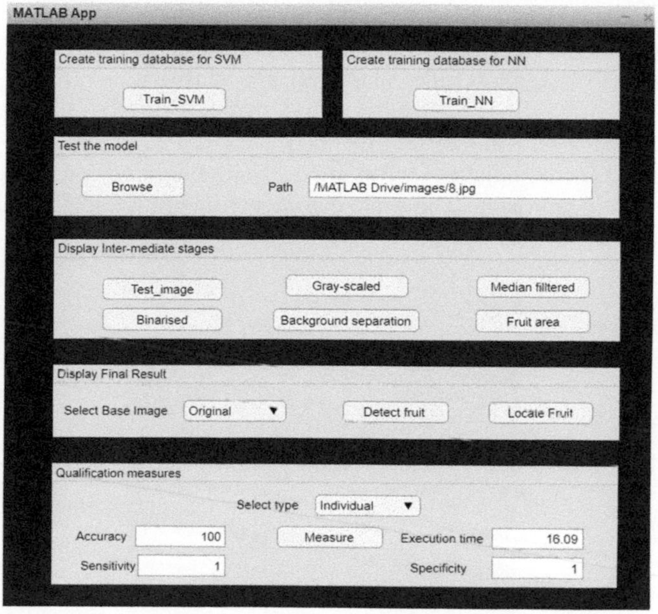

Figure 16.69   MATLAB app showing path and qualification results

Results
Reading the images.....

2 fruits detected before SVM Training the Data....

k =
  1
k =
  2
Testing the Data....
Training the Data....
k =
  1
k =
  2
Testing the Data....
Fruit–1 Location = 96.55889 173.3438 Length = 165.2242, Angle = 167.083
Fruit–2 Location = 189.4265 176.4399 Length = 82.2207, Angle = 196.89

Two fruits are detected by the system from this test case. The boundary box, centroid and three-dimensional fruit location are given. The test resulted in 100% accuracy, 16.09 s execution time, specificity and sensitivity equal to 1.

16.4.3.3   Class 3: bunch of fruits

This class includes the bunch of citrus fruits. There might be one or more bunches of fruit present in an image. The same can be verified in Figures 16.70–16.78.

Original RGB image

Figure 16.70   Test image

Grayscale image

Figure 16.71   Grayscaled test image

Median filtered image

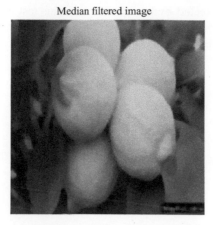

Figure 16.72   Median filtered test image

Binarised image

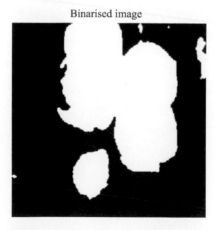

Figure 16.73   Binarized test image

Background   Fruit area

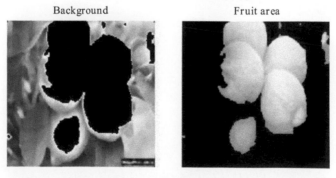

Figure 16.74   Separated background and fruit image

Fruit area after processing

Figure 16.75   Fruit area after morphological operation

Cropped fruit image

Figure 16.76   Cropped fruit from test image

Detected fruit with centroid   Detected fruit with centroid

Figure 16.77   Centroid and bounding box plotted on processed and original image

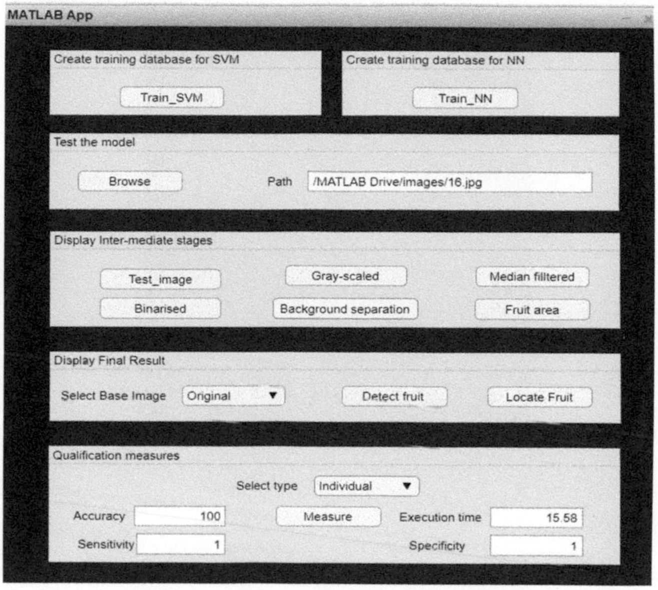

Figure 16.78 MATLAB app showing path and qualification results

Results

Reading the images.....
1 fruits detected before SVM Training the Data....
k =
    1
k =
    2
Testing the Data....
Fruit–1 Location = 135.0377 117.3232 Length = 121.9872 Angle = 132.1182

The single boundary box and centroid are detected for the entire bunch. The test gives the 100% accuracy, 15.58 s of execution time, specificity and sensitivity values equal to 1.

Failure cases

This is the case of false positive, where the leaf is getting detected as fruit. The reason for the same can be the leaf is being yellowish or the smoothness of the leaf. Thus after converting the image into grayscale the leaf was determined as fruit by the model as seen in Figure 16.79.

This is the case where the boundary box drawn cowers the whole image instead of covering only fruit. This case is also considered as false positive because background is considered as fruit area, as seen in Figure 16.80. This can be solved by better segmentation and robust image processing.

This is the case where one of the fruits is not identified by the model. The reason for the same is the fruit area is separated by leaf and thus the area is added to

Detected fruit with centroid

Figure 16.79   Failure case 1

Detected fruit with centroid

Figure 16.80   Failure case 2

background instead of fruit area. This is false-negative case where an actual fruit is considered as background, as seen in Figure 16.81.

16.5   Conclusion

Images from the natural scenes are taken and pre-processed and converted into grayscale image.

- Images are also filtered for noise using a median filter.
- The color, shape and texture features are calculated as stored in the database.
- The FFNN and SVM models are built and trained to perform designated tasks.
- The test image is selected, pre-processed, converted to grayscale, features are extracted.

Detected fruit with centroid

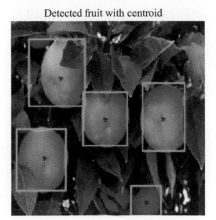

Figure 16.81   Failure case 3

- Test image is segmented, the area of fruits is separated from the background and leaves using SVM.
- The fruits from the images are extracted and false negatives are removed using SVM.
- Then, the centroid and bounding box for each of the fruit is located. If there is a cluster of fruits, then one centroid and bounding box is located for each cluster.
- A reference point is taken initially, from which the location of the identified centroid is calculated.
- The distance from the initial reference point to the identified centroid is calculated. Also, the angle to be deviated from the initial point to reach the centroid of the fruit is calculated in degrees.

16.5.1   Future scope

The proposed system illustrates a technique for identifying tree citrus fruits. This can be further enhanced for

- Better segmentation for extensive shadow conditions.
- Identifying separate individual fruit in a cluster of fruits by locating one centroid for each of the fruit in it.

References

[1]   Subhajit Sengupta, and Won Suk Lee, "Identification and Determination of the Number of Green Citrus Fruit in a Canopy under Different Ambient Light Conditions", Biosystems Engineering, 2014;117:51–61.
[2]   Lu Qiang, Cai Jianrong, Liu Bin, Deng Lie, and Zhang Yajing, "Identification of fruit and branch in natural scenes for citrus harvesting robot using machine

vision and support vector machine", International Journal of Agricultural and Biological Engineering, 2014;7:115–121.

[3]   Kyosuke Yamamoto, Wei Guo, Yosuke Yoshioka and Seishi Ninomiya, "On Plant Detection of Intact Tomato Fruits Using Image Analysis and Machine Learning Methods", Sensors, 2014;14(7):12191–12206.

[4]   Joanna Lado, Maria Jesus Rodrigo, and Lorenzo Zacarias, "Maturity indicators and citrus fruit quality", Stewart Postharvest Review, 2014;10(2):1–6.

[5]   Alireza Khoshroo, Jalal Khodaei, and Arman Arehi, "Detection of Red Tomato on Plants using Image Processing Techniques", Agricultural Communications, 2014;2(4):9–15.

[6]   Ding K. and Gunashekaran S., "Shape feature extraction and classification of food material using Computer Vision", American Society of Agricultural Engineers, 1994;37(5):1537–1545.

[7]   Han Li, Won Suk Lee, and Ku Wang, "Immature Green Citrus Fruit Detection and Counting based on Fast Normalized Cross Correlation (FNCC) using Natural Outdoor Color Images", Precision Agriculture, 2016;17:678–697.

[8]   Amrutha Jamkhandi, and Madhavanavar S. P., "Fruit Grading for Pomegranates: An Overview", International Journal of Recent Technology and Engineering (IJRTE), 2018;6(3):1–4.

[9]   Kavita Komal, and Sonia, "GLCM Algorithm and SVM Classification Method for Orange Fruit Quality Assessment", International Journal of Recent Technology and Engineering (IJRTE), 2019;8(9):697–703.

[10]   Kavita Komal, and Sonia, "Quality Assessment of Orange Fruit using Svm Classifier and Gray Level Co-Occurrence Matrix Algorithm", International Journal of Scientific & Technology Research, 2019;8(11):463–470.

[11]   Gururaj C. and Satish Tunga, "AI based Feature Extraction through Content Based Image Retrieval", Journal of Computational and Theoretical Nanoscience, 2020;17(9-10):4050–4054.

[12]   Sreekantha D. K. and Kavya M., "Agricultural Crop Monitoring using IOT - a study", International Conference on Intelligent Systems and Control (ISCO), January 2017, pp. 134–139, doi: 10.1109/ISCO.2017.7855968.

[13]   Dharun V. S., and Shijin Kumar P.S., "Extraction of Texture Features using GLCM and Shape Features using Connected Regions", International Journal of Engineering and Technology (IJET), 2017;8(6):2926–2930.

[14]   Gururaj C, Jayadevappa D, and Satish Tunga, "Fundus Image Features Extraction for Exudate Mining in Coordination with Content Based Image Retrieval: A Study", Journal of The Institution of Engineers (India): Series B, 2018;99:313–321.

[15]   Gururaj C, "Proficient Algorithm for Features Mining in Fundus Images through Content Based Image Retrieval", 2018 International Conference on Intelligent and Innovative Computing Applications (ICONIC), 2018, pp. 108–113, Plaine Magnien, Mauritius.

[16] Chowdhary C. L., and Mouli P. C., "Image Registration with New System for Ensemble of Images of Multi-Sensor Registration", World Applied Sciences Journal, 2013;26(1):45–50.

[17] Chowdhary C. L., Patel P. V., Kathrotia K. J., Attique M., Perumal K., and Ijaz M. F., "Analytical study of hybrid techniques for image encryption and decryption", Sensors, 2020;20(18):5162.

[18] Chowdhary C. L., "3D object recognition system based on local shape descriptors and depth data analysis", Recent Patents on Computer Science, 2019;12(1):18–24.

[19] Gururaj C., Jayadevappa D., and Satish Tunga, "Content Based Image Retrieval System Implementation through Neural Network", IOSR Journal of VLSI and Signal Processing (IOSR-JVSP), 2016;6(3):42–47, DOI: 10.9790/4200-0603034247.

[20] Gururaj C., Jayadevappa D., and Satish Tunga, " An Effective Implementation of Exudate Extraction from Fundus Images of the Eye for a Content Based Image Retrieval System Through Hardware Description Language", Third International Conference on Emerging Research in Computing, Information, Communication and Applications (ERCICA – 2015) published in Springer, ISBN: 978-81-322-2552-2, 31st July and 1st August 2015, pp. 279–290, NMIT, Bengaluru, India, DOI: 10.1007/978-81-322-2553-9.

Chapter 17

Automated detection of defects and grading of cashew kernels using machine learning

S.V. Veenadevi[1] and C. Srinivasan Padmavathi[2]

Abstract

Cashew quality is one of the significant parameter defining the rate of the product. The machine vision system is non-destructive, high-efficient substitute technology to the prevailing manual and mechanical methods to evaluate the quality of cashews. Leveraging image processing and machine learning techniques for cataloging cashew kernels quality plummets production expenditure escalates classification accuracy. Concoction of detection of cashew defects and grading cashew kernels is beneficial for the confection of the robust machine vision system [1,2].

An automated cashew kernel grading system using machine vision is proposed and presented, and a study of the effects of various preprocessing techniques in the grading process is made. The proposed work focuses on a cashew defect detector and segregation of high-quality cashew images, which primarily is based on leveraging image processing and machine learning techniques for cataloging cashew kernel quality that plummets production expenditure.

The cashew kernel quality is assessed using image processing and machine learning techniques. The various defects in the cashews are demarcated before the grading process, and the cashew kernels are classified into different grades (WW-180, WW-320, WW-450, splits, and SW-240). Image preprocessing and segmentation of cashew kernel is performed using the image processing toolbox of MATLAB®. The Lucy filter and Wiener filter are applied to eliminate blurring effects. Cashew image segmentation is performed by concoction of color threshold and Otsu's segmentation methods. Significant features, namely, color, size and shape, and texture features, are extracted from the segmented cashew kernel image. Texture features are extracted using the gray level co-occurrence matrix. The multi-class support vector machine (SVM) learning models and the

[1]Department of ECE, R V College of Engineering, Visvesvaraya Technological University, Belagavi, Karnataka, India
[2]Department of ECE, Sapthagiri College of Engineering, Visvesvaraya Technological University, Belagavi, Karnataka, India

random forest classifier are confected using training samples and different labels using the machine learning toolbox.

Cataloguing of cashew kernel quality is performed by the SVM classifier and random forest classifier based on trained models. The total training set comprising both defected and good quality cashews considered is 444 samples for training and 136 samples for testing. The defected and good quality cashew kernels are demarcated using the proposed methodology with an SVM classifier accuracy of 89.4% and with a random forest classifier accuracy of 94%. From results, it can be concluded that W-180, splits, and SW-240 are efficiently classified. Classifier accuracy can be improved by increasing the number of samples.

Key Words: Cashew grade; cashew kernel; image processing; gray level co-occurrence matrix; machine learning; support vector machine; random forest.

17.1   Introduction

The cashew quality determines the price of the product. India is one among the foremost exporters of cashew in the world. Most prevailing cashew nuts' quality detection and grading systems have the drawbacks of low efficiency, low cost, and complexity. A strategic delinquent in cashew kernel grading is the use of mechanical equipment and expensive color sorters; nevertheless, manual grading is performed. In general, cashew kernel grading presents many complications related to quality. Thus, it is having the requisite for a proficient and accurate quality regulator [1]. The cashew quality determines the price of the product, and still manual processing is performed to assess the quality and grades of cashew kernels. Research quantum in the field of machine vision-based assessment of quality, grading, and sorting of agricultural commodities is being escalated. Machine vision for automation of grading and assessment of several qualities associated to cashew kernel can plummet production expenditure and proliferates in quality, as it is non-destructive automatic detection technology [2,3]. Innovations in image processing and machine learning technology have become more effectual to assess cashew quality. Image processing is a tool adopted to evaluate the parameters correlated to agronomy with accuracy [4]. Image processing technique has been designated as the effectual machine vision system for the agriculture domain. Imaging techniques with distinct spectrum, such as X-ray, infrared and hyperspectral imaging, were beneficial in defining the vegetation indices, canopy measurements and irrigated land mapping with higher accuracies [5]. Machine vision-based sorting of agricultural commodities is a substitute to the conventional mechanical and electro-optical sorting techniques [6,7]. This technique offers high-speed multi-category cataloging by processing multiple-features acquired through image processing algorithms using trained machine learning models. Application of image processing and machine learning techniques in assessing cashew quality to detect cashew defects and to grade the cashews is presented in the chapter.

The Full chapter has been organized into various sections and each section has been explained briefly as follows: Section 17.1 briefed about the concepts of implementing Image processing and Machine learning techniques in assessing cashew quality, literature survey, motivation, problem statement and objectives, classification methodology. Section 17.2 caters an overview of the theory and fundamentals of defects and grades of cashew kernels. Section 17.3 briefs about the methodology of classification, development of machine learning models and the flowcharts describing the cataloguing procedure. Section 17.4 briefs about the classification results of SVM classifier, analysis of confusion matrix and efficiency of the classifier. Section 17.5 concludes the chapter by briefing the analysis of the results, overall classification accuracy of SVM classifier, Random Forest classifier and future scope.

17.1.1   Related work

A real-time cataloging system to automatically grade cashew kernels based on their color, texture, size, and shape is presented in [8]. Five grades (WW-180, WW-320, SW-320, SSW, and B) out of 26 available grades of cashew kernels are used for classification and support vector machine (SVM) classifier provides high accuracy than backpropagation neural network (BPNN). Automated cashew kernel grading system using machine vision is proposed in [9] and also presented the effects of various preprocessing techniques on grading process. Performance of classifiers namely BPNN, random forest, multi-class classifier using combinations of features is evaluated, BPNN provided optimal results with accuracy of 96.8%. Development of supervised intelligent classification model for white wholes (WW) grades of cashews kernels is discussed in [10]. Accuracy classification models to accurately classify WW grades ranged from 70% to 90%. Classification of cashew grades based on color, texture, and size using K-nearest neighbor (KNN) algorithm and a robust solution for object segmentation using K-means clustering is proposed in [1]. KNN classifier is used to catalog WW cashew grades with an accuracy of 87%. Associations of parameters of cashew kernel and development of the supervised learning model using decision trees, logistic regression, artificial neural networks, and support vector machines are presented in [2]. The average accuracy of the different classifiers is found to be 85%. A cost-effective, intelligent model to assess the quality of cashew kernels based on color features is developed in [3] and the model for six grades of cashews is evaluated. The congested model for six grades of cashews is evaluated, and the classification rate of the model is 80%.

Classification model of cashew nuts and analysis of shape parameters of cashew nuts is presented in [4] and it is showed the existence of a linear relationship between length and height of cashew nuts and also showed that the other parameters are not linearly related and [5] performed an investigation on the performance of different multi-class techniques including decision trees, multi-layer perceptron (MLP) and K-nearest neighbors for grading of cashew kernels. MLP method provides a high classification accuracy of 86%. Application of image processing and neural networks for detecting and cataloging areca nuts quality is presented in [6], the classification accuracy of the classifier is 90.9%, and [7] proposed a hybrid intelligent system for fruit grading and sorting using artificial neural networks. The neural network classifier achieved an accuracy rate of 93.3% more than BPNN (73.3%).

Advancements in machine vision systems escalated its implementation in various applications including quality detection of agro-products. Machine vision systems cater to non-destructive, cost-efficient methods compared to existing mechanical methods; still, manual processing is performed to assess the quality and grades of cashew kernels. Leveraging image processing and machine learning techniques in quality evaluation of cashew escalate productivity and plummets the production costs. Machine vision systems require being incorporate detection of defects of cashews along with the grading of cashews.

17.1.2   Proposed methodology

Automated detection of defected cashews is a prerequisite process before the grading stage. Integration of both stages, that is, detection of defects and grading processes makes machine vision system robust enough to substitute existing manual and mechanical methods. Incorporations of different cashew grades for training machine learning models are advantageous to the classifier for cataloging quality of cashew kernels. This method focuses on assessment of both defected cashews and grades of cashew kernels for developing machine learning models. The objective of the proposed method is: (i) To demarcate defected/damaged cashews (black/brown spots, discolored, mixed defects) before grading process. (ii) To extract relevant features from cashew images comprising of color, texture, and shape features. (iii) To train SVM machine learning models with training features and labels of both defected cashews and cashew grades (WW-180, WW-320, WW-450, splits, and SW-240). (iv) To classify quality and grade of cashew kernel based on trained machine learning models.

The different steps in classifying different cashews are: (1) Image acquisition process, apprehend cashew image through image acquisition tools. (2) Perform preprocessing on Cashew image using image preprocessing techniques. To eliminate the blurring effect, apply Weiner filter and Lucy filter. (3) Segmentation of the image with the help of Image segmentation techniques such as color threshold and Otsu's segmentation method to distinguish image pixels into Cashew kernel, and the background. (4) Extract RGB and HSV color moments for color analysis. Extract shape related and texture features using gray level co-occurrence matrix (GLCM). (5) Train support vector machine (SVM) classifier using training set features and Group labels. (6) Classify the cashew based on the trained SVM results to determine the quality and grade the cashews.

17.2   Defects and grades of cashew kernels

Cashew (*Anacardium occidentale*), the wondernut of the earth, was introduced to various parts of the world with principal objectives of afforestation and soil conservation [8]. India is the largest producer of raw cashew nuts (RCN). Indian cashew industry confronts many challenges associated with production of cashew kernel from raw cashew nut [1,2,9,10]. Several competitors have implemented modernized techniques to a superior range that their production expenditure is far low compared to Indian standards [1–3,10]. In India, cashew is a tradition and processing of cashews is more or less manual. India's cashew nuts market is the top producer in the world by absorbing over 25% of the supply. Up to 6% defective cashew nuts, which are lowering the price of good quality cashew nuts, due to unscientific separation and segregation. Cashew kernel processing and separation machines are available in the market, but they are separated only defects from the good cashew kernel. Market demands separation of cashew kernel based on quality and size to get more profit for farmers. Automation in India is to be implemented in the cashew industries to the effective employment of the full workforce with the escalation of throughput and quality of cashew kernels [3–7,11,12].

17.2.1　Cashew kernel manufacturing process

To produce a good cashew kernel from hard raw cashew nut, there is a traditional procedure incorporated. Processing of cashew nut involves skilled labor and machinery. The Cashew kernel manufacturing process comprises desiccation and calibration, roasting or steam cooking, shelling, peeling, grading or sorting, rehumidification, and packaging [13]. The initial stage in the cashew nut processing is to remove moisture content from raw cashew nut, in this stage the RCNs are Desiccated by scattering the RCNs on the drying yard under the sunlight for 1–3 days which removes the moisture content of nut to 6%–9% and calibrated by pre-cleaning and size grading of desiccated RCN. The impurities like plant debris, sticks/stones are also removed in this stage [13]. Once the RCNs are desiccated and calibrated the nuts are roasted and steam cooked, roasting process moderates the cashew outer shell. The roasting techniques in the cashew sectors [14] include fire roasting, steam cooking, drum roasting steam roasting and oil bath roasting. The roasting is followed by shelling process to extract cashew kernel from cashew nuts, and the extracted cashew kernel will have more moisture content which is roasted to remove the moisture so that testa can be peeled out efficiently using hot exchanger, steam, or electric hot house. This skin/testa from cashew kernel is detached using the peeling process. Cashew kernels are graded into white wholes, scorched wholes, splits, etc., based on the color, texture, size and shape after removing damaged /defected cashew kernels. Once the cashew kernels are sorted and graded, the excess moisture content is removed using rehumidification to reduce the damage during transport and the cashew kernels are fumigated before packing using aluminum phosphide. Cashew kernel packing requires inert atmosphere so the packages are vacuumed or infused with nitrogen.

17.2.2　Defects of cashew kernel

The quality of cashew kernels is degraded in many circumstances during each stage of manufacturing. The defects of the cashew kernels will be categorized into various groups and the defects differ for different grades. Defects comprise intrinsic and superficial damages that adversely impact the exterior part of the cashew such as immature, scorching or shriveled kernels, discoloration, blemishes, pitted black/brown spots on kernels which instigates eternal discoloration, scrapes, adhering testa, speckles, and flux marks.

Scorching is a discoloration due to overheating during shelling. Dark brown spots on the superficial part of the kernel when kernels are roasted but not from raw kernels are considered as spotting after roasting. Spots on the cashew which exceeds a level of 3 mm are termed as blemishes/discoloration defects [13,14]. Insect damages are the damages to the cashew kernel from living or deceased insects, visible mold, bird damage, decay or adhering dirt, rancidity, pest excreta or fragments, powdery residue, webbing, cast larval casings and/or the symptoms of pests or insect commotion in the container [15]. An off-flavor aroma or stink in the cashew kernel persist due to the presence of oil which is observed in those cashew kernel affected by rancidity, microbial activity, putrefaction, fermentation, plague or chemical blemish [13–15]. The cashew kernel becomes defected due to external materials such as industrial fibers, metals, shells, stones, mesocarp, muck, solder, stems, glass, straws, plastic, sticks, hairs, threads, and paper pieces. Superficial damages and internal scrapes on the natural curve of cashew are also considered as defects. Cashew kernels are categorized as first quality fancy, second quality scorched, third quality scorched, fourth quality, blemished wholes (BW), lightly blemished wholes (LBW), and dessert.

First quality fancy possess a uniform color of white or pale ivory. Second quality scorched may be light ivory, deep ivory or light ash grey, light brown in color [13]. Third quality special scorched possess brown, deep yellow, amber color and including characteristics such as slightly shriveled, light brown speckled, immature, discolored. Fourth quality cashew kernels have pitted spots, cashews lacking pitted spots would qualify as first or second quality. BW may be dark brown, deep yellow amber or light blue in color. Cashew kernels may be slightly shriveled, immature, or may be brown speckled or blemished on the superficial layer, constraining affected part not exceeding 60 percent of the kernels [12–14]. LBW possess color which may be light ivory, light brown, deep ivory, or light ash grey. Cashew kernels may have light brown speckles or blemished on the superficial layer of cashew, constraining affected part not exceeding 40% of the kernels. Dessert cashew kernels may be shriveled, scraped, shriveled, extremely scorched, deep brown/black speckled, blemished, or discolored [13,14].

17.2.3 *Grades of cashew kernel*

Different grades of cashew kernel and their characteristics currently available in the cashew industry market are summarized in Table 17.1. Totally five grades are considered in the chapter for the assessment of cashew kernel quality. Table 17.2 summarizes the defects and grades of the cashew kernels and their characteristics considered in the chapter. Three labels designated in the chapter encompass all the defects/damages of cashew kernel.

Table 17.1 Different grades of cashew kernel [14]

Sl. No.	Cashew kernel	Characteristics
White wholes (WW) grades		
01.	WW-180	White or light ash in color with characteristic
02.	WW-210	shape
03.	WW-240	
04.	WW-320	
05.	WW-450	
06.	WW-500	
Scorched wholes (SW) grades		
07.	SW	Darkened to some extent due to overheating
08.	SW-180	
09.	SW-210	
10.	SW-240	
11.	SW-320	
12.	SW-450	
13.	SW-500	
Other grades		
14.	Scorched small wholes (SSW)	Over-scorched, immature, spattered (karaniram), wrinkled (percival)
15.	Dessert whole (DW)	Deep scorched or brown, discolored and black spotted
16.	Butts (B)	Color – white or light ash or pale ivory and cross-wise equally or unequally fragmented parts are attached naturally
17.	Splits (S)	White or pale ivory or light ash in color with natural split lengthwise
18.	Large white pieces (LWP)	White or pale ivory or light ash in color
19.	Small white pieces (SWP)	
20.	Baby bits (BB)	
21.	Scorched butts (SB)	Darkened slightly and cross-wise broken kernel
22.	Scorched splits (SS)	Darkened slightly and split kernel lengthwise
23.	Scorched pieces (SP)	Darkened slightly (due to overheating)
24.	Scorched small pieces (SSP)	
25.	Scorched pieces seconds (SPS)	Over-scorched, wrinkled (percival), discolored, and immature.
26.	Dessert pieces (DP)	Deep scorched or brown, spattered, discolored, and black spotted.

17.3   Implementation of the methodology

The methodology involves image acquisition, image preprocessing and segmentation, feature extraction, and classification. The methodology involves tasks, such as acquisition, preprocessing, and segregation of cashew kernels. The initial task involved in the implementation of the methodology is the development of a vision system such as a 2D dimensional camera for acquiring images of cashew. Cashew images are apprehended using the image acquisition toolbox of MATLAB, with the same illumination, same canon camera exposure, and focus mode for all images of

Table 17.2   Defects and grades of cashew kernel

Label	Characteristics
Black spots	Dark brown/black spots on the superficial layer of cashew kernel.
Discoloration	Blemishes/discoloration, scorched kernels.
Mixed defects	Immature, shriveled, and other defects
WW-180	White or light ash with characteristic shape. No. of kernels per pound is 170–180
WW-320	White or light ash with characteristic shape. No. of kernels per pound is 300–320
WW-450	White or light ash with characteristic shape. No. of kernels per pound is 400–450
Splits	White or pale ivory or light ash in color with natural split lengthwise
SW-240	Darkened to some extent due to overheating. No. of kernels per pound is 220–240

cashews. The acquisition of cashew images is done to obtain the dataset by using a 12 MP digital camera. The dataset consists of top view images of cashews. The cashew image acquired is then preprocessed before segmenting the image and extracting the features, using techniques such as sharpening, cropping in order to enhance the quality of the image, and applying the Weiner filter and Lucy filter, to eliminate blurring. With the help of segmentation techniques, namely, color threshold using Otsu's method and clustering using k-means, the image pixels are distinguished into two categories: cashew kernel and the background. The preprocessed images are used to extract textural features from the segmented image using a GLCM. Shape and size features are extracted after binarizing the segmented image. Color features are extracted after transforming the RGB image into the HSV (hue, saturation, and value) color space. The significant features are used to train and evaluate the performance of classifiers, namely, support vector machine (SVM) classifiers and Random Forest. The complete preprocessor system will be trained by machine learning to make it intelligent.

The stages involved in the methodology are briefly described as below: 1. Image acquisition and processing toolbox of MATLAB provides vital tools for performing various operations on Cashew images. Apprehend Cashew image through image acquisition tools. (2) Image processing techniques such as sharpening, cropping is applied on cashew image to enhance the quality of image. (3) Processed image is subjected to segmentation using color threshold and Otsu's segmentation method. (4) From the segmented images, the shape, texture and color features are extracted using suitable wavelet transformation-based feature extraction methods. (5) Train the support vector machine and random forest classifier using features as the training test. The process involved in the methodology used to detect the defects and automatically grade the cashew kernel, that is, the stages involved in the process and the flow chart of the software implementation of the classification methodology employed is as depicted in Figure 17.1.

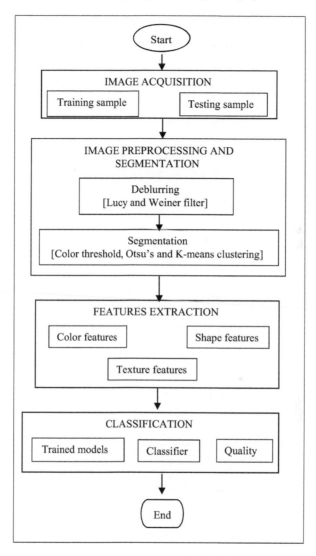

Figure 17.1   Process flow of the classification methodology

17.3.1   Image preprocessing and segmentation

Image preprocessing is a data processing technique to enhance images by adopting different filters. Figure 17.2 illustrates the preprocessing and segmentation method-ology adopted.

Image preprocessing is a technique to perform some relevant operations on an image, to enhance quality, and to extract significant features [8,9]. Cashew images are sharpened using an unsharp masking method. Image intensity and contrast

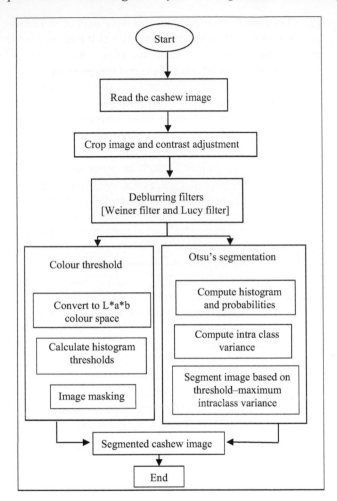

Figure 17.2   Process flow of the image preprocessing and segmentation

adjustment tools are applied to enhance the quality of the image. Weiner filter and Lucy filter are used for plummeting blurring effect. The mechanism of both filters is based on the principle of the deconvolution method, but Lucy filter works on Poisson noise and Weiner filter on Gaussian noise. In this processing, a myriad range of algorithms can be executed on the input data and can plummet signal distortion and build-up noise during execution. Contrast adjustment, image filtering, morphological operations, and deblurring are few methods of image pre-processing technique [1,10].

     The Lucy–Richardson algorithm, also known as Lucy-deconvolution, is a reiterative technique for recuperating a latent image that has been distorted by a cognizable point spread function, and works on Poisson noise statistics. In mathematics, Wiener deconvolution is an implementation of the Wiener filter to intrinsic noises in deconvolution [2]. This method attempts to plummet the impact of deconvolved noise at frequencies which have a weak signal-to-noise ratio as it executes in the frequency domain, and implements on Gaussian noise statistics. The Wiener filter is used extensively in image deconvolution applications, as frequency spectrum of most graphic images is equitably well scattered and may be evaluated efficiently [3,4].

Image segmentation is a technique of segregating an image into regions or fragments. This apportioning method into regions often depends on the characteristics of the pixels in an image [5]. For instance, assessing regions in an image is to evaluate abrupt discontinuities in pixel measurement, which characteristically designate boundaries/edges. It can explore distinct methods to image segmentation comprising multilevel automatic thresholding, reiterative approaches such as active contours and fast marching, and intensity-color-based methods. Another technique is segmentation based on color values, K-means clustering, color histogram threshold method, Otsu's segmentation method a few among many Image segmentation techniques.

Color threshold and Otsu's method, K-means clustering method are applied to segment the image into two fragments foreground (cashew kernel) and the background. Color threshold method constructs a segmentation mask by utilizing different color space histograms/representations. Otsu's threshold technique is used to automatically execute clustering-based image thresholding in computer vision and image processing applications [16]. This algorithm considers an image comprises of two-pixel modules centered on bimodal histogram (foreground pixels and background pixels), then it computes the optimal threshold extricating the two modules so that their intra-class variance (collective spread) is nominal, or equivalently their interclass variance is maximal [17]. Equation (17.1) represents intra-class variance expressed in terms of class probabilities ω and class means μ. Otsu's segmentation comprehensively examines for the optimum that plummets the intra-class variance, defined as a weighted sum of variance of the two classes (σ_ω^2).

$$\sigma_b^2(t) = \sigma^2 - \sigma_\omega^2(t) = \omega_0(t)\omega_1(t)[\mu_0(t) - \mu_1(t)]^2 \tag{17.1}$$

where class probability $\omega_{0,1}(t)$ is evaluated from the L bins of the histogram by

$$\omega_0(t) = \sum_{i=0}^{t-1} p(i) \tag{17.2}$$

$$\omega_1(t) = \sum_{i=t}^{L-1} p(i) \tag{17.3}$$

and class means $\mu_{0,1}(t)$ are represented by

$$\mu_0(t) = \sum_{i=0}^{t-1} \frac{p(i)}{\omega_0} \tag{17.4}$$

$$\mu_1(t) = \sum_{i=t}^{L-1} \frac{p(i)}{\omega_1} \tag{17.5}$$

Multi-Otsu method is the extension of original two class technique to multi-level thresholding. Image analysis is the extraction of significant statistics from segmented images, primarily from digital images by means of digital image processing techniques. Analysis of images encompasses processing an image into central constituents in order to extract statistical information [18].

The primary stage of color threshold method is conversion of color space from RGB to L*a*b*, it is performed to plummet the quantum of variables. Next stage is to evaluate histogram thresholds from three channels in the L*a*b color model and proceeds to the masking phase based on thresholds computed. Otsu's method evaluates histogram and probabilities of each intensity levels in the preliminary stage. Initialization of class mean and class probability to zero and assessment of all possible thresholds up to maximum intensity in the second stage. While assessing, it updates class mean and class probabilities and computes intra-class variance. The last stage includes the determination of desired threshold that corresponds to maximum inter-class variance. The segmented cashew image is acquired by a concoction of the above techniques, because some fraction of the defected cashew kernel is truncated by applying only one method. K-means clustering algorithm based on Euclidean distance is used which comprised both the saturation and value data. The algorithm worked with 2 or 3 clusters. Figure 17.3 shows the segmentation results obtained using K-means clustering. The results revealed that the optimal results were obtained with 3 clusters. Figure 17.3 shows the segmentation result obtained by using the K-means Clustering method.

17.3.2   Feature extraction

Feature extraction initiates from a preliminary set of evaluating data and constructs resultant values envisioned to be informative and non-redundant, assisting the consequent learning and generalization phases. Dimensionality reduction is interconnected to feature extraction methods. Input data of an algorithm can be transformed into a concentrated set of features if it is discovered to be too enormous to be processed and suspected to be consists of redundant values. Evaluating a subset of initial features is called feature selection. It is a method of dimensionality reduction that characterizes significant fragments of an image as a compressed feature vector with high efficacy. Color, size, shape, and texture features are the most significant features to evaluate the cashew grade.

The color space is defined by a range of colors, which are engendered by the principal colors of pigment. Color analysis is performed by extracting RGB and HSV color moments such as mean, standard deviation, and skewness. Color model (color space) is an abstract mathematical model, which primarily designates the range of colors as a tuple of numbers, typically as 3 or 4 values or color elements. The color model is an augmentation of the coordinate system and subspace, every color in the system is epitomized by a single dot. RGB (red, green, and blue) color space is basically interpreted as all possible colors, which used red, green, and blue colors to elaborate the color model. In such a conception, each pixel of an image is consigned intensity values of RGB components ranging from 0 to 255. The L*a*b

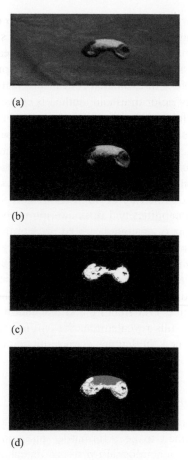

Figure 17.3   Image segmentation using K-means clustering [19] (a) cashew with black spots, (b) image after background subtraction, (c) segmentation with two clusters, and (d) segmentation with three clusters

elaborates mathematically perceivable colors in the three dimensions ('L' for lightness, 'a' and 'b' for the color opponents red-green and yellow-blue). HSV (hue, saturation, and value) color space model epitomizes the way human vision perceives color-making attributes and also represents the way points of distinct color mix together. Geometry features extraction comprises extracting size and shape information from the segmented image regions. The texture is one of the most significant outlining characteristics of an image and epitomized by the spatial distribution of gray intensities in a neighborhood. There are four varieties of texture feature extraction techniques used, namely, statistical, model-based, geometrical, and signal processing. GLCM is a statistical method of scrutinizing texture that contemplates the spatial relationship of pixels. Cashew image is converted into grayscale to decompose an input image using discrete 2D wavelet transform and derived co-occurrence matrices for frequency sub-bands of wavelets. Important texture features are extracted from these co-occurrence matrices.

Geometry attributes of connected components in an image can be evaluated by extracting shape and size features that comprises calculating axis length, area, perimeter, equivalent diameter, etc. Table 17.3 summarizes vital geometry related features extracted.

Texture is one of the most significant outlining characteristics of an image. It is characterized by the spatial distribution of gray levels during neighborhood. There are four varieties of texture feature extraction techniques used, namely, statistical, model-based, geometrical, and signal processing. The most extensively used method is statistical, which includes the co-occurrence matrix and pixel-value run-length methods for food processing [18]. Texture analysis includes generation of GLCM from the image, which symbolizes the texture based on the quantum of pixel pairs with particular intensity values configured in definite spatial relationships. It performs detection of boundaries of objects that characterized more by texture than by intensity. GLCM is a statistical method of scrutinizing texture that contemplates the spatial relationship of pixels. The GLCM characterizes the texture of an image with GLCM functions by evaluating how often pairs of pixel with particular values and in a quantified spatial connection ensue in an image, and extraction stages comprises constructing a GLCM, extracting statistical measures from this matrix [18,20]. Table 17.4 summarizes the significant texture features and their descriptive equations [20] that are extracted using GLCM.

Table 17.3   Geometry related features

Sl. No.	Feature	Description
01.	Major axis length	A major axis of the ellipse (in pixels) that has equivalent normalized second central moments as that of cashew kernel region [6]
02.	Minor axis length	A minor axis of the ellipse (in pixels) that has the same normalized second central moments as that of cashew kernel region
03.	Area	Total number of pixels contained within its cashew kernel boundary
04.	Perimeter	Total distance around the periphery of the cashew kernel region
05.	Equivalent diameter	Diameter of a circle which has the same area as the region of cashew kernel
06.	Aspect ratio	Ratio of major axis length and minor axis length
07.	Convex area	Total number of pixels in the smallest convex polygon that contain the cashew kernel region [5].
08.	Solidity	Proportion of the pixels in the convex hull (smallest convex polygon) that are also in the region
09.	Extent	Ratio pixels in the cashew kernel region to pixels in the total bounding box (smallest rectangle containing the region)
10.	Eccentricity	It is the eccentricity of the ellipse that has the same second-moments as that of cashew kernel region

Table 17.4   Textural features [20]

Sl. No.	Features	Equations
01.	Contrast	$\sum_{i,j=0}^{n-1} P_{i,j} \ \lvert i-j\rvert^2$
02.	Correlation	$\sum_{i,j=0}^{n-1} P_{i,j} \left[\dfrac{(i-\mu_i)(j-\mu_j)}{\sqrt{(\sigma_i{}^2)(\sigma_j{}^2)}} \right]$
03.	Angular second moment	$\sum_{i,j=0}^{n-1} P_{i,j}{}^2$
04.	Energy	$\sqrt{\text{Angular Second Moment}}$
05.	Entropy	$\sum_{i,j=0}^{n-1} P_{i,j} \ (-ln\,P_{i,j})$
06.	Homogeneity	$\sum_{i,j=0}^{n-1} \dfrac{P_{i,j}}{1+(i-j)^2}$
07.	Dissimilarity	$\sum_{i,j=0}^{n-1} P_{i,j} \ \lvert i-j\rvert$
08.	Cluster shade	$\sum_{i,j=0}^{n-1} \left[(i-\mu_i)+\left(j-\mu_j\right) \right]^3 \ P_{i,j}$
09.	Cluster performance	$\sum_{i,j=0}^{n-1} \left[(i-\mu_i)+\left(j-\mu_j\right) \right]^4 \ P_{i,j}$
10.	Smoothness	$1 - \dfrac{1}{(1+\sigma^2)}$
11.	Third movement	$\sum_{i,j}^{n-1} (P_{i,j}) \ (i-\mu_i)^3$
12.	Maximum probability	$max_{i,j}(P_{i,j})$

17.3.3   Classification

Machine learning is a statistical analytic technique that teaches computer systems to do what emanates naturally to humans and animals, that is, learning from experience. Machine learning algorithms use computational techniques to learn directly from information without depending on a preprogrammed equation as a model [21]. There are basically two types of machine learning techniques, supervised learning and unsupervised learning. A supervised learning algorithm takes a training set (known set of input data) and training labels (known rejoinders to the data) and trains a model to engender judicious predictions for the rejoinder to a new data [21]. Supervised learning uses classification techniques, which predict discrete responses and regression techniques predict continuous responses to develop predictive models [22]. Examples include neural networks, K-nearest neighbor, SVM, etc. Unsupervised learning discovers intrinsic structures or hidden patterns in data. This technique is used to envisage interpretations from an information set comprising input data without labels. Clustering is one of the unsupervised learning techniques, which is used for exploratory data analysis to discover consortiums or hidden configurations in the data. Hidden Markov model, K-means, hierarchical clustering are few examples of unsupervised learning techniques [21,22].

SVM is a supervised machine learning algorithm which classifies data into one or the other class (binary classification) [21,22]. Training features extracted from the cashew image are served to the SVM trainer for the confection of machine learning models along with training labels. New samples are cataloged based on these models. Classifier accuracy to detect defects of Cashew and cataloging of cashew kernels into different grades is evaluated. Binary SVM machine learning models are developed based on training features and training labels. A one-vs.-all strategy is adopted to develop models and classify them into different labels. Cataloging of new samples for the one versus all cases is performed by a winner takes all strategy, in which the classifier with the highest output function ascribes.

To start with the implementation of the SVM classifier the one vs. All approach is used as it failed to offer the desired accuracy, the one vs. one classification technique based on adaptive directive acyclic graphs as in [23–26] is applied to achieve the required accuracy. The classification is based on a 10-fold cross-validation process. To evaluate the performance of classifiers after the SVM classifier model was trained using the random forest classifier. Random forest classifier is based on ensemble learning that makes a group of decision trees from a randomly selected subset of the training set. It then aggregates the votes from completely different decision trees to select the complete test object class. The bagged ensemble for this study was trained with the hyper-parameters of 80 decision trees, maximum of six predictors for a decision tree and a minimum of two leaves, and an out of bag fraction of 0.2.

17.4   Results and discussions

The tasks involved in the proposed method such as image acquisition, preprocessing, segmentation, and feature extraction, classification are implemented using the MATLAB image processing toolbox. The morphology, texture, and color features are considered to get the optimum classification results. All the cashew samples are collected from Isha Cashew Kumbalgodu industrial area, Bangalore. Totally, five grades are used to study in this chapter, including White Wholes (WW-180), WW-320, WW-450, Splits, and Scorched Wholes (SW-240). Along with it, three different types of defective cashews, namely, black spots, discoloration, and mixed defects, were identified. The samples belonging to eight different grades were collected, labeled, and validated by the industry experts from the Isha cashew manufacturing plant. Total training sets comprising both defective and good quality cashews are 444 samples and 136 for the testing set.

Demarcation of defective cashews from good quality cashews is executed before the grading process. Overall damages/defects of cashew kernels are divided into three classes, namely, black spots, discoloration, and mixed effects. The black spots category encompasses black/brown spots on the superficial layer of cashew kernel. The discoloration label comprises dark brown colored cashews, and mixed effects cover immature cashews and concoction of other defects. For cataloging of defects, 129 samples are used as the training set and 35 samples for the testing set. The mixed defect label has more training set compared to other defect labels as more number of defects falls in this category. Grading is the process of cataloging cashew kernels into various class/grades based on color, texture, size, and shape. In all, 315 samples are used as a training set and 101 samples for the testing set for grading. Table 17.5 summarizes the training and testing set used for different defect

Table 17.5   Training and testing set of different defect labels/different grades

Label/class	Training samples	Testing samples
Black spots	29	9
Discoloration	38	10
Mixed defects	62	16
W-180	50	15
W-320	58	12
W-450	54	14
Splits	71	22
SW-240	82	38

labels and grades. Training features are extracted from total training samples including defective and good quality cashew samples and served to machine learning models including labels of training samples.

By trial-and-error approximation, the features required to get the good classification results are observed as follows: The WW-450, WW-320, and WW-180 grades had a distinct color when compared with other grades. The morphological features including perimeter, minor axis length, equivalent diameter and convex area were considered to easily differentiate among three classes. The color features including skewness of hue, saturation, standard deviation of hue, value, and red color dimension were chosen to be important for classification.

Figure 17.4 displays correctly the predicted output of the SVM classifier for the discoloration input sample, whereas Figure 17.4(a) shows the input sample and Figure 17.4(b) shows the correctly predicted output. Figure 17.5 displays the incorrectly predicted output for the discoloration input sample, whereas Figure 17.5(a) shows the input discoloration sample and Figure 17.5(b) shows the incorrectly the predicted sample. The classifier accuracy plummets as the quantum of the incorrectly predicted labels escalates.

Figure 17.6 displays the incorrectly predicted output of the SVM classifier for the blackspots input sample, whereas Figure 17.6(a) shows the input black spots sample and Figure 17.6(b) shows the incorrectly predicted output. Figure 17.7 displays the correctly predicted output for mixed defects input sample, where 17.7 (a) shows input mixed defect sample and 17.7 (b) shows correctly predicted output sample.

Figure 17.8 displays the correctly predicted output of the SVM classifier for the W-180 grade input sample, whereas Figure 17.8(a) shows the W-180 input sample and Figure 17.8(b) is correctly predicted output. Figure 17.9 displays incorrectly predicted output for the W-320 input sample, where Figure 17.9(a)

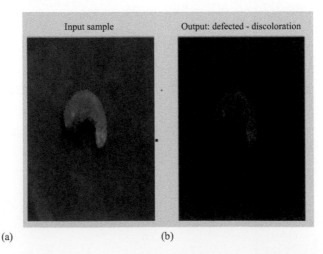

(a)   (b)

Figure 17.4   Correctly predicted output for the discoloration sample

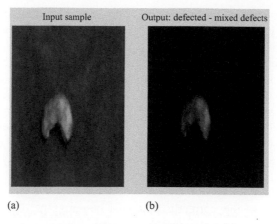

(a)   (b)

Figure 17.5   Incorrectly predicted output for the discoloration sample

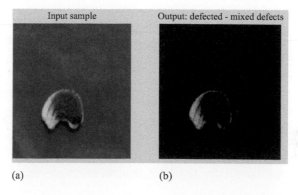

(a)   (b)

Figure 17.6   Incorrectly predicted output for the black spots sample

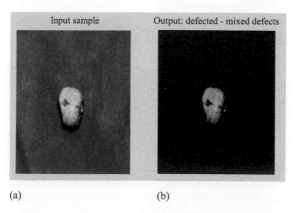

(a)   (b)

Figure 17.7   Correctly predicted output for the mixed defects sample

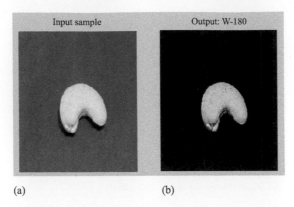

Figure 17.8   Correctly predicted output for the W-180 sample

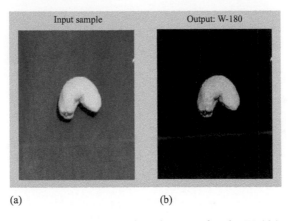

Figure 17.9   Incorrectly predicted output for the W-320 sample

shows the input W-320 sample and Figure 17.9(b) shows the incorrectly predicted output sample. Classifier accuracy for cataloging of Cashew kernels into different grades plummets as the number of incorrectly predicted labels escalates.

Figure 17.10 displays correctly predicted output of SVM classifier for the W-450 grade input sample, where Figure 17.10(a) shows the W-450 input sample and Figure 17.10(b) is correctly predicted output. Figure 17.11 displays correctly predicted output for W-320 input sample, where Figure 17.11(a) shows the input W-320 sample and Figure 17.11(b) shows the correctly predicted output sample.

Figure 17.12 displays correctly predicted output for splits grade input sample, where Figure 17.12(a) shows the splits input sample and Figure 17.12(b) is correctly predicted output. Figure 17.13 displays incorrectly predicted output for the SW-240 input sample, where Figure 17.13(a) shows the input SW-240 sample and Figure 17.13(b) shows the incorrectly predicted output sample. Color characteristic

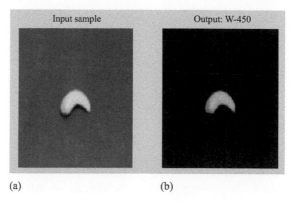

(a)   (b)

Figure 17.10   Correctly predicted output for the W-450 sample

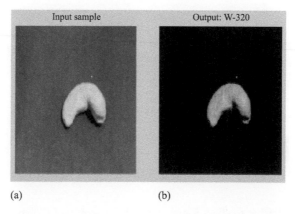

(a)   (b)

Figure 17.11   Correctly predicted output for the W-320 sample

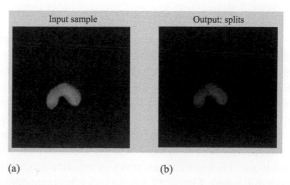

(a)   (b)

Figure 17.12   Correctly predicted output for the splits sample

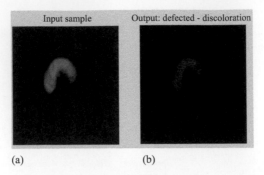

Figure 17.13   Incorrectly predicted output for the SW-240 sample

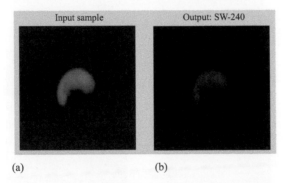

Figure 17.14   Correctly predicted output for the SW-240 sample

of SW-240 is similar to discoloration label. Figure 17.14 displays correctly predicted output for the SW-240 input sample, where Figure 17.14(a) shows the input SW-240 sample and Figure 17.14(b) shows the correctly predicted output sample.

SVM classifier is efficiently able to categorize W-180 grade as it is effortlessly distinguished. For cataloging of grades W-320 and W-450, the number of correctly classified samples are plummeted. Confusion matrix of SVM classifier is shown in Figure 17.15. Cataloging of SW-240 grade accurately confronted difficulties as some discoloration labeled cashews is almost parallel to SW-240 cashews. Overall statistical classification results of cashew kernels are summarized in Table 17.6.

The confusion matrix is plotted on the foundation of comparison between predicted labels and true labels ranging from 0 to 1. 100% accuracy will make all diagonal elements in the confusion matrix equal to 1. For instance, consider W-180 grade, 0.96 value indicates that several W-180 grades are accurately cataloged and 0.04 specifies the quantity of inaccurately predicted label of some samples as W-320 but a true label for those samples is W-180. Classifier accuracy is calculated as the ratio of correctly predicted labels to true labels. Classifier accuracy to demarcate defected cashews and good quality ones are proven to be 89.4%. The overall accuracy of the SVM classifier

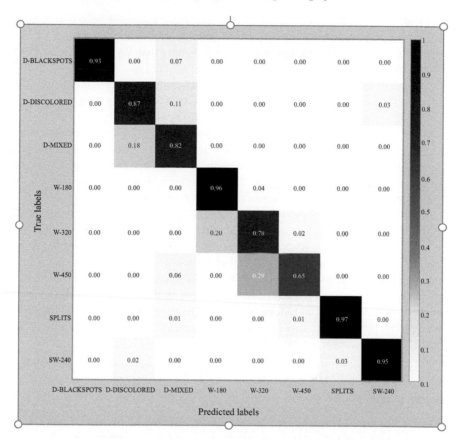

Figure 17.15   Confusion matrix of SVM classifier

Table 17.6   Statistical classification results

Label/class	No. of samples	Correctly classified	Incorrectly classified
Black spots	29	27	02
Discoloration	38	33	05
Mixed defects	62	51	11
W-180	50	48	02
W-320	58	45	13
W-450	54	35	19
Splits	71	69	02
SW-240	82	78	04

to assess the quality of cashews including grading of cashew kernels is found to be 87.2%.

Demarcation of defects of cashew kernels is performed initially before the grading process. Defects of cashews are cataloged into three classes. Totally five grades are used in this work to assess and classify cashew kernels into different grades. Training features extracted from samples are used for training machine learning models. Cataloging result analysis indicates that W-180, splits, and SW-240 are efficiently classified.

When compared to the multi-class SVM implemented the one-vs.-one SVM algorithm showed the classification accuracy of 90.6%, but the time consumed by the one-vs.-one algorithm to compute was found to be increased by a few seconds. So the same one-vs.-one algorithm was implemented based on the adaptive directed acyclic graph method, which showed a similar accuracy of 90.6% but at less computation time. The most vital set of features were selected and was used as a training set for the Random Forest classifiers. This classifier was able to distinguish among various grades and defects in cashew kernel more effectively with an accuracy of 94.28%. From the confusion matrix of the Random Forest classifier, it is revealed that the classes such as mixed defects and black spots showed the lowest precision, and the discoloration class showed better precision compared to other classes. However, the classifier results showed that the whole whites and scorched wholes were differentiated with high accuracy. From the classification results, the random forest classifier is proven to be a better classification model for differentiating five classes of cashew grades and identifying the defects in cashew kernels. The confusion matrixes for SVM (one-vs.-one) with accuracy: 90.6% and of random forest classifier with accuracy: 94.28% are depicted in Figures 17.16 and 17.17

		Actual Classification								Precision
		WW-450	WW-320	WW-180	SW-240	Splits	Black spots	Discoloration	Mixed	(Class-Wise)
Predicted classification	WW-450	15	0	0	0	0	0	0	0	1.00
	WW-320	0	11	0	0	0	0	0	0	0.84
	WW-180	0	2	11	0	0	0	0	0	1.00
	SW-240	0	0	0	32	1	0	0	0	0.97
	Splits	0	0	0	0	15	0	0	0	0.94
	Black spots	0	0	0	0	0	4	1	1	1.00
	Discoloration	0	0	0	0	0	0	5	0	0.50
	Mixed	0	0	0	1	0	0	4	4	0.80
Recall (Class-Wise)		1.00	1.00	0.85	0.97	1.00	0.67	1.00	0.44	

Figure 17.16   Confusion matrix for SVM classifier. Accuracy: 90.6%

		Actual Classification								Precision
		WW-450	WW-320	WW-180	SW-240	Splits	Black Spots	Discoloration	Mixed	(Class-Wise)
Predicted classification	WW-450	16	0	0	0	0	0	0	0	1.00
	WW-320	0	11	0	0	0	0	0	0	1.00
	WW-180	0	0	13	0	0	0	0	0	1.00
	SW-240	0	0	0	35	0	0	0	0	0.97
	Splits	0	0	0	1	14	0	0	0	1.00
	Black Spots	0	0	0	0	0	2	0	2	0.50
	Discoloration	0	0	0	0	0	2	4	0	0.8
	Mixed	0	0	0	0	0	2	1	4	0.67
Recall (Class-Wise)		1.00	1.00	1.00	1.00	0.93	0.50	1.00	0.57	

Figure 17.17   Confusion matrix for random forest classifier. Accuracy: 94.28%

17.5   Conclusion

This chapter focused on the automated assessment of the quality of cashew kernels, which is a step toward the automation of the Indian cashew industry, which still relies on manual labor for this task of grading the cashews and identifying the defects in cashew kernels. Image preprocessing makes the classification task more efficient. The leveraged image processing and machine learning techniques were applied to detect defects in cashews. Detection of cashew defects and cataloging of cashew kernels into five grades (WW-180, WW-320, WW-450, splits, and SW-240) is performed in this chapter. Most significant features, namely, color, texture, size, and shape features, are extracted and served for the confection of classifier models. Classifier accuracy to demarcate defected and good quality cashew kernels using multi-class SVM is 89.4%. Total accuracy to detect defects and also classify good cashew kernels into five grades is 87.2%. From cataloging results, it can be concluded that W-180, splits, and SW-240 are efficiently classified, accuracy can be escalated by increasing the number of the training sets. Classifier accuracy to demarcate defected and good quality cashew kernels using SVM (one-vs.-one) and using the random forest classifier is 90.6% and 94.28%, respectively. It can be concluded that random forest classification model can successfully segregate cashews into different grades and can be adopted in the cashew industry for grading.

Grading of cashew kernels is performed only for five grades, so all the commercially available 26 grades need to be utilized for developing machine learning models. Classifier accuracy depends on the number of the training samples; the training set requires to be escalated to efficiently classify all grades with high accuracy. Machine vision equipment can be constructed utilizing contributions of this work to employ intelligent machines in cashew industries to reduce manpower and time. Future scope lies in increasing the data set, with additional features such as the weight of the cashew, and the side-view of the kernel. To develop the cashew segregation machine (based on defects, quality, and grading based on machine learning, which is low computational complexity, accurate segregation, and grading ability for real-time), which is designed to process 10 kg of cashew kernels in 1 hour. To develop a hybrid algorithm that improves resolution works on highly non-linear based statistical learning principles, optimization technique, technology transfer, and publications. The machine operates on electricity and does not produce any waste product or harmful gas. Hence, it is environmentally friendly.

References

[1]   V. Nagpure, and K. Joshi, "Grading of cashew nuts on the bases of texture, color and size", International Journal on Recent and Innovation Trends in Computing and Communications, vol. 4, no. 4, 2016, pp. 171–175.

[2]   J. A. Kumar, P. R. Rao, and A. R. Desai, "Cashew kernel classification using machine learning approaches", J. Indian Soc. Agric. Statist., 2013, pp. 121–129.

[3]   V. G. Narendra, and K. S. Hareesh, "Cashew Kernels classification using Color features", International Journal of Machine Intelligence, vol. 3, no. 2, 2011, pp. 52–57.

[4]   Z. Lin, and Z. Qizhi, "Research and analysis of classification model based on the shape parameters of cashew nuts", Int. conf. on Consumer electronics, 2011.

[5]   P. K. Patel, M. Samvatsar, and P. K. Bhanodia, "Computer revelation system based classification of intact cashew grading system", International Journal of Engineering Sciences and Research Technology, 2012, vol. 8, no. 5, pp. 61–67.

[6]   K. Y. Huang, "Detection and classification of areca nuts with machine vision", International Journal of Computers and Mathematics with Applications, 2012, pp. 736–746.

[7]   J. Gill, A. Giridhar, and T. Singh, "A hybrid intelligent system for fruit grading and sorting", International Journal of Computer Science and Engineering vol. 9, no. 05, 2017, pp. 257–265.

[8]   A. Shyna, and G. Reena, "Machine vision based real time cashew grading and sorting system using SVM and back propagation neural network", IEEE Int. Conf. on circuits Power and Computing Techno., vol. 9, no. 2, May 2017, pp. 507–519.

[9]   M. O. Arun, G. Aneesh, and A. Shyna, "Automated cashew kernel grading using machine vision", IEEE Int. Conf. on Next Generation Intelligent Systems, vol. 3, no. 4, 2016, pp. 112–119.

[10] V. J. Narendra, and K. S. Hareesh, "Intelligent classification model for cashew kernel grades based on color, texture, and morphological features", Journal of Agricultural Engineering and Biotechnology, vol. 3, no. 3, 2015, pp.98–108.

[11] V. V. Singh, and A. K. Misra "Detection of unhealthy region of plant leaves using image processing and genetic algorithm", in Proc. of Computer Engineering and Applications (ICACEA), 2015 IEEE: 978-1-4673-6911-4, July 2015, pp. 11–15.

[12] N. Razmojooya, B. S. Mousavib, and F. Soleymani, "A real-time mathematical computer method for potato inspection using machine vision", Computers and Mathematics with Applications, 2012, pp. 268–279.

[13] G. Srivatsava, V. Meharwade, and S. Kulkarni, "Cashew Handbook 2014-Global Perceptive", 4th edition, June 2014.

[14] P. J. Patil, "Food processing technology and packaging: a case study of indian cashew industry", Journal of Nutrition and Health Sciences, vol. 3, no. 2, 2016, pp. 36–42.

[15] G. Muhammad, "Date fruits classification using texture descriptors and shape-size features", Engineering Applications of Artificial Intelligence, vol. 37, 2015, pp. 361–367.

[16] N. Otsu, "A threshold selection method from gray-level histograms", IEEE Transactions on Systems, Man, and Cybernetics Image, vol. 9, no. 5, 1979, pp. 62–66.

[17] J. H. Xue, and D. M. Titterington, "T-tests, F-tests and Otsu's methods for image thresholding", IEEE Transactions on Image Processing, vol. 20, no. 8, 2011, pp. 2392–2396.

[18] R. M. Haralick, K. Shanmugam, and I. Dinstein, "Textural features for image classification", IEEE Trans. on Systems Man and Cybernetics, vol. 3, no. 6, 1973, pp.610–621.

[19] D. Ilea, and P. Whelan, "Color image segmentation using a spatial k-means clustering algorithm", 10th International Machine Vision and Image Processing Conference, Dublin, Ireland, 2006.

[20] Y. Mingqiang, K. Kidiyo, and R. Joseph, "A survey of shape feature extraction techniques", Pattern Recognition Techniques, Technology and Applications, 2008.

[21] A. Padma, and R. Sukanesh, "SVM based classification of soft tissues in brain ct images using wavelet based dominant gray level run length texture features", Middle-East Journal of Scientific Research, 2013, pp. 38–44.

[22] J. Hu, D. Li, Q. Duan, Y. Han, G. Chen, and X. Si, "Fish species classification by colour, texture and multi-class support vector machine using computer vision", Computers and Electronics in Agriculture, vol. 88, 2012, pp. 130–140.

[23] B. Kijsirikul, and N. Ussivakul, "Multiclass support vector machines using an adaptive directed acyclic graph, in Neural Networks", 2002. IJCNN'02. Proceedings of the 2002 International Joint Conference, Vol. 1, IEEE, 2002, pp. 980–985.

[24] G. Thippa Reddy, R. M. Swarna Priya, M. Parimala, *et al.*, "A deep neural networks based model for uninterrupted marine environment monitoring", Computer Communications, vol. 157, 2020, pp. 64–75.

[25] N. Khare, P. Devan, C. L. Chowdhary, *et al.*, "SMO-DNN: Spider monkey optimization and deep neural network hybrid classifier model for intrusion detection", Electronics, vol. 9, no. 44, 2020, p. 692.

[26] R. M. Swarna Priya, M. Praveen Kumar Reddy, M. Parimala, *et al.*, "An effective feature engineering for DNN using hybrid PCA-GWO for intrusion detection in IoMT architecture", Computer Communications, vol. 160, pp. 139–149.

Index

access control through computer vision 11
accuracy (ACC) 346, 416
activation function 260, 367–8
AdaGrad approach 369
Adobe Photoshop 175
advanced driver-assistance systems (ADAS) 194
aerial video classification, challenges related to 359
agriculture, computer vision in 7–8
AlexNet architecture 61
AlphaGo 57
alternating direction method of multipliers (ADMM) method 94, 97
analysis sub-dictionary 93
animal identification and search 328–9
app() function 71
application-specific integrated circuit (ASIC)-based design accelerator 19–23
Arabic and Persian numbers 86
Argus Science LLC 196
artificial intelligence (AI) 2–3, 11, 57, 166
artificial neural network (ANN) 58, 87–8, 255
  working 256–8
AttnGAN based network 73
augmented reality (AR) 307, 313
autoencoders 166
  image retrieval using 67–74
automation, computer vision technology in 3, 5
  agriculture, computer vision in 7–8

automated automobiles 6–7
  classifying and detecting objects 10
  congregation data for training algorithms 10
  e-commerce industry, computer vision in 8–9
  face ID in mobile devices 6
  generating 3D maps 10
  health sector, computer vision in 8–9
  low-light mode with computer vision 10
automobile accidents 6
automobiles, automated 6–7

background separation 394–7
backpropagation neural network (BPNN) 441
backpropagation through structure (BTS) algorithm 353
bag of words (BOW) 213
banker's numerals 86
basis pursuit (BP) 90
benchmarked convolutional neural network 262
  Inception v3 262
  VGG16 262
Bengali handwritten number detection 88
bi-directional gated recurrent unit (BiGRU) 124
bi-directional LSTM 121
bilateral filtering 239
binarization 397–8
binary classification 364–5

  convolutional neural networks
    (CNNs) 152–3
  enhancing faster RCNN with
    MobileNet 155
  faster RCNN for object detection
    154
  object detection using deep
    learning 153–4
  in surveillance videos 272–3
  using deep learning 153–4
on-chip communication infrastructure
    32
online shopping 8
openweathermap API 323
opinion mining 204–6, 208
optical character recognition (OCR)
    84, 118, 307, 318–19
optimization techniques 368–9
Oriented Gradients 148
ORL database 68
orthogonal matching pursuit (OMP) 90
output stationary (OS) data-flow
    mapping methods 46

Palace Resorts and personalized
    marketing 197
parametric ReLU (PReLU) 124
peak signal-to-noise ratio (PSNR) 346
performance metrics 370–3
Persian HCR 88
photo-response nonuniformity noise
    (PRNU) 170
Picasa 175
Plant.id API 322–3
plant identification and search 328
plant identify (Plant.id API) 322–3
Poisson noise 448
pooling layer 260–1
precision 69
prefeature extracted images with CNN
    model 223
  bit plan slicing method 228–9
  datasets 226–7
  experiments and results 235–47

Gabor filter as a feature extractor
    229–30
Gaussian Canny filter 227–8
metrics
  accuracy 234–5
  cross-entropy loss 235
  model design 232–4
  preprocessing 227
  related work 223–6
  system configuration 235
  vehicle driver emotion recognition
    247–9
PReLU (Parametric Rectified Linear
    Unit) 121, 128
pre-processing 392
  background separation 394–7
  binarization 397–8
  finding the threshold of the
    grayscale image 397
  median filtering 394
  morphological operations 398
    binary opening 398
    erosion 398
  obtaining a standard format 399
  resizing the image 392
  RGB to gray conversion 392–4
  storing as training data 400
principal component analysis (PCA)
    46, 64, 225
processing-in-memory (PIM) method 23
productivity, increase in 281
Puigcerver model 119, 127
pupil center corneal reflection
    (PCCR) 185
Pupil Labs 196
PyTorch 147, 374–5

qualification measures 416
  accuracy 416
  confusion matrix 416
  execution time 417
  qualification results 417
  sensitivity 416
  specificity 417
quantization technique 267